From Infancy to Maturity

The History of the Department of Pediatrics,
The University of North Carolina
at Chapel Hill

1952–1995

Floyd W. Denny, Jr., *Editor*

Associate Editors
Harrie R. Chamberlin
Herbert S. Harned, Jr.
Ernest N. Kraybill
Judson J. Van Wyk

The Department of Pediatrics
The University of North Carolina
at Chapel Hill

Published by
The Department of Pediatrics,
The University of North Carolina at Chapel Hill
Wing C, Medical School
CB #7225, UNC-CH
Chapel Hill, North Carolina 27599-7225 U.S.A.
(919) 966-2504

Design by Erin L. Willder
Produced by B. Williams & Associates
Durham, North Carolina

Manufactured in the U.S.A.

First edition, first printing

Library of Congress Cataloging-in-Publication Data:

From infancy to maturity : the history of the Department of
  Pediatrics, the University of North Carolina at Chapel
  Hill, 1952–1995 / Floyd W. Denny, Jr., editor . . . [et al.].
      p.   cm.
  Includes bibliographical references and index.
  ISBN 0-9650394-0-4 (hard cover : alk. paper)
    1. University of North Carolina at Chapel Hill. Dept. of
  Pediatrics—History.   2. Pediatrics—North Carolina—
  Chapel Hill—History.   I. Denny, Floyd W., 1923– .
  RJ42.U5F76   1996
  618.92'00071'1756563—dc20   96-4620
                                                CIP

*To all of you who contributed
to the success of our department*

CONTENTS

PART NINE: BIOGRAPHIES OF THE EARLY GREATS OF THE DEPARTMENT

PART TEN: LOOKING TO THE FUTURE

LIST OF ACRONYMS

AAUAP	American Association of University Affiliated Programs
ABG	arterial blood gas
ABP	androgen binding protein
ACLS	Advanced Cardiac Life Support
AHEC	Area Health Education Centers
AIDS	acquired immunodeficiency syndrome
ALRI	acute lower respiratory infection
AOA	Alpha Omega Alpha
APCF	Ambulatory Pediatric Care Facility
APHA	American Public Health Association
ASO	Antistreptolysin O
BAL	bronchoalveolar lavage
B/D	Wards B and D
BPD	bronchopulmonary dysplasia
BSN	Bachelor of Science in Nursing
BSRC	Biological Sciences Research Center
BT	Bedtower
BWC	Burroughs Wellcome Company
CCC-SLP	Certificate of Clinical Competence in Speech/Language Pathology
CCSG	Children's Cancer Study Group
CDL	Center for Development and Learning
CF	cystic fibrosis
CGIBD	Center for Gastrointestinal Biology and Disease
CLD	chronic lung disease
CLIA	Clinical Laboratory Improvement Amendments
CSF	cerebrospinal fluid
DDDL	Division for Disorders of Development and Learning
DEC	Developmental Evaluation Clinic
DKA	diabetic ketoacidosis
DNA	deoxyribonucleic acid

DRG	Diagnostic Related Groups
ECG	electrocardiogram
ECU	East Carolina University
EdM	Masters in Education
EIS	Epidemic Intelligence Service
EKG	electrocardiogram
ENT	Ears, Nose and Throat
EPA	Environmental Protection Agency
EPDA	Educational Professional Development Act
ER	Emergency Room
FDA	Food and Drug Administration
FEP	free erythrocyte protoporphyrin
FHL	familial hemophagocytic lymphohistiocytosis
FISH	fluorescent *in situ* hybridization
FNP	Family Nurse Practitioner
FPG	Frank Porter Graham
FSH	follicle-stimulating hormone
FTE	full-time equivalent
FUO	fever of unknown origin
G6PD	glucose-6-phosphate dehydrogenase
GH	growth hormone
GI	gastrointestinal
HIB	*Haemophilus influenzae-type b*
HIV	human immunodeficiency virus
HLA	human leucocyte antigen
HMO	Health Maintenance Organization
HRSA	Health Resources and Services Administration
ICN	Intermediate Care Nursery
ICU	Intensive Care Unit
ID	Infectious Diseases
IGF	insulin-like growth factor
IOM	Institute of Medicine
ISCN	Infant Special Care Nursery
JAMA	*Journal of the American Medical Association*
JAR	Junior Assistant Resident
LCRC	Lineberger Cancer Research Center
LMD	Local Medical Doctor
LPA	Little People of America, Inc.
LPN	Licenced Practical Nurse
LRB	Laboratories of Reproductive Biology
LSU	Louisiana State University
MA	Master of Arts
MCH	Maternal and Child Health
MCMH	Moses Cone Memorial Hospital
MD	Doctor of Medicine

MGH   Massachusetts General Hospital
MOTT   mycobacteria other than tuberculosis
MPH   Masters in Public Health
MRRC   Mental Retardation Research Center
MS   Master of Science
MSN   Master of Science in Nursing
MSW   Master of Social Work
NADPH   reduced nicotinamide adenine dinucleotide phosphate
NARC   National Association for Retarded Children
NC   North Carolina
NCI   National Cancer Institute
NCMH   North Carolina Memorial Hospital
NCNB   North Carolina National Bank
NCSU   North Carolina State University
NHLBI   National Heart, Lung and Blood Institute
NICHHD   National Institute of Child Health and Human Development
NICU   Neonatal Intensive Care Unit
NIH   National Institutes of Health
NIMH   National Institute of Mental Health
NNP   Neonatal Nurse Practitioner
OCCHS   Orange Chatham Community Health Services
OI   osteogenesis imperfecta
OPD   Outpatient Department
OR   Operating Room
PALS   Pediatric Advanced Life Support
PFC   persistent fetal circulation
PGY   post-graduate year
PH   Pediatric Hematology
PhD   Doctor of Philosophy
PHO   Pediatric Hematology-Oncology
PI   Principal Investigator
PICU   Pediatric Intensive Care Unit
PIO   Pediatric Oncology
PKU   phenylketonuria
PL   pediatric level
RDEC   rabbit diarrhea *Escherichia coli*
RN   Registered Nurse
SAR   Senior Assistant Resident
SCOR   Specialized Center of Research
SICC   Special Infant Care Clinic
SPR   Society for Pediatric Research
SWOG   Southwest Oncology Group
TB   tuberculosis
TEACCH   Treatment and Education of Autistic and Related
            Communication-Handicapped Children

TF   testicular feminization
TGA   thymidine guanosine adenosine
TGG   thymidine guanosine guanosine
UAF   university-affiliated facility
UAP   university-affiliated program
UCLA   University of California at Los Angeles
UNC   University of North Carolina
UNC-CH   University of North Carolina at Chapel Hill
UNC-G   University of North Carolina at Greensboro
UP   University of Pennsylvania
UVA   University of Virginia
VA   Veterans Administration
VCUG   voiding cystourethrogram
VLBW   very low birthweight
WARI   wheezing-associated respiratory infections
WBC   white blood cell
WHO   World Health Organization
WTMS   Wake Teen Medical Services
WUNC   University of North Carolina Public Radio

PREFACE

THE Department of Pediatrics of the University of North Carolina began after World War II, when the people of North Carolina mandated its University to build a major teaching hospital in the village of Chapel Hill. The North Carolina Memorial Hospital was essential for the expansion of the University's two-year medical curriculum into a full-fledged four-year school of medicine. The Department of Pediatrics that emerged from this bold move is today recognized throughout the world as one of the premier centers of academic pediatrics. How this striking transition came to pass in such a brief span of years demands telling while those of us who witnessed these events are yet capable of recall. This volume represents our attempt to recreate the evolution of the Department of Pediatrics at the University of North Carolina from its nascent infancy to its full maturity and recalls the many people who played key roles in these developments.

The moving force throughout this project has been Floyd W. Denny, Jr., who had the vision to see the need for this history and who throughout has served as its chief editor and moving force. Dr. Chamberlin took on the challenge of securing pictorial documentation of our history. Dr. Harned did yeoman duties in getting together and editing manuscripts from our myriad contributors, and Dr. Van Wyk, not unexpectedly, was the gadfly of this group. It was initially considered prudent to limit the history to the eras under our first two chairs, Edward C. Curnen, Jr. (1952–1960) and Floyd W. Denny, Jr. (1960–1981). This decision was based on the fact that Dr. Boat was still chair of the Department and the Boat era was not yet "history." When Dr. Boat resigned in 1993, Dr. Ernest Kraybill was added to the group to oversee coverage of the Boat era from 1982 to 1993.

The history opens with a summary of the state of the Medical School in the early years written by Dr. William Blythe of the Department of Medicine, who was one of the first residents who trained in North Carolina Memorial Hospital and who has remained on the scene ever since. Blythe spent time on the pediatric service as an intern.

The first part of the book presents general accounts of the Department in the three eras. Large parts of the description of the Curnen years were derived from extensive taped interviews of Dr. Curnen by Dr. Harrie Chamberlin. A summary of the Denny years was taken from Denny's 1987 Berryhill Lecture, which described the Department into the 1980s. Dr. Boat summarized his administration during the 1993 meeting of the Denny Society; his talk was adapted for this publication by Dr. Jerry Fernald. Color was added to these three sections by several additional chapters, but particularly by reminiscences written by house staff members from each era, who were invited to "tell it like it was."

The largest segment of the book describes the development of the pediatric subspecialties and their role in the Department. During the Curnen years the primary responsibilities of the medical faculty members for teaching, service, and research were shared by the Department as a whole. The development of the subspecialties occurred during the Denny years; their maturation took place during the Boat years.

Subsequent sections address other parts of the Department that have been of particular importance to its development. These include "Partners in Pediatric Care," the "Pediatric Area Health Education Center Program," "Expanding Horizons: Our National Role," and "The House Staff." Several early faculty members were not available to make personal additions to this history so a special section has been included to highlight their contributions; this section is entitled "Biographies of the Early Greats of the Department." Finally, in "Looking to the Future" we express appreciation to Dr. Ned Lawson for leading the Department as interim chair after Dr. Boat resigned, and we welcome our new chair, Dr. Roberta Williams.

To complete the history we have assembled all the annual departmental photographs, some individual portraits, and snapshots of key events and other activities. We have listed all the residents, fellows, and faculty members as inclusively as possible. If any omissions occurred they were not intended.

During the course of these endeavors we accumulated a very large amount of archival material that could not be included in this volume. These archives are currently preserved in a file case dedicated to this purpose. Such departmental archives are unique in academic pediatrics and constitute a veritable treasure trove of records that may provide abundant thesis material for some future PhD candidate of the twenty-first or twenty-second century. We anticipate that future departmental chairs will add significant documents to this repository.

We want to acknowledge our great appreciation to the following for their gifts, which have made this book possible: the Floyd W. Denny Pediatric Society, the Department of Pediatrics, the dean of the School of Medicine, the executive director of the University of North Carolina Hospitals, and The Medical Foundation of North Carolina, Inc.

We cannot give proper credit to the many people who helped us with the preparation of the book, which we believe is unique in academic pediatrics.

Special typing and editing credit must be given to Betsy Chamberlin and Christine Reed. Extra special appreciation is expressed to Michele Eager for her many contributions in helping to bring our efforts to fruition and to Dr. Ernest Craige for the caricatures depicting the various eras in the development of the department. Finally, we express our thanks to Barbara Williams, Erin Willder, and Chris Crochetière of B. Williams & Associates; without their patience and careful guidance this history would not have been possible.

THE EDITORS

FOREWORD

THE original front entrance of the North Carolina Memorial Hospital faced north. And well it should have. For coming through it in those early days of 1952 were all sorts of people—faculty, staff, nurses, resident staff, and on and on—with the great preponderance of them coming from the North. They came from Boston, from New Haven, from New York; some others came from the Midwest—from St. Louis, Chicago, and Iowa City; and yet others came from closer to home. Most were coming to Chapel Hill for the first time; others were joyously returning. All were excited and expectant about what lay ahead of them. These were heady times!

I had the good fortune of having been born at the right time and having been at the right place to watch most, as well as participate in some, of what happened in those early days.

I was a Carolina undergraduate when the General Assembly of 1947 passed the bill with the recommended funds for the construction of the medical center.

I was a freshman medical student when the actual construction began and remember vividly a flatbed truck rolling up behind the Medical School (that is, between MacNider and University Infirmary), a bulldozer being unloaded, and shortly thereafter the first of many pine trees to go being pushed down.

I was in the last two-year class of the Medical School and therefore went away for the final two years.

I returned in July 1953 to begin a medical internship. By then the hospital had been open for about ten months. When the hospital first opened in September 1952, there were forty full-time members of the clinical faculty present and fifty-two part-time clinical faculty members who, according to Dr. Berryhill, "faithfully and competently assumed important teaching and clinical responsibilities." The basic science faculty totaled thirty-six full-time members.

Thus, at the time of the opening of the North Carolina Memorial Hospital, the entire full-time faculty was made up of 76 people and the total faculty—that is, full-time and clinical faculty—consisted of 130 people.

When nowadays we consider the size of the faculty then, the predominant feeling is one of quaintness. But the feeling at the time was amazement at the explosion in the number of people around and the size of the place. After all, the faculty had more than tripled, and there were all of the other people who are so vital in the operation of a medical *center* as contrasted to a two-year medical *school*.

So, one of the characterizing emotions at that time, certainly on the part of those who had been here for a while, was awe at what had happened to the place in such a short time.

An even more prevalent—and, in my judgment, more important—feeling on the part of everybody, ranging from the newly recruited maintenance men who had never been in a medical center to sophisticated faculty from famous medical schools, was a profoundly felt desire to have it succeed.

It was as if an innocent, rustic country bride suddenly found herself wed to an exotic man of the world, and both were determined to make the marriage work. Patience, understanding, exploration, hard work, refreshing rest, looks to the future and the past, excitement, outright pride, and even occasional outbursts of anger rising from righteous indignation all served in this early honeymoon period to make it go.

And go it did.

I was privileged to be a part of the Pediatrics Department for a very brief time (around Christmastime 1953), in a very low position. In the early years, straight medical interns spent a month or two as pediatric interns, a practice that at the time I thought was a good idea and one with which I still agree.

My most emphatic memory of that short period was of the kindness and helpfulness of the house staff and the faculty. George Summer was my resident and taught me many things, among them being a wariness of doing almost anything quickly.

Dr. Curnen was gentle, exceedingly kind to the house staff, and made me feel at home in the Department.

Thus, the preeminent feeling in the Department of Pediatrics in those early days was of mutual support and informality. It was indeed "like a family."

WILLIAM B. BLYTHE

PART ONE

The Curnen Years
1952–1960

CHAPTER ONE

General History

EARLY ORGANIZATION OF THE DEPARTMENT
AND BUILDING OF RELATIONSHIPS

D R. EDWARD CURNEN had outstanding credentials for the difficult job of
organizing a new department of pediatrics. He graduated from Yale College in 1931 and from Harvard Medical School in 1935. Following a year as
resident bacteriologist, he became a clinical intern and resident at Boston
Children's Hospital (1936–1939). He also gained a profound appreciation of
research from his years in microbiology, especially at the Rockefeller Institute
and as an associate professor of pediatrics and preventive medicine at Yale.
He served in the Navy during World War II and achieved the grade of commander in the Naval Reserve. These details of Dr. Curnen's background were
extracted from his curriculum vitae, but much of the historical information
to follow was derived from the insightful interview of Dr. Curnen by Dr.
Chamberlin (see archives).

Dr. Curnen begins by describing his decision to come to the University of
North Carolina. He received a compelling letter from Reece Berryhill inviting
him and his wife, Marian (known affectionately as "Manny"), to look over
the situation in the unfamiliar southland. Ed came to Chapel Hill following
a meeting in Virginia of the Society for Pediatric Research and the American
Pediatric Society, where he had presented a paper with Dr. Mary Godenne (his
second wife following Marian's untimely death). He met Manny in Chapel
Hill, where they experienced what they would later refer to as the "Chapel
Hill treatment." This active participation in the social and academic whirl
allowed them to learn a great deal about the Medical School, University, and
community in a short time. Upon returning to New Haven by train, they ana-

Edward C. Curnen, Jr. (1954), first Department chair

lyzed the situation and felt that this was an extraordinary professional opportunity for Ed that would allow him to "write on a clean slate," as well as enable them to live in an environment that would be pleasant for work and for the family. Ed had a prior knowledge of and respect for the two-year Medical School program at UNC, as several of his classmates at Harvard (including Isaac Manning in Durham and Monroe Gilmore in Charlotte) had been familiar with the programs of the preclinical years at Chapel Hill.

The main element of "culture shock" Ed encountered was that of the manifestations of racial discrimination, including separate drinking fountains, toilets, schools, and living and travel accommodations. Otherwise, the relatively liberal environment in Chapel Hill, where northerners were accepted, allowed the Curnens to feel comfortable. This same ambience aided later in the decisions of other northerners (Chamberlin, Ordway, Van Wyk, and Harned) to come to Chapel Hill.

Ed acknowledges his debt to Dr. Grover Powers and the Yale Department of Pediatrics for setting the tone of professional excellence combined with congeniality in his Department—"almost like a family." This influence of Powers also affected others Ed knew in New Haven who later became pediatric departmental chairmen, including Drs. Robert Cooke (Hopkins), Henry Kempe (Colorado), Richard Olmsted (Oregon), Donal Dunphy (Iowa), Victor Vaughan (Georgia and Temple), and William Nyhan (Miami and University of California at San Diego), among others. Harrie Chamberlin and Herb Harned also acknowledge the influence of Dr. Powers on their decisions to move to North Carolina. Powers may also have influenced Dr. Ordway to come.

Dr. Curnen recalls how helpful Dr. Arthur London was in acquainting him with the poor distribution of pediatricians in the state and with the political realities. Dr. London's importance to the Department during the Curnen years and thereafter is described by Dr. Herrington in a subsequent section (see "Biographies of the Early Greats of the Department"). Interestingly, there were only three pediatricians practicing east of Raleigh and no bona fide pediatrician was practicing in the Chapel Hill area. This created a major opportunity for the UNC Department to fill this vacuum and much energy was expended to train practitioners to fill this gap. As will be revealed later in detail, a large number of the straight pediatric house officers who trained at UNC-CH from 1956 to 1960 later practiced in North Carolina.

Dr. Curnen and Dr. Chamberlin both emphasized the importance of outreach visits to medical meetings in stimulating referrals to the fledgling Department. These often took place in "exotic" locations, such as "chick houses" and even a railroad restaurant. Dinner started after grace was said, which included such prayers as "Deliver us from the evil of socialized medicine."

The relationships of the Department of Pediatrics with the Medical School's administration and with other departments was probed in detail in Dr. Curnen's and several other interviews. In particular, the large size and subspecialty structures of the Department of Medicine were contrasted to the small size of the Department of Pediatrics. The chief of pediatrics had been appointed one year later than the chief of medicine and the Department of Medicine was well established even before Ed Curnen arrived. Rather than faulting Dr. Berryhill for conceiving of pediatrics as a small and minor department, Dr. Curnen felt that if he "had been Dean of the Medical School at that time he would have looked to the Department of Medicine for main strength and leadership." Dr. Curnen attributed the slower growth of the Department of Pediatrics to the state fiscal situation, where biennial budgets prevented rapid expansion of funding for salaries. Federal funding was also minimal during the early Curnen years.

Dr. Curnen had multifaceted relationships with many people who continued to advise him. He mentions specifically Drs. Thomas Rivers, Frank Horsfall, and Rene Dubos from Rockefeller and Drs. Kenneth Blackfan, Clement Smith, Charles Janeway, Max Finland, and William Castle from Harvard. Locally, the people he turned to most often were Drs. Sidney Chipman and Arthur London early on, and Drs. Chamberlin, Ordway, and Van Wyk later. Dr. Charles "Chuck" Burnett was especially close as a friend and advisor and, of course, Dr. Reece Berryhill was an admired and helpful person. Like every Department member who was interviewed, Dr. Curnen praised Sarah "Peaches" Dunlap, the executive secretary to the dean, for her administrative skills and delightful personality: "as an agent of communication she was superb."

The restrictions in funding limited allocations for faculty salaries. Dr. Van Wyk's initial annual salary of $6,000 was below even what was expected. A plan had been introduced by Dr. Nathan Womack, the chief of surgery, based on his experience in St. Louis, where each department contributed private practice income to the Dean's Office, and this was then parceled out to the various departments. The Surgery Department's salaries were always the largest and some of their excess monies were redistributed—with pediatrics always receiving the lowest amount. This supplement of basic salaries varied from month to month and thus often constituted a "surprise," not always pleasant.

Since money was scarce, Dr. Curnen had to establish each salary as a line

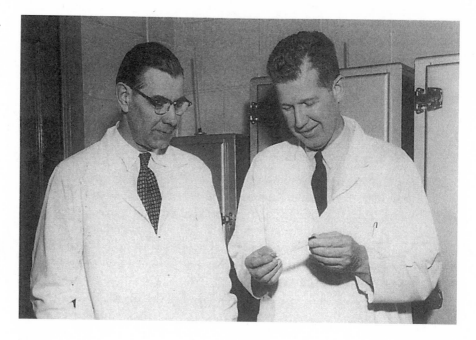

item in the biennial state budget and then be in a position to offer this salary
as an inducement for recruiting faculty members. This salary was fixed for
two years and attempts could be made to increase it only after this time interval. Dr. Curnen was indeed very restricted in his ability to increase salaries
during the interval between budgets, having to draw from the small pool of
funds available to him from the Dean's Office and from extramural sources.

Ed's cordial and cooperative relationship with Dr. Burnett and others in
the Department of Medicine permitted involvement of its subspecialists in the
care of children. He pointed out specifically the help that Drs. John Sessions
(gastroenterology), Jeff Palmer (hematology), and Ernie Craige (cardiology)
gave from that department. In addition, Dr. Doris Ahlee Howell from Duke
ran a clinic in pediatric hematology every week as a "labor of love," and Dr.
Ann Peters, who was trained in obstetrics, organized the nurseries. She and
Dr. Sidney Chipman were involved in the process of health maintenance, a
program with no counterpart in the Department of Medicine. Dr. Curnen
emphasized the different missions of the Medicine and Pediatrics Departments. "In Pediatrics, we are concerned about maintaining good health and
thinking of the needs of the patient, whereas in Medicine the mission was
viewed more as restoring good health or resisting the progress of deteriora-
tion and of the treatment of [the] specific diseases, rather than the overall
maintenance of health of their individual patients."

The relationship between pediatrics and medicine permitted the blending
of the two services for grand rounds at Thursday noon, when the natural histories of various disorders could be emphasized. These rounds and this useful
approach were shared by Drs. Burnett and Curnen, as well as others. Dr. Cur-

nen's broad-based background, with his appointments at the Rockefeller Institute as an assistant resident physician and at Yale in pediatrics and in preventive medicine, helped him in his professional and interpersonal relationships with internists.

The initial rotating internship, established by tradition and convenience, was replaced rapidly by straight internships in medicine, surgery, and pediatrics, as well as by that of the very successful mixed medicine-pediatrics internship, essentially sharing half time on each service. Most of these latter residents ended up as internists or pediatricians, but some proceeded into obstetrics or psychiatry, with very few entering surgery or its subspecialties. Interestingly, few of these interns entered general practice at that time. This mixed residency program became very popular and drew many applicants for the eight positions by 1960. (Incidentally, Dr. Curnen failed in an attempt to replicate this program when he was chairman of the Department of Pediatrics at Columbia University. He also felt that the warm relationship between the Departments of Medicine and Pediatrics in Chapel Hill avoided the separatism between these departments that he had experienced at Yale.)

Dr. Curnen described the development of the pediatric outpatient clinics from a general clinic perspective to specialty clinics as the caseload increased. The limited number of examining rooms in the fourth corridor of the Old Clinic Building were shared by other services. Inpatient facilities were also not well delineated and secretaries had to be ousted from the seventh floor to accommodate the initial pediatric patients admitted on January 9, 1953. Deliveries were performed in the operating rooms until several months after Dr. Chamberlin's arrival in January 1953.

EARLY GRADUATES OF THE RESIDENCY PROGRAMS

Dr. Curnen discussed the personalities of the initial residents who contributed so much, including Drs. William Davis and Earle Spaugh with their pragmatic approaches to medicine; Dr. Robert Winters's innovative and investigative ideas provided stimulating teaching. Although several times UNC did not "match" its full complement of pediatric interns, the straight residency program was built up gradually, aided by the popular mixed medicine-pediatrics internships.

Forty straight pediatric residents were trained from 1952 to 1960. Of these, eighteen have located pediatric practices in North Carolina, making up a "who's who" of practitioners in this state. Included in this group are Drs. Anne Askew, Richard Borden, Elwood Coley, Joseph Corpening, William Davis, Griggs Dickson, Hugh Hemmings, Victor Herring, James Morris, Frank Niblock, Richard Patterson, William Powell, Frank Shaw, Robert Senior, Martha Sharpless, Earle Spaugh, Charles Stamey, and James White. Several other pediatricians who have practiced in North Carolina served as rotating or mixed interns on the pediatric service, including Drs. Oliver Roddey, Franklin Stallings, Edward Thorne, and Malcolm McLean. This process of supplying primary care physicians to many regions of the state appears to have fulfilled in part the primary mission of the Medical School in its early years. There can be no question but that the physicians trained in the program played very active roles in initiating referrals and supporting the growth of the service. In contrast, very few pediatricians went from these programs to practice elsewhere in the nation during Dr. Curnen's tenure; only five individuals were identified as having done this.

A surprisingly large number of persons (fourteen) were identified as entering academic fields or hospital-based positions. Interestingly, except for Dr. Jacqueline Noonan, who was in the rotating program in 1954–1955 and later became a dominant figure in pediatric cardiology nationally as well as becoming the chair of the Department of Pediatrics at the University of Kentucky, these future academicians didn't appear on the scene until 1956.

RECRUITMENT OF FACULTY

A major part of Dr. Curnen's new job was the recruitment of faculty members who could aid him in establishing the desired ambience of the Department. In his interview, Dr. Curnen discussed the early recruiting of faculty, which was limited severely by lack of space as well as funds. He describes the assistance given to him by Dr. Loren MacKinney in 1952, when Loren stayed in Chapel Hill during his wife Delores's serious paralytic poliomyelitis. Six years later, Ed recruited Loren for a faculty position as chief of the outpatient department. He attempted unsuccessfully to recruit Bob Cooke and Donal Dunphy from Yale.

Judson J. Van Wyk

Dr. Van Wyk describes his own recruitment in his interview with Dr. Denny (archives). Jud had always been a person with a scientific bent, having majored in chemistry in college, but he left postgraduate studies at St. Louis University, where he worked with Nobel Laureate Dr. Edward Doisy, to enter Johns Hopkins Medical School. There he performed research with Dr. Mansfield Clark and was guided especially by Dr. Victor Najjar. He followed his residencies at Hopkins and Cincinnati Children's Hospital with NIH training under Dr. James Shannon for two years and then took fellowship training in endocrinology with Dr. Lawson Wilkins back at Hopkins. His recruitment to UNC was a two-way affair with Jud initiating the correspondence and later parlaying a UNC grand rounds discussion on rheumatoid arthritis into a focused discussion on the soft tissue swelling in the Bonnevie-Ullrich variant of the Turner syndrome. This led to a discourse on sex determination since Jud, along with Lawson Wilkins and Mel Grumbach, had recently found that two-thirds of the "girls" with Turner syndrome were chromosomal "males" (according to their understanding of the new sex chromatin technology). These unpublished data were not yet known in Chapel Hill. People therefore overlooked the fact that Jud knew almost nothing about rheumatoid arthritis, and he was hired soon thereafter. Jud always referred to this grand rounds as "turning water into wine."

The problems that Dr. Van Wyk encountered after coming to Chapel Hill were representative of those present at UNC in 1955. He had to scrounge funds for his own laboratory and, in order to accomplish this, took the advice of Dr. Charles Hooker in the Anatomy Department to approach the Elsa U. Pardee Foundation of Midland, Michigan. The $17,000 in funds that resulted from this unusual foray bypassed the Dean's Office and other administrative echelons. Despite his early meager salary and nonexistent laboratory facilities, Jud appreciated Dr. Curnen's vision and encouragement, and when Jud's Markle Scholarship came through his status locally improved significantly and basic starter funds were made available for his research. In describing these humble beginnings of his outstanding career, Jud acknowledges the wonderful support of Persis, his wife; everyone who knows her will understand his gratitude. A special chapter of the Department's early history could

Harrie R.
Chamberlin

be devoted to the role of the extra-ordinary wives who participated in its development during those trying times.

Dr. Chamberlin's background and recruitment are also detailed in the summary of his interview with Harned and on the tapes in the archives. Harrie had majored in biochemical sciences (a broad scientific mix) at Harvard College and had attended Harvard Medical School during wartime. After a year in neurological residency at Boston City Hospital with Dr. Denny-Brown and two years in the Army, he decided to change his career to pediatrics. His residencies at Massachusetts General and at Yale prepared him well for the type of program envisaged at UNC. His decision to come to Chapel Hill, after an additional six months at Boston Children's Hospital, was a difficult one, but he chose to join others who had come and whom he admired; he soon became Dr. Curnen's "man for all seasons." He signed on for two years before making a final decision and ended up staying a lifetime. His strong contribution to the program, including organizing teaching and participating in building up the clinical service and in developing the program in pediatric neurology are detailed in his interview and its summary.

Dr. Nelson Ordway's recruitment was unique. He came to UNC in the summer of 1954 from Louisiana State University, where he had been chief of pediatrics. Nelson's department at LSU was considered "too radical" during this period of McCarthyism and several of its members were under pressure to resign. Nelson, characteristically, couldn't abide this and became available for a move. He brought to UNC a broad scope of talents; he was extremely knowledgeable in treating seriously ill children with metabolic and cardiac problems especially, but he was also imbued with the same idealism that motivated Dr. Curnen. Clever in research techniques, he and Dr. Van Wyk supplemented the investigative spirit that Dr. Curnen possessed. Dr. Ordway's return to Yale in 1957, where he remained as the chief clinical pediatrician for sick children for many years, proved to be a major step up in his career, though a loss for UNC. More information about Dr. Ordway is included in chapter 3, "Faculty," and in his biography in part 9.

Dr. Herb Harned's recruitment in 1958 was aided by many of the same attractions that others had found: specifically, the sense of an expanding opportunity in a congenial atmosphere in a department emphasizing the same principles with which he was familiar. Harned's Yale background was extensive: there he had been a "faculty brat" since the age of seven, an undergraduate and medical graduate, a fellow in cardiology, and a faculty member for six years. He also knew Dr. Powers from childhood as a neighbor and was the caretaker of the Powers' yard during summers. His only training away from Yale had been at Hopkins as an intern and at Boston Children's as a resident for two years. The interchange of Ordway and Harned took place

Herbert S. Harned, Jr.

quite smoothly. Dr. Harned, in his interview, reveals how important this two-year period on Dr. Curnen's service was in his life and remembers many events vividly.

The Arnolds were recruited in 1958 as a "package deal." John had been recommended "warmly" by Dr. John Enders, the Nobel Laureate, who had instructed John in his laboratory at Harvard. Mary also had been highly recommended by those who knew her and proved to be a fine "bonus." John, who had been a pilot and then a POW in World War II, unfortunately developed malignant hypertension while at UNC and died prematurely from this disorder after the Arnolds moved to Brown University.

Dr. Ruth Dillard came in 1958, also as part of a husband and wife team since her husband, Arch, had an appointment in the Department of Obstetrics. Ruth became active in the outpatient department during her short stay and aided Dr. Chamberlin in the neurology clinic. Ruth and Arch spent time in Haiti and in Vietnam, and eventually Ruth became director of the outpatient clinic at the University of Texas in Galveston.

A particularly important person whom Dr. Curnen recruited was Dr. Annie Scott, who has been variously described as "one of a kind," "indestructible," "very special," and in other complimentary terms. She spent the earlier part of her career in China where, despite her lameness, she performed such feats as serving as pediatrician in chief in two major Chinese hospitals, moving these hospitals during wartime and treating hundreds of cases of diseases now very rare in the United States. She was a friend of Dr. Steven Chang, a personal physician of Chiang Kaishek and later a professor in Hong Kong. She came to UNC from Columbia University, in part because she loved this region of the world (her home was in High Point). Her skill and obsessive devotion in dealing with cystic fibrosis cases and in teaching about nutrition and childhood tuberculosis were appreciated along with her wonderful personal qualities. She is said to have "terrorized" the medical students and young house officers, but probably for their own good. Additional information about Dr. Scott's career is provided in chapter 3, "Faculty," and in her biography in part 9.

As has been emphasized, Dr. Curnen had a strong interest in scholarly research. He was able to set up his own virus laboratory on the fourth floor of the Old Medical School Building with the assistance of his research associate, Ms. Eru Tanabe, whom he brought down from Yale. Jud Van Wyk's ability to obtain outside funding permitted allocation of laboratory space in the Clinic Building, and Nelson Ordway established a blood gas laboratory in the restroom area of the Clinic Auditorium, fortuitously abandoned when duplication of restrooms ceased with racial integration. Herb Harned used a storage area and corridor in the Old Medical School Building until he worked out an arrangement to time his sheep experiments so that they would begin the day after the cadavers were removed from the dental anatomy laboratory. Such efforts and actions are indicative of the serious space problems that were not alleviated for many years.

DISTINGUISHED RESIDENTS

Several pediatric residents during the Curnen years have become especially prominent. In particular, two residents were brought to Chapel Hill who had obvious academic credentials and were regarded as potential faculty members. Dr. Robert Winters was an outstanding medical student at Yale; Dr. Curnen lured him to UNC from a West Coast residency. He was an excellent chief resident but also put enormous energy into scholarly investigations. He tracked down a huge family of patients with Vitamin D–resistant rickets, attending multiple family reunions where blood sampling was interjected between "hors d'oeuvres and entrees." This project became a classic study of the genetics of this disorder and was published with the assistance of Drs. Burnett, T. Franklin Williams, and John Graham. Bob worked as a fellow with Dr. Louis Welt for two years and then left for the University of Pennsylvania (before rejoining Dr. Curnen at Columbia).

Another outstanding resident was Dr. Harry Meyer, who later was jointly responsible for the development of the rubella vaccine. He had worked with a former colleague of Ed's, Dr. Joseph Smadell, at the Division of Biologics Standards in Bethesda. Dr. Curnen had to talk Dr. Meyer out of entering private practice in Arkansas with the inducement that he could participate in the ongoing coxsackie virus research in Ed's laboratory. After residency, however, Dr. Meyer accepted an attractive offer for a position at the Walter Reed Army Institute of Research. In 1972, he became director of the Biologics Division at Bethesda, a bureau of the Food and Drug Administration, and he is now the president of the Medical Research Division of Lederle Laboratories.

The list of practicing pediatricians and academicians includes many who have made important contributions after playing key roles in the development of the house staff program. In particular, Dr. Griggs Dickson was an outstanding chief resident toward the end of Dr. Curnen's tenure. Dr. Dickson practiced later in South Carolina and then in Charlotte, where he and Dr. J. C. Parke were instrumental in developing the pediatric teaching program at Charlotte Memorial Hospital. Dr. Robert Senior, another chief resident under Dr. Curnen, started the first pediatric practice in Chapel Hill in 1959, which has collaborated since with the Department on many projects. This important association reached its peak during the Denny years and will be detailed later.

In addition to the many contributions made by practitioners, it is important to recognize several academicians who proved to be especially notable products of the training programs of this era. Dr. Robert Herrington finished the residency program, returned for fellowship training in pediatric cardiology here, and was a faculty member for many years. Bob's skillful teaching has been recognized generally and he has received the Resident's Teaching Award twice. Dr. Martha Sharpless, after training at UNC, became the chief resident at Babies' Hospital in New York following Dr. Curnen's move to the chairmanship there. She returned to the Greensboro area and for many years was the mainstay in the pediatric residency teaching program at Moses Cone Hospital.

Dr. Robert Castle continued his academic career at Duke as a pediatric cardiac fellow and then returned for several years as a faculty member at UNC. Later, he became chief of pediatric cardiology at the University of New Mexico in Albuquerque and at one time was president of the New Mexico Heart Association. He has since practiced in Atlanta and Jackson (Mississippi) and is now in Austin, Texas.

Dr. Richard Patterson was chief of the hematology-oncology division at Bowman Gray School of Medicine before retiring in 1991. Dr. John Lukens is also a hematologist, now at Vanderbilt University School of Medicine, and has had an outstanding career. Dr. Faith Kung has also pursued this field and is a professor at the University of California (San Diego) Medical Center. Dr. Doris Ahlee Howell, who had graciously provided consultation in hematology and oncology while a full-time faculty member at Duke, must have inspired these physicians. She has recently retired after a distinguished career, including having served as a departmental chair. Her contribution to the Department was so unique and genuine that it will be treated separately later (see "Faculty").

Dr. Roland Schmidt completed pediatric cardiology training at UNC, was chief of pediatric cardiology at the University of West Virginia, and became an associate dean at that school. Roland now lives in retirement in Chapel Hill. Dr. Thomas Gardner also became a pediatric cardiologist, and after training at Yale became a faculty member at Boston University before moving west to practice in Evanston, Illinois.

Dr. Gerald Fernald was a first-year resident in 1960–1961 at North Carolina Memorial Hospital, completed his residency training at Boston Children's Hospital, and returned here as a fellow in infectious disease. He has had a distinguished career as an expert in chronic lung disorders and cystic fibrosis. He also has been associate chair of the Department for many years, bridging the gap between the regimes of Drs. Denny and Boat and acting as chair during this interval.

Dr. Paul Glezen also was a resident in 1960–1961 and continued as a faculty member here for many years before joining the pediatric infectious disease division at Baylor in Houston. Outstanding in his field, Paul has continued his connection with UNC as a loyal "alumnus."

Dr. Frank French shared the position of chief resident with Dr. Glezen, spending a very productive year in the laboratory of the pediatric endocrinology division. His outstanding career at the University of North Carolina has been chronicled in the section on the Laboratories for Reproductive Biology (part 4, chapter 17).

As one looks over the house staff lists in chapter 48, one can note the three-to-one preponderance of males over females among the Pediatric trainees during the Curnen years. The faculty ratio of seven males to four females reveals the respect in the Department for women as colleagues. Dr. Mary Arnold, in her interview, stated that at no time was gender a cause of unfair treatment during her years at UNC.

TEACHING PROGRAMS

The evolution of the teaching programs in the Department was primarily dependent on the faculty members and the excellent residents who participated on the teaching service. The early and formative first months of the Department were challenging and difficult, with only Dr. Curnen and later Dr. Chamberlin as full-time faculty members. However, much help was provided by Drs. Sidney Chipman and Arthur London.

Efforts were made early to coordinate programs with the Department of Pediatrics at Duke and were partly successful. Dr. Chamberlin had especially good relations with the Duke neurologists and Dr. Van Wyk benefited greatly from his relationship with Dr. Frank Engel, an endocrinologist there. However, early joint grand rounds in pediatrics foundered on lack of parking space there and other problems inherent in the relationships between the two departments.

Examination of the early teaching programs indicated that lectures were important because of the small faculty. For example, the second-year teaching program involved ten lectures yearly. Dr. Chamberlin presented a newborn at the first lecture and then showed the progress in its development at the last lecture, months later. He performed this feat with enthusiasm and even used his own daughter, as a toddler, in one series. This proved to be a very effective way to emphasize the importance of growth and development in pediatrics. This series of lectures was continued for at least ten years.

Early third-year bedside teaching by the attending faculty was arduous, since the entire service had to be covered by the small cadre of full-time attendings with the exception of six weeks each summer when Dr. Chipman volunteered to attend. Dr. Chamberlin attended for two-month stretches and for at least five months each year until Dr. Ordway arrived. The third-year program was designed on the models of the third-year Yale and fourth-year Harvard services, which were familiar to Drs. Curnen and Chamberlin. Evidence of this influence may be seen in the house officer/student manual *The Pediatric Patient*, which Dr. Chamberlin wrote and which was used for many years as the basic manual in pediatrics at this hospital (see archives).

Clinical rounds were supplemented very early by radiology and pediatric neurology teaching conferences. Initially, pediatrics, medicine, and surgery were involved in weekly combined staff conferences, but these later evolved into separate grand rounds, still frequently combining medicine and pediatrics. As has been mentioned, this type of interchange between medicine and pediatrics, which existed also among subspecialty groups as they developed, provided a basis for the establishment of the very successful mixed medicine-pediatrics residency at UNC and for its persistence over the years in various formats.

In 1956, admitting conferences in the early morning included all pediatric house officers, students on service, and attending staff. Following this, the students spent an hour with the assigned attending faculty member and then this attending rounded with the house staff. The only day each week that the attending did not round regularly was when he was assigned to see patients in his particular clinic. For several of the early years, weekly pediatric lectures were offered to the entire third-year class, but these were periodically discontinued and eventually dropped.

In 1959, with a much larger attending staff available, a curriculum committee was formed which included MacKinney as chair, Chamberlin, Harned, and Van Wyk. The report of this committee led to important changes, some of which have persisted to the present. The inpatient service was divided into two teams and the students were brought into these ward teams more actively. Frequent lectures about the newborn were delivered in 1955 for each of the six student groups who were on service during the school year. A student paper on a pediatric subject was required, but this was discontinued after several years as the clinical service expanded.

Conferences were frequent for the fourth-year students, who were involved then in an "outpatient" year. Each morning, one of thirty-eight topics over each six-and-a-half-week pediatric outpatient rotation was discussed, with two students presenting different aspects for fifteen minutes each, before the attending took over for an additional half hour. These sessions continued throughout the Curnen years. Initially, the subspecialty clinics were included entirely in the general clinic setting, with one day devoted to a specific discipline. Child psychiatry played an active role in the clinics held on Saturday mornings during the five-and-a-half-day working week. The important role of practicing clinicians in teaching in all of these clinics was stressed and some pediatricians drove long distances to help.

An important chart conference was held at Saturday noon luncheons where all discharges were reviewed as well as important OPD cases. These conferences were not always enjoyed by the house officers since they involved critiques. They were considered mandatory for all the attendings. Dr. Chamberlin indicates the intensity of these discussions by telling about the day that Hurricane Hazel came through Chapel Hill. The conference was held without a break throughout the period of the hurricane's passage and it was only when the participants left for home that they realized that roads were blocked, with trees down all over town and services otherwise disrupted.

Two innovative clinic programs were inaugurated. A "residents'" clinic, later termed "intermediate" clinic, provided inexpensive care by senior residents for the families of residents from all the hospital services and for medical students. There were no professional charges. This program still exists in modified form. Also, a "continuity" clinic was arranged with the Department of Medicine so that residents, including med-peds residents, could follow interesting child or adult patients throughout the year.

During the early years, a significant series of twenty to thirty lectures per year were given to the UNC student nurses by attendings and senior residents. Additional series of lectures to physical therapy students and to students in the division of maternal and child health were given, with both Drs. Curnen and Chamberlin playing especially active roles.

FACILITIES

Dr. Blythe describes the facilities of the new hospital with its northside entrance. The seventh floor was assigned to children from the very start, but clinical space had to be reclaimed initially from administrators. Deliveries initially were in the operating room and rooming-in was obligatory, since no round-the-clock nursery existed for the first three to four years. Interestingly, the first live baby delivered at North Carolina Memorial Hospital was the son of Delores and Loren MacKinney.

Improvements of facilities were slow to appear, but in 1956 the premature and infant special care nursery opened, and about a year later the newborn nursery began to be staffed around the clock. The fourteen-room pediatric clinic area, adjacent to the Medical School morgue's entrance, did not provide an ideal model for children's care, especially when the bodies were parked in a nearby hall. Also, since no state building in North Carolina was air-conditioned at the time the hospital was built, our seventh (top) floor achieved the distinction of being the hottest ward in the hospital. Dr. Harned has ascribed the "remarkable acuteness" of the staff in assessing the significance of fevers in our patients during those summers to the fact that most of the children on the seventh floor ran afternoon fevers.

RELATIONS WITH OTHER SERVICES

The Pediatrics Department had to stand up for its rights in its relations with other clinical departments in many instances. Two recurrent conflicts persisted during the Curnen years and afterward to a degree. The first resulted from Dr. Curnen's unshakeable belief that pediatricians should be present at all births and should be responsible for resuscitating the newborns. This, at times, resulted in matching a junior pediatric house officer against a relatively senior obstetrician, and conflicts subsequently arose. The only known altercation occurred, however, years later when pediatrician Hugh Bryan and obstetrician Stark Wolkoff squared off. Periodically, this policy would be reviewed, but pediatrics steadfastly maintained its jurisdiction over the newborn from the time of the exit from the birth canal.

Also, pediatricians were responsible for working up all infants below two years of age who were admitted to the surgical service (with the exception of orthopedic cases). Although the pediatrics faculty was unalterably committed to this concept (and still is, despite the erosion that has occurred over the years), the surgical staff resented the inference that they were not skilled in caring for infants. This persistent conflict may have contributed to the unwillingness of the surgeons at our institution to recognize the specialty of pediatric surgery until the 1980s.

Outstanding but formidable surgeons such as Drs. Nathan Womack, Gordon Dugger, and Richard Peters could intimidate some of the house staff and attendings, but Dr. Curnen beat back all challenges to his service's prerogatives. At Yale, Ed had been a distinguished member of the boxing team, indicating that behind his mild demeanor was a person made of stern stuff.

Other important persons in the medical complex at this time included Dr. Robert Cadmus, a tightfisted but able hospital administrator; Dr. "Daddy" Ross, chief of obstetrics and an outstanding raconteur; Dr. William Fleming, a hard-working, loquacious outpatient specialist; and Dr. Ernest Wood, a quiet and unaggressive chief of radiology. These individuals, especially, had many joint enterprises with pediatricians during these years. Many references to these and other important faculty members, including those who taught in the preclinical years, have been made during the taped interviews and in the descriptions of the subspecialties in part 4.

RACE RELATIONS

Despite its liberal reputation, Chapel Hill did not adapt easily to the Supreme Court's decision of 1954; schools, theaters, and buses were still segregated, as were facilities in the hospital such as the adult patient wards, dining halls, and restrooms. Thus, the integration of patients on the wards became an important issue and the Pediatric Department needed to exert leadership. Since the seventh floor for the most part was comprised of semiprivate rooms, the transition from separation of black and white patients to inclusion of both races in the same room could be made without involving many people, in contrast to how things had to be handled in large wards such as those that existed for the adult services.

Dr. Curnen describes integration as having proceeded unobtrusively and for the most part without serious complaints. The only incident he recalls was one involving the objections of an American Indian family to being grouped with blacks. Dr. George Summer, at the time a pediatric resident, also has provided additional information about this episode, which involved the additional problem of a black medical student examining a female patient of another race. In the academic year 1953–1954, a firm edict came down from the highest administrative levels that no white patients would be examined by black medical students. George found himself in the awkward position of having to assign a black student to examine a light-skinned Indian patient despite this ruling. Later, key faculty members, along with George, were summoned and were told in no uncertain terms by Dean Berryhill that this ruling was incontestable.* In marked contrast, Bill Blythe has described an incident in the mid-sixties when Dr. Berryhill personally backed him up in permitting a black student to perform a vaginal examination on a prominent North Carolinian. The affirmative action programs now in force at the Medical School also indicate the great changes in attitude that have occurred during the last forty years, which have been associated with appointments later of a black female chief resident and black faculty members in the Department of Pediatrics. One especially successful black medical student, James Slade, had been admitted to the Medical School during the Curnen years. Recently, as an outstanding pediatrician in Edenton, he received a coveted Distinguished Alumni Award.

The major general changes in integration occurred after the election of John Kennedy, but Chapel Hill soon reached the forefront of Southern communities in accepting integration. The Community Church, under the leadership of its minister, Charles Jones, had provided a place for the leaders of the civil rights movement to express their views. The Binkley Baptist Church, under the leadership of Robert Seymour, also followed this liberal perspective. A benign police chief in Chapel Hill permitted many marchers and organizers of the civil rights movement to practice passive resistance and to learn methods to maximize TV coverage.

ROBBIE PAGE MEMORIAL AND SUPPORT OF THE TRI SIGMA SORORITY

A very important contribution to supplement the core medical program of the Department was made by the national Sigma Sigma Sigma college sorority. This sorority has taken on major projects that have contributed to the care and comfort of children in hospital settings. Their ongoing philanthropy for many years at UNC focused especially on playroom programs, but also provided seed money for construction of facilities.

---

*Dr. Curnen claims that he "acquiesced to the 'ground rules,' only to ignore them in practice."

Drs. Curnen and Van Wyk played critical roles in the initiation of play therapy programs at UNC. Dr. Van Wyk, who was familiar with the play therapy program at Johns Hopkins Hospital, saw the deficiencies in the recreational facilities and programs here and proposed that money available for "rehabilitation" be used to plan a superior program at the North Carolina Memorial Hospital. Concurrently, the Tri Sigmas found that money they had visualized for research on poliomyelitis was now available for other projects. Robbie Page, the son of the national president of the sorority, had died at the age of five years of poliomyelitis, and the Tri Sigmas had been searching for a project where they could honor the memory of this lovely child who had "wished to help other children."

After a series of visits here by sorority members and other meetings, Dr. Curnen attended as the only man in a convention of five hundred sorority ladies and secured a pledge of $25,000 to seed the building of facilities for a play therapy program. Plans called for the "children's room" area on the east end of the seventh floor to contain a large playroom area and a small classroom for young patients. Supplementing this was a plan for a large conference room on the northeast corner of the seventh floor, later to be named after Dr. Curnen and destined to become the central teaching area of the Department.

The Tri Sigmas also contributed seed money in 1963 for an isolation unit at the western end of the seventh floor, supplemented by additional aid from Dr. Jack Lynch and his family. The Tri Sigmas have also been responsible for the establishment of a playroom in the outpatient department in 1969, for an intensive care area on the seventh floor in 1973, for a recreational area for older children on the ninth floor of the bed tower, and for a play area in the Jaycee Burn Center. Salaries and scholarships for the play therapy program have also been supported for many years.

Thus, from its origins during the Curnen era, the play program has progressed to become one of the best nationally and the Tri Sigmas' largesse has contributed greatly to many other departmental activities. (A complete description of the role of the Robbie Page Memorial is contained in part 5, chapter 29.)

INFANT SPECIAL CARE NURSERY

Dr. Curnen conceived of the idea of an infant special care nursery, to include both prematures and term newborns with special problems. Dr. Ordway wrote the following note on May 20, 1991, to corroborate this:

In my recorded interview with Harrie, did I comment on the Newborn Special Care Unit set up by Dr. Curnen? His concept was that all newborns needing special care—preemies, those with special medical and surgical problems—should be in a special area other than the ward or newborn nursery. Indeed, as I recall there was no normal newborn nursery at that time, because obligatory rooming-in was imposed on all mothers. I don't remember where the Unit was. It would accommodate about 4 newborns. I recall that Dick Peters made use of it. It is my impression that this was the first unit of this sort in the country—in the world? The large unit set up by Lou Gluck at Yale followed the Chapel Hill one by some years. [By 1958, after the opening of the normal newborn nursery, the Unit accommodated an average of fifteen prematures and other infants requiring special care.]

This unique idea could not be developed here as effectively as Dr. Curnen had wished because of limited space and difficulty in recruiting a neonatologist. After the development of Dr. Gluck's prototype unit, similar nurseries have been replicated in every major medical center.

MEDICAL MEETINGS AT THE UNIVERSITY OF NORTH CAROLINA

Important meetings held at UNC during Dr. Curnen's tenure included a meeting of the Interurban Clinical Club, founded in 1902 by Sir William Osler and composed of a select group of physicians from Baltimore, Philadelphia, New York, New Haven, and Boston and another important conference on the etiology of mental retardation. The former program took place in 1958 on one of Chapel Hill's beautiful spring days and provided an early opportunity for Dr. Carl Gottschalk to present his superb work on nephron collection techniques. Supplementing the scientific program was a presentation by Loren MacKinney's father, a University of North Carolina history professor, of interesting and beautiful medieval medical manuscripts.

The meeting on the etiology of mental retardation in 1956 was a landmark for the Department. This Ross conference was planned primarily by Dr. Curnen, aided by Dr. Chamberlin and by Dr. Richard Masland from Bowman Gray Medical School, and included presentations by a variety of pediatricians, neurologists, and basic scientists. Dr. Powers was made honorary chairman of this "star-studded" program. Dr. Curnen felt that "this [conference] has not been given much recognition as a seminal experience, but I think it brought a lot of people in diverse fields together and got them thinking about this matter and probably was very influential in the later developments which came along very rapidly and extensively in the early 1960s following the support and interest of the Kennedys." Dr. Curnen invited Dr. Jerry Harris (Duke) and Dr. Weston Kelsey (Bowman Gray) to share the leadership of this conference. Dr. Powers was chairman of the advisory board of the National Association for Retarded Children (later Citizens). Dr. Robert Cooke, who had two children of his own with cri du chat syndrome, attended this conference. He worked later with the Kennedys and was instrumental, along with others, in establishing the National Institute of Child Health and Human Development.

SOCIAL LIFE WITHIN THE DEPARTMENT

Since all work and no play makes for dullness of mind and spirit, some of the extracurricular activities of this time need to be mentioned. Many of those interviewed described the gracious and friendly entertaining of pediatric faculty members by Ed and Manny in their lovely colonial-style home in the Westwood section of Chapel Hill. Their children, Sheila, Tim, and Cotty, helped to make these occasions enjoyable. Usually these affairs took place when an appropriate distinguished visitor was matched with faculty members of like interests, but many times these gatherings just seemed to occur spontaneously and often they included children of the faculty.

Dr. Ordway was remembered for entertaining of a different sort. He believed in the "work party" that preceded festivities. However, these efforts were rewarded with warm hospitality from Nelson and Ernestine. This custom probably reflects Ordway's New England background, since those of us who trained at Boston Children's Hospital remember with some pain a similar commitment to the work ethic at the home of Dr. Charles Janeway.

The annual picnic was initiated during these years, but never reached the stage of "refinement" achieved during the Denny era. Harrie Chamberlin's lot on the other side of the bypass was used initially. Later the venue was changed to the Hogan's Lake area, where the yearly softball game was played on a field studded with cow flops, which helped to hone the skills of house staff, faculty, nurses, children, and others who participated in this classic contest.

During the first few years after the hospital opened, Mrs. Norma Berryhill served afternoon tea on Friday to the house staff in the hospital. This was a silver service, bone china "high tea" in the Southern manner and attendance was mandatory, as described by Dr. Summer, an early resident. He agreed that if nurses had been invited, as they were not, the inconvenient hour that had been chosen (when physicians were trying to complete their workups before the weekend) would have been more acceptable. These affairs emphasized the concept that "our doctors should be real gentlemen," and harmonized neatly with Dr. Berryhill's insistence that all physicians at NCMH should wear neckties at all times while on the premises.

DR. CURNEN'S DEPARTURE

A pivotal event occurred in 1960 when Dr. Curnen made the decision to assume Dr. Rustin McIntosh's important post as chairman of pediatrics at Columbia University. This represented a major event in each of our lives, but all realized that, characteristically, Ed was taking on a larger responsibility as chief of pediatrics at Babies' Hospital in New York, one of the most important jobs in pediatrics.

Those responsible for this history feel strongly that Dr. Curnen's original goal for this Department was achieved to the degree needed, creating a base for its maintenance and maturation over the years. He indicated his philoso-

phy and the difficulty of achieving this in his final statement of his last report
to the dean:

> The development and maintenance of an effective educational pro-
> gram in pediatrics includes the need for productive research, but
> depends in large measure upon the continuous provision of exemplary
> clinical services. This can and has been successfully accomplished with
> less than optimal physical facilities. Under such circumstances, how-
> ever, the requirement of high calibre personnel is even more evident
> and essential. It is apparent that all possible resources must continu-
> ally be cultivated if this paramount requirement is to be fulfilled.

PERSONAL QUALITIES OF DR. EDWARD CURNEN

Many insights into Dr. Curnen's personality and character may be derived
from the above summary of his tenure at the University of North Carolina
and from the numerous interviews on tape. Other impressions have been summarized by Dr. Chamberlin in his introduction preceding the complete interview reproduced in the archives:

> Ed has had considerable influence on all of those who have been priv-
> ileged to know him well. A true gentleman, in the finest sense of that
> term, he ranks among the most selfless people most of us have known.
> During the years between 1939 and 1952 he published prolifically and
> made significant contributions to the rapidly expanding field of clini-
> cal virology. Yet, after being called to Chapel Hill, he deliberately sac-
> rificed much of his research time to concentrate his efforts on the care-
> ful building of the new department. He set the highest standards of
> respect for patients and their families. He was careful to shield even
> his closest associates from the majority of problems encountered in
> building a new service and invariably showed deep and genuine con-
> cern for the welfare of each of his staff, in both their professional and
> personal lives.
>
> A man of sensitivity and gentleness, yet possessed of strength of
> purpose, utmost integrity, and steadfast firmness in what he believes is
> right—this is perhaps the best way to describe Ed Curnen.

Another appraisal of Dr. Curnen comes from Dr. Doris Ahlee Howell, an
"outsider" from the Department of Pediatrics at Duke. In response to a
request from Dr. Denny to assess Dr. Curnen's leadership, she called several
persons who shared associations with Dr. Curnen. We believe these insightful
comments are of enough historic value to be reproduced in some detail.

She summarizes these thoughts along with her own assessment:

> As you know, Ed led by kindly permissiveness and, at the most, gen-
> tle persuasion. What may not have been appreciated at first sight was
> his quiet role-modeling of intellectual curiosity, attention to detail,

responsiveness to the requests of his faculty and residents and, above all, love and concern for children. Whether in conference, seminar or a social event at his own home, Ed always played a low-key role and would direct the attention, praise and glory towards other people. He was never self-effacing, simply quietly modest; a little shy, but very comfortable in his own person. I think young faculty were sometimes frustrated by his refusal to tell them what to do, but like Gibran's poetic description of a teacher, he "leads you to the threshold of your own mind." His influence on the growth and development of young pediatricians was subtle, usually not recognized until years later when those very faculty found themselves emulating his examples. A truly sincere teacher, and kindly man! Ed was considerably different from the dynamic, over-achieving, impatient chairman of today—more of a throwback to the philosophical, reflective scholar of the previous generation.

HERBERT S. HARNED, JR.

CHAPTER TWO

Research During the
Curnen Years

Editors' Note: The following is based to a major extent on the annual reports submitted to the dean by the Department of Pediatrics. A listing of funding, publications, and other information abstracted from these reports may be found in the archives.

IF GREAT institutions are likened to the shadow of one man lengthened, the modern UNC School of Medicine is surely the shadow of Walter Reece Berryhill. Dean Berryhill loved the University of North Carolina with a passion, and he insisted from the beginning that anything less than the highest standards of excellence would be unworthy of either the University or the state of North Carolina. The establishment of the four-year medical school in Chapel Hill rather than in a metropolitan center reflected his conviction that high standards of scholarship could be better maintained in the environment of a great state university than in a metropolitan center. Although Dean Berryhill had had no personal experience with research, it was consistent with his personality that he would listen to Nathan Womack and other close confidants who insisted that research and research training programs be incorporated into the four-year school at the outset and not be deferred to a later and more convenient time. Berryhill's choice of Edward Curnen, Nathan Womack, and Chuck Burnett to head up the major clinical departments reflected this philosophy and created an environment in which creativity could flourish.

INFECTIOUS DISEASES

Edward C. Curnen, Jr., the first chairman of pediatrics, established a climate of scholarship that left an indelible imprint on the Department. His research was undoubtedly greatly influenced by the stature of his associates. Ed would frequently quote Oswald Avery, whose picture graced the departmental office. Curnen's coinvestigators in his early studies included some of the greatest names in research on infectious diseases, such as Maxwell Finland, Colin MacLeod, George Mirick, Lee Farr, Palmer Futcher, Kendal Emerson, Jr., Frank L. Horsfall, Jr., Lewis Thomas, and Joseph L. Melnick. Curnen's early work focused on the pathophysiology of bacterial infections, in particular the pneumococcus and streptococcus. By the mid-1940s, however, he had turned his attention to viral illnesses, beginning with "primary atypical pneumonia" with Lewis Thomas. (Although primary atypical pneumonia was then believed to be due to a viral illness, it was subsequently shown to be caused by *Mycoplasma pneumoniae*.) Curnen's research focus in 1952, when he came to UNC, was in tracking epidemics of nonparalytic viral infections of the central nervous system and on the clinical spectrum of diseases caused by the coxsackie viruses.

When Curnen arrived in 1952, the Medical School created some makeshift research space in the hospital and Curnen recruited Ms. Eru Tanabe to join him from Yale as head technician. Eru actually ran the Curnen laboratory during all the years that Curnen was in Chapel Hill, and she accompanied him to New York when he left in 1960 to take the chair at Columbia University; indeed, Dr. Curnen credits Ms. Tanabe for playing a key role in establishing the infectious disease laboratory in Chapel Hill and for most of its productivity.

Most of the early funding for Curnen's research program came from the National Foundation for Infantile Paralysis; $22,000 was granted in 1953 (an astronomical sum for those days), followed by $14,000 in 1954, $21,000 in 1955, and $25,200 in 1956. His polio funds dwindled after that, but Curnen then picked up support from the National Institute of Allergy and Infectious Diseases. In 1959, for example, he received a grant of $17,600 to study the role of viruses in aseptic meningitis and a three-year grant beginning at $21,000 to explore the feasibility of vaccinating against measles.

One of Dr. Curnen's achievements was to recruit Dr. Annie V. Scott to the Department as a clinical professor. Dr. Annie's unique background is chronicled elsewhere in these memoirs, but she enriched the research climate in infectious diseases by initiating studies of the incidence of childhood tuberculosis in Alamance County, as judged by tuberculin testing. She successfully carried out a prospective study of the prophylactic effect of isoniazid in a cohort of sixty-nine tuberculin-positive children. Annie was also responsible for instituting an aggressive attack on pulmonary infections in children with cystic fibrosis.

Although there is no record of a formal postdoctoral training program in infectious diseases during the Curnen years, it is of interest that the annual report of 1954 describes an investigation of the clinical manifestations of infections by coxsackie viruses in family units within a small residential community near Durham. The fieldwork was carried out by Dr. Hugh C. Hemmings, who was on a student fellowship from the National Foundation of Infantile Paralysis under the direction of Dr. Curnen. The follow-up to this story is that Hugh Hemmings finished his residency with distinction, became a pediatrician in Morganton, and his son is now a distinguished biomedical scientist at Yale!

Although Curnen found it very difficult to conscientiously carry out his duties as chairman of the Department and maintain an active research program, his research effort was given a boost with the recruitment of Dr. Harry Meyer to complete his pediatric residency at UNC and work part time in research with Curnen. Harry Meyer was a dogged investigator and indeed was responsible for correctly diagnosing the fatal rickettsial infection that hit the family of Jim Tatum, the UNC football coach, and which caused Tatum's death. Meyer later went on to head the Biologics Division Laboratory in Bethesda, Maryland, that developed the rubella vaccine and that was legally responsible for overseeing all of the vaccines in the United States.

In 1957, Curnen recruited Dr. John Arnold as an assistant professor of pediatrics. Arnold had been a house officer at Charity Hospital in New Orleans and had completed a fellowship in infectious disease at the Boston Children's Hospital under Nobel Laureate John Enders. Although Dr. Arnold initially assisted Curnen with his studies of echo virus and other projects initiated by Curnen, he also collaborated with Herb Harned in studies of the cardiac manifestations of viral illness and, in particular, the cause of idiopathic myocarditis. He was able to link idiopathic myocarditis in infants and students in the infirmary with an epidemic of Asian influenza. Other studies at this time included a comparison of the efficiency of intradermal versus subcutaneous routes of administration of influenza vaccine in infants under two years of age and clinical and laboratory methods for differentiating nonparalytic illnesses caused by poliomyelitis viruses from those attributable to coxsackie viruses and other agents. It was perhaps inevitable that friction would develop between the dynamic Harry Meyer and the more laid-back John Arnold and that this would adversely affect the productivity of the infectious disease laboratory. Curnen's greatest regret from this period is that the vast data that he had accumulated in his studies to delineate the viral etiology of aseptic meningitis and other diseases never were satisfactorily collated and written up for publication in a peer-reviewed journal. There is little doubt, however, that the research thrust in infectious disease during the Curnen years laid a strong foundation for the research in infectious disease that was brought into the Department by the recruitment of Floyd Denny as chairman of the Department of Pediatrics in 1960.

CARDIOLOGY

In 1954, Curnen recruited Dr. Nelson Kneeland Ordway as his third full-time faculty member. Ordway had very broad interests with a special focus on acid-base balance and congenital heart disease in childhood. He had received his clinical training at Yale and at the University of Pennsylvania Hospital, and had spent four years in the Department of Pathology at Yale, where he had investigated the physiology of war gas poisoning. In 1947 he went to Louisiana State University where he specialized in cardiology, and in 1952 he became chairman of the Department of Pediatrics. Although his principled defense of one of his faculty members, who had been attacked for unpopular political views during the McCarthy era, cost Ordway his position at LSU, it had a very salutory effect on the sparsely staffed Department of Pediatrics at UNC. Whereas at that time the Department of Medicine had been successful in recruiting vigorous chiefs for each of the major subspecialties (with the exception of endocrinology), the Department of Pediatrics had a total of two faculty members, and subspecialty consultation and care necessarily were dependent on internists, most of whom had had little previous experience in dealing with children. Ordway's expertise in pediatric cardiology, together with his good humor and consummate tact, made it possible for him to forge amicable and highly productive relationships with Ernest Craige and other cardiologists in the Department of Medicine and facilitated the establishment of a catheterization lab for pediatric patients. Although it is difficult to identify publications representing research efforts during this period, the annual report of 1957 describes studies of the physiology of congenital heart disease and mitral stenosis that were undertaken by N. K. Ordway in collaboration with Drs. Dan Young, Ernest Craige, and Richard Peters.

A significant accomplishment of Ordway during his short sojourn in Chapel Hill before returning to Yale in 1957 was that he established a favorable milieu for Dr. Harned to undertake research when he arrived in Chapel Hill in 1958 from Yale as a replacement for Ordway. Shortly after his arrival, Dr. Harned joined Dr. John Arnold in the latter's study of the effect of viral infection on cardiac function and as a possible cause of myocarditis. Harned's first funding came from the North Carolina Heart Association, a small grant to study "the importance of respiratory acidosis in infants with congenital heart conditions."

Harned lost little time in setting up a laboratory to continue the studies that he had begun at Yale on circulatory phenomena resulting from anoxia in the newly born lamb. The studies of neonatal asphyxia in newborn lambs attracted the attention of other researchers in the field and investigators such as Mary Ellen Avery made pilgrimages to Chapel Hill to observe Harned's methods so that they could carry out similar work in their own institutions. Harned's work was carried out in association with Drs. Loren MacKinney, Ken Sugioka, and Stark Wolkoff, a staff member in ob-gyn. The Ordway and Harned approach to cardiology was very attractive to residents of pediatrics, and some of their trainees from this source included Drs. Robert Herrington, Robert Castle, Thomas Gardner, Robert Abney, and Roland Schmidt. Among the earlier postdoctoral fellows attracted from other institutions was Robert Verney, whom Dr. Ordway attracted from France.

GENETICS/MINERAL METABOLISM/
ACID-BASE BALANCE

Although, as evident in the preceding sections, it is convenient to discuss research during the Curnen years by the specialties involved, there were no subspecialty divisions per se during these years. It is possible that this brought indirect benefits by increasing the cohesiveness of the Department and facilitating personal interactions without the inhibitory influence of divisional boundaries. The key player in studies on genetics, mineral metabolism, and acid-base balance was a pediatric house officer by the name of Robert Winters. Winters had been attracted to the University of North Carolina from Yale because of his respect for Louis Welt in the Department of Medicine. Winters was an exceedingly bright and dynamic young man whose curiosity and initiative left few individuals in the Department of Pediatrics untouched.

On one memorable morning rounds in 1956 Winters, who was then chief resident, presented a child with severe Vitamin D–resistant rickets (Ricky Edwards) to his attending, Dr. Van Wyk. Winters remarked that the mother was entirely normal and certainly did not have rickets. The attending pointed out, however, that the patient's incisor teeth showed evidence of severe intrauterine enamel dysplasia and wondered why the mother's normal calcium had not protected her son. It was an idle question, but one that Winters immediately picked up on. The child's mother soon became pregnant again and during her pregnancy her serum calcium fell to very low levels. This led to a major study on the genetics of Vitamin D-resistant rickets by Winters, together with T. Franklin Williams in medicine and John Graham in pathology. Winters went to family reunions throughout eastern North Carolina carrying with him a centrifuge which he placed on the kitchen table. He examined every member of the tribe, secured extensive pedigrees, and clearly documented that Vitamin D-resistant rickets was a sex-linked trait. Since the mothers of affected males were heterozygotic they were only mildly affected, whereas the homozygotic males were severely affected. These studies were eventually published in *Medicine*, and several medical schools were moved to assign this paper to their students as one of the classics in medical genetics.

The other love of Robert Winters was acid-base balance, and in this he found an eager coworker in Nelson Ordway. Ordway obtained a grant from the North Carolina Department of Health to establish a pediatric blood gas laboratory, one of the first such laboratories in the United States. This laboratory permitted close monitoring of children following surgery and other circumstances. Ordway and Winters collaborated in developing a nomogram for understanding the transitions between metabolic alkalosis, respiratory acidosis, and other metabolic disturbances and applied this to salicylism and other metabolic problems during childhood. Topics cited in annual reports to the University included "persistent respiratory alkalosis in patients recovering from metabolic acidosis" with Winters, Ordway, and Lowder, and "acid-base disturbance in salicylate intoxication" with Lowder, Ordway, and Winters.

Another resident who added to the research climate in the early years was Dr. George Summer. He was particularly interested in biochemistry and had managed to get some type of support for staying on as a fellow but did not have a laboratory home or preceptor. Dr. Curnen asked Dr. Van Wyk to serve in this capacity, although many of Summer's interests were out of Van Wyk's area of expertise and interest. In the departmental report of 1957, Dr. Summer reports the following work in progress: lipo-protein abnormalities in juvenile diabetes mellitus; heme pigment in bilirubin metabolism in erythroblastosis fetalis; studies in neoplasia; protein abnormalities in multiple myeloma and in solid tumors; and studies in hypogammaglobulinemic states. That year he listed as work completed: serum protein fractionation in nephritis and nephrotic syndrome; sweat electrolyte analysis in cystic fibrosis of the pancreas; and "protein fractionation in health and disease."

It was apparent that Summer's studies of protein metabolism required a sharper focus or hypothesis to attract any significant funding other than the $1,000 grants available locally as starter grants. Dr. Summer, therefore, appeared to be an ideal individual to follow through on a project of Van Wyk's that stemmed from Van Wyk's research at the NIH. While at the NIH between 1951 and 1953, Van Wyk had produced copper deficiency in dogs and demonstrated that they had a lesion of their bones with multiple fractures closely resembling the genetic disorder osteogenesis imperfecta. Since the lesion was similar to scurvy and both copper and ascorbic acid are cofactors of oxidative enzymes, Van Wyk postulated that the lesion of osteogenesis imperfecta might be due to failure to hydroxylate proline and lysine in collagen precursors. This research, to study human osteoporosis and experimental osteoporosis in dogs, was well funded by a grant from the Easter Seal Foundation to Van Wyk and Dr. R. Beverly Raney, chair of orthopedic surgery. While this work was inconclusive, subsequent results in other laboratories with molecular cloning techniques have confirmed the essential correctness of the hypothesis. In any event, it was apparent that Summer's heart was in the laboratory rather than in the clinics, and in the early sixties he left the Department of Pediatrics to take a full-time position in the Department of Biochemistry, where he eventually rose to the position of full professor.

NEUROLOGY

Dr. Harrie Chamberlin, the second full-time faculty member in the Department hired by Dr. Curnen, was recruited by Curnen immediately following his pediatric residency at Yale and had no opportunity to pursue research training. Chamberlin had had a year of adult neurological training at Harvard under Drs. Ray Adams and Denny-Brown and did some neurological consultation during his military service. Chamberlin was therefore able to establish an effective linkage with Dr. Thomas Farmer, who headed adult neurology. In the early years, Chamberlin collaborated with Drs. Waddell and Butler in pharmacology to study levels of anticonvulsants in children and also with

Curnen in a study of acute cerebellar ataxia in association with poliovirus infection. In addition, he became interested in the etiological factors in mental retardation. This interest was ultimately to play a major role in establishing the Biological Sciences Research Center for the study of neural development.

ENDOCRINOLOGY

Of Curnen's early appointees, Dr. Judson J. Van Wyk was clearly the individual, other than Curnen himself, who had received the most formal research training. Van Wyk's heroes in high school were Dr. Arrowsmith and the natural product chemists John Jacob Abel, Edward Kendall, and Banting and Best. Following his graduation from Hope College in 1943 as a chemistry major he enrolled as a PhD candidate under Nobel Laureate Edward A. Doisy in St. Louis. This was at the peak of the Second World War, and after one year Van Wyk abandoned his graduate studies to enroll in Johns Hopkins School of Medicine where, on the urging of Doisy, he became a de jure fellow of William Mansfield Clark, professor and chair of physiologic chemistry. Clark had little interest in biology or medicine, but filled in some major gaps in Van Wyk's background in physical chemistry and mathematics. After finishing his pediatric training at the Harriet Lane Home and Cincinnati Children's Hospital, Van Wyk spent two years at the NIH, where he was a member of the metabolism section in the National Heart Institute. He then spent two more years of formal postdoctoral fellowship under Dr. Lawson Wilkins, the father of pediatric endocrinology. So it was that when Van Wyk came to Chapel Hill, there were expectations that one of his primary missions would be to establish a viable research program.

At the time of Van Wyk's arrival in Chapel Hill there were no other faculty members either in the basic sciences or in the clinical disciplines who made any pretense of interest in endocrinology. This was the only subspecialty that was not represented in the Department of Medicine because Louis Welt espoused the philosophy of John Peters at Yale, who damned the discipline by quipping that "endocrinology is a sport, not a science." Thus, the Department of Medicine felt that endocrinology should be the province of experts in acid-base balance and intermediary metabolism. The resulting isolation for Van Wyk resulted in his spending a great deal of time at Duke, where his mentor was Frank Engel. Van Wyk is eternally indebted to Engel for his strong support during these early years and for introducing him to the national scene. Van Wyk repaid this debt, in part, by assuming a major role in helping Duke establish a division of pediatric endocrinology, first under Robert Stempfel and later under Stuart Handwerger.

In September 1957, Dr. Mary Arnold joined the Department on a part-time basis along with her husband, John. Mary was very much involved with nurturing a young family, but nevertheless was a great help in seeing patients and in providing empathy and moral support for the division. No longer was it nearly as lonely as it had been previously. Also, Van Wyk was able to help recruit Billy Baggett to the Department of Pharmacology from Frank Engel's brother, Lewis Engel, at the Massachusetts General Hospital. Baggett had also been trained by Doisy in St. Louis, and he and Van Wyk were able to initiate many productive collaborations before Baggett left to become chair of the Biochemistry Department at the University of South Carolina in Charleston. The story of the research interests of the division of endocrinology during the Curnen years is fully documented in the history of the Division and, to avoid repetition, will not be repeated here.

JUDSON J. VAN WYK

CHAPTER THREE

Faculty

Editors' Note: Several faculty members of the Curnen years continued to serve in the Department throughout the regime of Dr. Denny and even into that of Dr. Boat. Drs. Chamberlin, Van Wyk, Harned, and Herrington have contributed histories of their subspecialty programs, published in Part Four of this book, and thus receive considerable recognition for their work over the years.

Other individuals made significant contributions to the Department during the Curnen years, but the majority of their work was performed elsewhere. Several of these physicians made monumental contributions to pediatrics. The contributions of these individuals will be recognized in this section in alphabetical order and without subjective opinions regarding who made the greatest contributions to our program. Expanded biographies of each of these individuals are included in the archives, where many of their global accomplishments are described. The biography of Dr. Arthur London by Dr. Robert Herrington and those of Drs. Nelson Ordway, Annie Scott, and Sidney Chipman by Dr. Chamberlin are included in part 9, "Biographies of the Early Greats of the Department."

The periods of service of the full-time faculty are shown on the time line which extends into the early years of the Denny era. Also indicated on this figure is the part-time nature of some of the faculty appointments.

J OHN ARNOLD was an important workhorse of the Department in its early years. John demanded strong performances from the students and residents, thus acquiring the reputation of being a "Dutch uncle," but he related well as an advisor to these young people. Also, he was an effective devil's advocate at grand rounds and other teaching conferences and played an active role in their organization during the interregnum between Dr. Curnen's and Dr. Denny's regimes. Unfortunately, John developed malignant hypertension, requiring surgery while he was still a member of the Department and causing his early demise after he left.

John and Mary Arnold

Mary Arnold graduated from the University of Vermont College of Medicine and then trained in pediatrics at Babies' Hospital in New York and in endocrinology at Massachusetts General Hospital. She was an effective and popular teacher, especially when teamed with Dr. Van Wyk. Mary's Italian élan and outgoing nature helped her in communicating with associates and juniors. Any contact with Mary would undoubtedly be remembered for a lifetime. Drs. Mary and John Arnold left for Brown University in July of 1963, where she remains on the faculty and has received awards for her teaching.

Sidney Chipman, a Canadian by birth, received his MD degree from McGill. He left pediatric practice in Connecticut to receive an MPH degree from Yale after World War II. As founder in 1950 and chairman of the Department of Maternal and Child Health at UNC, he was under no direct

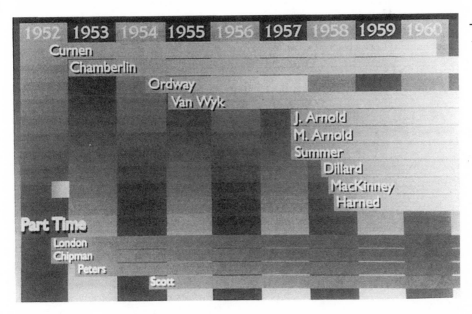

The Curnen years

obligation to aid in the launching of the new Department of Pediatrics here, but he participated very actively as a member of the attending staff. He "covered" the newborn service for long periods, regularly attended senior staff conferences and, for several years, carried full attending ward duties for six weeks in the summer. Despite his major involvement with the Pediatrics Department, "Chip" felt later that its relationship with the Department of Maternal and Child Health was "not entirely satisfactory" during his tenure. He questioned whether he may have failed to explain what his department "was all about." Dr. Ordway, a friend, commented on Dr. Chipman's "quiet, gentle and modest" demeanor and his "manners of a real patrician." He also stressed Chip's warmth and sense of humor. Dr. Chipman retired from his renowned department in 1970 and spent a year as the acting chairman of the analogous department at the University of Michigan. Dr. Chamberlin's interview of Dr. Chipman includes insights into the personalities and events of the early days of the Department of Pediatrics and is included in Part Nine, "Biographies of the Early Greats of the Department."

Ruth Dillard, a graduate of the University of Pennsylvania School of Medicine, left practice in Florida to serve here as a general pediatrician, attending on the wards, in the nursery, and in the outpatient department, especially in the neurology clinic. Her missionary spirit took her to Haiti and Vietnam with her husband Arch, a gynecologist, limiting her time at UNC to three and a half years. She has continued her interest in community medicine and was the medical director of the pediatric clinic at the University of Texas at Galveston for over ten years.

Doris Howell volunteered as a consultant in hematology-oncology at UNC while retaining her full-time status at Duke. She organized rotations at Duke Hospital for UNC residents and whetted their interest in her subspecialty. Drs. Faith Kung, Barbara Wilmer, and Wilma Castle pursued fellowship training with her at Duke and continued in this field. Dr. Howell was clearly more helpful to our Department than any other pediatrician at Duke, but was not able to persuade other Duke faculty members "to develop the same degree of camaraderie and collaboration." Her qualities of leadership have been recognized nationally as she has become a leader in her subspecialty and a departmental chair at the Women's Medical College of Pennsylvania.

Ruth Dillard (the oval shapes are from a mobile given to Ed Curnen on his move to Columbia University in 1960)

Arthur London deserves special mention both for his guidance and aid during the early years and for his long friendship with the Department. A biographical sketch by Dr. Robert Herrington is included in Part Nine, "Biographies of the Early Greats of the Department." His roles during the Curnen years were mainly as a teacher of practical pediatrics to medical students and residents and as an advisor to Dr. Curnen about the state of pediatrics in North Carolina, which he knew better than anyone. He also was important as a friend and advisor of Dr. Berryhill. He was deeply involved in the decisions relating to the location of the Medical School in Chapel Hill. The library in the pediatric clinic at UNC was dedicated to him in 1971, indicating the high regard in which he was held by his associates and students.

Loren MacKinney

Loren MacKinney, as shown on the time line, spent a period of three months as a part-time faculty member and then was appointed to the full-time faculty on May 1, 1958. A native of Chapel Hill, where his father was a professor of history, Loren was trained at Harvard and Boston Children's Hospital. His major roles at UNC were as director of the pediatric outpatient department and in the designing of the outpatient facilities for pediatrics in their Love Clinic location. Pediatrics fared far better than other services in this design. Dr. MacKinney served as a member and president (in 1966) of the national Association for Pediatric Ambulatory Services.

Nelson Ordway's service at UNC is recounted by Dr. Chamberlin in part 9, "Biographies of the Early Greats of the Department," in an excellent review of this key faculty member's contributions during the Curnen years. He helped to reinforce Dr. Curnen's emphasis on the science of pediatrics and added a broadly based scholarly dimension to the teaching program that appealed to colleagues, residents, and students. Despite its short duration, his period of service at UNC was very important during this formative period.

Ann Peters

Ann Peters had a broad background with degrees in social work and medicine and experience in obstetrics and in public health. As an associate professor of maternal and child health, she held a part-time appointment in pediatrics, where she was the primary attending physician for the nurseries. She brought broad-based ideas related to health care for children in the areas of prenatal care, day care advocacy, Head Start, and later the Children's Defense Fund.

Annie Scott's service at UNC, after a distinguished career as a missionary

George
Summer

physician in China, is also recounted by Dr. Chamberlin in a biographical sketch included in part 9, "Biographies of the Early Greats of the Department." Her great achievements during a long, productive life were recognized when her alma mater, the University of North Carolina at Greensboro, awarded her a doctor of science degree in 1975.

George Summer joined the Department in September of 1957 and remained until the mid-1960s, when he joined the Department of Biochemistry, leaving his clinical duties. Dr. Harned's interview of Dr. Summer in the archives has many insights into the problems encountered in the Medical School in its early years, viewed by one who was a resident, a fellow, a faculty member, and one who left the Department.

Pediatric practitioners also contributed to the Department, especially by attending in the outpatient clinics. Some of these pediatricians drove long distances to aid with the teaching. Perhaps the most faithful of these during the first eight years of the Department were Drs. John "Jack" Lynch from High Point, Emily Tufts of Pinehurst, James Lynn of Burlington, Sam Ravenel, James White, and Edward Benbow of Greensboro, Elwood Coley of Lumberton, Morton Pizer and Jimmy Rhyne of Raleigh, and James Morris of Goldsboro.

HERBERT S. HARNED, JR.

CHAPTER FOUR

Residents' Reminiscences

GRIGGS C. DICKSON (1955–1957, 1959–1960)

I GRADUATED from UNC School of Medicine in 1955 and entered the UNC pediatric program as a mixed medicine-pediatrics intern. I already had a broad exposure to all the ancillary services and professors at the Medical School—as well as house staff from other services. They were all important to my process of becoming a general pediatrician. We frequently shared patients as well as experiences and developed close friendships. A memorable episode developed when John Pender, a surgical resident, called the pediatric floor about 10 P.M. to get Earl Spaugh to see an ER patient with him. He asked to speak to the "biggest dog on pediatrics." The medical student who answered the phone summoned Dr. Ed Curnen, who was making late rounds. When John inquired if this was "the biggest dog in pediatrics," Dr. Curnen replied he didn't think he was "quite as big a dog as Dr. Spaugh." Dr. Pender has not yet forgotten this episode.

I especially remember my two-month stint learning practical bacteriology as a laboratory technician under the supervision of Charlotte Merritt. Newton Fischer and John Foust helped me sharpen my ENT skills in their clinic. Dr. Ernie Craige and his cardiology residents provided daily critiques of my readings of pediatric ECGs.

Metabolic rounds with Drs. Lou Welt, Walter Hollander, and Robert Winters were always awesome even though I remained lost in most of the discussions. The regular visiting professors were especially wonderful and challenging—who could forget Drs. Arthur London and Doris ("Ahlee") Howell and their practical applications of daily pediatric care.

In 1959, I returned as chief resident from a two-year Navy tour of duty at

Portsmouth Naval Hospital. I was in charge of a small house staff who met the challenge with hard work, overwork, and dedication. One intern presented special problems in "following." He had his own agenda and arrogance of anything concerning the South. This resulted in difficult interpersonal relations with his colleagues and patients, as well as the nursing staff. He had a particular aversion to being on call at night despite repeated specific "instructions" concerning this behavior. Needless to say, when he was found not available with an unlisted telephone number, a major confrontation occurred. I suggested his dismissal, but was overruled by calmer authorities. His attitude did improve and he completed his internship in a more responsible manner. I wonder what ever became of him.

During this year, we established a rotation for pediatric residents from the Portsmouth Naval Hospital—this lasted several years and at least one of these ultimately settled in North Carolina.

Dr. Denny arrived in Chapel Hill as I was departing. I was blessed to continue my contact with the Department for many years by returning as a visiting clinic attending. My house staff training continues.

W. PAUL GLEZEN (1960–1962)

Reminiscences of the Last Curnen Year and the First Denny Year

Editors' Note: Paul Glezen contributed other parts to this history, in addition to the following. He was vital to the establishment of the Gravely service for care of patients with pulmonary infections, to the creation of the studies at the Frank Porter Graham Center, and to the operation of the respiratory disease studies in the local pediatric practice. His contributions in these areas are included in the appropriate sections of the history.

I was assigned to the North Carolina State Board of Health by the Public Health Service in the late 1950s and immediately began an investigation of an outbreak of nonparalytic polio in Durham. Dr. Curnen's laboratory was testing the specimens for virus and quickly determined that the culprit was not polio but was coxsackie B5 virus. Thereafter followed a year when I would go to Chapel Hill each week to attend the combined medicine-pediatrics grand rounds, eat lunch with Dr. Curnen and other faculty, then work on "the paper" for the rest of the afternoon. (Unfortunately, "the paper" was never published.) I finished my two-year assignment and went off to Hurley Hospital in Flint, Michigan, for a year of pediatric training. I remember signing my contract for a second year of pediatric training at North Carolina Memorial Hospital and mailing it off. The next day I received a letter from Dr. Curnen telling me that he was going to Babies' Hospital in New York.

We didn't see much of Dr. Curnen during the last months of his reign in

Chapel Hill. I remember that he had established strict procedures for patient isolation and infant precautions. One late night, when I was the admitting resident on call, Dr. Curnen suddenly appeared on the ward just in time to catch Carlos Serrano flying down the hall in an isolation gown—a definite no-no. Dr. Curnen quietly reminded me of my responsibility to make sure that isolation procedures were adhered to. In the last conversation that I had with Dr. Curnen in an official capacity, he asked me to be co-chief resident with Frank French for the following year. For better or worse, Dr. Denny inherited the crew of French, Glezen, et al. Morning reports were instituted and they became an educational and confessional experience that we all remember fondly. Everyone on the faculty was supportive and provided the foundation for an excellent learning experience. However, the morning report, the weekly X-ray conference, and the infectious disease conference were the highlights, and Dr. Denny was at the heart of all three.

One experience of the chief resident year reminds us of the fledgling years of neonatology. (We will have to admit that North Carolina Memorial was not in the neonatology vanguard.) During my watch, Luther Hartwell Hodges III was unexpectedly born at NCMH. (His grandfather was a former North Carolina governor and the then secretary of commerce in the Kennedy cabinet.) Jud was attending in the nursery when Luke III began labored breathing. Jud called his friend in New York to ask him about the so-called Usher treatment for respiratory distress that we had heard described at the pediatric meetings during the previous spring. My recollection is that this consisted of glucose and a pinch of bicarbonate. Since we would not consider infusing this into the umbilical vein, it fell to my lot as chief resident to start the scalp vein infusion. And so, modern intrusive neonatology had come to NCMH. The next year, Bee Gatling came back to North Carolina to finish her residency after training in Denver and my recollection is that she started the first umbilical vein infusion in the premature nursery.

CHAPTER FIVE

The Legacy of Edward Curnen: Epilogue to the Curnen Years

THE RUMOR in 1959 that Ed Curnen had been offered the Carpentier Chair of Pediatrics at the Columbia University College of Physicians and Surgeons posed a severe threat to the small Department of Pediatrics at UNC. It was no secret that Curnen commanded the utmost respect among the top leaders of the pediatric academic community, including such important personages at the Babies' and Children's Hospital as Hattie Alexander, Dorothy Anderson, and William Silverman. Dr. Curnen was also very close to Rustin McIntosh, the venerated chairman, who was about to retire. Despite the fact that the chairmanship at Columbia was one of the most prestigious in American pediatrics, it was difficult to believe that Ed would leave Chapel Hill for New York City. Although the Department was plunged into gloom when his decision to leave became known, the farewell party for Ed and Manny proved to be a joyous celebration of wonderful years shared. This happy occasion is still warmly recalled by Ed and those that were present.

In eight short years Ed Curnen had built a tradition of excellence in patient care, teaching, and research. He had done this in spite of a parsimonious budget provided by the Medical School and with resources far below those provided to the Departments of Medicine and Surgery. Nevertheless, Curnen had established strong ties with pediatricians and family physicians throughout North Carolina; he had created respect among his peers because of his insistence on quality clinical care; he had established close collegial ties with the Department of Medicine and had laid the groundwork for the eminently successful joint medicine-pediatric residency; and he had accomplished all this while simultaneously creating a strong tradition of excellence in research.

Perhaps the most important of Ed's accomplishments was the strong sense

Manny and
Ed Curnen
at their
Department
farewell
party

of family that now existed among the few faculty that he had recruited. Ed was an English scholar and shared his love of English literature with his staff. Ed and Manny also mingled with many talented members of the local music scene and encouraged members of his staff to join them in their enjoyment of great music. Most important, Ed brought out the best in all of us and pointed out possibilities in each of us that were beyond our wildest imaginations. When Curnen left, the Department was still in its infancy, but it was a mighty, robust infant with huge potential!

JUDSON J. VAN WYK

Row 1: Harrie Chamberlin, Arthur London, Ed Curnen, Sidney Chipman, Ann Peters

Row 2: John Porter, Walter Feinberg, George Brice, Larry Gladstone, Jim White

Row 3: Lew Thorp, Earle Spaugh, Charles Starling, Dan Martin, Bill Davis, Charles Vernon, John Watters

1953–54

Row 1: Jim White, Arthur London, Ed Curnen, Sidney Chipman, Harrie Chamberlin

Row 2: Marilyn Michaels, Earle Spaugh, Bill Davis, Ben Johnson, Woody Coley

1954–55

Row 1: Ann Peters, George Summer, Ed Curnen, Jim White, Bob Winters, Charles Stamey

Row 2: Joe Corpening, Sidney Chipman, Harrie Chamberlin, Nelson Ordway, Dick Borden, Hugh Hemmings, Woody Coley, Annie Scott

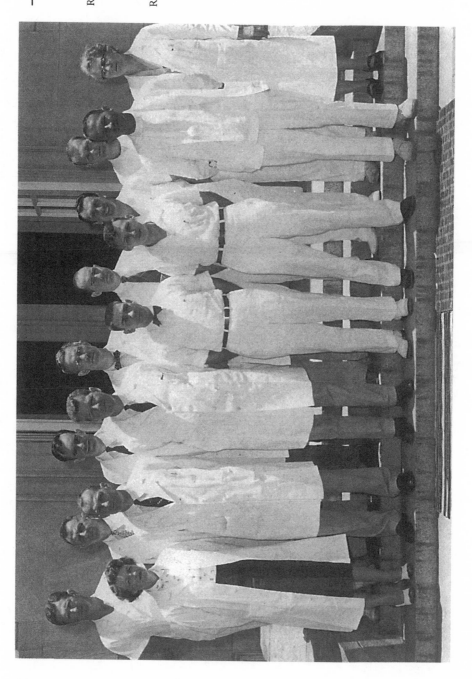

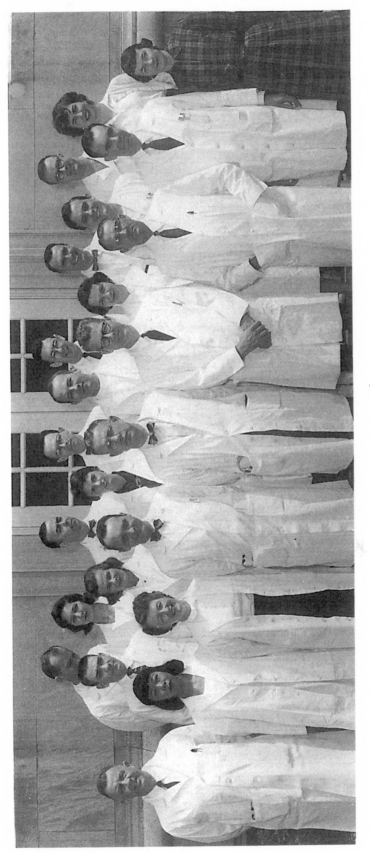

1955–56

Row 1: Sidney Chipman, Eru Tanabe, Ann Peters, Jud Van Wyk, Nelson Ordway, Ed Curnen, Arthur London, Harrie Chamberlin, Ann Edgerton

Row 2: Jim White, Sacha Field, Kathy McLaren, Charles Stamey, Sara Hoyt, Clarence Taylor, Marilyn Carrera

Row 3: George Summer, Pat Thompson, Jim Morris, Jim Grimes, Bill Powell, Hugh Hemmings, White Wellenborn

45

1956–57

Row 1: Ann Peters, Annie Scott, Jud Van Wyk, Ed Curnen, Nelson Ordway, Arthur London, Harrie Chamberlin

Row 2: Kathy Pritchard, George Summer, Bob Verney, Bob Winters, Pat Thomas, Sacha Field, Ann Fernald

Row 3: Griggs Dickson, Eru Tanabe, Anne Rogers, Wilma Castle, Ann Gardner, Virginia Tilley, Hugh Hemmings

Row 4: Bill Easterling, Clarence Taylor, Jim Morris, Lee Miller, Pat Thompson, Alfon Mosca, Florence Hoey, Bill Powell, Vic Herring, Tom Gardner, Bob Castle, Jim Grimes, Malcolm McLean

1957–58

Row 1: Annie Scott, Sidney Chipman, Loren MacKinney, Ann Peters, Ed Curnen, Jud
Van Wyk, Arthur London, Harrie Chamberlin, George Summer

Row 2: Alan Brown, Bob Herrington, Wilma Castle, John Arnold, Mary Arnold,
Boyd Cook, Ruth Dillard, Bryce Templeton

Row 3: Dick Patterson, Bob Senior, Martha Leas, Bob Castle, Barbara Wilmer, Tom
Gardner, Tom Dulin

47

1958–59

Row 1: Faith Currie, Mary Arnold, Ed Curnen, Marie Lipsett, Ann Ruhman

Row 2: Harrie Chamberlin, Jud Van Wyk, John Gaskin, Ruth Dillard, Herb Harned, Arthur London

Row 3: Bob Senior, Hervy Kornegay, Boyd Cook, George Summer, Loren MacKinney, Sidney Chipman, Harry Meyer, John Arnold, Bob Castle

· 1959–60 ·

Row 1: Annie Scott, Mary Arnold, Martha Sharpless, Maria Reyes

Row 2: Adrian Pollock, Jud Van Wyk, Carl Harris, Roland Schmidt, Herb Harned,
Harrie Chamberlin

Row 3: Loren MacKinney, George Summer, Bob Senior, Ed Curnen, Sidney
Chipman, Frank Shaw, Griggs Dickson, Charlie Waters

PART TWO

The Denny Years
1960–1981

INTRODUCTION

Editors' Note: For a general summary of departmental activities from 1960 to 1981 while Dr. Denny was chair, information was gathered from many sources. In this section, we have included the important Norma Berryhill Distinguished Lecture by Dr. Denny himself, given on September 30, 1987, and updated by him on March 28, 1995. This yearly lecture by an accomplished scientist and scholar of the School of Medicine is given in honor of Mrs. Norma Berryhill, who together with her husband, Dr. Reece Berryhill, contributed immeasurably to the development of the school and its faculty.

As a preface to Dr. Denny's own historical account of the Department, a short summary is presented, indicating the reasons for selecting him for this honor. Dr. Denny has modified his presentation appropriately; the earlier complete version of the lecture is available in the archives.

Dr. Van Wyk introduced Dr. Denny when he received the prestigious Howland Award on May 9, 1995. The complete nomination for this award, included here, reveals Dr. Denny's accomplishments as a leader, investigator, clinician, teacher, and as a personality. The reader also will find many more insights into his character and accomplishments in subsequent chapters in this book, especially the reminiscences by our house staff.

I N 1960, the Department of Pediatrics at UNC was a toddler poised to progress rapidly through childhood into an accelerated adolescence. There was an acute appreciation within the Department and throughout the school that the pediatric faculty was in urgent need of expansion to meet its responsibilities and challenges. Although there is no direct evidence on this point, it is likely that Dean Reece Berryhill recognized that the Department of Pediatrics had developed much more slowly than the Departments of Medicine and Surgery because of inadequate support, and he was now prepared to throw the resources of the school behind an aggressive new leader. To this end, Dean Berryhill appointed a

high-level search committee that included Charles Burnett, chair of medicine; Nathan Womack, chair of surgery; Logan Irvin, chair of biochemistry; and other leaders of the school. Berryhill, however, never allowed himself to be a slave to the democratic process, and in the end Floyd W. Denny was handpicked by the dean himself to become the Department's second chairman.

Floyd Denny met all the requirements of the job as perceived by Dean Berryhill: he came with an outstanding research background and had recently published the landmark study on the prevention of rheumatic fever. Although Denny had his primary academic appointment in a nonclinical department, his clinical skills were beyond question. He had been strongly recommended by Joseph Wearn, dean of Western Reserve and a longtime friend and confidant of Dean Berryhill. Most importantly, Denny had a burning desire to chair a department of pediatrics and a clear vision of what kind of department he wanted to develop. In particular, he was convinced that a modern department of pediatrics required organization into subspecialty divisions to which were delegated responsibilities for research and patient care.

Dr. Denny arrived in the late fall of 1960 and developed a very close relationship with Dean Berryhill, who served in some sense as a father figure. Floyd Denny came with the determination to build on the strengths that had been developed by Edward Curnen and the small faculty already on board. The results of his stewardship will be revealed in this section.

CHAPTER SIX

The Norma Berryhill Distinguished Lecture

INTRODUCTION OF THE LECTURER

D R. FLOYD W. DENNY, the 1987 Norma Berryhill Distinguished Lecturer, is Alumni Distinguished Professor of Pediatrics and Director of the School of Medicine Program on Health Promotion and Disease Prevention.

Dr. Denny joined the Medical School faculty in 1960 as chairman of the Department of Pediatrics and, during his twenty-one years as chairman, he built that young Department into one of the great leading departments of pediatrics in the world. A brilliant and devoted clinician, investigator, teacher, and administrator, he has made monumental contributions to this University, to medical science, and to the health care of children of the world.

A native of Hartsville, South Carolina, Dr. Denny received his undergraduate education at Wofford College and earned his medical degree at Vanderbilt University, where he served his internship and residency and where his subsequent career was profoundly influenced by the great pediatrician Dr. Amos Christie.

As a member of the U.S. Army Medical Corps, he was assigned to the Department of Preventive Medicine at Case Western Reserve University and worked in the Streptococcal Disease Laboratory in Cheyenne, Wyoming. It was there, working as a novice investigator with the renowned scientists Drs. John Dingle and Charles Rammelkamp, that he participated in the landmark studies of streptococcal infections that led to the prevention of rheumatic fever.

After three years in the Army, during which he rose to assistant director of the Streptococcal Disease Laboratory, Dr. Denny joined the Department of Pediatrics at the University of Minnesota as a clinician and investigator, where

Floyd W.
Denny, Jr.
[Credit:
Sam Gray]

he worked with Dr. Lewis Thomas. Two years later he returned to Vanderbilt as a member of the pediatric faculty and, after another two years, went back to Case Western Reserve, where he spent five productive years in the Departments of Pediatrics and Preventive Medicine.

A hallmark of his administration has been the successful recruitment of promising young faculty members and top candidates for house staff positions. An inspiring leader and teacher, Dr. Denny has earned the respect, affection and intense loyalty of a generation of house officers and students.

In 1981, former residents and students established the Floyd W. Denny Pediatric Society in his honor. He was chosen by the Medical School Class of 1965 to receive the Professor Award. Members of the Department of Pediatrics house staff have honored him with the Resident Award for excellence in teaching.

Major awards and honors include election to the Institute of Medicine of the National Academy of Sciences in 1980; the North Carolina Award in Science, presented in 1982; and, in 1985, an honorary degree from Wofford College and the Vanderbilt University School of Medicine Distinguished Alumni Award.

One of the great leaders of American pediatrics, Dr. Denny has served as president of the American Pediatric Society, the Society for Pediatric Research, and the Infectious Diseases Society of America.

Along with Dr. Berryhill, Dr. Denny understood that world-class schools of medicine are built upon a foundation of research. He championed the development of a strong, broad-based research program and personally directed the growth of his department's program of infectious disease research.

Some of Dr. Denny's most important scientific contributions have involved the epidemiology of childhood respiratory infections and the link between such infections and lung function problems later in life.

After successful careers as a researcher and a department chairman, Dr. Denny is in his "third career." In 1985, Dr. Stuart Bondurant, dean of the School of Medicine, asked Dr. Denny to serve as director of the school's new Program on Health Promotion and Disease Prevention. Under his leadership, the program has experienced remarkable growth and already has earned a national reputation for innovation and excellence.

Dr. Denny acknowledges that the "absolute, complete support" of his wife, Barbara, has been a crucial factor in the success he has achieved in all three of his careers.

Dr. Denny credits his friend and mentor, Dr. Reece Berryhill, with molding the School of Medicine during its formative years into the kind of institution to which the best people, those who have the most to contribute, can happily devote their professional lives.

Dr. Denny has been a powerful, principled, independent bastion of support for scientific and academic excellence applied without reserve to the health of the children of this state, the nation, and the world. He has been a leader in discovering and applying means of preventing illness and of limiting the impact of illness upon the physical, social, and intellectual development of children.

"THE GROWTH AND DEVELOPMENT OF PEDIATRICS IN NORTH CAROLINA AND AT THE UNIVERSITY OF NORTH CAROLINA SCHOOL OF MEDICINE"

Mrs. Berryhill, Chancellor Fordham, Dean Bondurant, Dr. Russell, Friends:

It is an honor, and a pleasure, to give the Third Annual Norma Berryhill Distinguished Lecture. With it we pay respect to this remarkable lady who did so much to help build our great School of Medicine. It is also an opportunity to honor and pay respect to those other spouses who contribute mightily to this institution. I will return later to this important subject.

When Dean Bondurant called to tell me of my being selected to give this lecture, my first reaction was immense pleasure at the honor. This was followed very quickly by an overwhelming feeling of horror and fright with the thought of what I must do today. After rereading John Graham's and Phil Manire's lectures, I became convinced that the cup, so to speak, should have been retired after the second lecture. Since then I have settled down a bit and the process of rethinking much of my time at Carolina and the hours I have spent discussing events with others have given me a lot of pleasure.

Now, a few words of explanation of the title. Growth and development are the stock-in-trade, the very life's blood of children, and, hence, pediatrics. This led quite naturally to my choosing this as the framework of my presentation. The first two lectures were historical in nature: John Graham's on the development of genetics at UNC and Phil Manire's on the development of UNC as a research university. It seemed appropriate, therefore, that I address some historical aspect of the University with which I am familiar.

After some thought it was obvious that I would talk mostly about pediatrics. After all, that is why I'm here today and how I got to North Carolina in the first place. North Carolina and this University mean so many things that it took some time to sort out how I wanted to organize my presentation. I finally decided on the following.

Using the Pediatric Department as the central issue I want to cover the period of time from the opening of the four-year medical school up to the present. This includes the stewardship of three individuals: Ed Curnen from 1952 to 1960, my time from 1960 to 1981, and Tom Boat from 1982 on. I want to make it clear that this is a story from my point of view. I've gotten help in many areas but inevitably what I tell you comes with all of my biases and prejudices and the coloring of memories that come with time. I am going to try to paint a picture that will include the following ingredients: The growth and development of the Department of Pediatrics will be the primary theme. I will emphasize the ambience or milieu of the early four-year school which will include the cast of characters in the School of Medicine who set the stage for its growth and development. I will describe what pediatrics was like when our school opened and how it has changed over the years. This will include the people, the house staff and faculty, who played such important roles. And finally, I will speculate about where we might be heading in the future.

Background

First though, a little of why and how I got to the University of North Carolina. The why is relatively easy—I wanted to be chairman of a department of pediatrics. I liked what they did and the opportunities a chairmanship presented. The how is more difficult to come by. [. . .]*

I thought I recognized here a place where I could be happy and do the things I wanted to do and, in addition, a fine place to live and raise a family. How right I was! I don't see how I could have found a better place for me. I have enjoyed it thoroughly, especially its "ups" and in spite of its "downs."

The Early Years

My first recollections of my entrance to this Medical School center mostly on the leadership of the institution. First, there was Reece Berryhill. My memory of Reece at that time includes his chain-smoking, his dark hair combed sharply back, and his complete attention to my problem. With him everything was on the table; I knew exactly where I stood at all times. He never told me what to do, and I felt I had his complete support. He was clearly the leader and the standard-bearer for the Medical School. For someone with my temperament, Dean Berryhill was ideal.

There were then those remarkable department chairmen. Charles or Chuck Burnett, chairman of medicine, was also a no-nonsense guy and nationally recognized investigator. He was known to the students as "Old Steely-Blue Eyes" because when Chuck fixed his gaze on you his eyes were indeed steely-blue and focused somewhere about your midbrain. He was one of the most well-rounded department chairmen I have ever seen. He was a brilliant clinician and teacher, an excellent investigator and administrator, and a very thoughtful and kind human being. Unfortunately, Chuck's health was bad and he relinquished the chair in 1964, to be replaced by Lou Welt.

Although he was not one of the original chairmen, I think it is proper to mention Lou at this time. An internationally recognized researcher and scholar, Lou was also somewhat of a character. He could be very tough on those around him but his standards were extremely high—for himself, his department, and the school. When he resigned in 1972 to take the chair at Yale, I missed him very much; I still do, as a matter of fact.

Nathan Womack, the chairman of surgery, was a giant among academic surgeons and, in my experience, a very wise man. He was of the old school; when he arrived at pre-op conference, the entire staff stood until he was seated. I, along with others, consulted Dr. Womack on occasion when we needed sound advice, and he never let us down. At times we got more than

---

*Indicates an omission from the original presentation.

we really wanted because he had a real way with words—and occasionally these got a little sharp. I still remember with some pleasure a time when I had sought his help. I was ready to leave; he stopped me and cautioned me to listen because he would not repeat what he was going to say. He then informed me that he thought I had done a good job since coming to Carolina. This surprised me greatly, and pleased me of course, and showed me a side to Dr. Womack that I had not experienced before.

Robert A. Ross was the first chairman of ob-gyn. Known to one and all as "Daddy," he was the local wag, always had some ready quip, and was full of homespun humor. It was with Daddy that I made a serious error in judgment. I thought at first that he was just a typical "good ole boy," only to learn that he was far smarter than I and that he was always ahead of me. Being a Southern boy I should have known better, but I didn't.

Bill Fleming was the chairman of preventive medicine. He was nationally recognized for his work on sexually transmitted diseases and was in charge of the ambulatory clinics at Memorial Hospital. By the time I arrived on the scene in 1960, there was emphasis here on ambulatory care that was far beyond anything that I had ever experienced before. This was under Bill's leadership and set the stage for the role that North Carolina has played subsequently in ambulatory medicine.

The clinical chairmen were rounded out with Ernie Wood as chairman of radiology and George Ham as chairman of psychiatry. Ernie subsequently went to New York in 1965 as chief of radiology at the New York Neurological Institute, which attests to his position in radiology in the country at that time. George resigned in 1962; I remember him as an exceedingly dynamic individual and the developer of a fine department. The first director of North Carolina Memorial Hospital was Robert Cadmus, who had an MD degree, which made him rather unusual as a hospital director. In 1964 he became the chairman of our Department of Hospital Administration, the forerunner of our Department of Social and Administrative Medicine. He left UNC in 1966 to become president of the New Jersey College of Medicine and Dentistry.

I am not going to include the basic science chairmen, not because they were unimportant, but because Drs. Graham and Manire have addressed their roles and because at that time they touched less on the newly accented sphere of clinical medicine.

To round out the picture in the school, I want to describe in greater detail the Department of Pediatrics. I had known Ed Curnen, the first chairman, for several years because of our mutual interest in infectious diseases. He was tall, soft-spoken, and nationally recognized as an infectious disease investigator. I very quickly learned that he was revered and loved by his faculty. The Department was small, only six strong without the chairman, but I liked the atmosphere in the Department and the standards of excellence that were present. It was rumored at that time that Dean Berryhill did not visualize a strong Department of Pediatrics, but if this was correct I never felt it in the least; and in my opinion, the Department received his complete and enthusiastic support.

This brief description of the Pediatric Department would not be complete without mention of several other pediatricians who played major roles in the early years. A cadre of practicing pediatricians in middle North Carolina came regularly to the Department to teach in the outpatient clinic. The most outstanding and loyal of this group was Arthur London, a practitioner of pediatrics in Durham. Arthur quickly took me under his wing and was my confidant and advisor until his death in 1976. Arthur was a remarkable individual, tough and acerbic, a fantastic clinician and teacher; he had complete and unswerving loyalty to our Department and to the University of North Carolina. Our conference room in the outpatient department has been named in his honor. There was also Sid Chipman, who was chairman of the Department of Maternal and Child Health in the School of Public Health at that time. Chip played an active role in the Department, especially in the nurseries, and was a loyal contributor to the Department as well as a close personal friend.

This is my memory of the leadership of the Medical School in its early years and the cast of characters who were responsible for laying the basis for its subsequent development. I find it hard to imagine a more impressive group of medical academicians, and I am still awed by the fact that Dr. Berryhill was able to attract faculty of such calibre to our fledgling School of Medicine. More important than the stature of these individuals is what they did and how they went about their business in those early years. What I want to stress here is the general atmosphere of the Medical School and hospital or the milieu of this academic environment. In my opinion, this will be the most significant thing that I will have to say today because I believe this is the most important part of our school and our hospital. I found at the University of North Carolina mutual respect among faculty that I had not experienced previously. There was an openness of negotiations, easy accessibility, and low departmental barriers which seemed to me to be almost unique. I detected a sense of humaneness and of collegiality that impressed me greatly. There was an aura about this institution that set it apart and made it a very special place to be. As we have increased in size, there are times when I fear we might be losing this remarkable characteristic; I urge those of you who are shaping the future of our school not to let this happen.

The Early Years in North Carolina

I would now like to turn to the broad picture of child care, or the field of pediatrics, as it existed then in the state of North Carolina. This is given as background to the development of our specialty at UNC. [. . .]

The picture of pediatrics as I perceived it in North Carolina and at UNC in the early 1950s with the opening of the four-year Medical School is as follows. Pediatrics as a specialty in North Carolina was quite new and relatively underdeveloped. The University of North Carolina School of Medicine had a new four-year school with a strong and imaginative dean and outstanding department heads. There was a small but well-founded Department of Pediatrics. It seems to me that the stage was set for the fantastically exciting days in academic medicine of the 1960s and '70s. I have often observed that we were limited at that time only by our imaginations and how hard we were willing to work.

The UNC Faculty

I would now like to fill you in on the growth and development of pediatrics at UNC in a number of different ways. I shall start with the faculty because that is certainly the most important and critical element in any department. It has been my philosophy that one should always, if at all possible, start with young faculty who give the signs of a promising career, protect them as much as possible so that they can develop, and then hold them accountable for what they do. We rarely hired new faculty at anything but the assistant professor level and this, by and large, has been successful.

In 1952–1953, the first year of the four-year Medical School, there were only two faculty members, Ed Curnen and Harrie Chamberlin, who recently retired. By 1955 the faculty numbered four and Jud Van Wyk had been added. In 1958 Herb Harned, also just retired, joined the faculty, which then totaled seven. This was the situation when I arrived on the scene in 1960. By the early 1970s we had seventeen full-time members, and by the mid-'70s this number had doubled and we had established twelve subspecialty divisions. In addition, we had initiated affiliated pediatric services at Wake Hospital in Raleigh, at Charlotte Memorial Hospital, and at Cone Memorial Hospital in Greensboro. By the early 1980s there were almost fifty full-time members, and, in the academic year 1984–1985 alone, there were eleven new appointments. This year there are seventy-five faculty members, including eleven on our AHEC faculty in the affiliated services. The faculty is replete with nationally and internationally recognized academic pediatricians who have assumed leadership roles throughout the world. As an example, we have eighteen members of the Society for Pediatric Research, including two of its presidents, and sixteen members of the American Pediatric Society, the two leading academic and research pediatric organizations. The research budget was listed as about $21,000 in 1952–1953 and in 1986–1987 was more than $5 million! The faculty have been very productive and, in 1986–1987, published ninety-four articles in refereed journals, fifty-seven book chapters, and one book. I don't want to bore you with figures but just want to point out that the Department was able to keep pace with the phenomenal developments throughout this country in academic medicine during these formative years.

It is much more difficult to evaluate our expertise and productivity in teaching and patient care but, in my opinion, our pace in these areas has matched that in research.

The House Staff

I have always thought that the house staff is an exceedingly important arm of any clinical department. Begetting our own kind is obviously one of our

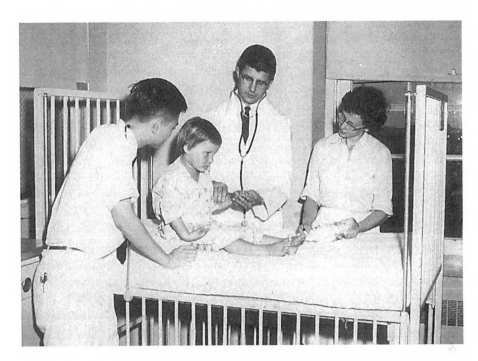

Floyd on resident rounds, with Brian Luke and Emmy Lou Cholak (1961)

chief reasons for being; but a good house staff also means several other things. It assures that patients are well cared for and that there is good student teaching. This goes a long way toward keeping a satisfied faculty which, as I have already mentioned, is equivalent to a good department. In addition, one of my greatest satisfactions has been in house staff teaching and watching the development of these remarkable young people. We have always had two types of teaching programs at the house staff level in the Department of Pediatrics. The straight training for pediatrics has been the mainstay of the Department. We also have a combined medicine-pediatric program, which entails equal training between the disciplines of pediatrics and internal medicine. This program lasts four years and leads to board qualification in both pediatrics and internal medicine. Our program is the forerunner of its kind in the country and is generally considered to be the best. Both the pediatric program and the mixed medicine-pediatrics program have been quite successful and popular. Let me give you some figures. There were four pediatric house staff the year the hospital opened. This increased in the early 1960s to twelve and by 1980 was thirty-four. In addition to these numbers there are variable numbers of house staff from other disciplines who came to us for periods of training. This year forty-four house officers will receive part of or a full year of training in pediatrics.

My memory is a bit vague on the numbers of applications we received in the early days, but I seem to remember that one of the first years when I was here we had fourteen applications for our four pediatric positions. For the

year 1987–1988 we had over three hundred completed applications for our
pediatric spots and ninety-three for our medicine-pediatric internships.

It seems appropriate at this time to reminisce a bit about the early house
staff. Although the numbers were small, the quality was outstanding. I recall
that for several years their scores on the American Board of Pediatrics examinations were tops, or very close to tops, in the country. There was a closeness
among the house staff and between house staff and faculty that I remember
with great pleasure. The devotion of the house staff is being demonstrated
by the attendance at a special luncheon for old chief residents during a forth-
coming meeting of the Pediatric Alumni Society next month. Thirty-two of
thirty-six will be with Ed Curnen, Tom Boat, and me.

Physical Growth: Offices, Laboratories, and Hospital Beds

Our physical growth has been less spectacular. The late 1960s found us
with eight thousand square feet for offices and research laboratories. This had
doubled by the late 1970s and this year finds us with about twenty-two thousand square feet, but this does not include small amounts of space at Frank
Porter Graham Child Development Center, the Biological Sciences Research
Center, or some space in North Carolina Memorial Hospital. Even so, the
acquisition of space has not kept up with our other growth and is a serious
impediment to our future productivity.

Our facilities for hospitalizing and caring for children have shown substantial growth. In the 1950s there were about thirty-five children's beds, a
newborn service, and a unit for prematurely born infants. We have continued
to grow over the years; how we did some of this will be covered shortly in
greater detail. We have now almost doubled our children's beds, increased our
newborn service, and have a modern neonatal intensive care unit and an up-
to-date pediatric intensive care unit. Our outpatient department contains a
drop-in clinic, which is open for twenty-four-hour care, a primary care unit,
and subspecialty clinics. [. . .]

These are markers of the growth and development of pediatrics at the University of North Carolina. Many, many people contributed greatly to these
developments; far too many for me to begin to recognize individually. These
occurred under three chairmen, a brilliant and dedicated faculty and house
staff, and a supportive administration. Before I go on to some of the pediatric
developments in the rest of North Carolina, I want to tell the stories of how
some of the other things that were important to our Department came into
being.

Saga of the Sigma Sigma Sigma Sorority

The first I have entitled the "Saga of the Sigma Sigma Sigma Sorority."
This begins in the 1950s when Drs. Curnen and Van Wyk conceived of the
idea that recreation for children who were hospitalized was the best form of
preventive medicine and rehabilitation. [. . .] This started a remarkable story
which has continued to this time. [. . .] Although none of the contributions

made at any one time by the Tri-Sigma sorority can be called enormous by present-day standards, their continuing support over a thirty-year period has resulted in almost unheard-of contributions to our service. I take this opportunity to salute them for what they have done for us.

The Child Development Institute

The next story I want to tell you about concerns the Child Development Institute. It all started in the early 1960s in the Department of Psychiatry when Dr. Rex Speers of the division of child psychiatry somehow engineered getting something over $100,000 from the legislature for establishing an inpatient child psychiatry unit. At the same time, President Kennedy, who had a retarded sibling, was sponsoring a congressional act entitled Mental Retardation Facilities and Community Mental Health Centers Construction Act of 1963. The carrot of this act was that the federal government would match local funds on a three-to-one basis for the establishment of such facilities and activities. The Department of Psychiatry recognized the wisdom of seizing this opportunity and changed their plans to encompass a more comprehensive unit in mental retardation. When Dr. Berryhill was made aware of what was happening, he made the decision to include the remainder of the School of Medicine in this process so that our application would be one that approached mental retardation from many different basic disciplines. [. . .] The funds from the Department of Psychiatry were parlayed through a variety of maneuvers to something over $600,000, which was then eventually matched on a three-to-one basis for the final grant. This all resulted in the establishment of what is called the Child Development Institute, which encompasses three separate centers: the Frank Porter Graham Center, which concerns itself largely with social and developmental matters; the Biological Sciences Research Center, which is composed of scientists, by and large in wet laboratories, who are interested in broader aspects of development; and the Center for Study of Development and Learning, which is largely a clinical unit assessing development. [. . .]

Programmatic and Other Growth

The Area Health Education Center Program

I also want to include a brief description of the Area Health Education Center Program, not because pediatrics had an unusual role in its development, but because, in my opinion, this has been one of the most important things that has happened to the School of Medicine, particularly to the Department of Pediatrics. It has allowed us to extend our influence far beyond the walls of the University. In essence, it has given us the state of North Carolina as our ballpark. Dr. Berryhill conceived the idea and was responsible for the early development of AHEC. Glenn Wilson engineered the program during its formative years, and Gene Mayer has been responsible during the past ten years for its continued growth, institutionalization, and consolidation as the prototype program in the country. During the early 1970s, I attempted to run the pediatric part of AHEC, but this proved too big a load with my other duties. Don Dunphy was persuaded to join us in 1974. The pediatric AHEC program has flourished under his direction since that time, resulting in clinical pediatric programs in all nine AHEC areas and academic teaching programs in three—Charlotte, Raleigh, and Greensboro. In the pediatric AHEC program we have twenty-four pediatricians who are full time and another fifty or sixty who work in a variety of capacities in the AHEC centers. All of this gives a flavor to our Department that is not only unusual in academic pediatrics but that has added a dimension that I think is tremendously important.

CHAPEL HILL PEDIATRICS

I want to describe, briefly, several other happenings or developments that have contributed in a significant way to our Department. In 1961 I was able to persuade Charlie Sheaffer, then the chief resident pediatrician at Babies' and Children's Hospital at Western Reserve, to join our Department, half time as director of our outpatient department, with the understanding that he would spend the other half of his time helping Dr. Robert Senior develop the first local pediatric practice. This resulted in the eventual establishment of Chapel Hill Pediatrics, a group practice, which has played an important role, not only in children's care in Chapel Hill, but in the evolution of our Department as well. The members of this practice play an important role in the teaching program of the Department and add a flavor only pediatricians in the active practice of pediatrics can give students and residents. For years, Charlie Sheaffer and I have given "dog and pony" shows twice a week in pediatric infectious disease to students and house staff in the outpatient department. This continues to be one of the highlights of my teaching experience.

AMERICAN BOARD OF PEDIATRICS

In 1978 I was contacted by Bob Brownlee, with whom I trained at Vanderbilt in the 1940s and who was the executive secretary of the American Board of Pediatrics, regarding relocating the main office of the board to the Chapel Hill area. There then followed negotiations that resulted in the moving of the board, the certifying body for pediatricians in the United States, to our midst. This has resulted in the further identification of the University of North Carolina as a significant site of pediatrics in the United States. The active participation of Dr. Brownlee and his staff in our program has been a significant and welcome contribution as well.

JOURNAL OF PEDIATRICS

Several years later, in 1984, arrangements were made for Dr. Joe Garfunkel, editor of the *Journal of Pediatrics*, to move to the University of North Carolina, along with the editorial office of the *Journal*. This marks us as the home of one of the most prestigious pediatric publications in the United States and has given us the valued addition of Dr. Garfunkel as a faculty member.

Department of Pediatrics at Duke

A description of these happenings would not be complete without mention of our associations with the Department of Pediatrics at Duke. This has been a warm one and, I believe, has been profitable for both of us. Early in our development Dr. Doris Howell, a well-known pediatric hematologist, came to Chapel Hill regularly to help us with our tough hematological problems. We have reciprocated in a variety of ways over the years and collaboration has prospered with Dr. Sam Katz as the pediatric chairman at Duke. The most tangible evidence of our recent collaboration is demonstrated by the recent establishment of a joint UNC-Duke Pediatric Rheumatology Research Center. This grew out of the help given to us by Dr. Deborah Kredich in establishing our own rheumatology program. After we obtained faculty in pediatric rheumatology, this association continued, and Drs. Kredich and Robert Warren are codirectors of this joint program.

Program for Health Promotion and Disease Prevention

I want to seize this opportunity to tell you about a relatively new program which I think is a good example of what can be done at the University of North Carolina, possibly in a unique way. I refer here to our new emphasis on health promotion and disease prevention. In the early 1980s Dean Bondurant put into motion planning activities that were designed to put greater emphasis in the Medical School on health promotion and disease prevention. This is in contrast to the universal emphasis in schools of medicine on therapeutic and curative medicine. At the same time that this planning was going on in the School of Medicine, the School of Public Health was doing the same. [. . .] The Schools of Dentistry, Nursing, and Pharmacy were included subsequently in the planning which resulted in the establishment of the University of North Carolina Center for Health Promotion and Disease Prevention in March 1985. The center is now one of three federally financed centers in the country and has fostered, along with the Center for Highway Safety Research, the development and the establishment of one of five Centers for Injury Prevention Research. A recent large teaching grant from the Pew Charitable Trusts will help us introduce health promotion and disease prevention into the curriculum. The Department of Pediatrics and many departments and faculty within the School of Medicine and the other schools in the Division of Health Affairs have given strong and enthusiastic support to this program.

Summary and Assessment of Growth

Growth in the State

Using all of these examples as markers of progress, I will now attempt to evaluate and summarize where I think we are today with pediatrics in North Carolina. It is obvious that I think that we have a fine Department of Pediatrics, which is well rounded in the areas of research, teaching, and patient care. In North Carolina there are three other well-recognized and excellent departments of pediatrics at Duke, Bowman Gray, and ECU. You will recall that the 1945 London Report listed 39 pediatricians in private practice in North Carolina. In 1986 the Board of Medical Examiners lists 739 pediatricians. The North Carolina Pediatric Society has seen similar growth. I have not been able to find precise figures for the past, but in a 1972 publication Dr. London notes that there were 255 pediatricians in the North Carolina Pediatric Society. This year there are 620 members. Activity within the North Carolina Pediatric Society has increased dramatically in the past decade. [. . .]

UNC Contribution to Growth

Since this is a presentation with major emphasis on what has gone on at the University of North Carolina, I have attempted to determine the contributions made by our School of Medicine to the training of pediatricians in the state. Figures for our participation were relatively easy to get, but the determination of the size of the group from the remainder of the state has proved to be difficult. In any event, among the pediatricians who are members of the State Medical Society and list themselves as pediatricians, 25 percent either went to medical school at the University of North Carolina, had their pediatric training on our service, or are members of our pediatric faculty. In the North Carolina Pediatric Society, 30 percent of the members have had or now have affiliation with UNC. Among pediatricians listed as certified or seeking certification by the American Board of Pediatrics, almost one-fourth have UNC attachments. I think these are remarkable figures in view of the relatively short period of time we have been in existence.

The Future

I would like to speculate briefly about what lies ahead for pediatrics. Good general pediatric care of children has changed little over the years and remains a large segment of what is anticipated of physicians who care for children. There is developing, however, a whole new dimension that increases the responsibilities of pediatricians. Certain chronic diseases, which in the past have played a relatively minor role in pediatric practice, are now becoming quite dominant. Examples are cystic fibrosis, leukemia, other cancers, prematures, AIDS, and alcohol and substance abuse. [. . .]

The effects of these changes on the practice of pediatrics and pediatric education will be great. [. . .]

We are faced with an equal number of perplexing problems in pediatric education. There is good evidence from several sources that we have too many physicians in the education pipeline and that there are far too many of certain types of subspecialists. It is not clear where pediatrics stands in this regard, but it seems that while there are not enough pediatricians in some rural areas and small towns, the larger metropolitan areas are adequately staffed or overstaffed. We must respond in our pediatric programs to the needs of the country, not only as far as numbers are concerned, but program content as well.

To the best of our abilities we must decide what pediatrics is going to be like in future years and adjust to these changes.

My greatest concern for academic pediatrics is even more basic and pertains to all universities in this country. This has to do with the financial and bureaucratic parts of medical academia today. Governmental regulations on the financing of medical care and the increasing necessity of paying for academic departments through the provisions of services have increased to the point that the scholastic and research productivity of our faculty is being seriously jeopardized. This is a particular problem with young faculty who are in the developmental phases of their careers. The rapid changes in the past few years in the social and scientific aspects of medicine make this an exciting period, but we must take care that we preserve those facets of academia that brought us to this point.

Denouement

Let me return now to the reasons that this lectureship was established. Its major objective is to honor Norma Berryhill because of her enormous contributions to the growth and development of our School of Medicine. Norma, we stand in eternal gratitude for all you have done for us. In addition, however, it means to me that this lectureship also honors all spouses who have helped their mates in their work. Accordingly, I want to pay tribute, not only to Norma, but also to my wife, Barbara. Without her I would have accomplished very little. With her, however, my professional career has been the most exciting, enjoyable, and meaningful experience I could possibly imagine. Of all my good fortune, the greatest was marrying Barb; she has been my companion, my advisor, and my friend for over forty years. She and I have also shared the pleasure and gratification of the growth and development of our three children into productive and successful adults. My absences have not always been easy for them, but they have always given me their support. I continue to be grateful for this.

Finally, this lectureship was designed to be a mechanism to welcome our new faculty as well, and I want to speak directly to them. In my opinion, you are joining the finest, the most thoughtful, and the most exciting medical academic faculty in the country. I welcome you to the University of North Carolina.

FLOYD W. DENNY, JR.

CHAPTER SEVEN

Nomination of Floyd W. Denny
for the Howland Award of
the American Pediatric Society

Editors' Note: Each year the American Pediatric Society honors one of its members with its highest award, the Howland Award, for his or her lifetime contribution to American pediatrics. The other editors of this history overrode the modesty of the senior editor to permanently record in this volume the role that Floyd W. Denny has played in American pediatrics and in the Department of Pediatrics at UNC. We believe that his accomplishments were accurately summarized in the letter that nominated Dr. Denny for the Howland Award. (JJVW, HSH, HRC)

I T IS with pleasure and enthusiasm that we nominate Floyd W. Denny, MD, for the 1995 Howland Award of the American Pediatric Society. Dr. Denny's entire career has been dedicated to the objectives of the society, namely: "advancement of the study of children and their diseases, . . . prevention of illness and the promotion of health in childhood, . . . and the promotion of pediatric education and research. . . ." We believe that his outstanding contributions in each of these areas and his prominent role as a pediatric statesman constitute compelling reasons to honor him with the highest award our discipline has to offer. In the following pages we wish to document the achievements and contributions that form the basis for this nomination.

FLOYD DENNY AS A LEADER

Floyd Denny was recruited at the age of 37 from Case Western Reserve University as the second chair of the Department of Pediatrics. Under his leadership the Department grew from 6 faculty and 12 house staff in 1960 to a leading Department of Pediatrics in 1981 with 40 full-time faculty in Chapel Hill and 10 Area Health Education Center faculty, 28 Pediatric house staff, 16 Medicine/Pediatric house staff, and nearly 20 fellows. At a time when pressures were mounting to emphasize clinical service, Floyd demanded high standards of scholarship as well as exemplary teaching and patient care from his faculty. At the end of his chairmanship, 7 of the 10 divisions within the Department had NIH-sponsored research programs and total extramural research support (direct costs) for the Department was approximately $2,500,000, in large part NIH funded.

Floyd Denny played a strong leadership role in the UNC School of Medicine during its formative years, always urging the highest levels of excellence. Floyd's efforts were responsible, in no small measure, for the fact that UNC's Health Care Complex is now a leader in medical education and one of the twenty largest recipients of NIH research funds.

Floyd also played an important advisory role in fashioning a statewide Area Health Education Center Program that links the medical schools of North Carolina with all health care regions. He had the vision to promote strong pediatric programs in Charlotte, Greensboro, and Raleigh which now serve as important community-based training sites for students and house staff.

After stepping down as Chairman of Pediatrics, Floyd took on the role of Director of a newly formed Program on Health Promotion and Disease Prevention (HPDP) in the UNC School of Medicine. He was a prime mover in the University's success in acquiring major federal funding for this center. Through his efforts HPDP has been identified as one of four major themes for the school's long-range planning process. His enthusiasm and keen interest in this area have stimulated numerous faculty colleagues to participate in disease prevention research and teaching. He has succeeded in fostering extensive collaboration among faculty in medicine and in public health. Dr. Denny would point out that his interest in disease prevention is not new. He began his career in the Department of Preventive Medicine at Case Western Reserve and has dedicated much of his effort to the epidemiology and prevention of respiratory infections.

For many years Floyd has been an articulate spokesman for pediatric issues in national and international forums. He served with distinction as President of both the Society for Pediatric Research (1968–1969) and the American Pediatric Society (1980–1981). Furthermore, he was elected to the American Society for Clinical Investigation, the Association of American Physicians and to the presidency of the Infectious Diseases Society of America (1979–1980), all clear indicators that he is held in high esteem by scientists and physicians outside the Pediatric academic community. Floyd also has been a leader in formulating research policy, serving as a member of the Advisory Council of the National Institute of Allergy and Infectious Disease (1979–1982). His prominence in national educational activities is exemplified by his membership on the National Board of Medical Examiners

(1971–1980). His work with the NBME included the chairmanship of the Part II Test Committee (Pediatrics) for several of these years. Floyd also played an important advisory role with the Armed Forces Epidemiological Board, Commission on Acute Respiratory Diseases, and Commission on Streptococcal and Staphylococcal Diseases.

Floyd has been a member of the Institute of Medicine (IOM) of the National Academy of Sciences since 1980. He is currently Chairman of the Board of Health Promotion and Disease Prevention for the Institute, and is a member of the IOM Program Committee. He was a key member and chairman of a National Academy of Sciences task force that examined data bearing on the possible relationship between aspirin ingestion and Reye Syndrome, and that published a statement warning the American public of the dangers of aspirin treatment. He currently chairs the FDA's Vaccines and Related Biological Products Advisory Committee. Through these efforts, Floyd has played and continues to play a substantial role in shaping health policy for this country.

Efforts to improve the health of people in other countries has also been an important component of Floyd's agenda. He has served as a member of the Advisory Board of the Biomedical Research Center in Cairo, as a member of the Technical Advisory Group for Acute Respiratory Infections of the WHO, and as a consultant to the Bureau of Technology for International Development, National Research Council.

Recognition for the quality of these efforts in Pediatrics and Infectious Disease Medicine has come in the form of numerous awards, some of which are listed below:

1. Phi Beta Kappa
2. Alpha Omega Alpha
3. The Lasker Award, presented to the Streptococcal Disease Laboratory Group (1954)
4. The Professor Award, UNC Medical School Class of 1965
5. The Outstanding Civilian Service Award, from The Surgeon General of the Army (1973)
6. The Resident Award for Excellence in Teaching, Pediatric House Staff, 1979–1980
7. The North Carolina Award in Science, the highest award given in this area by the Governor of the State (1982)
8. Honorary degree (DSc), Wofford College, 1985
9. Distinguished Alumnus Award of Vanderbilt University School of Medicine (1985)
10. The Distinguished Physician Award of the Pediatric Infectious Disease Society (1987)

11. Norma Berryhill Distinguished Lecturer, UNC School of Medicine, 1987

12. The O. Max Gardner Award of the University of North Carolina sixteen-campus system, to a faculty member who has made the greatest contribution to the welfare of the human race (1988)

13. Distinguished Faculty Award, UNC School of Medicine, 1988

14. James D. Bruce Memorial Award (for Distinguished Contributions in Preventive Medicine), American College of Physicians, 1993

15. Edward H. Kass Lecture: "A 45-year Perspective on the Streptococcus and Rheumatic Fever," the Infectious Diseases Society of America, November 1993

FLOYD DENNY AS AN INVESTIGATOR

Floyd was first author of his first paper: "Prevention of Rheumatic Fever: Treatment of the Preceding Streptococcic Infection," which appeared in the May 13, 1950, issue of the *Journal of the American Medical Association* (Denny, F. W., Wannamaker, L. W., Brink, W. R., Rammelkamp, C. H., Jr., and Custer, E. A., *JAMA* 143:151–153, 1950). This landmark communication was the first report of successful rheumatic fever prevention by effective treatment of streptococcal infection with penicillin. Now recognized as a classic in medicine, this article was republished in *JAMA* (254:534–537, 1985), as a "Landmark Article," and was the basis of the Lasker Award which was presented to Floyd and his colleagues in 1954.

Floyd's first publication of his scientific work foretold a productive career. Now numbering 120 reports, his research has focused in three areas.

First, Floyd continued his pioneering work on streptococcal infections and their consequences throughout the 1950s. He and his collaborators published a series of papers on the antibiotic treatment of streptococcal infections, and he has continued to pursue these issues actively. His interest in the epidemiology, pathogenesis and prevention of rheumatic fever has placed him at the forefront of this area throughout his career. Floyd's work on the classification of streptococci and measurement of streptococcal antibodies is recorded in several papers. This line of investigation has provided a basis for the modern management of Group A streptococcal infections and has contributed immensely to the health of children. Prevention of rheumatic fever has saved countless lives of children and adults throughout the world and has spared millions the debilitating effects of acquired heart disease. At this time, when the incidence of rheumatic fever is increasing, Floyd's contributions take on renewed importance.

Second, in collaboration with his long-time colleague, Wallace Clyde, and a number of young associates at the University of North Carolina, Floyd

Wally Clyde
and Jerry
Fernald

directed studies that defined the role of *Mycoplasma pneumoniae* as a respiratory pathogen. These studies have contributed greatly to current understanding of mycoplasma infections, the most frequent cause of pneumonia in older children and young adults, and have brought Floyd and his colleagues at the University of North Carolina international recognition in this area of investigation. Their research, which was carried out primarily in the 1960s and 70s, focused on properties of the mycoplasma organism and the immune response to mycoplasma. Although Dr. Denny currently is only peripherally involved with investigations of mycoplasmas, his trainees and coworkers have continued major efforts, culminating recently in the cloning and sequencing of the gene for the mycoplasma attachment protein and the successful insertion of this gene into adenoviruses, with the hope that the expressed antigen will serve as an effective immunogen.

Floyd's third and most recent research emphasis has been on the epidemiology of respiratory infections in children. Beginning in the 1960s, he and his colleagues established two sites, one in a community practice and the other in the Frank Porter Graham Day Care Center, to provide extensive long-term observations of respiratory infections in children. He organized a large team of collaborators including academic and practicing pediatricians, other health care givers, and laboratory assistants, to initiate longitudinal surveillance studies of respiratory infections. His research team was funded in 1976, through a Pulmonary Specialized Center of Research (SCOR) grant by the National Heart, Lung and Blood Institute, to investigate epidemiologic and biologic aspects of injury to airways by childhood infections. This grant has been funded continuously since that time. The results of these studies, now accepted as some of the best data available on the subject, have been published widely.

This work forms much of the current basis for understanding the seasonal variation in prevalence of many acute respiratory illnesses, the factors determining the susceptibility of groups of children, and the specific respiratory syndromes (nasopharyngitis, croup, tracheobronchitis, bronchiolitis, and pneumonia) caused by each of the most common microbial agents. Of particular note was the observation that acute otitis media is more closely associated epidemiologically with viral illnesses than with the bacterial flora in the upper respiratory tract. Floyd's work has covered almost the entire spectrum of infectious agents affecting the respiratory tract in childhood.

Floyd also has become an important spokesperson and consultant concerning the devastating effects of acute respiratory infections of childhood in third world countries and has provided several commentaries concerning the magnitude of this problem.

During the last four to five years Floyd has worked with pediatric and Public Health School colleagues in Chapel Hill to define the contribution of cigarette smoke exposure to the incidence and severity of respiratory tract infections in infants and to develop successful intervention strategies. Several publications document efforts to understand the spectrum of clinical manifestations and the extent of pulmonary dysfunction in childhood sarcoidosis. These papers contribute significantly to the comprehensive description of this condition, which is more common in the mid-Atlantic and Southern states than most realize.

Several points about Floyd's research career are worthy of emphasis. His scientific tools have been those of the epidemiologist. The questions he has attempted to answer have been in the mainstream of pediatrics. The results of his studies have had important and practical implications for the practice of pediatrics. The research goals that he has defined are still actively pursued under the direction of his former colleagues and trainees. This work continues to be energized by his insight and participation.

FLOYD DENNY AS A CLINICIAN

Floyd has been an outstanding clinician throughout his professional life. Within the state of North Carolina he has been a valued and highly sought after infectious disease consultant. Throughout his tenure as chairman, Floyd held Saturday morning ward rounds with the entire house staff and personally conducted morning report ("Denny Rounds"). Through these mechanisms he maintained a strong influence on the quality of patient care. In addition, his attending efforts characteristically have been enthusiastic and inspired by a deep sense of curiosity, as well as tempered by a logical and sensitive approach to the patient at hand. It is not widely appreciated that Floyd also has played a leading role in the care of children with a wide variety of pulmonary disorders (hence his fascination and involvement with childhood sarcoidosis) and rheumatologic conditions. In the early 1980s he established the UNC Pediatric Rheumatology Clinic and served as an attending physician in that clinic until a full-time rheumatologist was recruited in 1983.

In all of his clinical work Floyd has applied the principles of epidemiology to make decisions concerning the care of individual patients, and has insisted on a preventive approach to the care of children. His concern for preventive medicine has inspired a long-term involvement with the North Carolina Pediatric Society and with members of the State Maternal/Child Health Department and the Social Services Division to insure access to immunizations for all children.

FLOYD DENNY AS A TEACHER

Floyd has been a strong influence on the development of more than 300 pediatric residents and fellows during the 21-year tenure as Chairman of the UNC Department of Pediatrics. Many of these trainees now occupy academic positions in Departments of Pediatrics across the country. His trainees established the Floyd Denny Pediatric Society at the time he relinquished the Department chairmanship, and this society now provides a vehicle for postgraduate education of former residents and friends. At the last meeting 32 of his chief residents returned and personally attested to his powerful influence as their teacher.

Not often recognized is the fact that Floyd, together with Dr. Louis Welt, then Chairman of the Department of Medicine, conceived of a unique combined Medicine/Pediatrics training program and initiated that innovative program in the early 1960s. The Medicine/Pediatrics training program in Chapel Hill, along with the program in Rochester, N.Y., has been the front-runner in this post-graduate training effort for more than 25 years. Evidence for the wisdom of this approach comes from the increasing interest in combined Medicine/Pediatric training, which now takes place at 76 sites across the country.

Floyd Denny's trainees cite his teaching efforts as his most important contribution. They have documented this more eloquently than we can possibly do.

From a Professor and Chairman of a major Department of Pediatrics:

> It is clear to me that he has had the most influence on my career of any of my teachers. His greatness, I think, comes from the intensity he brings to his teaching and to his life. He was, I believe, the first of my teachers who was really comfortable—and even enjoyed—admitting what he didn't know. Floyd was also a model for the academic physician. He taught us of the tradition of academic pediatrics, instilling a sense of respect for those teachers who came before and after him. When I came to the program I had no intention of becoming an academician; when I left I could do nothing else.

From a former resident who is currently training for an academic career:

> The most striking feature about Dr. Denny is his integrity. He is rigid in believing that kindness and consideration is mandatory in caring for ill children and their parents; and that the most important thing that

the pediatrician-in-training must learn is how to keep on learning. Dr. Denny's energy level and his generosity with his time are seemingly limitless. I have never seen him put off someone who wanted to learn from him, and I have seen him fan some pretty unimaginative minds into creativity. Dr. Denny remains "my chairman," one of the most principled and best men I have ever known.

Floyd Denny following receipt of the John Howland Award (San Diego, 1995)

From an Associate Professor of Pediatrics, and Director of a Division of General Pediatrics in a leading medical school:

In recent years medical decision making and the teaching of medical decision making has been slowly transformed from an art to a science. What is so extraordinary about Floyd is that not once in three years did I see him fall into any of the traps that I have enumerated in my writings. Floyd had a virtually unique ability to treat each patient as a fresh, new, and exciting challenge. While he did not ignore his past experience or knowledge data base, he never generalized inappropriately or made faulty attributions because "this patient reminds me of someone I saw two years ago." He was never afraid to say he didn't know something. To this day I begin every introductory talk with new interns by putting up three words I expect to hear them say over and over again in our clinic: "I don't know." He was a man who was not only interested in his residents, but interested in the patients his residents were caring for. That caring about patients was imprinted upon me.

From a former resident in a group practice:

Dr. Denny's contributions to the medical education of so many of us is immeasurable. Never has there been a more dynamic teacher. In 1978, the three of us dedicated our practice to him and in the waiting room a plaque reads: "Floyd W. Denny, MD, Professor and Chairman of the Department of Pediatrics at the University of North Carolina School of Medicine, has been a profound influence on our professional careers. More than any other individual he has molded our approach to the health care of children. We aspire to have . . . Pediatric Associates reflect the principles of scholarship, intellectual honesty and love of children that he taught us by precept and example. To this end, and in appreciation, we dedicate this practice to him."

From a Director of a Public Health Unit:

He set the stage for my active pediatric life and I shall forever be in his debt. One tremendous attribute of Dr. Denny's is his humility. If he doesn't know something he will say so. As we were leading one of our morning resident rounds, after Dr. Denny said he did not know the answers to several questions, one of our more senior residents from Vanderbilt (who shall remain anonymous as he is now a professor in the department) said in extremely slow Southern drawl, "For the head of the Department of Pediatrics he knows virtually nothing."

This former resident shared with us a portion of a letter addressed to Dr. Denny when he stepped down from the chairmanship:

I want to thank you for so many things . . . for being strong and at the same time gentle; for being honest even when the truth hurt; for being wise when I was foolish, for setting an example that I could follow. You, Dr. Denny, and my dearly beloved late father, taught me what a man should be and I would like to tell you from the bottom of my heart, "thanks."

Collective recognition of Floyd's teaching efforts have come in the form of two awards, the Resident Award of the UNC Department of Pediatrics for excellence in teaching (1979–1980) and the Professor Award by the UNC Medical School Class of 1965.

There are many who make outstanding contributions in one or two areas of academic medicine. Few are unquestionably outstanding across a broad

Floyd and
Barbara
(1995)

spectrum of academic activities. In this respect, Floyd is exceptional! He has been a model clinician, a wise and revered teacher, an imaginative and productive investigator, a highly successful department chairman, an inspirational leader of American Pediatrics and Infectious Disease Medicine, and a shaper of health planning and policy for children everywhere. This amazing array of contributions has been fueled by his lifelong and uncompromising commitment to excellence. We believe that Floyd exemplifies all of the finest attributes of an academic pediatrician, attributes which the American Pediatric Society strives to foster. We propose him as a most fitting candidate for the Howland Award.

THOMAS F. BOAT
LOUIS E. UNDERWOOD
JUDSON J. VAN WYK

CHAPTER 8

Residents' Reminiscences

STEPHEN L. FRIEDLAND (1961–1962)

THANKS again for asking me to participate in the development of the Department history. I should caution you that my son, Michael, is the professional historian in the family, and that neither UNC nor anyone else has thus far asked to publish any of my work. However . . .

I spent only a year at Chapel Hill (1961–1962) and with the passage of this many years, it's hard to isolate the specific knowledge I acquired there from the material I've picked up before and since, with the specific exception, of course, of the MYCOPLASMA! That organism has become such a "signature" of Floyd's years with the Department that when, several years ago, Seth Hetherington—whom I had not known in Chapel Hill—came down from Albany to lecture to our Pediatric Department on infectious diseases, I had no difficulty whatever in knowing where he had trained.

When I arrived at Chapel Hill, after a year's residency with Sydney Gellis at Boston City Hospital and two years at a very small Air Force hospital in Greenville, Mississippi, it was a nice middle ground—as intellectually and academically challenging as Boston, but slower paced and, at least in those days, more relaxed and easy-going. I was in an Air Force-sponsored program—as was Bob Herrington—and drawing my regular captain's pay rather than the usual resident salary (I don't think I even knew what that amounted to), and since Anne and I lived in graduate student housing, we were a bit better off than many of my colleagues. I was only on call every fourth night (Bob, Frank Shaw, and Joanna Dalldorf were the other senior residents that year), which wasn't too much of a burden; Anne would bring dinner over for us, and then, unfortunately, I would have to take her home, check the apartment, and lock her in because there had been prowlers in the area.

Most of my other memories are anecdotal. I remember Brian Luke, with his rather heavily accented English, trying to make himself understood by and to understand families from the very rural parts of North Carolina, and, if memory serves, I remember the tragedy of an unimmunized child dying of diphtheria. I also remember well my nights on call with Bill Clarke and Dave Bruton, trying to set a new record with each child coming into the ER with meningitis for the shortest time from arrival through examination, lumbar puncture, exam of the CSF, and intravenous antibiotic therapy.

On a much more personal note I remember our first daughter Jane's birth at NCMH, with Joe Whatley in attendance. And I remember the genuine affection and respect that we had for each other—attendings and house staff—which is the primary reason we come back every three years.

ROBERT L. ABNEY III (1962–1964, 1966–1967)

House Staff in the Sixties

The old brick hospital blended nicely with collegiate buildings among the trees and winding streets. Small windows were made less functional by the air conditioning units. The inside decor was mainly yellow upper walls and dark brown "easy to clean" lower panels. The telephone and paging operators sat conveniently near the front door and knew everything about everybody.

The house officers' quarters were across the front drive, and rooms were available there for on-call house officers, with some even living there permanently. On-call rooms were fairly small and had upper and lower bunk beds, enabling the room to be shared by another physician (mainly medicine interns), who had smelly feet. This arrangement did have some educational value, in that it allowed the roommate to hear how the other person handled phone calls—"Start O_2 by mask, give 15 cc of paraldehyde PR, 5 mg Valium IV, I'll be right there," followed immediately by loud snoring.

Even then, there were signs of progress around the hospital. The cafeteria began opening for one hour between 10:00 and 11:00 P.M. to accommodate working house officers, and this was nice since the lunch and supper usually brought from home in one bag had completely run out, and the only snack available was canned baby food on the ward, unless you had a friend with keys to the kitchen at the clinical research unit.

Several house officers volunteered to help administer vaccines during the community oral polio, and later measles, immunization efforts. Absolutely no thought was given to any legal repercussions from this activity. WCHL radio was even on hand and gave several of the physicians their first live radio interview.

Bolin Brook Farm was the temporary home of at least three pediatric house officers, the site of several departmental picnics and at least one snipe hunt. It also hosted numerous unofficial retreats and gatherings with much conversation and rhetoric which ultimately did not amount to a hill of beans.

The combined pediatric-medicine grand rounds was very useful, in that it prevented the house officers from becoming too focused on their particular specialty, and it also gave a forum for the attending subspecialists to comment on similar problems in the adult and child. The interchange and forum for learning for the house officer were excellent. It also gave the intern a chance to learn that a referring physician was never referred to as an "LMD."

The seventh-floor house officers' lab, used by interns and medical students for admission laboratory work, gram stains, and plating cultures, was generally not a happy place, and all the above activity was called "scut." In retrospect, a great deal of basic learning was accomplished in this setting, but it was subsequently deemed an unnecessary part of medical education, especially when the hospital pointed out they could make a lot of money from laboratory procedures.

The resident's early morning report to the chief was nearly always a special treat. Admissions from the previous day and night were briefly presented, and it was nice to be able to bring an appropriate culture plate or gram stain for review and discussion. Many times this was the highlight of the day.

Amoxicillin emerged as the "wonder drug"—no more thinking, worrying, and guessing about triple therapy as initial treatment for meningitis. Some said then and still say now, "Everything that goes around comes around."

There are many good things that can be said about Bill Clarke, chief resident 1963–1964, a pediatrician whose career was cut short by early death to cancer, but one of his strongest attributes was that he was a realist who could cut right to the heart and truth of a matter in very short order. Once after hearing an attending go on and on about how wonderful a particular intern seemed to be, Bill muttered, "Give me a house officer who can tap a kid without muddying the water" and walked off. Night call in those days was every other night for interns and first-year ward residents, and there was rarely a complaint, but if so, Bill would simply say, "You're the one that signed on, and I can be the one to sign you off." (I'm not sure that would work in the '90s.)

John Stephenson was another memorable resident in the '60s. He was smart, steady, considerate, compassionate, and destined to become an ideal primary care pediatrician, whose career was also cut short by early death. He was single, and several females around the hospital felt him to be a good "catch." In those days the ID resident spent a fair amount of time in the bacteriology lab reading cultures, and one bacteriology technician was hot on John's trail. She asked him about his occasional cigar, and he described it as "ambrosia." She then spent several weeks looking for ambrosia cigars. (Of course, none existed.)

The continuity clinic was a mechanism where pediatric residents could see other house officers' children in the private clinic, and of course, consultation was available from among any of the attending pediatricians and other specialists. This was a very valuable experience for the pediatric resident, in that it exposed him to a much more informed and sensitive patient-parent practice relationship than he usually saw on the ward or in the outpatient clinic.

The feeling of the house officers in those days about Floyd Denny was that he was the soul, the glue, and the bottom line, and when he was out of town the morning report was not the same, grand rounds was not the same, and we all felt significantly deprived.

JOHN R. RAYE (1965–1968)

Pediatric Residency in the 1960s

Chapel Hill in the '60s was a beautiful, small college town and a perfect setting for the North Carolina Memorial Hospital. What was most notable on arrival as a new intern was the energy and spirit of the pediatric program. There was a real feeling of camaraderie in the residency. Everyone was there to learn to care for children. There was none of the sense of competition—one-upsmanship—that was present in so many programs. The faculty were stimulating and supportive, always encouraging you to do your best. This environment provided a great spirit of intellectual curiosity that was felt by residents and faculty alike.

This spirit was most manifest at Dr. Denny's morning report. This was a time when all the junior and senior residents (never the interns) met to discuss the cases from the day before. Each resident wanted to impress Dr. Denny by having the most complete differential diagnosis and treatment plan. This often meant long trips to the library after midnight to find new data to support your diagnosis. It meant bringing your culture plates from the incubators in the pediatric floor laboratory to look at the throat cultures, staph streaks, the results of the A disc or for the "sniff test." The discussions were lively and full of give and take; there were never any attempts made to belittle or embarrass anyone. Dr. Denny was always provocative and stimulating. There were always "pearls" to be had and new leads to follow. One of his greatest assets was his willingness to admit when he didn't know the answer to a particular problem. The famous Denny "I don't know the answer to that" led us to ferret out additional sources for the best solution. There were other pediatric faculty members, the library, trips to visit faculty of other departments; we never backed down from the challenge. We discussed, we argued, but we were always supported—supported by Dr. Denny, by other faculty members, and by our coresidents. We developed great respect for the faculty and worked hard to please them. This brought a great sense of shared responsibility to the program. When one of us needed extra help, everyone pitched in. When someone was sick, you stayed on the service and took care of "your" patients. There was no such thing as "someone else's problem." The program simply didn't work that way. This sense of responsibility derived primarily from the example set by Dr. Denny and was further enhanced by the chief residents.

The chief residents were special people. They frequented the floor and the nursery at night. They read your charts, made comments on the front sheet suggesting new diagnoses, more tests, and occasionally the error of your ways. They recalculated your drug doses, checked your signatures, and ensured that your discharge summary was complete. To an intern they were petrifying—they seemed to know everything! As a junior resident you looked to them for leadership and they were always there to support you. To senior residents they were colleagues, colleagues who were always ready to come in to help you with overwhelming problems and difficult diagnoses. They were there at morning report to keep the process moving. They were your inspiration and a source of knowledge. They plied you with articles, journals, and stimulating questions. As you moved through the residency, you found that while perhaps they didn't know *everything*, they would always work with you to solve the problems. Their welcoming picnic for the new interns was always a highlight of the year. Boiled shrimp. Beer in the bathtub! Some great times!

We worked hard in the '60s; in terms of hours, perhaps harder than now. While the acuteness may not have been as high, the patient stays were considerably longer, and we "lived" at the hospital. We worked a Monday-Wednesday-Saturday-Sunday or Tuesday-Thursday-Friday schedule. That meant everyone worked five and a half days at the hospital with long on-calls, starting Saturday morning and getting home Monday night or starting Thursday morning and getting home Saturday afternoon. We used to calculate that working around 120 hours a week at $2,300 a year meant that our take-home pay was about 30 cents per hour. On Saturdays, after rounds, we needed to finish our work before heading home for that all too brief "weekend off." These were long nights and busy days. I have already mentioned morning report. In addition, there were morning work rounds, daily attending rounds, and evening check-out rounds. Professor's rounds on Saturday morning were considered a highlight of the week. But why Saturday??? Dr. Denny "checked out the floor" and we all worked to keep it shined. These were the years of "Denny Dips," "sure as God made little green apples," and "gold-plated whirling tizzies." We would catch ourselves smiling at these Dennyisms, poking each other and readying our material for our theatrical sessions mimicking the boss. It was a time of learning, establishing great respect for our teachers, and high-spirited fun.

The pediatric floor was staffed with wonderful people. The nurses, the nurses' aides, the clerks, the playroom people: they all made the floor buzz. We all remember the diminutive aide, Mrs. Miles, who could hold the biggest and wildest child absolutely still for an LP or blood culture. The floor was busy, full of children with infectious diseases: meningitis, pneumococcal sepsis, *Haemophilis influenzae* invasive disease, "dew sores," and nephritis. We saw rheumatic fever, rickets, diphtheria, and pertussis. We cared for the children with sequelae of chicken pox and measles, mumps and rubella. We did careful physical exams, listened to murmurs, and thumped chests. Then we were off to the laboratory on the floor to do our own CBCs, spinal counts, and urinalyses. We did our own cultures and pour plates with subcultures, staph streaks, and A discs. The hospital lab didn't help you much at night— you *were* the laboratory. How many hours did we spend going over spinal counts and smears? looking for lancet-shaped diplococci and pleomorphic gram negative rods? Was it clumped stain or a bacterium?

On occasions when we actually had the opportunity to see a bed we would spend the night in an adjoining building. We played a little pool. Was there time to sleep or was the admitting resident "a sieve"? There were calls from referring physicians, from the nurses on the floor, and from our partners. I still remember some of the conversations. "She has no blood pressure at all? . . . (long pause) . . . Take it again and call me back." We ran to the floor and to the delivery room. We dreaded the new admission that would end all hope for sleep.

For many of us the nursery rotation was one of the program's highlights. The concept of neonatal intensive care was about to be born, but we had no faculty member with special training in this area. Here the resident had real responsibility with call for the entire month (day and night). We ventilated our first infant with respiratory distress syndrome in 1967. We wheeled up Herb Harned's Astrup machine from the sheep laboratory to do pHs and pCO$_2$s and thought we were hot stuff. We had no way to measure blood oxygen concentrations. Instead we watched the color, the temperature, and the baby. We thought the limit of viability was 1,250 grams. The smaller the baby, the longer we went before initiating feeds. That often meant two or three days before we started fluids or nutrition. We thought dropper feedings, Bird respirators, and Astrup machines were high technology. We did exchange transfusions by the dozen (no phototherapy). They were done with catheters with multiple metal stopcocks you hooked together. You had to learn how to turn each of the six or so stopcocks the right way so that it was 10 cc in and 10 cc out until the double volume exchange was finished. For apnea, we shook the incubator. We tied gauze around the feet and ran it out through the top so the baby could be stimulated. There were no fancy monitors to provide alarms and trends. But the nursery again was a place of teamwork. There were superb nurses who were always ready to help. Better still, they brought in hot baked pies and cakes on the evening shift and there was always coffee.

Other rotations included the clinic where Charlie Sheaffer oversaw the activities. The interns worked with different specialists on a weekly rotation. General ambulatory pediatric training was complemented by our own resident clinics where we took care of each other's children in addition to those of residents in other programs. The senior residents did the screening clinic for the walk-ins. Anything could turn up and often did. Nights were in the emergency room.

These were times that have made great memories. They are memories bred of hard work, great camaraderie, and a sense of purpose. This is where we learned intellectual curiosity and what mentoring was all about. This is where we developed a thirst for learning. The source of all this was Dr. Denny. He and the other faculty led us by example. They asked for our very best and we held them in such great esteem that we worked to please them. They were our teachers and our colleagues. We worked together and we played together. We went out together to the community and lectured around the state. We had continuing education programs in Pinehurst, where many would sneak out for a round of golf. We had some wild parties, yet somehow we always made it in to work the next day. This was a place where many of our own children were born. All of these memories, some great and some sad, tie us forever to Chapel Hill and to each other. To the people we counted on to take care of our patients when we were off. To the people we cheered with at Carolina basketball and football games. To the people who taught us Northerners that the Civil War wasn't entirely dead. These truly were great times.

The names we will not forget—Floyd Denny, Cam McMillan, Harrie Chamberlin, Jud Van Wyk, Herb Harned, Neil Kirkman, Bob Castle, Wally Clyde, Paul Glezen, Jerry Fernald, Frank French, and others. These were our mentors, people who have influenced the fabric of our lives in ways so subtle that they are truly a part of us. Floyd's leadership, the tone he set for the Department, his honesty, enthusiasm, and boundless energy shaped us all. This was the program's greatest gift.

HARVEY J. HAMRICK (1967–1971)

Reflections of a Pediatric Resident

As a fourth-year medical student in the fall of 1966, interest in a pediatric residency prompted a visit to the program at Case Western Reserve in Cleveland. My plane landed in the middle of a snowstorm with the outside temperature at five degrees. My winter coat was no match for the cold and the wind blowing off Lake Erie. After a quick reassessment of priorities, the UNC pediatric residency program was moved to the top of my match list. I started my internship in July 1967 and finished four years later after a year as chief resident. After one year of private practice in Winston-Salem, I returned to Chapel Hill in 1972 and have continued on the faculty until the present time. My fellow interns in 1967 were Mary Sugioka, Bill Keagy, Meade Christian, and Jack Kiesel.

Although these new interns were largely unaware (for obvious reasons), Chapel Hill was an interesting and exciting place in 1967. The town, the University, and North Carolina Memorial Hospital were just beginning to experience the initial phases of growth that transformed the entire community from a small college town to a thriving metropolitan area and major research university in the 1970s and 1980s. Between 1965 and 1971, the UNC student body increased from twelve thousand to over nineteen thousand, and between 1960 and 1970, the population of Chapel Hill doubled from twelve thousand to twenty-five thousand. The late 1960s and early 1970s saw vigorous expansion in commercial and residential development to accommodate the increased numbers of students and townspeople. The influx of outside commercial enterprises and development was a much debated topic. The first fast food restaurant (Hardees) arrived in 1965 at its present location amid much controversy about the detrimental effects of such an establishment on the "village character."

When Howard Lee succeeded Sandy McClamroch as mayor in 1969, he became one of a few black mayors in the South. Bob Scott was governor of North Carolina and J. Carlyle Sitterson was chancellor of UNC. Dean Smith had been head coach of the UNC basketball team for only six seasons and was not quite as well known then as he is today. At a university reception, he introduced himself to the wife of a prominent official who inquired "Mr. Smith, what are you dean of?" Members of the 1968 basketball team included Dick Grubar, Eddie Fogler, Rusty Clark, Bill Bunting, Larry Miller, and Charlie Scott, the first black basketball player at UNC. Bill Dooley was head football coach and Don McCauley was the star running back. James Taylor, a twenty-year-old native of Chapel Hill, made the big time in the music industry with the hits "Carolina on My Mind" and "Sweet Baby James."

Although pediatric residents were relatively insulated from outside events, we all knew that Chapel Hill assumed an important role in the social change, debate, and unrest which were associated with the continuing process of integration and with the Vietnam War. The Franklin Street peace vigils in front of the old post office started in 1967 and continued each Wednesday at noon until August of 1973. The Kent State incident in May of 1970 resulted in a huge march and demonstration involving four thousand UNC students two days later. During this time, medical students were cutting class to participate in such activities, causing some consternation among the faculty, where the traditional attitude was that doctors did not need to get involved in such things. Occasionally, the social unrest was evident in the Medical School when a student would challenge the traditional dress and appearance codes by showing up with sandals, long hair, and a casual shirt with no tie. Times indeed were changing.

The Medical School and hospital were much smaller in terms of buildings, personnel, and students. The student class size was between sixty and seventy. There were only fifteen pediatric residents (today there are forty-four), and fifteen to twenty full-time faculty members (today there are over seventy). Isaac Taylor was dean of the Medical School and Floyd Denny, Louis Welt, and Nathan Womack were chiefs of services. The pediatric faculty members included Drs. Van Wyk, Harned, Chamberlin, Herrington, Kirkman, Clyde, McMillan, Glezen, and Summer. Chapel Hill Pediatrics was the only pediatric group in town and the two pediatricians were Drs. Robert Senior and Charles Sheaffer. Drs. Senior and Sheaffer admitted their patients to NCMH and would often serve as the attending physicians. Dr. Sheaffer attended part time in the outpatient clinic and actually started the morning acute care outpatient conference. Dr. Senior taught office bacteriology to medical students for a number of years. Head nurses were Bonnie Beard (7E/7W), Margaret Adams (clinics), Elizabeth Warren (newborn nursery), and Martha Russell (premature nursery). There was no PICU. Also, there were no faculty members in neonatology, pulmonology, rheumatology, gastroenterology, nephrology, or critical care. Richard Morris arrived in 1971 as the first pediatric nephrologist. Dr. Joseph Whatley donated a half day a week from his practice in Durham to precept residents in a pediatric allergy clinic. Patients were transported in family cars or by private ambulance services, which usually were operated by funeral homes. There were no community rescue squads with their fully equipped vehicles and trained personnel. Medical air transportation started in 1975 when the first helicopter pad was built. In the hospital environment, physicians were paged by overhead speakers. Beepers did not appear until sometime in the early 1970s.

All resident rotations were in Chapel Hill. The Wake Hospital service did not start until 1974 or 1975. Rotations included the inpatient ward, the premature nursery, the newborn nursery, and the outpatient clinics. There were no resident continuity clinics. The various types of rounds and conferences were very similar to those today. One important difference was Saturday morning Denny rounds. These were high-adrenaline events. Nobody cut Denny rounds because the group was small enough that a missing person was conspicuous by being absent. The chief resident introduced each case and presenter. The interns were the presenters, having been tutored carefully by their respective junior assistant residents. A poor presentation by an intern reflected no glory on the responsible resident. High-profile cases were always infectious diseases—pneumonia, urinary tract infection, epiglottitis, meningitis, and osteomyelitis. The highest-profile cases were acute rheumatic fever and acute post-streptococcal glomerulonephritis. Cultures were incubated in a house officer lab on the seventh floor (remember the candle cans?). In a case of bacterial meningitis, the intern usually had inoculated and streaked the spinal fluid for culture and was programmed to produce the plates at precisely the right time in the presentation. Examination of the plates and the resultant commentary around management and antimicrobial therapy gave the young intern a very clear message: "There are two essential antibiotics. One is penicillin for everything streptococcal, meningococcal, or pneumococcal, and the other is chloramphenicol (never say Chloromycetin) for meningitis and Rocky Mountain spotted fever."

The call schedule for pediatric residents was rigorous. Interns were on call every other night, and on a busy service, this might mean thirty-six to forty hours in-house with only eight to twelve hours at home. Second-year residents had every third night call and senior assistant residents had every fourth or fifth night call. Interns and junior assistant residents wore white pants and short white coats and senior residents wore dark pants and short white coats. There were no blood drawing teams, IV teams, or respiratory therapists. Most IVs were scalp needles that were elaborately taped in place. The more reliable intracaths of today had not yet been invented. The premature nursery was a separate unit and Bird respirators were the standard. An old negative-pressure respirator was tried once on a small premature infant, but the violent motion and noise (which sounded like a broken sump pump) dampened our enthusiasm. Obviously, there were no CT scans or MRIs. Hydrocephalus was evaluated with the pneumoencephalogram. Some infants with diarrhea and dehydration arrived after having received a bolus of fluid in the form of clysis from the referring physician.

Children with pulmonary tuberculosis were admitted to a small pediatric tuberculosis unit on the first floor of Gravely. Part of the rationale for admission was to attempt to culture early morning gastric washings. The washings were obtained on three consecutive mornings. By the third morning, a child's response to the intern's appearance—NG tube in one hand and large syringe and basin in the other—was probably similar to the welcome received by agents of the Inquisition on morning visits to the dungeons. The prototype case for all house officers was bacterial meningitis. A new intern had achieved a medical rite of passage by taking care of a terribly sick child with meningitis.

Kawasaki disease, AIDS, and sexual abuse were not part of our clinical experience. We were just coming to grips with the "battered child" syndrome, and in 1971, Virginia Hebbert (the chief pediatric social worker) and the chief resident put together the first child abuse protocol for house officers. Hemolytic uremic syndrome was something reported in Argentina, and renal transplants were done in San Francisco. Many mothers smoked during pregnancy, but cocaine was not a problem. Most mothers bottle-fed their infants, and evaporated milk formulas were often used. I still remember the correct formulation: 13 oz. of Pet evaporated milk, 17 oz. of water, and 2 level teaspoons of Karo syrup. Children with cystic fibrosis were put in "mist tents." If you could see the child, the tent wasn't working well. I recall on many late night rounds sticking my head in a mist tent to listen to a tiny chest. Between coughs and through the moisture on my glasses and face, the infant's eyes and mine would sometimes meet in a moment of reflection. More than once, the infant seemed to be asking "Doc, is this thing really necessary?" A few years and a few studies later, mist tents faded from the landscape. Aspirin ingestion was fairly common because childproof caps and bottles had not been developed. Not everyone knew about Rocky Mountain spotted fever, so we occasionally got very sick children who had been misdiagnosed as having measles.

The screening clinic has not changed in concept since it remains the entry point for both walk-in patients and physician referrals. This was the area where we had the chance to see patients alone and make independent diagnoses. One of the nurses there, Mrs. Willis, had an observation that was accurate enough to be given the moniker of "Willis's sign." If a young infant presented to the screening clinic desk in the mother's arm with the blankets covering the head and face, you needed to check that infant immediately. By and large, such infants came from a long distance and were about 10 percent dehydrated and moribund. Children frequently presented unannounced to the screening clinic with referral information on a prescription blank. The basic message on the prescription blank was "Sick child, please treat." The more innovative and humorous referral messages were saved in a notebook in the clinic.

Most of the pediatric residents were married, white males with wives who did not work outside the home. Many had small children, and new children arrived during the three years of training. Glen Lennox was one of the few apartment complexes in Chapel Hill, and many resident families lived there. The wives had an active organization for social and child care purposes. No residents' children of that era were placed in day care. Favorite restaurants were The Pines and The Ranch House, where steak dinners were the custom. The Varsity and the Carolina were the only movie theaters unless you drove to Durham. Basketball games were played in Carmichael Auditorium and the Faculty/Staff Recreation Association was just getting started. University Mall was not completed until 1973, and WUNC radio did not begin broadcasting until 1976.

As a personal remembrance, my first night on call was probably the only night of my entire internship that I remember distinctly. I started on the ward service on the seventh floor and one of the patients assigned to me that day was an eleven-year-old boy with anorexia nervosa. He was terribly emaciated and psychotic, and, that night at 2 A.M., he proceeded to die. I will never forget trying to intubate him. I had sent the family home that day with a fairly optimistic outlook, but, at 4 A.M., I had to call them to report his death. Autopsy revealed an intestinal perforation of several days' duration leading to peritonitis and sepsis. To say the least, it was a humbling experience and a rather sobering way to start my internship. We learned a lot by trial and error, as all critically ill patients were taken care of on the seventh floor without the benefit of intensivists or specially equipped units. Medicine was changing, and our experiences with and inadequacies in caring for critically ill patients led to a recognition of the need for critical care units. Other memorable cases include a Lumbee Indian boy with intractable seizures who died before we could get him to the NIH for neurosurgery; a nine-year-old boy who survived thymectomy for severe myasthenia gravis but then had a fatal crisis at home in eastern North Carolina; a renal transplant patient (I think the first such child ever cared for at NCMH) who died of varicella complications; a teenage boy with G6PD deficiency who thought it was cute to ingest a mothball. He survived, but it was dramatic to watch his hemoglobin fall to 5 grams as his bilirubin rose to 15 mg/dl. Also, I'll never forget a child with sickle cell disease who developed acute post-streptococcal glomerulitis and died of renal failure. In those days, we performed peritoneal dialysis with the assistance of the adult nephrology service. Children with leukemia were placed on simple chemotherapy protocols, but the prognosis was usually grim. Children with hemophilia were treated with fresh frozen plasma, and, not infrequently, severe allergic reactions occurred or pulmonary edema resulted from the infusion of too much plasma.

Today the medical center is indeed complex—not only in terms of buildings and size but also in terms of types of patients and diseases, technical procedures, ethical and legal issues, and financial and insurance matters. Chapel Hill has a population of eighty thousand and is flanked by an interstate highway. However, it still is a place where ideas are born and basketball is played. James Taylor returned this spring and performed before a packed house in the Dean Dome. I suspect that if the five interns of 1967 had been there to hear "Carolina on My Mind" we would have returned briefly in our minds to a simpler time of white pants, mist tents, and Denny rounds.

WILLIAM C. HUBBARD (1966–1967, 1968–1969, 1971–1972)

In 1954, at the age of thirteen, I first dated my wife, Jane. She recalls that I told her at that time that I wanted to be a pediatrician. This early orientation toward a career in pediatrics was the result of the hero status of my pediatrician, Dr. Aldert Root, who was the first pediatrician in North Carolina. My parents' stories of how he saved my life when I hemorrhaged post-tonsillectomy, his reassuring diagnosis of mumps meningitis in the midst of the 1947 polio epidemic, and my memories of his manner during house calls resulted in a youngster's desire to be like him. My passage to pediatrics was sustained by enjoyable summers of working with children at camp and then profoundly influenced by my senior year in the UNC School of Medicine.

During my third year of medical school, like most students, I found that I enjoyed many of the clinical services. The enjoyment of a particular service depended largely on the attending professor, who served as the role model. Dr. Ernest Craige, a cardiologist in the Department of Medicine and the consummate teacher of physical examination of the heart, almost lured me down the path to a career in cardiology.

However, two experiences early in the fourth year of medical school got me back on track. Fourth-year students could elect to be an acting intern on a clinical service or subspecialty. I chose back-to-back rotations in the Pediatric Department. The first was an acting internship on the pediatric ward, while Dr. Campbell McMillan was attending. His impact on me was the same as his effect on every pediatric house officer. He did then, and henceforth has, set the standard within the Pediatric Department as the ideal physician-caretaker. He served as the model caretaker and the conscience for the Department.

The following month I was an acting intern on the pediatric infectious disease service when Dr. Denny was attending. The resident on the service was John Raye. I was swept along by John's intellect and wit and Dr. Denny's enthusiasm and knowledge. I'll never forget making rounds with John and then finding our way to the small microbiology lab in preparation for Dr. Denny's arrival to review the culture plates. By the end of the month, I could differentiate a colony of pneumococcus from alpha strep and, more importantly, had no further doubts that I wanted a career under the tutelage of this exciting professor.

I first joined the Department of Pediatrics July 1, 1966, as one of five straight pediatric interns. The house staff at that time consisted of five straight pediatric interns, plus three or four interns between the Departments of Medicine and Pediatrics in what was called the mixed program. There were five junior assistant residents, five senior assistant residents, and a chief resident position held by a fourth-year house officer, chosen by Dr. Denny. All of the pediatric house staff and faculty at that time were male.

During my first month of employment as a physician, I got a raise. Annual intern salaries at North Carolina Memorial Hospital were increased from $2,800 to $3,100. For this compensation, we took night call every other night. This meant spending thirty-six out of every forty-eight hours in the hospital for the entire year. In those times, no one questioned the rigor of that schedule. It was an understood part of the commitment to medicine.

To maintain some semblance of family life, wives would bring picnic baskets of dinner to the hospital cafeteria to steal some time with their house officer spouses. So ingrained in the UNC Department of Pediatrics was the importance of this commitment to medicine that Bill Kanto and I, who did our junior assistant residency year at the University of Virginia in Charlottesville, where interns were only required to be on call every third or fourth night, complained that under this "relaxed" schedule the interns there were unable to adequately keep in touch with their patients.

In the UNC Pediatric Department, one could identify the level of training of individuals by their dress. Fourth-year students were expected to wear short, white cotton coats, along with white cotton pants. The most popular shoes for students and house officers were Hush Puppies or dirty bucks, which quietly made the way along the halls late at night. The fourth-year students were further identifiable by the contents of their white coats. In one jacket pocket was a black vinyl notebook, known as the student's "peripheral brain." The other jacket pocket contained a stethoscope, reflex hammer, and several tourniquets used for the "scut work" of drawing blood for all lab work. The jacket breast pocket had several straight pins for sensory examination of the nervous system. Another pocket contained tongue depressors, a pen light, and Bic pens with red, blue, and black ink. It was the responsibility of the student to have immediately available any conceivable tool that a resident or attending might request during a patient examination.

Pediatric interns were required to wear white pants, but distinguished themselves by omitting the short white coats worn by students. Junior assistant residents wore white coats but regular civilian pants. Senior residents were not required to wear whites at all, though budgetary constraints resulted in many of them wearing their whites until the cuffs had shrunk well above the shoe tops. Attending physicians wore long white lab coats, one pocket containing their stethoscope and the other a small notebook. The contents of the notebook were a mystery, since I never saw an attending stoop to refer to this reference in the presence of students or house officers.

In the 1960s, pediatric house officers spent their training time divided among the newborn nursery, which was located on the fifth floor; the premature nursery, which was located on the fourth floor; the ward, which was on the seventh floor; and the clinic, which was located on the ground floor near the Medical School. There was also a small pediatric ward in Gravely Sanatorium where children with tuberculosis were admitted. Interns and first-year residents rotated through the newborn nursery and premature nursery. There was no neonatologist, therefore, attending in the nursery was shared among all the clinical faculty. Ms. Martha Russell, RN, the head nurse in the premature nursery, was the glue that maintained continuity of care as house staff and faculty moved through their nursery rotations.

Interns rotated through the general pediatric clinic which was under the supervision of Dr. Loren MacKinney (affectionately known as Mickey Mouse MacKinney). During the clinic rotation, interns took night call in the emergency room. The intern was responsible for walk-in patients throughout the night, with the senior resident on call serving as his back-up consultant. Clinic interns met each morning with Dr. Charles Sheaffer. It was at these morning reports that clinic and emergency room patients were presented and management discussed. Dr. Sheaffer was in private practice in Chapel Hill and brought important practical wisdom to the management of outpatient pediatric problems.

The pediatric ward service was split between two teams, each comprised of a first-year resident, two interns, and several third-year medical students. Each team had an attending who made rounds three to five times per week. Pediatric interns were in direct charge of and responsible for all patients on their service. The junior assistant residents oversaw their work and reported to the chief resident, who made check-out rounds with the house staff at the end of each day.

At night, the pediatric service was covered by an intern from each ward team, one of the junior assistant residents, and one senior resident who served as overnight consultant for the entire service.

On Mondays, Wednesdays, and Thursdays at 8:30 A.M., residents covering the ward and nursery had morning report with Dr. Denny in his office. These "residents' rounds" with the chief were the heart of the Department's teaching program. Early in the junior assistant residency year, these rounds were a bit intimidating. I felt like we all sat around Dr. Denny's office naked because there was no mantle to hide what we didn't know from the chief. You quickly learned that it was fruitless to try to bluff your understanding about clinical cases. To the tremendous educational benefit of all the residents, a level of intellectual honesty evolved in those rounds, exemplified by the chief. All of us learned from Dr. Denny that it was okay to say "I don't know the answer, but I would approach the problem in the following way." This exposure to his method of problem solving influences all of his house staff to this day.

By the senior residency year, the security of mutual respect had been achieved and morning report with Dr. Denny was warmly anticipated and enjoyed. Indeed, the game was always on and the goal was to scoop the chief.

Occasional instances when the house staff could entrap the chief at morning report were moments of great delight and continue to be fond "war stories."

One of my favorite recollections of these instances involved a febrile neonate, admitted with an unusual chest film. The right upper portion of the lung was opaque, suggesting consolidation. After the case was presented to Dr. Denny, the X-ray was placed on the view box. Characteristically, he leapt from his chair, studying the film at close range. Shortly thereafter he asked the resident in charge if he had aspirated the area of pulmonary consolidation to make a definitive bacteriologic diagnosis prior to starting antibiotics. The chief, known affectionately as "the Fastest Needle in the East" if there was a bacteriologic diagnosis to be potentially achieved, began his impassioned sermon on the importance of isolating an organism before beginning antibiotics. He ended the minilecture with the question, "Wouldn't you feel better this morning if you had stuck a needle in that baby's chest last night?" To the delight of the other residents who were in on the scam, the ward resident answered that he thought he would not feel better, since Dr. Scatliff, the chief of radiology, had clearly diagnosed the opaque shadow as a wing of the thymus gland and not pneumonia.

Dr. Denny's enthusiasm and commitment to teaching pervaded the whole Department, from the faculty through the house staff. I always felt the entire faculty was approachable and eager to share their knowledge. Whether it was Dr. Harned in the cath lab, Dr. Van Wyk in the wee hours of the morning in his research lab, or Dr. Kirkman in the clinical research unit, all made time to share their knowledge with the house staff and students. This attitude had a ripple effect on the house staff in their seriousness and commitment to learning. The commitment to excellence came from the top down.

Another characteristic of the teaching program in the '60s was the expectation that the house staff had a responsibility to teach each other. Senior residents taught junior residents, junior residents taught interns, and interns shared their knowledge with students.

After two years in the Air Force, I returned to the Department in 1971 as chief resident. Dr. Denny had spent the previous year on sabbatical in Great Britain. We both returned to Chapel Hill and the Pediatric Department to find that it was not insulated from the tumultuous upheavals among young people caused by the national turmoil over the Vietnam War. Like youth all over the country, the young pediatric house staff found themselves rejecting tradition and authority, which they identified with having resulted in the unnecessary deaths of many of their contemporaries in Southeast Asia.

Symbolizing this rebellion against authority and tradition was a change in house staff appearance, and in some cases commitment to work and to patient demands. House officers showed up at morning report in sandals, rumpled clothes, and no ties. As chief resident, I often thought the house staff had more passion for an antiwar march on Franklin Street than they did for staying late for check-out rounds. This casual demeanor and distraction with social issues outside of the Department was a stark and trying contrast from the tone of the house staff of the '60s.

The medical problems of patients admitted to the pediatric service and their management, of course, differed greatly in the '60s. There were no computers, no intensive care areas, not even a neonatal intensive care unit. Immature babies with hyaline membrane disease did not have the benefit of respirators or even a neonatologist. They were placed in an incubator, given oxygen and fluids by the "Gluck" formula. They either made it or they didn't.

On the ward, one would always see at least one patient recovering from acute rheumatic fever being pulled around the halls in a wooden wagon. Acute rheumatic fever patients were routinely admitted for one to two months until their sedimentation rates returned to normal. The ongoing debate was which child should be treated with steroids instead of aspirin and whether it made a difference in the long-term prognosis. Likewise, there was rarely a day without at least one hemophiliac on the ward. Pediatric house officers were skilled at walking the fine line between adequate quantities of fresh, frozen plasma to stop the bleeding without pushing the patient into pulmonary edema.

7–West rooms were characteristically filled with children with various types of bacterial meningitis and its complications of subdural effusions and hydrocephalus. In the summer, house staff struggled to differentiate Rocky Mountain spotted fever from meningococcemia. In the winter, they had their heads in the ultrasonic mist tent used to treat children with cystic fibrosis.

For house staff in the '60s, patient management was very much a hands-on endeavor. They were expected to do much of their own lab work. They drew blood, aspirated joint fluid and spinal fluid, and cultured specimens in the lab on the pediatric ward. Cultures plated in the seventh-floor lab included sheep blood pour-plates for detection of group A beta strep. The house staff read the cultures in the morning, prior to their being taken to the main hospital lab for official reading. Pediatric X-rays were read by the house staff and reviewed once weekly at the Pediatric X-ray Conference.

In summary, I remember the Pediatric Department in the '60s as a relatively small group of male faculty and house staff who were challenged to a commitment of excellence by Dr. Floyd Denny. The small size of the Department led to a close association between department members that has resulted in warm and lasting friendships. Likewise, common goals and experiences have forged a loyalty to each other and pride in the Department that has endured throughout our careers.

Hail to the Chief

It's 8:00 A.M. Saturday and pediatric chief resident Bob Abney is cleaning the seventh-floor conference room of crumpled paper and reference books that have been left on the black conference room table. He has already picked the cases to be presented to Departmental Chairman Dr. Floyd Denny by the interns who can be seen collecting their culture plates from the seventh-floor lab and quickly reviewing their notes. Attendance at Saturday morning walk rounds with Dr. Denny is required of all pediatric house staff. This begins sharply at 8:30 A.M., lest the tardy house officer wants to suffer through a lecture on timeliness from the chairman.

The view from the seventh-floor conference room reveals a beautiful fall morning. The leaves are just beginning to change and the sky is Carolina blue. Looking across the nurses' dorm, one can see Kenan Stadium, where the Tar Heels have a home football game with arch rival North Carolina State University. Already members of the marching band are filing in for their pregame practice. As house officers enjoy the view of the stadium on this crisp fall day, they hope they will make the game at 1:00 P.M.—not unlike their hope that some unwary nurse would leave her blinds open Friday night, which helps explain the popularity of the pediatric conference room as a gathering site (between the hours of 11 P.M. and 1 A.M.) for on-call male house officers from all clinical departments.

At 8:30 A.M. sharp, Dr. Denny sweeps into the conference room with his white lab coat flying and announces he's ready to "get going,". . . but not before spying a cup that Abney has missed on a book shelf and grumbling something about how "med students act like they were raised in pig sties." With that, Abney leads the group down the hall to the first room, where a new patient has been admitted with acute rheumatic fever. After a well-rehearsed presentation by intern Jack Benjamin, Dr. Denny pulls his antique stethoscope from his coat pocket and ceremoniously lays it on the child's chest. Soon, however, he is intently palpating the child's extremities. A look of satisfaction crosses his face. He bounds to the Venetian blinds to direct the light at precisely the right angle to show the subtle shadows of subcutaneous nodules. He is halfway through his discourse on the value of natural light and its angle when Harry Smith, a mixed intern recently rotated to pediatrics from medicine, blurts out that he can't see any shadows.

Waiting in the hall, the residents who have seen this nodule demonstration multiple times (though perhaps never a subcutaneous nodule) are scheming. The EKG of one of Dr. Van Wyk's hyperthyroid patients is opened, upside down, for the Chief's inspection. Resident Bob Kindley asks, "What do you think of the voltage criteria and ST segments in this tracing, Dr. Denny?" Not missing the smile on resident John Raye's face, the Chief hands the tracing to Jim Burke, asking him as the cardiology resident to interpret the strip for the group. Foiled, Jim quickly states it looks like a classic case of rheumatic carditis. The Chief, smiling his approval, has already started moving to the next room, signaling cessation of discussion.

The next patient is one of Neil Kirkman's admissions with an enzymatic defect in the urea cycle. Dr. Kirkman is just leaving the child's room as Dr. Denny and the team arrive. Upon request from the Chief, Dr. Kirkman, in his deep, monotone voice, begins a comprehensive stepwise review of each enzymatic reaction in every pathway influenced by this child's defect. Time drones on. Dr. Denny begins flexing and extending his fingers, then his arms, and has just completed two (back to the wall) deep knee bends when Dr. Kirkman breaks and asks if there are any questions. Dr. Denny quickly says, "No thank you, Neil" and starts moving down the hall muttering, "I'll be glad when someone discovers which GD virus causes those weird diseases."

The next patient has meningococcemia and a persistent fever one week after initiation of antibiotic treatment. Intern Bill Kanto presents the case and reports that he has repeated the lumbar puncture. The spinal fluid is reported by the lab technician to look improved. "Did you examine the spinal fluid yourself, Bill?" asks Dr. Denny. Kanto replies that he didn't have time and furthermore felt that the lab technician had more experience and expertise than he in identifying organisms in the CSF. Ten minutes later, with perspiration pouring down his flushed cheeks, Kanto reassures Dr. Denny that he will never again rely on a high school graduate technician to make critical decisions affecting the care of his patients and that he will find time to become intimate with the microscopic analysis of spinal fluid.

Attempting to rescue his intern, resident Thal Elliot ushers Dr. Denny to the patient's room. Elliot carefully washes his hands, but then uses his fingers to turn off the water. The Chief observes critically that Elliot will never make it as an infectious disease specialist unless he learns to turn off the spigot with his elbows. With that, the Chief is making his way into the room and exclaiming "As sure as God made little green apples, this patient has got loculated infection somewhere." Momentarily, he finds a warm and slightly tender knee. His eyes are ablaze. Everyone can see that he's fired up now. He has caught Elliot breaking sterile technique and scooped the A-Team in the space of five minutes.

One senses the game is on and the house staff is in trouble. I wonder if this is how opposing basketball teams feel when Charlie Scott swishes two long jumpers early in the contest. The Chief's eyes are sparkling. He takes two snorts from his Vicks nasal inhaler and quickens the pace to the next room.

A child with Rocky Mountain spotted fever is reported by intern Tom Digby to remain extremely sick two days after admission. Dr. Denny asks, "How are you treating him?" "With tetracycline," responds Digby hesitantly. "Our infectious disease consultant, Dr. Glezen [affectionately known as 'Small Paul'], recommends tetracycline." Dr. Denny scowls. He rubs his hand through his burr haircut and exclaims, "I don't believe in sending a boy to do a man's job. Damn shame, those hematologists raised all those fears about chloramphenicol. I'll tell you boys, when I get my Rocky Mountain spotted fever, I want you to treat me with chloramphenicol."

Giving himself a back rub against the door casing, Dr. Denny gets a faraway look in his eye and begins reflecting on a lesson from his mentor, Dr. Christie at Vanderbilt. "Dr. Christie (I could never call him Amos) taught me that every section of the country has its special infectious diseases. Southern California may have coccidioidomycosis, but here in Piedmont North Carolina we've got Rocky Mountain spotted fever. *Rickettsia, Rickettsiae*. Damn fine organism, Digby. You need to make friends with it."

Budding hematologist Dick O'Brien presents the next case of presumed lymphoma in a seventeen-year-old black male. O'Brien is concerned that the patient has impressive hilar adenopathy, but that the blood studies are normal. Furthermore, the patient has painful bruises on the anterior lower legs. After examining the patient's legs and looking at the chest X ray, Denny's eyes light up. "Boys, call off the oncologist. This is a gold-plated, revolving case of sarcoidosis with erythema nodosum. Pat Jasper, we need to know more about sarcoid in children. How about reviewing all the cases ever admitted to North Carolina Memorial Hospital and give us a report next week. By the way, did I ever tell you about the time my family was traveling to Atlantic Beach for vacation and my daughter asked me to look at the bites on her legs? The girl had erythema nodosum." Ten minutes later, after Dr. Denny has recalled a dozen more causes of erythema nodosum than the entire house staff can muster up, the group moves on. It's almost noon.

The next patient is a case of acute glomerulonephritis presented by intern Wally Brown, recently rotated to pediatrics from medicine. "Which type of streptococcus do you think caused this child's nephritis?" Dr. Denny asks Brown. Wally, nimble on his feet but a rookie in pediatrics, states he needs a refresher on the classification of streptococci. A faintly audible groan escapes from the senior resident row. "Follow me to the conference room, men. I need a blackboard to teach this poor intern a thing or two about streptococci."

The house staff is barely seated around the black onyx conference room table when Dr. Denny rolls up his sleeves and begins his emotional one-hour history of the streptococcus and its hemolytic and cell wall properties.

I rise quietly to open a window and steal a glance toward Kenan Stadium. What's that melody wafting up from the marching band? Could it be . . . ? Yes, I believe it is. "Hail to the Chief." I settle back in the black vinyl cushioned chair. Perhaps by second half . . .

WALLACE D. BROWN (1968–1970)

House Staff Memories

Memories are rather selective and pertain to the settings of the time and the individuals present. The following must be viewed in that context, and, for those that have interest, it will be because of those factors.

The house staff relationships were a special source of strength during the internship and residency years. During 1968, the on-call rotation was every other night, thirty-six hours on and twelve hours off, which has both negative and positive elements that are still debated today. However, the smaller band of house staff and the frequency of call also determined your social life, as there was minimal time to make other acquaintances. The spouses and children would congregate with basket dinners in the cafeteria each evening for those house officers on call. We all became acquainted with each other's families by this practice, and it was often the only time you would have contact with your own.

The apprehension of starting an internship was felt by all as we seemed to be "naked in the forest" and assisted each other in getting clothed with knowledge, information, and most importantly, confidence. Because of the intensity of call schedule, you knew everyone well, and success required team spirit with interdependence essential. It is interesting that I don't remember anyone not pulling his or her fair share, nor was there any question of someone leaving work undone for the next individual to pick up the pieces. There are always mind games that we play in such situations, and what is memorable to me is that at around 9:00 or 10:00 on the evening you were on duty, there began to be somewhat of a feeling of elation as you knew you would be off the next evening; however, at 9:00 or 10:00 on the evening you were off, there began to be a feeling of creeping depression as you knew you would be starting a thirty-six-hour stint the next morning. I think many of us, as I remember our discussions, had similar feelings.

The financial reward was limited, but since you were working all the time there was not much place to spend the money. The initial salary at that time was $4,000 for an intern, and many of us looked for other ways to earn money. One of the ways that we could do it was by using our medical affiliations to receive compensation for donating blood. Fortunately my blood was type O-negative with a low antibody titer and was desirable for exchange transfusions. This was especially important around Christmastime when the outlying pediatricians would send in to the nursery the ABO and Rh-incompatible infants who needed exchanges as the physicians themselves were trying to get a little relief during the holiday time. As a resident on the nursery, I knew when O-negative blood was needed, and this was my opportunity to donate and assist a child on its journey in life. It did not hurt at all to know that for this donation I also received $15 per unit that went to the home front.

There are also several salient memories of moments with attending staff that come to mind, and I must say that the spirit of assistance was ever present in the faculty and there was never any disregard for your most ignorant question.

One event occurred early in my house office training, and I remember it as follows: Each year before the start of the internship, Dr. Denny would have the interns over to his home for an informal meal and gathering to meet the faculty. The purpose, I believe, was for us to get to know people with whom we would be working on a more informal basis and also to allow the new interns to meet each other. As I drove there in my Corvair (Nader's claim to prominence), there was some apprehension, but the warm reception dispelled this concern quickly.

The rooms were laid out in somewhat of a circular pattern, with pizza, beer, soft drinks, etc. being served in the kitchen area and several other rooms for sitting and talking. True to my nature, I arrived at the pizza area first, and met my first faculty member, Dr. Harrie Chamberlin. We immediately engaged in an easy conversation, and since the University of Rochester was the source of my medical background, he began to name many common acquaintances. We subsequently compared stories of these individuals and his familiarity with where I had come from, and it was a very comfortable, warm interchange lasting at least twenty-five minutes. We then parted in opposite directions. As I was leaving the kitchen and walking the circle, I reached about 180 degrees from the starting point, and whom do I see coming toward me but Dr. Chamberlin. He had his usual broad friendly grin, and he extended his hand toward me, firmly grabbed mine and looked me in the eye and in his gentle voice said, "Hi, I'm Harrie Chamberlin, and you are. . . ?"!!!

Another faculty remembrance was working with Dr. Judson Van Wyk. As first-year residents, we had the responsibility of dictating discharge summaries and making sure the attending signed them once they were completed. It was told to me by multiple sources that Dr. Van Wyk was the most difficult person to track down and get this accomplished. Being young and not very polite at the time, I decided to tell Dr. Van Wyk that this was his reputation; however, I also told him I would dictate the summaries and get these all together in batches for him to sign to make this as efficient as possible. This worked beautifully, and we never encountered a problem. In addition, I had a most enjoyable, entertaining, and enlightening month with him as our attending.

Brevity has always been something I have admired, and during that month I did see the best example of that quality in an attending note. The patient was a child with hemophilia admitted for complications with bleeding. Our attending note read: "This patient with hemophilia is being cared for by the best pediatric hemophilia department in the world. I have nothing to add to the care they are giving." It was signed "Judson Van Wyk."

Finally, there are some individual and somewhat personal memories that are just a potpourri of mind expansion. Coming to Chapel Hill from the Northeast in 1968 revealed a distinctive difference in the roadside appearance as we entered what I first thought was red dirt but later learned was the red clay of North Carolina. The exposure to grits as a food source was also new, but I did convert to having a breakfast every other morning when on call of grits, baked apples, eggs, and orange juice, hoping to fool my body that it had received some rest that night. It always intrigued me that putting bourbon in a brown paper bag suddenly made it legal for social occasions. I also did not endear myself with the natives of North Carolina when we began watching the ACC basketball games and I commented that coming to the ACC is just coming "to watch New York area boys make good," as this was the time when Charlie Scott, Walter Davis, et al. were starring in the league.

Personally, there were some events that remained vivid between Dr. Denny and myself which I have shared with him in the past. The first involves the young intern in the process of applying for a residency program and realizing that he wanted to be at the Pediatric Department at the University of North Carolina. However, rumors were abounding about how Dr. Denny had been offered the chair at Western Reserve and would probably leave for that program. Again, with the naiveté of youth and not knowing the most appropriate approach, I went ahead and made an appointment with Dr. Denny. As always, he was accessible and easy to talk with, and I told him I desired to apply for the residency program in peds, but I had heard he might be leaving for Western Reserve. I wanted to know if that indeed were a fact because that might affect my desire to apply. As I remember, he responded first by moving around in his chair behind the desk and then said, "I am not in the habit of revealing my plans to everyone; however, I can tell you my family has never been happier than here in Chapel Hill." Well, I left, read between the lines, and took my chances.

Another most memorable event of the 1960s and 1970s was the tragedy, anxiety, and trauma of the Vietnam War. The Berry Plan was available for some, but my application did not qualify, and I was drafted into the Army as a general medical officer to undoubtedly go to Vietnam. As a father of two children with another on the way, and being made aware of what was happening by watching 400,000 people march on Washington, and beginning to develop convictions of my own, this was a most trying time.

Dr. Denny's advice to go to Washington and meet with people there proved to be correct and serendipitous. The sequence of events there did prove favorable for me and my family and helped avoid another personal encounter that would have been a distressing situation for all. I will never forget sitting in the park opposite the White House, with my suitcase, just totally confounded as to how I could be in this predicament. Fortunately, there were those that gave the right advice at the right time, which helped alleviate some of this bafflement.

JERRY C. BERNSTEIN (1971–1974)

Remembrances of the Department of Pediatrics

My first encounter with the Department as a medical student was in the trailer located where the current emergency room entrance exists. I was greeted by the then Peggy Davidson, who seven years later was to become my wife. I received instructions as to where to report, etc. The seventh floor was bright, shiny, and a happy-feeling place. I was impressed with the easygoing nature of all who worked there—house staff, nurses, etc. I recall the poster with our medical school pictures and our placement on either the Red or Blue teams. A list of our patients was to be marked under our pictures. If your patient had what I soon learned was one of the hot diagnoses, you were the lucky one to present at professor rounds before none other than the chief of the Department, Dr. Floyd Denny. Guess what those patients had?—bronchiolitis, acute glomerulonephritis, acute rheumatic fever, juvenile rheumatoid arthritis, osteomyelitis, meningitis, mastoiditis, etc. Well, it goes without saying that I ended up presenting at least three of those categories of patients to the Chief. I remember well the first one. I had the conference room all neat and straight, X-rays on the view box and my note cards discreetly out of sight. It would be impossible to tell you how my heart was beating when Dr. Denny strode into that conference room with lab coat flying, taking his seat at the head of the table, looking around at all of us, and then turning to me and telling me, "Shoot." I spit out the history and physical, turned to the X-rays, gave the lab data and differential diagnoses, treatment plan and outcome, and sat down. I can only remember feeling an out-of-body experience for the rest of the hour. I don't recall any criticisms so I must have done all right or so poorly that he recreated how the presentation should have been. Somehow I feel I did OK.

I was lucky to have had an inordinate amount of exposure to Dr. Denny on that first pediatric rotation. I was and still to this day am impressed by his excitement with teaching. I wanted to learn everything and had never felt that way before. The manner in which he made pediatric medicine come alive for me was "awesome," as they say in the vernacular of today.

George Hemingway was my chief resident and Harvey Hamrick my first senior resident. Both of them influenced me in my early experiences in pediatrics. Theirs was a practical approach to this specialty, unlike that of medicine or surgery. Somehow I knew that I was learning and having an impact on those patients I encountered.

As a fourth-year student, I included infectious disease as a pediatric elective. To my delight and anxiety, Dr. Denny was the attending. Fortunately, the resident had to take vacation during that month and there were no other house officers available to fill in. Dr. Denny and I were the consulting team. What an experience! I learned to sniff more blood agar places than I care to recount. We would go from the seventh-floor lab to the main lab downstairs, correlating patient histories with cultures obtained and treatments rendered. It was fascinating and I was on the way to becoming a pediatrician—not because of my love of children, but because of the excitement Dr. Denny showed me was there for the taking in pediatric medicine. The offshoot of that, of course, is the fulfillment of knowing that you have had a hand in the process of assuring the healthy growth and development of that child from neonate to adulthood.

When it came time to make a decision for internships, I still fancied myself a family physician and interviewed in both rotating 4 and straight pediatric programs. Each place I visited I was impressed with the degree of satisfaction exhibited by those in pediatrics, and thus, I assigned peds as my first choice in each program where I interviewed. Dr. Denny was taking a sabbatical in London during my internship year and I wanted to go away during that time, knowing that I wanted to return when he did. It was my good fortune to match with my first choice in the Department of Pediatrics at the University of Virginia. Dr. Denny's good friends Bob Merrill, Bill Thurman, and Mac Birdsong were all there. They gave me grief about returning to Chapel Hill, but they also gave me their support and a fantastic learning experience. In medical school I was certainly no scholar, but a year away enabled me to hone my talents and to bring a stronger physician back to the UNC program. It was the best thing that could have happened to me at that critical time in my training. I was determined to be a stronger physician for Dr. Denny. It was what he expected and what I wanted. And it worked!

Returning to the Department in July 1971 was difficult for me. I had such a positive experience at UVA that I had mixed emotions regarding my decision. Would I be remembered as the medical student or would I be appreciated as the young doctor who had grown in many spheres? It was not long before I realized the answer. As so many second-year residents experience, it was hard to turn the workup of our patients over to interns. But we learned. On the wards that year, the resident was on call *every other night*! That was especially difficult since I just had been on call every third night. Somehow this seemed primitive. I remember Dr. Denny saying one could not take care of patients without being on call every other night.

The gamut of diseases seen ranged from Rocky Mountain spotted fever, which had to be treated with chloramphenicol, to the many types of meningitis, to the respiratory illnesses that have not changed a great deal to this day—except that we don't see tuberculosis as we did then. What a great experience it was to rotate through Gravely with Drs. Clyde, Fernald, and Glezen. The seventh-floor lab seemed like a second home with all the plating of cultures we had to do, as well as doing WBCs, Hcts and differentials, gram stains, etc. What would CLIA say about that today?

The hematology service was quite a learning experience and was the one rotation where hope was at its lowest. Who could not help but feel a sense of dread when Dr. Mac along with Chaplain Todd Wolters entered a room? But then again, who better to give you a rainbow to hang onto than those two? It was 1972; patients with acute lymphocytic leukemia stayed in the hospital a month, which was the minimum amount of time it took for them to go into remission. And who could forget our putting rubber bands around those little heads during infusions of vincristine in order to save them from losing their hair? Somehow it didn't quite make sense that if we kept the medication from getting to the hair follicles some leukemic cells could be hiding there as well.

The endocrine service was always a treat! What an accumulation of characters. It was well known that Dr. Van Wyk roamed the labs and halls late at night. It was about midnight and I was the resident covering the wards when I heard my name being called to the treatment room on the seventh floor. It was none other than Dr. Van Wyk, who asked me to give him an injection of Bicillin. Before I could inquire as to the indications he had dropped his drawers exposing his buttocks. Here I am a scrubbed-faced resident with a syringe in hand facing the backside of a distinguished professor in the Medical School. What did I do? You're damned right: I gave him the Bicillin, he pulled up his pants and was on his way. As for me, I continued my rounds wondering if it all really happened.

I recall riding up in the elevator from the ground floor to the seventh with Dr. Kirkman. Known for his dry wit, he is equally well known for being somewhat less than outgoing. Having just been at UVA where house staff were on a first-name basis with most of the attendings, it was obvious that things were different here. I was determined in the elevator to see how long it would take for Dr. Kirkman to speak. As he was exiting the elevator after what seemed like the longest elevator ride in history, he turned to me and said, "Bernstein, I know who you are. Neil Kirkman here." It was great, and to this day I have always enjoyed the specialness that is Neil Kirkman.

The cardiology division was comprised of the gentle, unassuming Dr. Harned, who introduced me to catheterizations; Dr. Herrington, who ran the congenital defects clinic; and Stuart Schall, who introduced a new way of doing things. Yet, with all I learned, I still can't interpret EKGs worth a darn.

The endocrine division taught me everything I always wanted to know about thyroid disease and short stature. Drs. Van Wyk and French made me know that the growth chart was second only to the Bible in importance. Dr. Underwood in his own inimical manner taught me that diabetes was *not* an endocrine disease.

Dr. Cathy Taylor along with Virginia Hebbert and I teamed up as the maltreatment syndrome team and we saw all children who may have been abused and/or neglected. We put together a traveling show when I was chief resident that toured the state telling, and I think educating, folks of the existence of this disease. It was an experience that I will never forget, and to this day I have copies of our talks.

I remember Cathy in another way. A teenage girl was admitted because of rather strange behavior, and we all thought it was psychologic in origin and called for a psych consult. Not long after, Cathy emerged from the girl's room and acknowledged in her gentle way that we were right. This young lady did indeed have some psychologic component to her illness and the consult was appropriate. But, she asked, what had we planned to do about her myasthenia gravis? We had been royally scooped! To this day I admire her clinical acumen.

New faculty arrived during my tenure—C. Richard Morris in nephrology and Ernie Kraybill in neonatology. C. Richard with his staccato delivery taught us all we ever needed to know about looking at urines. Dr. Kraybill opened our eyes to a whole new world of the newborn. Prior to his arrival, the resident covering the special care nursery took call from home. Can you imagine that today? There were no monitors and yet there were certain monsters called Engstrom ventilators and negative-pressure ventilators. It was reminiscent of 20,000 *Leagues Under the Sea!*

Conditions that we treated were the various infections, but we saw lots of hemophilia and its complicating joint problems. Cystic fibrosis, thyroid and endocrine problems were in the house a lot. The malignancies occupied our beds for long periods of time. We did not see the neonatal problems that we do today because the preemies just did not survive. Asthmatics were not a large portion of our patient population.

Ampicillin, kanamycin, and chloramphenicol were our big guns. But I remember pen-in-oil! Gentamicin was new, as was methicillin. Ventilators for older kids were few, though I do remember one child on the vent who had meningococcemia. I recall that child arresting and Dr. Harned assisting in the resuscitation efforts. He impressed upon me to never count on memorizing dosages of drugs but to always have at hand the information you needed in situations that called for them. To this day I keep my meds and dosages in my wallet.

The facilities were the seventh floor, without what is now the bed tower. It seemed adequate at the time—as did the outpatient clinics. The nurseries were always less than adequate and played a far less important part in the training program than now.

The nursing staff was excellent. I remember fondly Bonnie Beard and her floor nurses, Annette Ayer and Dot Merrow as supervisors, Ida Hunter, Corinne Mayo, and Margaret Adams in the clinic.

When I returned to Chapel Hill, Bill Hubbard returned from the Air Force as chief resident. We forged a friendship and planned our future together practicing in Raleigh. Wally Brown, whom I had met during my med school years, had given me the opportunity to start my first IV on a patient. He, Bill, and I were to begin our practice together after I finished my last year of residency. However, Dr. Denny had other plans for me—the chief residency. I had heard rumors that I would be asked. Surely they would not think that I would give up the opportunity to start a practice by agreeing to spend a year making out night calls and arranging conferences as well as a variety of other sets of rounds, etc.? But when the Chief calls, you answer! So from July 1, 1973, to June 30, 1974, I was Dr. Denny's chief resident. What a year it was!

I guess the thing that stands out most for me about that year was not my being his first single chief resident (goodness, what wife would head up the pediatric wives group?) but was getting to know Dr. Denny in a most special way. His chief resident was an integral part of the Department. He not only taught medical students but the house officers as well. He was the physician in charge of the care rendered to all the patients in the house. He held the residents responsible for the care and they knew that. Prior to morning rounds, I had the opportunity to meet one-on-one with the most stimulating teacher I have every known. To have had that time was exhilarating. We would discuss issues of patient care and resident education, morals and ethics, and life in general. Dr. Denny is a demanding teacher. I had to make sure that my residents would come prepared for these rounds—lab data in hand, X-rays ready for the view box, and reports complete, yet less than three to four minutes in length. On more than one occasion he would just look over at me and I knew that he knew that I got the message, and that I would later pull the resident aside and gently offer constructive criticisms.

Arranging the Department conference schedule was often a pain and many a week I would panic and plead with any and all attendings to help me out with offering a topic for discussion. There were some changes I made during my year, none notable but they helped me. Everyone bitched about the night call, so I offered each resident the opportunity to make it out for any month they chose. That quieted lots of folks. Because there were few married couples (docs married to docs), the schedule was not nearly as complicated as it is today. In order to communicate better with referring physicians, I carried the admitting beeper every day during my year. In so doing, I was able to know who referred whom and saw that residents got back with those docs on a more timely manner regarding their patients. It also enabled me to better know physicians across the state, which has benefited me through the years.

Arranging grand rounds was the biggest conference planning the chief resident was responsible for: making sure the chairs were in neat rows, the curtains were even, and the projector and slides were ready. Many a time, if there were any pause or slight delay, you could count on seeing the Chief swivel in his chair in order to see his chief resident.

Eating meeting at noon on Friday required the chief resident's going to the cafeteria and making sure that sandwiches and tea were available because many times they were not delivered to the conference room. I chose to do something different by contracting with Mammy's Pantry to serve our eating meetings. What a hit! Although it necessitated an increase from twenty-five to seventy-five cents, attendance soared to an all-time high. What with a fare that consisted of pizzas, pastas, soul food, and a choice of three desserts, who could resist? Alas, all good things end. Mammy's went under and eating meeting returned to foil-wrapped sandwiches from the cafeteria.

My association with the Department continued through the Denny years and into the Boat years. I am comforted by the experiences I have had in the Department, not only during my formative years, but in the years since. As far as my development as a pediatrician, there are many who have contributed. Dr. Mac most assuredly is my emotional father, whereas Dr. Denny remains my intellectual father. In all that I do I hope to remain true to what they have taught and instilled in me.

I would be remiss if I didn't mention another benefit of being in the Department during the Denny years. Many of his office staff are responsible for much of what I accomplished during my chief residency. Harriett Dickey and Jean Culbertson were there to help me out lots. But also there was Peggy Davidson, who later was to become (and still is) my wife. Many a day I would settle in front of her desk and pour out my heart about all sorts of things. She'd listen and I would feel better. It's a wonder she agreed to marry me!

Later years would find us calling upon those with whom we worked to help us when our two-year-old daughter was diagnosed with leukemia. The love, trust, and skill that was shown us and her has made everyone in the Department through the years even more special to us.

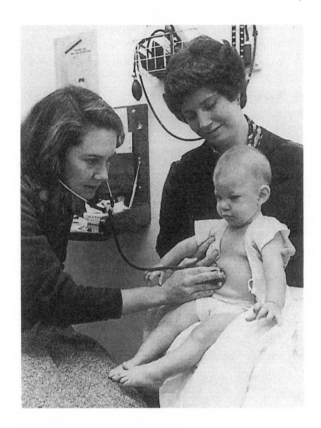

Muff Carr,
patient, and
mother

MARJORIE B. "MUFF" CARR (1976–1979)

A Look at the UNC House Staff: The Mid- to Late 1970s

In reflecting on life as part of the UNC house staff in the late 1970s, one of the first impressions that comes to mind is that of becoming a member of a large, diverse, and caring family—a family with many talents, medical and otherwise (there were several very musically talented faculty), varied personalities, and different perspectives on a variety of issues; but in essence it was a family with a common goal: that of supporting each other while providing the best and most up-to-date medical care for the patients for whom we were responsible. The attending staff seemed genuinely interested in the house staff, not only from the perspective of their hospital performance, but also as unique individuals with different talents, needs, and contributions that could be made both within and outside the Department.

It was apparent that the whole Department, from the secretaries to the nurses, from the PTs and recreation therapists to the nurses and doctors, all were operating as a team with a common cause—the care of the patient. There was good communication among the secretaries, the house staff, the nurses, and the therapists. There was seldom an air of one-upmanship among the house staff. No one ever said to a colleague, "That is your patient and your job—you do it." If someone could not get an IV in, another intern or resident was willing to try—many times, if necessary, until the job was accomplished.

If an intern had been up all night drawing ABGs in the nursery, there was an unwritten agreement that the other two interns would do that part of the work the next day—it was better for the house staff *and* the patient. If someone found *the* definitive article on a particular subject, it would get photocopied for several others—not just for the one who had discovered the article. If someone was having a terrible week, others noticed and inquired about ways that might help the person to improve the situation—whether it related to the care of the patients or to one's personal life. Occasionally, when admissions would multiply in logarithmic fashion, instead of following the typical rotation, the intern who was the least overwhelmed at that moment would take a patient out of rotation to allow the others to get caught up, or the clinic JAR would arrange for all the lab work, write the orders, and get the care going on the patient before the child ever arrived on the floor.

Holidays could easily have been difficult times to work, but generally were not. For those who were on call on a particular holiday, there was usually some form of in-house celebration, which would include the house staff, the nurses, the secretaries, and any pediatric physical or respiratory therapists who might have holiday responsibilities. It was planned in advance, with all of the on-call staff signing up for something to bring in order to avoid duplications; the most appropriate time, taking into account everyone's holiday schedule and patient responsibilities, was decided upon jointly. The schedule was flexible and allowed for unforeseen complications. Plates were saved for those who got tied up with emergencies.

On July 4, 1976, while the entire United States celebrated the two-hundredth anniversary of our independence with fireworks displays and parades from dawn to midnight, the workers on the seventh floor at NCMH held their own celebration in the Curnen conference room, timed so that a portion of the fireworks in Kenan could be enjoyed while sharing a covered dish supper with fellow workers. With the lights out in the conference room, we had the best seats in the house for the fireworks! It was a memorable experience.

On New Year's Eve one year, between 11:30 P.M. and 12:15 A.M. the on-call house staff (with spouses) and the nurses shared a few moments between patient care to bring in the New Year. In June of 1977, one of the female interns was on call for her second wedding anniversary; Bernie Branson, the JAR, and John Abramson, the other intern on the team, sent her flowers! After all, at that point in the training process she was spending more time with them than with her spouse!

Almost every Saturday night one could find house staff, spouses, and families sharing supper in the private dining room off the main dining area of the hospital cafeteria. Everyone knew everyone else, and it provided a brief and pleasurable respite from the world of sick children, with healthy children clamoring for attention while telling the on-call parent about all the events of the day. Those few moments helped to remind all of us that there were mostly healthy and happy children outside the hospital and that many of our patients would return to that world.

What could have been more special than the end-of-the-year picnic at Storybook Farm—with all the faculty and spouses and house staff and families gathered together to play and celebrate? There was good food, volleyball, and the rigged softball game with fearless Myron Johnson pitching and Dr. Denny umpiring. Dr. Denny was somehow able to defy the laws of physics and be several places simultaneously, making authoritative calls with his X-ray vision. The winner had self-proclaimed bragging rights for a year. The faculty almost always won. There were, of course, claims that the faculty were truly that good and the house staff that bad. Others argued vehemently that the chairman of the Department had selective vision. . . .Whatever, the day was great fun, and the game was *the* topic of conversation for weeks before, as the house staff plotted their collective strategy for winning that year, and for weeks after, as many recalled some special moment from the time shared together.

Life as a member of the peds house staff had a decided and comforting routine. On the floor on Mondays through Fridays the day began with 8:00 A.M. work rounds with the ward interns, JARs, and med students. New patients were presented briefly, overnight lab work reviewed, differential diagnoses expanded, and therapeutic strategies discussed. At 9:00 A.M., the ward JARs were expected at Dr. Denny's office to discuss the patients admitted the preceding night. It was always a helpful conference, as Dr. Denny usually had a clear grasp of the clinical problems and could offer helpful suggestions about the workup and the appropriate therapeutic modalities for most of the patients. While the JARs were conferring, the interns and med students were tracking lab results, ordering new tests, and doing quick checks on the patients before attending rounds, which began at 10:00 A.M. The attending staff took turns being responsible for a ward team, so that over the course of two years on the floor the house staff saw a wide range of in-house patients. This was especially true as patients with a specific problem would often be admitted to the team whose attending, whenever feasible, was an expert in that field. For example, when Art Aylesworth attended, one had a much higher possibility of being exposed to a wide range of exotic metabolic problems or a child with dwarfism. There was always a plethora of consultants to educate and guide the ward team when the patient's disease did not coincide with the attending's area of expertise. The consultants frequently taught the house staff new diagnostic procedures and skills, such as peritoneal dialysis, bone marrow aspirates, and other technical skills necessary to care for the patient. Between 10:00 A.M. and 12:00 noon patients were discussed and examined, diagnostic procedures planned, and treatment modalities mapped out. If there were doubts about a course of action, the appropriate consultants were decided upon. During the late '70s, the children older than five years were admitted to 7E, while all patients needing isolation were admitted to 7W. All the little ones under five years were on 7BT side B (west side) and there was a six-bed ICU which was hidden in the middle of the bed tower. A ward team would have patients in all of these locations at once, which could make rounding a challenge. Actually, rounding on 7BT could be a challenge any-time because during and after breakfast the halls could be filled with small people sitting in high chairs or walkers, or zooming over your feet in riding toys. Some were expert pickpockets and you could lose a reflex hammer in a matter of seconds! An occasional toddler might offer a favorite doctor or nurse a bite of breakfast or morning snack, but more often the outgoing tod-dlers would want to be held or pushed in a wagon or to actually "help" you with rounds! Despite the fact the toddlers were sick, 7BT was, for the most part, a happy and cheerful place to be.

Between 12:00 and 1:00 P.M. one generally had lunch, reviewed the day, and decided how best to accomplish all of the necessary jobs in the remain-ing portion of the day. It was also a good time to find articles in the library (if you were a JAR or SAR—as an intern one tended to rely on one's JAR) and photocopy them. There were also conferences to attend—X-ray confer-ence, grand rounds, eating meeting. The afternoons were spent doing careful assessments of the patients, tracking down new lab work, examining X-rays, possibly seeing a patient or two in the clinic, and if you were the admitting intern, beginning the workup of new patients.

Between 4:00 and 4:30 P.M. all of the house staff on the floor, plus house staff that were going to be on call for the night, met to discuss the patients on the floor and to sign out any potential problems. Signout rounds could get pretty rowdy depending on how tired the outgoing group was and how punchy the on-call group seemed to be. Things on occasion were noted to deteriorate rather rapidly. After signout, most of the time there were still sev-eral things that the interns needed to do before actually leaving the hospital. The amount of time spent depended on how sick the patients were, how orga-nized one was, and whether it was early or late in the year. Experience did help to shorten the days.

Somewhere between 5:00 and 6:00 P.M. the whole atmosphere of the day changed. The intensity of the day diminished, the patients became quieter, and the traffic on the floor decreased. The on-call interns were usually busy work-ing up the new patients and the JAR was either helping the ward interns or backing up the nursery intern. The SAR did whichever the JAR did not. On the rare night that things were truly quiet, one might find an intern or a JAR catching a show on the TV in the on-call room (especially during basketball season) or reading an article or discussing some aspect of medical care. The discussions at times were noted to be lively. The on-call room itself provided a graphic example of chaos and gave new meaning to a mother's claim that "My child would never do that! He/she was brought up to do better than this!" It was covered with clothes, books, bookbags, articles, partially read papers, and half-eaten lunches and snacks. Many days not even housekeep-ing would tackle it!

The on-call quarters were in fact a collection of three rooms—a "living" area, with three to four pieces of furniture (chairs, tables, and TV), most of which were totally unrecognizable because of the array of things that adorned them; a bathroom, which could have competed with the lab for having the most microbes growing in it; and the "sleep" room, which had two clearly delineated sides to it: the "residents'" side, with two single beds with a desk in between that held a phone, and the "interns'" side, which had a single bed and a set of bunk beds, with a chair that held a phone evenly spaced between the two beds. The first intern to get to bed at night had the distinct privilege of sleeping in the single bed with easy access to the phone, but not necessarily a good night's rest, depending on who the third intern was and what kind of night he/she was going to have. The last intern to retire was left with the top bunk—making it a virtual impossibility to get to the phone without getting out of bed every time the beeper went off, not to mention the noise one made when getting in and out of the bunk every time one needed to talk on the phone, which was of course several times a night.

One night Jay Poliner, a family practice intern and a quiet, reserved type of person, lost his beeper in the process of extricating himself from the top bunk. The beeper continued to be quite chatty and Jay, not wishing to turn on the light and wake the entire room, thoughtfully continued to crawl around on the floor looking for the talking beeper. When one of the other interns slowly awakened to a shadow crawling on the floor and someone talking (it was the beeper), she screamed. The other intern had awakened moments earlier, had perceived what was happening, and had been smothering giggles with her pillow in order to not awaken the residents. The longer Jay searched, the funnier it got. The drama must have gone on well over five minutes, and by that point everyone was awake. Those that were less sleep-deprived did not perceive the incident to be as amusing as did others more closely involved in the drama. This should be a clear indication that at 3:00 or 4:00 A.M. interns could be easily entertained!

On another night, so the story goes, the floor had been relatively quiet and two interns and a JAR (Denny Mayock) were in the on-call room resting as a tired and unsuspecting Dale Newton, the SAR of the night, was approaching from the nursery. An intern's beeper went off announcing a code and three bodies leaped from their chairs and flew out the door, flattening Dale in the process—not once, but three separate times. Dr. Newton was left to take care of his own wounds and to find the site of the code on his own.

The nursery was an entirely different world from the wards. Located at that time on the hall between 4W and MacNider, it was three rooms filled to the brim with sick infants, equipment, and competent nurses. It seemed totally isolated from the rest of the hospital—except for the blood gas lab! It was a community unto itself, a community in which, at least in the first few days to weeks of one's initial experience in the nursery, the nurses knew more than the interns did about the operations and care of the patients and could do the intern's job much more efficiently! The nursery was abuzz with the cacophony of monitors and ventilators, increasing the intensity of the nursery expe-

rience. Blood gases were drawn by the interns at that time and then run by
them to the ABG lab on the second floor, just inside the OR. One frequently
waited for the results before returning to the nursery, especially at night. One
would then make the necessary changes and begin the process again, with that
patient or with another one. Sometimes it seemed to be a continuous process.
Putting in an umbilical arterial line could be challenging under the best of circumstances. On one particularly long night a new intern was trying to put one
in for the first time. Craig LaForce was patiently trying to help. It was not
going well and it had been well over an hour in the attempting. Finally the
artery quit going into spasm, and the line went in. However, while suturing
the line in place, a suture was put *through* the line, and D10W began to
leak—everywhere. It must have been 3 or 4 in the morning. Any sane person
would have killed the intern and put in the line himself. Craig calmly stated,
"We will have to replace this line." From the intern's perspective, it probably
would have been easier to have been murdered.

Sleep was a precious commodity, not frequently acquired while one
rotated through the nursery. For some it was a powerful lesson in survival
techniques, while others happily thrived. There was a never-ending flow of
patients, ranging from the 500g "twenty-seven- to twenty-eight-weeker" to
the eight- to nine-pound "post-termer" with meconium aspiration or PFC,
from sepsis and meningitis to inborn errors of metabolism. Most of the time
the attendings were the neonatologists, with outside consultation from the
necessary disciplines for the basic problem if it was something other than prematurity and its accompanying complications. Occasionally others would
attend. One who did so with some degree of regularity was Dr. Harned. For
those of us who experienced him in the nursery, one of his best-remembered
phrases applied to the preemie growers: "He/she needs midget care."

As a JAR and SAR, one was expected to take transport call, which meant
that one was responsible for traveling by ambulance or helicopter, depending
on the distance, to the outlying hospital. A skilled nurse and respiratory therapist accompanied the house staff member and helped to stabilize the sick
infant (occasionally an older child) before returning to NCMH for further
care. If the distance was seventy-five miles or less, the transport was by land;
if it was greater than that, one flew by army helicopter, which came from Fort
Bragg. The transports had the potential to be anxiety-producing, depending
on the infant's problem, the distance, and one's level of training.

When flying, there would be two to three crew members from Fort
Bragg—a pilot, a copilot, and occasionally another crew member. They were
always congenial, and would sometimes demonstrate their piloting skills
when flying *to*, but never *from*, a transport. It was reported that one pilot, en
route to pick up a newborn with a diaphragmatic hernia, was notified that the
infant had died. Instead of quietly announcing this news to the transport
team, he simply turned the helicopter around—by turning it on its side so that
the entire transport team was looking at the ground!

It was not uncommon to be told by the pilots that they navigated by going from "golden arches to golden arches" or by following the railroad tracks! One pilot even flew briefly over the Atlantic before landing in Wilmington so that the transport team could see the full moon over the ocean.

The pilots were surprisingly knowledgeable about medical care—they certainly knew more about emergency care medicine than most of us did about piloting. Since all occupants of the helicopter were required to wear helmets for protection and several of the helmets had microphones, one could converse with some of the team members without screaming over the roar of the chopper. One night while returning from a transport to Wilmington, one of the house staff expressed concern to the pilot that the infant had had a change in status. This was done by stating that the resident hoped the baby did not "crash" before arrival at NCMH. The copilot, who was clearly not a seasoned veteran of the transport process, asked the pilot if the transport team thought that the helicopter was going to crash—to which the pilot calmly replied that the concern was that the infant not die before the transport was completed. The infant and the copilot both survived that transport.

The arrival of the helicopter in front of the hospital sent every child on 7BT who was not confined to a bed to the window to watch the helicopter land and take off. The helicopter created great excitement. Occasionally a patient would recognize his/her physician going or coming from a transport. If this happened, one could expect no less than nine million questions once one returned to 7BT to see the patients. On one particularly hectic day, a female SAR had two transports back to back. When Holcombe Grier, the admitting resident, came out to receive the incoming infant and inform the SAR that there would be another transport almost immediately, Holcombe hugged her in an attempt to soften the news. Sharp little eyes on the seventh floor immediately inquired if the hugger was the "huggee's" husband. When told that he was probably not, the patient stated emphatically, "Well, I'm telling!" One never knew when one's actions were being carefully scrutinized.

One Saturday morning after Denny rounds, a JAR was sent to Kinston to pick up a child who was suspected of having Reye syndrome. Kinston happened to be the home of the pilot, and somehow he radioed ahead to his family, who responded by having a picnic on the hospital lawn waiting for him upon his arrival. While he was dining, the critically ill child was being stabilized. Just before the child was to be transported to the helicopter, a physician other than the referring physician asked the resident to see another child who was also unresponsive and who was also suspected of having Reye syndrome. Before transfer of both children, the second child began to have a seizure. The resident calmly called for some phenobarbital to stop the seizure. The older LMD questioned the use of the drug, expressing concern that the child might stop breathing. The resident expressed supreme confidence in the drug, pushed the medication, and watched the child become apneic. The team calmly intubated the child and transported both children to the peds ICU, thereby assuring that there could be no further transports that day because both the PICU and NICU were filled to capacity.

An integral part of the house staff training was the months in the clinic. Each day began with an 8:00 A.M. conference in the London Library where the house staff, medical students, and attending staff met with Grover and Myra from the microbiology lab to review the cultures and identify the organisms growing on the plates. No one left that rotation without being able to identify the common organisms cultured from skin, throat, and urine. Cases were presented and discussed and topics reviewed. The conference provided a wealth of good practical knowledge about the day-to-day illnesses and procedures in pediatrics.

Around 9:00 A.M., the house staff dispersed to their assigned clinics— some to peds screening with Rita Brantley and Linda Boucher who kept things in order, some to the back in peds primary care with Mike Sharp and Harvey Hamrick, and some down the hall to assist in a specialty clinic, particularly if that clinic was low on medical staff. Each of the clinic nurses helped in either peds screening or primary care, as well as each having his/her own specialty clinic in which he/she assisted.

The nurses were experienced and patient and frequently had to work awfully hard to keep the house staff in line. The atmosphere was generally cheerful and warm. Linda and Rita ran an efficient clinic, while keeping their sense of humor. It was a fun place to work most of the time (except maybe during a flu epidemic when everyone was exhausted). Special occasions did not go unnoticed, and a luncheon celebration was not complete without one of Rita's Mississippi mud cakes, as anyone who rotated through the clinic would readily testify. It was here that many of the house staff most easily felt a part of the pediatric family.

Patients were seen in the screening clinic by the day crew from about 9:00 A.M. to 4:00 or 5:00 P.M., with the night team coming on at around 4:00 or 5:00 P.M. to see the night patients and emergencies. Admissions as well as walk-ins were handled through the clinic. Many nights Mike Carter, an English grad student, would work at the reception desk checking in patients, while Mike Bousman functioned as the nurse. If the on-call resident happened to be a female instead of a male on the nights that both of the Mikes worked, many of the patients would have difficulty with the break in the gender stereotype, and would tell the female physician that they had already given their history to the doctor (the receptionist) *and* had been seen by the doctor (the nurse that took vital signs)! At times it could be challenging to help the patients understand that men could be receptionists and nurses and that females could be doctors.

The average week was dotted with general conferences as well as specialty conferences, some of which were done with the Department of Medicine. All were designed to provide a wealth of information to the house staff. The major difficulty was fitting them into one's schedule.

There were three conferences that most of the house staff tried to attend with some degree of regularity. X-ray conference was a Tuesday midday event in which cases were presented briefly and the X-rays reviewed and discussed, with differential diagnoses and further workup elaborated. It could be a veritable gold mine for the intern. Infectious diseases were a prominent part of the conference, as well as classic radiographic depictions of certain disease processes. Dr. Denny was a dynamic part of that educational process.

Grand rounds were the most formal of the three big conferences and were held at noon on Thursday. The topics tended to be more academic, with an occasional "visiting fireman" discussing a favorite subject. There were, at times, some interesting and lively disagreements among the attending staff relating to a topic that had been presented. As a house staff member it was always fun to watch attendings defend their perspective and challenge the information presented based on their own area of expertise. Eating meeting was on Fridays and was more informal. As the name implies, food was allowed and the atmosphere was more relaxed. The subject matter tended to be more practical, leading at times to some lively conversations between the house staff and the attendings.

On Saturday mornings, the house staff spent one and a half to two hours trying to stump Dr. Denny. Rarely were they successful. Generally, two or three of the more interesting admissions or unusual cases from the preceding week were presented by the interns and discussed by Dr. Denny. The cases were generally a classic presentation of a disease process or an excellent example of the complications associated with a disease. On the rare times that a true unknown could be presented (i.e., a patient that was admitted very late on a Friday night—the later the better), Dr. Denny generally was able to out-think the house staff, provide a good differential diagnosis, and discuss the disease at length. At this conference, if it was possible, the patient and the family were examined in the flesh. The history was obtained from the patient, the child was examined, rashes were scrutinized, and lab work delineated (sometimes with the key piece withheld until asked for). It was always a tremendous learning experience for the house staff and a good chance to match wits with Dr. Denny.

One Saturday, an infant with an infectious process was presented. After extensive discussion of the disease process, the complications, the treatment course, and the probable outcome, some resident inquired about the rash the baby had, which was not related to the disease process. Undaunted, Dr. Denny replied, "It's baby rash!"

Wake rotation was a four-week experience in Raleigh with every-third-night call for all house staff, regardless of rank. At night there were two interns (one on the floor and one in the nursery) and a resident who floated between the two interns and also responded to problems in the ER and troubleshot admissions from the clinic. It was a busy time and a gold mine of practical experience. For the most part, the patients tended to be less sick, and the diseases tended to be more common. Many of us learned about diabetic ketoacidosis from one fifteen-year-old female who had about seventy admissions to Wake for DKA. Asthma and meningitis were also common admission diagnoses and allowed us to enhance our clinical skills with regard to those diseases. We learned ways other than the UNC way to deal with disease entities as we took care of other physicians' patients and were exposed to the family practice residents from Duke who also rotated through Wake. It was a good place for the exchange of ideas, and it was a time to become a little more self-reliant as there was not always an attending physician immediately available. It was also a time to learn to set priorities and to learn organizational skills, as one could not be in more than a place at a time. It was an integral and vital part of the house staff clinical education.

In the late '70s, Mike Durfee headed up the AHEC program at Wake. A sensitive and caring individual, Dr. Durfee was generally one who looked at each individual and the situation involved rather than always following the letter of the law in any particular situation. He felt comfortable at times with the bending of rules if this was beneficial for the care of the patient or for the education of the house staff. In August of 1977, the father of an adolescent who had been diagnosed at Wake in February of that year with a malignancy called to inquire if the house staff physician who had made the original diagnosis was at Wake. The resident was. The father had discussed the child's decline with Dr. McMillan and had requested that she not be required to return to NCMH to receive further chemotherapy or to die, but be allowed to die either at Wake or possibly at home. He was calling at that time to request that the resident come to see the child in her home in a small neighboring town. It was discussed with Dr. Durfee, who felt that it was not only a legitimate request from the family, but also a good learning experience. On the day the call came, Jay Poliner had actually driven his car instead of the van to Wake and so he took the resident to Zebulon after the workday was over for the first visit, sitting in the car while the patient was assessed. Two to three days later the father called again, stating that he felt the child was dying. He requested immediate support. Dr. Durfee was again consulted. He helped to arrange different in-house coverage so that the resident could leave the hospital and be at the bedside until the child died. He also provided keys to a state car so that there was transportation to and from Zebulon. It was a long, hot August day in an unairconditioned home. It was a different experience being alone and away from the hospital with all its support systems, such as chaplains and social workers, nurses and fellow house staff. However, it turned out to be an incredible learning experience, just as Dr. Durfee had expected it to be—not only for the resident that went, but also for the house staff that helped process the experience afterwards. Instead of complaining about all the extra work that had to be done over the course of one day with one MD gone, everyone was concerned about what happened, what it felt like, and what one did in that situation. Again, the house staff were working together for the good of all of the patients.

For most of the house staff who worked at NCMH in the late '70s, NCMH was a second home and our fellow residents, the nursing staff, the therapists, and the secretaries were all extended family. It was a happy and memorable experience—a time characterized by hard work, long hours, and intense learning experiences. Most of all it was a time of immense personal growth enveloped in an atmosphere of genuine care and concern, a time that prepared each of us for our chosen fields of endeavor—whether that be academics or general practice, subspecialty or administration.

ALAN D. STILES (1978–1982)

Denny Years: Resident Perspective

My contact with the residency program of the Department of Pediatrics at UNC began while I was a third-year medical student. I witnessed the close, supportive atmosphere of the pediatric resident group and saw the actions of a chairman who was closely and actively involved with the residents. These impressions returned as I decided on a medical field for further training.

As a pediatric intern, my first rotation was in the clinic. Each day started with the morning conference where all the patients seen in the screening clinic the day and night before were reviewed and Dr. Hamrick selected several patients for further discussion. Clinical pearls were dispensed and culture plates were read. After careful sniffing and looking, a few diagnoses were rendered. This conference was one of the most important places where the UNC "party line" was transferred to the house staff. For example, how to manage "sore" throats and the required steps to diagnose and treat "strep throat," when to admit a febrile infant and what workup should be performed, etc. The clinic was a reasonably slow-paced opportunity to see common illnesses and to spend a fair amount of time one-on-one with an attending. For the intern, this was the place where you learned to "look at ears."

Probably the most important lesson that residents learned in this setting was to live with the uncertainty of decisions as you sent out some patients and admitted others. Night call for the intern was on the ward, but for the resident, call was in the clinic. This brings back memories of the "private" sleep-room in the peds clinic "lounge," the "couch from hell," and the 3 A.M. buffing of the carpet in the hall by the diligent housekeeping staff. The other concept that all residents appreciated by the end of a clinic month was that some of the American public, those people who work second shift, live in a different world. These families would arrive for most routine or acute health care between 1 and 3 A.M., often with a child who had some real or perceived problem earlier in the evening—never witnessed because the parent(s) were at work. But because the family was worried and happened to be out, they decided to have it "checked." Interpersonal skills were occasionally taxed by these situations.

The wards were challenging because each team had ward patients and pediatric intensive care patients. The attending group was a combination of subspecialists and general pediatricians who were individually responsible for all the patients on the team. There were no attendings of record or subspecialty services at that time. This setup made rounds and patient care interesting, particularly with PICU patients or patients such as those receiving chemotherapy by protocol. Overall, this actually helped the team function as a unit and contributed to caring for the "whole" patient. There existed a true esprit de corps among the resident group working on the wards. Work rounds by the resident (always a junior resident), interns, and medical students occurred in the morning with walk rounds to visit each patient, bedside teaching for the students, and establishment of a plan for the day. Attending rounds were held in the late morning and the new admissions and other patients reviewed. Students presented their workups and generally some teaching conference by the attending or resident was done, targeting the students or the interns. The resident was responsible for communicating plans and problems to the attending and facilitating communication with the subspecialty services about consults or patient care issues. During the day, the teams (then Green, Blue, or Red) rotated admissions in order of arrival. The resident was responsible for seeing that the teams received a fair distribution of patients. There were the inevitable "discussions" about whether a re-admit "chemo kid" would count or not, or whether one team would receive all the PICU admissions. The diseases were frequently complex and many patients seemed to stay for extended times as diagnostic workups were carried out. Many of the patients cycled in and out of the hospital and were known to all the house staff. On the wards, pediatric house staff learned to love the sight of blood flowing back into the tubing of a "butterfly" or dripping from an IV catheter. Night call on the wards was also unique. It usually seemed quiet with the patients sleeping, but we knew that someone was out there sabotaging IVs (the bane of every house staff member's existence). It was known with certainty that no IV could last on 7W (the isolation ward) overnight and that at least one of the "impossible sticks" would lose an IV after midnight. I'm sure that another reason the house staff were so close was the sleep room accommodations. Where else could you find four bunk beds in a space too small for two beds, coed, and a single bathroom?

The NICU was intimidating for a lot of the house staff with its emergencies, procedures, sleep deprivation, and the open door from the delivery room. To add to the situation at that time, the attendings were a varied group: three neonatologists, two cardiologists, a geneticist, and even Dr. Denny once, making this a rotation of variety in teaching and "style." There was a perception that the success of an intern in the NICU was measured by success with intubations, and this led to a fair amount of anxiety for the house officers. Everyone felt a need to be able to intubate before becoming a junior resident at Wake because "at Wake you are it." For many of the house staff this was also the rotation where they lost their first patient and came face to face with "medical ethics."

The rotations on subspecialty services were almost always generally low key and fun. There were many interesting and complicated patients to see and notes to write. Who could ever forget the "easy to follow" and logical explanation of renal function and replacement therapy outlined by Dr. Morris?

Each of the services allowed the residents some latitude in the way the rotation was set up with teaching, often one-on-one, in areas that the resident chose. For example, I spent a fair amount of time with Dr. McMillan learning about neonatal coagulation problems. The other plus was that residents took vacation during subspecialty rotations.

Through part of my junior resident year, the transport team continued to have residents accompany a nurse and respiratory therapist. We flew on helicopters from Fort Bragg or drove in Orange County Rescue Squad ambulances to pick up patients. There were many stories of the "cowboy" pilots and medics and the zeal with which they approached a transport. Two of my transport experiences were particularly memorable. On one, we were picking up a set of premature twins, both intubated, being bagged and cared for in one isolette. As we approached the helicopter in the rain, one of the medics came out to help and accidentally released the leg lock on the cart, dropping the isolette (and me) to the ground and extubating both infants. The other experience was picking up a PICU patient at a small hospital near the coast. As we came in to land at the local high school football field, we found that the stands were full of children who had been bused over from the elementary school to watch the helicopter.

Wake Hospital was the only outside site where residents of my group rotated. The setup was similar to that still used, with rotations in the clinic, ward, and NICU. The physical facility was different (for example, the sleep rooms were in trailers on the north side of the hospital). We generally found Wake to be fun and challenging. Whether true or not, as junior and senior residents we frequently felt we were the "high-tech/latest therapy" consultants for sick patients on the ward, particularly in the two-bed "PICU" that operated sporadically in the room next to the nurses' desk. I suspect that this rotation was responsible for "maturing" many residents, especially on the nights when the resident covered the ER, plus either the ward or NICU, and cross-covered an intern on the other service. I certainly felt more "mature" after three continuous days and nights during the blizzard of 1980. Everyone had some experience with a bizarre patient or awful situation while on night call at Wake, but the hospital was a friendly place to work and the attendings were anxious to teach. Another high point of the rotation was the van ride to and from Wake. We had a chance to talk with each other while someone else did the driving, not to mention the fact that the van ran on a schedule so there was a near guarantee that you would arrive home at a known time!

Conferences haven't changed a lot, but grand rounds were held in Curnen conference room and the chief resident struggled with the slide projector. The residents were not responsible for as much of their self-teaching as occurs now with Journal Club and Friday conference. The one conference that was quite different was the Wednesday X-ray conference. It was typically animated by Dr. Denny and the pediatric radiologist in one-upmanship. Resident rounds (Denny rounds) were held by Dr. Denny in the chairman's office and all the residents on ward service and subspecialty services were "encouraged" to attend. If you missed a few, there was a gentle reminder from the chairman that you had not been there. The patient discussions often led to insight into problems, or occasionally led the group far astray from the real problem, but were always interesting and were another opportunity for contact with Dr. Denny in a small group. Saturday morning resident conference was held by Dr. Denny and all house staff were expected to be there. It consisted of two or three cases with discussions and the serious UNC indoctrination instilled in each of us about ASO titers, rheumatic fever, H. flu disease, osteomyelitis, influenza, respiratory syncytial virus infection, pneumococcal pneumonia, and so on. The cases were picked by the chief resident, and the intern caring for the patient presented to Dr. Denny. Though the format was that the case be an unknown, only unknowns in certain areas were fair game. This was the chairman with *his* residents. This single situation probably gave each of us that feeling of personal belonging that was so important to the UNC program.

1960–61

Row 1: Loren MacKinney, Jud Van Wyk, Arthur London, Floyd Denny, Ann Peters, Ruth Dillard, Carlos Serrano

Row 2: Jerry Fernald, Gus Conley, Martha Sharpless, Abe Mizrahi, Harrie Chamberlin, Paul Glezen

Row 3: George Summer, Frank Shaw, Ann Askew, Roland Schmidt, Herb Harned, Joe Swanton, Charlie Waters

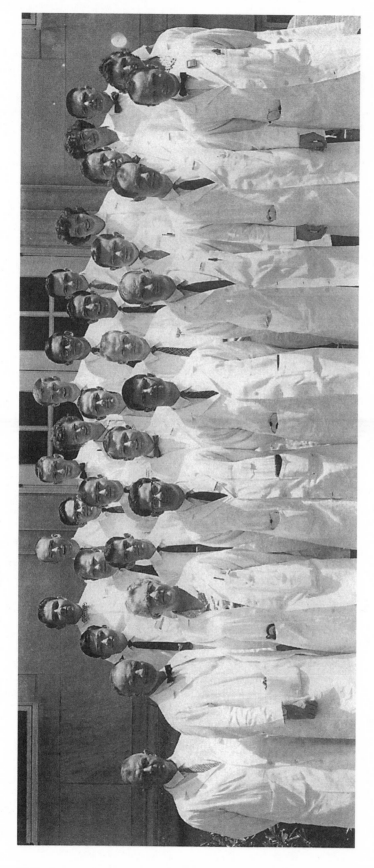

1961–62

Row 1: Sidney Chipman, Loren MacKinney, Annie Scott, Herb Harned, Floyd Denny, George Summer, Harrie Chamberlin, Jud Van Wyk

Row 2: Carlos Serrano, Paul Glezen, Gus Conley, Wally Clyde, Charlie Sheaffer, Mary Arnold

Row 3: Brian Luke, Dave Bruton, John Marchese, Steve Friedland, Ghody Rowshan, Bob Herrington

Row 4: Mike Bokat, Don Freeman, Bee Gatling, Roland Schmidt, Jo Dalldorf, Anne Askew

Row 5: Hubert Matthews, Bill Clarke, John Stephenson, Frank French

1962–63

Row 1: Mary Arnold, Jud Van Wyk, Floyd Denny, Herb Harned, Harrie Chamberlin, Sidney Chipman

Row 2: Cam McMillan, Gus Conley, John Arnold, Jo Dalldorf, Loren MacKinney, Bob Sanders, Wally Clyde

Row 3: Roland Schmidt, Fred Meyerhoefer, Adnan Dajani, George Branch, Dan Torphy, Mary Louise Smith

Row 4: Bob Herrington, Margaret Wyatt, Bee Gatling, Jasper Daube

Rows 5&6: Ed Shuttleworth, Forrest Weight, John Stephenson, Bill Clarke, John Fletcher, J. C. Pickens, Willie Peacock, Bob Abney, Leland Wight, Carl Phipps

1963–64

Row 1: Bill Clarke, George Summer, Jud Van Wyk, Herb Harned, Floyd Denny, Annie Scott, Mary Arnold, Sidney Chipman, Harrie Chamberlin

Row 2: Loren MacKinney, Margaret Wyatt, Roland Schmidt, Charlie Sheaffer, Frank French, Bob Castle, K. S. Kim, Wally Clyde

Row 3: Dick Honsinger, Conrad Andringa, Lou Underwood, Gabor Antony, Bob Shaw, John Arnold, Cam McMillan

Row 4: Bob Wilson, Fred Meyerhoefer, J. C. Pickens, Mike Durfee, Bill Cook, Dave Williams, George Branch

Row 5: Branch Fields, Bob Abney, Leland Wight, Larry Cutchin, Lloyd Tarlin, John Stephenson, Charlie Rathke

1964–65

Row 1: J. C. Pickens, Cam McMillan, Bob Castle, Loren MacKinney, Floyd Denny, Arthur London, Harrie Chamberlin

Row 2: Mike Durfee, Margaret Wyatt, Frank French, Charlie Hunsinger, Charlie Sheaffer, Wally Clyde

Row 3: John Raye, John Moore, Jane Kotchen, Bill Cook, Dave Williams

Row 4: Bob Wilson, Nick Beard, Ben Robbins, Bryan Simons, Leland Wight, Frank Loda, Dave Rosin, John Fisher, Bob Slotkin

1965–66

Row 1: Charlie Sheaffer, Jud Van Wyk, Mike Durfee, Floyd Denny, Herb Harned, Jim Etheridge, Cam McMillan, Paul Glezen

Row 2: Naomi Morris, Ray Antley, Charlie Hunsinger, Rich Doughten, Vasiliki Moscos, Thal Elliott, Neil Kirkman, Harrie Chamberlin

Row 3: Sidney Chipman, Nick Beard, Jo Dalldorf, Gene Lariviere, Loren MacKinney, Wally Clyde, Bob Castle

Row 4: Dave Williams, John Raye, Jerry Smith, Rich Doan, Jim Burke, Frank French, Dick O'Brien

Row 5: Bob Wilson, Earl Siegel, John Moore, Peter Dorsett, Bob Slotkin, Jerry Fernald, Frank Loda, Leo Van den Brande, Ralph Gibson

1966–67

Row 1: Neil Kirkman, Jud Van Wyk, Floyd Denny, Bob Abney, Paul Glezen, Jim Etheridge

Row 2: Earl Siegel, Dick Finch, Pat Jasper, Charlie Hunsinger, Herb Harned, Naomi Morris, Wally Clyde

Row 3: Frank French, Harry Smith, John Raye, Thal Elliott, Bev Raney, Leo Van den Brande, Mort Cohen, Sidney Chipman

Rows 4&5: Cam McMillan, Charlie Sheaffer, John Moore, Bob Herrington, Dick Lipman, Jim Burke, Bill Kanto, Tom Digby, Bill Hubbard, Dick O'Brien, Bob Kindley, Jerry Fernald

1967–68

Row 1: Cam McMillan, Mary Sugioka, Mort Cohen, Peter Krones, John Raye, Floyd
Denny, Jud Van Wyk, Wally Clyde

Row 2: Bill Kagey, Harry Smith, Larry Rankin, Paul Glezen, Herb Harned, Naomi
Morris, Earl Siegel, Charlie Sheaffer

Row 3: John Kiesel, Tom Digby, Thal Elliott, Pat Jasper, Lou Underwood, J. A.
Macfie, Sidney Chipman, Jerry Fernald

Row 4: Martin Woodall, Alva Strickland, Bev Raney, Meade Christian, Frank Loda,
Leo Van den Brande, Neil Kirkman

Row 5: Jim Burke, Jonathan Wise, Bob Kindley, Jack Benjamin, Bob Herrington,
Dick Lipman, Bob Abney, Frank French

1968–69

Row 1: Wally Clyde, Paul Glezen, Jim Etheridge, Bill Sayers, Floyd Denny, Neil Kirkman, Peter Dawson, Harrie Chamberlin

Row 2: Peter Zawadsky, Orene Vaughan, George Bensch, John Batjer, Tom Mettee, Chuck Post, George Hemingway, Ken Graupner, Harry Smith, Herb Harned, Earl Siegel

Row 3: Bob Herrington, Harvey Hamrick, Roberta Williams, Tom Saari, Phil Littleton, Jerry Fernald, Lou Underwood, Virginia Hebbert, Naomi Morris, Susan Davis, Elizabeth Woodell

Rows 4&5: Cam McMillan, Frank Loda, Meade Christian, Dick Lipman, Tom Bisett, Bill Hubbard, Tom Digby, Jack Benjamin, Frank French, Nick Beard, Al Collier, Sidney Chipman

1969–70

Row 1: Allen Cato, Bob Pantell, Najwa Khuri, George Hemingway, Floyd Denny, Arthur London, Jud Van Wyk, Harrie Chamberlin

Row 2: Abe Patterson, Robin Beck, Tom Saari, Neil Kirkman, Wally Clyde, Bob Herrington, Charlie Hunsinger, Herb Harned, Lore Knetsch

Row 3: Frank Loda, Earl Siegel, Marty Ulshen, Bob Richman, Lou Underwood, Frank French, Meade Christian, John Knelson, Paul Glezen

Row 4: Bob Shaw, Harvey Hamrick, George Bensch, Hugh Bryan, Martin Ritzen, Joe Russell, Roger Johnsonbaugh, Wally Brown

1970–71

Row 1: Myron Johnson, Paul Glezen, Susan Wolschina, Harvey Hamrick, Jud Van Wyk, Kathy Salter, Bob Herrington, Harrie Chamberlin

Row 2: Ross Vaughan, Wally Clyde, Jerry Fernald, Neil Kirkman, Bob Pantell, Robin Beck, Abe Patterson, Bob Richman, Gene Sherman

Row 3: Herb Harned, Al Collier, Bev Tucker, Peter Dawson, Jim Hampsey, Phil Moyer, Bernie Guyer

Row 4: Ellis Fisher, Willis Archer, Frank Loda, George Bensch, Hugh Bryan, Earl Bryant, Rick Suberman, Irwin Cohen

1971–72

Row 1: Kathy Salter, Sherry Bauman, Bill Hubbard, Floyd Denny, Cam McMillan, Harrie Chamberlin, Jud Van Wyk

Row 2: Bob Herrington, Jerry Fernald, Gene Borkan, George Bonham, Bob Pantell, Herb Harned

Row 3: Ellis Fisher, Paul Glezen, Jerry Bernstein, Benton Levie, Al Collier, Lou Underwood, Stewart Schall

Row 4: Neil Kirkman, Myron Johnson, George Miller, Ed Little, Richard Morris, Vernon Hunt, Bob Gould, René Duffourc, Bob Cohan, Mary Jo Freitag, Bill Webb, Irwin Cohen, Bernie Guyer, Charles Richman

1972–73

Row 1: Paul Glezen, Harrie Chamberlin, Ellis Fisher, Floyd Denny, Jud Van Wyk, Cam McMillan, Myron Johnson

Row 2: Emlen Jones, Wally Clyde, Bob Marshall, Lou Underwood, Frank Cashwell, George Miller

Row 3: Mike Gilchrist, Bob Gould, Peggy Falace, Bob Chevalier, Dan Barco

Row 4: Richard Morris, Lorcan O'Tuama, Mary Ann Williams Morris, Cathy Taylor, Bill Straughn, Ernie Kraybill, Susan Wolschina, Bob Little, Ed Little

Row 5: Jerry Fernald, Earl Siegel, Fred Henderson, Stan Lemon, Greg Hayden, Naomi Morris

Row 6: Al Collier, Herb Harned, Don Middleton, Tom Mettee, Bob Herrington

Row 7: Dwight Powell, Tom Murphy, Stewart Schall, Jim Smithwick, Bob Lister, Jack Benjamin, Harvey Hamrick

133

1973-74

Row 1: Paul Glezen, Greg Hayden, Susan Farrell, Neil Kirkman, Floyd Denny, Jerry Bernstein, Wally Clyde, Al Collier, Don Dunphy, Shirley Klein

Row 2: Sam Pepkowitz, Bob Chevalier, Phil Buchanan, Frank French, Susan Birkemeier, Ernie Kraybill, Myron Johnson, Carol Hagberg, Cynthia Worrell, Hal Woodward

Row 3: Naomi Morris, Tom Irons, Dave Clark, Lorcan O'Tuama, Anne Francis, Peggy Falace, Mary Pat Hemstreet, Joel Klein, George Broze

Row 4: Bob Greenberg, Ron May, Art Aylsworth, Dwight Powell, Ed Little, Hugh Bryan, Bob Little, Earl Bryant, Mike Bramley, Bob Gould, Stewart Schall

1974-75

Row 1: Herb Harned, Eleanor Weissberg, Carol Hagberg, Anne Scholl, Anne Francis, Bob Gould, Floyd Denny, Jennifer Margolis, Lou Underwood, Jerry Fernald

Row 2: Phil Buchanan, Dave Ingram, Ernie Kraybill, Mike Sharp, Bill Wilson, Rosemary Roberts, Jud Van Wyk, Wally Clyde, Frank Loda

Row 3: Jon Fusselman, Paul Sutton, Myron Johnson, John Myracle, Mike Bramley, Stewart Schall, Chuck Swisher, Neil Kirkman, Ron May

Row 4: Greg Hayden, Bob Little, Charles Yoder, Dave Clark, Peggy Falace, Steve Gehlbach

Row 5: Archie Johnson, Art Aylsworth, Cam McMillan, Ed Anderson, Dwight Powell, Don Middleton, Earl Bryant, Emlen Jones, Hal Woodward, Al Collier, Frank French

1975–76

Row 1: Neil Kirkman, Eleanor Weissberg, Susanne White, Sam Pepkowitz, Floyd Denny, Carol Hagberg, Lou Underwood, Jerry Fernald, Harrie Chamberlin

Row 2: Anne Scholl, Dave Ingram, Mary Ann Morris, John Myracle, Anne Francis, Cam McMillan, Ernie Kraybill, Jud Van Wyk, Al Collier

Row 3: Harvey Hamrick, Bob Dillard, Don Dunphy, Richard Morris, Frank Loda, Art Aylsworth, Hugh Wells, Myron Johnson, Dave Clark, Herb Harned, Frank French

Row 4: Jon Fusselman, Dwight Powell, Jerry Strope, Ed Anderson, Bob Herrington, Hal Woodward, Jeff Bomze, Tom Mettee, Doug Klaucke, Hugh Bryan, Bob Greenberg, Chris Snyder, Jeff Allen, Fred Henderson

1976–77

Row 1: Eleanor Weissberg, Karen McCoy, Karen Lowenstein, Don Dunphy, Hal Woodward, Floyd Denny, Jud Van Wyk, Cam McMillan, Harrie Chamberlin

Row 2: Jim Thullen, Dale Newton, Dave Tayloe, Kathy Salter, Steve Kahler, Ernie Kraybill, Chris Snyder, Paul Kaplowitz, Jennifer Margolis

Row 3: Bob Herrington, Earl Siegel, Fred Henderson, Bill Rhead, Rubin Maness, Joe D'Ercole, John Roberts, John Myracle, Lou Underwood, Terry Salter, Bernie Branson

Row 4: Phil Buchanan, Stewart Schall, Myron Johnson, Ron May, Peggy Zwerling, Jeff Bomze, Chuck Yoder, Jerry Strope, Mike Sharp, Mike McCauley, Brian Stabler, Richard Furlanetto

Row 5: Hugh Bryan, Bob Greenberg, Chris Snyder, Bill Wilson, Evan Pattishall, Rick Andringa, Jerry Hood, Art Aylsworth, Ken Whitt, Randy Forehand, Ray Isley

1977–78

Row 1: Terry Salter, Karen McCoy, Mary Sugioka, Hema Ghia, Don Dunphy, Jerry Fernald, Floyd Denny, Randy Forehand, Phil Buchanan, Ken Copeland

Row 2: Jack Dolcourt, Doug Willson, Melinda Paul, Muff Carr, Sandra Blethen, Herb Harned, Jim Thullen, Ernie Kraybill, Brian Stabler, Dave Stempel, Ned Lawson, Neil Kirkman

Row 3: Jud Van Wyk, Peggy Zwerling, Bob Hoyer, Frank Loda, Marty Ulshen, Paul Kaplowitz, Jerry Hood, Dennis Mayock, Bernie Branson, Ray Mitchell

Row 4: Nancy Chaney, Lorcan O'Tuama, Chuck Willson, Harrie Chamberlin, Rubin Maness, Mitchell Reese, John Shahan, Steve Kahler, Doug Clark, Chuck Lapp, Ross Vaughan

Rows 5&6: Wally Clyde, Al Collier, Cam McMillan, Stewart Schall, Jeff Bomze, Art Aylsworth, Dwight Powell, Arlen Collins, Fred Henderson, Myron Johnson, Bob Greenberg, Evan Pattishall, Joe D'Ercole, Hugh Bryan, Frank French

1978–79

Row 1: Jerry Hood, Stu Teplin, Mary Sugioka, Jeannine Leatherman, Muff Carr, Karen McCoy, Floyd Denny, Nancy Chaney, Jerry Fernald, Paul Kaplowitz, Phil Buchanan, Sharon Lail

Row 2: Juan Cardenas, Margaret Sanyal, Melinda Snyder

Row 3: Harrie Chamberlin, Dave Ingram, Susanne White, Diane Edwards, Wally Clyde, Al Collier, Lorcan O'Tuama, Lou Underwood, Dave Stempel, Doug Willson, Joe D'Ercole, Jud Van Wyk

Row 4: Rubin Maness, Mike Sharp, Frank Loda, Ernie Kraybill, John Roberts

Row 5: Kathy Chino, Tina Ciesiel, Holcombe Grier, Peter Morris, Ned Lawson, Marty Ulshen, Ken Whitt, Neil Kirkman, Harvey Hamrick, Bob Herrington

Row 6: Herb Harned, Brian Wherrett, Seth Hetherington, Richard Morris, Walker Long, Bill Turk, John Pecorak, Dwight Powell, Cam McMillan, Bill Wilson, Keith Hoots, Myron Johnson

1979–80

Row 1: Steve Kahler, Don Dunphy, Lou Underwood, Al Collier, Jerry Fernald, Floyd Denny, Chuck Willson, Shannon Kenney, Wanda Kotvan, Melinda Paul

Row 2: Herb Harned, Joe D'Ercole, Wally Clyde, Jack Dolcourt, Paul Kaplowitz, Frank Loda, Bruce Duncan, Pat Robinson, Terry Bilz, Carl Bose, Nita Coleman

Row 3: Cam McMillan, Jack Davis, Harrie Chamberlin, Jerry Strope, Dave Ingram, Ernie Kraybill, Jim Thullen, Harvey Hamrick, Margaret Sanyal, Stu Teplin, Arlen Collins, Rich Waller, John Grizzard, Jud Van Wyk

Rows 4&5: Walker Long, Steve Chernausek, Dana Ketchum, Alan Stiles, Seth Hetherington, John Bourgeois, Tom Miller, Mitchell Reese, John Pecorak, John Roberts, Randy Pasternak, Harry Guess, Stewart Schall, Fred Henderson, Jim Spaeth, Holcombe Grier, Keith Hoots, Alan Cross, Peter Morris, Marty Ulshen, Kathy Chino, Rick Sigmon, Stan Spinola, Michael Sargent, John Merritt

1980–81

Row 1: Marianna Henry, Jeannine Leatherman, Hugh Craft, Susan Hyman, Mary Sugioka, Don Dunphy, Doug Willson, Floyd Denny, Jerry Fernald, Stu Teplin, Richard Morris, Liliana Visscher, Susie Lipton

Row 2: Steve Chernausek, Ann Smith, Barbara Hodge, Ann Bailey, Peter Saviteer, Bob Valley, Steve Kahler, Paul Kaplowitz, Ray Mitchell, Randy Pasternak, Bob Greenberg, Bob Wells

Row 3: Harvey Hamrick, Harrie Chamberlin, Herb Harned, Wally Clyde, Harry Guess, Peter Morris, Ed Pattishall, Neil Kirkman, Ernie Kraybill, Alan Cross

Row 4: Bob Stifler, Bob Herrington, Alan Stiles, Marry Ulshen, Steve Trippel, Stewart Schall, Cam McMillan

Row 5: Mike Sharp, Rick Sigmon, Jerry Strope, Mike Fowler, Art Aylsworth, John Whisnant, Frank Loda, Craig LaForce, Seth Hetherington

PART THREE

The Boat Years
1982–1993

INTRODUCTION

Editors' Note: When the committee responsible for writing the history of the Department of Pediatrics began its work, Dr. Boat was still chairman. The decision was made accordingly to end the history in 1981 when Dr. Denny resigned. When Dr. Boat resigned in 1993 the committee reconsidered this matter and decided to add the so-called Boat years to the history. Since Dr. Boat was not available to supervise this section of the history, the committee, after much deliberation, decided on the following course of action. We asked Dr. Jerry Fernald to adapt Dr. Boat's presentation at the 1993 meeting of the Denny Society to a section on the history of the Department from 1982 to 1993, which follows the introduction. Drs. Kraybill and Denny interviewed Dr. Boat by telephone on April 26, 1995. The summary of this interview, supplemented with contributions from several administrative and faculty members, completes the history of the Boat years. The large section on the subspecialties was expanded to bring them up to date in 1993, including the marked influence of the Boat years.

B Y THE 1980s the winds of change were blowing through academic departments of pediatrics, as well as through the medical profession at large. The demands on a department chairman had increased tremendously since Dr. Denny became chairman in 1960. Still, his resignation, while in his prime, of the chairmanship he had held for more than two decades caught many by surprise. His own stated reasons for stepping down were that he had accomplished many of his goals as a chairman, fiscal matters were becoming more important than he found comfortable, and he did not wish to begin the planning for the children's hospital. Rather, he preferred a return to scholarly activities.

The search to replace Dr. Denny took place with little difficulty, and within sixteen months Dr. Thomas F. Boat arrived in Chapel Hill as the new chairman. The search had been chaired by Dr. Harold Roberts, professor of medicine, and had broad representation from the Medical School. Dr. David

Tayloe Sr. and Dr. J. C. Parke represented the practicing pediatricians of North Carolina and the AHEC faculty, respectively. The transition period for the Department was smooth due to the quietly effective leadership of Dr. Fernald as acting chairman, as well as Dr. Denny's remaining in the Department and taking an active part in resident recruitment.

Ernest N. Kraybill

CHAPTER NINE

UNC Department of Pediatrics, 1982–1993

I HAD the privilege of inheriting the leadership of a Department that in 1982 was strong, vigorous, and had been well run. The transition to new leadership was smooth, as most members of the Department were eager to build on the many strengths that existed and on traditions that were firmly rooted in rich academic soil. The accomplishments of this decade can be reviewed only with acknowledgment of the tremendous contributions made by Dr. Floyd Denny as chairman of the Department for the previous twenty-one years and Dr. Jerry Fernald, who had served as associate chairman of the Department under Dr. Denny, who had very capably guided the Department during the two-year transition period, and who provided vision, administrative capability, and a steady hand throughout the Boat era. In addition, the strong financial oversight, organization, and planning provided by Ms. Harriett Brewer Dickey before and during the tenure of Dr. Boat as chairman of the Department of Pediatrics allowed the Department to focus on program development. Dr. Jacob Lohr joined the administrative team as associate chair in 1990 and made important and insightful contributions to the organization of a modern ambulatory care program. Finally, the loyal and highly capable contributions of a remarkable faculty ensured the success of departmental endeavors.

The Department grew from thirty-nine total faculty in 1981–1982, including six AHEC faculty, to seventy-five total faculty in 1991–1992, including twelve AHEC faculty. In addition, adjunct faculty were added in a number of key areas, including three pediatric surgeons: Dr. Richard Azizkhan, who was recruited in 1985, followed by Dr. Stewart Lacey and Dr. Lesli Taylor. Late in the 1980s, Dr. Amelia Drake was recruited to provide pediatric ENT expertise. Dr. Richard Henderson was added early in the

Thomas F.
Boat
[Credit:
Sam Gray]

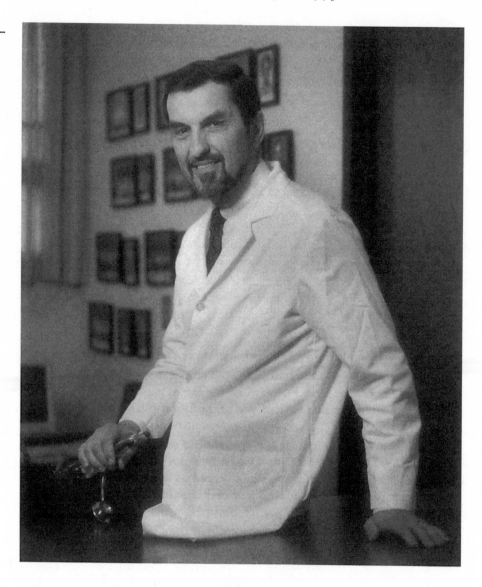

decade to assist Dr. Walter Greene as a second pediatric orthopedic surgeon. There was a complete turnover in pediatric radiology and expansion from one to two pediatric radiologists, the final duo being Dr. David Merten and Dr. Barbara Specter. Dr. Steve Resnick was recruited by the Department of Dermatology to serve as the pediatric dermatologist.

During this time, three new divisions were created. The first was the division of pediatric pulmonology, headed by Dr. Robert Wood, who arrived in Chapel Hill from the Rainbow Babies' and Children's Hospital (Cleveland) in 1983. By the end of the decade, that division was one of the biggest and most active in the Department, with six faculty members, an outstanding training program, and an active research effort. The division of rheumatology was created in 1984 with the arrival of Dr. Robert Warren. A second rheumatologist/

immunologist, Dr. Leonard Stein, was recruited from Toronto's Sick Children's Hospital two years later. Dr. Stein took over as chief of the division when Dr. Warren left for Texas Children's Hospital in Houston; he was subsequently joined by Dr. Ann Reed and on a part-time basis by Dr. Kathy Amoroso. In 1986, the critical care division was formed with recruitment of Dr. Arno Zaritsky. He was assisted at one point or another by Dr. Steven Lawless, Dr. Robert Kanter, Dr. Lewis Romer, and Dr. Lela Brink. The latter two were the major critical care participants at the end of the decade. During this decade, fifteen faculty left the Department, six through retirement and nine through resignation.

Gerald W. Fernald, associate chair of the Department during the Denny and Boat years

In 1982–1983, the total departmental budget was $5.8 million. This had grown to $19.1 million by 1991–1992. The largest gains by revenue source were clinical fees, which increased from $1.2 million to $5.5 million over this period of time, while direct-cost grant support increased from $2.8 million to $7.2 million over the ten-year period.

Although numbers of students taught remained constant over the decade, the clerkship was extended from a six-week to an eight-week rotation so that all of the students could receive four weeks of ward experience and four weeks of newborn and ambulatory experience. Greensboro (Moses Cone Hospital and the County Health Clinic) was added as a clerkship site, and through the efforts of Dr. Michael Sharp numerous community experiences throughout the state were offered on an elective basis, both to preclinical students and to fourth-year students. Over this decade, an average of 12 percent of the UNC medical students selected pediatrics as their training pathway. Dr. Harvey Hamrick provided creative and empathetic leadership to the student teaching program from 1983 to 1987, followed by Dr. William Coleman (when Dr. Hamrick took over the direction of resident recruitment and training from Dr. Robert Greenberg).

House staff training expanded remarkably during the 1982–1992 decade. At the beginning of the decade, house staff participated in the care of patients at both the University of North Carolina Hospital and at Wake Hospital in Raleigh. The Wake Hospital pediatric program was very capably led by Dr. David Ingram. By 1988, the formerly independent pediatric training program at Greensboro was folded into the UNC training program, providing a third training site, directed by Dr. Myron Johnson. Numbers of categorical pedi-

Richard
Azizkhan,
the Medical
Center's first
pediatric
surgeon

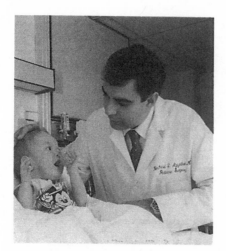

atric residents increased from a total of twenty-eight in 1981–1982 to forty-six in 1991–1992. During this time numbers of medicine-pediatrics residents remained stable at four per year, or sixteen for the entire program. Other training changes included expansion of coverage of Wake Hospital to include an adolescent medicine rotation and an emergency room rotation. During this decade, the community outreach program that was pioneered by Dr. Michael Sharp became an important part of the first-year training program. This experience included precepted activities at a number of community sites. A novel combined inpatient/outpatient rotation was initiated in hematology-oncology. Intensive experiences in critical care medicine were introduced into the program at the second-year (residency) level. The Department went from a single chief resident to two in 1988. Dr. Robert Greenberg was initially the director of house staff training and was replaced by Dr. Harvey Hamrick in 1987. Throughout this period, Ms. Sherri Davis, Pediatric Education Coordinator, was instrumental in keeping all trainees content and focused on their work.

The growth of fellowship training at both the MD and PhD levels was remarkable during the 1982–1992 decade. During the year 1981–1982, fourteen fellows were part of our training program, all of whom were MDs. By 1991–1992, there were forty-eight fellows including a number of postdoctoral PhD investigators. New training programs were introduced in behavioral medicine (for five years, after which federal support was withdrawn), critical care medicine, gastroenterology, general academic pediatrics, hematology-oncology, pulmonary medicine, and rheumatology. These seven new programs joined previously established programs in infectious diseases, genetics, endocrinology, neonatology, child development, and cardiology. The cardiology training program lost its accreditation in 1985. In addition, the preventive medicine training program was directed by pediatric faculty throughout the decade, first by Dr. Alan Cross then by Dr. Desmond Runyan. Institutional NIH or other federal training program support was available in the divisions of endocrinology, pulmonary medicine, infectious diseases, child development, gastroenterology, general academic medicine, and hematology-oncology.

The clinical service changed appreciably during the 1982–1992 decade. All of the space on the seventh floor of University Hospital was assigned to pediatrics to form the North Carolina Children's Hospital. The Children's Hospital also included the newborn unit and neonatal intensive care unit on the fourth floor and eventually a twenty-bed surgical unit on the sixth floor.

The intermediate nursery, which had ("temporarily") been on the seventh floor, was relocated adjacent to the NICU on the fourth floor. A new sixteen-bed pediatric intensive care unit was created on the seventh floor. The nursery was relocated to improved quarters in the middle of the obstetrics area on the fourth floor. In addition, general pediatrics' clinical activities were greatly expanded under the leadership of Dr. Jacob Lohr and moved to the ambulatory care building in 1992. Many of the subspecialty clinics remained in the first-floor clinical area, which was slated for extensive remodeling. Plans were laid for the construction of a semi-self-contained children's hospital in the mid-1990s.

Inpatient care evolved from a general attending orientation to a subspecialty orientation. A number of new techniques were introduced, including pulmonary endoscopy, interventional cardiology procedures for coarctation of the aorta and pulmonary valve stenosis, and organ transplantation which by 1992 included lung transplantation, heart transplantation, liver transplantation, and kidney transplantation. In 1993 a bone marrow unit including a pediatric service was opened. Major satellite activities were added, most notably a large cardiology program at Wake Hospital in Raleigh. By the end of the decade, satellite activities were conducted by the cardiology, pulmonary, rheumatology, hematology-oncology, and GI services at sites that included Raleigh, Wilmington, Laurinburg, Fayetteville (Fort Bragg), Charlotte, Asheville, and Greensboro.

Average medical/surgical bed occupancy on the general pediatric service increased from forty-three to fifty-eight, and PICU admissions increased from fewer than four hundred to more than seven hundred per year. Pediatric intensive care unit days per month increased from one hundred fifty to more than four hundred. NICU beds grew from a total of twenty-eight to thirty-six and were nearly always full, at times running over capacity. Outpatient visits grew from just over twenty thousand to more than thirty thousand, not including visits to satellite centers.

The research enterprise in the Department of Pediatrics grew considerably. In addition to the above-mentioned growth in external funding, numbers of research articles in peer-reviewed journals increased from 80 or 90 per year to approximately 160 per year, or approximately two research articles per active faculty member. The quality of research publications was impressive. The Department became more serious about recruiting and recognizing PhD investigators and promoting them into tenure-track positions. Major core activities were generated in the area of morphologic analysis (John Carson) and molecular biology (Ed Hu).

The Department of Pediatrics faculty members played key leadership roles in the UNC School of Medicine programs. Dr. Frank French was the director of the Laboratories for Reproductive Biology during the entire decade. Dr. Floyd Denny was director of the School of Medicine Program on Health Promotion and Disease Prevention, and Dr. Alan Cross headed the Center for Health Promotion, Disease Prevention program of the Health Sciences campus. Dr. Frank Loda assumed directorship of the Center for Early Adolescence. Dr. Melvin Levine was recruited from Boston to direct the Center for Development and Learning. Finally, Dr. Albert Collier was the associate director of the Frank Porter Graham Child Development Center and acted as interim director of that program for more than one year. Dr. Thomas Boat was the associate director of the UNC Lung Biology Center and followed Dr. Wallace Clyde as PI of the Pediatric Pulmonary Special Center of Research funded by the NHLBI.

THOMAS F. BOAT
ADAPTED BY GERALD W. FERNALD

Editors' Note: During the above presentation to the Denny Society on November 13, 1993, Dr. Boat asked two faculty members recruited by him to the Department to present information regarding their contributions. Dr. Robert "Bob" Wood described the development, growth, and accomplishment of the pediatric pulmonary division. This was chosen because of its excellence and because it encompassed Dr. Boat's clinical and research interests. A complete history of this division is included in the section on subspecialties.

Dr. Jacob Lohr was asked to describe the activities of the division of community pediatrics because of its remarkable growth and Boat's prediction of its importance to the future of pediatrics. The complete history of this division is also included in the section on subspecialties.

Dr. Boat also asked Dr. Thomas Ferkol, chief pediatric resident in 1988–1989, to present the house staff viewpoint during the Boat years. Ferkol made a delightful presentation on his impression of the important aspects of the Department during the Boat years: a strong interest in teaching and learning; an abundance of triple-threat faculty (research, teaching, clinical) to act as models for house staff; the UNC program's being the right size so the staff were not overcome with too many patients; and finally the congeniality of the whole Department.

Dr. Boat ended his presentation of the Boat years with a prediction for the future of the Department. He stated that the Department is in transition and that this is good. Since it has an excellent faculty, and is part of one of the best research medical schools in the country and at a leading university, its bright future is assured.

CHAPTER TEN

More on the Boat Years

Editors' Note: The preceding section portrays accurately many of the factual data showing the progress of the Department during the Boat years, but provides only glimpses of the chairman. The section to follow focuses on Dr. Boat himself and was gleaned from an April 1995 telephone interview of Dr. Boat by Drs. Kraybill and Denny and from impressions of key faculty members and administrators during the Boat years.

TOM BOAT—THE RELUCTANT CHAIRMAN

WHILE the search for a chairman in 1981–1982 had been relatively painless for the Department, the decision was not easy for Dr. Boat. Unlike Dr. Denny, Dr. Boat didn't have a burning desire to be a chairman. Just as the search was getting underway Tom was attending an NIH-sponsored meeting at the UNC Quail Roost Conference Center. When asked informally at that meeting whether he wanted to be a chairman, Tom replied that he didn't think so. He recalls vividly a later conversation with his wife Barbara:

> I came home and I talked to Barb. I remember she was standing in the kitchen. I said I got a call from Chapel Hill and they said that they wanted me to reconsider. And I said, "Well, maybe I will reconsider." I just remember she grabbed her stomach.

Tom recalls further:

> That was the start of a long process. It turned out that I wasn't able to say yes to this until Barb said yes. The first time we came down she

made the visit with me. The important thing was that it worked out and she saw an opportunity for herself. That certainly was a major part of the decision. The other was that I became aware of the strengths of the University and the School of Medicine and some of the collaborative programs—the School of Public Health and the Frank Porter Graham Child Development Center. I was also attracted by the work that was going on in cystic fibrosis. Ric Boucher and I spent hours talking together at a Gordon Conference. It became apparent to me that he was going to be a big mover in the CF field. I think that opened a door because it allowed me to think about moving without giving up being in the center of CF activities at a research level. Those are the things that certainly encouraged me to look further.

Tom recognized that he would be taking over the leadership of a strong, stable Department that had a good balance of teaching, clinical service, and research. He saw opportunities for collaboration with Dr. Albert Collier in investigations of lung infections, as well as with Dr. Boucher in studies of cystic fibrosis. Finally, Barbara, who had recently received her PhD in psychology, found an attractive position in the Department of Psychiatry.

TOM BOAT—THE MAN

The prospect of working in the shadow of a former chairman who was held in high esteem in the Department and nationally did not intimidate Tom, and he was strongly supported by Dr. Denny.

The faculty, residents, and students found Tom to be vigorous, aggressive, and intellectually honest. He set high standards for himself and expected the same of others. He was admired and respected by students, house staff, and colleagues in the School of Medicine and the University. Eric Munson, director of UNC Hospitals, with whom Tom negotiated for hospital resources, called Tom a "highly principled man who always behaved as a gentleman," "an effective advocate for the Department of Pediatrics," and "one of the more stylish chairs."

Tom became a strong administrator—unsentimental, unflappable, strong under pressure. He controlled his emotions; Harriett Brewer, administrative assistant in the departmental office, saw him visibly angry only once. She relates that "He just paced back and forth in his office; he wanted to 'kill' one of his faculty members." Harriett refuses to reveal who it was.

Though by nature a stern, reserved Midwesterner, Tom did not lack a sense of humor. His funny asides and easy laugh defused many a tense moment. He quickly learned the Southern idiom and used it to the advantage of the Department. But he remained impatient with the deliberate pace of change—especially when he wanted to implement new programs in pediatrics.

Tom was supported by an extraordinary wife who was developing her own productive career at UNC-CH. Barbara held her own in any conversation. A charming hostess, with her own sense of humor, she disarmed stuffed-shirt dignitaries with her "flip the spoon into a glass of water" trick. The "Boat House" on Eastwood Lake, sometimes with a tent pitched in the parking area, was the site of numerous parties that Tom and Barbara enjoyed as much as their guests. Both were skilled sailors and windsurfers. A competitive sportsman, Tom could hit a softball farther than any previous chairman and most house officers.

TOM BOAT'S LEGACY TO THE DEPARTMENT

Dr. Boat's resignation, like Dr. Denny's a decade earlier, caught many by surprise and caused consternation in the Department. Tom had a sense that "it was time." In reflecting on this later he said, "It was no one thing. It was hard—a very hard decision. I wasn't out looking for jobs but for me it really came down to what I would do with the last leg of my career. The option of staying in Chapel Hill was not to remain chair, in my mind." (Stuart Bondurant had recently announced that he would resign as dean and many encouraged Tom to throw his hat into the ring.) Tom observed, "I'm a reasonably good clinician, I like to do teaching, I'm pretty good at research, and I understand, I think, how to get things done and maybe I understand administration but, by God, I wasn't going to be a dean!" He considered taking a sabbatical to "retool" prior to resuming his laboratory research but rejected that as well. This all pointed to another chairmanship, if the right one were offered. The chairmanship of the Department of Pediatrics at University of Cincinnati and the directorship of the Children's Hospital Research Foundation seemed to be the challenge he was looking for, and he took it. After almost two years there he observed that "Only *some* of the grass is greener here."

By every conceivable measure, the Boat administration was a success. Tom continued and advanced the tradition of excellence in academic pediatrics at UNC-CH that had been established and maintained by Ed Curnen and Floyd Denny. While Denny had established the major divisions in the Department, Tom added three more and strengthened the existing ones. He also oversaw the implementation of much more direct involvement in patient care by the subspecialty groups, on the inpatient service as well as in the clinics. This was prompted by the increasingly complex nature of the illnesses of patients referred to the Department and the need of the subspecialists to deal more directly with referring physicians, as well as by the demands of third-party payers for shorter hospital stays. It was inevitable that this trend would diminish the autonomy of the residents—something that had been fiercely defended by past generations of house officers. Tom anticipated this impact and devoted many senior staff meetings to assuring that the education of residents wasn't jeopardized by the changes.

Dean Stuart Bondurant called Tom "one of the great chairs of pediatrics departments in the country, and indeed, for that matter, in the world." This

Tom and
Barbara Boat

opinion was shared by the committee that conducted the second five-year review of Dr. Boat's chairmanship. This panel of peers from within and outside the University unanimously recommended his reappointment "based on his exceptional record of energetic and productive leadership in academic pediatrics at local, state and national levels." The committee observed that "Under Dr. Boat's leadership the Department of Pediatrics has steadily advanced in delivery of patient care, clinical and basic research, medical student teaching, and residency/fellowship training. Additionally Dr. Boat has grown in stature as a national leader in pediatrics, and he has assumed a prominent role as a respected institutional leader."

   In Tom's own words, he left the Department "in transition, with an excellent faculty and a bright future."

ERNEST N. KRAYBILL

CHAPTER ELEVEN

Residents' Reminiscences

DAVID J. BURCHFIELD (1981–1984)

The Transition Years

"So you must be David Burchfield?" he surmised as he assembled the three new interns to assign them patients. That moment of astounding deduction immediately placed me in awe of Alan Stiles. But in retrospect, it mustn't have been hard for the chief resident to figure out who I was. Of the other two interns on the team, Larry Nickens had gone to Medical School in Chapel Hill and Karen Voter just didn't look like a David. However, at that moment, when I had just dropped my stethoscope and spilled the contents of my top pocket while bending over to pick it up, I was impressed.

"Yes, sir!" I replied from the crouch position. Reaching between Joan Fine's sandal-clad feet to fetch the last blank index card, I began to feel my face burn with embarrassment. What in the world are my chief resident and my first senior resident thinking about me right now as I grovel on the floor in response to such a simple salutation?

"You can cut the 'sir' stuff and just call me Alan," he soothed. "You're going to pick up Danny Green. Now Danny is an interesting patient who has A.L.L. . . ."

A.L.L.! my thoughts interrupted his discourse. *You know you've heard of that! Just THINK! You know he will probably ask you a question about it,* my paranoid mind convinced me, not ready to give up my just-completed medical student role.

" . . . and Sanfilippo mucopolysaccharidosis," he continued as I forced my mind back to his colloquy. "He probably won't do so well."

Unclear if the last statement referred to me or Danny, I mentally started kicking myself for ever wanting to leave Florida for my training. *You are in the wrong place*, I muttered.

Soon after that less than auspicious start, the true flavor of the training program under Dr. Denny began to take form in my mind. On rounds, Joan stressed that the intern was the patient's doctor and the decisions concerning the patient's management would be made by the intern. This became ever so clear that first afternoon when I gathered the courage to go meet Danny and his mother.

"Hello, I'm David Burchfield, Danny's new doctor," I announced, taking Mrs. Green's hand in mine in a well-rehearsed manner. I remember wondering if she noticed how sweaty it felt.

"Dr. Burchfield, Danny is not going to do well, is he?" she queried meekly.

Oh geez, this woman can read minds! I am in the wrong place! I thought. *Now what do I tell her?*

After a few seconds that felt like minutes I babbled, "Well, I don't think so, Mrs. Green." *That's the way to take charge, Burchfield*, I judged. *She has complete confidence in you now.*

"Well then, can I just take him home, Dr. Burchfield? I mean, if you don't think there is much to offer Danny, can't I just take him back home?"

Remembering what Joan had said just two hours before on rounds about the interns making decisions, I confidently responded, "I'll ask."

Here was my first opportunity to interact with one of the faculty and I wanted to make a solid first impression. I reviewed Danny's chart to make sure I had every detail. I went into the pediatric reading room and read all that *Nelson's* had to say about A.L.L. as well as Sanfilippo's. I cross-referenced the information in *Nelson's* with that in Danny's chart. Finally feeling prepared, I paged Dr. Fred Henderson, my attending. After introducing myself, I gave him the whole story in a perfect medical presentation format that went something like, "Danny has two bad diseases and his mom wants to take him home today. Is that OK?"

Over the next three years of residency and over the ten years since I left Chapel Hill, I have heard some truly great scientific discourses. David Ingram spoke about HIV before anyone knew AIDS was caused by a virus. A surgeon from Michigan explained how putting catheters into babies' carotid arteries could save their lives without causing a stroke. Joe D'Ercole expounded on the miracles of something called "growth factors." But to this day, no one has topped Dr. Henderson's so eloquently phrased, deeply thought-through response to my inquiry.

"Sure."

With that short but ever so persuasive oration, my first patient went home. And although the encounter was brief, my relationship with Danny typified the role of the intern under Dr. Denny's leadership. The intern was *the* doctor and everyone else consultants. The general attending was the attending of record on all patients admitted to the pediatric service regardless of whether they were admitted through a subspecialty service. This arrangement established and strengthened the doctor-patient relationship between the intern and the patient's family.

Of course, one quickly learned to use the consultants wisely. For instance, if a child admitted had been seen in Rutherfordton by Bob Herrington and was on digoxin, Lasix, and potassium, ninety-nine times out of a hundred the cardiologists were consulted. I often wonder where the intern who was the one in a hundred who failed to consult Bill Henry on an obvious cardiac patient wound up finishing his training.

I first knew that change was in the air during one of the Denny Saturday morning conferences. "Change is in the air," prophesied Dr. Denny. At the time, he was speaking specifically about intern recruitment, but the thought may have been more global. "We have to get more competitive with our house staff recruiting. The last few years have been hit-or-miss," he mused.

Talk about feeling self-conscious—I remember the interns staring down at their coffee cups, terrified that Dr. Denny's eyes would betray the secret of whether they were considered a "hit" or a "miss." After the conference, my heart started pounding as Dr. Denny stepped into the elevator with me and the door closed before I could make up an excuse to escape.

Mustering up the courage that one needs for true self-reflection but hiding it in the guise of humor I asked, "So Dr. Denny, I just have to know one thing. Am I a hit or a miss?"

I didn't know Dr. Denny as well as some of his trainees, but at that moment I thought I detected a flash of wit when he responded solemnly, "The jury is still out, Burchfield." Well, at least I like to remember it as wit.

Shortly after that Saturday, Dr. Denny announced that he was stepping down as chairman and the search was on. It was really an exciting time for the house staff, having all of these Who's Whos in pediatrics come through Chapel Hill to interview. Maybe it was the seminars given by these candidates that electrified us, but then again it could have been the invitations to lunch and dinner that lit our fires. Important in the process was the faculty bestowing a sense of involvement on the house staff.

From the resident's view during this process, the Department went along as usual under the direct supervision of Dr. Jerry Fernald. New interns were recruited using innovative ploys to weed out the "misses" and guarantee the "hits." Our group of interns had the last weekend of the academic year off to spend at the beach while the graduating PL-3s broke in the new recruits. Scheming to find a way to avoid an end-of-the-year "touchy-feely" session, someone forgot to tell our class advisor, Mike Sharp, where we would be meeting. As I said, things seemed to be transitioning smoothly.

Shortly after the arrival of Dr. Boat, things began to change. Change isn't all good, and it isn't all bad. And it isn't often comfortable, even if it is the correct course to take.

As a senior resident, I received a page from Gary Eddey, an extremely conscientious, bright, caring but worrisome intern. (Rumor has it that when Bob

Valley assigned patients to the interns on their first day, Gary dropped a pile of note cards at the mere mention of his name.) "Can you meet me on 7 West to work up the new GI patient?" he queried.

"Tell me about the patient," I interrogated.

"It is a little girl with hematochezia. She was seen in her physician's office several weeks ago with a poorly defined illness treated with amoxicillin and then a week or two afterwards she began having blood in her stool. Other than that, she has been completely healthy. She is being admitted to have a colonoscopy."

The adrenaline started rushing. This kid didn't need a colonoscopy, she needed a stool sample for C. *difficile* toxin. On arriving at the patient's room to discuss this with her mother, we found the little girl in that deep slumber brought on only by chloral hydrate or being post-call in the NICU. We guessed the former.

"Oh, hello. Don't worry about whispering because her doctor said that she will be out for several hours following the procedure," the mother apprised us. "But if she does wake up before 7 o'clock, we can go home."

If I reflect on all the changes in medicine that I've experienced, I point to that day as the day health care reform was born. The patient was admitted, medicated, instrumented, and discharged, all planned before the intern could ask if they used well water or city water. The referring physician had already been informed, and to top it off, the mother acted as satisfied as Mrs. Green two years earlier. I just wonder if Gary has learned how to evaluate a patient with hematochezia.

Since leaving Chapel Hill (and assuming a faculty position in Gainesville), I have become convinced that Dr. Boat's shift in focus, away from the intern and toward the attending physician as the primary physician, has value in the family's view. That system was used in most other universities, was cost effective, satisfying to referring physicians, and maybe the quality of care improved over the time when interns were the primary physicians ("The jury is still out, Burchfield"). However, lost was the autonomy and confidence in making decisions, vital components for physician training, and components that I will always hold dear in my memories of my internship.

N. REGINA RABINOVICH (1982–1986)

The Early Boat Years

Coming from a small, new medical school in the Midwest, I felt I had little hope of matching at Chapel Hill, but persevered because I had heard much about this institution from Drs. Joe Garfunkel and Robert Merrill, both then at Southern Illinois University. To make matters worse, I had arrived for my interview on the wrong day, which was hastily arranged with Ruth Etzel and Richard Morris (who I found out later was reputed to be a tough interviewer), and because I had added UNC at the last moment, it turned out none of my records were in place when the committee reviewed the files at Christmas. It was only my follow-up letter, indicating interest, along with a letter from my mentor making up the sole contents of my file that alerted Dr. Kraybill to a problem. He called my home during the holidays, and then the dean of the medical school read him my letter of recommendation. So I was rather shocked when I opened the envelope on Match Day!

The surprises continued. My only ambivalence about coming to a small town was that it seemed to be made up of a quiet group of married couples. Six weeks before internship began, I re-met and married my husband, Franco Piazza, in Lima, Peru (but that, as they say, is another story!). Coming from the Midwest, I thought "South" was Alabama and "East" was North Carolina (it's very close to D.C., right?), and I had never *heard* of the Tar Heels! It only took a day to realize that I had indeed moved south, and within a week I had adopted Chapel Hill and wanted all further passports for more incoming revoked—too crowded! Our older children were born and learned to speak in Chapel Hill, and still maintain vestiges of that wonderful accent. And of course, we all watch the Tar Heels whenever they play—we caught the Michael Jordan years and were forever converted.

As I sit and write this letter from the point of view of the enormous social and political upheaval that is Washington, D.C. in 1995, it seems clear to me that it *began* during our years at Chapel Hill. Undoubtedly, the changes in medicine have been on a continuum, but from the perspective of someone entering pediatrics in 1982, they began the day we arrived. Our intern group was rather unique in that we were all foreigners—that is, no one from UNC. Thus, we not only failed to have preconceived notions of how things "were done" at Chapel Hill, but our group brought extreme geographic diversity and historical perspective. Regardless of our individual reasons for selecting UNC, things changed under our feet. First, the wards we had visited during interviews had been left behind for the new wards on the seventh floor. Second, the famous Dr. Denny had left for an extended trip after stepping down as chair of the Department, and Dr. Tom Boat joined us in the middle of the first year. The third change appears more than a bit naive now: it was based on the reputation (among medical students) that UNC had as a "residents' hospital." That is, the residents were perceived to have a great deal of responsibility in the management of the patient, compared to "fellows' hospitals," where the subspecialty fellow reigned, or the "LMD hospitals," where the local physicians *let* you help with their patients.

Several months after we started, the Boats arrived and would both have a profound impact on our pediatric training. There was a cautious introduction at a picnic with this obviously young and attractive couple and rather reserved new chairman, then Tom proceeded to meet with faculty and, more slowly, with us. We met him wandering the wards with his own invention, the double-headed teaching stethoscope. We heard of his focus on research, grant-funded faculty, and molecular biology, which early on began to raise a ruckus with faculty. Already, the stories of Saturday morning rounds were ancient history, and although Tom immersed himself valiantly in our clinical activities, he obviously was reacquainting himself with general pediatrics after years as a successful investigator and clinical pulmonologist.

And that was just the beginning—for all of us. His vision of the changing needs in both research and clinical practice panned out. The "decade of the cell" indeed came true in terms of the focus of the NIH study sections and increased competition for research dollars. His perspective on the running of a referral hospital had immediate impact on house staff: he realized that general pediatricians rarely wanted to refer to hospital-based general pediatricians, but rather to specific subspecialties. Overnight, our "residents' hospital" was changed to a group of subspecialty services who contacted the referring physician directly. The general pediatric service was very small.

From our point of view, it left us with none of the responsibilities and all of the "scut" work, in danger of having to learn osmotically by running errands for the specialists. The changes over the three years can best be understood by remembering our starting point. We took call every third night, which felt civilized compared to the internal medicine ICU services of twenty-four on/twenty-four off, and of course stayed the following day until everything had been completed on our patients—hopefully by dinner. In the tradition of prior years, we were responsible for all the IVs of all pediatric patients twenty-four hours a day, and mixed our own patients' chemotherapy in the old "formula room" (something they had *not* taught me to do in medical school). The four ward residents on call slept in one large room, regardless of gender, where the six beepers (remember the code and admitting beepers) would wake all of us in a burst of epinephrine-induced tachycardia. The neonatal ICU was a very busy service, chronically at capacity in terms of available beds and ventilators. A 700-gram baby was considered at the border of viability—but you tried like hell anyway (and more and more often, succeeded). We lacked a full-time pediatric intensivist, but managed to take care of very sick children under the supervision of various subspecialists, like Drs. Bill and Marianna Henry (when did they ever see each other?). There was not a formal ACLS program, and pediatric house staff got training sometime during their second year—regardless of the fact that you ran codes from day 1. We were strongly discouraged from immunizing children in the walk-in clinic, since this was to be done only as a part of routine health care. Although there was a trained NICU nurse transport team, house staff provided coverage for PICU transfers by helicopter or ambulance. There were no tenured women on the pediatric faculty, but there was a Pediatric Women's Support Group. And I never remember fighting with insurance companies to get them to allow one more day of hospitalization.

As could almost have been predicted, our group rebelled. We just weren't going to take it anymore. I don't recall the straw that broke the camel's back, but the house staff gathered in the conference room on 7 East and just a few months after Tom Boat arrived, unanimously voted and signed a charter of sorts that created a Pediatric House Staff Council. I have no idea where this document is, but do recall that it indicated our willingness to work with the hospital administration and the Pediatric Department in improving patient care and the residency program. David Grossman, Bob Covert, and I signed the cover letter, and we sent the whole thing to the entire hospital. I'm sure we gave Tom more than a few sleepless nights, but somehow (perhaps with Barbara's input?) all that energy (ah, youth!) was channeled into fruitful activity over the next years.

Tom met with us and calmly welcomed our participation. Informal subcommittees were created and the work was divided. Some of the results, like talking the rest of the hospital house staff into equitable sharing of limited IV support services and lobbying for a PICU specialist, took about three years. The call room was divided into three areas—sometimes used along gender lines, other times along seniority. (Your major risk was being in the bottom bunk as both residents jumped to respond to a code—Franco almost killed Tom Monk.) A PICU call room was created—next to the PICU. Pharmacy began mixing up chemotherapy. A computer was purchased for house staff to use. House staff laboratories on the wards were defended but became less relevant—even before CLIA. ACLS training was instituted during the week of intern orientation. Mary Glenn Fowler, Marianna Henry, and Magee Leigh were tenured (through their own merit—but we applauded). And, with the support of subsequent chief residents, the internship was restructured to include clinic months *without* in-house night call—a true innovation.

Pediatric care continued to change. The level of intensity of each patient seemed to be ever increasing (as measured by the number of lines and monitors on each child), perhaps also reflecting that referrals were coming from a wider geographic area, in spite of the competition to the east and west. The tradition of house staff covering for each other took on a new meaning. The senior resident wore at least six beepers during interns' support group with Mike Sharp. I remember thanking my senior resident, Peter Saviteer, for letting me sleep for twenty minutes after twenty-one hours of an intense weekend night on call—and both of us realizing how ridiculous that really was! At the same time, there was a sense of an altered reality where what you did really mattered, and it was a privilege to serve.

And in spite of all of the change, we received a great education from a truly superb group. My memories can't really do justice to all of them. Dr. Denny did come back from leave, and thus we continued to benefit from his expertise and passion for medicine, streptococcus, and epidemiology. Dr. Mac taught me, by his every action, the inexplicable joy of helping very sick children, and compassion for dealing with their families. It didn't take long to figure out that Dr. Mary Glenn Fowler's quietly posed suggestions in the outpatient clinic were to be considered because she knew exactly what she was talking about. Mike Sharp enthusiastically redefined the outpatient clinic experience and helped us survive internship with his interns' support group. Alan Cross exposed me to the concept of public health and "prevention." Dr. Gronemeyer taught us always to seek new knowledge with his immediate diagnosis of the first case of infant botulism in North Carolina. New faculty arrived: Bob Wood with the lightning bronchoscope; Dr. Joe Garfunkel brought the *Journal* (one and only) to Chapel Hill. I can still place my hands to mimic the position of the heart and great vessels, as long as you don't ask me to read an EKG. Melody and the other nurses managed to not lose patience with us very often and taught us a lot.

We learned, we did have fun, and, I think, we left it a little better. . . . Flashbacks to canoeing down the Haw River; learning to windsurf from the Boats; interns' weekend at the beach. With the support of Tom Boat, my husband Franco was able to transfer to the pediatric service at UNC by the second year, and we spent our first seven years of marriage in Chapel Hill. Reflecting our diverse roots, our cohort is now geographically dispersed.

Speaking for myself, I was privileged to cross the Denny and Boat years. With both of their support, I pursued training in preventive medicine and epidemiology. Epi brought me to the NIH, prevention and public health training drew me to vaccine research, and now it's full circle—I just spent an intense weekend immersed in nucleic acid vaccine research, where I realized that industry is moving rapidly with product development, but what the NIH and FDA can do is to help elucidate the molecular basis for the mechanism of action *and* to develop the parameters for entry into clinical testing and the epidemiologic assessment of rare adverse events potentially associated with future products. And although I'm not clinically active right now (no one taught me how to balance one husband, three children, a very busy job, and also to maintain my sanity), that is about to change. Dr. Denny taught me that it was possible to go back and forth, always with the willingness to learn and relearn what you need, while Dr. Boat *keeps* trying to teach me not to try to do it all at once.

I keep trying to learn.

SUSAN W. DENFIELD (1983–1987)

The Boat People

When I think back to the four years (1983–1987) I spent at UNC with Dr. Boat as chairman the words that come to mind are *transition*, *change*, and *growth*. Those three words apply to the Department as well as to me personally.

For a Department, the period of transition from the "Denny era" to the "Boat era" appeared to me to be completed. Dr. Boat was clearly the boss, but Dr. Denny was (and is) a living legend. For an intern, presenting cases at the pulmonary conference with Drs. Boat and Denny there was very intimidating, but I must add that to this day I still consider it among the best conferences I've ever attended. In fact, about midway through the first year of my pediatric cardiology fellowship in Houston, one of the pulmonary fellows asked me where I ever learned so much pulmonary medicine. "Chapel Hill,"

I told him, "from Drs. Boat and Wood, and all the infectious disease part from Dr. Denny." There are, of course, others who deserve credit as well.

First years are always kind of tough—first year of medical school, first year of residency, first year of fellowship, and the first year of "ultimate responsibility" being an attending. We all go through a lot of first years, with new responsibilities. Those first years afford many opportunities for change and growth. I found myself learning a new language that year as well—"North Carolinian." I felt like an idiot when I could not make my Yankee ears understand what my patients or their parents were trying to tell me. I never dreamed I would need an "interpreter" to help with my history taking, but as time went on my ears adjusted and I could "mash" an elevator button and understand what y'all were telling me. By my second year of residency I could interpret for the new Yankee recruits who were struggling with the language barrier.

Even telling time can be a struggle during your first year. I started in the NICU the first month of my internship. I remember going home one night post-call and falling asleep; when I woke up it was twilight. I looked at the clock, and then outside, and couldn't figure out if it was 7 A.M. or 7 P.M. (I was too sleepy to sort out east and west by sun), but I knew that if Dan Rather was on the news it was evening and if Diane Sawyer was on it was morning. I have never been so glad to see Dan Rather in my life.

Later that year while on the wards I developed pneumonia. I coughed through rounds for at least a week and finally one morning when I got up I was too short of breath to walk to the bathroom to shower, so I figured I better stay home. That night when my fiancé (now husband of ten years) came over to check on me I told him I thought I needed to go to the hospital. He told me it was a good TV night (*Magnum, P.I.* and *Simon and Simon*), and couldn't I wait until the next day. However, I prevailed upon him to take a listen to my lungs, and being the astute clinician he is he said, "Geez, you've got crackles all the way up your back on the right—maybe you should go to the hospital." In the ER, I had an ABG and my pO2 was 50mm Hg. Being on the other end of the stethoscope is a very different experience. Although I did not have streptococci, I had the next best thing—*Mycoplasma pneumoniae*. To this day I can't say streptococci or *Mycoplasma pneumoniae* without hearing Dr. Denny's voice. I can still remember Dr. Tom Monk, one of my senior residents who was on the ID service at the time, coming up to me and saying apologetically that Dr. Denny told him I had to have an NP swab done (thank God I didn't have diarrhea), to document the infection. Erythromycin was prescribed, intravenously. I have never been so nauseated in my life—this includes pregnancy times two. Phenergan didn't help and, as I recall, Thorazine was eventually prescribed. I remember waking up with my fiancé and another resident, Dr. David Grossman, in the room saying, "Look, her eyes are going in different directions." Great, I thought, I am probably having a dystonic reaction and these guys are a big help.

The following morning as I sat mindlessly watching cartoons, Dr. Boat came by to check on how I was doing. I greatly appreciated his thoughtfulness and consideration in coming by, but was still rather "out of it" and forgot to turn off the cartoons. After Dr. Boat left, I realized the TV was still on and wondered what he must think of one of his interns watching cartoons. Several years later, when I was chief resident, I was talking with Dr. Boat about TV programming and discovered he liked watching those fishing shows where the guys sit around in boats, casting their lines and waiting for fish to strike. I didn't feel as bad about the cartoons after that.

Being a patient yourself gives you a much better understanding of what your own patients go through. Working with physicians like Dr. Campbell McMillan and Dr. William Gronemeyer also gave those of us who have had the privilege of working with them a greater understanding of our patients as well. Their approaches to patient care were always exemplary, from the "purely medical" to the psychosocial aspects, including the "care of the parents."

Just as our knowledge base was expanding and our ability to care for patients was growing, so too was the Department itself. New faculty were added in many areas including pediatric surgery, pediatric intensive care, and rheumatology, to name a few. Likewise the physical plant was growing. The seventh floor, the NICU, and the PICU were remodeled and expanded, and plans were under way to incorporate Moses Cone Hospital into the residency program.

Throughout the changes, though, one person has appeared to remain constant, the Rock of Gibraltar for all chief residents, Sherri Davis. I could always count on Sherri to come through in whatever crisis was arising, even if it was just the reassurance that we would survive it, whatever "it" was at the moment.

After I left and had been in Houston for about six months one of my attendings told me, "Gosh, we were real surprised you didn't have any trouble keeping up with the workload here, coming from such a small program." (You have to forgive Texans for their "Everything's bigger and better in Texas" attitude—they can't help it.) I must admit I was stunned by the comment, considering the growth that I knew had occurred in the Department and the astonishing array of pathology I had seen throughout my residency. In a way I considered the comment a backhanded compliment, and a tribute to the outstanding medical staff and the excellence of the residency program at UNC.

MARVIN N. HALL (1987–1991)

Remembrances of the Department of Pediatrics

Dr. Boat was, I think, fairly characterized by my mentors in the Department of Pediatrics at Emory University as one of the "new breed of chairmen." I didn't really know what this meant, but I was told that he was not only a proven clinician and researcher, but also a true administrator. He was ready to lead UNC into this new era when medicine would be increasingly recognized as a business. Dr. Boat had some large shoes to fill at UNC. My mentors had nothing but the highest regard for both Dr. Boat and the Department. UNC sounded like a place that I might want to explore.

I interviewed for residency on October 20, 1986. I remember many events of that day. Dr. Bill Coleman was perhaps the first faculty member I met at the morning information session. He was then, as he has been during our many subsequent interactions, vivacious, energetic, and a consummate and effective advocate for the Department. He could hardly contain his enthusiasm. One felt that any program that could generate that much excitement must be something exceptional. In the years since, Dr. Coleman has maintained that level of enthusiasm. As a resident and chief resident, one of the things I most appreciated about Dr. Coleman was that he remained a constant, unswerving house staff and medical student advocate. He had a dedication to the teaching components of the Department equaled by few. He routinely hosted either at his home or at the Chapel Hill Tennis Club the welcoming barbecue for the incoming interns. I think this was particularly appropriate. It allowed an early and thorough introduction to a faculty member who would certainly remain a confidant and ally throughout residency and subsequently. He constantly stressed the importance of growth and development, even in the tertiary-care setting. I still have the tape he gave to me, as my ward attending, to make sure that I measured head circumferences on all the patients I admitted.

Dr. Boat was one of my interviewers. What I remember most about our interaction was the tremendous sense of confidence he emanated (perhaps at the expense of my own). He seemed the perfect image of a department chair. Tall and a bit imposing at first, he laughed easily. We talked not only about research and his goals for the Department, but about his family, literature, and even windsurfing. Since then, I have been privileged to have many encounters with Dr. Boat. He remains for me the consummate image of a department chairman. I was repeatedly awed by the breadth of his medical knowledge. Of course, we all knew that he is an authority on pulmonary-related issues. More impressive were his discussions in "Boat rounds" with Tim Oliver or Dr. Garfunkel on issues related to general pediatrics. I remember well his probing one morning in Boat rounds to find out just how much I knew (and didn't know) about the pathophysiology of hemolytic-uremic syndrome. In his dealings with the house staff, he was sensitive and fair. One never doubted that his motivation was the betterment of the Department. He was up-front and decisive, often delegating responsibilities to others, but always acutely aware of all goings-on within the Department. When Laura and I were chief residents, he often asked for opinions regarding decisions he had to make — and what is more, he listened to what we had to say.

Bob Warren was my other interviewer. Unfortunately, he left UNC only a year or two after my arrival. I'll remember him, though, as one of the most savvy clinicians I have known. He was the person one consulted when the pieces just didn't fit. He could often put the puzzle together. I worked closely with him as an intern as we attempted to make a diagnosis in the first of our patients with FHL (familial hemophagocytic lympho-histiocytosis). It became quite a joke among the house staff that we seemed to treat so many patients with this very rare disease. We signed out FHL to our colleagues as easily as we did a patient with asthma.

Though that interview trip included several other programs, including that other place only eight miles away, my decision was an easy one. I just felt most comfortable with UNC.

My first rotation was in the neonatal intensive care unit. I remain convinced that this is the best place to begin a residency in pediatrics. One rapidly overcomes all inhibitions about actually touching and examining those tiny, fragile beings. It was here that I first met another jewel of the Pediatric Department, Dr. Ernie Kraybill. He manifests the kind of calm intuition regarding newborn infants that can be obtained only through thoughtful observation and caring over years. Regrettably, over my years at UNC, his career advancement meant that he was less often at the bedside with house staff, patients, and parents. He remains a role model as a humanist in intensive care medicine, to which I aspire. He appropriately became the resident medical ethics consultant. It was here in the NICU that I first realized that house staff are their own best educators. I learned so much that first month from my more senior residents, Karen Sennewald and Dean Meisel. Clearly, a great asset of the Department has been its ability to consistently attract house staff who are great teachers.

As I think about the NICU, my thoughts turn to our colleagues in the NICU at Wake Medical Center. By the time I began my residency, Wake was already an integral part of the teaching program. In particular, the NICU was a fun place to learn. I remember the first time I walked into the new NICU at Wake. What a contrast to the old, cramped unit! It was all glass and shiny. The colors were coordinated right on down to the nurses' uniforms. Drs. Thullen and Vaughn always kept their unique sense of humor. Then there was this new guy, Tom Young. It was always reassuring to the house staff to know that he was on service. We knew that he relished a good resuscitation. We could call on him whenever we needed help in the ER, ward, or elsewhere. I think one of the reasons we enjoyed working at Wake was that on any one night, we might see the entire gamut of pediatrics. One moment we might be intubating a "twenty-six-weeker," the next seeing an adolescent with pelvic inflammatory disease. It kept us on our toes.

No remembrance of Wake would be complete without the mention of Dr. Ingram. Several experiences are quite memorable. He loved to talk about group B strep and latex agglutination tests. I remember well his grand rounds on the use of steroids in bacterial meningitis back when that was "hot" news. He was willing, though, to give almost any topic of discussion "the old college try." One month when I was assigned to Wake, the medical students decided they needed more instruction in cardiology. He went on to give an admirable overview of congenital heart disease. He paused only occasionally for reassurance.

I can hardly proceed any further in my remembrances without mentioning the evolution of the pediatric intensive care unit. I arrived only shortly after Arno Zaritsky. He was the first at UNC of a new pediatric subspecialist, a pediatric intensivist. Until his arrival, there was no formal ICU rotation. Several subspecialists cross-covered as attendings in the PICU. He was immediately a hit with the residents. Just as Dr. Mac was a constant reminder that medicine is an art, Arno reminded us that it is a science as well. His answers to questions always began with a discussion of physiology or pharmacology. His attention to detail was a continuing testimony of a commitment to do no harm. Somehow, if he were around (and he usually was), even if things didn't turn out well, we were confident that the patient had received the best care possible. I have stood over so many critically ill patients with Arno—our first arterial switch, the first heart transplant, the first liver transplant. His clinical judgment and performance in crises are unequaled by anyone I know. He almost singlehandedly developed the ICU into a complete critical care program. It was not easy. The ICU changed locations multiple times during those years. One time it was split between the fourth and seventh floors. We might also have patients in the cardiothoracic ICU and the medical ICU. ICU rounds were sometimes like a track meet. Arno brought together not only the physical facility, but helped to develop appropriate nursing, pediatric transport, and physician education programs.

Another division that showed dramatic growth and improvement while I was at UNC was pediatric surgery. Richard Azizkahn was to that program what Arno was to the ICU. He too was a person who inspired great confidence. While an intern, I sat with him as he discussed with a family the pending surgery for their newborn premature son with a T-E fistula. It was a model presentation that combined sincere compassion and sensitivity with straightforward honesty. I later spent a month on the surgery service and witnessed firsthand his acclaimed technical skills.

As a reflection of the growing emphasis on outpatient pediatrics, the division of community pediatrics showed remarkable changes over my tenure at UNC. Dr. Jake Lohr was hired to oversee this evolution, which was still in progress when I left UNC. One remarkable change was the growing emphasis on evidence-based medicine and clinical epidemiology. This trend was a product of the growing affiliation with the School of Public Health and the Robert Wood Johnson Clinical Scholars program. Young faculty members, such as Des Runyan, Alan Cross, Peter Margolis, and Steve Downs, were the agents of this trend. Discussion at journal clubs gradually evolved from discussions primarily of the conclusions of articles into a dialogue about bias and research methodology. Residents were taught to be much more critical in their reading of medical literature.

Gratefully, one thing that did not change, though, was Harvey Hamrick:

he remained the epitome of the general pediatrician. He was, in fact, my children's pediatrician. I only once chastised my wife, Theresa, for calling Dr. Hamrick with a question. Shortly after the birth of my first son, she noticed that his urine had a peculiar odor. She became convinced that Jonathan had maple syrup urine disease. Perhaps as a reflection of her confidence in my medical acumen, instead of asking me, she called Dr. Hamrick. Though I think he was somewhat taken aback, I learned that his calming reassurance was much more effective than my own. After this, I referred all of my wife's medical questions regarding our children directly to Dr. Hamrick. Another of the many things that I quickly learned to appreciate about Dr. Hamrick was his eagerness for bedside teaching. He was the faculty member who, among other things, made it his personal mission to make certain that every house officer truly knew how to evaluate a tympanic membrane. He had a particular ritual. Carefully, he would assemble all of the required accouterments: two Kleenex, ear curette, appropriate sizes of ear specula (operating head style), and his trusty Welch-Allen otoscope. He would then appropriately restrain the patient, with assistance if needed, then carefully examine the ear and remove any offending cerumen. "You just can't practice pediatrics without owning a oo-Buck's ear curette," he would admonish. I still carry one in my briefcase.

As I think about Dr. Hamrick, I can't help remembering another gentleman of pediatrics at UNC to whom I owe a great debt of gratitude. Campbell McMillan was of course a favorite of an entire generation of pediatricians in North Carolina. My first patient who died was a long-time patient of Dr. McMillan's. He died abruptly in the middle of the night. I, of course, felt somehow responsible. What had I missed? Dr. McMillan came in to comfort the family. I don't know if he realized how much I needed consolation, but I took his words to heart. They were certainly appropriate for my feelings and I heard them as if they were meant for me. How appropriate it was to place that portrait of Dr. McMillan in the Curnen conference room with some of the other revered past faculty. I remain inspired by that friendly spirited sparkle in his eye.

Another faculty member who retired during my years at UNC was Bob Herrington. I will remember him with his left hand clasped around his right with the three middle fingers of his right hand pointed toward the left shoulder, as he demonstrated the anatomy of the heart. The left hand was the right ventricle as it wrapped around the left ventricle. The three fingers formed the aortic outflow tract. It was remarkable how this straightforward, readily available model seemed to make things so much more understandable. He continued to attend in the cardiology clinic at Wilmington long after his retirement. I'm not sure which he enjoyed more: teaching the residents, seeing his longtime patients, or the Stump Sound oysters he always picked up on the way back to the airplane.

There are many others I should mention as distinguished attendings at UNC whom I will always remember. Dr. Neil Kirkman retired during the Boat years. He would amble silently down the hallway, always looking at the floor. But when he had sufficient reason to speak, I learned to listen carefully. He could say very much in only a few words. Though Dr. Denny had stepped down as chairman, he remained an integral part of the teaching program. One could depend on him to liven up discussion during "Boat rounds" or chest conference. They were most lively and enlightening when he and Bob Wood disagreed. Dr. Denny and Dr. Hamrick equally taught us to read culture plates in outpatient conference, but unequivocally no one can wax eloquent about the streptococcus like Dr. Denny. I will think of him whenever I behold that distinctive, satisfying halo of beta hemolysis.

Many people contributed so much to us as house staff and fellows during the Boat years—not only attendings, but fellow house officers, nurses, and others. I cannot mention them all. I would be remiss, however, if I didn't especially mention Sherri Davis. She, perhaps more than any other single person, kept the day-to-day affairs of the house staff in order. More importantly, though, she served as a much needed surrogate mother figure for many of us. During those sometimes tumultuous years, she always had a ready ear to hear, a heart to understand, and a shoulder to cry on.

During those few, brief years, pediatric medicine changed in substantial ways. We were the first generation of house staff to witness the devastation of HIV infection in children. When I started my residency, pediatric AIDS was virtually unheard of in North Carolina. When I finished, an HIV test was considered early in any workup for failure-to-thrive, pulmonary infiltrate, FUO, or even protracted diarrhea. We were among the first to experience the cruel irony of AIDS. I remember one patient in particular who presented with pneumocystis pneumonia. His parents were virtually relieved when we discovered that he instead had a severe congenital immunodeficiency. As infants were diagnosed with HIV, we saw the parents struggle with the implications not only for their children, but for themselves and their spouses. We will remember the patients with hemophilia, as they began to experience night sweats, fevers, and weight loss. They and their parents felt betrayed by the medical establishment. And we were humbled once again by our uncertainty and vulnerability.

As we witnessed the onslaught of a great medical tragedy, we witnessed a substantial victory as well. Even before those landmark articles appeared in *JAMA*, we knew the impact the new HIB vaccine had made. It was amazingly rapid. H. flu meningitis became a rarity almost overnight, it seemed.

"I remember when. . . ." One can only hope that ours will be the generation that will one day be able to make such references to invasive HIV disease. We are reminded that prevention is the key to pediatrics.

DOUGLAS NELSON (1987–1992)

Memories of the Boat Years at UNC

I have many fond memories of my time in UNC's Department of Pediatrics during Dr. Tom Boat's years as chairman. Through a combination of good luck and extended medical education needs, I overstayed my welcome and spent a total of nine years in Chapel Hill. I had at least some connection with the Department of Pediatrics during each of those nine years, and the people and personalities of the Department were a consistently bright influence through good and not-so-good times as a medical student, med-peds resident, and chief resident.

My wife, Barbara, and I first came to Chapel Hill in 1983 as she began a master's program in English and I began medical school. I came to medical school planning at least tentatively to become a pediatrician, and I remember listening with extra attention when pediatricians lectured in our first- and second-year classes. I remember in particular being impressed with the gentle and compassionate way in which Dr. Campbell McMillan spoke of caring for patients, an impression that was to be reinforced many times during subsequent interactions with Dr. Mac. My first in-depth contact with the Department came, however, during my third-year pediatric clerkship at Wake Medical Center. During this and many later months at Wake as a resident I learned a lot about general pediatrics, the rewards and challenges of caring for kids, and of course many new strategies for playing Foosball in the ward playroom.

My first real contact with Dr. Tom Boat came as I began my med-peds residency. I started my internship on the UNC peds ward after a period of orientation during which all of the interns formed a bond based at least in part on shared anxiety about what we were about to do. The anxiety soon dissipated, however, and we settled into a very busy work schedule, but we did find some time for fun and recreation in the midst of long work hours. I remember admitting a child with cystic fibrosis who was a clinic patient of Dr. Boat's. The chief seemed very chairmanlike and intimidating to me, the inexperienced intern, as we discussed plans for the patient's care on the ward at night. I was doing my best to be professional, on top of things, and to at least appear intelligent when Janet Flaton's voice rang out over my pager, "Doug, *Moonlighting* is on TV in the call room!" Dr. Boat managed, I think, to feign that he hadn't understood the message and we carried on.

Through several subsequent months on the ward together and through the year that Maria Britto and I were cochiefs, my perception of Dr. Boat changed. He became in my mind much less an intimidating authority figure and much more a nice guy doing a pretty admirable job of balancing a huge number of sometimes conflicting responsibilities. His annual Christmas party for the house staff, faculty, and nurses was always a high point of the year, and the spring picnic was consistently a great time. The faculty–house staff softball game at the spring picnic provided a regular opportunity for the house staff to run roughshod over the woefully outgunned faculty team. With Dr. Boat as the faculty pitcher, many an intern and resident had a chance to take the chief "downtown."

There are many patients and events that run through my memories of my time at UNC. I remember in particular one eight- or ten-year-old boy on the pulmonary service who had recurrent pneumonias and was quite a diagnostic dilemma. Numerous diagnostic tests hadn't turned up an etiology, and the time had come for "Bronco Bob" Wood to perform a bronchoscopy. As the responsible intern, I was the official "immobilizer" during this procedure. After a struggle akin to a wrestling match the procedure was completed, and lipoid material returned on the BAL. It wasn't until later that the complete answer unfolded when someone extracted the history that this young fellow had been snorting WD-40 through the little red straw that comes with each aerosol can. This behavior was discouraged and he got better. I haven't been able to look at a can of the stuff since without thinking of him.

Many children with unusual and tragic illnesses were a part of all of our lives during those years. A little boy with persistent diarrhea whom we all cared for during our internship was later found to have been receiving surreptitious cathartics from his mother. A teenager recently diagnosed with pelvic Ewing's sarcoma, who was my first patient as an intern, appeared to have a complete remission with chemotherapy, but then had an unexpected and tragic recurrence during my last year at UNC. A little girl with a congenital airway abnormality was tracheostomy-dependent and needed to stay hospitalized for airway protection; we all watched her grow from a baby to a spirited child during the three or four years she was hospitalized. Several children with the horrible and somewhat mysterious familial hemophagocytic lympho-histiocytosis, a condition we all learned to let roll off our tongues as easily as "croup" or "meningitis." Many, many children with common and less memorable illnesses were also seen. We as house staff came to know and to joke about but also to truly care for these children during the many hours we spent with them.

But our experience was not by any means limited to inpatient care of exotic illnesses. As a future general pediatrician and internist, the place I felt most at home was in the pediatric screening ("screaming") and continuity clinics. Exposure to the "meat and potatoes" of pediatrics, with excellent clinicians and role models like Floyd Denny, Harvey Hamrick, Joe Garfunkel, Charlie Sheaffer, and many others, was a real pleasure. I learned to read throat and urine cultures, look in ears, and say endearing Southern phrases like "He looks like he's been rode hard and put up wet" and "Even a blind squirrel finds an acorn now and then." These phrases make up a disturbingly large part of my current vocabulary.

Many things changed in the Pediatric Department during the years I was at UNC. The Moses Cone Hospital pediatric service was incorporated as a part of our pediatric program. The Red and Blue teams became Ernie and

Bert. The pediatric ICU was greatly expanded under the leadership of Arno Zaritsky and became a favorite rotation of many of the residents. The neonatal ICUs at both UNC and Wake also expanded. The total number of pediatric and med-peds residents expanded greatly, and the department began selecting two chief residents per year rather than one. Several terrific faculty members retired, including Campbell McMillan and Henry Kirkman. Many new and talented faculty members came, however, including Stuart Gold, Bill Coleman, Tom Young, Ola Akintemi, and Wayne Price. My wife and I had our first child (Melanie) and found out firsthand about the joys and stresses of parenthood. Sherri Davis and Karen Kelly kept everyone sane and in the right place at the right time. Floyd Denny threatened to but never did get past strike two in umpiring softball games. A new shower was installed in the pediatric ward call room, sending thousands of bacterial, fungal, and protozoan organisms to unhappy deaths. Finally and most importantly, many children received excellent health care and many residents and students learned a lot about pediatric medicine and caring for both well and sick children.

In summary, I will never forget my time as part of UNC's Department of Pediatrics during Tom Boat's term as chairman. I learned a lot, had good times and bad times, developed from a neophyte to a practitioner of pediatrics, and had a chance to interact with a bunch of talented and delightful people. Pediatricians aren't considered the nicest type of physicians for no reason.

1981–82

Row 1: Ken Whitt, Joe D'Ercole, Karen Voter, Mary Sugioka, Al Collier, Floyd Denny, Jerry Fernald, Alan Stiles, Betsy Coulson, Bob Herrington, Susan Hyman, Ed Hu

Row 2: Frank French, Wanda Kotvan, John Santamaria, Peter Saviteer, Wally Clyde, Linda Goodwin, Ernie Kraybill, Bob Valley, Mary Glenn Fowler, Joan Fine, Steve Kahler, Richard Morris

Row 3: Sharon Foster, Johnny Carson, Mike Sharp, Harrie Chamberlin, Jerry Strope, David Pacini, Cheryl Kennedy, Stu Teplin, Pat Robinson, Bob Wells

Row 4: Elizabeth Wilson, Neil Kirkman, Don Dunphy, Ed Spence, Frank Loda, Elman Frantz, Art Aylsworth, Stan Spinola, Febe Brazeal, Larry Nickens, Richard Waller, John Grizzard, Harry Guess, Herb Harned

Row 5: Alan Cross, Dave Burchfield, Fred Henderson, Paul Sorum, Ruth Etzel, Cam McMillan, Tom Jones, Bob Stifler, Mike Schur, Paul Kaplowitz

1982–83

Row 1: Ed Hu, Al Collier, Floyd Denny, Tom Boat, Hugh Craft, Jerry Fernald, Ed
Spence, Marsha Davenport, David Pacini

Row 2: William Russell, Betty Wilson, Wally Clyde, Frank Loda, Dave Ingram, Bob
Valley, Mike Sharp, Stu Teplin, Diane Edwards, Ann Smith, Susan Pitts

Row 3: Frank French, Ned Lawson, Harrie Chamberlin, Herb Harned, Jerry Strope,
Mitchell Shub, Marry Ulshen, Ruth Etzel, Ed Pattishall, Jud Van Wyk

Row 4: Bob Wells, Dave Burchfield, Pi-Wan Cheng, Johnny Carson, Stewart Schall,
Neil Kirkman, Lou Underwood, John Santamaria, Alan Cross, Cam
McMillan, Steve Kahler, Brian Stabler

1983–84

Row 1: Carol Ford, Dr. Harikawa, Bob Wells, Ned Lawson, Bob Wood, Tom Boat, Bob Valley, Jerry Fernald, Floyd Denny, Ed Hu, Rupa Redding-Lallinger, Mary Glenn Fowler, Susan Pitts

Row 2: Wally Clyde, Harvey Hamrick, Mike Sharp, Ernie Kraybill, Ed Pattishall, Franco Piazza, Regina Rabinovich, Linda Goodwin, Tom Monk, Karen Voter, Jud Van Wyk, Mary Sugioka, Suzanne White, Gary Eddey

Row 3: Joe D'Ercole, Fred Henderson, Al Collier, David Goff, Marty Ulshen, Mitchell Shub, Nancy Charest, Jim Thullen, Carl Bose, Stu Teplin, Herb Harned

Row 4: Harrie Chamberlin, David Pacini, Jerry Strope, Johnny Carson, William Russell, Eric Smith, Jack Ho, Neil Kirkman, Pi-Wan Cheng, Elizabeth Wilson

Row 5: Charles Hargrove, Randy Hedgepeth, Bob Warren, Matt Gillman, Art Aylsworth, Stewart Schall, Cam McMillan, David Cook, Alan Cross, Frank French

177

1984–85

Row 1: Mary Sugioka, Neil Kirkman, Joe Garfunkel, Jerry Fernald, Tom Boat, Rupa Redding-Lallinger, Des Runyan, Bob Wells, Perry Futral-Almquist

Row 2: Susan Pitts, Doug Clark, Tom Monk, Linda Goodwin, Febe Brazeal, Joan Perry, Marsha Davenport, Stu Teplin, Carol Ford, Virginia Nichols, Sam Casella, Joe D'Ercole

Row 3: Bob Covert, Elizabeth Andrew

Row 4: Ed Hu, Jerry Strope, Ed Pattishall, Pi-Wan Cheng, Richard Morris, Patty Friedman, Greg Kirkpatrick, Franco Piazza, Gina Rabinovich, Al Collier, Wally Clyde, Laura Kierszenbaum

Row 5: Terry Murphy, Art Aylsworth, Cam McMillan, Eric Smith, Herb Cooper, Carole Lannon, Scott Buck, Bob Warren, Magee Leigh, Fred Henderson, Ernie Kraybill, Johnny Carson

Row 6: Jim Alexander, Randy Hedgepeth, Dave Joseph, Alan Cross, Frank French, Betty Wilson

178

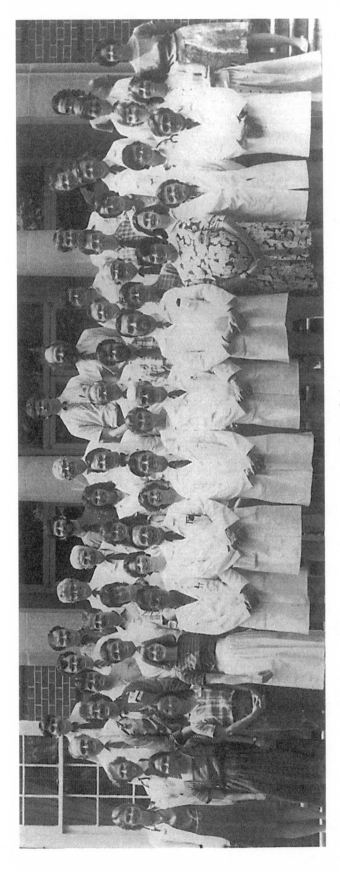

1985–86

Row 1: Shanti Reddy, Nancy Tang, Elizabeth Allen, Pi-Wan Cheng, Bill Coleman, Floyd Denny, Jerry Fernald, Tom Boat, Regina Rabinovich, Mary Sugioka, Ed Hu

Row 2: Michele Humlan, Susan Denfield, Karen Sennewald, Elizabeth Andrew, Greg Kirkpatrick, Marianna Henry, Steve Lichtman, Patty Friedman

Row 3: Frank Israel, Rob McClure, Doug Clark, Julie Kavanagh, Carol Ford, Stu Teplin, Frank Loda, Magee Leigh, Karen Voter

Row 4: Neil Kirkman, Jim Hubbard, Brent Weston, Joe Garfunkel, Jean Smith, Mike Sharp, Herb Harned, Wally Clyde, Rob Dunmire, Fred Henderson, Ed Pattishall, Mary Glenn Fowler

Row 5: Bob Warren, Jerry Strope, Marco Conti, Eric Smith, Frank French, Elizabeth Wilson

Row 6: Don Kees, Randy Hedgepeth, Terry Murphy, Cam McMillan, Jim Alexander, Bob Greenberg

1986–87

Row 1: Al Collier, Ed Ward, Steve Downs, Leonard Stein, Carl Bose, Floyd Denny, Jerry Fernald, Tom Boat, Susan Denfield, Susan Hall, Elizabeth Andrew, Herb Harned, Neil Kirkman

Row 2: Jean Smith, Pi-Wan Cheng, Elizabeth Allen, Robin Kelly, Marco Conti, Valerie Quarmby, Karen Voter

Row 3: Michele Humlan, Jackson Smith, Cathy Davis, Charles Toledo, Marty Ulshen, Ned Lawson, Wayne Rackoff, Joanne Dykas, Greg Kirkpatrick

Row 4: Mary Driebeck, George Retsch-Bogart, Jamil Khan, Ernie Kraybill, Wally Clyde, David Repaske, Alan Stiles, Frank Loda, Mary Glenn Fowler, Virginia Nichols, Kristen Moffitt, David Cook

Row 5: Elizabeth Wilson, Stu Teplin, Jerry Strope, Richard Morris, Ann Bates

Row 6: Frank French, Jim Hubbard, Mike Sharp, Cam McMillan, Joe Garfunkel, Terry Murphy, Magee Leigh, Rob Dunmire, Franco Piazza, Regina Rabinovich, Andy Muelenaer, Herb Cooper, Bob Wells

Row 7: Dean Meisel, Desmond Kelly, Jim Alexander, Fred Henderson, Art Aylsworth, Rob McClure, Tim Johanson, Don Kees

1987–88

Row 1: Jud Van Wyk, Wally Clyde, Al Collier, Bob Wood, Jerry Fernald, Scott Buck, Tom Boat, Marsha Davenport, Wayne Rackoff, Ed Hu, Deanna Mitchell, Frank Israel, Susan Hall

Row 2: Pi-Wan Cheng, Bill Coleman, Warren Bishop, Carl Bose, Karen Sennewald, Mary Glenn Fowler, Karen Kartheiser, Elizabeth Allen, Billie Moat-Statts, Maria Britto, Ernie Kraybill, Neil Kirkman

Row 3: Steve Lichtman, Marry Ulshen, Rob Dunmire, Sandra Botstein, Ann Bates, Nancy Charest, Brent Weston, Laura Noonan, George Retsch-Bogart, Magee Leigh

Row 4: Arno Zaritsky, Desmond Kelly, Eric Smith, Stu Teplin, David Repaske, Jim Hubbard, Tom Ferkol, Steve Downs, Tim Johanson, Art Aylsworth, Vanden Haar, Alan Stiles, Bob Wells

181

1988-89

Row 1: Leonard Stein, George Retsch-Bogart, Al Collier, Harriett Brewer Dickey, Jerry Fernald, Tom Boat, Tom Ferkol, Debra Shah, Christina Flannelly, Laura Noonan, Conleth Crotser, Jennifer Preiss, Sherri Davis

Row 2: Marc Rhoads, Steve Lichtman, Karen Kartheiser, Jean Smith, Ned Lawson, Charmian Quigley, Magee Leigh, Sharon Van Horn, Kristen Moffitt, Betsy Blair, Susan Hall, Regina Rabinovich, Richard Morris

Row 3: Herb Cooper, Wayne Rackoff, Joanne Dykas, Bonnie Hamilton, Nancy Charest, Ann Bates, Molly Froelich, Nancy Walton, Chris Foley, Dave Barnes, Carlos Perez

Row 4: Jim Crowe, Harvey Hamrick, Kim Kylstra, Steve Downs, Hank Shapiro, Terry Noah, Ernie Kraybill, Ken Whitt, Marvin Hall, Sandra Mattos

Row 5: Marco Conti, Frank French, Tim Johanson, Doug Nelson, Cam McMillan, Wally Clyde, R. Frerichs, David Repaske, Frank Loda, Dave Joseph, Franco Piazza, Pi-Wan Cheng, Art Aylsworth, Johnny Carson, John Simpson, Bob Greenberg

1989–90

Row 1: Al Collier, Sherri Davis, Sherrie Templeton, Kristine McVea, Yul Reinstein, Maria Portilla, Floyd Denny, Tim Johanson, Tom Boat, Ann Bates, Jerry Fernald, Christina Flannelly, Beth Dixon, Neil Kirkman, Renee Schust, Sharon Van Horn

Row 2: Conleth Crotser, Marsha Davenport, Diane Duffy

Row 3: Bill Coleman, Frank French, Steve Downs, John Hopper, Marc Rhoads, Jud Van Wyk, Alan Lamb, Nancy Charest, Vicki Teague, Deanna Mitchell, Robbie Couch, Adrian Sandler, Magee Leigh

Row 4: Ned Lawson, Ed Ward, Steve Lichtman, Jean Smith, Lou Underwood, Marguerite Oetting, George Dodds, Janet Flaton, Betsy Blair, Laura Noonan, Wally Clyde

Row 5: Marvin Hall, Chris Foley, Leonard Stein, Jennifer Preiss, Stuart Gold, Susan Cohen, David Repaske, Johnny Carson

Row 6: Fred Henderson, Mark Dickinson, Bryan Hollinger, George Retsch-Bogart, Gary Jones, Colleen Poprawa, Alan Stiles, Marco Conti, Shin-Ichiro Takahashi, Mary Ellen Dryden, Evonne Bruton

Row 7: Harvey Hamrick, Henry Akinbi, Doug Nelson, Herb Cooper, Marty Ulshen, Carl Bose, Art Aylsworth, Keith Marschke, Joe Garfunkel

1990–91

Row 1: Sherri Davis, Marc Rhoads, Yul Reinstein, Maria Portilla, Jake Lohr, Jerry Fernald, Floyd Denny, Tom Boat, Laura Noonan, Marvin Hall, Jud Van Wyk, Neil Kirkman, Cam McMillan

Row 2: Chris Rittmeyer, Sherrie Templeton, Susan Cohen, Al Collier, Marguerite Oetting, Molly Froelich, Bonnie Hamilton, Sefanit Fassil, Leonard Stein, Carl Bose, Anne Reed, Art Shepard, Harvey Hamrick

Row 3: Shelley Schoonover, Mia Amaya, Susan Albright

Row 4: Stuart Kupfer, Pi-Wan Cheng, Charmian Quigley, Kate Vaness-Meehan, Ned Lawson, Magee Leigh, Gary Jones, Colleen Poprawa, Art Shepard

Row 5: Marsha Davenport, Frank French, Bill Coleman, Stu Teplin, Peter Margolis, Stuart Gold, Henry Akinbi

Row 6: Arno Zaritsky, Gary Albers, Joe D'Ercole, George Retsch-Bogart, Alan Stiles, Joe Garfunkel, Herb Cooper, Hani Zreik, Ernie Kraybill, Bryan Hollinger, Adrian Sandler, Jon Klein

Row 7: Art Aylsworth, David Repaske, Keith Marschke, Mark Wright, George Dodds

184

1991–92

Row 1: Chon Lee, Doren Fredrickson, Bob Wood, Jerry Fernald, Maria Britto, Floyd Denny, Tom Boat, Doug Nelson, Jinny Brack, Sefanit Fassil, Barbara Dentz

Row 2: John Hopper, Harriett Dickey, Al Collier, Yul Reinstein, Doug Winesett, Marc Rhoads, Marsha Davenport, Diane Duffy, Jennifer Tender, Wally Clyde

Row 3: Leonard Stein, Marvin Hall, Steve Downs, Sherrie Templeton, Jean Smith, Huanshu Yang, Lou Underwood, Michele Larson, Renee Schust, Evonne Bruton, Jolanda Pucildwska, Ron Knight

Row 4: Bill Ashe, Magee Leigh, Ned Lawson, George Retsch-Bogart, Harvey Hamrick, Jean-Paul Thissen, Jeh Hoon Shin, Philippe Backeljauw

Row 5: Marty Ulshen, Joe Garfunkel, Noah Archer, Tim Garrington, Josephine Young, George Dodds, Frank French, Keith Marschke

1992–93

Row 1: Steve Downs, Jenny Hoare, Floyd Denny, Laura Bellstrom, Ned Lawson, Jerry Fernald, Jinny Brack, Joe Wiley

Row 2: Margaret Farmer, Stuart Gold, Steve Lichtman, Yul Reinstein, Brent Weston, Theresa Hamel, Hans Fundingsrud

Row 3: Teri Wooten, Laurie Beitz, Amina Ahmed, George Retsch-Bogart, Huanshu Yang, Terry Noah, Kate Vaness-Meehan, Herb Cooper

Row 4: Paul Monahan, John Hopper, Michele Larson, Marty Ulshen, Gary Jones, Ernie Kraybill, Mary Ellen Lane, Virginia Schreiner

Row 5: Pam Reitnauer, Magee Leigh, Anshu Batra, Peggy McCracken, Laura Heyneman

Row 6: Chris Rittmeyer, Mark Dickinson, Bassem Bejjani, Genaro Diaz, Aldon Collier, Martin McCaffrey

1993-94

Row 1: Rita Makhlouf, Jerry Fernald, Ned Lawson, John Hopper, Pam Reitmauer

Row 2: Frank French, Magee Leigh, George Retsch-Bogart, Bill Ashe, Lisa Patterson, Shannon Dudley, Paqui Motyl, Chris Tobin, Rachel Laramee, Kim McDermott, Bill Haddock, Dave Thies, Teri Wooten

Row 3: Alan Stiles, Marsha Davenport, Kenny Hefner, Tim Garrington, Melinda Taylor, Steve Downs, Brent Weston, Brenda Surles, Bassem Bejjani, Jim Kurz, Lynn Wegner, Barbara Hipp, Ron Kaplan, Barbara Dentz

Row 4: Stu Teplin, Steve Lichtman, Margaret Morris, Herb Cooper, Josephine Young, Richard Morris, Kim Buenting, Peter Michelson, Bob Krzeski, Carl Bose, Gary Jones

Row 5: Dorota Szczepaniak, Martin McCaffrey, Joe Wiley

1994–95

Row 1: Sherri Davis, Lynn Wegner, Marsha Davenport, Floyd Denny, Kim Buenting, Roberta Williams, Josephine Young with Alex, Jerry Fernald, Win Hauser

Row 2: Amy Fowler, Lars Savendahl, Sheila Knerr, George Retsch-Bogart, Carl Bose, Marianna Henry, Teri Wooten, Margaret Morris, Alexia Keller-Gusman

Row 3: Herb Cooper, Ali Calikoglu, Magee Leigh, Leonard Stein, Virginia Schreiner, Bassem Bejjani, Barbara Hipp, Jeff Johnson, Courtney Robertson

Row 4: Ron Kaplan, Hugh Black, Dan Via, Peter Chu, Hank Shapiro, Stu Teplin, Mark Ruggiero, Ed Pickens

PART FOUR

Pediatric Subspecialties

INTRODUCTION

The history of subspecialties in the Department of Pediatrics accounts for a large portion of the overall growth and development of the Department as a whole. As pointed out by Jud Van Wyk in the introduction to "The Denny Years," the Department was poised in 1960 for subspecialty development and Denny was anxious to take a leading role in this endeavor. At the beginning of this era three pediatric faculty stood out clearly as the backbone of this development and the members on whose shoulders it would take place. Harrie Chamberlin had great interest in child development and training in neurology; Herb Harned had extensive clinical and research training in cardiology; and Jud Van Wyk was clearly outstanding in endocrinology. These three quickly assumed leadership roles in developing active divisions that were responsible for clinical care, teaching, and research in their respective areas of interest. The development of child psychiatry should be included here as well because Dr. Lucie Jessner was very active in pediatrics at this time although not a member of this Department.

The subsequent development of the subspecialties was not so easy and certainly did not follow a straight line. Denny and Wallace Clyde began the development of the infectious disease division soon after Clyde's arrival in 1961, with Clyde taking a leading role. Hematology was developed next. Dr. Ahlee Howell of Duke graciously held this area together until we could coax Campbell McMillan to join us in the early 1960s. Dr. Neil Kirkman was the next addition, not because we thought that his expertise in genetics was critical to our Department at the time but because Denny and Van Wyk had independently been impressed with his potential as an academician. Rehabilitation was born in the mid-1960s. It had a rather slow and tortuous course until Dr. Robert Herrington assumed its controls and developed it into a functional unit. Community pediatrics was next to develop, out of the need to put emphasis on general pediatrics and health and medical care away from the hospital—Frank Loda was the ideal person for this area. In 1970 Dr. Richard Morris was recruited to develop pediatric nephrology, to complement the tremendous strength in this discipline in the Department of Medicine.

There were real problems in the development of neonatology, as chronicled by Dr. Ernie Kraybill. Efforts by the faculty to attract a neonatologist were thwarted by Denny, who, at the time, doubted the wisdom of the direction in which this discipline was heading. The faculty prevailed, however, and Dr. Kraybill joined us in 1972 to develop the strong unit we have today. Finally, for the Denny years, we were able to attract Dr. Marty Ulshen, who had had house staff training at UNC, to head a unit in gastroenterology.

This is a synopsis of subspecialty development between 1960 and 1982 when Dr. Thomas Boat assumed the chair of Pediatrics. The subspecialties mentioned above were strengthened and three divisions were developed under his leadership. Dr. Deborah Kredich of Duke gave tremendous help in rheumatology until Dr. Robert Warren could be recruited. Although expertise in lung disorders was well represented in the infectious disease division, it remained for Dr. Boat, a leading pulmonologist, to attract Dr. Robert Wood to UNC. They quickly developed one of the top divisions in the country. In the mid-1980s the need for intensive care of increasingly sick patients signaled the need to develop expertise in these areas; Dr. Arno Zaritsky was recruited to lead this effort.

The stories behind the development of all of these subspecialties are included in this section and are the hallmark of the growth of academic pediatrics during the halcyon days of the 1960s, 1970s, and early 1980s, especially as we experienced them at the University of North Carolina.

FLOYD W. DENNY, JR.

CHAPTER TWELVE

Pediatric Cardiology

T HE subspecialty of pediatric cardiology has evolved over the last forty years from a field in which the diagnostic and therapeutic modalities were relatively simple to its present very complex state. The history of our division reflects these changes, but also will reveal that we attempted to retain important associations with the central critical mass of pediatric care, training, and research in the Pediatric Department as a whole.

A relatively detailed, personal account of the division's history is available in the archives and may be of additional value to the historian; the following is a condensed version of this history.

Rather than attempt to create a large, autonomous cardiology unit at UNC Hospitals, comparable to those at larger, well-established children's medical centers, we strived to develop a superior teaching program within the confines of the Department of Pediatrics. During the Curnen and Denny years, the pediatric cardiologists of our small group—Drs. Harned, Castle, Herrington, and Schall—shared the concept of remaining active members of the Department by maintaining our expertise in general inpatient pediatrics and sharing the difficult general attending duties.

EARLY DEVELOPMENT OF PEDIATRIC
CARDIOLOGY AT UNC

While the Department of Pediatrics was being established in the early 1950s, events were taking place in preparation for the development of pediatric cardiology here. As chairman, Dr. Curnen brought a great deal of knowledge about streptococcal infection and rheumatic fever, as did Dr. Nelson Ordway later when he arrived on the scene in 1955. In addition, Ordway was familiar with congenital heart diseases, had performed cardiac catheterizations, and had established semimicro analytic methods at Yale. He transferred knowledge of these techniques to UNC and, working with Dr. Ernest Craige, the chief of medical cardiology, Dr. Richard Peters, the chief of cardiothoracic surgery, and Dr. Daniel Young, set up a cardiac catheterization laboratory.

Dr. Ordway's Influence

Ordway's role was important not only because he helped to set up the methods, but because during his short tenure at UNC, he inspired several members of the house staff to commit themselves to careers in pediatric cardiology. Both Drs. Robert Castle and Thomas Gardner went on to outstanding careers in this field. Castle, while he was a resident, combined with Craige to write a supplement to the journal *Pediatrics* entitled "Auscultation of the Heart in Infants and Children" (*Pediatrics* 26:511, 1960). This article was an outstanding contribution to the field and has been used as a teaching guide nationwide for many years (see archives). They used phonocardiograms to document the various cardiac auscultatory findings scientifically. Both Drs. Castle and Craige made the art of the cardiac physical examination the focus of their lifetime scientific contributions.

One of the first fellows in the Department of Pediatrics was Dr. Robert Verney, from France, who worked with Dr. Ordway. He is now a distinguished pediatric cardiologist in Lyon in his home country. Nelson's multilinguistic skills stood him in good stead in communicating with Verney and they periodically have renewed their friendship stretching across international borders. Ordway brought his research skills and creative mind to bear on other phases of the pediatric training program, contributions that are acknowledged in the history of the Curnen years. His collaborative efforts with the faculty of the Department of Medicine and with Dr. Peters helped to establish a base for pediatric cardiology that was in place when he left for Yale and Dr. Herbert Harned moved to Chapel Hill. Ordway served as the clinical chief of pediatrics at Yale for many years, where he was able to aid Dr. Norman Talner in developing an outstanding program in pediatric cardiology.

Cardiac Catheterization-Angio Studies at UNC after 1958

Before his arrival in 1958, Dr. Harned insisted on the installation of an image intensifier in the catheterization laboratory. Since this fit in with plans of the Department of Radiology, a rather primitive five-and-a-half-inch (in diameter) unit was obtained and was installed in 1959. Before this, Drs. Ordway, Dan Young, and Harned had to fluoroscope patients in the dark, with the help of an equally blinded anesthesiologist, often the talented Dr. Kenneth Sugioka. Short-acting IV barbiturates were usually employed and the procedures were generally kept short (one hour or less). A manifold, developed by Ordway and machined locally, permitted direction of the fluids appropriately for flushing, recording pressures, and withdrawing blood samples. An "electric eye" counted the drops of fluid as they passed through the fluid delivery system, causing a clicking sound that allowed the doctors to count the drops despite an inability to see them. A similar manifold has since been produced commercially, but Ordway did not obtain a patent for this as far as is known. Since coronary studies were not in vogue at this time and the cine unit was too small and low powered for use in many adult cases, pediatric cardiac catheterizations predominated for many years. Approximately three pediatric cases were studied per week.

Herb
Harned

Surgery at UNC

Dr. Richard Peters, trained in cardiothoracic surgery at Barnes Hospital in St. Louis, was brought by Dr. Nathan Womack in 1953 to be the first chief of cardiovascular surgery at UNC. Most of the operations at that time were performed on children with tetralogy of Fallot, patent ductus, coarctation of the aorta, or pulmonic stenosis, but Harned recalls that Peters had performed several inflow occlusion atrial septal defect repairs before 1958 and that this procedure was being done effectively during Harned's early years here. A "pediatric intensive care" area was set up on the seventh floor and specially qualified nurses were assigned to this area. The cardiac surgical team, led by Peters who was ably assisted by Drs. Robert Zeppa and George Johnson, supervised this area. This "intensive care" concept was later developed further and moved to various other locations in the hospital. The implementation of this idea permitted our hospital to lay claim to establishing the first intensive care unit in America.

Monetary Support for Children's Cardiac Disorders

Nationally, at this time, helping children with heart disorders became a strong priority of the Crippled Children's Division, a unit of the U.S. Labor Department. The original emphasis of this division had been on orthopedic cases, but the possibility of preventing and ameliorating rheumatic fever cases appealed to the "powers that be" in the 1950s. Rheumatic fever was still "childhood's greatest killer," its mortality rate being higher than that for accidents, malignancy, or other infections. In addition to this increase in federal funding, the dual development of improved diagnostic measures (Dr. Cournand and Richards won the Nobel Prize in 1955 for their roles in using cardiac catheterization) and new surgical therapeutic methods began to offer

Bob Castle

Bob
Herrington

opportunities for dramatically improving outcomes for children with congenital cardiac disorders.

PERSONNEL AT UNC DURING THE DENNY YEARS

Initially, our "division" of pediatric cardiology consisted solely of Herbert Harned, who was on perpetual call. Dr. Robert Castle was added in 1963 as an assistant professor and remained in the Department until 1966, when he left to direct the pediatric cardiology division at the University of New Mexico. Since then, Castle has also worked in Atlanta and Jackson and now practices in Austin, where he is director of pediatric cardiology at the Austin Children's Hospital.

Dr. Robert Herrington, after an initial fellowship in 1962, returned from military service in 1966 for further training in pediatric cardiology and later joined the faculty as an assistant professor in 1967. Herrington has made a lifelong contribution to the Department, bringing needed skills especially in the teaching of physical diagnosis. He also has been effective in teaching the spatial concepts of electrocardiography and has developed an interlocking hand model for demonstrating relationships of the cardiac structures. Herrington's confrontational and Socratic teaching methods have benefited hundreds of house officers and students during his long association with the Department and he has been awarded the Residents' Teaching Award twice.

As our outpatient projections grew, we added a third member of the division, Dr. Stewart Schall, in 1972. After medical school at the University of Pennsylvania and residency at Albert Einstein School of Medicine, Stewart followed Drs. Abraham Rudolph and Julien Hoffman to the University of

California at San Francisco as a cardiology fellow. He then worked as an associate in the office of Dr. Saul Robinson, who was the most important practitioner of pediatric cardiology in the Bay Area, as well as being president of the American Academy of Pediatrics. Schall, like Herrington, was a skillful and popular teacher, who used his delightful sense of humor to make the pediatric cardiology rotation a pleasurable one for the students and residents. He is now on the faculty of the University of North Carolina Area Health Education Center program at Cone Hospital in Greensboro as an associate professor and has continued his role as chief of pediatric cardiology at that institution.

Stewart Schall

Dr. G. William Henry was added as a fourth faculty member in 1983 and has succeeded Harned as chief of the division. Some of the accomplishments of Dr. Henry during the tenure of Dr. Thomas Boat will be considered later.

CLINICAL FACILITIES AND ORGANIZATION OF CARE

Viewed in the present context of the many new medical center "palaces," the buildings and facilities of the North Carolina Memorial Hospital were quite primitive in the 1960s, but this was true of the many underfunded hospitals in this country. In 1958, there were about forty beds on the seventh floor for children up to sixteen years of age. The playroom was soon to begin full operation, but the isolation unit was not yet available. A treatment room was used heavily for procedures such as lumbar punctures, infusions, and transfusions. Intravenous tubing and catheters were reused many times, so there was heavy reliance on the central supply section for cleaning of this equipment. The service, which converted from steam to gas sterilization techniques in the early 1960s, was an integral part of the hospital's operation.

The X-ray facilities in 1958, consisting of six diagnostic rooms, were supervised by Drs. Ernest Wood, William Sprunt, and Charles Bream. The cardiac catheterization room was at the end of this diagnostic corridor (room 6) and was used for a variety of purposes, especially since it soon contained the only image-intensified cine unit in the hospital. Therapeutic radiation took place also on the second floor off the south corridor. X-rays were stored below the second-floor diagnostic unit, which one reached by descending a tortuous spiral staircase.

Other facilities were very limited compared to those available today. The outpatient clinic area was shared by all clinical services, but pediatrics was usually assigned about eight rooms along the most western corridor of the Old Clinic Building. These limited facilities were markedly enhanced when the Love Clinic Building was built in the late 1960s, along with new operating rooms. The four-story Love Clinic Building represented a state-of-the-art facility for outpatient care, despite numerous mistakes in its fine planning which have plagued its occupants to the present day. Pediatrics fared relatively well in the distribution of facilities, having obtained rooms with windows, a playroom area, an adequate and reasonably attractive waiting room, and even a few offices for physicians, nurses, and other personnel. Also, a separate area for pediatric emergencies became available. This particular area has always been used for walk-ins, most of whom present with medical problems, rather than for surgical or traumatic cases.

The operating rooms, built where the entrance of the hospital had been (on the north side), consisted of only two floors and essentially blocked expansion of the hospital to the north in its central region, another major mistake in planning.

Early on, since pediatrics was involved in more catheterization procedures than medicine, we were assigned a central area that was used as a heart station for reading ECGs, teaching, and for staging cardiac catheterizations. However, when major changes in the design of the laboratories took place, we consented to move around the corner into rooms on the east side of the old Student Infirmary Building. This still provided a reasonably adequate heart station and a storage area for cine films, which could be retrieved immediately.

Facilities for medicine-cardiology were upgraded significantly when the new student infirmary was completed and the student health program was moved out of the Naval Building. ECG, echocardiography, exercise, Holter monitoring, and pacemaker monitoring laboratories were consolidated in this one area. With this, medical cardiology also assumed control over these functions, including the setting of physicians' fees for the procedures. We, as pediatricians, were able only to charge physicians' fees for ECG interpretations.

Until recently, the history of the development of cardiac catheterization at UNC could be discerned from lines on the floor of the catheterization lab (which now have been covered up). These lines represented previous walls of the room, visible because of the room's progressive enlargement. Dr. Harned can recall four expansions of this room, each accompanied by upgrading of the equipment. After two units of single-plane cine angiographic equipment became obsolete, biplane units were installed, culminating in the present C-arm Siemens equipment, which has proven very satisfactory. Dr. Schall participated with Dr. Popio in the selection of the latter machine during a trip to Paris. Monitoring and recording equipment progressed from initial direct writing to oscilloscopic representations. The Sanborn photographic recorder, used in Dr. Harned's research, served for many years (1959–1967) before improved Electronics for Medicine recorders became available and new instrumentation permitted wide-screen viewing of ECG and blood pressures. The growth of the Research Triangle directly benefited our equipment needs by bringing far better servicing and competitive pricing to the area.

Excellent technicians, who were mostly wives of struggling academicians, were available even during the early years. They worked hard and efficiently at the ridiculously low salaries set by the state at that time. Ms. Jacqueline Colley, Helen Clarke, and Bibba Montgomery come to mind as especially helpful persons in monitoring physiologic events and analyzing blood gases. When the oximeter became accurate enough for oxygen saturation measurements, the need for proficiency in blood gas analysis disappeared and cross-training as cardiac catheterization–radiological technicians became functional. For many years, one technician was assigned especially to pediatrics (and paid by state funds). Donald Jones filled the role with special distinction for about a decade before he took over the position of chief cardiovascular technician at Cone Hospital in Greensboro. From that time on, the technicians were under the jurisdiction of the chief of the cardiac catheterization laboratory—always a member of the Department of Medicine. The medical cardiologists in the cath lab held the purse strings for personnel, equipment, and fee setting, with pediatric cardiologists as outside consultants, but in exchange we avoided many of the problems and squabbles of the cath laboratory.

TEACHING PROGRAMS

The Department of Pediatrics and the division have always prided themselves on their teaching, which in large part has involved direct contact between teacher and student. Pediatric cardiologists have excellent props for their teaching—since the hearts of their patients have easily understandable anatomic characteristics whether they are relatively healthy or badly disordered. These hearts also project precise and meaningful noises, permit useful X-ray images and sharply defined echoes. They can be studied by accurate and definitive methods such as cardiac catheterization-angiography, echocardiograms, and nuclear magnetic imaging. Even in early days when these diagnostic methods were much less precise than they are now, they still were as refined as most other diagnostic tools in medicine that lend themselves to the teaching process. The parallel refinement of these diagnostic techniques with improvement in surgical methods has provided a fascinating chapter in medicine during our lifetimes.

Attending Duties

The pediatric cardiology faculty members all served as general attendings on the pediatric inpatient services. We also covered appropriate night and weekend call throughout the year for consultations relating to pediatric cardiac cases. Over the years, as more emergency cases of neonates were admitted, we spent many nights in the cardiac catheterization laboratory, at least until the use of IV prostaglandin E-1 became available to prevent closure of the ductus arteriosus. This treatment permitted delays in scheduling cardiac catheterizations so that they could be performed more electively during daytime. We involved fellows and house officers in these emergencies and other consultations. Of course, attendings were present at each cardiac catheterization procedure.

Student Teaching

A rotation through pediatric cardiology was organized in the early 1960s as a fourth-year elective long before the required fourth-year elective program went into effect. The aims of this program have remained essentially unchanged. We put the student into the role of "consultant" with daily A.M. and P.M. rounds on the cardiac patients in the house. The student accompanied the resident and fellow (if one of the latter was on the scene), and these reported back to the attending daily. The attending would then examine the patient with this information in mind. Since children with heart disease often demand immediate attention, we tried to anticipate consultations. This was often not difficult because we read all the ECGs and often a finding on the tracing would indicate that the patient needed attention. We had very few criticisms of being unavailable and probably erred on the side of being too intrusive.

We expected the students to acquire basic skills in interpreting ECGs, in developing skills in various aspects of the physical examination (especially auscultation of the heart), in understanding the basics of hemodynamics, in understanding the types of patients with heart disease encountered in children's inpatient and outpatient facilities, and in understanding how the basic tools of the cardiologist are used—i.e., ECGs, chest radiographs, angio-cardiograms, cardiac catheterizations, and echocardiograms.

We usually gave two or three lectures yearly to the entire second-year class. These evolved into a well-received one-day program on congenital heart disease, where we presented a basic lecture on cardiac physiology as demonstrated by congenital heart disease and followed this with a symposium involving cardiologists (Stewart Schall and Robert Herrington), a radiologist (usually David Delany), and a cardiac surgeon. A subsequent third session was held in the student laboratories where we presented "unknown" clinical cases, challenging the students to "diagnose" them. In the afternoon, the students were brought to the cath lab in small groups where the diagnostic equipment was demonstrated. We also assisted in discussing the excellent pathological specimens assembled by Dr. Frederick Dalldorf during a morning session which followed his lecture on congenital cardiac pathology.

Resident Teaching

The same aims listed for students were applied to teaching of the residents, but with a higher level of anticipated results. We expected residents to have good grasps of ECG and X-ray interpretations, to have refined their auscultatory and physical diagnostic skills, and to know enough about cardiac cases to write up at least one summary of a cardiac case study. We strongly emphasized house officer teaching, in line with many others in the Pediatrics Department, and generally felt this to be a rewarding experience for both parties.

Residents, students, and fellows participated in all of the outpatient clinics during the Denny era; eventually at NCMH (once weekly), Wake Hospital (twice monthly), Fayetteville AHEC (once monthly), Womack Army Hospital (every other month), Wilmington New Hanover Memorial Hospital (once monthly), Rutherfordton (once monthly), Greensboro Cone Hospital (once monthly), as well as several less frequent clinics in Lumberton and Sylva. We flew to the clinics in Wilmington, Rutherfordton, and Fayetteville-Womack Hospital and drove to the others. Each of these clinics had distinctive features relating to organization, personnel, and patient material. We supervised students, house officers, and fellows at the appropriate level of their knowledge. These clinics proved to be a popular part of the programs in our specialty at all levels, including that of fellows, and may have been partly responsible for the two residency teaching awards earned by Dr. Herrington and the one earned by Dr. Harned.

Formal teaching programs were quite limited during the Denny era since we generally believed individualized teaching was much more effective. We usually were responsible for three to four grand rounds each year, at times in association with the cardiologists in the Department of Medicine. During the early years we had to present at least one grand rounds session each year to promote the controversy over the use of steroids in the treatment of acute rheumatic fever. Drs. Harned, Herrington, and Denny favored this therapy with varying degrees of commitment. Endocrinologist Dr. Judson Van Wyk was adamantly opposed, stressing the bodily aberrations this treatment produced. Fortunately rheumatic fever, which had been responsible for a major component of our inpatient population, virtually vanished from the scene and this controversy never had to be resolved. Dr. Denny's classic contribution with Dr. Charles Rammelkamp, demonstrating the effectiveness of penicillin treatment of sore throat in preventing rheumatic fever, was responsible in part for the over sixtyfold decrease in this dreadful childhood disease.

Fellowship Training

A listing of the fellows trained by the division is produced at the end of this chapter. We always had a small program in terms of numbers of attendings, patients, catheterizations, and surgical procedures and we tried to devise programs to round out their training. This was not as difficult during the 1960s as it became later when the subspecialty programs became more fragmented. In the larger pediatric cardiology divisions in other departments, subsubspecialists appeared, including pediatric electrocardiographers, electrophysiologists, echocardiographers, specialists in cardiac diagnostic and later therapeutic catheterization procedures, exercise physiologists, etc. We attempted to compensate for this process by providing as much "hands-on" teaching as possible, and we were able to emphasize our strengths in outpatient diagnostic care and in direct participation of the fellows in the catheterization procedures. Most fellows personally performed over one hundred cardiac catheterizations during their training period with us. Toward the end of the Denny years, we began to consider fellowship training for one year, with additional training elsewhere. However, several of the best people completed their training in cardiology here, including Drs. G. William Henry and Walker Long, who were able to supplement their training in research in other divisions of the Medical School.

The loss of accreditation for the program, attributed by the board to overreliance on training arrangements with the Department of Medicine, was very disappointing, but understandable in view of the competitive advantages of larger programs where more compartmentalized training could be arranged more readily.

We projected our teaching to the medical community at large primarily through the AHEC programs, but have to admit a degree of disappointment in the rather minimal response of practitioners to the large pediatric cardiac outreach network. Two major teaching conferences had been organized with support of the Crippled Children's Division of the State Board of Health in 1959 and in the early 1960s with about forty interested practitioners in attendance at each one. However, as the subspecialty of pediatric cardiology became more complex, practitioners appeared quite willing to refer their patients for our continued care after having screened them initially. Along with this trend, practitioners appeared generally to have become less aggressive in their search for new knowledge about children's cardiac disorders.

RELATIONSHIPS WITH OTHER DEPARTMENTS

The division of pediatric cardiology at the University of North Carolina, like most divisions nationally, has remained a part of the Department of Pediatrics. Because of the relatively small size of our program during the Denny and Curnen eras, with its two to three faculty members, a more autonomous position was not possible. Other programs based on larger numbers of patients, cardiac diagnostic studies, and surgical procedures were able more readily to justify their own catheterization laboratories, inpatient suites, and special procedure areas for ECG, echocardiography, exercise studies, etc. Large pediatric cardiology programs are often built as a result of outstanding (or well-advertised) surgery. Reliance on cardiac surgery is built into this subspecialty and good relationships must be preserved.

The first chief of cardiothoracic surgery at UNC, Dr. Richard Peters, in addition to his performance clinically, energetically promoted and pursued profound cardiopulmonary research at UNC and later at the University of California at San Diego. As mentioned, he helped to establish the cardiac catheterization laboratory at UNC and he often helped pediatric cardiology to achieve its goals. He was a vigorous critic and insisted on excellence. He was very effective in stressing the importance of student research and in planning many of the teaching programs and expansions in facilities of the overall medical school program.

Dr. Benson Wilcox has been chief of cardiovascular surgery since Peters's departure and has been a very prominent academic surgeon. He improved his skills in congenital cardiac surgery as a result of his attention to anatomic details and is now recognized as preeminent in this aspect of his field. He has published several books recently, including the definitive text *Surgical Anatomy of Congenital Heart Disease*, written in association with the dynamic Dr. Robert Anderson. Dr. Wilcox has organized an excellent investigative program, relying heavily on the expertise of Dr. Carol Lucas, a PhD (computer science) in the Department of Surgery who is recognized internationally for her work on pulmonary circulation. Dr. G. William Henry developed his skills as a researcher by being a part of this program. Dr. Wilcox's knowledge of anatomy has stood him in good stead over the years and has enabled him to perform accurate procedures that have rarely had to be redone.

In addition to the importance of the division's relationships with cardiothoracic surgery, vital liaisons with the Department of Medicine's cardiology division were essential. The key persons involved in these associations were Drs. Ernest Craige and Daniel Young during the Denny years and Dr. Leonard Gettes during the Boat years. Various arrangements had to be made for these two divisions to operate effectively.

Dr. Craige's expertise in clinical diagnostic methods encompassed all of the noninvasive techniques—auscultation, electrocardiography, recording of precordial motions, M-Mode and cross-sectional echocardiography and combinations of these. He had international links, nurtured by his sabbatical leave to study with Dr. Aubrey Leatham in England. He assisted in the training of several outstanding cardiologists from that country, including Dr. Thomas Gibson, later a faculty member at Dartmouth Medical School, and Drs. George and Richard Sutton. He also brought outstanding young physicians into his division as faculty members, especially Dr. Charles Rackley (now division chief of cardiology at Georgetown), Dr. William Hood (now at Alabama Birmingham), Dr. Ellis Rolett (division chief at Dartmouth), and Dr. William Grossman (chief of the cardiac diagnostic laboratory at Peter Bent Brigham Hospital in Boston and author of the definitive text on cardiac catheterization methods). Dr. Daniel Young continued his career in cardiology at UNC and has become associated with many broad projects apart from cardiology. He was involved in the early liaison between the Medical School and East Carolina School of Medicine and recently has been elected president of the international organization of Physicians for Social Responsibility. (The taped interviews of Drs. Craige and Young are available in the archives.)

All of these individuals in the Department of Medicine had close contact with our division through joint meetings and use of facilities. We also worked with the electrophysiologists in that division, including Drs. James Foster and

Ross Simpson, who initially performed their procedures in the cardiac catheterization laboratory. Dr. Park Willis has been the director of the echocardiography laboratory since Dr. Craige retired (ca. 1984) and has been an important recent colleague. These individuals are highlighted because they worked even more closely with the persons in our division during its everyday operations than did the staff members of the Department of Pediatrics. On the other hand, our teaching responsibilities were directed more toward the pediatric residents and fellows than toward others.

We were involved, however, in teaching a great variety of other persons who rotated through our subspecialty service, including internal medical fellows, medicine-pediatrics residents, anesthesiology residents, medical students from other medical schools, and graduate nurse specialists.

Our relationships with the Department of Radiology were also very important. When Drs. James Scatliff and Orlando Gabrielle arrived from Yale–New Haven, they brought with them sophisticated know-how in interpretation of standard and angiographic films. Dr. Gabrielle was assigned as the primary cardiac radiographer and raised the level of programming and interpreting films to a state-of-the art position. He later became chairman of the Radiology Department at the University of West Virginia, but before he left he began the training of Dr. David Delany, who succeeded Dr. Gabrielle as our specialist in cardiovascular radiology.

Dr. Scatliff instilled in his associates, by his own example, the concept of consulting on the spot at any time of day or night. These radiologists were extremely helpful to have on hand during the procedures on our most difficult cases.

FELLOWS IN PEDIATRIC CARDIOLOGY

Because a major emphasis was placed on fellowship training, we shall describe some of the personalities and accomplishments of these especially interesting individuals.

The first fellow trained in pediatric cardiology after Dr. Denny became chief of pediatrics was Dr. Ghody Rowshan in 1960. Rowshan, an Iranian on a student visa, had attended medical school in Shiraz and entered this country as a resident at the Brooklyn Jewish Hospital. Many Iranians had followed this pattern of residency training during the reign of the Shah. Recommended quite highly, Ghody participated in all of the usual activities of the "division" (with its one faculty member), including its research programs. He taught us to sing the rousing Iranian national anthem during tense moments of sheep experimentation. He presented a paper resulting from these experiments at the Society for Pediatric Research meeting at Atlantic City, and later continued his training at UCLA for a year.

Dr. Roland Schmidt had left general practice in San Francisco to obtain additional training at UNC. He continued as a fellow in pediatric cardiology from 1961 to 1964. In addition to his clinical duties, Dr. Schmidt participated with Dr. Ernest Craige and their aspiring technician, Roberta Williams, in several studies involving external monitoring of cardiac impulses. After his training here, Schmidt became a faculty member at the University of West Virginia in Morgantown, where he worked with Dr. Russell Lucas, who later was chief of the division of pediatric cardiology at the University of Minnesota. Schmidt later became head of the division of pediatric cardiology in Morgantown and was an assistant dean. Subsequently, this somewhat peripatetic man of the West moved to Eugene, Oregon, where he participated in that state's outstanding Crippled Children's Program. He has subsequently retired to Chapel Hill.

Dr. Robert Herrington followed his fellowship training in the late sixties by becoming a faculty member and contributed enormously to the division's program over the ensuing years. He participated as a researcher and studied the response in newborn lambs to perfusion of their medullary respiratory centers with mock acidified cerebrospinal fluid. After that, he decided that he really was predominantly a "people person" and took on the position of chief of the outpatient clinics, while maintaining his interest in pediatric cardiology. Dr. Denny has credited him with changing the atmosphere of outpatient teaching of pediatrics at UNC so that it became an integral part of the teaching program, rather than its "Siberia." Dr. Herrington also took over the role of rehabilitation of children with spina bifida and other disorders, as has been described elsewhere. Later, he moved from being outpatient chief to becoming a more full-time member of the division of pediatric cardiology and played a very prominent role in developing our outreach clinics. Dr. Herrington has probably logged more air miles than any member of the Department of Pediatrics with his frequent flights to Wilmington, Rutherfordton, Fayetteville, and Fort Bragg. Robert Herrington has had one of the longest associations with the Department of Pediatrics of any faculty member. He retired just recently in September 1991 and plans to stay in Chapel Hill as a part-time faculty member.

Dr. Martin "Tony" Woodall's fellowship training was sponsored by the U.S. Navy, which was a direct result of the early relationship our Department had with the Naval Hospital at Portsmouth, Virginia. He remained interested in clinical pediatrics rather than research and went on to become the chief of pediatric cardiology at the San Diego Naval Hospital.

Dr. Robert Abney returned from military service for subspecialty training in our division. Abney had been a brilliant chief resident and performed equally well during his training in our program. An incisive thinker, he was destined for success in any field he chose to enter. Dr. Harned sent him to talk to Dr. Alexander Nadas in Boston with his highest possible recommendation, but after considerable soul-searching, Bob decided to return to Jackson, Mississippi, where he has been a successful practitioner of both general pediatrics and pediatric cardiology. He has participated actively in the teaching programs of the Department of Pediatrics at the University of Mississippi Medical Center.

Dr. Charles Bullaboy was a fellow from 1973 to 1975, after having been chief pediatric resident at Baptist Hospital in Winston-Salem. Bullaboy is a walking encyclopedia. For several years, he was assigned as the pediatric cardiologist at the Portsmouth Naval Hospital. When Dr. Harned attended that hospital as a visiting professor, he found that Bullaboy was universally admired as the person who knew the most answers. Bullaboy left the Navy to join the faculty of Eastern Virginia Medical School at the Children's Hospital of the King's Daughters in Norfolk. Charles is a careful and accurate writer and has published numerous clinical papers and book chapters.

Dr. Kathleen Salter was a fellow in 1974–1976, after having completed training in general pediatrics and pediatric neurology. She was especially effective as a liaison person with the cardiothoracic surgery division, where her husband, Dr. Blair Keagy, rose through the ranks to become chief resident. She joined the Geisinger Clinic in Pennsylvania where Blair became chief of vascular surgery, and at one stretch was chief of pediatric cardiology. She subsequently moved back to Chapel Hill to do general pediatrics associated with Chapel Hill Pediatrics.

Dr. John Myracle from Oklahoma trained in the general pediatric program here and then spent a year as a cardiac fellow in 1976–1977. This bright and talented person performed exceptionally well and was able to continue his training at Boston Children's Hospital. While there he was outstanding, as Dr. Harned learned later from Drs. Nadas, Roberta Williams, and Aldo Castenedo, and he was able to obtain a grant to study hypertension in children. Although they had plans for him to stay at Boston Children's, John decided that he really enjoyed general clinical pediatrics and its lifestyle. He moved to Winston-Salem and has been working in a large HMO since that time.

Dr. Hema Ghia was a fellow in 1977–1979, after having completed a year of training with Dr. McCue at the Medical College of Virginia in Richmond. Hema, a Hindu, handled herself very well in our strange, rural Southern location and showed intelligence commensurate with that of the other eight children in her outstandingly able family. (Five of her siblings are physicians and professors in this country, including Dr. Joe Ghia, who is a member of the UNC anesthesiology staff). Hema returned to India, where she is married to a pediatrician and continues her consultations in pediatric cardiology in Bombay.

Dr. Michael Sargent was a fellow from 1978 to 1980. This Princeton-educated person was the most articulate and precise trainee we ever had. He dictated notes that were grammatically correct and always on time. Sargent did not accept some of the premises of maximally intense medical care and early challenged the precepts of neonatal care especially. He has found his niche in sports medicine at the University of Maine in Orono.

Dr. G. William Henry overlapped for one year with Dr. Sargent and has remained with our program since 1979. Henry and his wife, Marianna, were students at UNC School of Medicine and both spent two years of residency at the Riley Hospital in Indianapolis (University of Indiana School of Medi-

Walker Long

Elman Frantz

cine). Returning to UNC, Henry has shown great talent both in clinical medicine and in the laboratory. He has worked well in the perisurgical area and soon involved himself with the cardiothoracic surgical research team, which has been conducting a variety of experiments especially related to the pulmonary circulation. Another key figure of this team, Dr. Carol Lucas, has teamed with Bill in increasingly complex studies of pulmonary hemodynamics. The evolution of Dr. Henry's research as he developed his own programs will be described later.

Dr. Walker A. Long, another extraordinarily able physician, added pediatric cardiology to his protracted period of training, which included mixed medical and pediatric residencies and subspecialization in neonatology. We arranged for Walker to continue his neonatal research program with Dr. Ned Lawson while he trained for two years in pediatric cardiology. He also participated in our program of studying the effects of indomethacin on ductal closure in prematures—a multicentered investigation piloted by Dr. Alexander Nadas of Harvard. In addition, he was closely involved with a pilot study of the use of prostacylin in neonates with persistent pulmonary hypertension syndrome. A book that he edited, *Fetal and Neonatal Cardiology*, published by Saunders in 1990, is comprised of remarkably detailed chapters by national and international experts in this field, in which he is also a recognized authority. Walker's return to academic pediatrics in 1994 has been welcomed by the Department.

Dr. Elman Frantz trained with us for one year pending an appointment with Dr. Abraham Rudolph's training program in pediatric cardiology at the University of California in San Francisco. Elman got a running start for entry into that program by being grounded in cardiac catheterization methods and clinical cardiology during his productive year with us. Recognizing Elman's well-rounded abilities and fine character, Dr. Henry insisted on an appointment for Elman as an assistant professor before agreeing to assume the position as chief of the division at UNC, rather than leave for Duke.

Of interest, two other outstanding chief residents from the general residency program have chosen careers in pediatric cardiology. Dr. Susan Warren Denfield pursued fellowship training in Houston in Dr. Daniel McNamara's program, and Dr. Scott Buck continued his training in Dr. Thomas Graham's program at Vanderbilt.

RESEARCH

The research program began quite soon after Dr. Harned's arrival at UNC and was supported early on by a grant from the U.S. Public Health Service and one from the Association for the Aid of Crippled Children. The funding, which permitted technicians' salaries, equipment purchases, and purchase of laboratory animals, was not very great by present-day standards. For example, the NIH grants provided $16,418 in 1960, $14,420 in 1961, and $16,721 in 1962; the present-day value of these amounts might be about $85,000 to $100,000 per year. Lacking adequate facilities, these studies were performed first in a small room on the fourth floor of the MacNider Building. Methods were developed for performing cardiac catheterization studies on fetal lambs and for evaluating the effects of head compression, painful stimulation, umbilical cord clamping, and terminal asphyxiation on their hemodynamics (Harned, H.S., Jr. et al.: *Amer J Dis Children* 102:180, 1961). When this study was presented at the plenary meeting of the Society for Pediatric Research in Swamscott, Massachusetts, it was well received despite the unbelievably bad facilities available for the presentation. At least our slides projected completely onto the small screen while those of other presenters projected onto the walls and professors who were seated nearby.

Studies involving this exteriorized preparation and those similar to it continued for many years under adequate federal and Heart Association funding. Also, for about ten years, part of Dr. Harned's salary was funded by the NC Heart Association for his role as "senior investigator" of this organization.

Later, emphasis was directed at finding the important mechanisms responsible for the initiation of breathing at birth. The articles that resulted from this support illustrate the nature of these studies and the collaborators who aided Dr. Harned (a list of these articles is included in the archives).

As these studies progressed, our physical facilities changed. The first change in venue was to the dental anatomy laboratory on the fourth floor of MacNider, then to a laboratory in the basement of this same building, both in its northernmost wing. This latter laboratory was shared with Dr. Rolett of the Department of Medicine. Finally, a very adequate laboratory was designed in the new Burnett-Womack Building on the third floor.

Several technicians, in particular Carolyn Holmes, Dr. Clarence "Nick" Griffin (later to become a medical student at UNC and an anesthesiologist in Denver), William Berryhill, and Jose Ferreiro, played vital roles in the conducting of these experiments. Another medical student who worked with us, Dr. Tift Mann, has now become a very successful cardiologist in Raleigh.

Of these, Jose Ferreiro made the greatest contribution by far and has continued to be a research associate with Drs. Wilcox, Henry, and Lucas. Jose, an extraordinary individual with many talents, was an irreplaceable associate who set up the experiments, learned difficult chemical methods, and applied statistical methodology. He has continued to grow as he has learned to establish the sophisticated methods of Dr. Henry's team, where he remains a central figure.

Concurrent with these studies, during the early Denny era, investigations were directed at human neonatal hemodynamic changes and the changing physical (auscultatory) findings after birth. An article by Craige and Harned on "Phonocardiographic and Electrocardiographic Studies in Normal Newborn Infants" (*Amer. Heart J.* 65: 180, 1962) summarized these studies.

An important publication from the division was the recent book *Pediatric Pulmonary Heart Disease* edited by H. S. Harned, Jr. (Boston: Little, Brown and Company, 1990). More than half of this text was written by Harned, but there were very significant contributions from G. W. Henry on "Peri-operative Management of the Child with Pulmonary Hypertension and Congenital Heart Disease," E. Frantz on "Pulmonary Arteriopathies Secondary to Toxic Ingestions" and on "Adult Respiratory Distress Syndrome," R. T. Herrington on "Clinical Examination and Cardiac Catheterization," W. A. Long on "Primary Pulmonary Hypertension," and Sandra Mattos on "Echocardiography of the Right Heart."

During the last few years of Dr. Denny's tenure as chief of pediatrics, a complex multicentered study of the effects of indomethacin on closure of patent ductus arteriosus in the newborn took up a major part of the division's investigative agenda. Our involvement as coinvestigators in this joint study with the neonatology division (under Dr. Ernest Kraybill's direction) resulted in part from Dr. John Myracle's associations with us and with the cardiology division of the Boston Children's Hospital, where he had been one of Dr. Alexander Nadas's fellows. This study provided excellent training for all those involved, including the attendings, acquainting them with the realities of comprehensive drug studies and preparing them for the major drug studies to follow at UNC. It was especially important for the fellows, Dr. Walker Long and Dr. Carl Bose (from neonatology), who attended the national meetings of this study group under Dr. Nadas's guidance with Drs. Harned and Kraybill. By their participation, they were able to learn firsthand some of the methods and pitfalls encountered in carrying out and completing such studies.

TRANSITION TO THE BOAT YEARS

In 1986, Dr. Henry was appointed chief of the division. Dr. Schall had already left for Greensboro and, despite its network of clinics, the number of cardiac catheterizations and surgical procedures had ebbed. As a new leader appointed by Dr. Boat, who beat off a frenzied effort by Duke to hire him, Dr. Henry had considerable leverage which he used effectively. With Harned's retirement in 1987, an opening became available for the hiring of Dr. Frantz. Bill's joint investigative program with the Department of Surgery provided funds for additional equipment and personnel. Perhaps most importantly, a degree of autonomy for the division was handed down by Dr. Boat to the new chief in relation to the division's fiscal operations.

But along with these positive features came increased responsibilities and additional demands placed on the division. The greater emphasis on generating money from patient care began to gather steam and the division members, along with others in the Pediatrics Department, were lectured on this aspect. New rules for monitoring and emphasizing the roles of the attending physicians to ensure payments for services, increasing concerns about the medicolegal aspects of care, pressures for shortening lengths of stay, and needs for precertifying certain procedures, including renderings of second opinions, began to plague those in the division more than during the kinder, gentler era of Dr. Denny's tenure. These changes impacted on the training of residents and students, as described ably by Dr. Burchfield of our house staff (see "Residents' Reminiscences"). The attending physician needed to have a more forceful (or at least more apparent) influence on all aspects of patient care, relegating the residents especially to less responsible and in many ways less rewarding roles.

Bill Henry

With the need to increase the numbers of patients, the division had to set about opening new clinics and referral patterns. The major thrust was to set up a sophisticated clinic in Raleigh and this was accomplished very successfully. This clinic required a great deal of time by Dr. Henry and his associates. Additional links were made with the Kaiser Permanente program to supplement the flow of referrals. Concurrently, cardiac surgery at the North Carolina Children's Hospital was upgraded. The addition of Dr. Michael Mill from Stanford with his specialization in heart transplantation provided this service for children. Dr. Benson Wilcox continued as the vitally important specialist in congenital heart surgery. The pediatric intensive care unit was enlarged and, under the care of Dr. Arno Zaritsky and his successors, provided more effective assistance to the pediatric needs of postoperative children with cardiac disorders.

Effective use of the Ronald McDonald House, which opened in 1988, permitted shortening of stays for children admitted for cardiac catheterizations, and many of these patients could be admitted on the day of the procedure. An effective network of operated cases was organized by Ms. Maggie Morris to provide information and psychological support for those children and families who were facing prospective surgery.

Along with the increased size of the program in pediatric cardiology and its increased complexity came need for additional personnel. With Dr. Herrington's retirement in 1991, his position became open. This was now a time to add new faculty positions and the division eventually enlarged to include five physicians.

As he began his tenure as chief of the division, Dr. Henry sought to develop a degree of subspecialization within it. Dr. Frantz assumed the major role in cardiac catheterization procedures and developed special skills in intervention techniques, including balloon valvuloplasties, coarctation of the aorta angioplasties, and nonsurgical closures of atrial septal defects and patent ductus arteriosus. Dr. Sandra Mattos, who had been recruited from London in 1988, had assumed a key role in echocardiographic methods, but only stayed for a year because of licensing difficulties.

Also destined to have a short stay in the division, Dr. Biadin Roldan, who had been trained at the Children's Hospital of Alabama in pediatrics and at the University of California at San Francisco in pediatric cardiology, succeeded her. His tenure at UNC was shortened by a lethal illness.

In 1991, Dr. James Loehr was brought in from an assistant professorship at the University of Colorado Health Sciences Center to a similar position here. A graduate of Stanford and the St. Louis School of Medicine at Washington University, Dr. Loehr was trained in pediatrics and pediatric cardiology at Colorado, where he developed his interests in cardiac metabolism of cardiomyopathies. While in the process of developing his research program, Dr. Loehr has contributed his excellent clinical skills in caring for the increased patient load.

Jim Loehr

The most recent new addition to the staff is Dr. Scott Balderston, a Phi Beta Kappa graduate of the University of Virginia and its Medical School, who was trained in pediatrics at the Portsmouth Naval Hospital. After a period of practicing pediatrics, he entered fellowship training at the University of Colorado and later served as a pediatric cardiologist at the Naval Hospital in Oakland, California.

Dr. Walker Long, who remained a member of the division while serving with distinction at Burroughs Wellcome, has returned primarily in a research capacity. His credentials are outstanding as an honors graduate at UNC as an undergraduate and medical student, as a fellow in neonatalogy and pediatric cardiology here, and as a recipient of a series of awards for excellence at Burroughs Wellcome. While with this company, he supervised the successful clinical trials for the use of the artificial surfactant, Exosurf, in the treatment of neonatal respiratory distress syndrome. He also has participated in projects relating to the use of prostacyclin for combating pulmonary hypertension. As an expert in pulmonary vascular disorders, he is in a position to wed this expertise with that of Drs. Henry and Lucas. Also, Dr. Carl Bose, who is coordinating neonatal research here on the use of nitric oxide inhalations to treat pulmonary hypertension, and Dr. Alan Stiles, who is addressing the basic chemistry of this disorder, should be in a position to augment Dr. Long's research efforts.

Dr. Henry has parlayed his research skills, acquired in part as a Morehead Scholar at the University of North Carolina as an undergraduate major in chemistry and as a Jefferson Pilot Fellow at our Medical School, into a sequence of research projects since his appointments here. Largely as a result of his associations with Drs. Carol Lucas and Benson Wilcox, these projects initially have included studies of velocity profiles in the aorta, main pulmonary artery, and branch pulmonary arteries in canine and lamb models. The effects of pulmonary hypertension and increased flow on these parameters and on input impedance have also been documented. With his associates and fellows, he has developed new techniques for multiangle visualization of pulmonary blood flow velocity patterns and for saccular aneurysms and bifurcations. His expertise in pulmonary vascular physiology has enabled Dr. Henry to lead meetings of the European Congress on Cardiology (in Düsseldorf), the World Congress on Medical Physics and Biomedical Engineering (in Kyoto), as well as meetings in Beijing, Madras, London, Hong Kong, and Bergamo. With Dr. Wilcox he cosponsored two conferences on surgical anatomy of congenital heart disease held in Chapel Hill. Dr. Henry is participating in a variety of ongoing projects featuring relationships with the University of Pittsburgh, Georgia Tech, and the Royal Brompton Heart and Lung Institute in London, which promise to add to the productivity of the division but will need to be detailed in subsequent histories. The archives reveal the important associations with Drs. Henry Hsiao, Carol Lucas, Blair Keagy, Robert Anderson, and others who have participated in these research enterprises and include listings of the studies performed with his fellows—Belinda Ha, M. Singh, and K. Katayama. Also included in the archives are the current curricula vitae of all the faculty members of the division during Dr. Henry's and Dr. Harned's tenures.

With the superior people on hand in the division and with a new departmental chair, Dr. Roberta Williams, herself a nationally recognized expert in pediatric cardiology, the prospects of melding this program into the projected major Children's Hospital organization seem especially bright at this time.

HERBERT S. HARNED, JR.

FACULTY

Balderston, Scott M. BA, Univ VA, 1976; MD, Univ VA, 1980; Asst Prof, Ped, 1993–94.

Castle, Robert F. AB, Case Western Reserve, 1953; MD, Case Western Reserve, 1956; Asst Prof, Ped, 1963–66.

Frantz, Elman G. BS, Manchester College, 1977; MD, Penn State, 1981; Asst Prof, Ped, 1987; Assoc Prof, Ped, 1993.

Harned, Herbert S., Jr. BS, Yale, 1942; MD, Yale, 1945; Asst Prof, Ped, 1958; Assoc Prof, Ped, 1961; Prof, Ped, 1971–91; Chief, Ped Cardiol, 1958–86.

Henry, George W. AB, Univ NC at Chapel Hill, 1973; MD, Univ NC at Chapel Hill, 1977; Asst Prof, Ped, 1982; Assoc Prof, Ped, 1987; Prof, Ped, 1994; Chief, Ped Cardiol, 1987.

Herrington, Robert T. BS, The Citadel, 1953; MD, Univ Wash, 1957; Asst Prof, Ped, 1967; Assoc Prof, Ped, 1972–93.

Loehr, James P. BS, Stanford Univ, 1975; MD, Washington Univ, 1987; Asst Prof, Ped, 1991.

Long, Walker A. BA, Univ NC at Chapel Hill, 1971; MD, Univ NC at Chapel Hill, 1976; Res Asst Prof, Ped, 1983; Res Assoc Prof, Ped, 1990.

Mattos, Sandra. BS, Collegio Nossa (Brazil), 1975; MD, Federal Univ (Brazil), 1981; Asst Prof, Ped,1988–89.

Roldan, Biadin G. BS, Univ SC, 1980; MD, Univ SC, 1984; Asst Prof, Ped, 1991–93.

Schall, Stewart A. BA, Rutgers, 1960; MD, Univ Penn, 1964; Asst Prof, Ped, 1972; Assoc Prof, Ped, 1978.

FELLOWS

Years	Name	Current Position
1960–61	Ghodratolah Rowshan, MD	Deceased
1961–64	Roland Schmidt, MD	Retired (in Chapel Hill — see *History*)
1962–63, 1966–67	Robert Herrington, MD	Retired (see *History*)
1964–66	Martin Woodall, MD	Ped Pract (Oklahoma City, OK)

1967–68	Robert Abney, MD	Ped and Ped Cardiol Pract (Jackson, MS—see *History*)
1973–75	Charles Bullaboy, MD	Assoc Prof, Ped Cardiol, Eastern VA Med School
1974–76	Kathleen Salter, MD	Ped Pract (Chapel Hill, NC)
1976–77	John Myracle, MD	Ped Pract (Winston-Salem, NC—see *History*)
1977–79	Hema Ghia, MD	Ped Cardiol Pract (Bombay, India)
1978–80	Michael Sargent, MD	Sports Med Pract, Univ of Maine at Orono
1979–92	G. William Henry, MD	Prof, Ped; Chief, Ped Cardiol, UNC-CH
1981–83	Walker A. Long, MD	Res Assoc Prof, Ped, UNC-CH
1984–85	Elman Frantz, MD	Assoc Prof, Ped, UNC-CH

CHAPTER THIRTEEN

Child Psychiatry and
Pediatric Psychology

THE collegial associations between the Departments of Psychiatry and
Pediatrics since the early 1950s have been a series of two "highs" and two
"lows." The first high was associated with the arrival of Dr. Lucie Jessner as
head of child psychiatry in 1955; the first low came with her departure in
1963. The second high came when Dr. Catherine Taylor assumed faculty status in psychiatry in the early 1970s and lasted for ten to twelve years. The second low followed that time and continues until the time of this writing in
1994. Because Jessner and Taylor are the star players in this drama this history will be centered around them and their associations with the Department
of Pediatrics. Because pediatric psychology, a part of the Department of Psychiatry at UNC, played a large role in all associations between the departments, its role will be emphasized. A variety of other disciplines and a large
number of people contributed significantly to all of these associations; they
will be recognized at appropriate times in the history.

Dr. Judson Van Wyk, who joined the pediatric faculty in 1955 and had
many interactions with Dr. Jessner, contributed his memories of this "high"
period in the next section.

THE JESSNER ERA: THE FIRST
"HIGH" AND "LOW" PERIODS

In the early 1950s, the major thrust of psychiatry was to identify and treat
"psychosomatic" illnesses. Clinically, psychoanalysis was riding on the crest
of its greatest popularity. Thus, the recruitment of George Ham as the first
chairman of psychiatry was thought by many to be one of Dean Berryhill's
more brilliant achievements. Ham was not only a card-carrying psychoana-

lyst in the best Freudian tradition, but also a fully credentialed internist and brother of the famed Thomas Hale Ham of Case Western Reserve University School of Medicine.

The Department of Pediatrics was a secondary beneficiary of Ham's appointment, since in 1955 he was successful in luring Lucie Jessner, a child psychiatrist from Harvard, to serve as liaison with the Department of Pediatrics. Jessner was a Viennese analyst who had been trained by Anna Freud. Lucie brought with her two fellows in child psychiatry, Harold Harris and Cornelius Lansing. Jessner interacted joyfully and enthusiastically with her pediatric colleagues, and the writer remembers Lucie wagging her finger at him and explaining in her Middle European accent that boys with delayed adolescence simply did not want to grow up because of a disordered relationship with their mothers (or was it with their fathers?). Lucie Jessner was a delight to work with and relished intellectual controversy. She was joined in 1957 by Dr. James Proctor, a psychoanalyst who was related to Nick Hilton of the Hilton Hotel chain. Proctor took his calling very seriously and was committed to educating his pediatric colleagues in Freudian doctrine. The writer vividly remembers a pediatric grand rounds in which a boy with a classic psychosomatic disease (asthma) was being presented. As the writer was taking his seat (late as usual), he heard Dr. Proctor earnestly explaining that the bedside humidifier with its elongated tube was making the boy anxious because it represented a penis. At that moment the late arrival had an allergic reaction and sneezed, but several in the audience thought that the sneeze sounded suspiciously like a scatological ejaculation that described horse feces. Other recruits at this time were David Freeman, who later worked part time with Harrie Chamberlin, and several pediatric psychologists including Lon Ussery and Ruth Falk.

In summary, under Ham's leadership, the Department of Psychiatry took seriously its commitment to provide patient care and teaching services to the Department of Pediatrics, although not everyone in the Department of Pediatrics was convinced of the soundness and value of the orthodox psychoanalytic approach. In 1963 Jessner departed and was succeeded by Rex Speers as chief of child psychiatry. An important achievement of Speers was his recruitment of Eric Schopler, a psychologist from Chicago, who has made major contributions to our understanding and treatment of infantile autism. Speers had little interest in a liaison with the Department of Pediatrics and the first "low" in associations began shortly after Jessner left.

Ham was followed in 1963 by John Ewing as chair of psychiatry. Ewing was a Scotsman and militant apostate from the Calvinism of his Presbyterian upbringing. Ewing never gave evidence of interest in the problems of children and took a more laissez-faire approach to pediatrics and child psychiatry than had Ham. Indeed, none of the individuals who chaired the Department of Psychiatry after Ham evidenced interest in providing the Department of Pediatrics with psychiatric services. That is not to say that there were no psychiatrists who provided services to children on the pediatric service: individual members of the Psychiatry Department who interacted with pediatrics in the

early years were Iverson Riddle,
David Freeman, Joe Allen, Bob
Reichler, John Boswell, Ray Schmitt,
and Herman Lineberger. Jorge Ferriz,
the child psychiatrist in the division
for disorders of development and
learning from 1964 to 1968, made
important contributions to that program. A trainee in psychiatry who
took additional pediatric training
was Maria Perez-Reyes.

Cathy Taylor

THE TAYLOR ERA: THE
SECOND "HIGH" AND
"LOW" PERIODS

The low of the late 1960s was
relieved in part by Schmitt's genuine
interest in providing psychiatric ser-
vices for children on the pediatric ward and clinics, but he opted to join Harrie Chamberlin full time in 1970, leaving a void filled subsequently by Dr.
Catherine Taylor. Taylor's contributions were immense and formed the backbone for the next "high" that was to last over a decade. Dr. Taylor, one of
four children of an East Tennessee farm family, graduated from the University of Tennessee College of Medicine in 1957. Following a year of a rotating
internship she spent two years in general practice in Harlan County, Kentucky. Her interest in children then directed her back to the University of Tennessee for a pediatric residency. She then practiced general pediatrics in Hickory, North Carolina, for three years before seeking psychiatric training at the
University of North Carolina. Following a child psychiatry fellowship she
became an associate in pediatrics and psychiatry at Duke, where she witnessed and became interested in the liaison between these two departments
which was supported by federal grant funds. In 1970 she returned to Chapel
Hill to begin the Taylor era, a decade of high points in the association of the
Department of Pediatrics and child psychiatry. We pick up this story in Cathy
Taylor's words.

As I entered the child fellowship at UNC in 1967, John Boswell had
just been appointed director of child psychiatry. Dr. Ray Schmitt, a
child psychiatrist, joined the child psychiatry faculty six months before
I completed my fellowship. During the next one and a half years, he
began to create a more active child psychiatry program in pediatrics.
He worked closely with Sandy Mills, who was at that time working
half time in the pediatric clinic as a child psychologist. As I indicated
my interest in returning to UNC from Duke, Ray Schmitt indicated his

desire to transfer to the DDDL with Harrie Chamberlin as their new and impressive "home" in the BSRC was completed. I was delighted to come back to UNC to child psychiatry and pediatrics and build on the foundation Ray had started.

One of the things I learned at Duke was that they had an NIMH child psychiatry consultation/liaison training grant for pediatrics. When I joined the faculty here in 1970 as an assistant professor in the Departments of Psychiatry and Pediatrics, I soon began to talk with Dr. Denny about trying to get a similar grant which would include a focus on training of medical students and pediatric residents on pediatric turf on the recognition and management of behavior problems they commonly see in practice. An additional focus on normal child development was needed. At that time I didn't know just how complex the business of putting together a "training" grant was. But Drs. Denny and Lipton were patient and very helpful and supportive. I finally got my first grant together in about 1972. Although we had a very favorable NIMH site visit and the enthusiastic support from the pediatric faculty and residents was duly noted by the site visitors, President Nixon impounded the NIMH grant funds which had been appropriated. After the impounded NIMH funds were finally released, the first funding was only $20,000. Even this small amount was helpful and later increased considerably as we resubmitted NIMH grants over the next ten to twelve years.

When I joined the faculty in 1970, Harvey Hamrick was the chief resident. Virginia Hebbert had been appointed chief social worker in pediatrics two or three years earlier; from day 1, she was attuned to the children and families in pediatrics. I considered Virginia one of my most valuable teachers in the real world of "knocks and bumps." Her love, kindness, patience, and knowledge were always so evident. But Virginia could also be tough as nails when a child was in danger or neglected. She was also able to see beyond the abuse and neglect and often see parents in need of support as well as the need to protect the child.

Child abuse and neglect was still a relatively new field in pediatrics. We were familiar with Kempe's work in child abuse but the child abuse laws in the state were almost nonexistent. A protocol on how to manage suspected child abuse and neglect in the hospital was needed. Harvey and Virginia tackled the job and asked for my involvement as well. Later chief residents carried on the program, with Virginia ever at their side—and they listened, too! We developed a weekly meeting chaired by the chief resident to discuss suspected abuse and neglect cases and be sure they were appropriately referred to the Department of Social Services. I participated in evaluations of children and their parents and also served as liaison between pediatrics and adult psychiatry for some of the parents. Some of the children were also evaluated and treated in the child psychiatry outpatient clinic. At times we all went to court. Any legal advice had to come from the attorney general's office in Raleigh since there was no UNC lawyer in the hospital. As the AHEC program was developing, the chief resident, Virginia Hebbert, and I were asked to make a number of presentations on abuse and neglect. Jerry Bernstein was just great on this road show! Seriously, Jerry and other chief residents and Virginia did more in the early days of making physicians and DSS aware of the detection and management of abuse and neglect than anyone in the state. Mason Thomas, from the Institute of Government, wrote and got into law the first child abuse law in North Carolina, which required mandatory reporting of suspected abuse. I was on a panel at the second Governor's Conference on Child Abuse in 1972.

As we formed the nucleus of a pediatric psychiatry/psychology consultation liaison program, I found that financial support from pediatrics was critical. John Boswell dates the beginning of a workable child psychiatry program in pediatrics to the time of Dr. Denny's commitment to the program, including partial funding of the program. Soon I began to bug Drs. Denny and Lipton about needing a full-time PhD psychologist. Both of them were supportive but there were no extra pennies. After receiving some grant funding, the first thing we did was to recruit Brian Stabler. Brian came from England to UNC where he earned his PhD in psychology. He later completed a postdoctoral psychology fellowship with Ruth Falk and was interested in pediatric psychology. He joined the faculty in 1973 and has continued throughout the subsequent twenty years to be a valuable part of the team. His enthusiasm and humor have always been special and quite effective in his role as an excellent teacher. His modeling for residents and students on interviewing children was invaluable. Brian also began a research program in endocrinology with a special focus on hypopituitary children. This has been a continuous focus of his research and grant funding. He also consulted in pediatric neurology, the cystic fibrosis clinic, the diabetic clinic, and other areas in the program. In recent years, after a sabbatical at Duke, Brian and Eric Jensen developed the Med Well program.

Brian Stabler

This biofeedback program has been a helpful treatment modality for many anxious children and adolescents.

As Frank Loda was developing and expanding the division of community pediatrics, he submitted and received a major statewide grant to develop a program in abuse and neglect. In 1975, Rosemary Hunter was completing her child psychiatry fellowship and was recruited to join the pediatric psychiatry/psychology program as well as the community pediatrics division to work with Frank Loda as he implemented this major program in child abuse. Nancy Kilstrom joined Virginia Hebbert as the social worker in this program. During her eight to ten years on the faculty before moving to New Mexico, Rosemary made a very real impact in the child abuse arena. We also developed a protocol for the management of raped/sexually abused children and adolescents. In all of these endeavors our top priority was the teaching and modeling of clinical evaluation and treatment techniques that medical students and pediatric residents could learn and take with them into practice.

Our group struggled together regarding the impact of the death of infants and children on the children's families, as well as on the house staff who were caring for the children who died. We developed a small conference chaired by the chief resident to go over the events surrounding the child's death and make plans to contact and usually meet with the parents. The nurses, chaplain, social workers, house staff, and others involved with the child tried to attend. Initially we called the conference the Death Conference, but Robert Gould, who was chief resident at the time, coined the name Survivors' Conference, a much better name since we focused on the survivors.

Early on, Brian and I also developed a behavior clinic. Mary Rogan, the pediatric social worker involved with the behavior clinic, again served as an excellent model for the residents as she demonstrated the importance of working with the parents. The residents interviewed the child/adolescent behind a one-way screen. I think the residents were often surprised to find out just how much a child can tell you in his play or by warming up and talking by utilizing puppet play.

In 1976 Ken Whitt completed his psychology internship and joined our pediatric psychiatry/psychology program. Ken initially focused primarily on the neurology clinics and neurology patients admitted to the wards. He also developed, with Des Runyan, a failure to thrive protocol. He later developed research and treatment programs with the sickle cell clinic, the oncology clinic, and more recently with the AIDS program. Melissa Johnson and Julie Juneuman were child psychologists who joined the faculty and were part of our program for several years. Dick Dalton, a child psychiatrist, was also on the faculty for two years in the early 1980s. He was well received by the pediatric house staff as he worked with us in the program. In the division for disorders of development and learning, Tom Gualtieri, an associate professor in the Department of Psychiatry, developed a busy research-oriented child neuropsychopharmacology clinic, which became of major importance in the management of many hyperactive and otherwise behaviorally disturbed children. Carolyn Schroeder, a child psychologist in the DDDL who was also on the psychiatry faculty, interfaced with our program and was known for her teaching skills and her work with residents and medical students. Bob Reichler and Eric Schopler continued their

Ken Whitt

development of the TEAACH program for autistic children and provided training opportunities for pediatric residents in their program.

Cynthia Wilhelm, a child psychologist with joint appointments in medical allied health, psychiatry, and pediatrics, has contributed her clinical/teaching skills to our program since the late 1970s. Cynthia has been primarily involved in the rehabilitation and rheumatology clinics but also contributed at various times to the endocrine and neurology programs and ward consultations. Barbara Boat made many contributions to the pediatric residency training in her work in Jean Smith's adolescent clinic, Des Runyan's sexual abuse clinic, Mike Sharp's community outreach program, and in her own sexual abuse program in child psychiatry.

As we created and expanded our program in pediatrics, Brian and I recognized early on that there were many key people who did a tremendous job in caring for the children and their parents. We needed their input, their expertise, and their help in caring for many of these children in need. We developed a weekly conference at which we sat down, ate a sandwich, and talked about these problems. I feel we also helped the house staff to learn just how important the observations of the nurses, the recreation therapists, the teachers, the chaplains, the social workers, the physical therapists, the occupational therapists, and others are to the comprehensive care of the children.

As I think back over the years, there was great satisfaction in being the pediatric faculty member who served as the liaison to the pediatric recreation program. Working with Howard West, Liz Cozart, Susan Gates, and more recently with Darl Pothover and Dick Hatfield has

meant so much to me. Those dedicated ladies in the Tri Sigma sorority who were responsible for the Robbie Page Memorial Fund contributed a great deal to the recreation program. The teachers! What
would we do without their help. Nathalie Harrison, Mary Lou Pollock,
Sheila Breitweiser, and all the others have given sick children a continuing link with their usual life outside the hospital. Their love, care,
and support are conveyed to the children as they teach them and keep
them up to date so that reentry when they return home is easier.

Elaine Hill and her many volunteers, along with nurses, including
Weiss Dykstra and Polly Johnson, worked with Virginia Hebbert and
others in developing a wonderful lap mothers' program. Sometimes
the name "lap mother" was modified as those volunteers became big
brothers and sisters. If those volunteers could only know how they
helped many needy, lonely children!

Virginia Hebbert, Mary Rogan, Marie Lauria, Marion Kalbacker,
and all the pediatric social workers have done a superb job in their
many roles in the Pediatric Department.

Brian and I had the support from Dr. Denny and so many of the
pediatric faculty—Jerry Fernald, Cam McMillan, Mike Sharp, Harvey Hamrick, Al Collier, Neil Kirkman, Jud Van Wyk, Lou Underwood, Herb Harned, Harrie Chamberlin, Ernie Kraybill, and so many
more. They made each of us feel very much a part of the Department
of Pediatrics. This left us in an enviable position, seldom found in child
psychiatry programs in the country. It made working with and teaching the students, the residents, and the faculty fun and exciting and
easy.

I do want to close by describing briefly how my own clinical focus
has changed in recent years. About a half dozen years ago, at the time
of a rather mass exodus of psychiatry faculty from the adult consulta-
tion/liaison service, I was asked to come on board and became a member of the adult psychiatry consultation/liaison faculty. I agreed to help
out in the near crisis situation.

Dr. Taylor's story and the decade of very excellent relationships
between pediatrics and child psychiatry and pediatric psychology ends at
this point. The last sentence in the above paragraph is classic Cathy Taylor—
always ready to help when needed though this meant leaving her first
love—children.

Funding of the liaison program became a problem in the early 1980s.
This, coupled with the actions of the new chair in the Department of Psychiatry who abolished the pediatric liaison, signaled the beginning of a
new "low" in the relationships between pediatrics and child psychiatry
which continues to this day. As this is written in late 1993 the pediatric
psychologists, headed by Dr. Kenneth Whitt with the additional faculty
support of Teresa Pawletko and the psychology fellows, give vital help to

the children on the pediatric service but there is no organized help from child psychiatrists.

CATHERINE A. TAYLOR
JUDSON J. VAN WYK
FLOYD W. DENNY, JR.

FACULTY

Jessner, Lucie N. MD, Univ Koenigsberg (Prussia, Germany), 1926; Prof, Psychiat, 1955–62; Dir, Child Psychiat Sect, 1955–62.

Proctor, James T. MD, Univ Kansas, 1946; Assoc Prof, Child Psychiat, 1954–62.

Stabler, Brian. BA, Univ Durham (England), 1967; PhD, Univ NC at Chapel Hill, 1971; Asst Prof, Psychol in Psychiat, Ped and Fam Med, 1973; Assoc Prof, Psychol in Psychiat, Ped and Fam Med, 1979.

Taylor, Catherine Anne. BS, Carson Newman College, 1950; MD, Univ Tenn, 1957; Asst Prof, Psychiat, Ped and Fam Med, 1970; Assoc Prof, Psychiat and Ped, 1976; Chief, Ped Psychiat/Psychol Serv, 1970–91.

Whitt, J. Kenneth. BA, Univ Virginia, 1968; PhD, Univ Texas at Austin, 1976; Asst Prof, Psychol, Psychiat and Ped, 1976; Assoc Prof, Psychol, Psychiat and Ped, 1983; Chief, Div Ped Psychiat/Psychol, 1991.

FELLOWS

Years	Name	Current Position
1979	Marjorie Carr, MD	Priv Pract, Ped (Raleigh, NC)
1979–80	Margaret Zwerling, MD	Pract, Child Psychiat (Camden, ME)

CHAPTER FOURTEEN

Community Pediatrics

IN THE late 1960s, Dr. Denny began to explore the idea of establishing a
division of community pediatrics which would probe societal issues affecting the health of children. A search was established for an appropriate leader.
However, this appeared to be futile as all the candidates lacked training, especially in research. Fortuitously, Dr. Denny decided to interview one of "our
own," Frank Loda, who shared Dr. Denny's research vision and who wished
very much to accept the challenge of establishing such a division. Dr. Denny
later felt that this was one of the most important appointments that he made
as a departmental chairman.

In a revealing interview of Dr. Loda by Dr. Denny (which is available in
its entirety in our archives), the wisdom of this decision is apparent. Dr.
Loda's background, training, and social philosophy prepared him for successful leadership.

Dr. Loda described his boyhood and assisting his father in community
affairs. As director of the Community Chest in the small city of Texarkana,
Arkansas, Frank's father needed to be involved in frequent fund-raising cam-
paigns; but beyond this, he exposed young Frank to other community activities, such as campaigning for chest X rays for detection of tuberculosis, dis-
tributing food to drought-affected farmers, and visiting an industrial school
whose student girls were suffering from very bad health. These activities
alerted Frank to some of the societal forces influencing health.

Initially interested in politics, Frank attended Harvard and then chose
Vanderbilt Medical School, where his interest in infectious disease flourished.
He received additional medical training at Vanderbilt, the University of
Washington in Seattle, the NIH with Dr. Vernon Knight, and then at UNC
with the pediatric infectious disease group, where he completed his pediatric

residency training. A fellowship followed with Professor Stuart-Harris
in Sheffield, England, where Dr. Loda
worked in a family practice, studying
transmission of respiratory illnesses.
Acquaintance with the medical system of Great Britain and the activities of the pioneering center for social
pediatrics at Newcastle upon Tyne
strengthened Dr. Loda's own knowledge of social medicine. After he
returned to UNC, he found the ongoing experiments at the Frank Porter
Graham Child Development Center
on the effects of social and economic
deprivation on child development of
great interest. He became the director of the health component of the
center from 1967 to 1970.

Frank Loda

Several needs of the Department
in 1970 were critically important and contributed to the development of the
division of community pediatrics. The pediatric outpatient department needed
to be organized more effectively, especially in the area of general pediatrics,
where there was heavy reliance on part-time teachers. Also at this time, the University developed a commitment to begin training family nurse-practitioners
who require considerable exposure to ambulatory pediatrics. In addition, the
Orange Chatham Community Health Services (OCCHS) was established,
with three clinics scheduled to offer primary medical care. This was a critical
time for appointment of a leader from pediatrics to synthesize these developments and to work politically with the many disparate groups in the University and community. Dr. Loda was appointed in 1970 just before Dr. Denny
started his sabbatical year in England.

Critical decisions were made then as to the nature and mission of the community pediatrics division. Rather than just becoming a clinical service to
process the moderate pediatric outpatient load, the program was to be
designed as an instrument for social research in medicine that could contribute to the intellectual life of the University.

As the Medical School's designs for a new residency in family medicine
were being formulated, Dr. Loda flew to England with Drs. Robert Smith,
Louis Welt, and Glenn Wilson to discuss these plans with Dr. Denny, as well
as to attend an important Anglo-American Conference on Health Care. In his
interview with Dr. Denny, Dr. Loda described the flight: "The plane was practically empty and so I went to a back seat and outlined what I was going to
tell you about my plans for community pediatrics. I obviously had been thinking about it, but I outlined it all on that flight and considered things like the

relationship of our division to the study of children's behavior and the relative importance of behavioral issues. That eight hours or so as we flew into the gathering dark was when I really put it together."

Dr. Loda has since defined community pediatrics as "that branch of pediatrics concerned with the role of social institutions, social policy, social mores in the health of children and what health professionals can do to affect these relationships in a positive way." He augments this: "Clearly, in that definition the social institutions would include the family, educational institutions, and day care; social policy would include issues like government regulations and funding; social mores would include attitudes toward violence, sexual stereotyping, and racial stereotyping. All of those things really do affect the health of children in a very profound way. Later, we came to add to that definition the concept of the physical environment as being something that we were uniquely concerned about."

Despite incorporation of understanding of psychological factors into the "new pediatrics" of the '50s and '60s and the later melding of these factors with the biological, *sociological* factors were still underemphasized. Loda concludes: "What wasn't being added was the third leg of the stool. It is sociological phenomena, the way society interacts with children and families," that needed proper emphasis. Dr. Loda stresses that "children are particularly vulnerable to sociological phenomena; institutional failures impact much more on children because they lack the resources to cope if their families are not supportive."

Dr. Loda entered into a review of some of the resources of this institution which favored development of a successful program. The state and the University were involved in organizing rural health centers and promoting new ways of delivering health care, such as the use of nurse-practitioners. Dr. John Cassel, in the School of Public Health, was a pioneer in the field of social medicine, and he and his colleagues provided research tools and vision for promotion of the ideas expressed above. This depth of available expertise helped Dr. Loda rapidly establish a fellowship program that has attracted many skillful and highly motivated young people over the years.

The first two fellows in the program were Drs. James Schwankl and Greg Liptak, who were funded partly by OCCHS, where they worked while obtaining degrees in epidemiology from the School of Public Health. Soon the Robert Wood Johnson Clinical Scholars program became available at UNC, permitting creation of models for training physicians in a new specialty of community pediatrics. With funding from this program available, the division of community pediatrics was able to recruit some of the best residents from our own Pediatrics Department, as well as from other institutions.

In addition to the resources provided for training by the School of Public Health, other University resources were utilized. Dr. Loda indicated the excellent early support given to the division by Glenn Wilson in the Department of Social Medicine of the Medical School, which took the form of philosophical and psychological support, as well as shared facilities, financial help, and "driving the wedge for us in many ways."

The division was heavily involved in the clinical training of the pediatric house staff. The AHEC program also provided additional resources for the training of residents and medical students in general pediatrics. The division was involved in the decision to extend the teaching of general pediatrics through residency programs at Wake Medical Center and participated in these programs after their establishment.

Bob Greenberg

Dr. Loda, in his interview, discussed the attendings who have helped to create this preeminent division:

Dr. Robert Greenberg started as an instructor in 1971, working in the Prospect Hill Clinic serving Caswell and northern Orange Counties. He was soon also involved in the total pediatric residency teaching program as its director and as a member of the House Staff Selection Committee. This intimate association of the division with pediatric house staff training was continued after Dr. Greenberg left by Dr. Harvey Hamrick and others. In addition to Dr. Greenberg's role as counselor to the house staff, he generated additional respect as a result of his research studies on the roles of nurse-practitioners as purveyors of health care and his studies of the passive effects on health of inhalation of cigarette smoke. It was a great loss to the division when Dr. Greenberg left to join his wife in Louisiana, where he is now director of maternal and child health for that state.

Dr. Harvey Hamrick, who completed his medical school and pediatric resi-

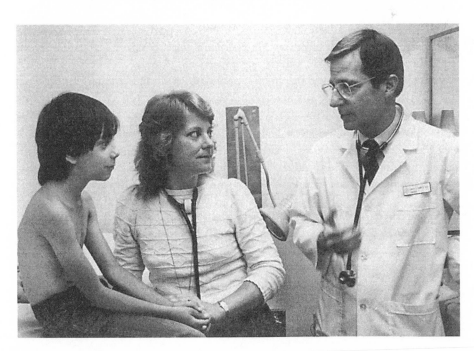

Harvey Hamrick as a mentor in the clinics

Mike Sharp

dency training at UNC, returned from a year of practice to become a fellow in 1972. During his fellowship, he concentrated on learning the theories of medical education, which have proved useful as he has become a pivotal member of the division and the Department. Dr. Loda has emphasized the exemplary manner in which Dr. Hamrick has designed and conducted the teaching program in the general pediatric outpatient department.

Dr. Donal Dunphy, as the director of the pediatric component of AHEC, played an extremely important role in projecting the activities of the community pediatrics division onto the statewide level. As one of the founding fathers of the national Ambulatory Pediatric Association and one of its former presidents, Dr. Dunphy provided a historical perspective for the division. Don was one of the members of the division who taught students and house staff in the newborn nurseries. The division has assumed a major responsibility for this, supplementing its role in providing inpatient ward attendings.

Dr. Michael Sharp joined the division in 1977. As a fellow, he enrolled in the core curriculum of the Robert Wood Johnson Scholars program. He has been interested in empowering families to involve themselves more profoundly with their children's health care and, as part of this, has set up networks of families with child health problems whereby they can interchange information and establish support systems.

Dr. Alan Cross joined the faculty in 1978 and has provided an international arm for the division through his interest in the health care of Kenya. Dr. Cross's broad-ranging interests and "global" talents have continued as he has pursued his present role as UNC director of the Health Promotion Disease Prevention Center. One of his research activities keyed on defining appropriate measures for children's health examinations.

Dr. Desmond Runyan joined the division in 1979 and has provided expertise in adolescent medicine in addition to his primary interest in child abuse. His research has been directed at studying the labyrinth of legal procedures for foster home placement, as well as the long-term consequences of child abuse on the emotional health of the victims.

Dr. Jean Smith joined the faculty in the early 1980s, adding a female perspective to considerations of child abuse, sexual abuse, and the care of adolescents.

Dr. Mary Glenn Fowler completed a fellowship in the DDDL and became a member of the teaching faculty. Her research was directed to the study of children with chronic diseases and developmental disabilities, generating several well-received national workshops and presentations.

Alan Cross

Dr. William Gronemeyer joined the division in 1978 in a part-time capacity. As a retired practitioner, he provided many years of seasoned judgment and practical knowledge for the teaching program in the outpatient department. He was admired greatly by the pediatric house staff, who awarded him their coveted Teacher of the Year Award in 1981.

Dr. Susanne White, after completing her residency at UNC, obtained an MPH degree in 1981. She became the director of the pediatric outpatient department at Wake Hospital. She was the first African American tenured professor in the Department of Pediatrics at UNC. She now holds a very important position at Louisiana State University.

With this outstanding and imaginative faculty, the division was awarded the national Outstanding Teaching Award by the Ambulatory Pediatric Association in 1984. This national recognition mirrored the high regard in which the teaching program has been held locally. Teaching of general pediatrics in an outpatient setting is far from being a "step-child" when organized as well as has been done at the UNC Hospitals. Primary care is detailed skillfully in the daily morning sessions by Dr. Hamrick and his associates, building on the traditions of Drs. Arthur London and Charles Sheaffer. Additional strength in teaching has been provided by members of the American Board of Pediatrics after its move to Chapel Hill. Drs. Robert Brownlee and Harold Meyer were the first of this group to participate. Dr. Joseph Garfunkel, the editor of the *Journal of Pediatrics*, has been a particularly outstanding addition to this teaching program and has been another of the division's members to be awarded the Outstanding Teacher Award.

The effectiveness of teaching of general pediatrics at UNC has been verified by the high scores recorded on the examinations of the American Board of Pediatrics. Often the figures for general pediatrics have been better than those for subspecialties, but generally all the scores have been in the top 5 percent nationally. Rather than taking his share of credit, Dr. Loda attributes these high scores to the high quality of people we have been able to recruit.

The teaching program of the division has extended well beyond the confines of taking care of the children brought to the OPD. For example, residents have been involved in home visits in rural Orange County as part of

Des Runyan

Mary Glenn
Fowler

the Adolescents-in-Need program and have participated in health education in middle schools in Chatham County. Outpatient rotations at Wake Hospital and as part of the Greensboro AHEC program have provided enriching experiences.

Of course, any successful program is bound to have some disappointments. One major disappointment for Dr. Loda was the failure of the OCCHS program to become a major part of the teaching program despite the early role it played in the development of the division. In addition, the program of following children of house officers and medical students sequentially, known as the continuity clinic, had a "bumpy" start because of scheduling difficulties and the multiple demands on the residents' time. Over time, however, this clinic has gained acceptance and is now a valued part of the resident training experience.

In a more recent communication, Dr. Loda has described the diversification of the division during the Boat years. Two additional sources of funding have been used to expand the fellowship training program. In 1986, the division of community pediatrics, along with the Center for Development and Learning, received a grant for faculty development in behavioral pediatrics. In 1988, in coordination with the Department of Family Medicine and the Department of Internal Medicine, the division was awarded a National Research Training grant in primary medical care research from the National Health Service. In addition, there were funding opportunities through the preventive medicine residency program in the Department of Social Medicine and through National Research Training grants in health care research to the Sheps Center; these provided a variety of sources to expand the number of fellows in the division. These training programs have produced a steady stream of able young people prepared to conduct research in community and primary care settings, have provided the division with a number of new faculty members, and have allowed UNC to send well-trained future leaders to other academic institutions.

Bill Gronemeyer

Two major areas of research during this period deserve particular attention. In 1984, the division received a large grant from the National Heart, Lung, and Blood Institute to design an intervention program to reduce infants' exposure to second-hand smoke. As mentioned, this project was led initially by Dr. Robert Greenberg and included participation by other faculty members from the division, from the Department of Psychiatry, and from the Department of Health Behavior and Health Education in the School of Public Health. These studies, and projects related to them, have had a significant effect in increasing awareness of the hazards of passive smoking to infants.

Dr. Loda emphasized also the major program on child abuse and neglect that he initiated and that now is primarily directed by Dr. Des Runyan and his colleagues.

This work represents a good example of the effective integration of academic clinical service and basic epidemiologic research with leadership in public health at the state level. In the area of child abuse, a large clinic has been developed here, and the division has been involved also in the formation of a very effective statewide network for evaluating these children. Dr. Runyan has obtained continuing substantial support for national studies of the long-term effects of child abuse and neglect. Dr. Runyan has his primary appointment in the Department of Social Medicine; his work in clinical pediatrics through the division also provides an outstanding example of the type of interdepartmental collaboration that has marked the history of the division during this period.

In August 1988, Dr. Loda assumed the directorship of the Center for Early Adolescence while continuing as chief of community pediatrics. This center had been established in 1978 by Dr. Joan Lipsitz as a unit of the School of Education at UNC-Chapel Hill. It was the first center in the nation devoted to promoting healthy growth and development of ten- to twenty-year-old children. Before leaving the center to join the staff of the Lilly Endowment in Indianapolis, Dr. Lipsitz had created a strong emphasis on middle-school education and on involving the support of youth-serving agencies in the community.

Jake Lohr

Major initiatives related to middle-grades education, the preparation of middle-grades teachers, literacy programs, and programs for young adolescents after school hours have been continued and strengthened, as have efforts to develop comprehensive, coordinated, community-based services for this age group. Dr. Loda has extended these efforts statewide and, with the involvement of the Sheps Center for Health Policy Research, has engaged in national projects relating to the health needs of adolescents.

It soon became clear that the Center for Early Adolescence required a full-time director and Dr. Loda asked to be relieved of his responsibilities as chief of the division of community pediatrics. After a national search, Dr. Jacob Lohr, who was a graduate of our Medical School and had been a professor at the University of Virginia, was appointed. Dr. Loda, continuing as a member of the division, has made sure that the clinical activities of the Center for Early Adolescence remain closely linked to the division.

Looking to the future, Dr. Loda sees great potential in the Greensboro program under Drs. Myron Johnson and Jane Foy and believes that this indeed can be developed into a teaching program comparable to that at Wake Hospital. Dr. Foy already has a school-based program in place at a Greensboro high school.

Although the program in community pediatrics has been very advanced, the Medical School generally has been slow in following its lead. However, Dr. Loda has been encouraged by recent attitudinal changes in the Departments of Medicine and Family Practice. The links with the Department of Maternal and Child Health in the School of Public Health have been strengthened, especially since Dr. Desmond Runyan has been here, and this linkage may again approach the very successful earlier liaisons that were promoted by Drs. Naomi Morris and Earl Siegel. The leadership provided by Drs. John Cassel and Bernard Greenberg in amalgamating these mutually beneficial relationships has been sorely missed since their untimely deaths.

Dr. Denny has stressed the favorable ballpark for developing a successful program in this state and this University community. Still, there are many untapped resources that will permit additional achievements. Perhaps even the physical location of the division may be improved with concentration of activities at fewer sites.

Before concluding the interview with Dr. Denny, Dr. Loda reemphasized several programs of which he is especially proud. The child abuse program, initiated from early insights by Dr. Rosemary Hunter, has become a national model. Statewide medical evaluations have been established for child abuse and sexual abuse cases. The family nurse-practitioner training initiatives, the establishment of rural health centers, the promotion of the Adolescents-in-Need programs have all been influenced strongly by physicians in the community pediatrics division. He also emphasized his pride in the accomplishments of the many persons who have been trained in the division and who are listed at the end of this section.

Peter
Margolis

With rapid changes occurring nationally in the delivery of health care for children, new challenges are facing the division now under Dr. Lohr's direction. A far more important role is envisaged for primary care physicians and training of general pediatricians must keep pace with these new demands. The division has undergone considerable expansion, with the addition of new faculty members whose impact on the division and Medical Center is beginning to be felt.

Since this historical account has focused primarily on the origins and development of the program of community pediatrics, we cannot do justice to the promising ongoing activities and projects of the present faculty and staff. Newer members of the division include Steven Applegate, Clay Bordley, Barbara Dentz, Steven Downs, Gary Freed, Carole Lannon, Peter Margolis, and Rebecca Socolar. In addition to being the largest division in the Department, community pediatrics will be in a position to compete in creativity with the other divisions, while contributing an increasingly larger share in the care of children by the Department.

Dr. Denny's presidential address for the American Pediatric Society in 1981 stressed the importance of outreach into the community. It is gratifying for the Department that a curriculum has been defined to address societal problems relating to child health and that this important division has contributed so imaginatively to the creation of this new perspective.

FRANK A. LODA
HERBERT S. HARNED, JR.
FLOYD W. DENNY, JR.

FACULTY

Brownlee, Robert. AB, Erskine Coll, 1943; MD, Vanderbilt, 1945; Clin Prof, Ped, 1978.

Cross, Alan W. BA, Yale, 1966; MD, Columbia, 1970; Inst, Ped, 1978; Asst Prof, Ped and Commun and Admin Med, 1979; Assoc Prof, Ped and Social and Admin Med, 1986; Dir, Ctr for Hlth Promot and Dis Prev, 1992; Prof, Ped and Social Med, 1994.

Downs, Stephen M. BA, Univ Colorado, 1980; MS, Stanford, 1986; MD, Stanford, 1986; Visit Clin Prof, Ped, 1991; Asst Prof, Ped, 1992; Asst Prof, Biomed Eng, 1995.

Dunphy, Donal L. BA, Holy Cross, 1939; MD, Yale, 1944; Prof, Ped, 1973–87; AHEC Liaison, Ped, 1973–89; Acting Chair, Fam Med, 1975–76; Spec Asst to Dir AHEC, 1979–89; Dir, Med/Ped Resid Train Prog, 1982–87; Clin Prof, 1987–89; Prof Emerit, Ped, 1989.

Fowler, Mary Glenn. BA, Univ Washington, 1968; MD, Univ Oregon, 1972; Inst, Ped, 1977; Asst Prof, Ped, 1979; Assoc Prof, Ped, 1986–88.

Freed, Gary L. BA, Univ Texas at Austin, 1983; MD, Baylor, 1987; Asst Prof, Ped, 1992; Adj Asst Prof, Hlth Policy and Admin, Pub Hlth, 1992.

Garfunkel, Joseph M. MD, Temple Univ, 1948; MS, Temple Univ, 1953; Editor, *Journal of Pediatrics*, 1977; Visit Prof, Ped, 1984; Prof, Ped, 1985; Clin Prof, Ped, 1991.

Greenberg, Robert A. AB, Harvard, 1960; MD, Penn, 1964; MSPH, UNC Sch Pub Hlth, 1982; Inst, Mat and Child Hlth, 1971; Asst Prof, Mat and Child Hlth and Ped, 1972; Assoc Prof, Ped, 1977; Prof, Ped, 1985–90.

Gronemeyer, William H. MD, Case Western Res Univ, 1935; Clin Prof, Ped, 1978–82 and 1985–87.

Hamrick, Harvey J. AB, UNC-CH, 1961; MD, UNC-CH, 1967; Inst, Ped and Fam Med, 1972; Asst Prof, Ped and Fam Med, 1974; Assoc Prof, Ped and Fam Med, 1979; Prof, Ped, 1987.

Hunter, Rosemary. AB, Wellesley, 1963; MD, Univ Washington, 1967; Asst Prof, Ped and Psychiat, 1976–83.

Lannon, Carole M. BA, Macalester Coll, 1976; MD, Univ Minn, 1982; MS, UNC Sch Pub Hlth, 1993; Clin Inst, Med, 1990; Visit Clin Asst Prof, Ped and Med, 1991; Clin Asst Prof, Ped and Med, 1992.

Loda, Frank A. AB, Harvard, 1956; MD, Vanderbilt, 1960; Asst Prof, Ped, 1967; Asst Prof, Mat and Child Hlth, 1967; Dir, Div Comm Ped, 1971–90; Assoc Prof, Ped, 1972; Prof, Ped, 1980; Adj Prof, Mat Child Hlth, 1983.

Lohr, Jacob A. BA, UNC-CH, 1962; MD, UNC-CH, 1967; Prof, Ped and Dir, Div Comm Ped, 1990.

Margolis, Peter A. AB, Dartmouth, 1976; MD, NYU, 1980; PhD, UNC Sch Pub

Hlth, 1990; Clin Inst, Ped, 1987; Asst Prof, Ped, 1990; Adj Asst Prof, Epidem, 1991.

Meyer, Harold. AB, Penn, 1943; MD, Jefferson, 1946; Clin Prof, Ped, 1980–87.

Runyan, Desmond K. AB, Macalester College, 1972; MPH, Univ Minn Sch Pub Hlth, 1975; MD, Univ Minn, 1976; DrPH, Mat and Child Hlth, UNC-CH, 1983; Asst Prof, Ped and Soc and Admin Med, 1981; Clin Asst Prof Epidem, Sch Pub Hlth, 1983; Assoc Prof, Ped and Soc and Admin Med, 1988, Assoc Prof, Ped, 1988; Clin Assoc Prof, Epidem, 1988; Prof, Ped and Soc and Admin Med, 1995.

Sharp, Michael C. BA, Amherst, 1968; BMA, Dartmouth, 1972; MD, Harvard, 1974; Inst, Ped, 1977; Asst Prof, Ped, 1980; Dir, Fam Support Network of NC, 1986; Assoc Prof, Ped, 1987; Dir, Office of Comm Educ, 1993.

Smith, Jean. BA, Univ Missouri at Columbia, 1971; MD, Univ Missouri, 1975; Clin Asst Prof, Ped, 1984; Asst Prof, Ped, 1987; Clin Assoc Prof, Ped, 1994.

Socolar, Rebecca S. AB, Bryn Mawr, 1979; MD, UNC-CH, 1984; Visit Res Asst Prof, Ped, 1992; Clin Asst Prof, Ped, 1994.

White, Susanne T. BS, Bennett Coll, 1971; MD, UNC-CH, 1975; MPH, UNC-CH, 1981; Dir, Teens Clinic, Wake AHEC, 1981–88; Asst Prof, Ped, UNC-CH, 1982–88; Dir, Ped Outpt, Wake AHEC, 1982–88.

PRIMARY CARE FELLOWS

Year	*Name*	*Current Position*
1989–90	Peter A. Margolis, MD, PhD	Asst Prof, Ped and Clinc Asst Prof, Epid, UNC
1990–92	Amy A. Levine, MD	Clin Asst Prof, Ped and Nutrit, UNC

BEHAVIORAL PEDIATRICS FELLOWS

Year	*Name*	*Current Position*
1987–90	Conleth Crotser, MD	St. Luke's Med Ctr, Cleveland, OH
1988–89	Jennie McLaurin (Smith), MD	Adj Clin Asst Prof, Ped, UNC; Med Dir, Migrant Hlth Prog, Office of Rural Hlth and Devt
1990–93	Sharon Van Horn, MD	Adolesc Clin, Orange Cty Hlth Dept

MISCELLANEOUS FELLOWS

Year	Name	Current Position
1971–72	Robert S. Thompson, MD	Dept Prev Care, Grp Hlth Coop, Seattle, WA
1972–74	Harvey J. Hamrick, MD	Prof, Ped, UNC
1972–74	James E. Schwankl, MD	Pract, Ped, Siler City, NC
1980–82	Jack A. Land, MD	Pract, Ped, Festus, MO
1981–83	Steall Tsitoura-Lykopoulous, MD	Academic Ped, Greece
1987–88	Francis E. Onyongo, MD	Prof and Chair, Ped, Univ Nairobi, Kenya

ROBERT WOOD JOHNSON CLINICAL SCHOLARS

Year	Name	Current Position
1973–75	Gregory S. Liptak, MD	Assoc Prof, Ped; Med Dir, Easter Seal Ctr, Strong Mem Hosp, Univ Rochester
1974–76	Tom Mettee, MD	Pres, Cuyahoga Fam Phys, Inc; Asst Clin Prof, Case West Res Univ
1974–77	Thomas M. Boyce, MD	Dir, Div Behav and Dev Ped; Prof, Ped; Adj Assoc Prof Epid, UC-SF
1975–77	Earl W. Bryant, MD	Med Dir, Emerg Rm, Carolinas Hosp, Florence, SC
1975–77	Michael F. Durfee, MD	Phys, Stud Hlth Svc, NC St Univ
1976–78	Patrick H. Casey, MD	Dir, Div Dev Ped; Prof, Ped, Univ Arkansas
1976–78	Wendy G. Mitchell, MD	Assoc Prof, Ped and Neurol, USC
1977–80	John M. Pascoe, MD	Head, Gen Ped and Adolesc Med; Assoc Prof, Univ Wisc
1978–80	Edward P. Ehlinger, MD	Dir, Pers Hlth Svcs; Adj Asst Prof, Ped and Pub Hlth, Univ Minn
1978–80	Anthony C. Kimbrough, MD	Dep Dir, Ped Ed; Dir, Amb Care, Child Hosp, Austin, TX
1979–81	Carolyn L. Gould, MD	Staff Phys, Rutgers Comm Hlth Plan, NJ

1979–81	Desmond K. Runyan, MD	Prof, Ped and Soc Med; Prin Inv, LONGSCAN, UNC-CH
1982–84	Thomas M. Jones, MD	Clin Asst Prof, Psychiat, UNC-CH
1983–85	Ruth A. Etzel, MD	Chief, Air Poll and Resp Hlth Branch, CDC&P
1984–86	Charles J. Homer, MD	Dir, Clin Effect Prog, Child Hosp; Asst Prof, Ped, Harvard
1987–89	Peter A. Margolis, MD, PhD	Asst Prof, Ped, UNC-CH
1988–90	Jonathan D. Klein, MD	Asst Prof, Ped and Prev Comm Med, Univ Rochester
1988–90	Carole M. Lannon, MD	Clin Asst Prof, Ped and Med, UNC-CH
1989–91	Stephen M. Downs, MD	Asst Prof, Ped, UNC-CH
1990–92	Gary L. Freed, MD	Asst Prof, Ped and Hlth Pol Admin, UNC-CH
1991–93	W. Clayton Bordley, MD	Visit Asst Prof, Ped, UNC-CH
1992–94	Elizabeth Dixon, MD	Priv Pract (Sylva, NC)

CHAPTER FIFTEEN

Critical Care

S OME would say that critical care is a concept that was invented at UNC. One of the first "special care units" was developed at NCMH in the early 1950s to accommodate adult medical and surgical patients with intensive care needs. Also, the "premature nursery" was a unique departure from the routine care nurseries of the past and served the Departments of Pediatrics and Ob-Gyn up until the 1970s, when the neonatal intensive care unit (NICU) was developed. Nevertheless, most of our readers who received their training before the 1970s will remember that critically ill children received their intensive care on an ad hoc basis. That is, resuscitation and other critical care treatments were carried out in the patient's ward room, which became a beehive of activity during the short period of time required to restore the patient's vital functions or to determine that no further efforts would be beneficial.

The first formal pediatric intensive care area was located on the south side of 7 West, circa 1973. In the large ward room formerly occupied by boys with orthopedic problems, a four-bed unit was created, with a fifth isolation room in the corner intersecting with the 7 West isolation unit added later. Patients placed in this unit received an increased level of nursing care from the 7 West unit but were cared for by the pediatric house staff under direction from whichever attending was engaged in that patient's care. Bob Herrington was in charge of the initial planning of this "intermediate" care unit with final planning, equipping, and coordinating of nurse training for the unit carried out by Stewart Schall after he joined the cardiology division in 1972.

In 1975, at about the time the Gravely Children's Chest Unit closed and all of pediatrics was returned to the seventh floor, the newly constructed six-bed ICU in the center of the bed tower addition was opened with June Schakne and, later, Louise Taylor as head nurses. Again, patients transferred to this unit were cared for by whichever medical or surgical team they were on, the main advantage being the location of the beds around a central nursing station which provided an increase in level of staffing and a certain amount of expertise. Many of the pediatric surgical patients were admitted to this ICU but cardiothoracic patients usually remained in the cardiothoracic ICU with pediatric cardiology consultations being provided by the members of the pediatric cardiology division. Dr. Bill Henry, during his fellowship and early junior faculty days, developed special expertise in perisurgical cardiovascular care.

In the late 1970s, the chief residents requested a formal resident rotation in the new ICU. As part of organizing this new rotation, Stewart Schall asked Ned Bowe and Bud Klein to become codirectors when they expressed interest. Drs. Bowe and Klein were anesthesiologists with pediatric and intensive care experience and special interest. Dr. Schall, with the approval of the codirectors, pressed for the recruitment of an intensivist to head the unit.

In 1981, Dr. Geoffrey Barker, who was director of the pediatric intensive care unit at Toronto Sick Children's Hospital, served as a visiting professor sponsored by the Denny Society. His review and recommendations served as the basis for defining the future needs and direction of development for critical care in the Department of Pediatrics before Dr. Boat arrived. Dr. Robert Valley, who was senior resident and chief resident in 1983 and 1984, played a large role in coordinating the activities of the various services and attendings working in the unit. Dr. Terry Bilz Hansen, one of our pediatric residents who had trained in pediatric critical care, assumed leadership of the unit in July 1984. We were greatly saddened to lose her to rapidly progressive melanoma shortly thereafter. Subsequently, Dr. Jerry Strope, our first pediatric pulmonary trainee, Dr. Bob Wood, who arrived in 1983 to develop the new pulmonary division, and Dr. Marianna Henry, one of its first fellows, provided much of the attending coverage for the unit, while a full-time intensivist was being recruited. Others who contributed their time and talents to the PICU attending roster during these difficult years were Drs. Margaret Leigh, Fred Henderson, C. Richard Morris, Robert Warren, Stewart Schall, and Robert Herrington.

In 1985, Dr. Arno Zaritsky arrived from D.C. Children's Hospital to head a new division of critical care medicine in the Department of Pediatrics. For the first time, we had an expert in the area of pediatric critical care in our Depart-

Arno
Zaritsky

Lew Romer

Lela Brink

ment. Arno's "people skills," as well as his technical expertise, were invaluable in working with the hospital to develop a new ten-bed critical care unit on the site of the former 7 bed tower A toddler unit. The problem of filling beds and justifying adequate nursing coverage, which had plagued us for the previous ten years, was gradually resolved as patients were attracted to the unit from the pediatrics medical and surgery services and by direct referral from surrounding hospitals. Input from the pediatric transport service under the direction of Dr. Carl Bose also began in July 1986. The level of care delivered personally by Dr. Zaritsky to the unit, with supporting attending coverage provided by Drs. Bob Wood, Des Runyan, Steve Downs, and others with sufficient critical care skills, attracted the cardiothoracic patients to the PICU, where combined direction of their care was shared by the two services. As faculty trained in pediatric critical care were recruited, the attending roster became exclusively critical care oriented and relieved other members of the Department from their difficult but much appreciated voluntary coverage. Dr. Steve Lawless was the first pediatric intensivist to be recruited by Dr. Zaritsky. Drs. Robert Kanter, Eugene Freid, Lewis Romer, and Lela Brink were all recruited after Dr. Lawless moved on in July 1990.

In addition to elevating the level of intensive care available for children throughout the state, development of the critical care division had a very significant impact on other aspects of the developing North Carolina Children's Hospital. Training in pediatric advanced life support (PALS) was directed by Dr. Zaritsky and his colleagues, and all new house staff regularly received PALS training as they began their internship. Since critically ill patients were directed to the PICU, the ward service rarely was faced with critically ill patients on admission. The new generation of house staff was taught critical care by pediatric experts and, although the various subspecialty groups consulted on patients in the PICU, they were no longer directly responsible for resuscitation and life support technology.

As the Boat era drew to a close, Dr. Zaritsky summarized the recent history of the PICU under his direction. He emphasized the increasing critical nature of referrals, especially the addition of liver transplants (and subsequently bone marrow and heart transplants). PICU nursing became independent from the adult critical care services and expanded from twelve to fifty-one FTE positions. A fellowship training program was initiated in July 1990, training one fellow that year (Cecelia Rave Caldwell) and another in 1991 (Marvin Hall). Future plans included development of an intermediate care unit, expansion of the faculty to four full-time positions, and support for the fellowship from the hospital. Unfortunately, Arno Zaritsky withdrew from the directorship of the critical care programs and moved to Norfolk in July 1992. The program continued under the direction of Drs. Lewis Romer and Lela Brink as the Department began to search for a new chair with Dr. Boat's departure in June 1993.

GERALD W. FERNALD

FACULTY

Editors' Note: Many attendings, as mentioned above, participated in teaching and patient care in the years before and after the PICU was formally organized. If we have failed to recognize an individual's contribution of time and effort, we apologize for the oversight.

Bowe, Edwin A. BS, Trinity Coll (CT), 1971; MD, Univ Missouri, 1975; Asst Prof, Anesth and Ped, 1979.

Brink, Lela W. BS, Univ Wisc, 1972; MD, NJ Med Sch, 1977; Asst Prof, Ped, 1992; Acting Dir, PICU, 1992.

Freid, Eugene B. BS, Rockford Coll (IL), 1979; MD, Chicago Med Sch, 1984; Asst Prof, Anesth and Ped, 1990.

Henry, George W. AB, UNC-CH, 1973; MD, UNC-CH, 1977; Clin Inst, Ped, 1981; Asst Prof, Ped, 1982; Assoc Prof, Ped, 1987; Chief, Div Ped Cardiol, 1987.

Kanter, Robert K. BA, Univ Penn, 1971; MD, Univ Penn, 1976; Assoc Prof, Ped, 1990–92.

Klein, Elmer F., Jr. AB, Univ Missouri, 1962; MD, Univ Missouri, 1965; Prof, Anesth, 1979.

Lawless, Stephen T. BS, Fordham Univ, 1977; MD, Rutgers, 1981; Asst Prof, Ped, 1988–90.

Romer, Lewis H. AB, Dartmouth, 1977; MD, Dartmouth, 1981; Asst Prof, Ped, 1990; Acting Dir, PICU, 1992.

Schall, Stewart A. BA, Rutgers, 1956; MD, Univ Penn, 1960; Asst Prof, Ped, 1972; Assoc Prof, Ped, 1978.

Strope, Gerald L. BA, Houghton Coll (NY), 1965; MD, Univ Rochester, 1974; Asst Prof, Ped, 1979; Assoc Prof, Ped, 1986–87.

Wood, Robert E. BS, Stetson Univ, 1963; PhD, Vanderbilt, 1968; MD, Vanderbilt, 1970; Assoc Prof, Ped, 1983; Prof, Ped, 1988; Chief, Div Ped Pulm and Allergy, 1983–94.

Zaritsky, Arno L. BA, Univ Penn, 1972; MD, Univ Maryland, 1976; Asst Prof, Ped and Dir, PICU, 1986–92.

FELLOWS

Years	Name	Current Position
1990–93	Cecelia Rave Caldwell, MD	Dir, PICU, Mem Mission Hosp (Asheville, NC)
1991–94	Marvin N. Hall, MD	Asst Prof, Crit Care, TC Thompson's Child Hosp (Chattanooga, TN)

CHAPTER SIXTEEN

Developmental Pediatrics

Editors' Note: The history of this important aspect of pediatrics at the University of North Carolina can be conveniently and appropriately divided into two separate stories. The first is the story of the division for disorders of development and learning from its inception in the early 1960s until the middle 1980s. This picture is vividly painted by Dr. Harrie Chamberlin, the founding father of developmental pediatrics at the University of North Carolina. When he retired in 1984 Dr. Melvin Levine became director of this subspecialty. At that time the division was made a freestanding center within the University, thus changing somewhat the approach to developmental pediatrics at UNC. That story is told by Dr. Levine in the second part of this section.

DIVISION FOR DISORDERS OF
DEVELOPMENT AND LEARNING

THE division for disorders of development and learning (DDDL) was founded as a developmental evaluation clinic (DEC) in January 1962. Originally a part of the Department of Pediatrics, it became a separate entity and the clinical arm of the Biological Sciences Research Center (BSRC) in 1970. DDDL pediatric faculty members, however, maintained their faculty appointments in the Department of Pediatrics so that, while the pediatric section remained an integral part of the DDDL, it also continued as a departmental division.

From the beginning the program goal was the establishment of an effective interdisciplinary setting on behalf of developmentally handicapped children for the training of students and practicing professionals, for exemplary service including both evaluation and treatment, and for research. The degree of handicap could range from various forms of learning disability to profound involvement, as with spastic quadriplegia, severe mental retardation, and inability to communicate. The "whole child" was to be considered, along with his/her family and the extent of community support. Demonstration throughout of true interdisciplinary activity was an imperative—not mere parallel activity by members of several professional disciplines; the environment thus established was, above anything else, the hallmark of the DDDL.

Background of the Director

Dr. Harrie Chamberlin's interest in developmentally handicapped children can readily be traced to his contact with Dr. Grover Powers, chairman of the Department of Pediatrics at Yale when Chamberlin arrived in July 1949. A year of internship in neurology under Dr. Denny-Brown on Harvard's neurological unit at the Boston City Hospital also contributed. But exposure to mentally retarded persons, who were to become Chamberlin's focus, was minimal during that year, absent during two subsequent years while a medical officer in a large Army hospital, and minimal again during a year's pediatric internship at the Massachusetts General Hospital. In fact, his only real exposure came during the neurology year on a visit to the "living museum" of mental retardation syndromes at the Fernald School in Waltham, then a series of ancient factory-like buildings that comprised the oldest residential institution for retarded persons in the United States. Never were the moderately and severely involved adult unfortunates whom Chamberlin saw referred to as people: they were "tuberous sclerotics," "mongolian idiots," "nonverbal quadriplegics," or "gargoyles."

In 1938 Powers persuaded Connecticut's Governor Cross to place a new state facility for the mentally retarded, the Southbury Training School, within a half-hour's drive of New Haven. Dr. Herman Yannet, an associate professor on Dr. Powers's staff, was medical director, all medical students made at least one visit to Southbury, all pediatric interns spent seven weeks there, and a six-month residency rotation was available. But the resident about to take over, having just finished an Army tour of duty in Korea, had telegraphed Powers for permission to go to Peking to photograph the city before Mao's approaching Red armies engulfed it. Powers telegraphed "yes" and Chamberlin temporarily became the resident.

Southbury at that time was the most forward-looking facility of its kind in America and Chamberlin's few weeks there, combined with a regular six months' rotation chosen in the following year, instilled an abiding interest in mental retardation. Yet he did not realize how thoroughly this would shape his career until some seven years after becoming the second member of the new Department of Pediatrics in Chapel Hill, in January 1953, under one of his former mentors at Yale, Dr. Edward Curnen.

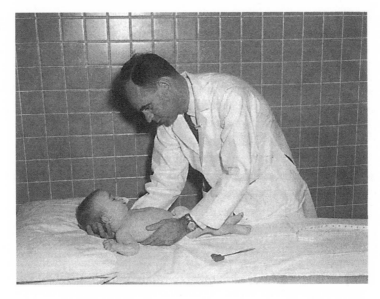

The Curnen Years: Preparation

During the Curnen years, Chamberlin's efforts were concentrated primarily on two major tasks: sharing in the development of the service and teaching functions of the new Department and initiation of a program in pediatric neurology. Yet additional influences were gradually steering him toward his eventual focus on infants and children with mental retardation and overall developmental handicaps.

Almost from the start, the high proportion of infants and children referred to Chapel Hill with developmental problems was somewhat of a surprise. That Chamberlin was the only academic pediatrician with some neurological background in the state until the late '50s (pediatric neurology was not defined as a subspecialty by the American Boards of Pediatrics and Neurology until 1957) and virtually the only academic pediatrician with interest in mentally retarded children played some role. But the numbers merely increased in the years that followed.

Most important was the decision to hold a Ross Pediatric Research Conference on "Etiologic Factors in Mental Retardation" in Chapel Hill in November 1956. Organized to honor Dr. Powers primarily by Dr. Curnen, with help from Chamberlin and others, it drew outstanding clinicians and researchers in various fields from around the country, plus contributors from England and Japan. Probably the most important conference to be hosted by the Department during the Curnen era, it was the first major symposium on this topic to be held in the United States.

By now Chamberlin had become involved in helping to develop an Orange County chapter of Parents and Friends of Retarded Children, a national organization soon to be called the National Association for Retarded Children

(NARC). By 1959 he was a member of the executive committee of the NARC's state chapter.

By the time Dr. Curnen moved to Columbia (1960), Chamberlin had become increasingly concerned by an inability to give adequate service to children with developmental handicaps and their families in the pediatric neurology clinic setting. Psychological and physical therapy consultations were carried out in other areas of the Medical Center. There was inadequate time to review problems in any depth with parents and almost no opportunity to plan adequate support of families in their communities or to be certain of appropriate follow-up. For the demonstration of an integrated overall approach to such problems the environment was totally inadequate.

The Denny Years: Initiation and Growth of the Program

THE DEC

In January 1962 a developmental evaluation clinic (DEC) was initiated within the Department of Pediatrics. Directed by Dr. Chamberlin, it utilized Children's Bureau funds channeled through the State Board of Health and was staffed by a part-time social worker, a part-time psychologist, a part-time child psychiatrist, and a part-time pediatrician (Chamberlin). Initially only one child and his/her family were studied per week, with all pediatric residents and all neurology residents rotating through the program. The DEC proved to be popular as a training site and, a few months later, occasional psychology trainees were assigned.

By 1965–1966 the staff had grown to eight professionals, representing pediatrics, child psychology, child psychiatry, communicative disorders, social work, and nursing, plus two support persons. In addition, trainees from pediatrics, neurology, psychology, child psychiatry, social work, nursing, physical therapy, special education, maternal and child health, the chaplaincy, and the Medical School fourth-year class were sharing in the DEC and a true interdisciplinary program had been established.

ACTIVITIES AT THE STATE AND FEDERAL LEVELS

In October 1962, the North Carolina Governor's Commission for the Mentally Retarded, to which Chamberlin had been appointed by Governor Terry Sanford, recommended the establishment of a permanent North Carolina Council on Mental Retardation which would report to the governor's office. Upon its initiation, Chamberlin became chairman of the Medical Committee and would remain an active member of the council, later known as the Council on Developmental Disabilities, for twenty-three years. He finally stepped down in 1986, two years after his retirement and four years after taking on the chairmanship of a newly formed offshoot of the council, the North Carolina Task Force on Prevention of Developmental Disabilities.

By early 1963, North Carolina's programs for the retarded had attracted the interest of the Kennedy administration. The President's Panel on Mental

Retardation had just completed its report. Chamberlin was asked to review the state's activities with Mrs. Sargent Shriver, the president's sister, and was subsequently appointed to the White House Advisory Committee by Dr. Stafford Warren, the president's special assistant for mental retardation. This committee, which was charged with the job of implementing as many of the recommendations of the President's Panel as possible, soon swung into vigorous action. Little did the members know at the time that the urgency was real, for by late November Kennedy would no longer be president. Dr. Donald Stedman, later an associate vice president of the greater University of North Carolina and then dean of the School of Education at Chapel Hill, played a major role, particularly in the development of a highly successful White House Conference on Mental Retardation held at Airlie House in September. North Carolina's Terry Sanford gave the gubernatorial address.

Although much was accomplished by the White House Advisory Committee, from the point of view of universities its most important activity was that which led to Public Law 88-164, Title I of which, the Mental Retardation Facilities Construction Act, provided the groundwork for two forms of university-based programs. Part A authorized grants for the construction of centers for research "on mental retardation and related aspects of human development" (MRRCs). Part B authorized grants for the construction of so-called university-affiliated facilities (UAFs) for the mentally retarded, "clinical facilities affiliated with universities in a position to develop programs for training professional personnel in the field of mental retardation." Chamberlin witnessed the signing of this legislation by Kennedy in late October and was given one of the thirty-three pens used in the ceremony.

Twenty UAF awards and twelve MRRC awards were made to universities across the country during the next five years. Ten universities, including the University of North Carolina at Chapel Hill, received both awards. From early 1965 through 1968, Chamberlin, as a consultant to the Division of Mental Retardation of the Rehabilitation Services Administration, shared in many site visits, chairing four of them. In 1968–1971 he was a member of the original Executive Committee of what was to become the AAUAP (American Association of University Affiliated Programs for the Developmentally Disabled) and was a member or chair of one or more committees of that organization from then until his retirement in mid-1984.

NORTH CAROLINA'S UAF AND MRRC AWARDS

It was natural for the University of North Carolina at Chapel Hill to apply for both a UAF and an MRRC award. The DEC was a natural base for the former, as its makeup and goals fitted closely with the concept put forward for the character of a UAF. At the same time, Dr. Floyd Denny, Dr. Morris Lipton, and others developed a proposal for a biologically oriented MRRC, while Dr. Halbert Robinson, a psychologist, developed a proposal for an MRRC with a psychoeducational base. It later became necessary to combine the two MRRC proposals, with the vice chancellor for health affairs becoming the titular director. While the grants were for construction of facilities, on a three-to-one federal-to-state matching basis, a construction award virtually automatically also led to an award for program from the Office of Maternal and Child Health for UAFs, and from the National Institute of Child Health and Human Development for MRRCs.

Following two extensive site visits at Chapel Hill (one for the UAF, which was to become known as the division for disorders of development and learning or DDDL, and one for the MRRC, which was to become the Biological Sciences Research Center or BSRC and the Frank Porter Graham Child Development Center), award letters were received, that for the UAF dated August 10, 1966, and that for the MRRC dated September 1, 1966.

While these construction awards could be very large, they were limited by the amount of state monies that the University could pull together to cover 25 percent of the overall cost. Obtaining adequate state funds for the University of North Carolina was a difficult, complex, and prolonged process. Suffice it to say that $620,000 was finally pulled together toward what was to become the BSRC, designed to house both the UAF and the biological portion of the MRRC. After a two-year delay, the building was finally completed in January 1971. Administratively the program was now the clinical division of the BSRC with Chamberlin responsible to Dr. Lipton, the latter's director, as well as to Dr. Denny for the DDDL's pediatric section.

SPACE

Having initially had no specific space of its own, in 1964 the DEC acquired a small trailer for four of its staff. By 1966, and by then designated as the DDDL, the program had expanded into four large trailers interconnected by catwalks. But even these facilities were overcrowded within two years. Moreover, during rainy weather they proved to be located in a sea of mud. On rainy days a staff member could often be seen carrying an infant or young child across a series of stepping stones while the parents teetered along behind! By early 1971, when the DDDL took over most of the two lower floors of the new four-floor BSRC building, it consisted of thirty-five professional and ten support personnel. At last, with multiple examination and observation rooms, three large classrooms with observation areas, a large playroom, conference rooms, student offices, a library, a shared auditorium, and a large media and studio area, the program had all the space that it needed. Yet by 1976 the total professional and support staff had reached its maximum at fifty-five and short-term students were often sitting on the corridor floors.

FUNDING (TO 1984)

The DDDL training budget, increasingly derived from multiple sources, grew steadily from the inception of the DEC in 1962 until it reached a peak at about $940,000 in 1976. From then on inflation, rising salaries, and increased social security withholding forced some pruning of training activities.

By contrast, research grant input increased steadily during the last few years of Chamberlin's tenure, in large measure through the efforts of Dr. Stephen Schroeder, a psychologist and assistant director for research development. By 1984, $350,000 was derived from research grants that either belonged entirely to the DDDL or for which a member of the DDDL staff was the principal investigator.

The DEC grant from the State Board of Health had reached $72,000 in 1966, when funding was shifted to the Maternal and Child Health Service of the U.S. Public Health Service. This source, always the core of DDDL's funding, leveled off at $630,000 in 1971. Fortunately, beginning in 1969, additional funds for varying periods came from a variety of sources: the Bureau of Education for the Handicapped; the Administration on Developmental Disabilities; the Chapel Hill school system to support one, and often two, teachers in the DDDL's specialized classroom projects; and the North Carolina Division of Health Services for further training of personnel in the developmental evaluation clinics around the state. Most satisfying, in view of constant uncertainty due to dependence on such generous federal funding, was the awarding of a "change budget request" for permanent state funding for the DDDL in 1973. Beginning at $76,000, this had reached $159,000 by 1984 and is now (1993) well above $200,000 each year.

Interestingly, the DDDL initially was not allowed to charge patient fees, on the grounds that its staff were funded by federal tax dollars. This injunction was relaxed in the early 1980s, but extensive charges were not made prior to 1984. In many ways this was a blessing, for it was possible to keep the client load at an optimal level for training and avoid the pressures that all staff feel now to see more and more clients in order to support the budget.

ADMINISTRATIVE STRUCTURE

With a professional faculty holding academic appointments in seven schools and at least twelve departments, and with graduate students from up to eighteen University departments, the DDDL administrative structure was necessarily complex. Chamberlin was indirectly responsible to seven deans, all of whom seemed to have different salary scales, different guidelines for promotion, and often different philosophies. The network of interactions surrounding the DDDL in time became so involved that it was eventually formalized by no less than twenty-four separate contracts with other University and state department programs. An able full-time administrator was essential and Chamberlin was fortunate to recruit just such a person, along with an equally able administrative assistant.

The pediatric section was but one cog of a dozen in an integrated whole. With four staff, including the DDDL director, the pediatric section (in 1976) had fewer personnel than three other sections (psychology, social work, and special education), the same as one (communicative disorders) and more than the remaining seven (physical therapy, occupational therapy, nursing, pedodontics, nutrition, child psychiatry, and the chaplaincy). Overall DDDL philosophy, by which disciplines were considered coequal, was totally different from that of most earlier programs for persons with handicaps.

Thus the DDDL pediatric section did not stand on its own. To understand it and its role as a part of the Department of Pediatrics, it is necessary to gain a clear picture of the full DDDL program. The remainder of this report is therefore divided into two sections: the overall DDDL, its faculty and staff makeup and its service, training, outreach, research, and publication activities; and the pediatric section itself.

The Overall DDDL (to 1984)

FACULTY AND STAFF

As with any organization, the quality of the overall DDDL program, considered exemplary by many outsiders, was due to the vision, ability, hard work, and ease of personal interaction that characterized virtually all DDDL faculty. A dozen or more persons were outstanding, some of them destined to become known at the national level. Chamberlin believes that his primary contributions to the program were his good fortune at recruiting and his efforts to see that all faculty, as well as students, were treated with respect and a sense of equality regardless of the depth of their training. In the early years, recruiting decisions were especially demanding since, for several disciplines including pediatrics, appropriate training opportunities had barely begun to appear. Thus several faculty developed expertise while adapting to DDDL requirements "on the job" or during training as a DDDL student or fellow.

Over the twenty-two years from the initiation of the program until Chamberlin's retirement, approximately 150 professionals were DDDL faculty members. Most remained five to ten years, a few for twelve to eighteen years, and four for even more. A few had already gained a feel for interdisciplinary activity while pursuing an MPH degree at UNC's School of Public Health. Overall academic appointments were spread through all schools in the Division of Health Affairs except the School of Pharmacy, and also in the School of Education, the School of Social Work, the Graduate School of Arts and Sciences, and an important adjunct appointment even came from the Institute of Government. A PhD candidate in sociology under the wing of the Institute for Research in Social Sciences in the 1960s based his dissertation on the DDDL, and there were constant interactions with other divisions of the Biological Sciences Research Center and with the Frank Porter Graham Child Development Center.

It is appropriate to identify the subsequent status of certain DDDL faculty and staff, though several others are doubtless equally worthy of mention: a former DDDL nutrition section head (Elizabeth Brannon) is now in charge of maternal and child health core training grants in all UAPs in the United States (since the late 1970s these programs have been designated as UAPs, for university-affiliated programs, rather than as UAFs); a former assistant director for research development (Dr. Donald Routh) has chaired the Behavioral

Medical Study Section at the NIH; another former assistant director for research development (Dr. Stephen Schroeder) has directed the UAP at Ohio State and now directs the large tripartite UAP at the University of Kansas; a former special education section head (Dr. Ann Turnbull) and a former DDDL adjunct faculty member (Rutherford Turnbull) codirect the Beach Center on Families and Disability at the University of Kansas; a former communicative disorders section head (Dr. Patricia Porter) is chief of Developmental Disabilities Services for North Carolina; the founder of the chaplaincy section (William Gaventa) has headed the chaplaincy division of the American Association on Mental Retardation and is one of the few leaders in this field in the United States; a former DDDL psychologist (Dr. Frances Campbell) now directs the important Abecedarian Project at the Frank Porter Graham Child Development Center; and another former DDDL psychologist (Dr. Gary Mesibov) now directs Project TEACCH, the internationally recognized program for autistic children.

Among DDDL support staff, the former DDDL administrator (J. Robert Gray) became administrative director of the Lennox Baker Children's Hospital; Harriett (Dickey) Brewer, Chamberlin's secretary in the late 1960s, has been the invaluable administrative manager of the Department of Pediatrics under Drs. Denny and Boat for a quarter of a century; and another Chamberlin secretary and subsequently, for fifteen years, DDDL's able administrative assistant (Carolyn Elfland) is now the University's associate vice chancellor for business affairs.

SERVICE

During the DEC period and the earliest years of the DDDL, persons with any of the full range of developmental handicaps were eligible for evaluation with the exception of those with so-called learning disabilities, which were only just beginning to be partially understood. Patients (or clients, as representatives of most disciplines called them) would vary from those with mild mental retardation associated with little or no physical handicap to profoundly handicapped infants and children with severe cerebral palsy and little ability to communicate. In the 1970s, a small proportion of children with a variety of manifestations of the learning disabilities were accepted and clearly aided by the therapeutic approaches developed for them. It is of interest that, following Chamberlin's retirement and the arrival of Dr. Melvin Levine to direct what was renamed the Clinical Center for the Study of Development and Learning, there has been a marked shift in the spectrum of types of clients accepted. The full range of the traditional "low frequency, high intensity" problems are still seen, but, because of Dr. Levine's primary interest in children with learning disabilities and related problems, a greatly increased number of "high frequency, low intensity" clients are now accepted.

Initially emphasis was placed on the evaluation of infants and children under the age of three. This was the age group in which Chamberlin had greatest interest, and it was felt that if one could start remedial approaches early for both the infant and its parents the chances of a better outcome were enhanced. A thorough home visit, documented by an extensive report, was always made before the evaluation, which generally extended over two and a half days with a return some ten days later for the interpretive conference with the parents. In time, the length of the typical evaluation was reduced to two days and later, to accommodate short-term students, a one-day model for the less complicated referrals was developed. As the DDDL staff grew in size, a typical week would involve one one-day and two two-day new patients, plus a host of return evaluations and additional returns for a wide variety of individual and group treatment programs.

The makeup of the team that saw each child and its family, initially in individual evaluation settings by discipline, was tailored to the known needs of that child (largely determined at the home visit) and usually comprised of faculty from five or six disciplines, often with almost as many students. A family advisor from an appropriate discipline was assigned. That individual greeted the family on arrival, introduced it to other staff, checked on progress from time to time, and saw to it that reports from all disciplines had been received before the interdisciplinary evaluation conference the following week. In addition, he or she was chairperson of that conference, shared in the subsequent interpretive conference with the family, made certain that all follow-up arrangements and community support/treatment contacts had been made, filled out a code sheet on the patient (eventually for a computerized database), and dictated the final overall summary of the case. Appropriate local therapists and community support people from schools, day care centers, and other programs were invited to the evaluation conference.

By the early 1980s evaluation services were beginning to coalesce around four specialized teams concerned with (1) developmental problems of infants, visually handicapped youngsters, and persons in need of augmentative communication systems; (2) learning and behavior problems of school-aged and older persons; (3) assessment and development of programs for multihandicapped persons; (4) situations best met by a special needs team and requiring special planning for particularly complex cases.

DDDL clients were accepted from many sources, especially in later years when they involved all childhood and adolescent age groups plus an occasional young adult for specialized services (such as augmentative communication). Most were from North Carolina but there were significant numbers from other states. As North Carolina's regional system of eighteen developmental evaluation clinics matured, the DDDL's burgeoning waiting lists were largely kept under control by suggesting evaluation of the less complicated cases in a DEC closer to home. But, at the same time, the DDDL was regarded by the DECs as a tertiary referral center for particularly complex problems, such as severely multiply handicapped infants and children.

In addition to evaluation, other levels of DDDL service included treatment, outreach consultation, and technical assistance. Treatment programs have included a "prescription generating center" for short-term study in a

DDDL classroom of handicapped children with difficult management problems from the Chapel Hill public schools, an infant treatment group (whose published curriculum has brought it national recognition), an augmentative communication clinic which utilizes advanced microelectronic techniques (the DDDL was among the first interdisciplinary programs in this country to develop this field), a specialized classroom for multihandicapped children, a preschool program for visually impaired children, a clinic for severe motor handicaps, a behavior modification program, a specialized biofeedback program, a feeding clinic, parent counseling groups, and a detailed parenting program. Other treatment programs that centered in the pediatric section will be described later.

INTERDISCIPLINARY CLINICAL TRAINING

Early DEC staff were surprised at the interest shown by several University departments in exposing their students to the interdisciplinary process. As mentioned earlier, by 1976, when the number plateaued, graduate students and some undergraduates from eighteen different departments located in seven different schools in the University had regular training experiences in the DDDL, though a few were largely observational. In addition, occasional short-term specialized programs were arranged for small groups of students from half a dozen community colleges and technical schools who planned to work in Head Start programs or day care centers. While many staff in the state's DEC system had already been exposed to the DDDL during their training, several others arranged short-term ad hoc experiences there each year.

The length of assignment to the DDDL varied markedly from brief exposures of a day or less to fellowships of a year or occasionally two years (in psychology, pediatrics, pedodontics, and infrequently in communicative disorders and nutrition). In 1978–1979, for example, a total of 509 students received training, of whom 82 spent a month or more in the program. Among the fellowships, those in psychology were the most competitive with 58 applications for the two new positions available during that particular year. Although the majority of students were assigned from University departments at UNC-Chapel Hill, each year an average of ten or twelve made special arrangements for rotations of differing lengths from other universities. Occasionally these trainees came from as far away as Hawaii, Australia, Europe, or South America.

The character of the student training programs varied widely, depending on each student's discipline and the length of the assignment. Yet the core experience for most involved participation on one or more interdisciplinary evaluation teams, precepted by an appropriate team member. DDDL faculty clearly recognized that the service models used for training, at least the two-day model, were representative of a fairly ideal situation and far from cost-effective. But this was not a concern. It was also clear that a well-trained professional would be far better prepared to know how and where to compromise in a real world. Indeed, exposure within the DDDL itself to the one-day model, more akin to that in most DECs, already gave some experience with partial compromise.

Further training was gained from sharing in one or more of the DDDL's many treatment programs (described earlier under "Service"). In addition, long-term trainees, particularly fellows, occasionally participated in one or more of the DDDL outreach programs, to be described below. Supplementing these experiences was the DDDL's interdisciplinary core course, fourteen semi-weekly lectures taught by senior members of the DDDL faculty, repeated twice and sometimes three times a year and listed in the offerings of three University departments. A wide variety of DDDL in-house seminars and workshops was also available, ranging from a popular behavior modification seminar to a perceptual-motor workshop to in-service training in statistics. The regularly held "Tuesday noon meeting," a kind of grand rounds, should be mentioned, as well as the popular annual Interpretive Workshop, which employed role play with astonishing effectiveness.

At least three important DEC/DDDL symposia are worthy of mention. In 1963, when the DEC was still in its infancy, it presented one of the first major conferences on mental retardation anywhere to combine consideration of both biomedical and environmental factors. Some ninety-five physicians, primarily academic or practicing pediatricians, were among the attendees. A young special educator from the University of Illinois, Dr. James Gallagher, gave a fine banquet speech. It was his first visit ever to North Carolina. He was impressed and so were we. Some years later he became the able director of the Frank Porter Graham Child Development Center.

In 1974 the DDDL shared with the rest of the Child Development Institute in the symposium in Chapel Hill for a meeting of the President's Committee on Mental Retardation. The DDDL's 20th Anniversary Symposium in 1982 was a particularly happy occasion. Dr. Josef Warkany, research professor of pediatrics at the University of Cincinnati, gave the major presentation on his early research on endemic cretinism. Long revered by many of us, he had returned to Chapel Hill twenty-six years after his first visit, when he had shared in the Ross Conference on Etiologic Factors in Mental Retardation.

A review in 1983 of the status of former DDDL trainees found their wide distribution across the United States on staffs of developmental evaluation centers, in social service, health, and mental health departments, in various administrative positions dealing with the handicapped including several state-level positions, and in all professional ranks on the faculties of seventeen different universities, including a chairman of a department of psychology and faculty members in six different UAPs. At this writing, ten years later, no exact data are available, but it is known that former trainees hold several departmental chairs, that a former psychology fellow (Sam Thios) has been acting president of Denison University, that another former psychology fellow (Philip Davidson) is founder and director of the UAP at the University of Rochester, and that a former pediatric fellow (Mark Swanson) has directed the UAP at Southwestern in Dallas and now directs the new UAP at the University of Arkansas. A former long-term special education trainee from Australia (Tony Shaddock) has founded and directed something very similar to a UAP at the University of New England in New South Wales. In addition, as mentioned, among former DDDL faculty, Dr. Stephen Schroeder, former assistant director for research development, later headed the Nisonger Center, the UAP at Ohio State, and now directs the Schiefelbusch Institute, the UAP at the University of Kansas. Thus former DDDL faculty and students have directed the equivalent of six UAPs other than the DDDL.

OUTREACH

Within the University itself, DDDL faculty conducted many courses and provided many individual lectures. During 1979–1980, for example, in addition to the popular DDDL core course, they were directly responsible for twenty-three different courses in a dozen departments and presented over sixty lectures in other courses throughout the University. They also were members of a large number of M.A. thesis and Ph.D. dissertation committees.

Beyond Chapel Hill, with continuing maturation, the DDDL reached out to provide consultation and technical assistance to communities, to the state, and frequently to programs in other states. Recipients of these activities included developmental day care centers, group homes, residential centers, schools, Head Start programs, the state's Division of Health Services, and the Department of Public Instruction. As many as seventy seminars and workshops in locations outside Chapel Hill were presented annually, in addition to individual lectures. DDDL faculty were members of group-home boards and many other local and state committees. Several were active on various relevant national committees and, in addition to the DDDL director, the DDDL administrator (J. Robert Gray) and associate director (Dr. Calvin Knobeloch) each served on the Executive Committee of the AAUAP.

The adjunct DDDL faculty member from the Institute of Government (Rutherford Turnbull) conducted a complete review of laws relating to children in North Carolina and then battled for changes that resulted in the legal structure for a model limited guardianship program for handicapped children, a model that has since been copied in other states.

The DDDL's media services program, important to both its training and outreach functions, made unusual contributions far beyond the University on at least two occasions. One was a special audiovisual program, produced at the DDDL to illustrate various forms of developmental disability, presented to the Appropriations Committee of the North Carolina General Assembly at its request. Another was the appearance of DDDL training tapes on the CBS *Evening News* with Dan Rather on three consecutive nights; the subject was tardive dyskinesia in childhood, a program in part presented by Dr. Thomas Gualtieri, who ran the DDDL's neuropharmacology clinic.

RESEARCH

In its earliest years the DEC/DDDL was heavily preoccupied with the development of its service and training programs. Research activity was largely limited to individual case reports, occasionally written jointly with personnel from other divisions of the BSRC, and to the longitudinal studies of selected patients led by Dr. Marilyn Erickson, the first psychology section head. The DDDL director, who had had no research training, was acutely conscious of the need to stimulate increased research activity. Thus, when Dr. Donald Routh arrived in 1971 to head the psychology section he was appointed to the new position of assistant director for research development. Routh and, perhaps even more, Dr. Stephen Schroeder, who succeeded him in that position in 1977, did much to add several major long-term projects to the variety of small clinical studies that were ongoing.

It will be quickly recognized that much of DDDL research was interdisciplinary, as it should have been. Although many valuable studies did center in other sections, the large research projects that centered in the psychology section were among the most important and often included extensive interaction with other divisions of the BSRC or with other important research programs elsewhere in the University.

By the early 1980s two definite foci of research had emerged. They were well summarized by Dr. Schroeder in 1983:

1. The Neurobiology of Developmental Behavior Disorders—(a) Methylphenidate Pharmacokinetics in Central Disorders: Drug differentiation of cognitive and adaptive behaviors. (b) Stereotyped Behavior and Thioridazine Pharmacodynamics: Drug-behavior interactions. (c) The Psychopharmacology of Tardive Dyskinesia: Neuroleptic withdrawal and behavior supersensitivity. (d) Neurochemical Correlates of Self-Injurious Behavior. (e) Developmental Neurobehavioral Toxicology: Neurobehavioral assessment of low-level lead exposure in children.

2. Early Screening and Assessment with Biologically At-Risk or Handicapped Infants and Young Children—(a) Non-Traditional Assessment of Cognitive Abilities in Handicapped Infants. (b) Special Infant Care: Social competence in blind infants; Stress and temperamental factors. (c) Augmentative Communication: Research and development of interface devices. (d) Pediatric Audiology: Audiological assessment of high-risk infants.

PUBLICATIONS

During the five years prior to 1983 (when the assessment was made), DDDL faculty published an average of eighteen articles in refereed journals and seven book chapters annually. Three DDDL faculty were journal editors or associate editors, and five were on the editorial boards of ten different journals.

The Pediatric Section (to 1984)

BACKGROUND

The DDDL pediatric section was always small, never exceeding four persons and not over three after 1976 (10 to 12 percent of the total DDDL faculty). The presence, however, of a full-time fellow, and occasionally two fellows, after 1974 increased the section's effectiveness. Initially this small size was relatively deliberate, to allow balance throughout a program of a dozen sections, but growth was planned when pediatric neurology was added, producing greater teaching strength and research potential. Unfortunately this was not to last, for reasons to be described below.

The size of the section was thoroughly adequate for a strong interdisciplinary program. As the anchor for a strong training site for pediatric residents it was less adequate, unless the resident had developed considerable interest in handicapping conditions and in the interdisciplinary process. This degree of interest was there for the pediatric fellows, for a few of the UNC pediatric residents, and for the occasional pediatric trainees who eagerly rotated through the DDDL from other universities. For them there seemed to be a basic enthusiasm for what the DDDL had to offer. It should be recognized that, well into the 1970s, mental retardation in general, and many other developmental handicaps for which there was no obvious biomedical cause or treatment, often received minimal attention on pediatric wards and even in some general pediatric clinics. There was little glamour associated with these cases for most residents or their attendings. But, as more and more of these conditions turned out to have an associated genetically inherited metabolic abnormality or a subtle cytogenetic defect and as questions concerning them, as well as more detailed questions on normal child development, began appearing in pediatric board examinations, the situation changed.

FUNDING

With the exception of its pediatric neurologists and a constant 25 percent contribution to Chamberlin's salary from the Department of Pediatrics, the salaries of all pediatric section faculty and for one position for a pediatric fellow were always funded from DDDL grants or from the DDDL's small but important core state budget. Fringe benefits, however, which were significant, were paid by the Department of Pediatrics. A second fellow was funded from outside sources on two occasions, once by the Navy and once by Michigan State University.

Although the salary for Dr. Charles Swisher, in the DDDL's new pediatric neurology position, was paid from grant funds during his first two years (1972–1974), a tightening DDDL budget at the end of that period led, in 1974–1975, to valuable additional support from both the Departments of Pediatrics and Medicine (division of neurology), where he held joint appointments. When Dr. Jeffrey Allen took over the pediatric neurology position in

1975–1976, the DDDL's financial situation was even tighter; Allen was thus generously funded for a third of his salary by pediatrics and a third by medicine, leaving only a third for the DDDL to cover.

But, from the DDDL's point of view, the end of that academic year brought catastrophe: all pediatric neurology funds were withdrawn by Dean Fordham to help build a base for the new Department of Neurology. Though the actual figures continued to rise, the overall worth of the DDDL grants was now leveling off and, with rising salaries and fixed costs, would soon begin to decline. Over the next several years all but one of the media staff, the record librarian/data collector, and then the training coordinator had to be dropped, leaving a single individual, Dr. Calvin Knobeloch, as the DDDL associate director, the training director, and a communications disorders specialist, with no staff for the complex job of planning and monitoring the many interdisciplinary training programs. Several junior professional staff positions were not refilled, and eventually the DDDL child psychiatrist, Dr. Raymond Schmitt, who had been a full-time DDDL faculty member for eleven years, had to be returned to his home department. Finally J. Robert Gray, the DDDL's able and effective assistant director for administration, was required to leave (fortunately, for an equally challenging job), and Dr. Kenneth Jens, special education section head, who had had considerable administrative experience, was transferred into that position. Under these conditions of continuing belt tightening, any revival of pediatric neurology or addition of another pediatrician, a relatively expensive professional, was out of the question if the overall balance of disciplines was to be maintained.

FACULTY

By 1984 eleven pediatricians had been members of the pediatric section:

Harrie R. Chamberlin (DDDL director), 1962–84	Charles N. Swisher, 1972–75*
	Jeffrey C. Allen, 1975–76*
Mary H. Sugioka, 1968–71 (half time), 1980–91	Robert D. Chessin, 1976–78
	Mary Glenn Fowler, 1977–79
Charles Hunsinger, 1969–70	Stuart W. Teplin, 1978–
Joanna S. Dalldorf, 1969–77	John M. Pascoe, 1979–80
Carole M. Stuart, 1971–76	

With the exception of Dr. Chamberlin and Dr. Stuart Teplin, who joined the DDDL pediatric staff in 1978 and who was promoted to an associate professorship before Chamberlin's retirement, all pediatricians in the pediatric section were junior faculty members, either instructors or assistant professors. Some, though excellent teachers, showed little interest in research; several others would likely have risen to a higher rank in the Medical School had

---

* with joint appointment in the division of neurology

Stu Teplin

Mary
Sugioka

they stayed longer. Of the latter, most remained only one or two years and Swisher for three. Two others who might have produced more research were married to able research-minded full professors in other Medical School departments; as one of them put it, "One research physician in a family is enough."

But during the early years, when interest in the field was minimal for most physicians and when there were almost no appropriate training programs, the challenge was primarily to find someone interested enough in the interdisciplinary process to share physician service and training responsibilities with the DDDL director. Among these was Dr. Mary Sugioka, who did so on a half-time basis for three years, even before completing her pediatric residency. Seven years later, she returned for a two-year fellowship and then became the second DDDL pediatrician to have experienced full fellowship preparation in child development and developmental handicaps. Dr. Joanna Dalldorf, also an early member of the section who had previously worked with Chamberlin in the pediatric neurology clinic, remained for eight years, making valuable service and training contributions.

Jo Dalldorf

The first major advance in building the section came with a telephone call to Chamberlin from Dr. Philip Dodge, a pediatric neurologist and chairman of the Department of Pediatrics at Wash-

Chuck
Swisher

ington University in St. Louis. He felt that Charles Swisher, a McGill medical graduate who had just finished a pediatric neurology fellowship on his service, would be an ideal addition to the DDDL faculty. After joining the DDDL in 1972, Swisher proved to be just that. His broad approach to children and his interest in the interdisciplinary process were unusual for pediatric neurology trainees of his day. A fine clinician and teacher with strong clinical research interests, he soon attracted more pediatric residents to the DDDL. In addition he was primarily responsible for the superior reputation of the DDDL pediatric fellowship, initiated in 1974. Under his guidance four pediatric neurology fellows rotated through the DDDL as well, for shorter term experiences. Also a good teacher of professionals in other disciplines, Swisher was respected and admired by the entire faculty and staff. At this point the potential for strong bonds between the DDDL, the Medical School, and specifically the Department of Pediatrics seemed to be blossoming.

Thus it was a heavy blow when Dr. Linda Swisher, Chuck Swisher's wife and an outstanding speech pathologist, was offered an important position at Northwestern University in 1975. She had followed her husband from St. Louis to Chapel Hill and he now felt obliged to follow her. That July he became director of pediatric neurology at Michael Reese in Chicago. Dr. Jeffrey Allen, who took over, was also an able pediatric neurologist and a good teacher who effectively utilized the Socratic method. But he was less enthusiastic about the DDDL setting and the interdisciplinary process. After barely a year, when his son developed a rhabdomyosarcoma, he returned to New York so that the boy could be treated at Sloan-Kettering, close to Allen's home. He is now head of pediatric neurological oncology and a professor of pediatrics at New York University. As recounted under "Funding," the DDDL, having been the first UAP after that at Hopkins to have a pediatric neurologist on its staff, now relinquished the position for good.

Of the five subsequent pediatricians who became members of the DDDL's pediatric section (including Sugioka, who was returning), all but two (Chessin and Pascoe) had had fellowships in developmental pediatrics. But these two were also valuable assets. Bob Chessin (1976–1978), who had just finished the chief pediatric residency at Duke, now practices in Connecticut with an emphasis on developmental problems and is on the clinical faculty at Yale. Jack Pascoe (1979–1980) came from the University of Michigan, had done research on family support systems, and has been active nationally in developmental and behavioral pediatrics. He is on the faculty at the University of Wisconsin and was president of the Ambulatory Pediatric Association in 1994–1995.

Of the remaining three (Mary Glenn Fowler, Teplin, and Sugioka), Fowler (1977–1979) was the first of the DDDL pediatric faculty to have had a fellowship background in developmental handicaps, in her case at the DDDL itself (1976–1977). She had come to the DDDL highly recommended by Jimmy Simon, pediatric chairman at Bowman Gray. After two years as a valuable member of the pediatric section she moved on to our Department's division of community pediatrics and is now doing AIDS research at the NICHHD.

By mid-1984, when Chamberlin relinquished the DDDL directorship, two thoroughly trained and effective developmental pediatricians had helped guide the pediatric section for four and six years respectively and the fellowship recipients had continued to be of high caliber (see "Clinical Training"). Sugioka would finally depart in 1991 and is now on the staff of the Durham Developmental Evaluation Clinic, along with Dr. Nancy Johnson-Martin, a former DDDL psychologist. Teplin, well trained in Dr. Arthur Parmelee's excellent program at UCLA, now holds tenure and has made valuable contributions across the full gamut of teaching, service, and research.

SERVICE

All DDDL pediatricians who held appointments above the level of instructor in the Department of Pediatrics took on their share of attending responsibilities on the wards and/or in the nurseries, by nature both a service and a teaching function. Swisher and Allen had additional demands, as they were expected to attend on both the pediatric and adult neurology wards. All members of the pediatric section shared in the role of the physician on the DDDL's interdisciplinary evaluation teams, including the handling of an occasional family advisorship. As in any academic medical center environment, all service activities also generally involved training.

Consultation in the clinics and on the wards was an important function of the DDDL pediatric staff. When professionals from other DDDL disciplines were involved, most of whom did not have formal hospital privileges, these consultations were under the supervision of a DDDL physician. Beginning in the early years while Chamberlin was still teaching in the pediatric neurology clinic, various DDDL consultants were often called in for problems in speech and language, audiology for small infants, occupational therapy, and special education. Specialized behavior modification was later introduced in the pedodontic clinic of the Dental School by Dr. Carolyn Schroeder under Dr. Thomas McIver, the half-time DDDL pedodontist. DDDL staff, including a DDDL nutritionist, also regularly consulted for Dr. Kirkman in the pediatric genetics clinic. On the wards, guidance in behavior modification programs and in the use of augmentative communication devices, as well as a variety of other special services not available from official hospital personnel, could be brought to appropriate patients.

Within the DDDL itself a section pediatrician also frequently shared directly or consulted for many of the treatment programs. While specialized classroom programs were usually founded and run by professionals from other disciplines, Teplin played the major role in the establishment of a class for visually impaired preschoolers.

Despite its interdisciplinary setting, at least two clinics within the DDDL were almost totally medically oriented. One was the medical consultation clinic, where a pediatrician, working alone or with a pediatric trainee, could follow DDDL patients who required frequent visits for specific medical problems such as seizure management. This clinic could also be used to demonstrate the brief evaluation of a new patient using screening techniques, much as might be done in a physician's office.

The other unidisciplinary setting was Dr. Thomas Gualtieri's neuropharmacology clinic. While Gualtieri, a research child psychiatrist with an adjunct appointment in the DDDL, was supported by his research grants and by his own department, he fortunately spent considerable time in the DDDL, where his clinic, in which other DDDL staff and trainees often shared, was situated. Providing a highly specialized service function, pharmacotherapy in behavioral and cognitive disorders, the clinic's training and research activities were even more important.

Significant service was also provided through the joint follow-up of specific cohorts of patients with Drs. Kirkman and Aylsworth in the Department's division of genetics and metabolism. The location of their offices and laboratories, directly above the DDDL, made this a particularly happy relationship. Examples were the phenylketonuria follow-up clinic run for Dr. Kirkman by the DDDL and, later on, follow-up of patients with fragile X syndrome. Chamberlin, and later Sugioka, were particularly involved in following patients with phenylketonuria. In the 1950s Chamberlin had diagnosed the first cases to be recognized in North Carolina and was the first in the state to use the low phenylalanine diet. In the early '60s, before Dr. Kirkman's arrival in 1965, through his role on North Carolina's old Council on Mental Retardation, Chamberlin had persuaded the State Board of Health to use Dr. George Summer's and Dr. John Hill's automated application of the photofluorometric measurement of phenylalanine levels for the proposed statewide phenylketonuria screening program. The alternative was the Guthrie method, which the Children's Bureau was pushing and to which almost all other states were turning. As had been anticipated, the photofluorometric method proved to be far more accurate, a happy bonanza for Kirkman, who was able to carry out a series of extremely useful and important studies on phenylketonuria management because of the accuracy of the data available on such a vast scale.

By the late 1970s, because the proportion of pediatric residents who were choosing the one-month DDDL elective had become disturbingly low, increased efforts, beyond mere consultation, were made to draw certain DDDL activities into the main body of the Department's pediatric clinics. It was hoped that this might provide some help toward overcoming the effect of the geographical, and often the philosophical, gap between the two areas. Sugioka began to share with Dr. Robert Herrington in the birth defects clinic. In 1979 Teplin joined Dr. Ernest Kraybill as codirector of the special infant care clinic (SICC) for the follow-up of high-risk newborns who had been cared for in the newborn intensive care unit (NICU). Dr. Knobeloch, DDDL's associate director and an expert on hearing in small infants, provided audiology assessments. This arrangement, which is still ongoing (1993), has provided new dimensions to the follow-up of these infants and enhanced the training and research potential of that program.

The shift by Mary Glenn Fowler from the DDDL pediatric section to the division of community pediatrics, while a major loss in one respect, was also a boon in that it strengthened relationships with the pediatric clinics where Fowler spent considerable time. She became a valuable salesperson for the DDDL and helped develop activities that increased the residents' consciousness of it. Among these activities was the establishment of a school function clinic in the main pediatric clinic area where she, Sugioka, and Dr. Michael Sharp were preceptors, occasionally drawing in psychologists and special educators from the DDDL faculty. While efforts of this sort were important, there was no way to transport a major segment of the DDDL program into the departmental core clinic area. Although the popularity of the one-month DDDL elective among UNC pediatric residents may have increased slightly, the lure of the program never returned to the level it had enjoyed up until the mid-1970s.

CLINICAL TRAINING

An extensive range of training opportunities and sites for DDDL pediatric trainees has already been described. In order to prevent bewilderment due to this wide array, handouts that included a descriptive list of the most appropriate opportunities were given to all pediatric trainees of a month or more and each was assigned a specific advisor from the pediatric section faculty to facilitate guidance.

The core experience for virtually all pediatric trainees, from the medical student to the fellow, was preceptored participation on the interdisciplinary evaluation teams and, following observation and careful advice, sharing in interpretive conferences with the parents. In addition, all pediatric trainees were expected to share in the weekly pediatric section meeting. There a specific topic was presented on some aspect of child development or developmental handicap each week, usually based on a library search and sometimes opening with one or more brief DDDL case presentations. These presentations were made by all members of the pediatric faculty and the pediatric fellows, with all one-month trainees, whether fourth-year students or residents, responsible for one of them. All faculty and trainees whenever possible also

attended the previously mentioned DDDL Tuesday noon meetings in the auditorium, a kind of interdisciplinary grand rounds, in later years under the
guidance of Dr. Stephen Schroeder, at which DDDL clinical research studies
were often presented or visiting speakers discussed their work.

Among the most sought-after experiences during the DDDL pediatric elective was participation in the pediatric liaison clinic, a program initiated at the
offices of the Chapel Hill pediatric practice of Drs. Sheaffer, Conley, Christian, et al. and organized by Dr. Carolyn Schroeder with the help of a DDDL
social worker (Elaine Goolsby) and a DDDL nurse. Here the trainee observed,
and often shared in, telephone calls and direct visits for infants and children
with developmental and behavioral problems in a practice setting. This innovative program so enhanced patient service that Dr. Schroeder recognized it
as an opportunity to demonstrate that a good psychologist could be cost-
effective when operating within a pediatric practice. After more than a dozen
years as one of the outstanding members of the DDDL faculty, she eventually decided to devote full time to the project to prove this. In addition, exposure to the project was considered so valuable for pediatric residents, who
previously had experienced it only on a DDDL elective, that it was built into
an ambulatory clinic rotation to which all pediatric residents were assigned
under the direction of Dr. Sharp in the division of community pediatrics.

Other experiences built into the one-month elective were a visit to an outstanding developmental day care center and to a nearby exemplary sheltered
workshop in Burlington; training in proper administration of the Denver
Developmental Screening Test; learning more about assessment of high-risk
infants with Teplin in the special infant care clinic; observing the evaluation
of an autistic child in the TEACCH program; and others. Several trainees,
including at least one medical student, took the opportunity to be the
overnight "sitter" for a carefully chosen multihandicapped child while the
parents were away. Other than being handicapped oneself, this is perhaps the
best way to learn what being handicapped can mean to an individual. It took
a bit of fortitude to choose this opportunity, but the next morning each
trainee, though sobered and perhaps a bit more mature, was enthusiastic.

Another element of the new ambulatory rotation set up by Dr. Sharp was
a one-day exposure to the DDDL for all pediatric residents. For this, the one-
day evaluation model was modified so that the evaluation conference could
be held on the same day. While on occasion less satisfactory for trainees from
other disciplines because of lack of time to prepare their reports, this modified evaluation sparked interest among many residents who otherwise would
have known virtually nothing about the DDDL.

The changes in the sources of the one-month elective pediatric trainees
over the years is of interest. For several years after 1962, all neurology residents and all pediatric residents alternated as the medical trainee concentrating on the single weekly patient. The eventual one-month DDDL elective was
initially relatively popular among both fourth-year students and pediatric residents and there frequently were two trainees during each month. With the

section strengthened by the addition of Swisher, for several years many UNC family medicine residents chose the rotation and also, over two or three years, half a dozen Duke family medicine residents took part. After the numbers of pediatric residents declined to only five or so a year, trainees began to rotate from the Navy's pediatric residency program in Portsmouth, Virginia. On average, they were more knowledgeable and more sophisticated in the field of developmental handicaps than the average UNC resident at that time (the late 1970s). This culminated in funding by the Navy of one of their own as a full-time fellow (Douglas Gregory) for 1979–1980. Each year, in addition, two or three medical students from schools scattered widely across the country also chose the one-month rotation, and each year or two a physician from overseas participated (Mexico, Venezuela, Argentina, England, and Germany come to mind), usually for a specially tailored program.

From the start, in 1974, the full-year pediatric fellowships were popular. Each was formulated in large measure according to the wishes of the incumbent. Each fellow spent at least a month on a rotation through the division of genetics and metabolism and another month in the division of pediatric neurology. Although most became involved in a clinical research project or shared in an ongoing DDDL project, this was not universal. But each became a fine clinician for the handicapped. (A list of all fellows and their current positions is included at the end of this chapter.)

Of the eleven fellows, eight joined or returned to the faculties of eight different universities other than UNC (two have since entered practice), two (Fowler and Sugioka) joined the DDDL faculty, and the eleventh (Gregory) returned to the Navy. Of the eight who went to other universities, one has been the director of two UAPs (Swanson at Southwestern in Dallas and now at the University of Arkansas as previously mentioned), a second is now helping the state of Wyoming develop a UAP (Edwards), and a third is now a pediatric department chairman (Wherrett at Queens University in Kingston, Ontario).

In addition to their responsibilities to medical trainees, DDDL pediatric faculty, and often the pediatric fellow, shared in the teaching of DDDL trainees in other disciplines. The faculty also presented regularly to fourth-year medical students in the London Library, and Chamberlin and Teplin, along with Dr. Carolyn Schroeder, taught in the developmental biology course for medical students in the first year.

OUTREACH

DDDL pediatric faculty, and also often the pediatric fellow, shared with their counterparts in other disciplines in many of the outside seminars, workshops, and consultation activities outlined under "Outreach" for the overall DDDL. In addition to individual lectures, there were state-level committee assignments, such as the North Carolina DEC Directors Committee, which allowed the DDDL to be an integral part of the state DEC network. From the beginning, the DDDL had played a significant role in the planning, training for, and replenishing of that network.

In addition to outreach responsibilities by pediatric faculty mentioned under "Activities at the State and Federal Levels," Teplin made significant contributions at both these levels on planning committees for infants and children with visual handicaps. For the American Academy of Pediatrics, Chamberlin was a member of and then chaired the Committee on Mental Retardation in the late 1960s and later sat on the section committee for the Section on Child Development (1977–1980). More importantly, during 1982–1984, he chaired the steering committee of the Maternal and Child Health Consortium, a national project that sought to strengthen the linkages between the country's UAPs and state Maternal and Child Health and Crippled Children's programs. At the state level, he chaired (1982–1986) the North Carolina Task Force on Prevention for the Council on Developmental Disabilities, which developed the North Carolina state plan for the prevention of developmental disabilities ("A Healthy Start") and mounted a major statewide conference on this subject in late 1985.

RESEARCH AND PUBLICATIONS

Despite miscellaneous ongoing minor research projects, research by members of the pediatric section was not the section's strong suit. This fact stands out markedly when the section's research activity is compared with the increasingly prolific output of worthwhile publications centered in the considerably larger psychology section during the late 1970s and early 1980s. Any approach to a parallel increase in the pediatric section resulted largely from Teplin's follow-up work on retrolental fibroplasia and on the importance of psychosocial as well as biologic factors in the development of small high-risk infants being followed in the special infant care clinic.

Among the pediatric fellows, Dr. Ave Lachiewicz expanded her original study of a fragile X family that Chamberlin had been following to include other families with this syndrome, a study that led to her coauthoring two publications by 1985. Following an additional fellowship with Drs. Kirkman and Aylsworth and another year in the CDL, she capitalized on these studies by setting up the excellent fragile X program at Duke, where she is now a member of the Department of Pediatrics. Dr. Jack Dolcourt, a medical student at the University of Colorado, first came to North Carolina in 1975 to take the DDDL elective and then applied for an internship. While at the DDDL he became familiar with the studies on environmental lead in which Dr. Stephen Schroeder was sharing. Later he coauthored, with other members of the group, two articles on this subject. He is now on the faculty at the University of Utah.

Chamberlin had authored or coauthored, between 1952 and 1971, reports on several clinical research studies (on organic phosphate insecticide poisoning, anticonvulsant drug therapy, acute cerebellar ataxia, and hydranencephaly). But, aside from sharing with Summer and Frazier in the BSRC in a study of the metabolic aspects of siblings with hyperglycinemia, he wrote more book chapters than articles in the later years (mainly on medical assessment of the mentally retarded and on the interdisciplinary process). His survey chapter of the whole field of mental retardation became steadily more complex as the field evolved over two decades and three editions of Dr. Thomas Farmer's textbook of pediatric neurology, one of which was also published in Spanish.

Swisher, coauthor of an article on the pathology of Hallervorden-Spatz disease, was interested in the neuropathology of several other central nervous system abnormalities. He was conducting an interesting neurogenetic study among the Lumbee Indians with Dr. Alexander Todorov which was cut off when he left for Chicago. Others in the pediatric section coauthored an occasional clinical study, such as that by Dr. Carole Stuart on a patient with methylmalonic acidemia and two or three shared articles by Dr. Joanna Dalldorf.

Had the pediatric section been larger it would have been possible to set aside more time from the heavy demands of service and teaching, for these were greater than in many pediatric specialty clinics. But in the early 1980s, of the three members of the section only Teplin had had real research experience. Though often stimulated by the research of others, each section member found it difficult to build any consistent momentum in this direction. It is a paradox that, in 1984, because of more research in other sections, primarily the psychology section but shared with others, the DDDL ranked close to the top of the few UAPs that were publishing significant numbers of research reports in refereed journals.

Summary

The DDDL has clearly demonstrated the effectiveness of a balanced interdisciplinary process in providing a high level of evaluation and management to developmentally handicapped children and their families. That message has been transmitted to hundreds of trainees who are now scattered across the state and nation.

Yet that very approach, coupled with relatively low research productivity in the pediatric section, may have been the Achilles' heel in the attempt to make the DDDL setting truly popular for many medical trainees below the fellowship level. Their sudden shift to a situation in which the physician often was not at the center of the wheel and where the detail of each evaluation sometimes seemed overly time-consuming did not fit the temperament of many of these trainees. But others were enthusiastic.

Despite these problems in its pediatric section, the DDDL can be said to have played an important role during the period of society's awakening to its responsibilities to persons with developmental handicaps.

HARRIE R. CHAMBERLIN

FACULTY

Allen, Jeffrey C. BA, Oberlin, 1965; MD, Harvard, 1969; Inst, Ped, 1975; Asst Prof, Ped and Med (Neurol), 1976.

Chamberlin, Harrie R. AB, Harvard, 1942; MD, Harvard, 1945; Inst, Ped, 1953; Asst Prof, Ped, 1955; Assoc Prof, Ped, 1959; Prof, Ped, 1970; Prof Emerit, Ped, 1984; Dir, DDDL, 1966–84.

Dalldorf, Joanna A. AB, Cornell, 1954; MD, Cornell, 1958; Clin Inst, Ped, 1962–63, 1965; Clin Asst Prof, Ped, 1967; Asst Prof, Ped, 1969–77; Clin Asst Prof, Ped, 1984.

Fowler, Mary Glenn BA, Univ Wash, 1968; MD, Univ Oregon, 1972; Asst Prof, Ped, 1979; Assoc Prof, Ped, 1986–88.

Schroeder, Carolyn S. BA, Thiel Coll, 1961; MS, Univ Pitt, 1963; PhD, Univ Pitt, 1966; Clin Prof, Ped and Psychiat, 1983–92; Sctn Head, Psychol, DDDL, 1975–82.

Sugioka, Mary H. BS, Duke, 1959; MD, Duke, 1967; Clin Inst, Ped, 1968–71; Clin Asst Prof, Ped, 1980; Clin Assoc Prof, Ped, 1989–91.

Swisher, Charles N. AB, Harvard, 1961; MD, McGill, 1965; Asst Prof, Ped/Med (Neurol), 1972–75.

Teplin, Stuart W. BA, Brandeis, 1969; MD, Penn, 1973; Asst Prof, Ped, 1978; Assoc Prof, Ped, 1985.

FELLOWS

Year	Name	Current Position
1974–75	Irwin L. Schwartz, MD	Assoc Clin Prof, SUNY-Stony Brook; Priv Pract, Dev Ped
1975–76	Nancy L. Golden, MD	Priv Pract (Orleans, MA)
1976–77	Mary Glenn Fowler, MD	Natl Inst Allergy and Infect Dis (AIDS Research)
1977–78	Mark E. Swanson, MD	Assoc Prof, Ped; Dir, UAP for Dev Disab, Univ Arkansas
1978–79	Brian Wherrett, MD	Prof and Chair, Ped, Queen's Univ (Kingston, Ontario)
1978–80	Mary H. Sugioka, MD	Pract, Durham Dev Eval Clinic
1979–80	Douglas B. Gregory, MD	Priv Pract, Dev Ped, US Naval Hosp (Portsmouth, VA)
1980–82	Robert B. Stifler, MD	Chief, Ped, Kaiser Permanente, Durham and Chapel Hill Branches
1981–82	David Sciamanna, DO	Pract, Neonatol, N Mich Hosp (Petosky, MI)
1982–83	Diane R. Edwards, MD	Coord, State of Wyoming Hlth Svcs, Div Dev Disabilities
1983–84	Ave Lachiewicz, MD	Asst Clin Prof, Dev Ped, Duke

THE CLINICAL CENTER FOR THE STUDY OF DEVELOPMENT AND LEARNING

A History since 1985

Mel Levine

In July 1985 Dr. Melvin Levine assumed the directorship of the division for disorders of development and learning. Soon thereafter the division was made a freestanding center within the university. The Clinical Center for the Study of Development and Learning (CDL) thus became one of three centers within the Child Development Institute (the others being the Frank Porter Graham Center and the Biological Sciences Research Center).

The new center continued to pursue the integrated missions of training, research, technical assistance, and exemplary service for individuals with developmental disabilities. The clinical services within the CDL were reorganized in 1985 into a series of problem-oriented programs. These included an assistive technology service (to apply the latest communication and other techniques to aid severely handicapped persons), a preschool evaluation program, a series of multidisciplinary clinics to serve children and adults with learning disorders, and an infant program. The number of patients served within these domains grew substantially during the 1980s, such that clinical revenues increased from $40,000 per year to nearly $400,000 with many more clients being evaluated and offered follow-up services. As the reputation of these clinical services grew, the CDL became an international resource, as patients were referred from all over the world.

The CDL rapidly intensified its efforts at community outreach. Affiliations were established with several school systems. Consultation services were offered in these sites which also were used for the education of trainees from the CDL. Among the more notable outreach achievements was a preschool program for visually impaired children. This program represented a prototype that eventually was adopted by the state of North Carolina. During the late 1980s and early 1990s affiliations were established with the Governor Morehead School, the Wright School, and a number of other specialized agencies dealing with problems related to developmental and behavioral dysfunction.

In 1991 the CDL initiated its Agent Orange Program, which offered outreach services to the children of veterans of the war in Vietnam. The program has also offered public education and advocacy services.

Bill
Coleman,
a CDL
pediatrician
and director
of the
pediatric
clerkship

Project Impact, a statewide effort to offer training and technical assistance in the application of the latest techniques in assistive technology, comprised another important outreach effort from the CDL. In addition, during the 1990s the center has implemented a series of nutrition outreach programs geared to at-risk and underserved populations in North Carolina.

The CDL launched a substantial research effort during the late 1980s. The projects fostered the development of a number of new diagnostic instruments that are currently in use throughout the world. A series of pediatric neurodevelopmental examinations, developmental assessment tools for young children with chronic illnesses (Toll Control Project), and a standardized interview for adolescents with learning disorders (The Strands) were developed with the support of private foundations (including the Robert Wood Johnson Foundation and the Smart Family Foundation) and the federal government (Administration on Developmental Disabilities).

The center has also engaged in considerable outcome research. CDL investigators published studies of developmental outcomes in low-birthweight infants and neuropsychological outcomes in closed head trauma and in AIDS. The center has collaborated actively with the Frank Porter Graham Center and the Department of Psychiatry on a number of other major investigations of this type.

In 1987 the center received a $1.2 million grant from the Geraldine R. Dodge Foundation to initiate a project called SCHOOLS ATTUNED, which represented an attempt to reform middle and junior high schools throughout the United States by sensitizing them to and informing them of issues related to neurodevelopmental variation among early adolescents. The project entailed the design of curriculum materials for teachers, new diagnostic tools for use in schools, and management systems for children with learning disorders. Studies of the project's effectiveness have yielded evaluation data that have been reported. The U.S. Department of Education funded "Developmentary Schools" in 1993 in order to implement an elementary school version of SCHOOLS ATTUNED. Additionally, the center won a five-year competitive grant from the U.S. Department of Education to develop curriculum materials on the subject of attention deficits.

The communications section of the CDL was funded in 1994 to study critical mechanisms related to normal and aberrant processing of language sounds in developing children. This research is likely to be especially valuable in helping with the understanding of youngsters who have trouble learning to read.

The training activities in the CDL continued to expand in the 1990s. Educational programs were implemented in fourteen different professional disciplines at multiple levels of training. Postgraduate (CME) courses and a unique series of minifellowship programs were offered and well attended by physicians, mental health professionals, and educators from throughout the world. In 1994 a special training program was established for clinicians from Croatia to assist them in managing the childhood victims of the war in Bosnia. This collaboration has continued and flourished.

Adrian Sandler, CDL fellow and faculty pediatrician, 1987–94

In the mid-1990s the Clinical Center for the Study of Development and Learning continued to design and implement new forms of training throughout the United States. In many cases these educational initiatives were integrated with research projects studying the effectiveness of various demonstration models. In these and other efforts the CDL has continued to receive support from the Administration on Developmental Disabilities and the Bureau of Maternal and Child Health as well as a number of private foundations and donors.

MELVIN D. LEVINE

FACULTY

Coleman, William L. BA, Univ of the Americas (Mexico City, Mexico), 1967; MA, Univ Calif at Berkeley, 1969; MD, Univ New Mexico, 1979; Asst Prof, Ped, 1986; Assoc Prof, Ped, 1993.

Levine, Melvin D. AB, Brown Univ, 1961; MD, Harvard, 1966; Prof, Ped, 1985; Chief, Ctr for Devt and Learning, 1985.

Sandler, Adrian D. MA, Univ Cambridge, 1980; MB, BCh (MD), Univ Cambridge, 1982; Asst Prof, Ped, 1990–94.

Sugioka, Mary H. BS, Duke, 1959; MD, Duke, 1967; Clin Asst Prof, Ped, 1980; Clin Assoc Prof, Ped, 1989–91.

Teplin, Stuart W. BA, Brandeis Univ, 1969; MD, Univ Penn, 1973; Asst Prof, Ped, 1978; Assoc Prof, Ped, 1985.

FELLOWS

Year	Name	Current Position
1985–86	Ave M. Lachiewicz, MD	Asst Clin Prof, Ped, Duke
1986–88	Desmond P. Kelly, MD	Assoc Prof, Ped; Dir, Developmental Diagnostic Ctr, South Illinois Univ
1987–90	Adrian D. Sandler, MD	Med Dir, Ctr for Child Dev and Rehab, Thoms Rehab Hosp (Asheville, NC)
1988–90	Thomas H. Kuhn, MD	Dev Ped, Area Mental Hlth, Preschool Svcs, Ctr for Human Devt (Charlotte, NC)
1990–91	Ricardo Halpern, MD	Dir and Asst Prof, Dev Clinic at Univ Pelotas (Brazil)
1990–92	Ronald L. Lindsay, MD	Pract, Knights of Columbus Dev Ctr, Cardinal Glennon Hosp; Asst Prof, Ped, Univ St. Louis
1990–92	Theodora Y. Phea, MD	Asst Prof, Ped, Vanderbilt Univ; Developmental Ped, United Way "Success by 6" Program
1990–93	Michelle M. Macias, MD	Dir and Asst Prof, Ped, Genetics & Child Devt, Med Univ of SC
1991–92	William T. Read, Jr., MD	Dir, Ctr for Child and Adoles Dev and Behav, Middleford Clinic (Eau Claire, WI)
1992–94	Michael W. Knudsen, MD	Priv Pract (Raleigh, NC)
1993–95	Henry L. Shapiro, MD	Asst Prof Ped, Univ S Florida; Developmental Ped

CHAPTER SEVENTEEN

Endocrinology

Editors' Note: The history of the division of pediatric endocrinology falls naturally into two sections. The first section contains the complete story of the division from its inception in the early 1960s. The second is the related story of the Laboratories for Reproductive Biology. Dr. Judson Van Wyk, the father of pediatric endocrinology at the University of North Carolina, paints the graphic picture of the entire division in the first part. He then changes hats and relates the story of the Laboratories for Reproductive Biology and how they relate to the parent division and to the Department of Pediatrics.

PEDIATRIC ENDOCRINOLOGY:
A PERSONAL PERSPECTIVE

MY appointment as the fourth member of the pediatric faculty at UNC did not arise from any perceived need for a division of pediatric endocrinology, but rather from a mandate to make basic research an integral part of the Department. We describe here how that came about and what became of that mandate.

The UNC School of Medicine was already establishing traditions of excellence when it graduated its first four-year class in 1955. Dean Reece Berryhill understood very clearly that this medical school would never measure up to the lofty standards of its parent university unless a serious commitment to research were embedded within the very foundations of the clinical departments and not postponed until a more convenient time when the clinical services were well established. This philosophy was reflected in his choices of Burnett, Womack, and Curnen to head the principal clinical services. The first chair of pediatrics was Edward C. Curnen, who was a product of Yale and the Rockefeller Institute, where he had been associated with such giants as Frank Horsfall, Lewis Thomas, and Oswald Avery, the discoverer of DNA. Avery had been Curnen's mentor, and his photograph graced Ed's wall.

Imagine the frustration of Ed Curnen in 1954: Although the school was about to graduate its first four-year class, the Department of Pediatrics had so far been allocated only two full-time faculty slots besides his own, and, to make matters worse, only one additional permanent faculty position had been allocated for the next biennium.

Although it may be that Ed appointed an endocrinologist to this precious faculty position because he believed that endocrinology would form the core on which medical science would advance, the truth was probably somewhat different from that. At mid-century, endocrinology had failed to meet the promise of its early pioneers who had envisaged a ubiquitous system of chemical messengers that were produced by virtually every cell type and that governed the growth and functions of all tissues. Regrettably, endocrinologists spent the better part of this century in diminishing this global concept of chemical mediation to the point where the concept of hormonal control became limited to substances produced by a half dozen or so glands of internal secretion. As a consequence, endocrinology was slow in being integrated into the mainstream of biomedical science, and clinical endocrinology was left with a very limited purview.

On my first visit to Chapel Hill, I was asked to conduct grand rounds, presumably to see what kind of a clinician I was. The subject was a seven-year-old girl with rheumatoid arthritis and markedly swollen joints. I was terrified, since I could say everything that I knew about rheumatoid arthritis in five minutes, and that was if I talked *very, very slowly*. It so happened, however, that my old preceptor, Lawson Wilkins, together with Melvin Grumbach and I, had a paper in press that reported for the first time that many of the girls with the syndrome of gonadal dysgenesis (now popularly referred to as the Turner syndrome) were actually genetic males since their somatic cells lacked the nuclear sex chromatin dot that distinguishes females from males. (Of course, when karyotype analysis became available a few years later, we learned that these girls were not really XY males.)

In any event, I started grand rounds by pointing out that the swelling of the hands and feet in rheumatoid arthritis might possibly be confused with the peripheral edema seen in some patients with the syndrome of gonadal dysgenesis. After this outrageous leap of non sequiturs, I then gave my grand rounds on mechanisms of sex differentiation rather than on rheumatoid arthritis. The audience was titillated and apparently forgot that the grand rounds was supposedly on rheumatoid arthritis. In any event, I got the job!

Ed Curnen, of course, was not fooled. He did not hire me because he needed an endocrinologist; he had grilled me very thoroughly on my scientific

Jud Van Wyk assuming his typical office crouch

background and aspirations, and hired me with the hope that I might help fulfill his mandate to develop a research-oriented Department of Pediatrics.

The Preparative Years

My interest in biomedical research had been kindled early by a small book entitled *Chemistry in the Service of Medicine*. This monograph told about the isolation and structural analysis of epinephrine by John Jacob Abel at Johns Hopkins, and of thyroxine by Edward Kendall at the Mayo Clinic. This stimulated me to major in chemistry at Hope College, and, when it came time to enter graduate school, I enrolled in the Department of E. A. Doisy at St. Louis University. Doisy was an international leader in the chemistry of natural products and the first to isolate an estrogen. He was awarded the Nobel Prize for his isolation of vitamin K.

Research on antibiotics had one of the highest priorities in wartime research and as a first-year graduate student I worked side by side with Doisy in his small laboratory attempting to isolate an antibiotic from the mold *Aspergillus clavatus*. Although this invaluable learning experience would pay rich dividends in the years to come, I soon became disenchanted with Doisy's Prussian approach to research, and after a few months of soul searching, I made a major career shift by deciding to go to medical school. I chose Johns Hopkins because of its reputation for treating medical students like graduate students.

In 1944, two days after D-Day, I wed my college sweetheart, Persis Parker, and together we set out for Baltimore and Johns Hopkins. Doisy had arranged for me to continue in chemistry under his friend, William Mansfield Clark, who was chairman of the Department of Physiological Chemistry at Johns Hopkins. Although Clark was then secretary of the National Research Council and spending only a few days a week in Baltimore, he agreed to precept me on a project in physical chemistry through my first three years of medical school. Although this project had little relevance to biology or medicine, it filled major gaps in my knowledge of physical chemistry and taught me much about experimental rigor. Medical school was a joy for me and I particularly liked the "people" aspect of medicine, although intellectually I was more stimulated by laboratory research. For the rest of my life I would never be happy doing either exclusively.

I was turned on to pediatrics by such exciting people as Victor Najjar, who ran the pediatric OPD and later became chairman of microbiology at Vanderbilt; Harold Harrison, who was my mentor throughout medical school and house officer training; Horace Hodes, who exemplified the complete pediatrician and who was head of the Sydenham Infectious Disease Hospital; and lastly by Lawson Wilkins, who kindled my interest in endocrinology. After two years of house officer training at Johns Hopkins, I completed my last year of pediatric residency at Cincinnati Children's Hospital.

Because the Korean War was then making military service inevitable, I joined the Public Health Service for a two-year stint at the NIH. These two years were devoted to studying a bone and connective tissue lesion in dogs caused by copper deficiency. The condition in these dogs was remarkably similar to osteogenesis imperfecta (OI) in children. Because copper and ascorbic acid were known cofactors for the oxidative enzymes involved in the hydroxylation of proline in collagen, I postulated that the abnormal bone matrix in children with OI might be due to a genetic error in the apoenzymes involved in collagen formation. This was to form the basis of one of my earliest research projects when I arrived in Chapel Hill.

After two years at Bethesda, I was ready to go back into clinical training and pediatrics, and, together with Melvin Grumbach, joined the program of Lawson Wilkins at Harriet Lane Home in Baltimore. Clinical endocrinology was in its infancy, and these were exciting days in the Wilkins unit. Lawson Wilkins had been a private pediatrician for twenty-five years and had entered full-time academic medicine after the age of fifty, when Edwards Park invited him to head up a new endocrine clinic at Johns Hopkins. Although Wilkins was not scientifically trained, his inquiring mind made him one of the great scientists in our field. Wilkins had recently demonstrated that cortisone would control the overproduction of androgens in the adrenogenital syndrome and much of my time was spent measuring pregnanediol and pregnanetriol in urine from these patients. Wilkins's insights on sex differentiation (based on Jost's embryonic castrations) led him to postulate that some of the girls with the syndrome of gonadal dysgenesis (Turner syndrome) would prove to be genetic males. Mel Grumbach and I were able to confirm this prediction by using the sex chromatin method recently described by Murray Barr. Wilkins's interest in potassium led him to purchase one of the first flame photometers on the East Coast, and I broke in his balky machine to study a dwarfed boy with hypokalemic alkalosis. The patient proved to have a renal tubular lesion that led to great losses of potassium in his urine. This lad and other patients of mine were later described by Fred Bartter at the NIH, and this condition became known as Bartter syndrome. Lawson also had purchased a binary counter, and we were among the first to use radioactive iodine in the diagnosis of thyroid disorders.

I would have been happy to remain in Baltimore, but Wilkins had no job for me. My associate Al Bongiovanni had developed great respect for Ed Curnen while they were coworkers at the Rockefeller Institute and suggested that I try to get a position in the new department that Dr. Curnen was organizing at UNC. Al introduced me to Dr. Curnen at a Ross Conference, and this led to the visit that culminated in the famous grand rounds on rheumatoid arthritis mentioned above.

On one of my early visits to Chapel Hill I learned that no research space and only a meager start-up fund for buying equipment were available. On one of these visits, Charles Hooker, chairman of anatomy, told me about the new Elsa U. Pardee Research Foundation in Midland, Michigan, and wrote down the name of its secretary, Mr. Carl Gerstacker. Hooker did not know the mission of the foundation. I finally secured an appointment for an interview in Midland following my pediatric board examinations in Detroit. Only on the way in from the Midland airport did I learn from my cab driver that Gerstacker was the financial genius behind the Dow-Corning empire. I was interviewed at length by Gerstacker and his brother-in-law William Allen, who headed the agricultural division of Dow, and whose wife, Elsa, was a twin of Gerstacker. Mr. Allen told me that the Pardee Foundation was a foundation to cure cancer, but only recently had he learned that children got cancer(!). I was also interviewed by Dr. William Gronemeyer, who was the Allens' pediatrician. (Dr. G later retired in Chapel Hill and taught in our division of community pediatrics.) I had no clue what the outcome of this strange interview might be, but a few weeks later, after returning to Baltimore, I received a call from Reece Berryhill saying that he had a check for $17,000 on his desk and what the hell was this all about? He lectured me about breaking University rules by soliciting funds on behalf of the University without authorization (he did not, however, return the check). As a result, I went to Chapel Hill on July 1, 1955, with a credit line of $17,000, with which I built a laboratory on the fifth floor of the Old Clinic Building and hired Anne Fernald as my first (and probably best) research technician.

Early Years in Chapel Hill

When I arrived in 1955, I became not only one-fourth of the pediatric faculty, but one of only four pediatricians in a town populated by a fertile young faculty. This made it hazardous to attend cocktail parties where we were more likely to be questioned about bedwetting than our opinions about a new television personality in Raleigh by the name of Jesse Helms.

The concept of an endocrine division was, at that time, nonexistent. The entire ambulatory clinic was housed on the ground and first floors of the Old Clinic Building. William Fleming, who was in charge of ambulatory clinics, had initially planned that the ambulatory services would be integrated into a general clinic with no subspecialty groups. Thus, a patient could be seen by any subspecialist on demand. This idea was already dying before I arrived. I rapidly developed a large clientele of faculty kids as well as patients with general pediatric problems ranging from cardiac disease to allergies, neoplasms, and snakebite. Each faculty member was expected to serve as ward attending on the general pediatric service three months of the year.

Because NCMH and the four-year school were new in Chapel Hill, it was necessary to obtain referrals by an aggressive approach to practicing physicians throughout the state. Accordingly, we were on a regular lecture circuit to county medical societies and other groups from Asheville to Wilmington. Since these trips had to be made by car, I generally asked one of the residents to accompany me and became very close to residents Charles Stamey, Griggs Dixon, and Hugh Hemmings. Such barnstorming across the state began to pay off, and slowly my clinic became populated with more endocrine patients than general pediatric patients.

In 1957, Ed Curnen recruited John Arnold to help him in infectious disease and his wife, Mary Arnold, who had been trained by Nathan Talbot in Boston, joined me in endocrinology on a part-time basis. Although she was very busy with child rearing at that time, she was a great help in the clinic and alleviated some of my scientific loneliness.

During these early years I received many requests from the other clinical services to consult on patients with endocrine disorders. Although each of the other subspecialties was well represented in the Department of Medicine, endocrinology was conspicuous by its absence. This was because Lou Welt echoed the claim of John Peters at Yale that endocrinology was a sport and not a science. Thus, by default I became the school's all-purpose clinical endocrinologist. This situation continued for the next eleven years, until the Department of Medicine hired Robert Ney to head its own endocrine division.

Relationships with Duke

During my early years, I was not only the solitary endocrinologist on the clinical services, but there was virtually no ongoing interest in endocrinology in any of the basic science departments. This void would have been fatal to my career were it not for Frank Engel, who was chief of endocrinology in the Department of Medicine at Duke and a member of their Department of Physiology. I regularly attended Frank's evening journal club and seminar groups and many of his clinical conferences. Frank introduced me to the national endocrine scene and frequently invited me to his home to meet visiting scientists, including his brother Lewis, who was a distinguished steroid biochemist at Harvard, and his identical twin George, who was (and is) a distinguished psychiatrist/internist at the University of Rochester. Frank and Lewis Engel helped us recruit Billy Baggett for our Department of Pharmacology. Baggett was one of the most able postdocs in the laboratory of Lewis Engel. In return, I helped Frank recruit Robert Stempfel (and later Stuart Handwerger) to head Duke's pediatric endocrine division. After Frank's premature death in 1962, I forged another relationship with Jack Kostyo, whom Frank had recruited to physiology at Duke. Jack and I organized a highly successful evening seminar series that alternated between Durham and Chapel Hill.

The Division of Pediatric Endocrinology Takes Shape

Floyd Denny arrived as the second chair of pediatrics in 1960 with a commitment to build the Department around strong subspecialty divisions. A turning point for our program came in 1962, when the NIH awarded me both a career research award and an endocrine training grant. The career award supposedly guaranteed lifetime support, but this program was quickly terminated when it was discovered that only members of the judiciary could receive lifetime appointments. Furthermore, these grants were hated by deans and department heads because recipients became too uppity and refused to do the more menial departmental chores. Nevertheless, NIH continued to honor their commitment to me until I voluntarily relinquished it a few years ago.

The Endocrine Faculty

Our training program has provided postdoctoral training for most of our endocrine faculty. My first fellow supported by the training grant was Frank French. As a medical student at the University of Rochester, he had undertaken research under the guidance of the distinguished pathologist George Whipple; he had taken his internship and junior residency in Cleveland under Fred Robbins. I first met Frank French in 1958 in Kinston, where I was giving a talk to the county medical society. Frank was then carrying out his military obligation at the Seymour Johnson Air Force Base, and out of boredom had decided to attend my talk on disorders of sex differentiation. I invited him to visit Chapel Hill, and Dr. Curnen was successful in persuading him to complete his pediatric residency in Chapel Hill rather than in Durham. Dr. French

Lou
Underwood

eventually became chief resident in pediatrics, and in 1962 he was the first to enroll in our new endocrine training program. In 1982 Frank was appointed chief of the UNC-wide Laboratories for Reproductive Biology (LRB) and successfully assembled a consortium of scientists in the Research Triangle area. The administrative office of the LRB, a number of its laboratories, and its molecular biology core facilities are physically located within the Department of Pediatrics and adjacent to the rest of the division of endocrinology. His group is now recognized as one of the premier laboratories for the study of male reproduction. He has been ably assisted in his research by a number of young investigators. Dr. Elizabeth Wilson, who, after receiving her PhD in biochemistry from Vanderbilt, received her postdoctoral training in our endocrine training program under the preceptorship of Frank French, is now internationally recognized as one of the leading investigators in the androgen field.

Dr. Louis E. Underwood graduated from Vanderbilt School of Medicine and elected to take his senior residency in Chapel Hill. During his elective in endocrinology, Underwood became a collaborator with Dr. Gabor Antony, one of our endocrine fellows, who was undertaking studies of hypoglycemia on the clinical research unit. When Lou returned to Vanderbilt as chief resident he studied additional patients who were then included in the series. After two years in the Navy in Boston, Underwood returned to Chapel Hill as a postdoctoral fellow. His outstanding qualities were particularly recognized by Frank French, who served as Underwood's preceptor while I was away on sabbatical, and Frank persuaded Dr. Denny to recruit Underwood as a permanent faculty member. This was a wise decision. Lou Underwood has done much to ensure the clinical integrity of the division and has established himself as one of the most respected investigators in growth hormone research. His laboratory research has been at the interface between nutrition and endocrinology, and in 1994 he was awarded the prestigious Award in Nutrition by the American Academy of Pediatrics. In 1988 he succeeded me as chief of the endocrine division and head of our combined pediatric-medicine training program in endocrinology.

Joe D'Ercole

Dr. A. Joseph D'Ercole, a graduate of Notre Dame and Georgetown University School of Medicine, had been an outstanding pediatric resident under Dr. Sydney Gellis at Boston Floating Children's Hospital and had spent two years in the Public Health Service studying the effect of prenatal exposure to agricultural pesticides on fetal development. D'Ercole was one of the most outstanding fellows that we have had, and at the completion of his fellowship it was obvious that we should make a strong attempt to keep him on our staff. Although it was no longer possible to tell Dr. Denny that we needed another pair of hands to treat our diabetics (that argument had been used twice before in urging the hiring of Drs. French and Underwood), there was a strong need for a research-based neonatologist. D'Ercole had done much of his work in the area of fetal growth and it was natural that we approach him to see whether he was willing to accept an assistant professorship while at the same time serving an apprenticeship in neonatology sufficient to make him board certifiable. Joe agreed to do this and then returned to our division with a mandate to develop a subspecialty of fetal and perinatal endocrinology. D'Ercole's achievements have won international recognition and have created a school of thinking that has in turn attracted many fellows with a neonatology background.

Dr. Marsha Davenport, a graduate of Harvard and University of Kentucky School of Medicine, came to UNC as a resident in pediatrics and then enrolled in our training program as a postdoctoral fellow. During her fellowship, Marsha was precepted by Kay Lund, Jane Azizkhan (who was a member of the Lineberger Cancer Center), and Lou Underwood. After completing her fellowship, she was appointed by Dr. Boat as the fifth clinical faculty member in the endocrine division. Her area of research is on the relationship between nutrition and IGF-I and its binding proteins, and she has enlarged our clinic by providing comprehensive care for a large cadre of patients with Turner syndrome.

A most important addition to our division was the recruitment of Dr. P. Kay Lund to the Department of Physiology in 1982. Kay had received her

Marsha
Davenport

Kay Lund

PhD in gastrointestinal physiology from the University of Newcastle upon Tyne. She received her postdoctoral training in molecular biology at Massachusetts General Hospital, where she was the first to clone the gene for preproglucagon. When Dr. Perl recruited her for our Physiology Department, I succeeded in persuading her to turn her attention to the molecular biology of growth factors. Since then, Kay has become an international authority on the genes for IGF-I and has played a major role in training some of our postdoctoral fellows. She is now applying her skills to her original field of gastrointestinal physiology and is an active collaborator with our gastroenterologists, in particular Martin Ulshen and Steven Lichtman. She is also precepting the research of several pediatric GI fellows. In 1991 she was awarded UNC's Hettleman Award for creative research by a junior faculty member. Dr. Lund is also a caring and inspiring teacher, and in 1994 the freshman class awarded her all three of its teaching awards.

Dr. David R. Clemmons, chief of the endocrine division in the Department of Medicine and codirector of the endocrine training program, has played an important role in the pediatric endocrine division. After his second year of medical school David took a year off to do research in our division. He showed exceptional talent for research and was one of those who first demonstrated that somatomedin-C (IGF-I) cross-reacts with the insulin receptor. After returning to medical school and graduating at the top of his class, David took his medical residency at Massachusetts General Hospital and Johns Hopkins and several years of endocrine fellowship at MGH. He then returned to Chapel Hill for an additional year of fellowship in our division, where he worked in the laboratory of our colleague Jack Pledger. After returning to the

Department of Medicine as a faculty member, Dr. Clemmons has continued his research on insulinlike growth factors and is now an internationally recognized authority on the IGF binding proteins.

Two other faculty members are deserving of special mention because of their contributions to our division as research collaborators and preceptors of postdoctoral fellows. Dr. W. Jackson Pledger was recruited from the Farber Cancer Center at Harvard as chief of the division of cell biology in the Lineberger Cancer Center. He added an important dimension to our research in the mechanisms of cell replication. He is now director of research at the Moffitt Cancer Center at the University of South Florida. Dr. Marco Conti was recruited by Frank French from the University of Rome as a member of the Laboratories for Reproductive Biology. Dr. Conti's focus was on intracellular mechanisms of signal transduction, and he was an important teacher, collaborator, and preceptor. Dr. Conti is now a faculty member at Stanford University School of Medicine.

Expansion of the professional staff of the endocrine division required additional space for our activities. Space was found for Joe D'Ercole in the Burnett-Womack building, and our initial eight hundred square feet of the fifth floor in the Old Clinic Building gradually expanded by appropriation of toilets and other spaces, often through a process of "Sturm und Drang." Finally, in 1980 we were granted relief by being assigned space on the third floor of the Medical Research Wing of MacNider Hall and were able to redesign a suite that would bring together all of our existing personnel. In the 1990s we again find our expanded space totally inadequate for our activities and are once again petitioning for more adequate quarters.

The Training Program

Without question our training program has been the source of my greatest professional and personal satisfaction, and continues to thrive under the leadership of Lou Underwood. The pediatric endocrine division, including the Laboratories for Reproductive Biology under the leadership of Frank French, has provided postdoctoral training for fifty-seven physicians. Of the fifty-two who have completed their training, forty-five now hold full-time academic positions, and fifteen of these are now division heads. We have provided postdoctoral training for twenty PhDs and have had nineteen predocs, thirteen of whom have received a PhD for research carried out in our division.

Our first trainee, Frank S. French, was followed by Dr. Gabor Antony, who is now head of endocrinology at the University of New South Wales. Our third recruit was Dr. J. Leo Van den Brande, a Flemish physician who had been trained in Groningen but who had had minimal research training. Leo was responsible for the initiation of our research on the sulfation factor (which later became somatomedin-C and even later insulinlike growth factor-I). As will be detailed later, the somatomedins have shaped a great deal of the subsequent research of the division of pediatric endocrinology, and in 1988 I was privileged to be present in Jerusalem when Leo was awarded the Andrea

Prader Award as the outstanding pediatric endocrinologist of the European Society of Pediatric Endocrinologists.

In 1969, while on a sabbatical leave at the Karolinska Institute in Stockholm, Sweden, I met Dr. Martin Ritzen, a pediatrician with a PhD in cell biology, and arranged for him to take his training in endocrinology in Chapel Hill. He elected to work with Frank French, and Frank subsequently took his sabbatical with Martin at the Karolinska. This further cemented a very close linkage between the Karolinska Institute and the division of endocrinology in Chapel Hill.

Although it is not possible to detail here all of the marvelous fellows that have been trained in our program and their subsequent achievements, a complete roster of our trainees and their present status is provided at the end of this chapter.

Research and Scholarship in the Division of Endocrinology

The Early Years

From the beginning Dr. Curnen encouraged me to give research a very high priority at a time when clinical demands made this a seeming impossibility. He did not demand that I pay my keep by seeing more patients or by getting a grant to pay my salary. (The truth was that there was very little salary to pay since my salary was less than my previous fellowship stipend had been!) When Ed Curnen left in 1960 to accept the chair at Columbia, his policies were continued by Floyd Denny and subsequently by Tom Boat. These three men provided an environment within the Department of Pediatrics in which basic research and exemplary clinical care could flourish side by side.

When I arrived in Chapel Hill, Dr. Curnen asked me to serve as preceptor for a former resident, Dr. George Summer, who was interested in genetic abnormalities of proteins in a wide range of diseases. Dr. Summer took on the osteogenesis imperfecta (OI) project that had evolved from my research at the NIH. Dr. R. Beverly Raney, professor of orthopedics, joined us in an application to the Easter Seal Foundation for a grant to support this research, and from then on George was funded from this source.

Soon after arriving in Chapel Hill, I applied for my first NIH grant to study "The Role of Hormones in Growth and Development." This proved to be a salutary title because it funded a long-running grant that covered a multitude of projects.

My first laboratory objective was to establish methods for measuring a wide range of steroids in order to follow patients with errors in sexual differentiation, including children with congenital adrenal hyperplasia, and to provide tools to study the regulation of adrenal function by the pituitary. Later, the grant funded studies in thyroid disease, pituitary stalk section, growth hormone physiology, and finally in growth factors. In 1991 Kay Lund, my long-term associate in the Department of Physiology, took over as the principal investigator on this grant.

In 1958, I became a John and Mary R. Markle Scholar in Medical Science. The procedure for these coveted awards was for each medical school to nominate one candidate; these nominees were in turn interviewed for three days by prominent nonmedical personages. Although winning this award provided only $30,000 for a five-year period, it made it possible for me to remain at Carolina and it put me in the prestigious company of John Graham, Ike Taylor, George Penick, T. Franklin Williams, and Walter Hollander.

One of my early research interests was in thyroid disease and particularly in separating genetic from environmental causes of simple goiter. To study this I teamed up with Bill Deiss at the Durham VA and later with Jim Wynn when Deiss took the chair in medicine at the University of Indiana. I also collaborated in this research with John Graham and his team of genetic technicians.

Thyroid research required moving into the isotope era. The tight regulation of isotope usage by the Atomic Energy Commission after the Second World War required investigators to have special training and a special license to use them in their research. I spent six weeks in Oak Ridge in 1960 to obtain my certification; similar training was also taken by Frank French and Lou Underwood. The Pardee Foundation gave us another sizable grant to purchase a gamma counter with automatic changer, a counter for doing radioactive iodine uptakes in patients, and other equipment. Indeed, for a time we performed all of the ^{131}I uptakes in the hospital. Our Oak Ridge training was overkill insofar as isotopes were concerned, and I even ended up working with the nuclear reactor at NCSU in Raleigh in an attempt to measure thyroid hormones in prematures by neutron activation analysis.

Some of my most fruitful early studies in Chapel Hill were in women with breast cancer who were being treated by our neurosurgeon, Gordon Dugger, by pituitary stalk section. The concept that certain types of cancer are hormonally dependent was still in its infancy, although some success had been reported with hypophysectomy in women with metastatic breast carcinoma. Dugger postulated that the benefits of hypophysectomy could be gained by simply sectioning the pituitary stalk to prevent the hypothetical hypothalamic releasing hormones (their isolation came much later) from reaching the anterior lobe of the pituitary. The results obtained from the endocrine function studies that we carried out before and after stalk section in sixty-six women provided some of the most complete documentation then available of the role of the hypothalamus on pituitary function in humans. Stalk section, however, had little, if any, effect on the progress of metastatic breast carcinoma and is no longer performed.

BOOK CHAPTERS

When Lawson Wilkins died in 1962, I inherited his chapter on the thyroid in the old Holt & MacIntosh *Textbook of Pediatrics*. I wrote this for several editions under the editorship of Henry Barnett and Abe Rudolph. I finally asked Del Fisher to collaborate with me, and subsequently turned the chapter over to him.

As a postdoctoral fellow with Lawson Wilkins I had become intrigued with the theoretical aspects of sex determination and was pleased when the late Robert Williams asked me to develop a chapter on this subject for inclusion in the third edition of his famous *Textbook of Endocrinology*. Up until that time, no attempt had been made to integrate clinical disorders of sex differentiation with the rapidly evolving theoretical concepts of sex differentiation based on steroid biochemistry and the recently developed techniques of cytogenetics. I later asked Mel Grumbach to join me in revising this chapter in the fourth and fifth editions.

I relinquished my authorship of the chapter on sex differentiation to Mel Grumbach when Bob Williams asked me to write a chapter on growth for the sixth edition. I was willing to undertake this new challenge only if Lou Underwood would join me in creating such a chapter and take primary responsibility as senior author. This proved to be a very fruitful enterprise since we attempted to accomplish the same thing as in the sex chapter, integrating theoretical concepts of growth regulation at the cellular level with the many clinical syndromes of normal and aberrant growth. The third revision of this chapter was published in December 1991 in the eighth edition of Williams's text, now under the editorship of Jean Wilson.

In 1979 Dr. George Cahill asked me to contribute a chapter on peptide growth factors to a new three-volume *Endocrinology* text edited by Lester De Groot. I asked Ray Hintz, a former fellow and chief of pediatric endocrinology at Stanford, to assist me. Dr. William Russell, a former trainee and a member of the Pediatric and Cell Biology Departments at Vanderbilt, collaborated with me in rewriting this chapter for the second and third editions. The explosion of research on peptide growth factors has led to a commitment by the editors to devote an entire volume to this subject in future editions.

RESEARCH ON MECHANISMS OF HORMONAL ACTION

After the rather diffuse research efforts in the early years described above, the major research thrust of the endocrine division turned toward how certain hormones produce their biological effects. Research on how testosterone acts has been carried out by Frank French and Elizabeth Wilson with their associates in the Laboratories for Reproductive Biology, whereas research on growth hormone and peptide growth factors has been the focus of the rest of us.

Mechanisms of Androgen Action. The award of the NIH training grant in 1962 placed on us a serious responsibility to provide our trainees with adequate training in all aspects of endocrinology. Accordingly, shortly after Frank French began his fellowship, Billy Baggett and I organized a course in steroid biochemistry that convened every Thursday evening at 7:00 P.M. and continued into the wee hours. Since Frank was the only postdoctoral fellow, we managed to entice a variety of technicians and faculty members to enroll in the course, including Luther Talbert, who had been hired by "Daddy" Ross to head up gynecologic endocrinology.

While this course was in progress, a gynecologist in Texas referred to us a sixteen-year-old girl with the syndrome of testicular feminization (TF), a condition that I had written about in Williams's *Textbook of Endocrinology*. These patients are genetic males with testes but are normal females externally. Our patient was a beautiful fashion model. Since the etiology of TF was unknown at that time, we admitted our patient to the clinical research unit to investigate the etiology of this condition. Baggett and I immediately changed the format of our steroid course from a rather sterile exercise of analyzing unknown mixtures of steroids to answering the question: "What is wrong with this girl?"

Each of us took a different hypothesis to test. Frank chose to test the hypothesis that she was insensitive to testosterone. This hypothesis had been first advanced by Lawson Wilkins but had subsequently fallen into disfavor. Frank used the metabolic balance technique to demonstrate that she did not retain nitrogen or phosphorus following the administration of testosterone. The results of this exercise provided the first hard evidence that TF is due to androgen insensitivity.

Since one could not understand testicular feminization without understanding the action of androgens, Frank French went into the laboratory and spent the next twenty-five years studying this subject. He took a year in Billy Baggett's laboratory and returned as an assistant professor of pediatrics. During the course of these studies, Frank, together with Shihadeh Nayfeh and Martin Ritzen, demonstrated the presence of an androgen binding protein (ABP) in the testes and epididymides and traced the origin of ABP to the Sertoli cell. He later showed that ABP is under the control of FSH and androgen.

Finally, in 1988, Frank, together with David Joseph, succeeded in cloning the gene for ABP. That year, together with Elizabeth Wilson, Dennis Lubahn, David Joseph, and other colleagues, Frank also cloned the gene for the androgen receptor. The latter accomplishment made it possible to demonstrate that patients with TF either lacked the androgen receptor gene or had mutant genes that blocked androgen binding or interaction with DNA. In fact, one of the proofs that the gene coded for the androgen receptor and not for some other substance was his demonstration that one of our original patients with TF had a deletion of this gene.

This is the most dramatic example I know of where a clinical observation was taken to the laboratory and, after twenty-five years, brought back to the bedside to answer the original question. These findings are now providing an important tool in studying prostate cancer and other diseases of the male reproductive tract.

Research on Growth Hormone and Somatomedins. The focus of our division on growth hormone (GH) began in the early '60s when it became possible to measure GH in blood by radioimmunoassay. At about this time our clinic had started to treat dwarfed patients with GH deficiency by giving them injections of crude pituitary extracts. We collected pituitary glands from local pathologists and shipped them to Morris Raben in Boston. Raben would process the pituitaries and send us a portion of the extracted GH. These preparations were extraordinarily crude and arrived as a green powder which we dissolved in saline and injected into patients. Surprisingly, we achieved rather startlingly good rates of growth with minimal side effects.

Studies of how growth hormone acted were very rudimentary at that time. One of the main investigators was Jack Kostyo, my colleague in the Department of Physiology at Duke. Kostyo believed that growth hormone acted directly on muscle and bone, whereas the studies of Daughaday and Salmon in 1957 suggested that the action of growth hormone was indirect through an unknown "sulfation" factor or factors.

It was this controversy that stimulated Leo Van den Brande to begin his historic investigations in 1966 on the mechanism of growth hormone action. This research eventually led to the isolation and sequencing of somatomedin-C (Sm-C), a peptide hormone that is the major effector of GH action. (Stan Bennett, a noted linguist and chair of our anatomy department, suggested the name somatomedin, which means "to mediate the action of somatotropin." The C, of course, stands for Carolina.) We showed that many of its actions are similar to those of insulin, and demonstrated that not only is Sm-C itself structurally similar to human proinsulin, but that its receptor is homologous to the insulin receptor. We developed the first radioimmunoassay for Sm-C, and this permitted us to document the hormonal dependency of this peptide and its relation to nutritional status.

Needless to say, we were not alone in this search. Howard Temin, who received the Nobel Prize for reverse transcriptase, was trying to identify the substance(s) in blood that are necessary for cells to grow in culture, and termed these substances "multiplication stimulating activity." At the same time, a group of diabetologists in Zurich were trying to identify the insulin-like substances in blood that differ from insulin. In fact, the Zurich group determined the sequence of what they then referred to as "non-suppressible insulin-like activity" before we completed the amino acid sequence of Sm-C. We had to content ourselves with showing that the two molecules were identical. We agreed with the Swiss that both names be abolished, and that the names of specific members of this family be renamed "insulin-like growth factors" and that these substances be known generically as somatomedins. Thus "somatomedin-C" became "insulin-like growth factor-I" or simply "IGF-I."

Somatomedin research has been the dominant theme of our division since the late 1960s. Leaving details aside, the somatomedins have come to occupy a position of importance in biology far beyond the wildest dreams of Leo Van den Brande and me twenty-seven years ago. The somatomedins are produced in many different tissues and have proven necessary for the division of most cell types and for a host of differentiated cell functions. Thus, they are helping to fulfill the concepts of the endocrine system that were postulated by Starling and his contemporaries at the turn of the century. Gone forever is the idea that hormones are only produced by a few discrete glands of internal secretion. By 1992, 10 percent of the nearly two thousand abstracts at the annual meeting of the Endocrine Society were related to the somatomedins.

Lou Underwood, Joe D'Ercole, Kay Lund, and David Clemmons, together with countless postdoctoral fellows, have played major roles in these developments. Lou Underwood and David Clemmons are now undertaking clinical studies with the somatomedins. Lou, for example, is studying the effects of IGF-I in severely dwarfed children with genetic forms of GH insensitivity. These children have very high levels of growth hormone but have various defects of the growth hormone receptor so that they are unable to produce IGF-I in response to growth hormone. Although these children are as severely dwarfed as if they had no growth hormone, all have responded dramatically to the administration of IGF-I. One boy from Poland continues to grow at an accelerated rate after three years of treatment; his parents have immigrated to Chapel Hill.

David Clemmons has become a world leader in defining the role of the somatomedin binding proteins and in exploring the use of IGF-I in catabolic conditions such as malnutrition, AIDS, and various other chronic diseases.

Kay Lund together with Martin Ulshen in our pediatric GI division are studying the role of growth factors in bowel regeneration after injury or partial resection. It is conceivable that this new knowledge of how gut regenerates might improve the outlook in malabsorption syndromes or in necrotizing enterocolitis in premature infants.

Joe D'Ercole is using transgenic animals to determine the physiologic roles of the IGFs and their binding proteins. His work is revealing the very important role that these peptides and their binding proteins play in neural development. Alan Stiles and his group in neonatology are studying the role of growth factors in lung growth. This approach could have important ramifications in bronchopulmonary dysplasia and similar disorders.

My own research has been directed toward the mechanisms of IGF-I action at the cellular level. This work was initiated in collaboration with Jack Pledger in the Lineberger Cancer Center and more recently with Marco Conti in the Laboratories for Reproductive Biology.

Summary

This has proven to be a very brief and somewhat disjointed sketch of the history of the division of endocrinology, which started as a nondivision and ended up as perhaps one of the premier pediatric endocrine divisions in the world. Certainly it has always been more highly oriented toward basic research than is customary in a clinical department, and this reflects, I think, the imperative of Berryhill and Curnen to incorporate basic science into the core of the Department. This led to the selection of Van Wyk as the fourth faculty member and shaped the subsequent course of the endocrine division. To accomplish our goals, we have practiced strict control on the number of patients that we see and have attempted to maintain a model clinic in which we provide exemplary clinical services without being burdened unduly with excessive patient demands. Our research funding has grown by leaps and bounds and we have received many honors and recognitions. We came into biomedical research at a moment that astronomical progress was being made, and we were supported by a Department that gave us full encouragement and support.

The emphasis in this review has been on the early years, because that is the era that will soon be forgotten. The current era is vibrant with activity, and the ongoing story needs to be told by someone else.

JUDSON J. VAN WYK

LABORATORIES FOR REPRODUCTIVE BIOLOGY: ROLE OF PEDIATRICS

Early Years of the Laboratories

The UNC Laboratories for Reproductive Biology (LRB) were established in 1968 at a time when there was great public concern over the adverse effects of the global population explosion on human civilization. The UNC Population Center (Pop Center), which had been established earlier, was heavily engaged in the epidemiologic aspects of population control, and there was a perceived need for the research community to focus more specifically on more basic issues of reproductive biology. The recruitment of Dr. Stanley Bennett as chairman of the Department of Anatomy was facilitated by the added inducement of a sizable grant from the Rockefeller Foundation if Dr. Bennett would also serve as director of a new institutionwide program of research on reproductive biology. The chronology of the early events in the life of the LRB are recounted in a memorandum from Dr. John B. Graham to Dr. Isaac Taylor, who was then dean of the medical school.

The history of the first eleven years of the LRB under the leadership of Dr. Bennett are beyond the scope of the present history. Suffice it to say that following the retirement of Dr. Bennett in 1982, Dean Bondurant appointed Dr. Frank S. French, professor of pediatrics, to direct and restructure the LRB to better fulfill the mission for which it had been initially funded.

Dr. Frank S. French: The Years of Preparation

Dr. French was born in Missouri and received his baccalaureate degree from the University of Kansas and his medical degree from the University of Rochester. While in medical school French had his first taste of research from a summer project under the tutelage of Dr. George Whipple, professor of pathology. After one year of pediatric internship on the service of Fred Robbins at the Cleveland Metropolitan Hospital, Dr. French was obliged to fulfill his military obligations in the U.S. Air Force at the Seymour Johnson Air Force Base in Goldsboro, North Carolina. Good fortune brought Frank and Jud Van Wyk together in Kinston, North Carolina, where Jud was addressing the local medical society. As a result of this encounter, French finished his

Frank
French

pediatric training at UNC. He served as cochief resident with Paul Glezen in an arrangement that permitted him to spend six months' research time in the Van Wyk laboratory, and that made it possible for Paul Glezen to spend six months of research time in infectious disease. In 1962, following his residency, Frank became the first postdoctoral fellow in Van Wyk's endocrinology training program, which had just been funded by the National Institute of Arthritis and Metabolic Diseases.

Although Van Wyk's primary interest at that time was in thyroid disease and sex differentiation, he thought the training program should offer a formal laboratory course in steroid biochemistry. To this end he teamed up with Dr. Billy Baggett in the Department of Pharmacology to conduct an evening course in which unknowns were analyzed by every available technique. In 1962 Van Wyk was referred a sixteen-year-old patient from Laredo, Texas, who had no sexual hair, had never menstruated, but who nevertheless had well-developed breasts and had worked as a model. She proved to have an XY karyotype and testes but no uterus. Although she fit existing clinical descriptions of the syndrome of testicular feminization, there was considerable confusion at the time about the etiology of the defect. She and a phenotypically similar control patient were therefore hospitalized on the clinical research unit and each member of the steroid class along with their instructors was asked to devise and test a hypothesis to answer "What is wrong with this girl?" French took the hypothesis that the basic lesion was end organ resistance to the actions of androgens and proceeded to prove his hypothesis in a series of now classic metabolic studies.

It was obvious to French that in order to fully understand the molecular basis for androgen insensitivity in such patients, it would first be necessary to understand how androgens produced their effects at the cellular level. Thus, after completing his fellowship in pediatrics, Dr. French took an extra year in the laboratory of Dr. Billy Baggett in the Department of Pharmacology. In 1966 Dr. French returned to the pediatric endocrine division as its second full-time faculty member.

Revitalization of the LRB

Dr. French was a charter member of the UNC Laboratories for Reproductive Biology, and his appointment to succeed Dr. Bennett was based on his outstanding research accomplishments in the area of male reproduction. In the years following his demonstration that the syndrome of testicular feminization resulted from peripheral insensitivity to the effects of androgen, French and his colleagues had discovered the androgen binding protein, shown that in the rat it was made by Sertoli cells, and delineated many of its properties. They had discovered and characterized several androgen-dependent proteins in the male reproductive tract and had made great progress in characterizing the androgen receptor. Thus, when a search was mounted by the School of Medicine to find an eminent scientist to succeed Dr. Bennett as head of the LRB, the foremost candidate proved to be Dr. French, and in 1982 he became the second director of the LRB.

Although the LRB is a separate administrative unit under the direct jurisdiction of the dean of the School of Medicine, Frank French lost no time in putting his imprint on its direction. He reorganized it so that its major focus should be the study of male reproduction, with the long-range goal of building a larger clinical component on a strong foundation of basic research. He persuaded Dean Bondurant to assign approximately eight thousand square feet of space on the third floor of the Medical Research Wing of MacNider contiguous to the existing space of the division of pediatric endocrinology. This space was designated to house the administrative offices of LRB, the molecular biology core facility, and a few smaller laboratories. This arrangement permitted Drs. French, Elizabeth Wilson, and others to remain in laboratory space already allocated to them by the pediatric endocrine division.

French further organized the LRB to include additional core facilities in the areas of histochemistry/microscopy, radioimmunoassay, and tissue culture. Other activities sponsored by the LRB have included seminars, workshops, and a training program for predoctoral PhD candidates, and postdoctoral training for physicians and PhD scientists from the United States and other countries.

The LRB now includes twenty-five research projects at UNC that interact with ten projects located in other Triangle institutions: Duke University, NC State University (Department of Biology and the Veterinary School), and National Institute for Environmental Health Sciences. It is supported by a population research core grant from NICHHD (1992–1997), a training grant in the reproductive sciences from NICHHD (1991–1996), and a training and faculty development grant from the Andrew W. Mellon Foundation (1991–1993). In addition, individual research grants total nearly $4 million a year.

Major Research Achievements

As head of the LRB French never lost focus on his quest to understand the mechanism of androgen action. An early focus was on the androgen receptor, and work from several laboratories confirmed that the defect in testicular feminization lay in abnormal binding of testosterone to target cells. In 1988 these lines of research culminated in cloning the genes for both the androgen binding protein and the androgen receptor. Since the syndrome of testicular feminization had been determined to be an X-linked disease, the strategy used for cloning the receptor was to screen an X-chromosome library with a probe based on a consensus sequence found in other steroid hormone receptors. This was far from a foolproof approach, however, and one of the proofs that the cloned gene was that of the androgen receptor was the finding that this gene was deleted in one of the original patients studied by Van Wyk.

The cloning of the androgen receptor represents a prototypic example of a physician investigator taking a clinical question to the laboratory and then after twenty-five years using the laboratory findings to answer the initial question posed by the proband and to shed light on other clinical problems. French was soon collaborating with various groups around the world who wished to correlate clinical findings with specific mutations in patients with testicular feminization and other disorders of sex differentiation. Furthermore, now, for the first time, clinical fellows were brought into the LRB to study our own patient population. Other groups are using the tools of the LRB to study such disorders as prostatic carcinoma. Indeed, the LRB has now emerged as one of the premier centers of excellence for research in male reproduction.

Impact of the LRB on the Department of Pediatrics

The most obvious benefit of the LRB to the Department of Pediatrics has been its working side by side with the pediatric endocrine division in its research and training activities. Dr. French has remained an active clinical member of the endocrine division and the LRB has provided primary research training for several postdoctoral fellows in the endocrine division. These include Drs. Eric Smith and David Repaske, who are now on the staff of Cincinnati Children's Hospital; Dr. Nancy Charest, who is on the faculty of Yale University; and Dr. Stuart Kupfer, who was awarded an NIH Clinical Investigator Award at UNC and is now an assistant professor of pediatrics at Washington University in St. Louis. Several investigators in pediatrics such as Johnny Carson and Ping Chuan Hu have been partially supported by the LRB by supervising various of their core facilities.

The Department of Pediatrics, in turn, has provided an invaluable service by extending courtesy academic appointments to LRB appointees concurrent with or in anticipation of an appointment in a basic science department. Some of the basic scientists given appointments in the Department of Pediatrics have included Drs. Elizabeth Wilson, Laura Tres, David Joseph, Marco Conti, Susan Hall, and Deborah O'Brian.

In summary, for the past dozen years the Laboratories for Reproductive Biology and the Department of Pediatrics have enjoyed a mutually productive relationship and continue to demonstrate the importance of close bridges between the basic medical sciences and the clinical practice of medicine.

Judson J. Van Wyk

FACULTY, INCLUDING THE LABORATORIES FOR REPRODUCTIVE BIOLOGY

Arnold, Mary B. AB, Vassar, 1945; MD, Vermont, 1950; Inst, Ped, 1957; Asst Prof (part-time), Ped, 1960–65.

Davenport, Marsha L. AB, Harvard Univ, 1977; MD, Univ Kentucky, 1982; Asst Prof, Ped, 1991.

D'Ercole, A. Joseph. AB, Univ Notre Dame, 1965; MD, Georgetown Univ School of Med, 1969; Asst Prof, Ped, 1978; Assoc Prof, Ped, 1981; Prof, Ped, 1986.

French, Frank S. BA, Univ Kansas, 1951; MD, Univ Rochester, 1956; Asst Prof, Ped, 1966; Assoc Prof, Ped, 1969; Prof, Ped, 1976; Dir, Lab of Repro Biol, 1982.

Lund, Pauline K. BSc, Univ Newcastle upon Tyne, 1975; PhD, Univ Newcastle upon Tyne, 1979; Asst Prof, Physiol, 1988; Assoc Prof, Physiol, 1989; Joint Appt Assoc Prof, Ped and Physiol, 1993; Dir, Molecular and Transgenic Mouse Core Facility, Ctr of Gastrointestinal Biol and Res, 1989.

Underwood, Louis E. AB, Univ Kentucky, 1958; MD, Vanderbilt Univ, 1961; Instructor, Ped, 1969; Asst Prof, Ped, 1970; Assoc Prof, Ped, 1975; Prof, Ped, 1980; Chief, Div Ped Endocrin, 1989; Prof, Nutrition (School of Public Health), 1991.

Van Wyk, Judson J. AB, Hope College, 1943; MD, Johns Hopkins Univ, 1948; Asst Prof, Ped, 1955; Assoc Prof, Ped, 1959; Prof, Ped, 1962; Kenan Prof, Ped, 1973; Prof, Biol, 1986; Chief, Div Ped Endocrin, 1959–89.

Wilson, Elizabeth S. BA, Ohio Western Univ, 1970; PhD, Vanderbilt Univ, 1974; Res Asst Prof, Ped and Biochem, 1979; Assoc Prof, Ped, 1983; Prof, Ped and Biochem and Biophysics, 1990.

POSTDOCTORAL FELLOWS (MD)

Years	Name	Current Position
1956–57	Patricia Z. Thomas, MD	Unknown (previously Res Assoc, Worchester Inst)

1957–59	George Summer, MD	Prof, Biochem (emeritus), UNC-CH
1962–64	Frank S. French, MD	Prof, Ped; Chief, Lab of Reproductive Biol, UNC-CH
1963–65	Gabor Antony, MD	Prof, Ped; Chief, Div Ped Endocrin (emeritus), Univ New South Wales (Sydney, Australia)
1965–68	J. Leo Van den Brande, MD	Prof and Chair, Dept Ped, Utrecht (Netherlands)
1967–68	Jeffries Macfie, MD	Surg in Priv Pract (Spartanburg, SC)
1967–69	Alva Strickland, MD	Endocrinologist (Spartanburg, SC); Clin Prof, Ped, Univ SC at Columbia
1967–70	Louis B. Underwood, MD	Prof, Ped; Chief, Div Ped Endocrin, UNC-CH
1969–72	Roger Johnsonbaugh, MD	Clin Research, Smith, Kline & French
1969–70	Martin Ritzen, MD	Prof, Ped; Chief, Div Ped Endocrin, Karolinska Inst (Stockholm, Sweden)
1969–71	Robert Richman, MD	Prof, Ped; Chief, Div Ped Endocrin, SUNY Health Sciences Center (Syracuse)
1970–72	Raymond Hintz, MD	Prof, Ped; Chief, Div of Ped Endocrin, Stanford Univ School of Med
1972–74	Robert Lister, MD	Tripler Army Hosp (Honolulu, HI)
1972–74	Robert Marshall, MD	Chief, Dept Ped, Chattanooga Child Hosp
1973–74	Vidar Hansson, MD	Prof, Pathol and Molecular Biol, Univ Oslo (Norway)
1974–77	A. Joseph D'Ercole, MD	Prof, Ped, Div of Endocrin and Neonatol, UNC-CH
1974–77	Mary Ann Morris, MD	Asst Prof, Ped, Duke Univ School of Med
1976–78	Richard Furlanetto, MD	Prof, Ped; Chief, Div Ped Endocrin, Univ Rochester School of Med
1977–78	Minuto Francisco, MD	Prof, Med; Asst Prof, Ped; Chief, Div Endocrin, Univ Genoa (Italy)
1977–79	Sandra Blethen, MD	Prof, Ped; Chief, Div Ped Endocrin, Univ NY at Stoneybrook
1977–79	Kenneth Copeland, MD	Assoc Prof, Ped, Baylor Univ School of Med

1978–80	Pierre Chatelain, MD	Prof, Ped; Chief, Div Ped Endocrin, Univ of Eduard Heroit (Lyon, France)
1979–80	David R. Clemmons, MD	Prof, Med; Chief, Div Endocrin, UNC-CH
1979–82	Steve Chernausek, MD	Prof, Ped, Cincinnati Child Hosp at Univ Cincinnati
1979–82	Paul Kaplowitz, MD	Assoc Prof, Ped; Chief, Div Ped Endocrin, Med College of Virginia
1980–82	Michael Foster, MD	Assoc Prof, Ped, Univ Louisville School of Med
1981–82	Steve Trippel, MD	Asst Prof, Orthoped, Harvard Med School, Massachusetts Gen Hosp
1981–84	Ann T. Smith, MD	Private Ped Pract (Traverse City, MI)
1982–83	Alan Stiles, MD	Assoc Prof, Ped, Div Neonatol, UNC-CH
1982–84	William Russell, MD	Assoc Prof, Ped, Vanderbilt Univ School of Med
1982–85	Eric Smith, MD	Asst Prof, Ped, Cincinnati Child Hosp at Univ Cincinnati
1983–85	Victor Han, MD	Assoc Prof, Ped, Univ Western Ontario (Canada)
1983–89	Nancy Charest, MD	Asst Prof, Ped, Yale Univ School of Med
1984–87	Sam Casella, MD	Assoc Prof, Ped; Acting Chief, Div of Ped Endocrin, Johns Hopkins Univ School of Med
1985–88	Marsha Davenport, MD	Asst Prof, Ped, UNC-CH
1986–87	Jeanne Hassing, MD	Asst Prof, Ped, Univ Nebraska School of Med
1988–90	Cecelia Camacho-Hubner, MD	Res Assoc, St Bartholomew's Hosp (London, UK)
1988–90	George Retsch-Bogart, MD	Asst Prof, Ped, UNC-CH
1988–90	Jan Walker, MD	Asst Prof, Ped, Univ New South Wales (Sydney, Australia)
1988–92	David R. Repaske, MD	Asst Prof, Ped, Cincinnati Child Hosp at Univ Cincinnati
1988–93	Wayne Price, MD	Asst Prof, Ped, UNC-CH
1988–93	Charmian Quigley, MD	Asst Prof Ped, Univ of Indiana

1989–90	Patrizia Del Monte, MD	Staff Endocrinologist, Dept Endocrin, Univ Genoa (Italy)
1989–91	Dorothy J. Eicher, MD	Asst Prof, Ped, Univ SC School of Med
1989–92	Alessandra DeBellis, MD	Asst Prof, Med, Univ Florence (Italy)
1990–92	J. Hoon Shin, MD	Prof, Ped, Univ Seoul (S. Korea)
1990–92	Jean-Paul Thissen, MD	Prof, Ped, Univ Catholique de Louvain (Belgium)
1990–93	Jolanta Pucilowska, MD	Res Assoc, Dept Physiol, UNC-CH
1991–93	W. Jackson Smith, MD	Asst Prof, Ped and Med, Univ Kentucky
1991–94	Philippe Backeljauw, MD	Chief, Ped Endocrin, Carolinas Med Ctr (Charlotte, NC)
1991–94	Charlotte Boney, MD	Asst Prof, Ped, Brown Univ School of Med
1991–94	Philippa Charlton, MD	In training, Genetics, UNC-CH
1992–94	Stuart Kupfer, MD	Asst Prof, Ped, Washington Univ School of Med
1992–94	Steven G. A. Power, MD	Asst Prof, Ob-Gyn, Univ Western Ontario
1993–	Barbara Chrzanowska, MD	Guilford County Health Dept
1993–	Ali Calikoglu, MD	In training, UNC-CH
1993–	Cathy Choong, MD	In training, UNC-CH
1993–	Lars Savendahl, MD	In training, UNC-CH
1995–	Dionisios Chrysis, MD	In training, UNC-CH
1995–	Daniel Gunther, MD	In training, UNC-CH

Postdoctoral Fellows (PhD)

1969–70	James Coffey, PhD	UNC Dental School; Retired
1975–77	Elizabeth Wilson, PhD	Prof, Ped and Biochem, UNC-CH
1977–78	Oscar Lea, PhD	Univ of Bergen (Norway); Deceased
1977–78	Ariane Plet, PhD	Staff Scient, Faculte Cochin, Saint Vincent de Paul (Paris, France)
1977–79	Marc Feldman, PhD	Asst Prof, Med, Albert Einstein School of Med
1979–83	Paul Ordronneau, PhD	Res Scientist, Burroughs Wellcome (RTP, NC)

1980–83	Richard Bartlett, PhD	Assoc Prof, Neurol, Univ Miami
1981–85	Stephanie Perry, PhD	Asst Prof, NC School of Veterinary Sci
1983–92	Valerie Quarmby, PhD	Res Scientist, Endocrin Sci Lab (Los Angeles, CA)
1984–92	Kuo-Chieh Ho, PhD	Prof, Botany, Taiwan National Univ (Taipei, Taiwan)
1985–89	Susan Hall, PhD	Res Asst Prof, Ped, UNC-CH
1987–88	Michael Vanderhaar, PhD	Asst Prof, Nutrition, Michigan St School of Agricult
1987–89	Silvia Migliaccio, PhD	Asst Prof, Histol, Univ Rome (Italy)
1988–91	Dennis Lubahn, PhD	Assoc Prof, Biochem, Univ Missouri College of Agricult
1988–91	Debbie Rountree, PhD	Asst Prof, Zool, Univ Louisville
1988–91	Shin-Ichiro Takahashi, PhD	Assoc Prof, Nutrit Biochem and Human Genetics, Univ Tokyo School of Agricult (Japan)
1989–92	Catherine Jin, PhD	Res Assoc, Glaxo
1989–	Zhong-Xun Zhou, PhD	Res Assoc, Peds, UNC-CH
1993–	Maria-Christina de Avelar, PhD	In training, UNC-CH
1993–	Christophe Gregory, PhD	In training, UNC-CH
1993–	Ping Yi, PhD	In training, UNC-CH

Predoctoral Fellows

1969–72	Roger Johnsonbaugh*	See under Postdoctoral MDs
1971–74	Donald Tindall*	Assoc Prof, Reprod Biol, Mayo School of Med
1971–77	Albert Smith*	Unknown
1972–73	David R. Clemmons	See under Postdoctoral MDs
1973–75	Samuel Weddington*	Deceased
1974–78	Nicholas Kotite*	Amer Univ Beirut (Lebanon)
1978–81	Edward Leof*	Assoc Prof, Molecular and Cellular Biol, Mayo School of Med
1979–83	Dennis Colvard*	Asst Prof, Reproductive Biol, Mayo School of Med
1980–88	Victoria Davis*	Staff Scient, NIEHS (RTP, NC)
1982–87	Billie Moats-Staats*	Res Asst Prof, Ped, UNC-CH
1983–87	David B. Cooke, III*	Asst Prof, Biol, Morehead Univ

1983–87	David H. Viskochil*	Asst Prof, Ped and Genetics, Univ Utah School of Med
1984–93	Jian-an Tan*	Postdoctoral fellow, UNC-CH
1985–89	Wendell Yarbrough	Resident, ENT, UNC-CH
1986–88	Raoul Rooman	Medical student, Univ Antwerp (Belgium)
1986–91	Johannes Swinnen*	Postdoctoral fellow, Univ Antwerp (Belgium)
1987–91	Yan-min Wang*	Postdoctoral fellow, UNC-CH
1988–93	Cindy Zahnow*	Postdoctoral fellow, UNC-CH
1989–93	Jorge Simenthal	Medical student, UNC-CH
1989–93	Patrick Sullivan*	Postdoctoral fellow, UNC-CH
1990–93	Zhonghan Dai*	Postdoctoral fellow in pharmacology, Duke Univ
1991–94	Keith Marschke*	Res Scient, Ligand Pharmaceuticals (Los Angeles, CA)
1994–	David Fenstermacher	In training, UNC-CH

---

* received PhD

CHAPTER EIGHTEEN

Gastroenterology

FOR the first twenty-five years after the opening of North Carolina Memorial Hospital, children with gastrointestinal problems were under the care of the general pediatricians with the advice and consultation of gastroenterologists from the Department of Medicine. Liver biopsies were done with trepidation and standard GI procedures were avoided whenever possible. A division of pediatric gastroenterology came into existence in 1977 with the recruitment of Dr. Martin Ulshen, who, on his arrival, became the first fully trained pediatric gastroenterologist in the state of North Carolina.

DR. ULSHEN: YEARS OF PREPARATION

Dr. Ulshen grew up in New York City and its suburbs. The fact that, until his internship, he had never traveled farther south than Washington, D.C., did not suggest that he would ultimately settle in Chapel Hill. Although he had always liked the sciences best, especially biology, it was not until college and some early thoughts about veterinary medicine that he decided on a career in medicine. He attended college and medical school at the University of Rochester in New York. In 1969, when he graduated from medical school, a special relationship existed between the Departments of Pediatrics at the University of Rochester and the University of North Carolina, largely through the professional interactions of the chairmen, Dr. Denny and Dr. Robert Haggerty at Rochester. North Carolina Memorial Hospital had one of a handful of outstanding mixed medicine-pediatrics training programs at that time. Dr. Ulshen had narrowed his choice to Chapel Hill and Cleveland, a place more in keeping with his early years; but good fortune brought him to Chapel Hill. During his internship year, he chose to enter the U.S. Public Health Indian Service to have more experience before choosing between medicine and pediatrics. Early in his internship, he had arranged to be stationed at the Indian Hospital in Phoenix, Arizona. A position as field health officer, running clinics throughout the local reservations, seemed like an ideal opportunity to experience the "real" practice of medicine and pediatrics. Senior officials at Phoenix were delighted to promise this position, one for which they said no one ever volunteered.

The internship year had been exciting. With some misgivings and regret, Dr. Ulshen headed out to Arizona in July 1970, fully planning to return to Chapel Hill for residency training at the end of his tour of duty. After driving that distance, he was the last of the general medical officers to arrive in Phoenix; by then, all of the field health officer positions had been taken by the early arrivers. In fact, the only position left was in pediatrics, and he was asked whether he would be willing to take it. He agreed and this turned out to be one of the best decisions of his life. Not only did this turn out to be a fantastic clinical experience, but it was a strong influence to enter pediatrics and abandon internal medicine.

At Phoenix, he worked as a junior associate with four fully trained and dedicated pediatricians and two pediatric residents. There was much opportunity to work in the clinic and one could often follow one's own patients after admission. The hospital was a referral center for the Indian Service in Arizona; tuberculosis, meningitis, and Valley fever were among the problems seen. What proved to shape his future, however, was a large experience with chronic diarrhea and chronic malnutrition. While at North Carolina, he had helped with the care of a patient of Dr. Neil Kirkman's with intractable diarrhea. She was the daughter of a prominent member of the University community. Despite much thought and concern, the etiology of her disorder remained a mystery. As her condition deteriorated, Dr. Kirkman decided to try a new mode of nutritional support, parenteral nutrition, just described the same year in the *New England Journal of Medicine*. In the tradition of "see one, do one," Dr. Ulshen had the opportunity to try this therapy again in several infants approaching death from malnutrition in Phoenix. Although the girl in Chapel Hill eventually died, the Indian children in Phoenix had self-limited protracted diarrhea of infancy and recovered once the cycle of malnutrition was reversed.

After completion of his duty in Phoenix, Dr. Ulshen decided to complete his residency at the University of Colorado to stay in the West and to train in its topnotch nursery. Late in his residency, he decided to continue with clinical subspecialty training in the relatively new field of pediatric gastroenterology and remained at Colorado for the first year of fellowship. At this time, he noticed an advertisement in the *New England Journal of Medicine* for pediatricians to supervise house staff in the pediatric clinics at North Carolina Memorial Hospital. Individuals would be expected to carry on other scholarly activities; this seemed like a good opportunity to mesh general pediatrics with gastroenterology and gastrointestinal research as well as to return to

Chapel Hill. Dr. Ulshen visited the Department of Pediatrics with this plan in mind. Fortunately, two senior faculty encouraged him to complete a full fellowship in order to be adequately trained for an academic career. These individuals were Dr. Denny and Dr. John Sessions, the chief of gastroenterology in the Department of Medicine. Although impatient to start, Dr. Ulshen transferred to a laboratory research program at Boston Children's Hospital, becoming one of the first group of fellows to be completely trained in a pediatric gastroenterology program. In Boston, he studied regulation of activity of the intestinal enzyme sucrase under the direction of Dr. Richard Grand. About six months into this year, it became evident that laboratory research was a lot more interesting than the laboratory sessions he had experienced in medical school and, further, that a single year of laboratory training was not going to be adequate. With Dr. Denny's blessings, he remained at Boston an additional year and arrived back in North Carolina in late summer 1977.

EARLY LONELY YEARS

Although Dr. Denny had made the offer of the opportunity to do only laboratory research with no clinical commitments during the first year back at Chapel Hill, it was impossible for Dr. Ulshen to resist doing some consultations in the clinic and on the ward. To this day, it is not clear whether Dr. Denny was bluffing! Fortunately, the service began slowly, as pediatricians in North Carolina had no previous experience referring to a pediatric gastroenterologist. In addition, in the early years at Chapel Hill, endoscopic procedures were not as easily performed in children and were, therefore, done infrequently. This was especially true for colonoscopy, which was performed only once or twice a year in children at North Carolina Memorial in the late '70s. As a result of these circumstances, Dr. Ulshen had adequate time to begin a research career that might have easily foundered in a less protective academic environment.

When Dr. Ulshen first arrived, a very small endoscopy unit was shared with the adult gastroenterologists. There was one procedure nurse, Meredith Reinhold, who had taken the position partly because the patient load was light and it offered the opportunity to take call from home, coming in when a procedure was needed. By 1993, when Meredith retired, she headed a group of ten nurses and aides who staffed an active combined pediatric and adult endoscopy unit. The pediatric GI service had similar steady growth. Initially, there was no designated GI clinic and patients were seen ad hoc. But both outpatient and inpatient services grew steadily. In 1993, the GI clinic had increased to a day and a half weekly with patients often seen urgently on other days. Fourteen hundred patients were seen in the pediatric GI clinic that year.

EXPANSION OF THE DIVISION: THE BOAT YEARS

At the time that Dr. Denny stepped down from the chairmanship, it was becoming apparent that the GI service was too large for one individual who had any hopes of continuing scholarly activities. Expansion awaited the prerogative of the new chairman. Dr. Boat agreed with the need even before arriving at Chapel Hill. He had been in the process of recruiting Dr. Mitchell Shub from his training at Massachusetts General Hospital to go to Cleveland as a pediatric gastroenterologist in order to collaborate with Dr. Boat in studies of the structure of intestinal mucins. When Dr. Boat accepted the chairmanship at North Carolina, it was not difficult to persuade Dr. Shub, who had done his pediatric residency at Duke, to join Dr. Ulshen in the GI division. Dr. Shub remained from 1983 to 1985, when he moved to Phoenix for personal reasons. During this period a retired pediatrician from Wayne State in Detroit, Dr. Les Pensler, moved to Raleigh. He had provided outpatient pediatric GI care at Detroit Children's Hospital for many years and, in fact, had done a clinical gastroenterology rotation at Boston Children's Hospital at the same time that Dr. Ulshen was in training there. Dr. Pensler began to attend the pediatric GI clinic at NC Memorial and continued to volunteer his time for nearly ten years. Even before Dr. Shub contemplated moving, the service had grown to a size to justify expansion to three faculty.

Dr. Steven Lichtman was recruited from Canada in 1985. Despite the fact that Dr. Ulshen's car broke down while returning Dr. Lichtman to the airport on his initial visit, he accepted the position and arrived several months after Dr. Shub left in 1985. Chapel Hill provided a change after spending nearly all of his life in Toronto (except for a year as a pediatric resident in Sydney, Australia), but Dr. Lichtman and his family soon began to enjoy the rural pleasures of North Carolina. Initially, he held a position of visiting assistant professor but entered the tenure track in 1987, when he became a permanent resident (retaining his Canadian citizenship). During this period of transition, Mary Driebeck (a physician's assistant) worked in the division and helped maintain the clinical activity.

The third position was filled the following year when Dr. Marc Rhoads was convinced that the research environment and excellent diversity of clinical diagnoses made Chapel Hill an ideal opportunity. Like Dr. Lichtman, he had completed his training at the outstanding pediatric GI fellowship program at Sick Children's Hospital in Toronto. In 1991, Dr. Rosalind Coleman moved from the Department of Pediatrics at Duke University to the newly revived Department of Nutrition in the School of Public Health at UNC. She was given a joint appointment in the Department of Pediatrics, division of gastroenterology, because of her interest in metabolic liver disease.

In 1992, the division became a component of the first active pediatric liver transplant service in North Carolina. The program has been under the direction of Dr. Hartwig Bunzendahl in the Department of Surgery at UNC. By 1994, fourteen children had received orthotopic liver transplants, eleven of

The Gastro-
enterology
division
(1989):
Mary
Driebeck,
Marty
Ulshen,
Steve
Lichtman,
Marc
Rhoads, and
(kneeling)
Warren
Bishop

whom are alive and well. The division began its first outreach clinic in Wilmington in 1993.

RESEARCH

On arrival at Chapel Hill, Dr. Ulshen's initial research interest was regulation of mucosal digestive enzyme activity. One of the attractions of Chapel Hill was the opportunity to work with Dr. Bill Heizer from the division of gastroenterology, Department of Medicine, who was identifying and characterizing intestinal peptide hydrolases. During these studies, Dr. Ulshen became increasingly interested in regulation of growth of the small bowel mucosa. This interest led to studies of epidermal growth factor, a peptide growth factor found in the small bowel contents that is relatively resistant to digestion. He was aided by discussions with Dr. Ed O'Keefe in the Department of Dermatology and Dr. Shelley Earp in the Department of Medicine.

The digestive disease groups at the University of North Carolina and NC State University have had a unique relationship, developing in 1985 an NIH-funded core center for the study of intestinal function and pathology called the Center for Gastrointestinal Biology and Disease (CGIBD). Dr. Don W. Powell, who had become head of the division of digestive diseases in the Department of Medicine in 1977, spearheaded the creation of this center, one of only six NIH-supported digestive disease centers in the country at that time. His goal was to unify the strengths of the three major universities in the Research Triangle in the area of digestive diseases. However, the gastroenterologists at Duke decided to develop their own center (they were unsuccessful). Members of the pediatric gastroenterology group have been active investigators in the CGIBD. The relationship with the center has led to a number of strong collaborations with members of other departments, including Dr. P. Kay Lund, a molecular biologist in the Department of Physiology; Dr. John LeMasters, a cell physiologist in the Department of Cell Biology and Anatomy; Dr. Robert Sandler, an epidemiologist in the Department of Medicine; Dr. Robert Argenzio, a GI physiologist at the NC State School of Veterinary Medicine; Dr. Jim Lecce in the Department of Animal Sciences at NC State; and Dr. David Brenner, new chief of the division of digestive diseases in the Department of Medicine.

As Dr. Ulshen's interest in intestinal growth increased, he developed a collaborative effort with Dr. Kay Lund, who was also interested in gut hormones and regulation of bowel growth. Together, they have subsequently studied local expression of the enteroglucagons and insulin-like growth factors in the intestine and accessory digestive organs and their potential role in bowel development and recovery from injury. In addition, they have looked at the effects of nutrient on peptide hormone production in the small bowel. Dr. Ulshen has also collaborated with Dr. Robert Sandler in the identification of altered epithelial proliferation in the colon as a marker of premalignant change in the colon.

Dr. Lichtman arrived at Chapel Hill having studied the secretory IgA response to bacterial overgrowth in the small bowel at Toronto with Dr. Gordon Forstner. He joined a group interested in the role of bacterial cell components in inflammatory diseases of the bowel which included Drs. R. Balfour Sartor and John H. Schwab from the Departments of Medicine and Immunology-Microbiology, respectively. Within a short time after moving to Chapel Hill, he made an important observation that had a profound influence on the direction of his research: In certain strains of rats with small bowel bacterial overgrowth, resulting from surgical creation of a blind loop of small bowel, the animals developed abnormal serum liver enzyme levels. The histologic appearance of these livers was abnormal, and subsequent studies of cholangiograms in these animals demonstrated a picture typical of sclerosing cholangitis. It had been known that in man sclerosing cholangitis is commonly associated with chronic inflammatory bowel disease. This observation in animals provided a possible link between bowel disease and this biliary tract disorder. Dr. Lichtman's subsequent studies have focused on understanding the pathogenesis of this lesion, the relationship of bacterial components to progression of this lesion and methods of prevention. As a part of these studies, he has collaborated with Dr. John J. LeMasters to isolate Kupffer cells from the livers of these animals in order to explore the role of these cells in the pathogenesis. He has studied the effects of bacterial cell wall polymers (endotoxin, peptidoglycan) on Kupffer cell activation and is beginning to look at intracellular signaling following endotoxin stimulation. During the course of this work, he received the James W. Woods Junior Faculty Award in 1991; this is a Medical School award for outstanding research potential given annually to junior faculty and is quite competitive. A recent observation by Dr. Lichtman of reactivation of arthritis by bacterial overgrowth in the small bowel has moved his work into the field of arthritis. He is currently studying what component of bacterial overgrowth leads to the reactivation. This work has direct relevance to the arthritis associated with bowel disease (e.g., inflammatory bowel disease and various intestinal infections).

Dr. Rhoads came to Chapel Hill with experience studying small bowel epithelial electrolyte transport during recovery from viral gastroenteritis with Dr. Richard Hamilton in Toronto. He collaborated from the start with Dr. James Lecce and more recently with Dr. Guillermo Gomez in the Department of Animal Sciences at NC State University to study the effects of specific micronutrients on intestinal recovery from piglet rotavirus infection in colostrum-deprived piglets. Along with Dr. Ulshen, they studied the effects of oral administration of exogenous growth factors on recovery. Dr. Rhoads has also collaborated with Drs. Robert Argenzio and Helen Berschneider at the Veterinary School at NC State University in studies of regulation by glutamine and eicosanoids of intestinal transport and epithelial cell proliferation in vitro. He has collaborated with Dr. Tony Paradiso of the pulmonary division in the Department of Medicine in studies of enterocyte pH and Ca^{++} regulation. He has had a special interest in glutamine as a stimulator of neutral NaCl absorption and as a growth potentiator in the small bowel mucosa. He has found that glutamine metabolism stimulates enterocyte proliferation through the action of mitogen-activated protein kinases (MAP kinase) and Jun kinase. Dr. Rhoads has also been involved in interesting studies of acute diarrhea in Pakistan and India.

Dr. Sherif Gabriel joined the division in late 1994 as a research assistant professor. He had earned a PhD in biochemistry at the University of Saskatchewan and then had a postdoctoral fellowship in the cystic fibrosis center at the University of North Carolina. His interest in mucosal transport in the intestine fit in well with the interests of the division. As a fellow, he had performed outstanding electrophysiologic studies of the action of CF transmembrane regulator, the CF effector protein, in Cl^- transport, working with isolated intestinal epithelial cells, isolated membrane patches, and a transgenic mouse model of cystic fibrosis developed at UNC.

Dr. Don Powell was a very strong supporter of the pediatric GI training program during the early formative years. He also was an important mentor for Dr. Rhoads, providing guidance in starting his laboratory and successfully competing for NIH funding. In 1992, Dr. Powell left UNC to become head of the Department of Medicine at the University of Texas, Galveston. He was replaced in 1992 by Dr. David Brenner. Dr. Brenner's interests are in the mechanisms of development of liver fibrosis, and he has a strong background in molecular biology, which has benefited the entire digestive diseases program.

The division's clinical research effort began when Dr. Ulshen made a serendipitous finding that ultimately led to his describing a new mechanism of pathogenesis of *E. coli* enteritis in the *New England Journal of Medicine.** He subsequently reported studies of esophagitis in children and collaborated in multicenter studies of the treatment of inflammatory bowel disease. Dr. Rhoads was fortunate to have the opportunity to study in vitro mechanisms of diarrhea in the small bowel of children with a rare disorder of congenital diarrhea, microvillus inclusion disease.

TRAINEES

From the start, the training program in pediatric gastroenterology had a close relationship with that of the Department of Medicine. Fellows in each program received training in the other. Joint conferences have been a strength of the program. In 1982, the first postdoctoral fellow in pediatric gastroenterology, Dr. Charles Hargrove, began his training sponsored by the U.S. Navy. The following year Dr. Henderson Rourk came to UNC from Duke University to do a year of clinical training with funding from the Medical School at Duke. Dr. Rourk had been a pediatric pulmonologist and his mission was to return to Duke to begin a pediatric GI service. The next fellow was Dr. Rick Sigmon, who had done a medicine-pediatrics residency. He completed one year of gastroenterology training in the Department of Medicine and one in the Department of Pediatrics. He is among a very small group of individuals with board certification in pediatrics, internal medicine, gastroenterology, and pediatric gastroenterology.

Dr. Warren Bishop was the first of a group of subsequent fellows to complete a three-year training program in the expanded pediatric GI division. He

---

*Several mechanisms have been described to explain the pathogenesis of diarrheal disease caused by *E. coli*. In 1977, a laboratory colony of rabbits was reported with nosocomial diarrhea that was found to be caused by a strain of *E. coli* (RDEC-1) that adhered to the intestinal mucosa, thereby damaging microvilli (*J Infect Dis* 1977; 125:454–462). This was the first description of a new mechanism, enteroadherence of *E. coli*, but it had no counterpart in human disease. Dr. Ulshen in collaboration with a pathology postdoctoral fellow, Dr. John Rollo, described findings in a seven-week-old infant with chronic diarrhea, enterocolitis, and *E. coli* overgrowth in the small bowel (Ulshen MH, Rollo JL. Pathogenesis of *Escherichia coli* gastroenteritis in man—another mechanism. *N Engl J Med* 1980; 302:99–101). The unique characteristic of this enterocolitis was the presence of brush-border damage associated with adherent bacteria (identified on electron microscopy), remarkably similar in appearance to the *E. coli* RDEC-1 infection in the rabbit, in the absence of findings of enterotoxin production or invasive properties. This proved to be the first report of enteroadherent *E. coli*–associated diarrhea in man, a mechanism of human disease subsequently confirmed in a number of publications. It seems likely that this mechanism of diarrhea was an important cause of the outbreaks of enteropathogenic *E. coli* described in previous years in young infants, an entity in which the mechanism of pathogenesis had been a mystery.

received an NIH National Service Research Award to study the epidermal growth factor receptor in the small bowel. His research mentors were Dr. Ulshen and Dr. Shelley Earp of the Department of Medicine. Dr. Bishop is now an assistant professor at the University of Iowa and chief of the division of pediatric gastroenterology. Dr. Yul Reinstein finished the training program in 1993 after completing studies of protection of the liver against injury with Drs. LeMasters and Lichtman and went into practice in the Children's Hospital, St. Petersburg, Florida. Dr. Doug Winesett also has been sponsored by the U.S. Navy, entering the program in 1991. His research interest was in the role of IGF-I in growth of the small bowel. He finished his U.S. Navy obligation at the Naval Hospital in Bethesda, Maryland, although his interest was to enter academics. Dr. Ellen DeFlora entered the pediatric GI fellowship program in 1992 and has begun in vitro studies of Kupffer cell function with Drs. Lichtman and LeMasters. The newest fellow, Dr. Chris Rittemeyer, entered the program in 1993. He has an MPH from Johns Hopkins and plans to do studies of the prevention of necrotizing enterocolitis with oral gammaglobulin and enhancement of premature infant gut function with parenteral glutamine.

TEACHING

The GI service has been an active clinical training program for the Department of Pediatrics because of the very active clinical service. Pediatric gastroenterologists contribute to the preclinical training in nutrition and gastrointestinal biology and pathophysiology each year. In addition, members of this division have contributed to the training of gastroenterology fellows in the Department of Medicine. Faculty have contributed chapters to over a dozen textbooks. The faculty frequently lecture around the state and country and have national recognition in the areas of adaptation to short bowel, oral rehydration, and the liver disease associated with inflammatory bowel disorders.

OTHER ACTIVITIES

Dr. Ulshen has served as an associate editor for the *Journal of Pediatrics*, first starting in 1985. He also was on the staff of contributors to the selected summaries section of *Gastroenterology* from 1984 to 1989. In the late 1980s a new Sub-board for Pediatric Gastroenterology of the American Board of Pediatrics was begun, and in 1989 Dr. Ulshen became the medical editor for this sub-board. In 1993, Dr. Ulshen also became a member of the American Board of Pediatrics. With the arrival of Dr. Steve Zeisel as the new chair of the Department of Nutrition in the School of Public Health, this department was revitalized. As part of this effort and with the plan to ultimately make this a joint department with the School of Medicine, Dr. Zeisel started to bring into the department individuals in the health sciences outside of the School of

Public Health with interest in nutrition. Dr. Ulshen was appointed to this department and helped with the early work of rebuilding.

Dr. Rhoads has headed the Pediatric Nutrition Support Team and is a member of the Advisory Board of the North Carolina Institute of Nutrition. Dr. Lichtman became editor of the selected summaries section of the *Journal of Pediatric Gastroenterology and Nutrition* in 1993. He has been a board member of the Crohn's and Colitis Foundation of America.

MARTIN H. ULSHEN

FACULTY

Gabriel, Sherif E. BS, Univ Saskatchewan, 1984; PhD, Univ Saskatchewan, 1990; Res Asst Prof, Med, 1994.

Lichtman, Steven N. MD, Univ Toronto, 1978; Vis Asst Prof, Ped, 1985; Asst Prof, Ped, 1987; Assoc Prof, Ped, 1992.

Rhoads, J. Marc. BA, Johns Hopkins Univ, 1976; MD, Johns Hopkins Univ, 1980; Asst Prof, Ped, 1986; Assoc Prof, Ped, 1992.

Shub, Mitchell D. BSEE, Northeastern Univ, 1972; MD, Univ Vermont, 1976; Asst Prof, Ped, 1982–85.

Ulshen, Martin H. BA, Univ Rochester, 1965; MD, Univ Rochester, 1969; Asst Prof, Ped, 1977; Assoc Prof, Ped, 1983; Prof, Ped, 1993; Chief, Div Ped Gastroenter, 1977; Assoc Prof, Nutrition, 1991; Prof, Nutrition, 1993.

FELLOWS

Years	Name	Current Position
1982–84	Charles Hargrove, MD	U.S. Navy (Bethesda, MD)
1983–84	Malcolm Rourk, MD	Assoc Prof, Duke Univ
1983–85	Richard Sigmon, MD	Priv Pract (Charlotte, NC)
1986–89	Warren Bishop, MD	Assoc Prof, Univ Iowa
1990–93	Leon Reinstein, MD	Priv Pract (Tampa, FL)
1991–94	Douglas Winesett, MD	U.S. Navy (Bethesda, MD)
1992–	Ellen DeFlora, MD	In training, UNC-CH
1993–	Chris Rittmeyer, MD	In training, UNC-CH
1994–	Ming Wora, MD	In training, UNC-CH

CHAPTER NINETEEN

Genetics and Metabolism

I N 1965, less than ten years after the human chromosome number was determined to be forty-six and barely a half-dozen years after the discovery that Down syndrome is caused by an extra copy of chromosome 21, Neil Kirkman was recruited to join the UNC pediatric faculty. His proposal that medical genetics be taught to pediatric residents and medical students probably marked the beginning of our division of genetics and metabolism.

To be sure, genetic concepts were in place for specific disorders in such fields as endocrinology and hematology. Endocrinologists understood the autosomal recessive nature of adrenocortical hyperplasia and hematologists did not need to be told that factor VIII deficiency was an X-linked recessive condition. Indeed, some of the pioneering work on those disorders had been done in Chapel Hill. As in other medical centers, however, malformation syndromes, chromosomal abnormalities, and techniques of genetic counseling were among the subjects for which there seemed to be no formally assigned diagnostic or educational responsibility.

Dr. Kirkman proposed that members of a medical genetics division have two responsibilities: (1) diagnosis and teaching of certain disorders that "fell between the cracks" of other medical disciplines; and (2) teaching young physicians how to incorporate genetic principles into their own practices. It became apparent during the '60s that genetic disorders account for 20 to 30 percent or more of the pediatric inpatients in teaching hospitals, and genetic predisposition was being recognized as underlying many of the common disorders in adults. Neil suggested that medical geneticists could fill a role analogous to that of faculty in a division of infectious disease. Infectious diseases are much too common for all patients with infections to be under the care of members of such a division. Rather, the task of members of such divisions is

Neil
Kirkman

to train physicians to deal with common problems and know when they need help and to provide such help when needed.

In the subsequent thirty years, medical genetics has grown from almost "interest group" status into a full-fledged medical specialty. The American College of Medical Genetics, with a membership of over a thousand, has been admitted as the twenty-fifth full member of the Council of Medical Specialty Societies, and medical genetics residencies are being established through the Accreditation Council for Graduate Medical Education. The history of our division parallels the exciting development of this new specialty of medical genetics.

After his residency in pediatrics, Neil received research training in enzymology and biochemical genetics at the National Institutes of Health in the laboratories of Gordon Tomkins and Herman Kalckar, where the basic defect of galactosemia was discovered. Using parents of galactosemic children, he developed one of the first enzymatic tests for identifying heterozygotes for a recessive disease. His work with galactosemia included developing enzymatic assays for red cell galactose-1-phosphate for monitoring the management of children with galactosemia.

Neil also reasoned that deficiencies of red cell glucose-6-phosphate dehydrogenase (G6PD) would be lethal, if complete, and that the small amount of residual G6PD might have abnormal properties, according to the nature of the mutation in each male with this sex-linked disorder. Deficiencies of G6PD are now recognized as the most common, and genetically heterogeneous, of the known human enzyme defects. Studies of purified G6PD led Neil to recognize and name the more common of the G6PD variants worldwide, as well as rare variants giving rise to chronic hemolytic disease. His findings preceded that of later DNA workers in showing that distinct variants existed even among those that were electrophoretically normal. He and his associates used the close linkage between G6PD and factor VIII deficiency to provide one of the first prenatal diagnoses through genetic linkage. Work on red cell G6PD by Dr. Kirkman, with his former postdoctoral fellow Gian Gaetani, subsequently led to identification of one of the most commonly cited studies in medicine (concerning how hydrogen peroxide is detoxified in mammalian cells) as being in error. They discovered that catalase has tightly bound NADPH, which catalase uses to keep itself active in the presence of its own toxic substrate, hydrogen peroxide. The correct identification of the way that hydrogen peroxide is handled has assumed new importance, as derivatives of oxygen, especially hydrogen peroxide, are being increasingly recognized as toxic intermediates in a wide variety of human disorders.

When Neil came to Chapel Hill in the mid-1960s, the state of North Carolina was ahead of most other states in developing programs to deal with genetic diseases, with significant consequences for our division of genetics and metabolism. The first effect on this division was an indirect one occurring in 1965. Through the efforts of Dr. Harrie Chamberlin, who was serving on an advisory council, the state avoided two traps that other states fell into when pressure was being put on legislators to begin newborn screening for phenylketonuria (PKU). First, no state testing law was approved. Rather, funds were authorized for a high-quality state newborn screening laboratory, for education of North Carolina physicians, nurses, and nursery staff about the importance of such screening, and for what was later to become a follow-up program. Justification for not mandating testing became apparent when, in 1982, the compliance rate (for newborn testing) was shown to be higher in North Carolina than in most states with a state testing law. In addition, the conclusion of a review of newborn screening at the 1982 International Congress on Birth Defects in Strasbourg, France, was that many states had erred in putting the emphasis on mandated testing rather than on the means for implementing the testing and following up on the results.

Another difference in PKU programs between North Carolina and other states was the use, from the very beginning, of an automated, quantitative (fluorometric) assay for phenylalanine in the state laboratory, rather than the Guthrie microbiological assay. The automated fluorometric method is more accurate than the Guthrie method, and this accuracy has become extremely important as infants have begun to be discharged home earlier after birth. The difference in concentration of blood phenylalanine between affected and normal infants is much less for one-day-old infants than for three-day-old infants.

The test was developed in 1964 by two UNC (Chapel Hill) physician-biochemists, Dr. John Hill and Dr. George Summer.

After the onset of newborn screening in the mid-1960s, state administrators at the newborn screening laboratory and PKU program began referring increasing numbers of the phenylketonuric infants to our division for (a) confirmation of the diagnosis, (b) education of the parents, and (c) long-term dietary management. By 1980, essentially all infants in the state suspected of having PKU, as well as many diagnosed with galactosemia, were being referred to our division for evaluation, counseling, and management. Through a legislated supplement to our state grant, Dianne Frazier, PhD (biochemistry) and registered dietitian, was hired to follow our children with inborn errors of metabolism receiving special diets and to deal with the gradually increasing problem of maternal PKU. Neil has continued, until his recent semiretirement, as principal consultant and advisor to the state newborn screening laboratory in Raleigh. Dianne has worked closely with Neil in this capacity and also in research on techniques used in newborn screening for galactosemia. Among other contributions, they have identified some of the causes of the problems in galactosemia screening that were being experienced nationwide and developed improvements in these techniques.

The foresight of North Carolina legislators and state administrators affected our division and medical center in a second major way. In 1968–1969, Dr. Ted Scurletis, of the North Carolina Board of Health (as it was then called) announced that the state was interested in funding a genetic counseling program, preferably one at a university medical center. Through the efforts of Dr. Nash Herndon and Dr. H. O. Goodman, there had been training of junior-level assistants in genetic counseling and emphasis on education of medical students about medical genetics at the Bowman Gray School of Medicine. But Dr. John Graham pointed out that UNC had the only program for providing a PhD in genetics in North Carolina at that time, and that we were an appropriate site for such a state-funded program. When our request was approved and assigned to be administered through the Department of Pediatrics, we became one of the first state-funded medical genetics programs in the country. Justification for state support included the fact that decreasing the frequency of genetic disease, even slightly, through genetic counseling was very cost-effective, given the extreme cost of some of these chronic disorders. Moreover, the families most in need of genetic services were often young couples, just getting started, whose meager savings were rapidly depleted by the expense of managing a child with a chronic or costly disease, while older, more financially secure adults were less in need of such services. Another justification was the lack of third-party coverage for testing and counseling at that time. Although some of these inequities have been corrected in recent years, many still exist.

Neil's early success in obtaining funding from the North Carolina Board of Health for one of the first state-funded medical genetics programs in the country was a major turning point. Funding began in 1968, the laboratories were established, and soon afterward the UNC Genetic Counseling Program officially opened its doors. Continuous funding of this grant has at least partially supported most of the service and educational activities in the division since then.

From the very start, Dr. Kirkman felt that the following features of a genetic counseling program were essential for effectiveness, for medical-legal protection of the medical center, and for maintaining good relations with the public: (a) establishing a cytogenetic laboratory under the full-time directorship of a doctoral-level person trained in clinical cytogenetics; (b) sending patients summaries of what was said during genetic counseling sessions; and (c) avoiding directive counseling (i.e., telling patients what to do). In addition, division policy stated that diagnostic activities not related to genetic disease should be avoided. As a consequence, members of the division have not been directly involved in such practices as determining paternity, race, or fetal sex for selective abortion solely on the basis of sex.

In 1971, a building was completed for the new Biological Sciences Research Center (BSRC). This was designed to be the laboratory research arm of the UNC Child Development Research Institute, one of twelve national research centers established in 1966 by federal and state grants. Neil moved into this building, where the division has been based ever since.

In his report to the state for the period 1/1/71 to 6/30/71, Dr. Kirkman wrote a brief paragraph about each of thirty families that received genetic counseling services during that time. At the time of this writing, members of the division sometimes see that many patients in one week.

Shortly after state funding began, a cytogenetics laboratory was established. In the 1960s there were very few, if any, doctoral-level individuals who had been specifically trained in what would now be called clinical cytogenetics. Most laboratories were small and were under the part-time supervision of a physician, generally in a division of pediatric endocrinology or a department of pathology. At UNC, Dr. Wilma Castle had set up a small blood karyotyping laboratory which was assumed by Dr. Margaret Swanton of the cytology laboratory in the Department of Pathology. As a temporary measure, some of the new state funds went toward the support of Dr. Swanton's laboratory. Being unable to find a person who had been trained specifically in clinical cytogenetics, Dr. Kirkman recruited Dr. Phil Buchanan, who had just received his PhD at North Carolina State. For his initial training in clinical cytogenetics, Dr. Buchanan was sent to spend time with Dr. H. O. Goodman at Bowman Gray. In the following two to three years he also received training, several months at a time, with Dr. Fred Hecht at Oregon, Dr. John Littlefield at Harvard, and Dr. Art Bloom at Michigan. With both blood karyotyping and later amniotic cell karyotyping, Dr. Goodman kindly provided confirmation of our early abnormal results.

Dr. Kirkman began to meet with the residents assigned to the genetic-metabolic rotation each week before clinic to go over the patients who were to be seen. Much of the time spent in these sessions was devoted to discussion of basic concepts of genetics and the disorders expressed in the patients, rather than only specific plans for evaluation or management, the number of patients being so small as to allow this. With time, this weekly session eventually evolved into two sessions: a weekly preclinic conference and a separate teaching conference and journal club.

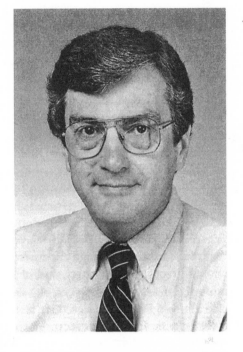

Art Aylsworth, successor to Neil Kirkman as director of the Division of Genetics and Metabolism

Dr. Kirkman recruited Art Aylsworth, a pediatrician with postdoctoral training in biochemical genetics and metabolism, to the genetic and metabolic division in 1973. Art had gained an introduction to the fields of clinical genetics and dysmorphology as well as additional experience with inborn errors of metabolism during two years in the Air Force at Wilford Hall Hospital. During a recruiting visit, Neil showed Art a patient with an undiagnosed storage disease which eventually turned out to be the eighth reported case (second American case) of mannosidosis. This was a fortuitous encounter since Art had just been involved in identifying the first American case of mannosidosis in a baby who had been brought to his clinic at Wilford Hall for a six-month well-baby check.

In 1974, Art was asked to organize a medical meeting in conjunction with the week-long annual meeting of the Little People of America (LPA), Inc. at Asheville's Grove Park Inn. It was through examining adults and children at these meetings that Dr. McKusick and his retinue of faculty, fellows, and ex-fellows from Johns Hopkins were able to clinically delineate dozens of different types of dwarfism and characterize their natural histories by following them longitudinally. A clinic for western North Carolina patients was held the first afternoon and a nice (free) dinner and program on skeletal dysplasias arranged at the Inn for the evening, with commitments to attend from over a dozen local physicians. Unfortunately, only two showed up, leaving us in the somewhat embarrassing position of throwing the party to which no one came. But Dr. McKusick and the other speakers proceeded with the program as if nothing were unusual, even though most of the attendees were from the Hopkins group. In spite of this somewhat shaky start, Art continued to work with the LPA Medical Board for a number of years, establishing our division as a referral center for skeletal dysplasia diagnosis and management.

Art's interests in clinical genetics and dysmorphology developed along with a growing need in the program for more emphasis in these areas, and he became the director of the state-funded Genetic Counseling Program in 1977. The role of the "clinical geneticist" has evolved gradually over the past three decades, nationally as well as in our division. Along with an exponential increase in our knowledge about the genetic underpinnings of human diseases during this time, a parallel need has grown for delineation and classification of clinical phenotypes to facilitate genotype-phenotype correlation and interpretation of the new molecular data. The "clinical geneticist," therefore, has an opportunity to be involved in both basic and applied research as well as patient service and teaching. Accordingly, while our service activities have provided much needed genetic diagnoses, counseling, and clinical management for families and practicing physicians across the state, the clinics also have been a rich source of patients and extended families for research studies.

The teaching of medical genetics to preclinical medical students here began with lectures by Dr. John Graham and Dr. Kirkman. Each was able to "bootleg" lectures through the foresight and generosity of Dr. Fred Dalldorf, course director of pathology, and of Dr. Harry Gooder, course director of cell biology. Dr. Logan Irvin, then chairman of the Department of Biochemistry, also allowed Dr. Kirkman to give lectures in the biochemistry course for medical students. In a recent lecture at UNC, Dr. Francis Collins, now internationally famous for his work in molecular genetics, attributed his beginning interest in medical genetics to his hearing Dr. Kirkman at these lectures. The present second-year course in medical genetics came into being because the dean of the School of Medicine was asked for it by a delegation of medical students who seemed to be more aware of the importance of genetics in medicine than were the dean and department chairmen themselves.[1]

Dr. Kirkman believed strongly that the preclinical lectures to medical students should not be an advanced version of undergraduate genetics. Rather, the lecturer should use clinical problems to illustrate the nature, application, and usefulness of genetic principles. Indeed, the many clinical problems appearing in the syllabus have come almost entirely from the experiences of members of this division with thousands of patients over the past twenty years. Over the years, this successful course has been produced through the cooperation of over a dozen people from five departments, with our division of genetics and metabolism providing most of the instructors, lecturers, and syllabus material.

Although a division of the Department of Pediatrics, this division became heavily involved in assisting members of the Department of Obstetrics and Gynecology in developing genetic prenatal diagnosis at UNC. This involvement came from the necessary use of a high-quality cytogenetic laboratory (administered through this division), from the general genetic nature of many of the fetal defects, and from the requirement for genetic counseling techniques in dealing with such couples. In keeping with the policy stated earlier,

---

1. A classic Kirkman reaction. (FWD)

Dr. Kirkman—and later Dr. Aylsworth—saw to it that ample time was spent with each couple before the prenatal test, explaining the advantages, risks, and limitations of the test. Moreover, this information was summarized as a written communication to the patients. Our cytogeneticist saw to it that prenatal diagnostic samples were obtained in a way that would maximize successful growth of cells and accurate diagnoses. As the volume of prenatal diagnosis patients became large, the perinatal medicine staff of the Department of Obstetrics and Gynecology began to assume responsibility for counseling couples whose reason for prenatal diagnosis was solely maternal age (risk for Down syndrome). They recruited two master's-level counselors for the task. They have also provided the counseling for results from their alpha-fetoprotein laboratory, which is one of two laboratories partially funded by the state.

Members of our division have continued to provide counseling and follow-up for most other prenatal diagnostic patients. Drs. Aylsworth and Kirkman have strongly advocated an autopsy when there has been death of a fetus or neonate with malformations or suspected metabolic defect. This has necessitated their examining the deceased fetus or neonate and helping the pathologists in evaluations. For many years, Drs. Kirkman and Aylsworth, together with our genetic counselors, have had a routine of sitting down with couples, reviewing the autopsy, and providing genetic counseling for couples who have lost a fetus or infant. These are usually couples referred to us or couples with whom we have had earlier contact. As with other couples, a letter summarizing the session is sent to the couple and the referring physician.

Events at other medical centers subsequently justified our initial decision here to have the cytogenetic laboratory under full-time supervision of a technically proficient clinical cytogeneticist. Although this was originally thought to be important primarily for prenatal diagnosis, the policy proved to be equally important for blood karyotyping. Parents were deciding on future pregnancies, or prenatal diagnosis, based on the blood karyotyping results on a malformed or retarded child.

In the early 1980s, some restructuring took place in the division. After a brief hiatus when there was no cytogenetics laboratory director, a new era emerged with the recruitment of Dr. Kathleen Rao as our new director of cytogenetics in 1984. Kathleen had been the first senior technician and laboratory supervisor in our original cytogenetics laboratory in 1971. After sev-

Kathy Rao

eral years in the lab, Kathleen left to obtain her PhD in the UNC genetics curriculum, and then went on to establish a very successful cytogenetics laboratory program at the new East Carolina University Medical School in Greenville. After we recruited her back to Chapel Hill, the sample volume in our laboratory more than quadrupled because of Kathleen's well-deserved reputation for extraordinary quality. Under the direction of Dr. Rao, this facility has distinguished itself as one of the outstanding clinical cytogenetics labs, not only in the Southeast but in the country. Kathleen was recognized for her expertise by being asked to serve on the cytogenetics review committee for a national collaborative cancer study group, and by being asked to run the proficiency testing for all cytogenetics laboratories in the southeastern United States after recording a perfect score in the first round of testing. When proficiency testing was transferred from regional programs to the College of American Pathologists, Kathleen's lab became one of fifteen cytogenetics programs in the country designated as "referee" laboratories, against which all others undergoing testing are compared. The laboratory now routinely uses molecular techniques to characterize chromosomal structural rearrangements that previously could not have been identified. It also collaborates with other genetic research labs on campus, helping to map newly cloned genes with molecular cytogenetic fluorescence in situ hybridization (FISH) technology. Kathleen is also active in training graduate students, residents, and postdoctoral fellows while directing a laboratory that performs over two thousand procedures each year.

Research from the cytogenetics lab illustrates an oft-quoted principle attributed to Dr. Van Wyk that one can learn a lot by carefully studying one or only a few well-selected patients. When Laurel Estabrooks was a trainee in the lab, she and Kathleen identified an extremely small terminal deletion on the long arm of chromosome 21 in a patient with holoprosencephaly. Aside from being only the second such case reported and, therefore, confirming distal 21q as another "holoprosencephaly locus," this patient contributed a "genetic reagent" through her blood sample which continues to be useful in mapping that region of chromosome 21. (Kathleen reports continued insistence by one group of collaborators in California that this deletion is too small for our lab to have seen cytogenetically, and yet it was identified through a "routine" study in the lab.) Numerous other patients with rearrangements of similar research interest have been identified by Dr. Rao's lab, including several under active investigation at the time of this writing, such as a 6p rearrangement involving the cleidocranial dysplasia locus, an 8q deletion involving the branchio-oto-renal syndrome locus, an Xp deletion involving the Goltz focal dermal hypoplasia region, and an Xq deletion involving the choroideremia locus. Laurel's thesis work with Dr. Rao involved molecular mapping of several deletions on the region of chromosome 4p associated with the Wolf-Hirschhorn syndrome, some of which were from our patients here, with others being sent in by collaborators who learned of Laurel's project. This work led to important mapping information and to Laurel's being asked by Dr. Hirschhorn to help organize and cohost with him a symposium on the Wolf-Hirschhorn syndrome.

In the early 1970s directors of clinical genetic services began to appreciate the need for assistance in the task of genetic counseling. It soon became apparent that the clinical geneticist's time was more efficiently used if someone else obtained medical records, took a detailed family history, and dictated the initial draft of a letter of summary. Such an assistant could also spend more time than the physician detecting concerns, misconceptions, and relevant psychosocial issues. The assistant could also provide much of the counseling for common disorders after the diagnosis was established, while physicians could continue to have the responsibility for physical examinations, clinical diagnoses, and some of the communication with physicians, parents, and patients.

Filling the role of such a genetic assistant early in the program here were two consecutive, part-time social workers and one person with an MS in genetics. Later in the 1970s, we recognized that the appropriate person for the task was the "genetic associate" (now called genetic counselor) who was a graduate of a two-year program such as that at Sarah Lawrence College. These individuals take courses in genetics with emphasis on medical genetics, have supervised training in genetic clinics, and receive an MS degree. The division has been fortunate to recruit an outstanding succession of such counselors, beginning with Debbie Timmons from the Sarah Lawrence program. Debbie and another of the counselors from our division have subsequently entered medical school and become physicians. One of our genetic counselors, Mrs. Nancy Callanan, provides most of the counseling for molecular diagnostic (DNA) studies done by the hospital laboratories section of molecular pathology under Dr. Larry Silverman, for the cystic fibrosis and muscular dystrophy clinics. Our counselors have assisted Jewish groups in several communities in setting up Tay-Sachs carrier testing drives, with the laboratory work being done in our biochemical genetics laboratory.

The state of North Carolina, through our division, was one of the first to establish genetic satellite clinics. Dr. Kirkman argued that satellite clinics are especially appropriate in the practice of medical genetics for the following reasons: (a) often the condition is sufficiently severe or chronic to justify deferring the evaluation until a clinic can be held near the home of the family; (b) holding the clinic near the home of the patient increases the likelihood that necessary relatives will be available for examination, for family history information, and for counseling; and (c) our division was initially responsible for providing genetic services for the entire state, which is of such a size and shape as to make it impractical for some families to drive to Chapel Hill.

These satellite clinics were started in the early 1970s with funds from the March of Dimes. From the beginning, these were "fly-in" clinics, utilizing the Medical Air Operations service at nearby Horace Williams Airport to serve areas at a moderate distance from Chapel Hill in the eastern and western parts of the state. Colonel Provancha, then head of the Medical Air Operations service, was an enthusiastic and memorable pilot. Sometimes his enthusiasm exceeded ours, as when he would dip down to fly through the valleys in the mountains on the way to and from autumn clinics in Asheville, just so we could have a closer view of the apple orchards and changing leaves. The early clinics were held in Asheville, Charlotte, Jacksonville, and Elizabeth City. With the establishment of other state-funded genetic programs, first in Winston-Salem and later at Charlotte and Greenville, members of our division now limit our satellite clinics to the central and south-central part of the state. The frequency of these clinics has gone from three to six per year initially to more than fifteen per year currently. It was at one of these satellite clinics in the mid-1980s that we discovered a young boy with neurofibromatosis who happened to have an unusually extensive family history of many other affected relatives. Eventually, over seventy relatives were examined and sampled, and linkage data from this family were used in mapping the NF1 locus to the pericentromeric region of chromosome 17.

At the request of black community leaders in North Carolina, members of this division provided medical genetic advice and help for some of the early efforts to deal with sickle cell disease. We advised them on techniques of informing people as to their being carriers of a recessive gene, providing three separate genetic training sessions for the state sickle cell workers. Dr. Kirkman, along with Dr. Campbell McMillan of the hematology division, testified before the legislature in support of a bill that would prohibit insurance companies from denying coverage to people with sickle cell trait. Dr. Kirkman was also asked to testify on several other occasions regarding bills before the legislature having bearing on other genetic issues.

The first certifications of the American Board of Medical Genetics were in 1982. Considering the small size of our division of genetics and metabolism, an unusually large number (twelve) of the candidates passing their board examinations that first time were people who had trained or worked in this division. By 1990, twenty-one such candidates from the division had successfully taken their boards in medical genetics. (Thinking this was a notable achievement considering the failure rate for these examinations, Dr. Kirkman performed a quick statistical analysis on his pocket calculator, as he often has done in the Thursday teaching conferences, and announced that the probability of this success rate being achieved by candidates of average ability was <0.0025.)[2] A postdoctoral program administered through this division has been accredited for training since 1986 in biochemical genetics, clinical genetics, and cytogenetics, and since 1991 for molecular genetics and PhD medical genetics.

By 1970, pediatric residents were routinely taking one-month rotations in the division. Five of these former pediatric residents are now medical geneticists. Fourth-year students were also choosing the elective in genetics by the

---

2. Another classic Kirkman performance. (FWD)

early 1980s. Approximately a dozen have coauthored papers with members of the division.

The history of a division is largely the stories of the people who have enlivened it during their training years. Postdoctoral fellows are listed elsewhere. Students receiving their PhDs in genetics through work with Dr. Kirkman in this division have included Mary Ella Mascia Pierpont, MD-PhD (now professor of pediatrics at the University of Minnesota), Patricia Stubblefield, Kathleen Rao, and Charles "Tim" Timmons, MD-PhD (now a pediatric pathologist at the University of Texas-Southwestern, Dallas). A number of people who worked as technicians with Dr. Kirkman subsequently went on to more advanced degrees and contributions in the field of health: One is a nutritionist, another a genetic counselor, one is now a dentist, and four became physicians.

During Tim and Kathleen's memorable years as "lab rats," a significant proportion of our small division was named "Timmons" (Tim, Chrys as a postdoc, and Debbie, our first genetic counselor), causing secretaries and callers perpetual confusion. Tim could not be present at Neil's retirement party in 1991, but instead sent a long, marvelous recollection of his years here which we read at the evening party. Following are some excerpts from Tim's letter.

My memories of being a graduate student under Dr. Kirkman leave me filled with wonder; chiefly, wonder that he did not pitch me out on my ear. The rational mind requires a logical explanation for such super-human endurance, and in the years since I have formed the theory that he had unwisely bet someone that I would finish the program. He looked the other way when we hung Christmas stockings on the fume hoods. He never flinched when the word processor incarcerated my dissertation. Why, he was even implicated in the corruption of the ice machine, which periodically yielded up a cache of soft drinks or even white wine or champagne. (Of course, now, as a member of the College of American Pathologists, I shudder to think of discovering such atrocities on a lab inspection.) Despite most intense provocation, I cannot remember him ever raising his voice—even to normal speaking levels. I believe it was Kathleen Rao who said, when I thought I heard him out in the hall, "Don't be silly. If you heard him, it can't be Dr. Kirkman." His displeasure was subtle. His mere glance had us quaking after Jean Shearin, with an unfortunately directed stream of water, destroyed the electrical mechanism of his recording spectrophotometer. After Kathleen Rao and I methodically incinerated his two electrophoresis power sources in two days, he actually said, "This has got to stop." We were devastated.

I think he had hoped that bringing Kathleen Rao into the lab as my fellow graduate student would teach me good work habits. She arrived as a model of decorum, industriousness and scientific sensibility.

Unfortunately, Dr. Kirkman was in Scotland on sabbatical at the time and by his return, she had been lured into such dubious partnerships as constructing an 18-channel preparative electrophoresis chamber of twine and dialysis tubing that looked like some extraterrestrial milking machine. All too soon the poor woman was giving human names to her cloned cell lines and was finally reduced to such a state of distraction that she was observed wearing a fully stained acrylamide disc gel across the instep of her shoe for three days without noticing. It is to Dr. Kirkman's great credit that her career was saved.

Reflecting back now, I realize that Dr. Kirkman had a remarkable ability to be understanding toward us. He taught us well, much of it by example. We learned scientific method by watching his patient, methodical research. We learned human genetics at his clinical conferences. We learned ethics from his firm stands on counseling issues. We learned involvement from his own with the PKU children, who to him were not just numbers and plasma levels but actual children who were constantly being slipped wienies by well-meaning grandmothers. And we learned humanity from his closeness to his family and pride in his children. We all change the things we touch. In my own way, I suppose I left my mark on Dr. Kirkman's laboratory, and I don't just mean that piece of starch gel that may still be stuck to the ceiling. Certainly, Dr. Kirkman and the wonderful people I worked with in his laboratory have left their mark on me, stored in my heart with the warmest of memories.

On June 14, 1991, a symposium was held in honor of Neil Kirkman on his retirement (semiretirement, actually), and a number of former trainees returned for the occasion. The afternoon program included the following speakers and topics:

Professor Gian Franco Gaetani came all the way from the University of Genoa, Italy, and talked about his long-term collaboration with Neil in a presentation entitled "From G6PD to Catalase: A Twenty-Year Friendship." When informed of the meeting by telephone, he had replied, "I wouldn't miss it!" Bill Wilson, a faculty member in the pediatric genetics division at the University of Virginia in Charlottesville since completing his fellowship here, spoke about the "Long-term Sequellae of Treated Inborn Errors of Metabolism." Bill has established a solid career in both clinical genetics and biochemical genetics as well as pediatric resident education. Steve Kahler, at Duke University in pediatric genetics and metabolism since his fellowship here, talked about "New Developments in Fatty Acid Oxidation Disorders." Steve also fills dual roles at Duke as clinical geneticist and specialist in genetic metabolic disorders. Ave Lachiewicz, also on the pediatric faculty at Duke, presented her material on "Behavior of Young Children with Fragile X." Ave had spent a postdoctoral year with us after her fellowship in developmental pediatrics in the division for disorders of development and learning. During that year she studied the longitudinal developmental records on over twenty patients we had diagnosed with fragile X syndrome, providing the first data showing declining IQ with age in most affected boys. Cora Jean Edgell, on the research faculty in our UNC-CH Department of Pathology, presented her work on "Differentiated Gene Expression in Endothelium." And Laurel Estabrooks, finishing her work in Dr. Rao's lab, presented data from her project in a talk entitled "Characterization of Chromosome 4p Deletions and Rearrangements."

Dr. Kirkman took partial, early retirement in 1991 and continues to work in the division with primary research and clinical interests directed toward the large patient population with PKU and galactosemia he follows.

In 1993, two new faculty members were recruited to the division. Joseph Muenzer, MD, PhD (biochemistry), became the new director of the biochemical genetics and metabolism section. Joe received postdoctoral training in medical genetics and endocrinology at the National Institutes of Health in Bethesda, where he trained with Dr. Elizabeth Neufeld and developed an interest in the lysosomal storage diseases. He is working closely with the metabolism section in the UNC Hospital laboratories to enhance the detection of inborn errors of metabolism, and consulting with the state newborn screening laboratory on patients identified through that program. His laboratory research is focused on the molecular genetics of MPS II, Hunter syndrome. Joe is also pursuing studies related to gene therapy for storage diseases and other inborn errors of metabolism and is developing a mouse model for Hunter syndrome.

Cynthia M. Powell, MD, joined us in 1993 after having completed a post-doctoral fellowship in medical genetics at the National Institutes of Health and the Children's National Medical Center. Cindy is board certified in both clinical genetics and cytogenetics and is helping to further develop our research efforts in the cytogenetics laboratory.

Currently, the division provides evaluations, counseling, and management services to over twelve hundred patients and families each year at UNC Hospitals and several satellite clinics. We now have over twenty-five years of data collected through the clinics on patients with a variety of birth defects and other genetic diseases. This is an exciting time in medical genetics, as some families that were seen over ten years ago are coming back to have samples taken for molecular studies and some former pediatric patients are bringing their own children back to see us, allowing for longitudinal evaluation of natural history and intrafamilial variability of expression. Areas of interest other than the inborn errors of metabolism mentioned above include the genetics of laterality determination, neurofibromatosis, neural tube defects, birth defect epidemiology, skeletal dysplasias, delineation of mental retardation/malformation syndromes, phenotype delineation for gene mapping studies, and phenotypic delineation and cytogenetic characterization of patients with novel chromosomal rearrangements.

In all sections of the division, there is significant potential for further growth in research, service, and teaching activities. The Human Genome Project is generating a wealth of new genetic data that will need to be applied to patients in all medical disciplines. As this new information becomes available for clinical application, we will need to be active in providing continuing genetic education for North Carolina's physicians and other health professionals. This body of new genetic information can be expected to grow in an almost exponential fashion and it will be our job to make sure it is used correctly and efficiently in patient evaluation and counseling. Our division has been involved in one of the half-dozen Human Genome Project grants that were given to study the efficacy of different methods of population-based screening and counseling for cystic fibrosis, and we will be called upon to apply what we have learned from that project for many different conditions in the future. The advent of gene therapy will also bring new opportunities and challenges. We anticipate that well-trained clinical geneticists will be needed throughout the health care system to bridge the gap (in both directions) between research laboratories and clinical practice, defining phenotypes, collecting families for genetic studies, and then interpreting research results for patients and families in the process called genetic counseling.

Into this brief history has gone the information that is not readily obtainable in an annual report or a curriculum vitae.

HENRY N. KIRKMAN, JR.
ARTHUR S. AYLSWORTH

FACULTY

Aylsworth, Arthur S. B Eng Phys, Cornell Univ, 1963; MD, Univ Pennsylvania, 1967; Inst, Ped, 1973; Asst Prof, Ped, 1975; Assoc Prof, Ped, 1980; Prof, Ped, 1993; Dir Gen Couns Prog, 1977; Acting Chief, Ped Div Genet Metabol, 1991; Chief, Ped Div Genet Metabol, 1995.

Frazier, Dianne M. AB, Drew Univ, 1964; PhD, Duke, 1969; MPH, Univ NC, 1983; Inst, Biochem, 1972; Asst Prof, Biochem, 1975; Asst Prof, Ped, 1986.

Kaiser-Rogers, Kathleen. BS, St. Andrews Presbyterian Coll, 1983; PhD, Univ NC, 1991; Clin Asst Prof, Ped, 1995; Asst Director, Cytogenetics Lab, 1995.

Kirkman, Henry N. BS, GA Inst of Tech, 1947; MS, Emory Univ, 1950; MD, Johns Hopkins, 1952; Prof, Ped, 1965–91; Clin Prof Emeritus, Ped, 1991; Chief, Ped Div Genet Metabol, 1965–91; Dir Gen Couns Prog, 1970–77.

Muenzer, Joseph. BA, Kalamazoo Coll, 1970; PhD, Case Western Res Univ, 1976; MD Case Western Res Univ, 1979; Assoc Prof, Ped, 1993.

Powell, Cynthia M. AB, Cornell Univ, 1976; MS, Sarah Lawrence Coll, 1978; MD Med Coll of VA, 1987; Asst Prof, Ped, 1993.

Rao, Kathleen W. BS, William and Mary, 1970; PhD, UNC, 1980; Asst Prof, Ped and Pathol, 1984; Assoc Prof, Ped and Pathol, 1991; Dir, Cytogen Lab, 1984.

FELLOWS

Years	Name	Current Position
1968–69	Gian F. Gaetani, MD	Prof, Med (Hematol), Univ Genoa (Italy)
1973–74	Peggy B. Falace, MD	Priv Pract (Lexington, KY)
1975–76	Cora Jean Edgell, PhD	Assoc Prof, Pathol, UNC-CH
1977–82	Stephen G. Kahler, MD	Assoc Clin Prof, Ped, Duke Univ Med Ctr
1978–79	William G. Wilson, MD	Assoc Prof, Ped, UVA
1979–81	M. Chrystie Timmons, MD	Assoc Prof, Ob-Gyn, Duke Univ Med Ctr
1981–82	Gail E. Herman, MD, PhD	Assoc Prof, Inst for Mol Genet, Baylor
1981–82	Jean Shearin, PhD	Res Staff, Burroughs Wellcome (RTP, NC)
1982–83	Eugene R. Soare, MD, PhD	Priv Pract (Dover, NH)
1984–85	Ave M. Lachiewicz, MD	Asst Clin Prof, Dev Ped, Duke Univ Med Ctr
1986–89	Patricia A. Friedman, MD	Priv Pract (Chevy Chase, MD)
1987–91	Laurel Estabrooks, PhD	Lab Dir, Integrated Genetics (Santa Fe, NM)
1987–91	Allen N. Lamb, PhD	Lab Dir, Integrated Genetics (Santa Fe, NM)
1988–90	Theonia K. Boyd, MD	Asst Prof, Pathol, Tufts
1991–94	Kathleen Kaiser-Rogers, PhD	Clin Asst Prof, Ped, Asst Dir, Cytogen Lab, UNC-CH
1992	Ilana Kepten, PhD	Israel (current position unknown)
1992–94	Ruth Heim, PhD	Div Molec Pathol, Dept Hosp Labs, UNC-CH
1992–94	James Tepperberg, PhD	Asst Dir, Cytogen Lab, Roche Biomed Labs (RTP, NC)

CHAPTER TWENTY

Hematology-Oncology

HISTORY OF THE DIVISION

AT THE outset it should be pointed out that "hematology-oncology" as a medical specialty had not yet evolved when our Medical School was expanded to a four-year institution with clinical departments in 1952. The specialized practice of hematology became well recognized by the 1940s, especially among internists responding to the rapidly growing knowledge about nutritional anemias at that time. However, the practice of oncology did not emerge until at least a decade later in the wake of several promising advances in the treatment of cancer. Specifically, gains in treating Hodgkin's disease and childhood leukemia strongly promoted the combined practice of hematology and oncology by the late 1960s among both internists and pediatricians. Thereafter, the first certifying examination for the subspecialty "pediatric hematology-oncology" was offered by the American Board of Pediatrics in 1974. By then the new subspecialty was off and running in the world at large and also fully represented in the Pediatric Department of the School of Medicine, UNC-CH. In the last two decades pediatric hematology-oncology (hereinafter, PHO) has been a single subspecialty with respect to board certification and also to program organization for the most part. On the other hand, separate divisions of hematology and oncology have been customary in most departments of medicine for about a decade, matched by separate boards in these subspecialties for qualified physicians taking care of adult patients. This difference from pediatrics is largely the result of a fifty-fold greater prevalence of cancer in adults than in children.

The history of PHO in our Department of Pediatrics will be described in sections corresponding to those periods of time served by our three departmental chairmen from 1952 to 1993: the era of Edward C. Curnen, 1952–1960; the era of Floyd W. Denny, Jr., 1960–1981; and the era of Thomas F. Boat, 1982–1993. During Dr. Curnen's era clinical services for children with blood diseases and cancer were provided by the general pediatric faculty and house staff, utilizing selected consultants from other departments and Duke University. The major features of these services will be outlined. Thereafter, steps leading to the formation of a PHO division were initiated upon the arrival of Dr. Campbell McMillan in 1963, three years into the era of Dr. Denny. Dr. McMillan provides the story of the PHO division from the very beginning until the end of the Denny era. Dr. Herbert Cooper, who became the director of the division in 1985, has provided the subsequent history.

The Edward C. Curnen Era: 1952–1960

A pediatric hematologist for the Department of Pediatrics was not recruited during the Curnen era, in line with the custom of most departments at that time. On the other hand, state-of-the-art clinical services for children with hematologic and oncologic diseases were carried out by the pediatric attending physicians and house staff with definitive assistance from three sources. First of all, Dr. Jeffress G. Palmer was regularly consulted as needed, both for inpatient and outpatient problems. Dr. Palmer finished his hematology fellowship with Dr. Maxwell Wintrobe at Utah in May 1952 and joined the Department of Medicine at UNC-CH as its first hematologist in September 1952. Because Dr. Wintrobe's program served children as well as adults, upon his arrival in Chapel Hill Dr. Palmer was familiar with blood problems in children and also with questions about these problems from pediatricians. In particular, he helped with bone marrow and blood studies on new cases of leukemia and with the institution of appropriate treatment. Dr. Palmer was the only faculty member of the division of hematology in the Department of Medicine until he was joined by Dr. John C. Herion in 1957. Second, helpful assistance with hemophilia and other clinical coagulation problems was consistently available to the Department of Pediatrics from members of the world-renowned coagulation research programs of Dr. Kenneth M. Brinkhous in pathology and Dr. John H. Ferguson in physiology. Third, Dr. Doris Ahlee Howell was invited by Dr. Curnen to be a regular consultant at UNC-CH in 1955 when she joined the Department of Pediatrics at Duke University School of Medicine. Dr. Howell, generally known as "Ahlee" to her host of friends, came to Duke after completing a fellowship in pediatric hematology and oncology with Dr. Louis K. Diamond at Boston's Children's Hospital and the Department of Pediatrics of Harvard Medical School. She brought enormous talents in clinical scholarship to her work at Duke and Chapel Hill and is the acknowledged founder of pediatric hematology-oncology in the state of North Carolina. Ahlee Howell is still fondly remembered by colleagues and family members with whom she worked.

In response to a request for her impressions of PHO at Chapel Hill during the Curnen era, Dr. Howell provided an account in a letter dated April 8, 1993, from which the following slightly edited portions are taken:

> My alliance with UNC was strengthened through the enthusiastic generosity and cordiality of Drs. Ed Curnen and Jeff Palmer. It soon became evident that Ed was delighted to have someone worry about the hematologic problems which were growing by geometric progression, particularly with the increasing attention to childhood cancers and the new chemotherapies and radiologic techniques. The house staff was eager, hungry and hard working. Although now it seems impossible to believe we could function with only one afternoon a week, the telephone was always available and I could run over at other odd times if necessary or the faculty or house staff would bring slides over to Duke when they were coming for another reason. During those Curnen years, there were several house officers who developed a particular interest in hematology and the growing field of oncology. Two of these in particular, Dr. Faith Kung and Dr. Dick Patterson, spent elective time with me at Duke and then followed on with careers in hematology-oncology. Both remained in academic medicine and have made names for themselves in the field. Two others, Dr. Wilma Krause-Castle and Dr. Barbara Gibson, also put additional time into trying to extend my services to the UNC patients.
>
> Probably one of the strongest ties I had in those early years was actually with the Department of Pathology and the generosity and largesse of Dr. Ken Brinkhous. Being faced with an ever-growing pool of hemophilic children at Duke and no one there at that time to turn to I naturally took the 11-mile trip to Chapel Hill frequently, both with blood samples and an inquiring and worried mind. Ken and his associate John Graham were constantly generous, helpful and kind. My peer support came through Gus Johnston, who was a fellow with Dr. John Ferguson of the Department of Physiology. At the same time it was a tremendous boon to have Dr. Phil Webster, a dentist committed to improving the care of hemophilic children, develop a dental clinic to which I constantly ran back and forth with my patients to enhance their care.
>
> One of the most valued experiences was the warm friendship of the faculty during those early years who every other day of the week in their attending rounds had to be the know-all and end-all of hematology-oncology but, on Thursday, would always graciously accede to my experience and contributions. The house staff were top-notch and really stretched themselves to fill the gap. Jeff Palmer and his team were always cooperative and responsive to requests for help.

The Floyd W. Denny, Jr. Era: 1960–1981

FACULTY AND STAGES OF PROGRAM DEVELOPMENT

At the outset of his chairmanship Dr. Denny was unmistakably committed to the development of strong subspecialty divisions within the Pediatric Department, including a program in hematology-oncology. He was firmly supported in this regard by Dr. Ahlee Howell, who added consultation on recruitment of a full-time faculty member to her ongoing help with management of patients.

In the summer of 1961, Dr. William L. London instituted a weekly PHO clinic in the Old Clinic Building in connection with joining the pediatric group practice in Durham of his uncle, the late Dr. Arthur London. Dr. Will London had graduated from the School of Medicine of UNC-CH in 1955, followed by three years of residency in pediatrics at Children's Hospital in Boston and a single year of fellowship in PHO with Dr. Louis K. Diamond. By the time Dr. London completed his fellowship on June 30, 1961, arrangements had been made with Dr. Denny for him to develop a PHO teaching clinic that would serve patients, medical students, and pediatric house staff alike. He was at work within two weeks of moving from Boston to Durham. This first-ever PHO clinic was separate from Dr. Howell's continuing Thursday afternoon consultations, which thereafter emphasized inpatients.

In the process of exploring the field of candidates for a full-time PHO faculty position at UNC-CH, Dr. Denny was referred in the fall of 1961 to Dr. Campbell McMillan, who was in practice in Laurinburg, North Carolina, at that time. The referral was made by Dr. Richard T. Smith, then chairman of the Department of Pediatrics at the University of Florida, who had recently recruited McMillan for such a position. Prior to completing a three-year PHO fellowship with Dr. Diamond at Boston in the summer of 1961, McMillan withdrew his acceptance of the PHO position in Florida. This difficult decision was reached because of extenuating circumstances developing after the death of McMillan's father in North Carolina. (It should be noted that McMillan referred Dr. Smith to a Dr. Howard Pearson at that time, a young hematologist in the U.S. Navy who had decided to seek civilian life. The rest, as they say, is history.)

In October 1961, McMillan received a letter from Dr. Denny at Chapel Hill, inviting mutual exploration of a PHO position in the Department of Pediatrics here. This prospect was very attractive to McMillan, not only because of the uniformly strong reputation of Dr. Denny and the Department but also because of the prestige of coagulation research at Chapel Hill. The major focus of McMillan's work during his fellowship was clinical research involving children with hemophilia, largely consisting of studies on an early factor VIII concentrate. Nonetheless, in view of just settling in Laurinburg, he declined the prospect at that time. However, communications did continue and intensified in the spring of 1962 when Dr. Denny, Dr. Wallace Clyde, and McMillan met at the pediatric section meeting of the North Carolina Medical

Society in Pinehurst, where Wally Clyde and McMillan were both on the program. An immediate and warm sense of connection among these three men developed at this meeting. Specifically, McMillan was irreversibly caught up in the spell of Dr. Denny's legendary enthusiasm. Thereafter, following two visits to Chapel Hill in the summer of 1962, McMillan began to attend Dr. Will London's PHO clinic at least once a month. His gentle reentry into academic waters was combined with a variety of activities that were both gratifying and stimulating. These included renewing links to his old friends Ahlee Howell and Will London, developing strong relations with persons in coagulation research (especially Drs. Harold Roberts of the Department of Medicine and Phil Webster of the Dental School), and continuing to interact with Dr. Denny and the rest of the pediatric faculty.

By November 1962 McMillan had fully rediscovered academic pediatric hematology-oncology and found it to be irresistible. Furthermore, previous problems on the home front had stabilized and the pediatric practice was well within the reach of Dr. Purcell alone. Accordingly, McMillan contacted Dr. Denny about the availability of a PHO job in the Department. At that time the ongoing search for prospects had not yielded a bumper crop. Indeed, there were *very* few PHO candidates in those days. Thus, after consultation with other appropriate persons and well before Christmas of 1962, Dr. Denny made a firm offer to McMillan, which was gratefully accepted. In the middle of January 1963 McMillan along with his wife, Florence, and children loaded their worldly goods into a Volkswagen bus with a trailer attached and headed out from Laurinburg to Chapel Hill on a chilly day featuring a classic Carolina blue sky. The worldly goods included a small -30°C freezer given by Dr. Diamond to McMillan at the end of his fellowship in the summer of 1961. This freezer was immediately taken upon arrival in Chapel Hill to a room on the fifth floor of the Old Clinic Building, where it became the first piece of equipment in McMillan's new laboratory. This room, which served the purposes of both laboratory and office for the next five years, was adjacent to the office and laboratories both of Dr. Judson Van Wyk and his pediatric endocrinology division and of Dr. Jeff Palmer and his medical hematology division. The location was truly optimal.

During the period 1963–1970 McMillan was the only full-time faculty member in pediatric hematology-oncology. Dr. Will London continued to attend the weekly outpatient PHO clinic along with McMillan. However, in the summer of 1963 Dr. Ahlee Howell left Duke, and therefore Carolina as well, to become the chair of pediatrics at the Woman's Medical College of Pennsylvania in Philadelphia. Upon her departure, McMillan went to Duke on a weekly basis as a consultant until Dr. Stanley Porter came from the University of Arkansas in 1964 to be the next chief of PHO at Duke.

Even though McMillan worked alone during the period in question, this was a happy and productive time with respect to PHO program development. Standard approaches to treatment of children with frequently encountered diseases of the subspecialty were developed, including protocols for hemophilia, sickle cell anemia and its variants, leukemia, and Wilms' tumor. Teaching of medical students was variously fitted into existing departmental systems, and an elective in PHO for senior medical students was well subscribed after its institution by the School of Medicine in the fall of 1968. Also, earlier in 1968 a monthly PHO clinic at New Hanover Memorial Hospital in Wilmington, North Carolina, became one of the first of its kind in the newly developed AHEC system. A minifellowship in PHO was designed and offered to house officers taking the monthly rotation on this service. It was gratifying that the PHO month was heavily singled out by residents from the U.S. Naval Hospital in Portsmouth, Virginia, who spent three-month periods in our Department for subspecialty experience in those days. It should be noted that three residents participated in significant clinical studies leading to senior or second authorship of articles in major journals.

Cam McMillan

McMillan applied to the National Heart and Lung Institute in 1963 for funds to study factor VIII in the newborn. The research was designed to establish the relative roles of factor synthesis in the newborn versus placental transfer of factor from the mother, using dogs in Dr. Brinkhous's hemophilic colony. The grant was funded in full for three years and the research question was answered: All factor VIII in the newborn is derived from the newborn. More importantly, the grant enabled McMillan to set up his own coagulation research laboratory. It is a striking reflection of the slower pace of research in the 1960s as compared even to the 1970s that the tools for his research project were entirely usable without change after a complete hiatus of almost three years. In 1966 McMillan was appointed associate director of the clinical research unit, located on the fifth floor of South Wing, to serve with the director, Dr. William B. Blythe. Accordingly, McMillan's office was moved to that location and he began an immensely rewarding association with the Clinical Research Unit (CRU) that would continue until 1979. Thereafter, in the fall of 1969 the CRU was moved from 5 South to the recently completed third floor of the new hospital bed tower being constructed above the J. Spencer Love Ambulatory Patient Care Facility (APCF). Accordingly, McMillan's office and laboratory were moved, along with the office and laboratory of Bill Blythe, to these very generous new quarters. Previous laboratory space was vacated in time for appropriate renovations to accommodate its use by Dr. A. Myron Johnson, who would join McMillan as a second member of the PHO faculty in late 1970.

In contrast to the relatively quiet and steady progress of the PHO program from 1963 to 1970, the period from 1970 to the end of the Denny era in 1981 was characterized by substantial fluctuation. During the first seven years of this period continuing growth and development of the program led to a well-defined PHO division with new faculty and activities in patient care, teaching, and research. However, at the end of 1977 a cluster of serious setbacks required reorganization of the division in a series of steps extending from the end of the Denny era into the Boat era. These changes within the division occurred in a setting of overall medical progress that had accelerated since the early 1970s with profound effects on academic medicine in general and PHO at UNC-CH in particular. Salient examples of such progress included quantum leaps in the field of molecular biology and very promising results from applying collaborative clinical research to cancer treatment. In addition, at our Medical School the annual admissions increased from 65 students in 1965, to 100 students in 1970, and then to its final level of 160 students in 1976.

Dr. Myron Johnson had been recruited primarily for his potential contributions to laboratory research. He had just completed a two-year fellowship in immunology and hematology with Dr. Chester A. Alper at the blood grouping laboratory of Children's Hospital at Boston and Harvard Medical School. His training and research had been largely concerned with the genetics, control of synthesis, and function of the acute phase reactants, particularly antiproteases. His research interests were specifically pertinent to the institutional programs in coagulation research where the roles of various antiproteases, serving to regulate the formation and removal of blood clots, were not a major focus of investigation at the time. In addition, Dr. Johnson constituted a significant resource for development of a PHO fellowship program for which there was definite need.

Dr. Johnson was not able to obtain support for collaborative studies within the NHLBI-funded hemorrhage and thrombosis program project of the Department of Pathology. However, he did secure funding from the NIH thereafter for his independent research. In due course he acquired international recognition for his work on antiproteases, notably alpha-1 antitrypsin.

In 1972 the PHO program changed its identity from a departmental teaching service dominated by clinical hematology to a division of pediatric hematology-oncology by virtue of two major events. First, Dr. John T. Benjamin, a former resident in our Pediatric Department from 1966 to 1969, became the first fellow in our PHO program. Second, in order to strengthen its increasing activities in clinical oncology, PHO at UNC-CH joined the pediatric division of the Southwest Oncology Group (SWOG) as a probationary member in March 1972. These two events are summarized as follows in slightly edited excerpts from a document provided by Dr. Benjamin, dated March 21, 1993.

After three years as a pediatrician in the Army, I returned to Chapel Hill for a year of pediatric hematology fellowship. I had decided that I would go into practice after my year with Dr. McMillan and try to practice in an area where I could continue to stay involved with hematology.

The Division was now called "Pediatric Hematology-Oncology." The Division consisted of Dr. McMillan, Dr. Myron Johnson, who was busy with research most of the time, a med tech (Elizabeth Little), a resident, and now me—the fellow. At first it was somewhat difficult to distinguish the resident's duties from my own, but after a month or so that didn't present too much of a problem.

My time was divided into three areas. First, I helped establish our membership in the Southwest Oncology Group. Dr. McMillan had realized that we should get involved in such a group and therefore had registered with it. He had sent away for the protocols that we would be using. The first day I walked into the office I remember seeing this huge stack of paper in the corner. In response to my question, I was told, "I was hoping you might help organize our protocols." The treatment of cancer had changed. No longer was it the decision of the attending to choose how a child would be treated; the protocol would determine the treatment.

Second, I became involved in three clinical research projects that ultimately got published, including the follow-up on a Wilms' tumor protocol that I had designed and instituted before I went into the Army, Clinical Research Unit–based studies on a child with congenital dyserythropoietic anemia and another child with congenital osteopetrosis.

Third, I helped see patients in the clinic, on the ward, and emergencies in the ER. All cancer and leukemia patients were seen in the clinic on a regular basis (largely in accord with protocol requirements). They had many interventions done such as bone marrows, intrathecal, and intravenous meds that hadn't been done in the past. I believe that one clinic day became two days a week and finally three days a week during my stay there.

With the added emphasis on protocols and paperwork, the relationship between the patient and the doctor changed. In the early years, the parents of a child would hear the child's diagnosis and be assured that the child would receive the most up-to-date treatment available which would start immediately. Now, the parents would come to the hospital and, after hearing the diagnosis, be told that their child would be randomized to one of two treatments. The parents always asked which treatment might be the better one. If the child came in on a Saturday, the parents might need to wait until Monday morning (when the SWOG statistical office at Houston opened for patient registrations) before finding out which treatment the child would get. As the treatment progressed, each relapse, each problem would be dictated by the protocol. While all this information was ultimately necessary for determining optimal treatment, something seemed to go out of the doctor-patient relationship.

In the late summer of 1973 Dr. Benjamin and his family left Chapel Hill for him to join Pediatric Associates of Charlottesville, Virginia, in the general practice of pediatrics. He overlapped with Dr. J. Hugh Bryan, who joined our PHO division as the next fellow in July 1973 after completing two years as a clinical associate in the pediatric oncology branch of the National Cancer Institute (NCI). Dr. Bryan graduated from the UNC School of Medicine in 1969 and followed this with two years of pediatric residency in our Department before going to the NCI.

Dr. Bryan brought to his fellowship at UNC-CH a remarkable blend of his previous top-flight training in clinical oncology with his own natural talents and interest in this field. His entry into the routines of our affiliation with the pediatric division of SWOG strongly resembled the likes of Van Cliburn sitting down at the piano. The fellowship provided Dr. Bryan an ideal arena in which to exercise his considerable abilities in pediatric oncology with accompanying benefits to patient care and teaching of students, residents, and attending physicians. In turn, his skills in hematology were enlarged and sharpened. At the end of his one year of fellowship at UNC-CH, Dr. Bryan accepted an offer to join the Department of Pediatrics as the third faculty member in the PHO division.

There were other notable events in 1974. In that year Dr. Herbert A. Cooper became an official consultant to the PHO division when he joined the Department of Pathology as an assistant professor with a secondary appointment in the Department of Pediatrics. These appointments followed his four-year postdoctoral fellowship from 1971 to 1974 in hemostasis and thrombosis in the Department of Pathology under the direction of Drs. Robert H. Wagner and Kenneth M. Brinkhous. Dr. Cooper received his MD degree in 1964 from the University of Kansas School of Medicine at Kansas City. From 1964 to 1971 he took a year of rotating internship at Charles T. Miller Hospital and the Children's Hospital at St. Paul, Minnesota, followed by two years of pediatric residency and two more years of hematology and oncology in the Mayo Graduate School of Medicine. His period of training was interrupted from 1967 to 1969 by military service as chief of pediatrics at Beale Air Force Base, California. Dr. Cooper's joint appointment in pediatrics merely formalized collegial connections with Drs. Myron Johnson and Campbell McMillan that had been established after he first came to Chapel Hill in 1971.

In February 1974, the University of North Carolina at Chapel Hill, represented by the PHO division, was approved by the pediatric division of SWOG for full membership. Critical to this approval was the registration of eighty-eight patients on protocol at UNC-CH during the probationary period. In June 1974, the PHO division forwarded its first grant application to the National Cancer Institute, requesting $139,070 for three years of support for collaborative studies with SWOG, beginning January 1, 1975.

In August 1974 the PHO team was enlarged by the addition of two persons indispensable to the delivery of optimal clinical services to children with cancer and their families. Marie M. Lauria was recruited as a clinical social worker. She had received a Master of Social Work degree from UNC-CH in May 1974. Patricia E. Greene, RN, was recruited as a clinical nursing specialist in pediatric oncology by the Department of Nursing, North Carolina Memorial Hospital. She had been awarded a Master of Science in Nursing at the University of Florida in 1973. Her record included nursing experience with childhood cancer not only in Gainesville, Florida, but also at St. Jude Children's Research Hospital in Memphis and at Grady Memorial Hospital in Atlanta.

In November 1974, McMillan extended the trends of a favorable year up to that time by traveling to Philadelphia to take and also to pass the first certifying examination in PHO offered by the American Board of Pediatrics. On the other hand, in a letter dated December 4, 1974, the acting program director of the Cancer Cooperative Clinical Trials Program of the NCI informed McMillan that his application to support studies with SWOG was approved but could not be funded by 1/1/75 as requested. Fortunately, funds did become available in due course and the grant was initiated on 6/1/75, with proportional reduction in the first year but full funding in the last two years up to 12/31/77.

The period of time from June 1975 to the end of 1977 was a uniformly busy and productive time for the PHO division. Selected highlights were as follows: First, the offices and laboratories for Drs. Johnson and Bryan were then located in excellent quarters on the third floor of the newly constructed Burnett-Womack Clinical Sciences Building within the growing medical center complex. This space also accommodated the division secretary and a study area for students, residents, and fellows. Second, two former UNC pediatric residents served as research fellows from July 1975 through June 1977: Drs. Ronald B. May and Mary Jo Freitag. Dr. May had just completed his residency while Dr. Freitag had served on the UNC pediatric house staff from 1970 to 1972 before moving out of state with her family. In addition, Dr. Jean B. Belasco served as a research fellow from July 1976 through June 1978, thereby overlapping for a year with Drs. May and Freitag. Dr. Belasco received her MD from Temple University School of Medicine and completed her pediatric residency at St. Christopher's Hospital for Children in Philadelphia. Third, the rate of new pediatric oncology patients at UNC-CH increased in 1975 upon the departure from Duke of Dr. Stanley Porter. Because of the resulting needs for help with PHO at Duke, Dr. Will London discontinued coming to clinic at Chapel Hill at that time in order to serve over there. (It should be noted that Duke's share of the pediatric oncology pie was abundantly reclaimed by Dr. John M. Falletta after he came to Duke in 1976. He was recruited from the Baylor College of Medicine at Houston, where the PHO program, as in the cases of UNC and Duke, belonged to the pediatric division of SWOG.) Fourth, in January 1976 Dr. Hugh Bryan instituted a monthly pediatric oncology clinic in Charlotte. Developed at the request of Dr. James C. Parke, Jr. of the Pediatric Department at Charlotte Memorial

Hospital, this clinic became the second one (after the Wilmington clinic, ongoing since 1968) to be served by the PHO division within the AHEC system. The Charlotte clinic was instantly and enormously successful, both as a resource for patients and families and as a vehicle for educating students, residents, and pediatricians in the community. Also, within a year of its inception this clinic was a source of about twelve new patient registrations with SWOG, supported by a modest supplementary grant from the NCI through the central office of SWOG at Kansas City. Fifth, the PHO division was deeply involved in a series of initiatives leading to the development of two major institutional programs: the Cancer Research Center, beginning in 1975 and headed by Dr. Joseph S. Pagano of the Department of Medicine; and the Comprehensive Hemophilia Diagnostic and Treatment Center, beginning in 1978 and headed for the next five years by Dr. Philip M. Blatt of the Department of Medicine. Sixth, and finally, in accord with a deadline of February 1, 1977, the PHO division forwarded to the NCI an application for renewal of its grant for collaborative studies within SWOG. The application described a multidisciplinary plan for diagnosis and management of approximately sixty children with cancer per year, utilizing research protocols designed by collaborating investigators. The application requested $670,410 for five years of support, beginning January 1, 1978. Dr. Bryan was the major architect of this proposal, both in its conception and in its final assembly. Furthermore, in August 1977 this proposal was modified for incorporation as a pediatric oncology section into the renewal application to the NCI by Dr. Pagano for the UNC Cancer Research Center. The purpose of the proposal was to demonstrate the need for a full-time basic scientist to join both the PHO division and the community of basic scientists within the Cancer Research Center. The need for such a scientist was keenly felt among the PHO faculty, particularly in the face of thriving psychosocial services, educational programs, community outreach, and clinical research in the division.

In a letter from the NCI dated October 3, 1977, McMillan was informed that the renewal grant application for collaborative studies in SWOG had been unanimously recommended for approval by the Cancer Clinical Investigation Review Committee. However, the high hopes generated by that letter were dashed by a subsequent letter from the NCI dated November 4, 1977, that the grant could not be funded. Altogether, six institutions in the pediatric division of SWOG were not funded at that time, including UNC-CH. These programs represented approximately one-third of the total group. Officials of the NCI were hopeful that funds might be available later in the fiscal year but were unable to provide any interim financial assistance. Dr. Barth Hoogstraten, chairman of SWOG at Kansas City, sent a spirited memorandum to all principal investigators in the pediatric division, exhorting everyone to "hang in there." It should be noted that eighty-four patients were registered on SWOG studies by UNC-CH in 1977 alone, whereas eighty-eight patients were registered during the initial two-year probationary period from March 1972 to February 1974.

Within one month of the negative verdict from the NCI, both Drs. Bryan and Johnson decided to change the direction of their careers from PHO, to radiation oncology in the case of Dr. Bryan and laboratory medicine for Dr. Johnson. Accordingly, they both resigned from their positions in the Pediatric Department, effective July 1, 1978. (Thereafter Dr. Bryan began a fellowship in radiation oncology at the University of Pennsylvania in Philadelphia and Dr. Johnson became associate director of the Blood Bank at UNC-CH with a primary appointment in the Department of Pathology.)

Beginning in November 1977, a series of specific steps were taken by McMillan and Dr. Denny to adjust the PHO program to the reductions in financial and faculty resources that would occur in the next year. Despite warm support from Dr. Hoogstraten and the pediatric division of SWOG, it was decided that continued membership of UNC-CH in that organization would not be feasible. Therefore, in a letter to Dr. Hoogstraten dated December 5, 1977, McMillan submitted resignation of the PHO division from SWOG, effective upon termination of its grant at the end of 1977. McMillan decided to continue the Wilmington AHEC clinic on a bimonthly basis but not to attend the Charlotte AHEC clinic after Dr. Bryan's departure until the needs of the PHO program at Chapel Hill were clarified. The needs in question involved not only the program in general but also two new research fellows: Drs. W. Keith Hoots and Melinda S. Snyder, due to begin their training on July 1, 1978. In connection with Dr. Bryan's final clinic at Charlotte, Dr. Parke of the Pediatric Department there telephoned McMillan to request that Dr. Falletta and the PHO division at Duke manage this clinic in the interim. Dr. Parke pointed out that this arrangement would prevent loss of the considerable momentum that had been gained by the clinic. Also, the grant from SWOG funds for support of the clinic would not be lost because the Duke PHO program had not lost its funding. McMillan agreed to this proposal; his telephone conversation with Dr. Parke took place in the late spring of 1978.

Drs. Keith Hoots and Melinda Snyder began their research fellowships in the PHO division in July 1978. Dr. Hoots was a Morehead Fellow in the UNC-CH School of Medicine, from which he received his MD in 1975. He then completed three years of pediatric residency at the Parkland Memorial Hospital in Dallas. Dr. Snyder received her MD from Ohio State University School of Medicine in 1974, followed by three years of pediatric residency at the North Carolina Baptist Hospital in Winston-Salem and a single year of PHO fellowship at Children's Hospital in Cincinnati. During their fellowships at UNC-CH from 1978 to 1980 both Drs. Hoots and Snyder provided invaluable help with clinical and educational needs of the PHO program at a time of major changes and relatively decreased resources. In addition, they contributed effectively to a variety of hemophilia-related projects on the Clinical Research Unit, and Dr. Hoots investigated a unique coagulation disorder in the pathology research laboratories of Drs. Jan McDonagh and Herbert Cooper. Thereafter the fellowship program was discontinued in connection with an extended process of redefining and rebuilding the PHO division within the Department of Pediatrics.

In the aftermath of the "Crash of '77" Drs. Denny and McMillan agreed on the need to recruit a pediatric oncologist who would help restore strength, direction, and appropriate funding to the oncologic component of the Department of Pediatrics. Furthermore, McMillan was entirely willing for such a person to become the new head of the division, to head a separate division for oncology, or simply to join the existing division. It should be pointed out that the UNC Cancer Research Center was not a resource in these regards. The NCI did not fund the proposal in the center's renewal grant application for a basic scientist who would join both the PHO division and the research community of the center.

While the search for a new oncologist was proceeding within the Pediatric Department there were several important changes affecting the PHO division. In the summer of 1979 McMillan resigned his thirteen-year position as associate director of the clinical research unit and moved his office and laboratory to existing PHO space on the third floor of the Clinical Sciences Building. Concomitantly, the clinic for the Comprehensive Hemophilia Diagnostic and Treatment Center was moved from the Clinical Research Unit (where it began) to the medicine clinic on the first floor of the Ambulatory Patient Care Facility (APCF). Also, Patricia Greene left the PHO team in June 1979 for a nursing position with the American Cancer Society in New York City. By the time of Ms. Green's departure, the inpatient nurses had been trained in state-of-the-art management of pediatric oncology patients, including the use of research protocols. Outpatient nursing services in this regard were capably taken over by Margaret E. Adams, RN; she was already the nursing supervisor for the constellation of pediatric clinics, including those of the PHO division, all held on the first floor of the APCF.

The search for an oncologist was culminated in September 1979 when Dr. John K. Whisnant accepted an offer from Dr. Denny to head a new division of pediatric immunology-oncology within the Department of Pediatrics. The guidelines for this division were not rigidly specified by Dr. Denny in order to allow for maximal development of the division and its adjustment to existing programs. In general, Dr. Whisnant was expected to develop a departmental program in immunology and oncology that would closely interact with the ongoing program in hematology headed by McMillan. Thus, the PHO division was divided into "PIO" and "PH" divisions. (It should be noted that the PHO division in the Department of Medicine at UNC-CH had been divided into divisions of oncology and hematology in 1977.)

At the time of Dr. Whisnant's appointment he was head of the immunology section in the medical division of the Burroughs Wellcome Company (BWC) at Research Triangle Park, North Carolina. He initially joined BWC as a clinical research physician in the immunology section in June 1973. This position followed a final year of pediatric residency and coincided with a final year of fellowship in pediatric immunology, both at Duke University Medical Center. In January 1976, he began to participate in the emerging program in immunology and rheumatology at Chapel Hill as a clinical assistant professor of pediatrics. Then, in March 1976, he became head of the immunology section at BWC, a position he maintained in addition to his new role as head of the PIO division at UNC-CH, beginning in September 1979.

As for his earlier education and training, Dr. Whisnant was a Richard J. Reynolds Scholar at the Bowman Gray School of Medicine of Wake Forest University, from which he received his MD in 1968. After a year of internship in pediatrics at North Carolina Baptist Hospital in Winston-Salem, he had a year of pediatric residency with the Albert Einstein College of Medicine at the Bronx Municipal Hospital in New York City. Then, from 1970 to 1972 he was a research associate in developmental immunology at the NICHHD in Bethesda, Maryland, followed by his final year of residency at Duke from 1972 to 1973.

The appointment of Dr. Whisnant as head of the PIO division is obviously relevant not only to the history of oncology in the Department of Pediatrics but also to that of immunology. This narrative will be limited to a description of his very substantial contributions to the reorganization of pediatric oncology within the Department.

Office and laboratory space on the sixth floor of the Clinical Sciences Building was assigned to Dr. Whisnant for the new division. Concomitantly, this space was shared with Dr. McMillan, his secretary Wanda Braxton, and the fellows Drs. Hoots and Snyder, who moved up from previous quarters on the third floor of the same building. Ms. Braxton provided secretarial services both for immunology-oncology and for hematology. Patient care and teaching responsibilities, the existing schedules for ward rounds, clinics, and conferences were not changed significantly. Thus, the functions and supportive structures of the PIO and PH divisions were closely linked.

Dr. Whisnant served as chief of the PIO division from September 1979 near the end of the Denny era to July 1982, when the Boat era began. The following contributions to pediatric oncology at UNC-CH were highlights of his tenure. First, in 1979 he recruited Dr. Thomas E. Williams to BWC as a senior clinical research scientist. Shortly thereafter Dr. Williams was appointed clinical associate professor of pediatrics at Chapel Hill. He was a valuable resource for developing the PIO division, having been chief of the PHO division at the University of Texas Health Sciences Center at San Antonio since 1969. This position followed research fellowships at the University of Virginia from 1967 to 1969, including one year of PHO fellowship and a year of laboratory-based cancer research. Also, before going to Texas in 1969 Dr. Williams spent a month in the coagulation research laboratory of McMillan at Chapel Hill for an introduction to the investigation of coagulation disorders. Dr. Williams received his MD from the University of Texas Southwestern Medical School at Dallas in 1962 and completed his pediatric residency at the Children's Medical Center of Dallas in 1965.

Second, on behalf of the Department of Pediatrics at UNC-CH, Dr. Whis-

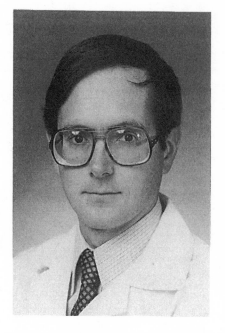

Bob Wells

nant recruited Dr. Robert J. Wells to the PIO division as an assistant professor of pediatrics. Dr. Wells started in July 1980. He had just completed three years of PHO fellowship in the program of Dr. Robert L. Baehner at Indiana University in Indianapolis. He received his MD in 1972 from the School of Medicine of the University of California, San Diego, and completed his pediatric residency in 1975 at the Children's Medical Center in Cincinnati. He was a base pediatrician with the U.S. Air Force in Turkey for two years before beginning his PHO fellowship in 1977. As soon as Dr. Wells arrived in Chapel Hill, he convincingly demonstrated his impressive skills in all phases of pediatric hematology and oncology as he joined Drs. Whisnant, Williams, and McMillan.

Third, Dr. Whisnant played a pivotal role in paving the way for the pediatric oncology program at UNC-CH to join the Children's Cancer Study Group (CCSG). In regard to the question of getting back into such a group, Drs. Whisnant, Williams, and Wells unanimously agreed that CCSG was the best way to go and that the process of applying should begin promptly. Dr. McMillan was less sure than they, both about timing and about the relative merits of CCSG versus the Pediatric Oncology Group (POG), the new name of the reorganized pediatric division of SWOG. In the fall of 1980, Dr. Whisnant arranged a memorable evening at the Chapel Hill Country Club when the four faculty members of the PIO and PH divisions met with Dr. G. Denman Hammond, chairman of CCSG. It should be noted that Dr. Hammond, an internationally respected leader in pediatric oncology who was in the area for another conference at that time, completed his undergraduate education at UNC-CH in 1944. At the beginning of the meeting in question, he approached the group in a reserved and guarded manner and frankly promoted the merits of exploring POG rather than CCSG for membership. And then Dr. John Whisnant went to work. In a virtuoso performance, he vividly portrayed the benefits that CCSG would derive from the membership of UNC-CH with not only its own scientific resources but also those of many collaborative programs in the area, including BWC. At the end of the evening, one could practically hear the equipment beginning to move earth for the new road between Chapel Hill and CCSG. More specifically, Dr. Tom Williams assumed the responsibility of putting the application together during subsequent months. In 1982 UNC-CH became a probationary member of CCSG;

full membership followed in 1985. (These outcomes will be considered in more detail below, in the summary of the Thomas F. Boat era.)

Fourth, and finally, Dr. Whisnant quickly became involved in the institutional Clinical Cancer Education Program, based in the Department of Surgery and directed by the late Dr. James F. Newsome. In January 1980, Dr. Whisnant was named associate director of this program and served until the beginning of the Boat era in July 1982.

In a letter dated January 11, 1993, Dr. Whisnant provided his impressions of pediatric oncology and hematology, from which the following slightly edited portion is taken:

> I would only hope that we include some commentary regarding the great opportunity that we had during our time together. Not only were the four of us [Whisnant, Williams, Wells, and McMillan] different enough to form a strong team playing different positions, but we had wonderful contributions from Marie [Lauria] and from Margaret [Adams] also. I think our interface with the pharmaceutical industry is also worth some discussion. This was a unique opportunity with 50% of our senior staff actually employed by and paid for by another organization. For better or for worse, this relationship emphasized our research content and encouraged our cooperative group participation [in CCSG]. I honestly believe we made substantial gains in the quality of programs and I would emphasize our progress and positive memories. Perhaps our group also made progress in the larger arena of the Medical School and the Cancer Center. I remember fondly the cancer education program that Turk [James F.] Newsome and I led and successfully renewed [through a competitive grant application]. Certainly, the summer intern program for students was one of the enjoyable and rewarding activities during my time at "The Hill."

The above account from Dr. Whisnant concludes the major section of this historical narrative, dealing with faculty and stages of PHO program development during the Denny era from 1960 to 1981. Subsequent sections will briefly summarize the ingredients in selected components of the overall PHO program during the Denny era.

CLINICAL SERVICES

At UNC-CH, as elsewhere, the characteristics of clinical services for children with hematologic and oncologic disease constantly changed from 1960 to 1981 in step with medical progress. Up to 1967, the PHO division conducted a single half-day clinic each week in the pediatric section of the Old Clinic Building, serving five to ten patients per session. Also, consultation was provided to the ward team for one to three children who would be in the hospital most of the time. These services were quite sufficient to handle both initial and subsequent needs of twenty to twenty-five new cancer patients annually and about the same number of new hematologic cases. In those days virtually all children with cancer, regardless of type, failed to survive for more than a year or two. However, when the PHO clinic moved into the pediatric section of the newly constructed Ambulatoty Patient Care Facility in 1967 the demands of clinical oncology were beginning to increase because of favorable trends in cancer treatment. Likewise, plasma fractions for treating patients with hemophilia were improving rapidly and the concept of home therapy for these patients was emerging. The annual number of new cancer patients doubled to about forty by 1974, doubled again to more than eighty in 1977, and then settled down to about forty patients thereafter. The number of new hematology patients per year did not change appreciably, remaining at an estimated twenty-five patients.

By 1973 the PHO division was conducting the following clinics each week: an all-day oncology clinic, a half-day general hematology clinic, and a half-day hemophilia clinic in collaboration with Dr. R. B. Raney, chief of the division of orthopedics, and his staff. In 1978 an all-day comprehensive hemophilia clinic was initiated on the Clinical Research Unit and then moved to the medicine clinic in the APCF the following year. In this clinic children and adults underwent hematologic, psychosocial, and dental evaluation in the morning and orthopedic evaluation in the afternoon. Hospitalized patients were managed by the ward teams in consultation with the attending physician and staff of the PHO team. This approach was customary for all subspecialty divisions in the Department of Pediatrics except, of course, for the division of neonatology, which Dr. Ernest Kraybill initiated in 1972.

EDUCATIONAL PROGRAMS

Apart from customary participation of the PHO faculty in educational programs of the Medical School and Department of Pediatrics at UNC-CH, the division provided training for seven research fellows from July 1972 through June 1980. Of this group five are certified in the subspecialty of PHO by the American Board of Pediatrics, three are full-time academicians, and one is practicing pediatrics with a clinical appointment in a medical school. Two training grants to which the PHO division had access were crucial for the support of these research fellows. First, the clinical cancer education program, supported by a grant to UNC-CH from the National Cancer Institute (NCI) beginning in 1966, provided funds for four of the PHO fellows. As noted previously, Dr. John Whisnant was associate director of this program from January 1980 to July 1982. Second, an ongoing NIH grant for research training in hematology, awarded to the division of hematology in the Department of Medicine, supported two of the PHO fellows. Finally, in one instance fellowship funds were provided by the NCI grant to the PHO division for collaborative studies in the pediatric division of SWOG from 1975 to 1977.

Two other educational initiatives during the Denny era should be cited here. On March 28, 1975, the Ninth Annual Malignant Disease Symposium of the School of Medicine, UNC-CH, was presented in Berryhill Hall by the PHO division, supported by the clinical cancer education program and BWC.

The topic was "Childhood Malignancy" and the speakers, selected by Drs. Bryan and McMillan, were definitive national authorities on leukemia and solid tumors at the time. Finally, in connection with commencement exercises for the School of Medicine in 1977, the David A. Mayberry Award was presented for the first time to graduating seniors Will Ryan and James Patterson, who were declared cowinners. This award, ongoing since then, is derived from a fund established in the PHO division with a generous donation by Dr. A. Ray Mayberry in memory of his son David, who had died of Hodgkin's disease. The award was designed to honor that senior medical student who, in the opinion of the PHO team, had demonstrated the best clinical scholarship while learning about children with cancer.

RESEARCH

In general, research carried out in the PHO division during the Denny era was directed along three tracks, corresponding to the primary interests of the several faculty members. McMillan's work emphasized clinical research in coagulation disorders, particularly hemophilia. His major project was a cooperative study (with ten other institutions across the nation) of the natural history of factor VIII inhibitors acquired by patients with classic hemophilia. This NIH-supported, CRU-based study began in July 1975, ended November 1979, and yielded a variety of significant findings. Furthermore, this study provided an organized group of 161 patients for the formation in 1978 of the Comprehensive Hemophilia Diagnostic and Treatment Center at UNC-CH. Dr. Johnson's research was supported by two grants while he was in the PHO division: A study of genetic antiprotease variants in disease was funded by the National Institute of Allergy and Infectious Disease, and a study of induction of liver disease by proteolytic enzymes was funded by the National Institute of Arthritis, Metabolic and Digestive Diseases. The research of Drs. Bryan, Whisnant, Williams, and Wells was largely directed to clinical studies on treatment of children with leukemia and solid tumors, including a variety of projects carried out on the Clinical Research Unit.

Two private sources of funds were invaluable to the PHO division for support of miscellaneous studies that could not be covered by regular grants. The David A. Mayberry Fund was cited in the preceding section of this narrative. In addition, the Larry Silver Fund was available to the PHO program from 1963 to 1969. This fund was established by Dr. and Mrs. Marvin Silver of Chapel Hill in memory of their son Larry, who had died of acute leukemia. Interestingly, the Silvers first contacted Dr. Ahlee Howell at Duke about their wish to make a donation; they were referred by Dr. Howell to McMillan since she was leaving for Philadelphia in the summer of 1963. That's the way things were back in those days! A particularly helpful purchase with the Larry Silver Fund was a scintillation counter that was used for many years in projects on the clinical research unit, including erythrokinetic studies by Dr. Jack Benjamin and protein turnover studies by Drs. Johnson and McMillan.

CAMPBELL W. MCMILLAN

Editor's Note: Dr. McMillan has given a very factual and complete history of hematology and oncology in the Department of Pediatrics. Characteristic of the quality of the man, he has not left those of us compiling this history with enough "essence" of his true qualities, of which there was an enormous amount. In a department heavily salted with research and researchers he was always a little uneasy that he was not doing enough original investigation. This was not an accurate assessment because his research was very good. In addition, as another marker of the esteem with which he was held, he was the associate director of the Clinical Research Unit and director of the Comprehensive Hemophilia Center. His true claim to stardom and perfection, however, was as a teacher and as a clinician. In large groups his presentations were models of organization and simplicity that were delivered with colorful words and stories, occasionally accompanied with biblical quotes or Southern homilies. He was particularly masterful in one-on-one sessions—always thorough, patient, and thoughtful. He was a caring and compassionate clinician, loved by his patients and their parents, and a model of the caring physician for literally hundreds of students and house staff.

This description of the qualities of Campbell McMillan would not be complete without describing his role as a Pediatric Department member. For twenty-eight years he served as the "conscience" of the Department. We could always be certain that he, in his humble way, would let us know if we were showing any tendency to make any move that was not in the best interests of children. (FWD, Jr.)

The Thomas F. Boat Era: 1982–1993

At the outset, it should be noted that the entry of Dr. Boat in July of 1982 was associated with two other significant events in that year. First, Carolina won the NCAA basketball championship in New Orleans on March 29, 1982, with a 63-62 victory over Georgetown. (As true aficionados will recall, the winning basket was made by a freshman from Wilmington named Michael Jordan.) Second, a somewhat analogous achievement for the PHO program in October 1982 was its induction into the Children's Cancer Study Group (CCSG) as a probationary member, especially gratifying to Dr. Tom Williams, who was the major architect of the application.

In the section that follows, the history of PHO in the Boat era will be outlined chronologically by means of selected highlights. As indicated in the preceding section, Dr. Whisnant resigned his position as chief of the PIO division at UNC-CH, effective July 1, 1982, to devote more time to his position as head of the immunology section, medical division at BWC. He continued to work with the ongoing immunology and oncology programs through his appointment as a clinical associate professor of pediatrics. Accordingly, Dr. Boat instituted search committees for new chiefs of two departmental divisions: a reconstituted PHO division and a new division of rheumatology and immunology.

In a memorandum to the faculty of the Pediatric Department, dated January 28, 1983, Dr. Boat officially announced that hematology and oncology would be recombined administratively and functionally as a single division. In addition, he designated Dr. Robert Wells the interim director of this division until a new chief was appointed. Later in 1983 Dr. Robert W. Warren accepted Dr. Boat's offer to head the new division of pediatric rheumatology and immunology. His office and laboratory were located in renovated space on the fourth floor of the MacNider Building. In the same year Dr. Warren was joined in adjacent space by the PHO faculty (Drs. Wells, Whisnant, Williams, and McMillan), who moved from the sixth floor of the Clinical Sciences Building. A final major event of 1983 was the resignation of Dr. Philip Blatt as director of the Comprehensive Hemophilia Center to go into the private practice of adult hematology-oncology in Delaware; he was succeeded by McMillan.

Under the direction of Dr. Wells, the PHO division delivered an excellent performance as a probationary member of CCSG. Also, referral of new patients increased and pediatric residents were progressively involved in the overall PHO program. Finally, Dr. Wells was very successful in promoting collaborative clinical research within the School of Medicine at UNC-CH. For example, he was largely responsible for enlisting the help of Dr. J. Kenneth Whitt of pediatric clinical psychology in a variety of projects, leading to an established role for Dr. Whitt in the PHO program. A key project in this regard was a CRU-based evaluation of the psychological effects of prophylactic whole brain radiation in children with leukemia.

The search for a new chief of the PHO division ended in 1985 when Dr. Herbert A. Cooper accepted Dr. Boat's offer of this position. As noted in the previous discussion of faculty during the Denny era, Dr. Cooper became an official consultant to the PHO program after completing his postdoctoral fellowship with Drs. Wagner and Brinkhous in 1974. At that time he joined the medical faculty with a primary appointment in pathology and a secondary appointment in pediatrics. When Dr. Cooper became chief of the PHO division in 1985 the department of his primary appointment was changed to pediatrics. Thereafter, UNC-CH achieved full membership in the CCSG in October 1985 and Dr. Cooper also became the principal investigator for this major component of the PHO program.

There were other important developments regarding PHO faculty in 1985. First, Dr. Tom Williams resigned both his position with BWC and his clinical appointment at UNC-CH and returned to his former PHO program at San Antonio to initiate a bone marrow transplant program there. Second, Dr. Jane Azizkhan was added to the PHO faculty when she joined the institutional cancer research program as a molecular biologist with joint appointments in the

Herb Cooper, successor to Cam McMillan as director of the Division of Hematology-Oncology

Departments of Pediatrics (primary) and Pharmacology. Her office and laboratory were located in the recently constructed Lineberger Cancer Research Center (LCRC), first occupied in 1984. Furthermore, her husband, Dr. Richard Azizkhan, was recruited by the Department of Surgery to become the first chief of a division of pediatric surgery at UNC-CH. Truly, Rich Azizkhan was manna from heaven for the entire Department of Pediatrics. Possessing boundless energy and formidable talents both as a pediatric surgeon and as a person, he quickly became an invaluable resource for the PHO division and for the institutional contribution to CCSG. Finally, soon after taking office in 1985 Dr. Cooper recruited two persons who played major roles in the patient care and teaching functions of the PHO division: Rose P. Dunaway, RN, pediatric oncology nurse; and Mary Sue Van Dyke, MSN, family nurse-practitioner and clinical assistant professor of pediatrics. In the following year the clinical capabilities of the PHO team were significantly further enlarged when UNC Hospitals formally designated Gwen K. Konsler, BSN, a pediatric oncology nurse.

At the time of Dr. Cooper's entry into the PHO program, outreach consisted of an ongoing bimonthly clinic in Wilmington and a newly established clinic at the Moses Cone Hospital in Greensboro, North Carolina, both parts of the AHEC system. Within a year of his arrival Dr. Cooper added a monthly PHO clinic at the Asheville (North Carolina) AHEC, which he attended regularly. The clinics at Greensboro and Wilmington were largely covered by Drs. Wells and McMillan, respectively. It should be noted that the Greensboro program was supported by a modest grant for cancer control from 1985 to 1987. Thereafter this clinic was discontinued because of its relative proximity to Chapel Hill as well as problems with maintaining adherence to protocol among children with cancer treated over there.

In 1986 Dr. Cooper became codirector of a new UNC sickle cell program along with Dr. Eugene P. Orringer of the division of hematology, Department of Medicine. A comprehensive clinic, analogous to the previously established hemophilia clinic, was developed to serve both children and adults with sickle cell anemia as well as variants of this disease. The clinic was instituted on Tuesday afternoon of each week and held within the pediatric outpatient area on the first floor of the APCF; it followed an existing PHO morning clinic.

In 1987 all PHO clinics were moved to renovated space on the second

floor of the Gravely Building. This space was adjacent to a section on that floor that had been occupied recently by oncology and hematology clinics for adult patients. The sickle cell clinic was relocated in the PHO outpatient area rather than the adult section. On the other hand, the hemophilia clinic remained within the medicine clinic on the first floor of the APCF.

Another significant event for the PHO program in 1987 was the inauguration of the Webb Award. This award was derived from a trust fund created in the PHO division by the family of William E. Webb to support the care of children with cancer and blood disease. The Webb Award was established in order to honor that second-year pediatric resident who, by consensus of the PHO team, had made the most significant contribution to the care of PHO patients and their families. The first awardee was Dr. Brent W. Weston, who joined the pediatric house staff at UNC-CH after receiving his medical degree from Duke University School of Medicine in 1985. Recipients have been selected and honored each year since 1987 at the time of the annual spring picnic for the Department of Pediatrics.

In 1988 a distinct era of the PHO division came to an end when Dr. Bob Wells resigned his position at UNC-CH to join the PHO program at the Children's Hospital Medical Center in Cincinnati, Ohio, as an associate professor of clinical pediatrics. It should be noted that his faculty colleagues were no less than *three* former division chiefs when he served as the acting chief of the PHO division from 1983 to 1985. Indeed, Dr. Wells successfully guided the PHO program through a period of major transition with remarkable skill and understanding. The following is a slightly edited excerpt from a letter by Dr. Wells, written in response to a request for his impressions and dated December 30, 1992:

From my current perspective as I think back on my time at Chapel Hill, (especially) 1982–1983, I think to a large extent we were in a

Stuart Gold

Gary Jones

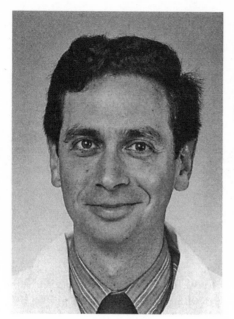

sense victims of a system under stress that was breaking down. On the other hand, once you understand the problems and stresses that you face you are in a better position to estimate the likelihood of solutions on a near-term scale and to evaluate realistically your own performance and that of others. So on this basis I can look back on the Chapel Hill experience and feel quite good about it. I miss the consistent resident exposure and teaching that allowed one to see the development of physicians and I miss living in Chapel Hill although things are very nice in Cincinnati too.

In July 1989 Drs. Stuart H. Gold and Gary R. Jones joined the Department of Pediatrics as new members of the PHO faculty. Dr. Gold was recruited from the University of Colorado Health Sciences Center at Denver, where he had completed both his pediatric residency (1981–1985) and PHO fellowship (1985–1989). He received his MD in 1981 from the Vanderbilt University School of Medicine in Nashville, Tennessee. Dr. Jones came from the Children's Hospital Medical Center at Cincinnati, Ohio (even as Dr. Wells went there), where he had been a William Cooper Proctor Research Scholar in the PHO program from 1986 to 1989. Dr. Jones received his MD in 1980 from the University of Oregon Health Sciences Center in Portland, followed by pediatric residency at the University of Minnesota in Minneapolis from 1980 to 1983. He completed his PHO fellowship at the Children's Hospital of Los Angeles in California from 1983 to 1986, from where he went to Cincinnati.

In addition, Colleen S. Poprawa, MSN, joined the PHO division in 1989, and Bernard E. Weissman became a major resource to the division the same year when he joined the Lineberger Cancer Research Center with appointments in pathology (primary) and pediatrics. Ms. Poprawa, a clinical nurse specialist, was recruited by Dr. Cooper to fill the PHO nursing position vacated in 1989 by Ms. Niles, who returned to private life with her family. Appointed a clinical assistant professor of pediatrics upon coming to UNC-CH, Ms. Poprawa had previously been a pediatric nurse at Yale–New Haven Hospital. As for Dr. Weissman, he came to Chapel Hill from the University of Southern California School of Medicine at Los Angeles. There he had earned international recognition for his work on the genetic control of tumor expression with an emphasis on childhood malignancy. His recruitment by Dr. Joe Grisham, chairman of pathology, was actively supported by Drs. Boat and Cooper. Also, Drs. Weissman and Gary Jones had collaborated during their overlapping years in Los Angeles.

As evident from the highlights summarized above, significant growth and development of resources within the PHO division took place during 1989. Accordingly, Drs. Cooper and McMillan decided to apply for accreditation of a PHO fellowship program. In September 1989 a formal application in this regard was submitted to the residency review committee for pediatrics of the Accreditation Council for Graduate Medical Education in Chicago, Illinois. A site visit to the PHO division was conducted at Chapel Hill on February 15, 1990, by William I. Staples, MD, field representative of the Accreditation Council. The proposed fellowship program was approved.

There were two other highlights for the PHO team in 1990. Rose P. Dunaway, RN, was honored by UNC Hospitals as Nurse of the Year. Marie E. Lauria, MSW, was named Oncology Social Worker of the Year by the National Association of Oncology Social Workers. And there was a loss: At the end of 1991 Dr. McMillan fully retired from the Department of Pediatrics and the PHO division.

Beginning in January 1992, Dr. Stuart Gold assumed direction of the PHO clinic at the Wilmington AHEC. In accord with requests from the medical community there, this clinic reverted to its original monthly schedule and services to patients were expanded. In July 1992, Dr. Brent W. Weston joined the Department of Pediatrics as a new fourth member of the PHO faculty. As noted previously, Dr. Weston was the first recipient of the Webb Award in 1987. After completing his residency at UNC-CH in 1988, he went to the University of Michigan at Ann Arbor for a three-year PHO fellowship in the program of Dr. Laurence Boxer. He then remained at Michigan for another year beginning July 1991 to extend his productive research on human fucosyltransferase genes, sponsored by Dr. John B. Lowe. Another major event for the PHO division in 1992 was the acceptance by Dr. Paul Monahan of an offer from Dr. Cooper to become a research fellow in the program beginning July 1993. Dr. Monahan began his pediatric residency at UNC-CH in June 1990, following his graduation from the School of Medicine of the University of Virginia at Charlottesville.

As the Thomas F. Boat era drew to an end in 1993 there was a cluster of significant gains and losses. First, Dr. Joseph M. Wiley joined the Department of Pediatrics and the PHO division as head of the pediatric component of the newly established bone marrow transplantation program at UNC-CH. He was recruited from the renowned oncology center of Johns Hopkins University School of Medicine in Baltimore, Maryland, where he had been assistant professor of pediatrics and of oncology since 1989. After Dr. Wiley received his MD from the University of Maryland School of Medicine at Baltimore in 1982, he completed his pediatric residency (1982–1985) and PHO fellowship (1985–1988) at Johns Hopkins Hospital. In 1988 he joined the faculty of the medical school there as an instructor with joint appointments in the Departments of Pediatrics and Oncology.

On the other hand, the departures from Chapel Hill of Drs. Jane and Richard Azizkhan in 1993 constituted major losses to UNC-CH in general and the PHO division in particular. They and their children moved to Buffalo, New York, primarily because Dr. Richard Azizkhan accepted a position there as the chief of pediatric surgery at Children's Hospital of Buffalo. Dr. Jane Azizkhan transferred her research program to Roswell Park Cancer Institute in Buffalo.

Finally, the end of the Boat era was signaled—as it was in the beginning—by an NCAA basketball championship for Carolina at New Orleans. This time the prize was achieved by a dramatic 77-71 victory over Michigan on April 5, 1993, and the star was a sophomore from Garner named Donald Williams. As always, the beat goes on!

HERBERT A. COOPER

FACULTY

Bryan, J. Hugh. BA, Univ NC, 1965; MD, Univ NC, 1969; Fellow/Inst, Ped, 1973; Asst Prof, Ped, 1974–78.

Cooper, Herbert A. BA, Univ Kansas, 1960; MD, Univ Kansas, 1964; Asst Prof, Ped and Pathol, 1974; Assoc Prof, Ped and Pathol, 1977; Prof, Ped and Pathol, 1985; Chief, Div Ped Hem/Onc, 1985–95.

Gold, Stuart H. BA, Vanderbilt, 1977; MD, Vanderbilt, 1981; Asst Prof, Ped, 1989.

Johnson, A. Myron. AB, Asbury College, 1955; MD, Vanderbilt, 1959; Asst Prof, Ped, 1970; Assoc Prof, Ped, 1976–78; Prof, Ped, 1989.

Jones, Gary R. BS, Oregon State, 1976; MD, Univ Oregon, 1980; Asst Prof, Ped, 1989.

McMillan, Campbell W. BS, Wake Forest College, 1948; MD, Bowman Gray, 1952; Asst Prof, Ped, 1963; Assoc Prof, Ped, 1968; Prof, Ped, 1972–91; Chief, Div Ped Hem/Onc, 1963–79; Chief, Div Ped Hematol, 1979–83.

Wells, Robert J. BA, Grinnell College, 1968; MD, Univ Calif at San Diego, 1972;

Asst Prof, Ped, 1980; Assoc Prof, Ped, 1987–88; Chief, Div Ped Hem/Onc, 1983–85.

Weston, Brent W. BA, Duke, 1981; MD, Duke, 1985; Asst Prof, Ped, 1992.

Whisnant, John K. AB, Duke, 1964; MD, Bowman Gray, 1968; Clin Asst Prof, Ped, 1976; Asst Prof, Ped, 1979; Clin Assoc Prof, Ped, 1981–86; Chief, Div Ped Immunol/Oncol, 1979–82.

Wiley, Joseph M. BA, Loyola College, 1978; MD, Univ Maryland, 1982; Assoc Prof, Ped, 1993; Chief, Div Ped Hem/Onc, 1995.

FELLOWS

Year	Name	Current Position
1972–73	John T. Benjamin, MD	Prof, Ped, Med College of Georgia
1973–74	John H. Bryan, MD	Dir, Dept of Radiation Oncol, Cape Fear Valley Med Ctr (Fayetteville, NC)
1975–77	Mary J. Freitag, MD	Homemaker (Madison, WI)
1975–77	Ronald B. May, MD	Assoc Prof, Ped, ECU School of Med
1976–78	Jean B. Belasco, MD	Clin Assoc Prof, Ped, Univ Penn School of Med
1978–80	William K. Hoots, MD	Assoc Prof, Ped, Univ Texas School of Med
1978–80	Melinda S. Snyder, MD	Attending Phys, Med Unit, John Umstead Hosp (Butner, NC)
1988–91	Cheryl A. Miller, MD	Asst Prof, Ped, Med College of Wisconsin
1993–	Paul E. Monahan, MD	In training, UNC-CH

Editors' Note: The 1990 meeting of the Denny Society was dedicated to the retirement of Dr. McMillan as an active faculty member. In response to this recognition he delivered the following talk. Its poignancy so impressed the editors that we thought it should be included in this history. We believe you will agree.

REFLECTIONS ON THE NATURAL HISTORY OF PROGRESS

by Campbell W. McMillan

During the period from my entry into the Bowman Gray School of Medicine in 1948 to my winding down in pediatrics at Chapel Hill in 1990, it has

Cam
McMillan
with an
admirer

been my good fortune to have a ringside seat at a drama of medical progress
more spectacular than anything I could have ever imagined at the beginning.
Specifically, in the field of coagulation and its clinical disorders, which I
entered as a hematology fellow with Dr. Louis K. Diamond in Boston during
1958–1961, the treatment of hemophilia in its various forms has changed in
a mind-boggling fashion. In the case of classic hemophilia, treatment with
fresh frozen plasma has given way to the use of factor VIII extracted by monoclonal antibodies and clinical trials with recombinant DNA factor VIII
secreted by Chinese hamster ovary cells are nearing completion.[1,2,3] Other
such products are waiting in the wings.[4] In the course of it all, half of our
overall hemophilia population and a majority of persons with severe classic
hemophilia were infected with the Human Immunodeficiency Virus (HIV)

1. Brinkhous K. M.: Hemophilia. *Bull NY Acad Med* 30:325, 1954.

2. Zimmerman T. S.: Purification of factor VIII by monoclonal antibody affinity
chromotography. *Sem Hematol* 25:25, 1988.

3. White G. C. II, McMillan C. W., Kingdon H. S. et al.: Use of recombinant antihemophilic factor in the treatment of two patients with classic hemophilia. *N Engl J
Med* 320:166, 1989.

4. Kim H. C., McMillan C. W., White G. C. et al.: Clinical experience of a new
monoclonal antibody purified factor IX: half-life, recovery, and safety in patients with
hemophilia B. *Sem Hematol* 27:30, 1990.

between about 1975 and 1985.[5] This outcome was unquestionably influenced by our well-intentioned but ill-fated efforts to treat hemophilic patients aggressively. Fortunately, the window of infection began to close in 1984 when HIV was discovered and appropriate steps could be taken to deal with this truly nasty virus.[6,7] Also, spectacular advances in our understanding of the molecular biology of clotting factors at that time set the stage for development and provision of highly purified and essentially risk-free products for treatment of our patients.[8,9] The bottom line of all this is that the prospect for a genetic cure of hemophilia is no longer a pipe dream as we close out this century and head for the next one. Furthermore, as I am sure you realize, what I have outlined about hemophilia is merely a biopsy of scientific advance as a whole.

And so, with this brief introduction as a background, let me ask you this: What is progress? For the purpose of this discourse with you, I choose to define progress as a natural process in which human beings variously convert the unknown to the known. Because this process occurs over time, it would appear logical to presume that progress is characterized by a natural evolutionary history of which we catch only a relatively brief glimpse during our lifetimes. On the basis of this brief glimpse, what can we guess about the origins and destiny of progress? More importantly, what does progress have to tell us, if anything, about the way we organize our daily lives?

Before we address these questions, let us examine the notion that progress is mediated by an act in which a human being somehow manages to extract from the unknown a fragment that proceeds to be known. I strongly suggest that these acts are not the exclusive province of persons who are engaged in research but rather are the property of everybody. These acts range from the very large and important discoveries that may lead to a Nobel Prize all the way to the very small and unnoticed exercises of daily problem-solving by the likes of butchers and bakers and candlestick-makers—and of course, all pedi-

---

5. Johnson R. E., Lawrence D. N., Evatt B. L. et al.: Acquired immunodeficiency syndrome among patients attending hemophilia treatment centers and mortality experience of hemophiliacs in the United States. *Am J Epidemiol* 121:797, 1985.

6. Galo R. C., Salahuddin S. Z., Popovic et al.: Frequent detection and isolation of cytopathic retroviruses (HTLV-III) from patients with AIDS and at risk for AIDS. *Science* 224:500, 1984.

7. Vilmer E., Barre-Sinoussi F., Rouzioux C. et al.: Isolation of a new lymphotropic retrovirus from two siblings with hemophilia A, one with AIDS. *Lancet* 1:753, 1984.

8. Smith K. J., Lusher J. M., Cohen A. R. et al.: Initial clinical experience with a new pasteurized monoclonal antibody purified factor VIIIC. *Sem Hematol* 27:25, 1990.

9. Kaufman R. J., Wasley L. C., and Dorner A. J.: Synthesis, processing, and secretion of recombinant human factor VIII expressed in mammalian cells. *J Biol Chem* 263:6352, 1988.

atricians! Thus, I suggest that the act of converting the unknown to the known is a fundamental characteristic of the human condition and is, collectively, the central ingredient of all human progress. Furthermore, I suggest that the process of wrestling with the unknown is motivated by an instinct that is so important that it fully matches our more recognized instincts for self-preservation and propagation of the species.

How might we describe the natural history of progress with respect to its apparent movement and the reaction of us human beings to it? It would be fun to define the kinetics of progress if there were enough meaningful data to do such a thing. Intuitively, I suspect such an attempt would be doomed by semantic obstacles. Nonetheless, in my lifetime progress has proceeded with a clearly exponential enlargement of knowledge. There seem to be at least two components to the enlargement: a relatively steady state of progress alternating with bursts of acceleration. The bursts of activity have been particularly impressive and have occurred both in connection with response to major emergencies and in the aftermath of major scientific discoveries. Salient examples of emergencies that have stimulated progress include World War II and the advent of AIDS, the admitted devastation of these events notwithstanding. As for spontaneous scientific discoveries, representative examples in the area of coagulation research include the development of the partial thromboplastin time by Langdell, Wagner, and Brinkhous[10] here in Chapel Hill in 1953 and the elegant discovery of cryoprecipitate by Pool and Shannon[11] at Stanford in 1965. Within the past fifteen years the era of molecular biology has truly come of age with the likes of techniques for raising monoclonal antibodies and for direct analysis of genes.[12,13] These recent breathtaking discoveries have not only revolutionized the field of coagulation but the rest of biological science as well.

As I look back over the years since I came to Chapel Hill in 1963, I can give personal testimony to the accelerating pace of progress that has occurred. After I finished my hematology fellowship with Dr. Diamond in 1961, for personal reasons I joined Bill Purcell in practice in Laurinburg, NC. I had a marvelous time in practice but the lure of academics proved to be more than I could resist. Accordingly, after appropriate negotiations with Floyd Denny, I gratefully accepted his invitation to join the Department here. Thereafter, I

---

10. Langdell R. D., Wagner R. H., and Brinkhous K. M.: Effect of antihemophilic factor in one-stage clotting tests. *J Lab Clin Med* 41:637, 1953.

11. Pool J. G., and Shannon A. E.: Production of high-potency concentrates of antihemophilic globulin in a closed-bag system: assay in vitro and in vivo. *N Engl J Med* 273:1443, 1965.

12. Kohler G. and Milstein C.: Continuous cultures of fused cells secreting antibody of predefined specificity. *Nature* 256:495, 1975.

13. Southern E.: Detection of specific sequences among DNA fragments separated by gel electrophoreses. *J Mol Biol* 98:503, 1975.

was able to apply for and get my first NIH research grant on the basis of fellowship skills that were *still* competitive after a hiatus of about eighteen months. In 1990 there is absolutely no way you could go into hibernation for a year or so and expect to pick up where you left off. You can feel the train moving faster.

Now let us consider how we human beings regard the progress that is all around us. Let me touch on two issues that are interesting to me. First, at most individual points in time progress tends to be overshadowed by the appearance of disaster and chaos. Take right now, for example. We are in the process of having to reach way down within ourselves to pay the piper for a catastrophic joy ride in which our country has been caught up during the past decade. And no sooner had we become firm allies of Russia and the countries of eastern Europe than we found ourselves drawn into a strange and dangerous caper in the Middle East. But, folks, it is always that way. In the same way that you cannot appreciate the curvature of the earth without watching a ship gradually disappear over the horizon, you cannot appreciate progress fully unless you take stock of things over a period of time. Our present problems notwithstanding, I believe the natural history of progress tells us that we will get through this in due course and reap the harvest of better things, with or without a war. A second issue regarding the perception of progress by us humans has to do with a tendency for us to be afraid of it even though, as I have already assured you, we are all a central part of the very progress that some of us fear. As you know full well, human beings have assigned the term "God" to that part of the unknown around and within us which we have variously chosen to approach through reverence and worship rather than scientific exploration or customary problem-solving. There is no doubt that many look with fear and trembling on the outcome of fooling around with the power of the atom, the cloning of genes and that sort of thing. On a lighter note, I like what Jim Croce had to say about confronting higher powers: "You don't tug on Superman's cape, you don't spit into the wind, you don't pull the mask off that ol' Lone Ranger and you don't mess around with Jim!"[14] More specifically, the coming of age of ethics as a discipline has, without question, paralleled the acceleration of progress in medical science over the last three decades. Medical ethics has arisen in connection with a generally perceived need to deal responsibly with the tension existing between rapid medical progress and our limited understanding of human life. When you move into uncharted territory, it follows that new ground rules need to be developed.

To illustrate my point let me share with you a statement that summarizes the issue at hand unusually well, in my opinion. This statement is taken from a 1976 monograph entitled *The Doctor as Judge of Who Shall Live and Who*

---

14. Croce J.: You Don't Mess Around with Jim. In *Jim Croce Photographs and Memories*. Lifesong Records (No. 35010), Cashwest Productions, New York, 1974.

Shall Die by Helmut Thielicke,[15] a distinguished authority on theological ethics from the University of Hamburg.

> Medicine has made such tremendous advances in the modern period that there seems to be almost no limit to what it can do. This very fact raises a host of fundamental questions, chief of which is probably the question concerning the nature and destiny of man himself. In the field of medicine this question becomes quite specific: Is there something about man that dare not be changed—something in his very nature that dare not be violated—if he is to remain human? And if there is this fixed and inviolable something, then to what extent dare we manipulate man? To what extent dare we implement the technical capacity of modern medicine to transform him, to change the way he functions, indeed to alter his genetic constitution?. . .
>
> It is important for us to understand that, as regards the control and management of our enhanced knowledge and refined technical capabilities, we stand indeed at a historical juncture. . . .

You will recall that I earlier defined progress as a natural process in which we human beings variously convert the unknown to the known, a process that has a natural history of which we catch a glimpse. If that is true (and I fully recognize that it may not be), then let me ask you this: Why are we driven to convert the unknown to the known?

Without the benefit of any serious scholarly pursuit on this question on my part (at least not yet), I submit that the need to convert the unknown to the known, like the need to propagate the species, is a fundamental property of all protoplasm. I further submit that this property has steadily evolved over all of time and has clearly achieved its highest expression in us human beings. Is it possible that this property is recapitulated, at least in part, in the natural and wondrous evolution of curiosity in children that we pediatricians are privileged to see every day?

Reasons for such instincts as self-preservation and propagation of the species are intuitively easy to understand. Now, if the urge to explore and understand the unknown is also an instinct as I am suggesting, what—may I ask—is the fundamental purpose of this instinct? Let me suggest three possibilities. First, converting the unknown to the known may promote a sense of safety. A monster in a child's room may be quickly banished when it is learned that it is only the shadow of a tree limb, waving in a gentle breeze outside the child's window on a bright, moonlit night. The fact is, the unknown is capable of creating serious disturbance in anyone's mind. Without any question, a major source of the power resting with any physician is his or her endowment with the authority to define and explain a given clinical problem, quite

---

15. Thielicke H.: *The Doctor as Judge of Who Shall Live and Who Shall Die.* Fortress Press, Philadelphia, 1976.

apart from whatever treatment may be given. Second, converting the unknown to the known may be a means of overcoming our mortality. Although we properly resist preoccupation with the death that will eventually come to each of us, the fact is that we know it will come in due course. Steps for trying to preserve oneself both now and even in the hereafter and for having children through reproduction or adoption are obvious instinctual ways to deal with this problem. I suggest that successful exploration of the unknown is another fundamental way that we seek to achieve immortality. In this regard, I would like to tell the whole world, especially those who are depressed because they feel insignificant, that the act of converting the unknown to the known does not have to be big in order to be important. Indeed, I like to think that a single transaction characterized by heightened perception such as genuine hugging of a loved one may be more than enough to leave behind, even if it is never recorded anywhere. Third, converting the unknown to the known may have no purpose apart from being a central necessity for the natural history of progress. I am fascinated by a memorable line from the movie *Breaking the Sound Barrier* which I think I saw while I was in medical school. I don't recall who was in it. Anyway, at one point the daughter says to the scientist, "Daddy, why do you want to break the sound barrier?" He quietly replies, "Because it has to be done." Maybe that is all there is to it.

So much for possible reasons why we are led to come to grips with the unknown. How do we go about it? Let me briefly touch on certain obvious approaches. The various religions and mythologies that have proliferated throughout all of recorded time represent an approach based on worship. Genuine agnostics appear to be well outnumbered by variously faithful followers of countless religions. Literature and the fine arts, including painting, sculpture, music, dancing and drama, represent—as I see it—an approach to the unknown based on enlargement of our understanding of human existence with all its goodness and badness, its hopes and its fears. There is no question: Genuine art is truly capable of seizing one's mind and soul. By the way, with respect to seizing of one's mind and soul, I would definitely add Carolina basketball. My family and I can directly attest to the certainty that Dean Smith has provided a genuine art form for us and for many others throughout his years at Chapel Hill. Finally, scholarly investigation, including medical research, is a particularly obvious means for wrestling with the unknown. By way of synthesizing all of this, I pass on to you the admonition of Max Planck in his essay "The Meaning and Limits of Exact Science"[16] that we explore the explorable and venerate the unexplorable. But let me reiterate my firm conviction that the urge to come to grips with the unknown is a property of everybody, not just monks, sculptors, and scientists.

Now let me ask you this: Can you identify in your mind an act of suc-

---

16. Planck M.: The meaning and limits of exact science. In Planck M.: *Scientific Autobiography and Other Papers*. Philosophical Library, New York, 1949.

cessful exploration of the unknown? Mind you, I am talking about daily problem-solving just as much as a research project you may have carried out during a summer in medical school. Let me suggest two basic components of the process that was carried out, whatever your specific act might have been. First, there was a burst of insight that may have been spontaneous, derived from someone else, or acquired at some point in a deliberate search for something. The burst of insight, whatever its source, is characterized by a sense of asking the right question and of heading in the right direction. It is a good feeling and I am sure that all of you have felt it and know what I am talking about. Second, the insight is translated into substance. In classic terms this second stage is expressed in disciplined scholarship, quality craftsmanship, and determined goal-seeking behavior. Whether the task is major or minor, this stage simply consists of getting the job done, preferably done right.

And now, to wind down, let me summarize certain favorable and unfavorable factors that might influence the outcome of the natural history of progress with respect to us human beings. On the good side, there is unmistakable evidence that human knowledge expands continuously. Indeed, the expansion appears to be exponential at the present time. Furthermore, if the unknown is infinite and human penetration of the unknown is inevitable, then it follows that the potential for enlargement of human knowledge is also infinite.

On the other hand, there appear to be some definite obstacles to progress as well. After all, the unknown is not readily penetrated in terms of really major discoveries. I suggest that the bursts of insight that I mentioned earlier come more through random events than through deliberate searching. Above all, we human beings are all fraught with limitations, characterized—I would say—by about 95–99 percent foolishness and no more than 1–5 percent genius. For the most part, our foolishness (which may actually be a useful buffer of sorts) is expressed in an endless variety of wasteful though non-violent ways as in the likes of too many distraught people in our society, Saddam Hussein, or the chilling Grand Inquisitor described in *The Brothers Karamazov* by Dostoyevsky.[17] And so, where will the natural history of progress take us all? I have assured you that the potential for successful human conquest of the unknown is infinite. Does it follow that human beings in generations to come will not only know more than we do but also be less foolish than we are? Is it possible that the exponential growth of our knowledge is actually a prelude to our self-destruction like one of Mr. Phelps's tapes in the recent television series *Mission Impossible*? If we are not destined to self-destruct, will enlargement of our knowledge ever be matched by enlargement of the human spirit? Where does love fit into all of this?

I do not know where humanity is heading. But I am immensely grateful

---

17. Dostoyevsky, F.: *The Brothers Karamazov*. North Point Press, San Francisco, 1990.

for being alive in spectacular times and for being me instead of many other possibilities that I can think of. Actually, as I have said earlier, I do not believe that the world will self-destruct, I regard our current problems as more or less par for the course, and I have all the faith in the world that the natural history of progress will take future human beings into marvels that we cannot now fully envision. But even in those days, I guarantee that persons will be complaining about problems and feeling that the world is about to come to an end. The French author Alphonse Karr[18] said it best back in 1849: "Plus ça change, plus c'est la même chose," which being translated is to say, "The more things change, the more things stay the same."

Finally, in closing, let me remind you that 1990 is the year of Ryan White and Jim Henson as well as Saddam Hussein. When Elton John[19] sang and played "Skyline Pigeon" at the memorial service for Ryan White I could feel a chunk of the unknown break loose in my mind through a surge of revelation about the power of the human spirit. And, if you listen carefully, you can get the same kind of revelation from Kermit the Frog:[20]

> It's not easy bein' green;
> Having to spend each day the color of the leaves,
> When I think it could be nicer bein' red, or yellow, or gold—
> Or something more colorful like that.
> It's not easy bein' green.
> It seems you blend in with so many other ordinary things.
> And people tend to pass you over 'cause you're not standing out
> Like flashy sparkles in the water—
> Or stars in the sky.
> But green's the color of spring
> And green can be cool and friendly-like.
> And green can be big like a mountain, or important like a river,
> Or tall like a tree.
> When green is all there is to be
> It could make you wonder why; but why wonder, why wonder?
> I'm green and it'll do fine. It's beautiful!
> And I think it's what I wanna be.

18. Karr A.: Les Guepes, 1849 (Jan). In Bliss A. F.: *Dictionary of Foreign Words and Phrases*, E. P. Dutton, New York, 1966.

19. John E.: Skyline Pigeon. In *Elton John Here and There*, MCA Records (No. MCA-2197), Universal City, California, 1976.

20. *Bein' Green*, words and music by Joe Raposo. © 1970 Jonico Music, Inc. All Rights Reserved. Used by permission. Warner Bros. Publications U.S. Inc., Miami, FL 33014.

CHAPTER TWENTY-ONE

Infectious Diseases

HISTORY OF THE DIVISION, 1960–1993

THIS section highlights the very extensive and productive history of the pediatric infectious disease division during the years that Denny and later Boat served as chairs of the Department. The material is organized into segments dealing with the early development and early years of the division, some special study resources in Chapel Hill, research in the division, influence of the division on other programs, and the faculty and trainees.

Development and Early Years of the Division

A history of the pediatric infectious disease division for 1960–1993 would not be complete without mention of the role of infectious diseases in the Department between 1952–1960 when Dr. Edward Curnen was chairman. This is well chronicled by Judson Van Wyk in chapter 2, "Research during the Curnen Years." In that chapter Van Wyk describes Curnen's career in infectious diseases at the Rockefeller Institute and at Yale, first in bacterial infections and then in viral infections, especially the enteroviruses. After coming to the University of North Carolina Curnen, with the help of Ms. Eru Tanabe, established a laboratory for the study of enteroviruses. This would be the primary site of infectious disease research during the Curnen years. Funds were received from the National Foundation for Infantile Paralysis and the National Institutes of Health for a study of the role of viruses in aseptic meningitis, a study exploring the feasibility of vaccinating against measles, and an investigation of the clinical manifestations of coxsackie virus infections. Harry Meyer, later to become well known for developing the rubella vaccine and as director of the Bureau of Biologics of the Food and Drug

Administration of the U.S. Public Health Service, was recruited to the pediatric house staff and participated in Curnen's studies. John Arnold, recruited to the pediatric faculty in 1957 after a fellowship with Dr. John Enders, also participated in these investigations. Arnold remained on the pediatric faculty until several years after Denny's arrival, when he moved to Brown University. Van Wyk summarizes the salutary effort of these early years on the subsequent development of infectious disease research as follows: "There is little doubt, however, that the research thrust in infectious diseases during the Curnen years laid a strong foundation for the research in infectious disease that was brought into the Department by the recruitment of Floyd Denny as chairman of the Department of Pediatrics in 1960."

Curnen left Chapel Hill in the summer of 1960, but Denny, although appointed chairman on November 1, 1960, did not make the move to Chapel Hill until January 1, 1961. The press of departmental duties precluded any research activities on his part until the arrival of Wallace A. Clyde, Jr. in the summer of 1961. In the meantime the virus laboratory remained in operation under the direction of Dr. Arnold, though at a reduced level of productivity. The arrival of Clyde, who had been a research fellow with Denny at Western Reserve University (now Case Western Reserve University) School of Medicine in Cleveland, marked the beginning of a new era of infectious disease research at the University of North Carolina. First, though, more about the backgrounds of Clyde and Denny that prepared them for this venture.

Denny received his medical education at Vanderbilt University at the Army's expense during World War II. Thus, in 1948 following his pediatric residency he reentered the Army as a medical officer to repay his service debt. For reasons still unknown to him he was assigned to the Department of Preventive Medicine at Case Western Reserve University to "study acute rheumatic fever." It was there that he came under the tutelage of Drs. Charles Rammelkamp and John Dingle and began his long association with Dr. Lewis Wannamaker. After six months of laboratory training in Cleveland in Rammelkamp's laboratory, Wannamaker and Denny, along with another young medical officer, William R. Brink, assisted Rammelkamp in establishing the Streptococcal Diseases Laboratory of the Armed Forces Epidemiological Board at Warren Air Force Base in Cheyenne, Wyoming. This laboratory was to stay in operation for five years and was the site of much of the research that clarified the epidemiology, clinical manifestations, and antibiotic management of streptococcal upper respiratory infections and rheumatic fever. Paramount among these accomplishments were the studies that demonstrated that adequate treatment of streptococcal infections prevented the occurrence of rheumatic fever; the laboratory received the Lasker Award in 1954 for these studies. Denny served as the assistant director of the laboratory under Rammelkamp from 1949 to 1951; Rammelkamp maintained his home office and laboratory in Cleveland, spending approximately one week each month in Wyoming. These administrative duties were important as learning experiences for Denny's future chairmanship. Denny left the Streptococcus Laboratory in

September 1951 and went to the University of Minnesota to work with Dr. Lewis Thomas, then a research professor of pediatrics in the Heart Hospital. Research experience there consisted of further work on streptococcal antibodies and on the Shwartzman phenomenon. After two years in Minnesota he returned to Vanderbilt, where he had more clinical duties but was able to continue his interest in the clinical and epidemiological aspects of streptococcal infections. After two years the chance to apprentice himself to Dr. Harry Ginsberg in virology and to be the assistant to Dr. John Dingle, who was president of the Armed Forces Epidemiological Board, lured Denny back to the Department of Preventive Medicine of Western Reserve University, where he remained until his move to North Carolina. Laboratory research was directed toward the basic aspects of the infection of cells with adenoviruses. Considerable experience was also gained in the now famous Cleveland Family Study during the 1957–1958 epidemic of influenza; over 50 percent of the Family Study population was infected during that time. Denny remained active in clinical infectious diseases at Babies' and Children's Hospital and had an exciting one-half day each week working with Dr. Ben Spock in the pediatric family clinic.

Of special importance to the subsequent time in North Carolina were the experiences at Western Reserve University with Dr. Wallace A. Clyde, Jr. and Dr. Charles I. Sheaffer. Wally Clyde, a former medical student and pediatric resident at Vanderbilt, entered a fellowship with Denny in 1959 after a tour of Navy duty and was lured to North Carolina in the summer of 1961. This gifted researcher was destined to be a major factor in the division of infectious diseases and in the Department of Pediatrics at North Carolina. Charlie Sheaffer was a pediatric resident at Babies' and Children's Hospital. His abilities as a pediatric clinician were so outstanding that he was also lured to North Carolina, where he also played a key role in infectious diseases and in clinical practice.

When Clyde arrived in Cleveland in 1959 he was given the task of sorting out the relationship of the "Eaton agent" to an agent which had been demonstrated by work of the Commission on Acute Respiratory Diseases to cause a type of "atypical" pneumonia in volunteers at Fort Bragg in Fayetteville, North Carolina. At that time the Eaton agent was thought to be a virus, but its relationship to human disease was controversial. Work by Liu using recently described fluorescent antibody techniques developed by Coons and Kaplan had provided a means of studying antibody responses to infections with the agent. These methods were extremely cumbersome, requiring growth of the organism in embryonated eggs, preparing frozen sections of the lungs and trachea and localization of specific antigen by fluorescent antibodies. Fluorescence microscopy is in common use today but at that time was very difficult, including the building of very crude fluorescent microscopes. Clyde proved to be unusually adept in the laboratory. His studies clarified the relationship of infections with the Eaton agent to the development of cold hemagglutinins which were shown to be related in a positive way to the sever-

Wally Clyde

ity of illness. These studies also propelled Clyde into the forefront of studies of the Eaton agent which was shortly shown by Marmion to be a pleuropneumonia-like organism (PPLO), now called mycoplasma. While still in Cleveland Clyde demonstrated that the mycoplasma could be grown in tissue culture, thus considerably simplifying appropriate laboratory studies. Clyde continued his work with this mycoplasma, now called *Mycoplasma pneumoniae*, after moving to North Carolina. His work formed the basis for much of the work of the infectious disease division over the next three decades. (The nature of this work will be described in detail later in this history.) During his Cleveland fellowship Clyde became familiar with the laboratory techniques of respiratory virology from studies taking place in Denny's laboratory. Thus, he was prepared to play a major role in establishing at North Carolina a laboratory for studying the major respiratory pathogens and their relationship to infections. (This will be described in detail in a later section.)

With the arrival of Clyde in Chapel Hill in the summer of 1961 the "new" infectious disease "division" began to take place. It was several years before a formal division was formed but the infrastructure was being established. Newly described techniques for growing mycoplasmas in artificial media were put into place, along with a new method for their identification developed by Clyde. The virus and tissue culture laboratory was adapted to the respiratory viruses, and a bacteriology section for studying *Streptococcus pneumoniae* and *Haemophilus influenzae* was started. These endeavors were facilitated by the very able assistance of a research associate, J. B. Kirkman. While the laboratory was being developed Charlie Sheaffer was getting established as part-time director of the outpatient clinic and in half-time practice with the only practicing pediatrician in Chapel Hill at that time, Dr. Robert Senior. Dr. W. Paul Glezen, recruited to the pediatric house staff by Curnen, shared the chief residency with Dr. Frank French (1961–1962) and spent his six months working with Curnen in the enterovirus laboratory. As a former Epidemio-

Paul Glezen

logical Intelligence Service (EIS) officer in the U.S. Public Health Service he was interested in respiratory infections and was an early member of the budding group. Thus, all of the pieces of the future infectious disease division were in place.

The Division from the Early 1960s to 1992

The arrival of Clyde, Denny, and Sheaffer in Chapel Hill by 1961, and the presence of Glezen on the house staff, heralded a new era in pediatric infectious disease at the University of North Carolina. Teaching programs for students, house staff, and fellows were developed, as well as provisions for infectious diseases services for the children admitted to the ambulatory clinic and inpatient wards at NC Memorial Hospital. Research into the basic, epidemiological, and clinical aspects of acute respiratory infections, however, was the principal focus of the division during this time. The following sections will describe various aspects of the division of pediatric infectious diseases over the ensuing years.

SPECIAL STUDY RESOURCES

Laboratories. The research laboratory was always the center for infectious diseases activities. Clyde's office was always immediately adjacent to the work areas. Although Denny's office was located in the departmental suite in a different location he spent most of his lunches and as much free time as possible with the division. Over time the laboratories were located first in Mac-Nider Building, next in the Medical Sciences Research Wing, and finally in its present location in the Burnett-Womack building. This last space was the first that was planned completely by the new division personnel and was designed so that it was in close proximity to the Pediatric Department offices, allowing Denny access to the division. Laboratory space was also developed in the Frank Porter Graham Center, located first in temporary quarters on Cameron Avenue and then in the present location on the 15-501/54 bypass. (Further details of these laboratories and the accompanying office space will be included in descriptions of division research.)

Chapel Hill Pediatrics. A private pediatric practice in Chapel Hill—Chapel Hill Pediatrics—was the site over many years for the study of acute respiratory infections in nonhospitalized children. The practice was started in 1959 by Dr. Robert Senior. Dr. Charles Sheaffer joined the practice in 1961, spend-

Charlie Sheaffer

Meade Christian

ing half time in the practice and half time coordinating the outpatient clinic in the Department of Pediatrics. The series of clinical studies was begun in 1964, with these two pediatricians making the clinical observations; the laboratory observations were performed in the division laboratory. This was an exceedingly rewarding venture for the practitioners and the academicians. Seminal observations were made about the epidemiological and clinical aspects of acute upper and lower respiratory infections which led to many publications in journals and in textbooks (these will be reviewed in the next section). For the practitioners, their practice was enriched with the development of a new approach to clinical practice. For example, the pediatrician was able to tell parents that their six-month-old baby with bronchiolitis almost certainly had a respiratory syncytial virus infection, which could be confirmed in a few days. Dr. Gus Conley joined the practice in 1966 and Dr. Meade Christian in 1973, rounding out the group who worked with the division in these studies over twelve years. Later, the data took on new importance. Work was begun on the long-term consequences of respiratory infections in early childhood. Patients from the practice who had specific respiratory syndromes due to defined agents years before could be recalled for evaluation.

North Carolina Memorial Hospital Children's Ward. The seventh-floor pediatric ward of NC Memorial Hospital was the site of early studies on children with acute lower respiratory infections severe enough to require hospitalization. These studies showed clearly the epidemiological differences in mild and severe disease in small children and, along with the private practice studies, helped form the basis for innovative clinical management schemes. The studies of hospitalized children with respiratory infections were not pursued as vigorously (though over four hundred cases were studied) as were those on infections in nonhospitalized children, reflecting clearly the interests of the research team in this important part of respiratory infections. (The reported studies on hospitalized children will be described below.)

UNC Student Health Service. The UNC Student Health Service was also the site of studies on acute respiratory infections in college-age students. At that time this service was located on the second floor of the Old Clinic Building in space now occupied by the outpatient cardiology service. Although these studies resulted in several publications and interesting observations, infections in this group of patients were not pursued as vigorously as were those in younger children.

Frank Porter Graham Day Care Center. When the Frank Porter Graham Child Development Center was established in 1966, a day care center was opened for the study of the development of very young children brought together in this organized way. The division immediately seized upon this opportunity to organize a systematic study of acute respiratory infections in these children who were six weeks to five years of age and separated into groups by age of about twelve children. The power of research in this setting was not the numbers of subjects to study, but that the same child could be observed and studied repeatedly over time, both when ill and when well. Dr. W. Paul Glezen became the first director of divisional activities at the FPG Center in 1966. He was followed shortly by Dr. Frank Loda and then Dr. Albert Collier, who has directed these activities since 1972. (Special attention is given later in this history to the scientific productivity of this endeavor.)

The Gravely Children's Chest Disease Ward. Children hospitalized because of or with infectious diseases occupied beds on the pediatric isolation unit or on one of the other children's wards where they could be isolated adequately. The division staff did not have primary responsibility for these children (unless they were the regular attending pediatrician) but acted as consultants. The exception to this was the Gravely Children's Chest Disease Ward. This was a ten-bed unit located on the first floor of what was then the Gravely Sanatorium. This service grew out of Dr. Annie Scott's 1950s interest in childhood tuberculosis and cystic fibrosis. Dr. Paul Glezen seized upon Dr. Scott's interest, and with the help of Mr. Ben Clark, administrator of the North Carolina Sanatorium System, designed and had the first-floor area remodeled to house this service. Patients could be hospitalized here for extended periods at very nominal cost. Availability of patients over time made possible various research pursuits, such as quantitative bacteriology in cystic fibrosis and differential antigen skin testing in patients with mycobacterial infections. This was an ideal situation at the time and the opportunity to have its own service unit in a small and easily manageable ward provided an ideal working situation until the Gravely Hospital was closed as a state-operated tuberculosis and chest hospital in 1974. (The Gravely ward is also described in greater detail later in this section.)

The Pediatric Isolation Unit. Before Dr. Curnen left UNC in 1960 he had obtained contributions from the Robbie Page Memorial of the Sigma Sigma Sigma sorority to use as start-up funds to construct an isolation ward on the west end of the seventh floor of NC Memorial Hospital. This Sigma Sigma Sigma gift was later augmented by funds from the University of North Carolina, the North Carolina Medical Care Commission, Dr. and Mrs. John F. Lynch, Jr., and the Women's Auxiliary of the North Carolina Memorial Hospital to build a ten-bed unit consisting of single-bed rooms each with toilet facilities, air-conditioning, and exhaust systems designed so that the most contagious of diseases could be contained. Admissions to this isolation unit were not controlled by the infectious disease division; beds were used to hospitalize children with noninfectious diseases needing single-bed rooms when there were vacancies. The division staff did act as consultants regarding proper isolation techniques and care of individual patients. Over the years the use of the unit for isolation of children with contagious diseases has diminished with the decline in the occurrence of these infections, but the unit is still utilized frequently for isolation purposes.

TEACHING IN THE DIVISION

From the division's inception its staff assumed responsibility for the educational programs for pediatric infectious diseases for medical students, house staff, fellows, and practicing pediatricians. Division staff assisted in the lecture and laboratory courses for preclinical science students. Teaching of the third-year students while they were on their pediatric rotation was done in small groups or individually at the bedside. For many years Dr. Robert Senior held frequent sessions with third-year students when he would discuss the many values and joys of office bacteriology. Teaching of the house staff was intense. In addition to the usual contact with staff from the division, Denny held intake rounds with the resident staff three mornings each week and with the entire house staff on Saturday mornings, during which there was always emphasis on infectious diseases. Much of the infectious diseases teaching was incorporated into patient care rounds (described in the next section on clinical services). The teaching of fellows was done individually and during the almost daily luncheon sessions when research and clinical problems were discussed. Continuing education of pediatric infectious diseases was incorporated into the usual departmental activities in that endeavor.

PEDIATRIC INFECTIOUS DISEASE CLINICAL SERVICES

The pediatric infectious disease clinical service after 1960 had patient care duties significantly different from those of some other subspecialties. The cardiologist had patients with heart problems that required his expertise, as did the nephrologist, the neurologist, and the endocrinologist. While some children were admitted to the hospital solely with an infectious disease problem the great majority of infectious disease problems occurred in patients with other significant basic problems. Thus, the division was not faced with the management of a large cadre of patients to be cared for in hospital or in the outpatient department. Attempts to establish an active pediatric infectious disease outpatient clinic were never very successful. The number of inpatients with infectious disease problems, such as the interpretation of culture results and the proper choice of antibiotics, however, was always quite large. Thus the greatest clinical service provided by the division was on a consulting basis. There was one exception to this. The Gravely ward for children with chest problems was solely the responsibility of the division staff and for six years this unique service was a significant addition to the care of this special group of children. (This unit will be described in detail below.) Consulting duties were assumed in rotations of one month by the infectious disease faculty, accompanied usually by a pediatric resident and one or more fourth-year students. Daily routines usually consisted of an early morning review of patients and culture results and patients from the preceding day in the clinic, bacteriology rounds in the laboratory, patient rounds on the wards, and consulting on patients on other services when requested. Telephone consulting with practicing physicians was always a significant duty as well. Particularly difficult cases were always reviewed by the entire group at the luncheon meeting.

Pediatric Infectious Disease Research 1960–1993

Throughout its history the area of greatest emphasis by the infectious disease division has been research. This has consisted of a balance of basic, clinical, and applied studies. The following section provides a sketch of the research activity, divided into that which took place during the Denny years and that which took place during the Boat years.

THE DENNY YEARS

The MacNider Days. The research space allocated to the infectious disease division consisted in 1961 of an area that had been used initially by the first pediatric chairman, Dr. Edward Curnen, for his enterovirus studies. The location was on fourth-floor MacNider, where today the offices of the pediatric hematology-oncology division may be found. The largest of three rooms was a square area divided roughly in half with filing cabinets to create an office with two desks and a long bench bearing two homemade glass isolation hoods (open front, ultraviolet lights), centrifuges, assorted tables, and storage cabinets. A glassed-in cubicle served for sterile cell and tissue work. An adjacent half-laboratory was equipped for nonsterile operations, including microscopy and serology. The last room was a utility area containing a steam-operated manual autoclave, an egg incubator, racks for mouse boxes, large cans for animal feed, a deep sink for glassware washing, and containers for disposal of contaminated materials. It was said that Curnen had planned this area so that it would be self-contained and well away from the traffic of Mac-Nider Building, to safeguard work with cell cultures and provide containment for the enteroviruses being studied, including poliomyelitis and coxsackie viruses.

A visitor entering the main room in those days in early 1961 might encounter John Arnold at his desk, his technician, Judy, at work isolating enteroviruses from clinical specimens, and Curnen's technician, Eru Tanabe, busily packing data sheets and virus stocks for moving to New York City. To be left behind, under a desk, was a battered valise containing all the raw data concerning a survey for enteroviruses in North Carolina. Paul Glezen had assisted with this study and continued to come to the laboratory to work on it during the half of the year he shared the chief residency with Frank French. Often diverse faculty members would visit for consultations, particularly Bill Blythe and Chris Fordham of the medicine nephrology division, who were attempting to maintain renal tissues in a culture system. These discussions, usually held in the isolation cubicle, were wide ranging but occasionally touched on the subject at hand.

On his arrival in Chapel Hill in July 1961, Wallace Clyde was met by the scene described above. He set about to organize and store various materials mailed or hand-carried from Case Western Reserve University in Cleveland, including seed samples of the parainfluenza viruses, a variety of adenovirus types, chick embryo passage samples of the Eaton atypical pneumonia agent, immunofluorescence reagents, rabbit antiviral sera, and a collection of his and Denny's data books. Denny had arranged for some major equipment purchases so that these would be on hand for immediate use. A state-of-the-art Zeiss photomicroscope with ultraviolet, brightfield, darkfield, and phase contrast lighting was the centerpiece of this equipment. This microscope served the infectious disease division for about twenty-five years, finally succumbing to the lack of replacement parts and accessories. The other major item was the Harris microtome cryostat (described by Coons et al. in 1951) for preparation of frozen tissue sections. This purchase introduced Clyde to the North Carolina state bureaucracy. Investigating a long delay in shipment of the cryostat, he learned that, as in standard purchasing procedure, the machine had been advertised in quest of three bids. This was rather futile in this case, since the unit was custom built by the Harris Refrigeration Co. of Boston, and there were no distributors.

After a period of adjustment and equipment rearrangement, new research projects would begin in the MacNider quarters. The enterovirus studies of Curnen ended, as his technician completed transfer of all material to New York. Arnold engaged primarily in clinical virology and oversaw a complex project by medical student James White concerning a case in which primary maternal *Herpes simplex* virus infection resulted in fatal congenital infant disease. This was a unique case for the time, which won the student first prize in a paper contest sponsored by the *New England Journal of Medicine*.

Initial research funding, which began in September 1961, was through a contract provided by the U.S. Army Medical Research and Development Command, under auspices of the Commission on Acute Respiratory Diseases of the Armed Forces Epidemiological Board. The work that had been done in Cleveland, and that would be continued in Chapel Hill on atypical pneumonia, was of interest to the military establishment due to the frequency of this syndrome among military recruits. Some of the first new work in the laboratory involved continuation or extension of work begun at Case Western Reserve. In virology, the growth cycles of parainfluenza type 3 virus in HeLa cell cultures were studied. Viral antigens appeared in the cytoplasm just following the eclipse phase and before the release of new virus, which corresponded to the onset of hemadsorption. This work was later to be extended to an animal model. The most significant work of this period concerned the Eaton agent of atypical pneumonia—work that was to engage many investigators in the laboratory for years to come, and by which several careers were made.

The Eaton agent arrived from Cleveland in the form of frozen chick embryo lung suspensions. Successful growth of the agent in artificial medium (which also proved it to be a new *mycoplasma* species) had just been reported from the National Institutes of Health, but Clyde's attempts to reproduce this before the move from Cleveland had failed. The secret ingredient turned out to be the yeast extract—rather than the commercially available brewer's yeast powder, which had been tried, it was necessary to prepare an aqueous extract of fresh baker's yeast. The laboratory had been joined by J. B. Kirkman, an experienced bacteriologist, and with his help proper mycoplasma media were compounded following a trip to a local grocer to purchase envelopes of Fleischmann's active dry yeast. This was then tested with chick embryo cultured material. Recognition of the tiny mycoplasma colonies was initially difficult, but the effort was greatly aided by the consultation of Harry Gooder. Gooder had recently joined the (then) Bacteriology Department and had worked extensively with bacterial L-forms, which share some properties with mycoplasma species. Very soon the growth of the Eaton agent, now known as *Mycoplasma pneumoniae*, became routine. Studies on its biological properties, including the observation that it produced *beta*-hemolysis of sheep erythrocyte agar overlays on plate cultures, characteristics of growth in broth, and antibiotic sensitivity patterns, were accomplished. This laboratory was first to note the exquisite sensitivity of *M. pneumoniae* to the macrolide group of antibiotics, especially erythromycin, which later was to become the standard of therapy.

As the culture capability for *M. pneumoniae* came on line, a pediatric resident, David Bruton, reported to the emergency room with high fever and signs of pneumonia. Sputum samples from him were placed in monkey kidney cell cultures (which had been used before the artificial media were described) as well as on the new agar medium. Both of these yielded pure cultures of *M. pneumoniae*, providing the first isolate of this organism in the state of North Carolina. This culture was deposited with the American Type

Culture Collection and has been one of the reference strains used by a number of investigators over the years.

During this period Denny, in particular, began discussions about the desirability of conducting some comprehensive clinical/epidemiological studies of children's acute respiratory infections. An ally in this planning was Paul Glezen, who had Epidemic Intelligence Service (EIS) training before completing his pediatric residency. He was due to give PHS service time after residency, and an effort was made to allow him to stay in Chapel Hill as a fellow while he organized the respiratory infection research. Unfortunately this plan was rejected by his superior, Alexander Langmuir (who even made a site visit to the MacNider facility), and the clinical studies had to be put off for a time for lack of direction and manpower.

During the MacNider days, there were sounds of construction behind a plywood partition just fifty feet north of the laboratories. A new six-level wing had risen over a two-year period, which would provide laboratory space for individuals in the Departments of Pathology, Physiology, Pharmacology, Anatomy, and Bacteriology, and the pediatric infectious disease division. The move to more suitable and expanded facilities was eagerly anticipated for many months by the division staff. This represented the first new research space that had been built in the medical complex since completion of North Carolina Memorial Hospital in 1952.

Due to construction time lag, the new infectious disease space had been designed by Curnen prior to his departure from the University of North Carolina School of Medicine. However, the design had been made sufficiently versatile that it served the needs of the new infectious disease division quite well for about a dozen years.

The Medical Sciences Research Wing Days. The physical proximity of the MacNider quarters and the new space made moving relatively simple. The staff savored not only clean surroundings, but a feeling of great spaciousness. The pleasant sensation of space lasted about two weeks, as all furniture and equipment found their places. Curnen had taken a rectangle of 950 square feet, dividing it into an office, three glassed-in isolation cubicles, a large preparation and heavy equipment room, and a room with tiled floor and drain that could be used for small animal work. The cubicles and the larger rooms at either end were connected by an internal hallway which was wide enough to hold small equipment along one side.

The elevator of the new wing had stops from basement to third floor; it did not reach to the fourth floor. There were two versions of the explanation for this anomaly. In the first, it was said that Curnen had asked that it be done this way, to limit access to the area of his enterovirus laboratory. As in the MacNider facility, reduction of traffic and containment of pathogenic human infectious agents were important safety measures. The other explanation concerned the architects. This was one of the last classical colonial structures built on the campus. There were five floors above ground, topped by a gabled slate roof. Had the elevator gone to the top floor, the roof lines would have been ruined by the overhead housing. It is likely that architectural esthetics were the more important considerations over biohazard concerns.

The design of the laboratory was ideal for projected work of the division. Since there would be comprehensive microbiological studies of respiratory infections, one cubicle was set aside for mycoplasma studies, one became the bacteriology laboratory, and the third was reserved for virology. The connecting hallway provided space for centrifuges, refrigerators, and a small secretarial station, ably staffed by Sherri Davis, who was destined to have a long and distinguished association with the Department of Pediatrics.

A number of events set the infectious disease program in motion. Clyde received a National Institutes of Health Career Development Award entitled "Mycoplasmas and Human Disease" (which was to extend for ten years). This had the ambitious goals of speciating and characterizing the mycoplasmas of man and exploring for any disease associations that these might have. At this time, the only diseases known were pneumonia caused by *M. pneumoniae*, and the tenuous connection of nongonococcal urethritis and *Ureaplasma urealyticum* (then called "T" strains). Because of the divisional interest in respiratory diseases, an early activity involved collections of throat swabs from a large number of normal faculty, staff, and students to characterize the mycoplasma flora. Isolates from a number of subjects, together with known species from the American Type Culture Collection, were used to prepare rabbit antisera for serological identification of the organisms. This early work led to recognition of a new, nonpathogenic human mycoplasma species, for which the name *M. pharyngis* was proposed (but, later, not accepted by the nomenclature committees). A method of speciation also was developed which greatly facilitated and simplified identification of isolates. This involved placing small filter paper discs saturated with different antisera on an inoculated agar plate, then incubating the plate to allow growth of organisms. A given mycoplasma species was inhibited in growth in the vicinity of homologous antiserum, providing species identification. This method became very popular with other workers in the field; it was to be recognized, twenty years later, as one of the ten most cited papers in the *Journal of Immunology*.

After a stint in the Public Health Service, Glezen returned to Chapel Hill to join the infectious disease faculty. He organized the first clinical study of serious respiratory disease, which involved pediatric inpatients. These studies were all designated by letters, and thus this first one became known as the "A Study." The patients were cultured for bacteria, mycoplasmas, and viruses, and paired sera were collected for antibody tests against a battery of agents. The study revealed the variety of viruses, *M. pneumoniae*, and fungi that caused pediatric admissions. Another important finding was the multiplicity of agents sometimes involved in an infectious episode: for example, one child with pneumonia yielded *Streptococcus pneumoniae* from the blood, *M. pneumoniae* from his throat, and developed an antibody rise to parainfluenza virus type 3. Over four hundred patients ultimately were enrolled in the "A Study."

The move into the Medical Sciences Research Wing provided space in which postdoctoral fellows could work. The first at this site were Robert Sanders, a recent Vanderbilt graduate and pediatric trainee, and Adnan Dajani, who had worked earlier as a pediatric resident with Denny at Rainbow Babies' and Children's Hospital in Cleveland. Sanders studied disease caused by parainfluenza virus type 3 in guinea pigs. Because of the ubiquity of this virus, antibody-free stock could be obtained only from the garage of a homemaker in Beltsville, Maryland. Sanders completed this project and returned to Tennessee after one year. Dajani also worked with an animal model, reproducing and extending the findings of Eaton with cultures of *M. pneumoniae* in the hamster. This work paved the way for a number of future antibiotic and immunologic studies using this model. Because of his interest in pursuing an academic career, Dajani spent two years in training that encompassed basic diagnostic bacteriology, mycoplasmology, and virology. Mycology was provided by Dr. Conant's summer course at Duke. Some training in microbiology enabled an MS degree. He also organized a clinical/microbiological study of respiratory disease among university students admitted to the Student Infirmary (this became the "B Study").

The studies on the etiology and epidemiology of children's respiratory diseases were greatly expanded through the addition of two new populations. The first group was constituted by the patients of the only pediatric group practice then in Chapel Hill. These studies were organized by Glezen and facilitated by all fellows and faculty of the division. This was known as the "C Study." This study was to last for eleven years, with etiologic studies of croup, tracheobronchitis, bronchiolitis, and pneumonia—6,165 illnesses in all. The publications on these four respiratory syndromes and on approaches to the management of acute lower respiratory tract infections in nonhospitalized children have been widely quoted and used in pediatric and infectious disease textbooks. The material was also an important base for future grants. The C Study was supported first by the Armed Forces Research and Development Command and later under contracts from the Vaccine Development Board of the National Institute of Allergy and Infectious Diseases.

The large population of normal, middle-class children enrolled in the C Study also was used in various other projects, such as the "D Study." This particular study involved the investigation of causes of pharyngitis in 715 children over one calendar year. Results revealed the epidemiology and relative importance of group A *beta*-hemolytic streptococci, viruses, and mycoplasmas in the causation of acute pharyngitis in childhood. *M. pneumoniae* was found to be associated with some pharyngitis cases; no association, which others had suggested, was found for *M. hominis*.

In 1965, Gerald Fernald, returning from military service, set out to characterize the human immune responses following *M. pneumoniae* infections as his chief fellowship research project. This work has yet to be equaled in terms of its detail and temporal understanding of the natural immune process in this common infectious disease. Acquisition of a room in MacNider, which backed up to the Medical Sciences Research Wing space, had allowed development of an immunology laboratory used by Fernald for his fellowship work, and for other research after he joined the infectious disease division faculty. This same room had been used earlier by Charles Sheaffer for chromosome preparations and by Clyde for immunofluorescence microscopy and photomicrography. Today, this space has been replaced by a walk-in cold room.

Also returning from the government service and soon joining the pediatric faculty was Frank Loda. In 1966, a longitudinal study of children and learning was organized at the Frank Porter Graham Center of the Child Development Institute. This program was housed in two large mobile homes located on Cameron Avenue next to the University power plant. A third, smaller trailer served as an infirmary, for collection of study specimens, and also provided on-site facilities for bacteriology and virology. Soon after the program began Loda became medical director of the unit and thus was in a position to oversee medical research projects conducted there. Although the program was small (ten to twelve new subjects entered each year as infants), the power of observation was great since the children could be observed eight hours a day, five days a week, and were available for repeated studies. All respiratory illnesses were characterized and studied etiologically. This became known as the "K Study."*

In 1977, the longitudinal study was moved to more permanent quarters provided by a new research building that was located at highway 54 West and Smith Level Road on the campus of the Frank Porter Graham Elementary School. Albert Collier became the medical director, and the respiratory disease studies continued. Ample space was available on the building's fourth floor to provide staff offices, self-contained bacteriology and virology laboratories, conference space, the division's reprint library, and nursery facilities for the youngest recruits joining the research program. The lower floors of this building housed the preschool- and kindergarten-age subjects, while those in grades 1–6 came to the adjacent school building. A notable addition to the experimental resources was a complete pulmonary function laboratory, which permitted plotting of lung growth in subjects studied repeatedly; any effects of intercurrent respiratory disease also could be evaluated.

The unique nature of the Frank Porter Graham research population enabled a wide variety of multidisciplinary studies over subsequent years. In addition to studies of respiratory infections, other examples included work in educational psychology and evaluation of the effects of indoor air pollution. The prospective, longitudinal design of the study made possible special work

---

*The missing study letters beyond the pharyngitis study "D" included "E" for reference cultures, "F" for a short-term study in the nurseries, "G" for a study of *Herpes gladiatorum* in football players, "H" for a longitudinal study in a fraternity and a sorority, "I" for an influenza vaccine trial, and "J" for a study of lower respiratory tract illnesses in college students.

in infection that would not have been possible otherwise: Examples include evaluation of the interplay between viruses and respiratory bacterial flora in the pathogenesis of otitis media; the occurrence, epidemiology, and clinical expression of *Mycoplasma pneumoniae* infections in very young children; and changing patterns in respiratory flora typing and antibiotic sensitivity over time, including comparison of strains from the same subject.

Development of the Frank Porter Graham laboratories now meant that the infectious disease division was operating on two sites, which enhanced the possibilities for fellowship research, expanded the kinds of clinical studies that could be done and increased laboratory personnel and equipment needs. In the context of these pages it would be difficult to mention all the projects of the postdoctoral fellows and the faculty research that occurred during the Medical Sciences Research Wing days. Both names and topics are reflected in the division's publication list in the archives, between the years of 1963 and 1976, and in the list of trainees at the end of the division history.

Many new developments characterized the division during the early 1970s. Albert Collier and Dwight Powell completed fellowships and joined the faculty. There were four sabbatical leaves: Fernald to the immunology program at Duke; Denny to the Medical Research Council in London; Clyde to the Department of Pathology at Yale; and Glezen to Boston Children's Hospital. With the expanding faculty, more space was badly needed. This came in the form of three contiguous rooms in MacNider. These were not configured for laboratory space due to previous renovations, but were ideal for offices. Clyde, Glezen, and our first administrative assistant set up shop here, freeing up space for others in the Medical Sciences Research Wing area just around the corner.

It was in the new office spaces that developments heralding new research initiatives took place. Clyde studied an announcement from the National Heart, Lung and Blood Institute (NHLBI) for Pulmonary Specialized Centers of Research (SCOR). This was the second generation of the special program, the first having been announced in 1971. The concept of the program was that there be a multidisciplinary approach, including both basic and clinical science, on a central theme of interest to the Institute. Clyde saw little here that would be pertinent to the interests of the infectious disease division, but happened to show the announcement to Glezen, who reacted much more positively. The ensuing discussions resulted in the development of ideas in which the most common lung problem of children—infection—would be evaluated in terms of long-term effects on pulmonary health. The work would "package" all the research activity of the division, through studies of inpatients, outpatients, normal children studied longitudinally, high-risk nursery babies, and in vivo and in vitro experimental model systems including bacterial, mycoplasmal, and viral agents. This certainly seemed to be an ambitious proposal, yet it encompassed many interests of the investigators, and there was a good record of previous productivity in all areas of the proposed work.

Behind MacNider Building and the Dental School a major building project was underway. This nine-story building would be the next home of the pediatric infectious disease division. The relocation would be different from earlier ones, for now the division members had the opportunity for the first time to plan and tailor the assigned footage to best suit the anticipated work. John Herion had the onerous task of being the building coordinator for the faculty, and discussions with him were very helpful to our group. The increased space and improved facilities would be an important boost also for the pending SCOR program.

The Burnett-Womack Clinical Sciences Building Days. The new home of the pediatric infectious disease division was on the fifth and sixth floors of the new building, which was planned to provide offices and research laboratory space for faculty of the clinical departments. The division's allotment of three thousand square feet included a suite of five offices plus clerical support space on the front (south) face of the building on the fifth floor. The windowless laboratories (greatly hated by the technical staff) in the building's center were of modular design and measured fifteen by twenty feet each. One of these was a preparation/storage area, one a conference room/library unit, and the main laboratory space was a quadruple module with a one-hundred-square-foot isolation cubicle at each corner. A mechanical chase behind the rear wall of each laboratory carried all utilities and made modifications in the laboratories relatively simple. Two additional modules on the sixth floor were equipped as immunology laboratories for Fernald.

Having settled into their new space, the infectious disease faculty (Collier, Clyde, Powell, Fernald, and Denny, in the chairman's office on the back side of the fifth floor; Glezen had departed for Baylor University by this time) were anxious to begin some of the work proposed in the SCOR program. As always with pending grant applications, much time passed without any indication of where the proposal stood. However, contact was made seeking Clyde's help in codirecting and organizing a workshop on bronchiolitis sponsored by the agency which was to be held in Bethesda in 1976. We had gotten the agency's attention. Later an NHLBI staff member visited Chapel Hill to discuss content and contributors for the workshop. In relation to questions about the frequency of bronchiolitis, she asked for a source of the information and was told it was our work, used as background for the SCOR application. Extracting a copy of the application from her briefcase, the next question was "What page?" Our prospects heightened.

The workshop was unique, focusing just on the syndrome of bronchiolitis and involving a multidisciplinary group of investigators from several countries. From the Chapel Hill program participants were Denny, Collier, Henderson, and Clyde. Glezen also contributed to the workshop, but as a representative from Baylor University, where he had relocated following his sabbatical period. So little had been written about bronchiolitis prior to this workshop that it was very useful to have group discussions. In 1977, the workshop was published in *Pediatric Research*, stirring further interest in the scientific community.

At last, word came that the Lung Division of NHLBI had selected our proposal for funding. With a great sense of relief the investigators began to think in real terms of what they had proposed to do and how to accomplish this work. The application had been written in such a way that practically all manpower and facilities were already available, and start-up could proceed expeditiously. It therefore was quite disappointing to learn that the grant, while approved, would not be funded for another six months for NIH fiscal reasons. This did allow time for a key investigator, a virologist, to be recruited in the person of Ed Dubovi, who was a recent graduate of Wagner's program at the University of Virginia in Charlottesville. Dubovi's charge was to head the diagnostic virology effort at the Frank Porter Graham Center and to initiate more basic research in respiratory virology. Also, it was necessary to identify a biostatistical collaborator for the clinical/epidemiological work. This post was filled initially by Roger Grimson; Grimson was soon replaced by Ron Helms, who established a long-term and productive relationship with the SCOR. As the program began, Dwight Powell left to accept a position in infectious diseases at the Children's Hospital in Columbus, Ohio.

The Pediatric Pulmonary SCOR officially began on December 1, 1976, and included the following projects:

1. A longitudinal study of respiratory infections and lung growth in normal children (Collier, Fred Henderson, Russ Pimmel). Subjects from the pediatric group practice, whose respiratory disease history was known from previous studies ("C Study"), would be recalled for pulmonary health assessment and further follow-up.

2. A study of the natural history and host defense defects in children with chronic or potentially chronic pulmonary disease (Fernald, Powell, Denny). Thorough evaluation of patients referred to the clinic for chronic or recurrent pulmonary symptoms would be conducted to learn which tests were most informative and to seek ways to place patients into categories for therapeutic and prognostic considerations.

3. A questionnaire survey would be designed to determine the frequency of chronic respiratory diseases among children in North Carolina (Loda, Robert Chapman).

4. Development of experimental model systems of several kinds was proposed to facilitate understanding of the pathogenesis of different respiratory infections (Clyde, Henderson, Collier, Joel Baseman). Intact animals, organ cultures, and cells were to be used for work with respiratory viruses, bacteria, and *M. pneumoniae*.

5. Immunologic studies in models of lower respiratory tract infections were planned to define mechanisms involved (Fernald, Powell,

Henderson). Initially the models chosen were *M. pneumoniae* and human parainfluenza type 3 virus, with future plans to include *Bordetella pertussis*.

6. Ultrastructural studies of host-parasite interactions involved both transmission and scanning electron microscopy (Collier, Kenneth Muse). Initial work examined *M. pneumoniae* and *B. pertussis* in hamster tracheal organ culture.

7. A final project examined metabolic pathways of normal and injured respiratory cells (Baseman, Collier, Eric Hansen). A major goal of this work was understanding how different infectious agents alter differentiated respiratory cells.

The seven projects outlined above were supported by several core units designed to provide common needs rather than have them duplicated in each project. These units were administrative support core (Clyde), clinical support core (Fernald), and laboratory support core (Denny).

As the program developed, several new investigators were recruited who would propose new projects later on. Productivity of the program was considerable; twenty-five to thirty publications annually were not unusual. The first SCOR cycle ended on November 30, 1981.

THE BOAT YEARS 1982–1993

With the support of the SCOR program, active basic and clinical research continued during the years of Tom Boat's chairmanship, and his active sponsorship and direct participation augmented the goals. Renewal of the grant provided for a five-year continuation starting in 1981; a third application also was successful, in 1986; and a fourth cycle began in 1991. Although a requirement of these grants is that they be multidisciplinary, the infectious disease division played a central role throughout the history of the program. With time, the nature of the research evolved away from the clinical/epidemiological studies of the 1960s and 1970s that had required faculty group efforts to individual projects of more limited scope, in which faculty members served as the principal investigators. Therefore, accomplishments of this decade are best summarized with a brief statement of each investigator's work, in alphabetical order.

Melinda A. Beck, PhD Beck is a research virologist at the Frank Porter Graham Child Development Center. Her interests are in the nutritional aspects of the pathogenesis and immunology of infections due to viruses, especially the enteroviruses. This is pertinent to the mission of the Center because of its relevance to the study of the development of children and common childhood infections.

Johnny L. Carson, PhD In direct support of the SCOR program, but serving the Department of Pediatrics broadly as well, a Cell Biology and Ultrastructure Research Center was organized, with Carson as director. This permitted centralization of activities, much of which had taken place in other departments in the past, and upgrading and/or acquiring equipment. Many kinds of research applications were conducted by Carson, often with the collaboration of other faculty, postdoctoral fellows, and students. Research focused on the development and function of the airways' epithelia and their response to infectious or noxious agents. The objects of study were cells, tissues in organ cultures, animal models, and human patients or volunteers. Many new concepts emerged from this work, especially the evidence that cilia may be damaged transiently by infection or noxious injury. Also noteworthy has been the extensive

Johnny Carson

experience with patients having primary ciliary dyskinesia.

Wallace A. Clyde, Jr., MD During the 1980s Clyde's main research activities related to the SCOR program and to a number of collaborations for studies on mycoplasmas. He was the overall director of the SCOR program through its first three cycles (Boat directed the fourth) and functioned also as a project

director and participating investigator at various times. The most significant collaborative results were identifying *Mycoplasma pneumoniae* as an agent of pericarditis in adult patients together with a group of internists at Duke; and extension of data showing that many patients with *M. pneumoniae* infections develop antibodies against the mitotic spindles of dividing cells, in conjunction with workers at the Statens Seruminstitut in Denmark.

Al Collier

Albert M. Collier, MD During the 1980s Collier held a variety of administrative positions simultaneously: infectious disease division chief, Frank Porter Graham Center medical research director (acting center director for a time),

Center for Environmental Medicine and Lung Biology associate director, and codirector of the SCOR program. Accordingly, his research relationships are to a diverse group of programs. A close connection was maintained to the ultrastructure/cell biology operation of the SCOR. Among studies in which he participated is one in which urinary cotinine (a nicotine metabolite) excretion by children was shown to be a reflection of passive tobacco smoke exposure. Studies also were conducted on effects of indoor air pollution, ozone, or infection on pulmonary function of children, and on respiratory epithelial ultrastructural changes in volunteers exposed to various inhalants.

Floyd W. Denny, MD After leaving the pediatric chairmanship, Denny had time for research pursuits in conjunction with the infectious disease division program, particularly the SCOR activity. He helped design and analyze the clinical/epidemiological projects and served as director of the biometry core unit, which encompassed data management and analysis functions for the SCOR projects. Unfortunately, the SCOR interaction had to be terminated when the opportunity arose for him to assume the full-time position of director in developing the School of Medicine Health Promotion Disease Prevention Program.

Gerald W. Fernald, MD Fernald served as acting chairman during the Denny to Boat transition, but completed and published a study of chronic pulmonary disease in children, which was a SCOR project he had directed. Later, work was accomplished on certain immunologic aspects of *M. pneumoniae* and respiratory syncytial virus infections. During 1982–1987 an epidemiologic study of mycoplasmal pneumonia in the UNC Student Health Services was conducted and compared to a similar study in this population during the 1960s.

Fred
Henderson

Beyond this point Fernald turned his attention away from research and to the administrative jobs of associate pediatric chairman and directing the rapidly growing UNC Cystic Fibrosis Center.

Frederick W. Henderson, MD Henderson's long-term commitment to the study of viral etiology, immunologic response, and epidemiology of respiratory infections characterized his research contributions during the 1980s. Emphasis was placed on otitis media and on chronic respiratory disorders of children, particularly concerning persistent middle ear effusions and childhood asthma. Subjects for the research included the population of children attending the Frank Porter Graham Child Development Center program and others from two large private pediatric practices. Among the many research topics addressed were the importance of respiratory syncytial virus infections to the etiology and epidemiology of otitis media and persistent middle ear effusion in infants and toddlers; developmental consequences of prolonged middle ear effusion; antigenic subtype-specific immune responses to respiratory syncytial virus by young children; spread of antibiotic-resistant *Streptococcus pneumoniae* among children in group day care; the relationship between lower respiratory tract infections and developing lung function in infants and young children; the epidemiology of recurrent wheezing and asthma in elementary school children; and the immunologic characteristics that distinguish allergic children with and without asthma.

Ping-chuan ("Ed") Hu, PhD Resignations of key faculty in the SCOR program and the need for new research initiatives led to the recruitment of Hu in 1982. He applied for the first time contemporary technology to studies on pathogenesis of *M. pneumoniae* disease, especially the Western blot technique and monoclonal antibodies using hybridomas. Important discoveries included the identification of the P1 protein structure on the attachment tip of the organism, and that the P1 function could be blocked by monoclonal antibody to the protein. Subsequent research emphasized disease pathogenesis at the molecular level, with efforts to clone and sequence the P1 protein. Initial difficulties were found related to the unusual genetic situation in which the TGA stop codons were used as TGG tryptophan codons. Following complete sequencing of the P1 gene, complexity of the organism's attachment process became apparent, in that the attachment moiety was composed of multiple components. These findings have been extended toward the possibility of developing a vaccine that would stimulate an immune response capable of inhibiting attachment of the mycoplasma to the respiratory epithelium.

Ed Hu

David L. Ingram, MD Ingram, as director of the AHEC teaching service at Wake Medical Center, continued his research interests, primarily in group B streptococcal infections in neonates, in sexually transmitted diseases in children, and in antigen detection in the diagnosis of bacterial infections. The group B streptococcal studies involved the use of antigen detection in body fluids for diagnosis. The role of *Chlamydia trachomatis*, *Neisseria gonorrhoeae*, *Ureaplasma urealytium*, and large colony mycoplasmas, *Gardnerella vaginalis*, and

Wilma Lim

human papilloma virus infections were studied in sexually abused girls. He also studied the role of antigen detection in type b *Haemophilus influenzae, Streptococcus pneumoniae,* and *Neisseria meningitidis* infections.

Wilma Lim, MD Lim joined the pediatric infectious disease faculty in 1990 to lend her expertise in pediatric HIV infection to the growing problem of AIDS in infants and children attending the clinics and wards of UNC Hospitals. In addition to organization of clinical care protocols, she established research collaborations with the AIDS Clinical Trials Group in the Department of Medicine, allowing pediatric-age patients to be participants. Later, the affiliation with Medicine was terminated and a new collaboration was established with Duke Medical Center to create the North Carolina Children's AIDS Network, a more advantageous arrangement for acquisition of NIH research support.

Influence of the Infectious Disease Division on Other Programs

Many programs and work of individual faculty members, both within and outside the Department of Pediatrics, were affected by activities of the pediatric infectious disease division. This was particularly true in the research arena; the division had the largest research funding in pediatrics for many years and ranked among the top programs in the School of Medicine as well. The breadth and multidisciplinary nature of the studies created alliances with other clinical and basic science departments, other schools within the University, and with outside organizations such as the U.S. Environmental Protection Agency. Major impact occurred in three particular areas which will be discussed in more detail: pediatric pulmonology (and development of a pediatric pulmonary division); a children's chest disease unit at Gravely Sanatorium; and research projects involving the population of children attending the Frank Porter Graham Child Development Center.

PEDIATRIC PULMONOLOGY

In the early 1960s, a focus of interest in pulmonary disease developed as acute lower respiratory tract infections (ALRI) became a major interest of the division of infectious diseases. With the addition of Paul Glezen in 1965, the group strengthened its interest in the etiology, epidemiology, and pathogenesis of ALRI. What they lacked was expertise in lung physiology, but this was generally unavailable as a pediatric subspecialty at that time. Dr. Annie Scott had been caring for cystic fibrosis and tuberculosis cases in the Department since the middle 1950s, assisted by George Summer, who ran the sweat tests in his laboratory. By 1964, Dr. Scott had retired and Dr. Summer became full time in the Department of Biochemistry. Dr. Joanna Dalldorf, who had just finished her pediatric residency, took over the CF patients, and Dr. Glezen began to follow TB as well as sarcoidosis and other chronic lung problems in the Gravely clinic.

In 1968, a children's chest unit was opened in Gravely, fulfilling a dream often expressed by Dr. Scott. This ten-bed ward provided a first-floor area with adjacent outside playground for care of children with tuberculosis, cystic fibrosis, and other lung problems. House staff from the Department rotated on a monthly basis and the resident worked in clinics with Dr. Glezen. A weekly X-ray conference was soon developed for review of cases with the house staff. It was attended by members of the pediatric infectious diseases group, Dr. Thomas Barnett from adult pulmonology, and Dr. Cooper, who was the Gravely radiologist. Later on, in 1975, Dr. Frank Volberg arrived as the first pediatric radiologist at NCMH. This weekly chest conference was moved back to the NCMH children's floor in 1975 when the seventh floor was expanded and Gravely closed. It survives to the present time as one of the more popular weekly ward conferences in the Department.

In 1967, care of the CF patients was assumed by Jerry Fernald, who had just finished his ID fellowship in the division. A CF nurse was provided by the hospital and patients were seen in the Old Clinic Building once a week along with other patients in the infectious disease clinic. When the new Love Clinic opened in 1970 in the bed tower, a mix of infectious disease, cystic fibrosis, and juvenile rheumatoid arthritis patients were moved to the new site, where they were followed by Drs. Denny and Fernald. In 1974, application for CF center status was approved by the Cystic Fibrosis Foundation with Jerry Fernald as director and Alan Cato as backup physician. When the Gravely clinics closed in 1974, the TB and other chest patients were transferred to this ID/chest clinic.

In 1967, John Knelson, a neonatal physiologist, was recruited to work part time in the Department. John was an employee of the U.S. Environmental Protection Agency, recently located in the Research Triangle Park. In addition to supervising the neonatal program, John set up a pulmonary function laboratory at the Frank Porter Graham Day Care Center assisted by Dr. John Brooks, a pulmonary fellow at EPA. Not only did these efforts provide physiologic measurements of lung growth in children for the FPG studies, they also provided the first expertise in pediatric pulmonology for the Department.

As interest in pulmonary physiology developed in the division, fellows were recruited to pursue research projects. The first was Cynthia Worrell (1973–1974) from the Department of Pediatrics, University of Arkansas School of Medicine. During her year at the FPG site, Cynthia worked on experiments to measure lung compliance in hamster lungs.

In 1977, Gerald Strope began to train as the first pulmonary fellow in the Department. He had completed a medicine-pediatric internship and two years of pediatric residency at NCMH. In the absence of a pediatric pulmonary program, he received formal training in the pulmonary division of the Department of Medicine. His first research project was to measure pulmonary functions in hamsters, an animal model already in use in the division. In 1978, he assumed responsibility of the pulmonary physiology core in the new SCOR program while continuing to complete his fellowship training under the mentorship of Dr. Philip Bromberg. Upon completion of his fellowship in 1979, Jerry joined the faculty as the first full-time pulmonologist in the Department.

Dr. Marianna Henry, who completed her residency training at NCMH, began training as a pulmonary fellow under Dr. Strope in 1980. While pursuing research and formal teaching under members of the pulmonary division of the Department of Medicine, she received clinical training in the ID/chest clinic and on the pediatric inpatient services. The pulmonary laboratory at FPG provided opportunities to expand the studies of lung growth in childhood, which has been a major area of Dr. Henry's interest in subsequent years as a faculty member. Fred Henderson has been a long-time collaborator in these studies, supported by the pediatric SCOR.

In 1982, Dr. Margaret Leigh joined the ID division as a fellow under the mentorship of Drs. Denny, Henderson, and Strope. She had served as a CF center director at the University of Kentucky for the previous two years but wished to pursue an academic career focusing in the area of pulmonology. During her first year she developed a ferret model of influenza and launched a research program which was to continue successfully for the next decade. The next year she became one of the first fellows in the newly formed pulmonary division under the leadership of Dr. Robert Wood.

Another group that contributed to the development of pediatric pulmonology at UNC was the allergists. A residents' clinic had been in place under the part-time direction of Joseph Whatley for many years. In 1973, Dr. Mary Pat Hemstreet completed her allergy-immunology training at Duke and joined the full-time faculty to run the allergy program and to work in the primary care clinic part time. Dr. Hemstreet's presence provided a readily available allergist to work with many of the patients followed in the ID/chest clinic, particularly those with reactive airways disease. She was the first to use a spirograph in clinic so that pediatric patients could avoid going to the adult pulmonary function laboratory. Dr. Hemstreet left the program in 1976 when she and her husband moved to Birmingham. David Stempel was recruited from fellowship at Stanford to take over the allergy program. During his four-year tenure, he further developed the clinical program and carried out studies relating IgE and wheezing-associated respiratory infections (WARI).

In 1982, with the arrival of Tom Boat as chairman of the Department, the time had arrived for a pulmonary division. Dr. Robert Wood joined Dr. Boat from Cleveland to head the new division and Drs. Strope, Henry, and Leigh were its first members. Interaction between the ID and pulmonary divisions remained strong, with the weekly chest conference and pulmonary clinics the main focus. The few ID patients not followed in the pulmonary clinics comprised a small but continuing pediatric infectious disease clinic population. All members of the pulmonary group joined in caring for cystic fibrosis patients, laying the groundwork for future growth of both the pulmonary division and the cystic fibrosis center. This growth eventually established these programs as preeminent in the southeastern United States.

GRAVELY PEDIATRIC FACILITY

A precise history of the pediatric service at Gravely Hospital is not possible because accurate records were not kept and Dr. Annie Scott, responsible for its early years, is dead. Dr. Scott joined the Department in 1954, had her office in Gravely Hospital, and until her retirement in 1964 assumed primary responsibility for the clinical care of children with cystic fibrosis and tuberculosis. Thus, she was the pediatric liaison between North Carolina Memorial Hospital and Gravely Sanatorium, then a member of the North Carolina Sanatorium System but affiliated with the University of North Carolina. Dr. Scott held weekly clinics for follow-up of patients with primary tuberculosis, children who were contacts of patients with open tuberculosis, children with infections with mycobacteria other than tuberculosis, and patients with blastomycosis, histoplasmosis, and sarcoidosis. One of Dr. Scott's dreams had been the establishment of a pediatric inpatient service at Gravely, but there is no record of her taking an active role in the planning of the Gravely unit. Dr. Paul Glezen, then a young faculty member in the division of pediatric infectious diseases, played the major role in this service and contributed most of the information presented here.

The first mention of a separate pediatric unit at Gravely is found in departmental meeting minutes of October 1, 1963: "Plans were shown of the area in Gravely Sanatorium which is to be converted into a Pediatric Chest Disease Unit. Drs. Arnold and Clyde are to participate in developing plans for this conversion although other members of the department were invited to offer any suggestions they might have."

These plans developed slowly; after several years arrangements were made through the North Carolina Sanatorium System to proceed with the necessary physical changes in Gravely Hospital. Through the efforts of Mr. Ben Clark, administrator of Gravely Hospital, and his assistant, Mr. Earl Hartsell, Jr., a ten-bed pediatric ward was built and opened on July 29, 1968. It was located on the first floor away from adult patient areas. Dr. Glezen was chief of the service and the only attending pediatrician for the first two years of the unit's existence. Later the faculty members of the infectious diseases division shared in the attending responsibilities. Pediatric house officers from North Carolina Memorial Hospital rotated through the service and the resident on the infectious disease service worked in the Gravely clinic and ward.

Dr. Glezen did retain records of admissions to the pediatric unit for one year and these are recorded here to give the "flavor" of the patients admitted. He wrote:

> During 1973, 130 patients were admitted to the Gravely Pediatric Ward, but only 42 had a final diagnosis of infection with *M. tuberculosis* or mycobacteria other than tuberculosis (MOTT). Twenty-five patients with cystic fibrosis were admitted for pulmonary toilet and another 12 patients with pulmonary disease of unknown etiology were admitted for workup. A protocol for study of the latter group had been developed. The protocol included etiologic studies for agents in all classes—mycobacteria, fungi, viruses and mycoplasmas as well as routine bacteriology; anatomic studies; metabolic studies (sweat C⁻ and alpha-1 antitrypsin); studies of host defense mechanisms; atopy and pulmonary mechanics. All of the resources of NCMH were available, including excellent support from the other Pediatric sections, ENT and thoracic surgery. A variety of diagnoses was made; for instance, 6 patients with sarcoidosis were admitted in 1973 alone. Other fascinating cases were recognized, including patients with bronchial adenoma, pulmonary actinomycosis, chronic granulomatous disease, Kartagener's syndrome, cor pulmonale from upper airway obstruction, blastomycosis, histoplasmosis and coccidioidomycosis.

Notations appear occasionally in Pediatric Department minutes after the 1963 item until the closing of the unit in 1975, and then periodically after that when the Department of Pediatrics considered other plans for Gravely Hospital. These notations, as incomplete as they are, do paint some pictures of the pediatric involvement in Gravely Hospital.

On March 11, 1969, just one sentence: *The sixth intern will divide her responsibilities between Gravely Sanatorium and the Pediatric Out-Patient Department.*

On June 9, 1970, a longer entry:

> Members of the faculty noticed that the attending at Gravely Sanatorium actually represented a fifth person. With Dr. Glezen's pulling regular attending duties on the seventh floor and continuing to serve as attending on the Gravely Service, some of us felt that Dr. Glezen may be carrying an unfair load. When asked if he would like to be relieved of his attending duties on the seventh floor, however, Dr. Glezen pointed out that he is responsible for the third year teaching program and has attending duties on the seventh floor so as to keep in touch with the students and with the progress of their teaching program. He expressed a strong wish not to be excused from the seventh floor attending duties. The faculty then wondered if some rotation might not be set up for the attending responsibilities at Gravely.
>
>   Dr. Glezen mentioned that many interesting patients, such as children with cystic fibrosis, will be almost entirely on the Gravely service.

He wondered if some formal assignment of Gravely patients to third year students should not be undertaken. Several expressions in favor of this were given. One possibility which was mentioned was that third year students should be assigned Gravely patients in the same manner as their assignment of patients on the seventh floor. No strong views were expressed on this point, however.

The fate of these suggestions is unknown. Those of us involved at the time cannot recall what action was taken.

On June 1, 1971, an entry showed growth of the unit:

House Staff Coverage of Gravely for the coming year—Dr. Glezen emphasized the increased patient census at Gravely during the past year. Restrictions on the kind of admissions has been eased with only one-half of the patients admitted for tuberculosis. The hospital now has an intensive care ward which will allow the admission of sicker children (with respiratory disease) to this facility. During the past year the intern on call for Gravely at night and on weekends covered both the Emergency Room and Gravely. The Gravely intern was also expected to work part time in the OPD during the week. The salary for two house officers has been obtained from Gravely for the coming year and Dr. Glezen stated that Gravely should have an intern with no other responsibility for night coverage.

On April 4, 1972, Dr. Glezen proposed and the staff approved a formal alignment of one of the ward teams with a Gravely rotation. The infectious diseases service would provide the attending on this service.

On May 30, 1972, along with some administrative reorganization of the Department, Dr. Glezen was given responsibility of "Gravely Service Professional Administration."

On October 29, 1974, the end of the Gravely pediatric service was approaching:

The Fate of Gravely Hospital. Dr. Denny informed the staff that on 1 November Gravely Hospital would become a part of NCMH for administrative purposes. This means that the Department can determine the type of patients admitted to Gravely. It was pointed out that the use of Gravely as a pediatric pulmonary disease center would not change but empty beds could be filled with patients with other diseases. The only limitation at present would be that only patients needing minimal care can be admitted to Gravely.

On November 11, 1974, the Gravely service was closed:

Dr. Denny brought the group up to date on the Pediatric Service at Gravely. This service will be closed later this week; this will be temporary in that the administration is waiting for the Pediatric Department to present a program for the use of this space in the future. Dr.

Denny has set up a committee comprised of Hugh Bryan, Bob Greenberg, Harvey Hamrick, Hal Woodward, and Jim Schwankl to come up with a program for this space which will be presented to the faculty at a Senior Staff meeting in the future. Hugh Bryan requested that any suggestions as to staffing and the type of patient to be admitted to this service be forwarded to this group in the very near future.

On January 14, 1975, Paul Glezen's resignation from the Department was announced. Because his interest in the Gravely service was so crucial to its success his leaving clearly affected greatly the decisions that were made, as shown in the following entries.

On June 24, 1975, future plans for Gravely were discussed:

Gravely Hospital: A report concerning the utilization of Gravely Hospital was recently presented to the Patient Care Council of NCMH. This recommended that the second and third floor of Gravely be used as a rehabilitation and intermediate care facility for adults. No mention was made of the children's beds on the first floor. Dr. Denny inquired of Mr. Berry as to the state of these beds. It was indicated to him that there appeared two options for the utilization of children's beds: (1) Keep this service as is with a ten to twelve bed intermediate care unit. (2) Close as a patient care unit and open a minimal or intermediate care unit on the seventh floor.

Notations appear in departmental meeting minutes from 1978 to 1982 about the possible establishment of the pediatric service at Gravely into a minimum-care unit or even the conversion of the entire Gravely Hospital into a pediatric hospital. All of these discussions proved fruitless because of a general lack of enthusiasm for either one. No mentions of Gravely appear after March 1982.

In 1993 Dr. Glezen concluded his memories of the Gravely service with these words:

In its time the Gravely Pediatric Unit served a useful purpose for tuberculosis control and diagnosis and management of all types of chronic pulmonary disease. It provided house officers with a unique educational experience that may be of increasing value during the coming years. The closure of the Gravely Hospital as part of the State Hospital system coincided with the decision of the Public Health Service to severely cut the national tuberculosis control program. The people in charge stated that the program was no longer cost effective, not realizing that as cases decreased in number the cost of finding the few remaining cases must rise. After many years of declining rates, the decrease in funds allowed the tuberculosis case rate to plateau for a few years and then begin to climb. Now we are confronted with a crisis in many of the urban areas with rapidly rising case rates, multiple drug resistant organisms and rapidly fatal infections in immunocompromised patients. With this has come a recommendation for *directly observed therapy*. The problem is to find sufficient personnel to observe all of the patients needing therapy. Some have even gone so far as to suggest that we might need specialty hospitals to care for recalcitrant patients!

FRANK PORTER GRAHAM CHILD DEVELOPMENT CENTER

In the summer of 1966, a grant to Dr. Ann Peters, with collaboration of Drs. Halbert and Nancy Robinson, allowed initiation of what became a long-running study of childhood development and effects of special educational efforts. The general design of the research involved recruiting subjects before birth and applying the educational intervention strategies throughout infancy, preschool years, kindergarten, and elementary grades. A comparable control group not receiving the interventions also was recruited. This work became the backbone of the Frank Porter Graham Child Development Center, which was one arm of the UNC Child Development Institute.

The infectious disease division was fortunate in being involved with medical aspects of this program from the beginning; provision of free medical care for the subjects was the principal inducement for parental consent. From the infectious disease standpoint, access to this population of children permitted a unique opportunity to follow and characterize intercurrent illnesses in the same child over time (attendance at the center was 0800–1700 hours, five days weekly except holidays and vacations). The focus of these studies was respiratory infection, the most common medical problem of young children in the United States. Infectious disease studies were facilitated through service of division members as medical directors: first Dr. W. Paul Glezen, then Dr. Frank Loda, and finally (to the present) Dr. Albert Collier.

Initially the center was housed in three doublewide trailers next to the old University laundry and power plant on Cameron Avenue. A smaller trailer was equipped as an examination room and microbiology laboratory, so that respiratory specimens could be collected on site and subjected to preliminary examination for viruses and bacteria, including mycoplasmas. Initially there were four cohorts of eight children each, ranging in age from birth to three years. Continuous observation of these subjects by the teachers enabled early referral for any illnesses to the medical/research staff for evaluation.

As conceived originally by Dr. Robinson, the small program in the Cameron Avenue trailers was to be extended to include a large population of 240 infants and children in buildings to be constructed on the campus of the Frank Porter Graham Elementary School, located on the NC 54 bypass and Smith Level Road. The association of this study with a component of the Chapel Hill–Carrboro school system would allow continued access to study children moving from day care through kindergarten to the elementary school grades. A four-story research building adjacent to the classroom buildings was completed and occupied. Unfortunately, Robinson left Chapel Hill before these ambitious plans could be accomplished. Dr. Earl Siegel became center director for a time, to be followed by Dr. James Gallagher as long-term director. During these transition periods medical care of the children and research on the etiology and epidemiology of respiratory infections was continued by the infectious disease division. A smaller population of subjects, mainly infants and prekindergarten children, were housed on three floors of the research building, which also contained self-sufficient microbiology laboratories. A small number of the original recruits were followed through the school system.

At the time these studies were begun, information about illness in day care was quite limited. Therefore, the infectious disease staff was relieved that while respiratory illnesses were more common than might be seen in a home-care setting, the illnesses were not as severe as had been feared.

The small size of the population attending the center prevented some types of studies; however, the fact that each child could be followed closely and studied repeatedly counterbalanced this limitation. For example, during the period 1970–1980 children had respiratory tract cultures made every two weeks when they were well, with additional studies during illnesses. This made possible better interpretation of the possible etiologic role of bacterial flora, the shedding patterns of viruses, and evidence that most *M. pneumoniae* infections in these subjects were asymptomatic.

No effort will be made here to summarize the many research reports that appeared describing the center studies, which are included in the bibliography in the archives. Of note are papers on the acquisition, carriage, elimination, and reacquisition of *Streptococcus pneumoniae* and *Haemophilus influenzae* strains, and the role of humoral immunity in infection and reinfection with respiratory syncytial virus.

The laboratory staff and facilities kept pace with the ongoing work at the center and even provided the technical resources for other studies of the infectious disease division, such as the major evaluation of respiratory disease seen in a pediatric practice, which is described elsewhere. Generally the staff consisted of two or three research technicians, a laboratory aide, and a full- or part-time laboratory director. In the clinical arena, examination of the children and collection of specimens was done by a nurse (the first, Wendy Barksdale), and later by a nurse-practitioner (first, Jessie Watkins), assisted by several aides. Dedicated equipment, including incubators, water baths, centrifuges, and microscopes, were available for respiratory virology and bacteriology. Mycoplasma cultures were planted here and transported to the central research laboratory for processing.

A major addition to the laboratory facilities was provided in the early 1970s in the form of a pediatric pulmonary function laboratory, through assistance of Drs. John Knelson and John Brooks and with support of the U.S. Environmental Protection Agency. The laboratory was updated several times to maintain its state-of-the-art characteristics. Children at the center were trained to perform reproducible spirometry, a feat that proved possible beginning around age three. New studies could be accomplished, such as evaluation of the growth of lung function in individual children and the physiologic effects of characterized upper and lower respiratory tract infections.

The studies of children's respiratory infections, which continue today at the Frank Porter Graham Child Development Center, have greatly increased our understanding of these infections in young children, particularly in the day care setting. In all publications and reports dealing with these subjects appreciation has been expressed to the parents for permission for participation of their children, and to the children for their willing cooperation.

WALLACE A. CLYDE, JR.
FLOYD W. DENNY, JR.

FACULTY

Arnold, John H. BS, Tulane, 1948; MD, Tulane, 1951; Inst, Ped, 1957; Asst Prof, Ped, 1959–65.

Beck, Melinda A. BA, Calif Polytech State Univ, 1983; PhD, Ohio State Univ, 1987; Visit Asst Prof, Ped, 1991; Asst Prof, Ped, 1992.

Carson, Johnny L. BS, West Carolina Univ, 1971; PhD, Univ NC at Chapel Hill, 1975; Res Asst Prof, Ped, 1980; Asst Prof, Ped, 1985; Assoc Prof, Ped, Cell Biology and Anatomy, 1989; Dir, Ped, Cell Biol/Ultrastructure Facility, 1989.

Clyde, Wallace A., Jr. BA, Vanderbilt, 1951; MD, Vanderbilt, 1954; Inst, Ped, 1961; Asst Prof, Ped, 1962; Assoc Prof, Ped and Bacti, 1967; Prof, Ped and Microbiol, 1972; Chief, Div of Ped Inf Dis, 1962–80.

Collier, Albert M. BS, Univ Miami, 1959; MD, Univ Miami, 1963; Inst, Ped, 1970; Asst Prof, Ped, 1971; Assoc Prof, Ped, 1976; Prof, Ped, 1981; Chief, Div of Ped Inf Dis, 1980; Assoc Dir, Center for Environ Med and Lung Biol, 1980.

Denny, Floyd W., Jr. BS, Wofford College, 1944; MD, Vanderbilt, 1946; Prof, Ped, 1960; Alumni Dist Prof, Ped, 1973; Chair, Ped, 1960–81.

Dubovi, Edward J. BA, Univ Penn, 1967; PhD, Univ Pitt, 1975; Res Asst Prof, Ped and Bacti, 1977–81.

Fernald, Gerald W. BS, Univ NC at Chapel Hill, 1957; MD, Univ NC at Chapel Hill, 1960; Asst Prof, Ped, 1967; Assoc Prof, Ped, 1972; Prof, Ped, 1980; Assoc Chair, Ped, 1972; Acting Chair, Ped, 1981–82; Dir, UNC CF Center, 1975.

Glezen, W. Paul. BS, Purdue, 1953; MD, Univ Ill, 1956; Asst Prof, Ped, 1965; Assoc Prof, Ped, 1969–75.

Henderson, Frederick W. BS, Univ NC at Chapel Hill, 1967; MD, Univ NC at

Chapel Hill, 1970; Asst Prof, Ped, 1977; Assoc Prof, Ped, 1984; Prof, Ped, 1989.

Hu, Ping-chuan (Ed). BS, Natl Taiwan Normal Univ, 1956; MS, Northwestern Univ of La., 1966; PhD, Mich State Univ, 1973; Res Asst Prof, Bact and Immunol 1976–1980; Res Assoc Prof, Ped, 1982; Assoc Prof, Ped 1985; Prof, Ped, 1991.

Lim, Wilma A. BS, Univ San Carlos (Philippines), 1979; MD, Cebu Inst Med (Philippines), 1983; Clin Asst Prof, Ped, 1990.

Loda, Frank A. AB, Harvard, 1956; MD, Vanderbilt, 1960; Asst Prof, Ped, 1967; Assoc Prof, Ped, 1972; Prof, Ped, 1980; Asst Prof to Adj Prof, UNC Sch of Pub Health, 1967; Chief, Div of Comm Ped, 1971–90; Dir, Center for Early Adoles, 1988.

Powell, Dwight A. BS, Univ Ill, 1965; MD, Univ Ill, 1969; Inst, Ped, 1973; Asst Prof, Ped, 1975–79.

Strope, Gerald L. BA, Houghton Coll, 1958; MD, Rochester, 1974; Asst Prof, Ped, 1979; Assoc Prof, Ped, 1986–87.

FELLOWS

Year	Name	Current Position
1960–62	W. Paul Glezen, MD	Prof, Microbiol, Baylor Univ
1962–63	Robert S. Sanders, MD	Dir, Wilson Cty Hlth Dept (Lebanon, TN); Retired
1962–64	Adnan S. Dajani, MD	Prof, Ped; Chief, Ped Inf Dis, Wayne State Univ
1964–65	Kwang S. Kim, PhD	Sen Res Assoc in Virol, NY State Hlth Dept
1964–66	Robert I. Slotkin, MD	Ped Pract, Charlotte, NC
1965–66	Jacob A. Lohr, MD	Prof, Ped; Chief, Div Comm Ped; Assoc Chair, Ped, UNC-CH
1967–69	Richard P. Lipman, MD	Ped Pract, Lynn, MA; Clin Att Staff, Boston Child Hosp Med Ctr
1972–75	Dwight A. Powell, MD	Prof, Ped; Chief, Ped Div Inf Dis, Ohio State Univ
1973–74	Cynthia Worrell, MD	Ped Pract, Panama City, FL
1973–75	Joel D. Klein, MD	Chief, Div Ped Inf Dis, A. I. DuPont Instit (Wilmington, DE)
1974–75	Katherine Strangert, MD	Ped Assoc, Karolinska Instit (Stockholm, Sweden)

1975–76	Edwin L. Anderson, MD	Prof Staff, Cardinal Glennon Child Hosp (St. Louis, MO)
1975–77	Frederick Henderson, MD	Prof, Ped, UNC-CH
1975–77	Kenneth E. Schuit, MD	Deceased
1978–80	Thomas F. Murphy, MD	US Air Force, Wright-Patterson AFB, Ohio
1978–80	Margaret Sanyal, MD	Clin Assoc, Yale–New Haven Hosp
1978–80	Gerald L. Strope, MD	Assoc Prof, Ped, E Virg Med School; Dir, Div Pulmon Med and Med Dir, Trans Care Pav, Child Hosp of the King's Daughters (Norfolk, VA)
1980–81	Holcombe E. Grier, MD	Acad Inst, Harvard Univ and Dana Farber Cancer Res Instit (Boston, MA)
1981–83	S. Cecilia Hutto, MD	Asst Prof, Ped, Univ Miami
1981–84	David L. Pacini, MD	Ped Pract, Grand Junction, CO
1982–84	Timothy P. Denny, PhD	Assoc Prof, Plant Pathol, Univ Georgia
1982–84	Margaret Leigh, MD	Assoc Prof, Ped; Chief, Div of Ped Pulmon, UNC-CH
1983–85	Nancy Hinshaw, PhD	Res Asst Prof, Ped, Duke Univ Med Ctr
1984–86	John D. Chapman, PhD	Res Scient, Roche-Hoffman Res Lab (Nutley, NJ)
1984–86	Ulrike Schaper, PhD	Homemaker (Ames, IA)
1985–87	Penny Mulenaer, MD	Asst Prof, Ped, Univ Virginia; Consult Inf Dis, Comm Hosp of Roanoke Valley (Roanoke, VA)
1986–89	Julia M. Inamine, MD	Asst Prof, Microbiol, Colorado State Univ
1986–89	Lisa Simpson, MD, MPH	Speech Writer for Hillary Clinton (Washington, DC)
1989–90	S. Philippe Simoneau, PhD	Asst Prof, Laboratoire de Phytonique LFR Sciences (Angers Cedox, France)
1991–93	Lance Miller, PhD	Res Assoc, Univ Kansas
1992–	Nana K. Kufuor, MD, MPH	In training, UNC-CH
1992–	Thomas S. Lucier, PhD	In training, UNC-CH
1994–	Shi-Kau Liu, PhD	In training, UNC-CH

CHAPTER TWENTY-TWO

Neonatal-Perinatal Medicine

BACKGROUND: THE CURNEN ERA (1952–1960)

PRIOR to 1960, neonatology had not been recognized as a pediatric sub-specialty; indeed, the word "neonatology" had not yet been coined. Other fields of pediatrics such as cardiology were becoming functionally distinct but, in general, academic departments were not organized into divisions. The Department of Pediatrics in Chapel Hill was no exception. The Department was small, patients were treated in general wards and clinics, and there was not a formal division of labor among the faculty. All of the senior faculty members helped take care of the newborns.

December 7, 1956, marked the opening of the first nursery in the North Carolina Memorial Hospital. Prior to this, healthy full-term newborns roomed in with their mothers, sick full-term infants were treated on the general pediatric ward, and prematures were transferred to Duke University Hospital. Dr. Curnen had planned carefully for the new unit, which he called "The Premature and Infant Special Care Nursery." Prematures, sick full-term infants, and infants needing surgery would all be treated in the same unit. This was an innovative concept (see "Facilities" below). Until the opening of the newborn nursery about a year later, all the apparently healthy full-term babies, as well, were admitted there for the first twelve to fifteen hours or until they had tolerated the first feeding. Thus, the first nursery of the new four-year school was prepared to deal with virtually any newborn problem.

Dr. Curnen recruited Miss Martha Russell to become the head nurse in the new unit. She had been recommended to him by Dr. Harry Gordon, a pediatrician on the faculty of Johns Hopkins University with a special interest in prematurity. Miss Russell, a native of North Carolina, had gone to Johns

Hopkins Hospital in 1950 for an eight-week course in caring for premature infants, then stayed as a staff nurse and eventually became head nurse. Before coming to Chapel Hill to be in charge of Dr. Curnen's new nursery she had worked at Duke University Hospital, Sinai Hospital in Baltimore, Rex Hospital in Raleigh, Vanderbilt University Hospital in Nashville (where she worked with Dr. Mildred Stahlman), and Charlotte Memorial Hospital.

Miss Russell recalls that the Premature and Infant Special Care Nursery on 4 West had three rooms, with a capacity of fifteen babies. The room charge was $18 per day. The unit was approved by the State Board of Health for three "premature" beds that were supported by state funds. The unit was staffed by residents and interns, with one attending physician. The residents rotated every two months. The first admission was that of a term baby having seizures, referred by Dr. Emily Tufts from Moore County Hospital in Pinehurst.

THE DENNY YEARS (1960–1981) AND
THE BOAT YEARS (1982–1993)

Faculty

The Denny years were marked by growth in the number of pediatric faculty members and their organization into subspecialty divisions. The development of the major subspecialties was consistent, in general, with that in other academic departments of pediatrics. But neonatology was a curious exception; it developed considerably later. The reasons may be complex, but they surely had to do, at least in part, with Dr. Denny's philosophy of pediatrics. He was skeptical of an organizational plan based on arbitrary age limits. He believed that newborn infants with health problems were served best by pediatricians with knowledge and skills relevant to the problems at hand. The Department was well staffed with experts in cardiology, infectious diseases, neurology, endocrinology, and metabolic disorders. These specialists were all involved in the care of prematures and other infants with special problems of the newborn period. The Denny philosophy, though responsible for some delay in establishing a conventional division of neonatology, resulted finally in a division that was integrated more successfully into the Department than was the case in many university departments. The isolation of neonatology from general pediatrics that was seen in some departments a decade later did not occur in Chapel Hill.

Dr. Denny's ideas about how newborns should be cared for in his Department received strong support from one of the founding fathers of neonatology, Dr. William Silverman of Columbia University. Dr. Silverman was a pioneer in the development of clinical trials to test proposed new treatments of premature infants. In a two-day consultation visit to Chapel Hill in September 1966, Dr. Silverman concluded that the Department was doing an excellent job of taking care of newborns. He shared Dr. Denny's view that the entire Department should remain involved in the Premature and Infant Special Care Nursery. Thus, while other departments such as the one at Duke University were recruiting full-time directors for their newborn programs, the Denny model continued to serve the UNC Department well.

It was the rapidly accumulating advances in treatment of hyaline membrane disease, particularly the use of respirators, that began to strain the ability of the Department to stay at the forefront of neonatal care. Dr. Herbert Harned, chief of the division of pediatric cardiology, and successive chief residents became the de facto neonatologists. They were aided, early in 1972, by the arrival from the University of Michigan of Bruce Steinbach, a talented and experienced respiratory therapist. Even several years before that, infants with respiratory failure were treated with mechanical ventilation, using both negative-pressure and positive-pressure equipment. But Dr. Denny saw the handwriting on the wall. Faculty members and residents were beginning to suggest, and in some cases to demand, that a neonatologist be recruited. Denny began seeking a faculty member who could provide some oversight and establish policies for the care of ill newborns.

The decision of the National Air Pollution Control Administration (forerunner of the Environmental Protection Agency) to establish research laboratories in Chapel Hill coincided nicely with Denny's search for a neonatologist. Dr. John Knelson had been offered the directorship of the laboratories but wanted an appointment in a department of pediatrics. Dr. Denny needed someone to organize and coordinate neonatal care but did not have sufficient funds in his budget to hire a full-time person, nor was he convinced that he needed one.

Dr. Knelson came with excellent credentials for both jobs. In college he had majored in chemistry and graduated with honors. Between college and medical school he had been honored with a Fulbright scholarship at the Sorbonne and the Pasteur Institute in Paris. After graduation from the Northwestern University School of Medicine, he had received training in pediatrics, pulmonary medicine, and epidemiology at the University of Michigan. Then he had taken a fellowship in neonatology with Dr. Mary Ellen Avery at Johns Hopkins University. He had even lived in the Tar Heel State; his academic preparation had been interrupted by a two-year military obligation that took him to Fort Bragg, North Carolina. He was ideally suited for the job in the Department of Pediatrics in Chapel Hill.

Dr. Knelson was hired by the EPA with the understanding that he would spend about 15 percent of his time in clinical neonatology at NCMH. The arrangement was easy on Dr. Denny's tight budget. Knelson's entire salary came from the EPA; the Department of Pediatrics provided him with research funds. Knelson was appointed assistant professor of pediatrics in July 1969.

In addition to developing the research program in air pollution at the EPA and overseeing the nurseries at NCMH, Knelson initiated perinatal research in collaboration with Dr. George Brumley at Duke University. Dr. Brumley, the first neonatologist at Duke, had also had his training in neonatology with

Dr. Avery at Hopkins. They pursued research into questions of neonatal lung physiology—questions that had been generated in Dr. Avery's laboratory at Hopkins. Knelson recalls wrestling pregnant sheep into the back elevator of Duke Hospital and smuggling them into the X-ray Department to determine whether the ewes were carrying twins.

As the EPA air pollution research grew, so did the needs of the nurseries at NCMH. By 1971 it became apparent that a full-time neonatologist was needed, and a search was begun. Dr. Tim Oliver, the chairman of pediatrics at the University of Pittsburgh, recommended that Dr. Denny consider Dr. Ernest Kraybill, a neonatologist who had recently completed a fellowship in neonatology with Dr. Gordon Avery in the Children's Hospital of the District of Columbia and had taken a position in Avery's division in the George Washington University School of Medicine. Kraybill and Oliver had rubbed elbows during a two-week period in 1969 when Kraybill had been a visiting fellow in Oliver's nursery in Seattle while Oliver was chief of neonatology at the University of Washington. The visit had been sponsored by Dr. Judson Randolph, chief of pediatric surgery at the Children's Hospital of the District of Columbia. He had seen some procedures and equipment in Oliver's nursery in Seattle that he thought should be brought to the Children's Hospital nurseries. While Denny was relying on Oliver's judgment about Kraybill, Kraybill sought out Oliver to find out if Denny would be a good boss. Oliver characterized Denny as a "straight shooter." That was good enough for Kraybill. Additional favorable review of Denny as a chairman came from Dr. Robert Parrott, chairman of the Department of Pediatrics at George Washington University and, like Denny, an infectious disease specialist.

Kraybill was appointed assistant professor of pediatrics with responsibilities to head a new division of neonatology in September 1972. The unofficial title "director of nurseries" was attached to the position, as well. Dr. Denny's job description was succinct: "I want you to take responsibility for everything having to do with newborns in our Department."

The differences in background between Kraybill and Knelson indicated the shift that had occurred in Dr. Denny's thinking. Kraybill, a graduate of the University of Pennsylvania School of Medicine, was a general practitioner turned pediatrician turned neonatologist. His rotating internship in Lancaster, Pennsylvania, had caused him to change his mind about becoming an internist and turn instead toward pediatrics. This change of heart came late in the internship year; it was too late to do the necessary traveling to find the right training program in pediatrics. He canceled his residency in internal medicine at the Mayo Clinic and accepted a position in the Stuart Clinic. There, in the Appalachian foothills of Patrick County, Virginia, he became a country doctor, satisfying the urge toward general practice that had taken him to medical school in the first place. Two years of this confirmed his belief that internal medicine was largely geriatrics and solidified his interest in pediatrics as a field where a doctor could really make a difference. During his pediatrics residency at the Children's Hospital of the District of Columbia he came

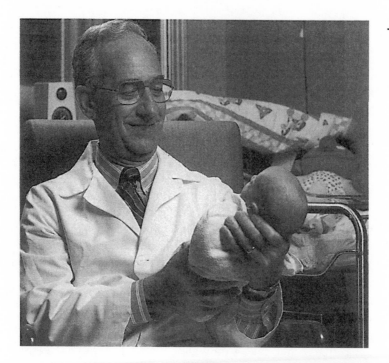

Ernest
Kraybill

under the influence of Dr. Gordon Avery, one of the pioneers in neonatology. Once again, Kraybill's interests changed, this time from general pediatrics to neonatology. He stayed at the DC Children's Hospital for a fellowship in neonatology, then took a position on the faculty of George Washington University.

Kraybill had no laboratory research training but had taken part in a number of clinical studies as a resident and fellow at the D.C. Children's Hospital. These had been important learning experiences. An early pilot study of a primitive extracorporeal membrane oxygenator to treat hyaline membrane disease showed the need for more basic research as well as animal experimentation. Another project illustrated the need to be prepared for the unexpected result. During the winter of 1966–1967, Dr. Robert Parrott and coworkers had begun clinical trials of an experimental vaccine against the respiratory syncytial virus—the etiologic agent in most cases of bronchiolitis. The bronchiolitis epidemic that winter was unusually widespread and severe. Paradoxically, the children who had received the vaccine were the sickest of all. One of them died, despite mechanical ventilation, one night when Kraybill was the supervisory resident on the respiratory ward.

The appointment of a person with no laboratory research background to develop a new division was without precedent for Dr. Denny and the Department of Pediatrics. This fact was not lost on either Denny or Kraybill. They discussed it at length. Before Kraybill was offered the job there was a very clear understanding that while Kraybill's first responsibility would be to develop the clinical and teaching program in neonatology, neonatal research would not be foregone; it would only be postponed. There was a clear and nonnegotiable agreement that the second position that would be created in the division would be filled by a researcher.

It was more than three years before the search for the second neonatologist began. It was not immediately successful. A number of unsuitable candidates were not invited to return for second visits. One or two promising candidates chose not to consider a professional move. It was Dr. Judson Van Wyk who proposed the recruitment of Dr. A. Joseph D'Ercole, then a fellow in pediatric endocrinology under Jud's tutelage. After medical school at Georgetown University, Joe had taken a residency in pediatrics at Tufts University in Boston, where he had been chief resident under Dr. Sydney Gellis. He then spent two years in the Mississippi Delta investigating pesticide poisoning for the U.S. Public Health Service before coming to Chapel Hill for a fellowship in pediatric endocrinology at UNC. Joe was doing research in the area that Jud had pioneered—the study of growth-promoting peptides that are under the control of human growth hormone. Jud observed that Joe's research was concerned with control of fetal and neonatal growth, a problem of utmost importance to neonatology. That Joe had not had formal training in neonatology was of no consequence to Jud and was brushed aside as a "minor" problem: "Kraybill can teach D'Ercole the necessary clinical skills in a few months." It was proposed that Joe be appointed to the faculty with joint responsibilities in two divisions—endocrinology and neonatology. Kraybill was skeptical. He was concerned about whether a faculty member could be productive in two divisions, but even more about whether one could become a competent neonatologist without a formal fellowship. Denny recalls that Kraybill became convinced on this point during the 1977 Merrimon Lecture. Kraybill and Denny happened to be sitting side by side in 103 Berryhill Hall. The Merrimon Lecturer was Dr. Charles Janeway, renowned former chairman of the Department of Pediatrics at the Harvard School of Medicine. Denny leaned over and pointed out, from Janeway's résumé that was printed in the program, that Janeway had never had a residency in pediatrics. Kraybill responded, "I get the point. That's what you've been trying to get across to me." To clinch the lesson, Denny reminded Kraybill that Denny himself had had only twenty-seven months of pediatrics training—less than the required amount for board certification. He divulged that Irvine McQuarrie, his former chief at the University of Minnesota, had to "lie" in order for Denny to become board eligible.

So, after the appointment of a neonatology division chief without laboratory research training, Denny next appointed a neonatologist without clinical training in neonatology. D'Ercole became an assistant professor in July 1977, with responsibilities in two divisions—endocrinology and neonatology. It was a brilliant move. Joe's research leadership established a base for other young investigators who were to join the division later. But he also became a valued attending in the NICU. While other attendings asked the residents mundane questions about blood gases and respirator settings, Joe asked more fundamental questions: "Why isn't this baby growing?"

Ned Lawson

Almost simultaneously with the appointment of D'Ercole, a third faculty member was recruited. Dr. Edward E. Lawson came to UNC from the Boston Children's Hospital, where he had received residency training in pediatrics, then fellowship training with Dr. Mary Ellen Avery in the joint program in neonatology. Finally Denny had hired a conventionally trained neonatologist, with a background in laboratory research as well as clinical training. Ned's research background was in neural control of respiration. He was appointed assistant professor in January 1978. His physiology research laboratory, using animal models, complemented D'Ercole's molecular biology laboratory.

Ned had North Carolina roots. His father, Dr. Robert Lawson, had been on the faculty of the UNC School of Public Health before the UNC School of Medicine became a four-year school. Then he had become chairman of pediatrics at the Bowman Gray School of Medicine in Winston-Salem, where Ned was born. During Ned's second recruitment visit, as Kraybill was driving the Lawson family from the airport to Chapel Hill, Dr. Lawson's wife, Rebecca, observed: "Now Ned can be happy—he has red mud on his shoes again!"

This trio—Kraybill, D'Ercole, and Lawson—comprised the division of neonatology in the Denny administration. Because D'Ercole and Lawson devoted 60 to 70 percent of their time to laboratory research, Kraybill continued to rely on several of the "old-timers," including Harned, Herrington, Kirkman, McMillan, and Underwood, to attend periodically in the Premature and Infant Special Care Nursery. Once, in 1982, after he had stepped down as chairman, Dr. Denny agreed to attend for a month, under the condition that an experienced house officer would handle the details of all but the infectious disease problems. Dr. John Grizzard, a third-year resident who was about to begin a fellowship in neonatology, relished the role. The residents and nurses declared it one of the unit's finer months. It was a fitting performance by a chairman who viewed neonatology as part and parcel of pediatrics.

The next appointments in neonatology took place during the Boat administration. Dr. Carl Bose, the second fellow to complete neonatology training at UNC-CH, was recruited back to Chapel Hill from the University of Utah to fill some urgent needs in the division. He was appointed assistant professor in 1983. His background and interests fit nicely with the needs of the division. Both D'Ercole and Lawson had received substantial grants in support of their laboratory research and therefore needed to devote less time to nonresearch activities. Carl was able and willing to fill the void. In addition to his patient care and teaching, Carl was given administrative responsibilities including directing the infant transport program—which under his leadership became the pediatric transport service—and the development, with nurse clinician-educator Karen Metzguer, of the educational outreach program. He would make a major commitment to clinical research as well.

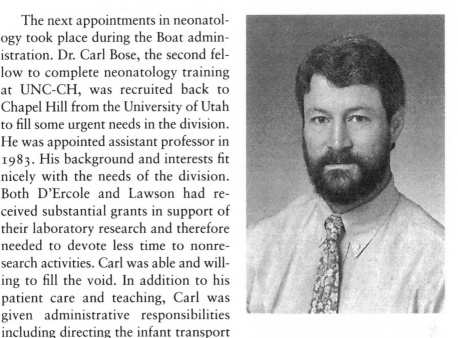

Carl Bose

In 1986 Dr. Alan Stiles, a former chief resident in pediatrics at NCMH, was recruited back to UNC and appointed assistant professor after a fellowship at the joint program in neonatology in Boston. A protégé of Joe D'Ercole, Stiles set up a molecular biology laboratory to study growth and differentiation of the lung. Like Bose, he eventually took on significant administrative responsibilities within the division. These included directing the neonatal nurse-practitioner program and directing the fellowship training program.

In 1990, Dr. Kathleen Veness-Meehan was appointed assistant professor, adding to the division's expertise in developmental biology of the lung. She had recently completed her fellowship training in neonatology at the University of Rochester, where she remained for another year as senior instructor in order to gain additional research experience. She brought to the division strong clinical skills as well as a background in basic research relating to lung injury. During the first several years of her appointment her broad interests in the social context of prematurity and neonatal illness became apparent. She became a strong advocate of families. These interests led to the development of a number of clinical research projects that ultimately helped infants and their stressed parents.

The last appointment to the division faculty during the Boat administration was that of Dr. Wayne Price in 1991. Wayne had come to Chapel Hill in 1988 to begin a fellowship in neonatal-perinatal medicine after training in pediatrics at the D.C. Children's Hospital with Dr. Kraybill's former mentor,

Alan Stiles

Kate Veness-
Meehan

Dr. Gordon Avery. As a fellow, he learned molecular biology in Dr. D'Ercole's laboratory. His appointment was as research assistant professor, but his duties included teaching and patient care as well. The division that started with one part-time faculty member in 1969 now had seven full-time neonatologists.

In 1987, after fifteen years as chief of neonatology, Dr. Kraybill concluded that the division would benefit from new leadership and resigned as chief. He wanted to pursue some other interests, particularly studies of developmental outcomes of the smaller babies surviving the neonatal period. He assumed new responsibilities in the North Carolina Area Health Education Centers (AHEC) program, serving as liaison for pediatrics and AHEC associate director for medical education. In 1992 he was appointed chairman of the Committee on the Protection of the Rights of Human Subjects—the IRB of the UNC-CH School of Medicine, the UNC-CH School of Pharmacy, and the UNC Hospitals. When this task soon required a 50 percent time commitment, he needed no coaxing to reduce his attending commitment to three months per year in the intermediate care nursery and a half-day a week in the special infant care clinic.

Dr. Boat appointed Dr. Lawson as chief of neonatal-perinatal medicine in 1987. He served in that capacity until June 1993. Dean Bondurant had appointed him interim chair of the department of pediatrics in January 1993, upon Dr. Boat's resignation and move to Cincinnati. Dr. Bose, who had just returned from a sabbatical in the United Kingdom, was appointed interim chief of the division in June 1993 so that Dr. Lawson could devote his full attention to administering the Department. During Lawson's administration as chief, the division experienced significant growth in clinical activities as well as research productivity. Lawson was the key person responsible for the planning that permitted consolidation in 1991 of the newborn intensive care nursery and intermediate care nursery on the fourth floor of UNC Hospitals, adjacent to expanded division offices.

Clinical Services

The establishment of the division of neonatology at UNC coincided with the development of regionalized perinatal health care services in North Carolina. In 1972 Governor Robert Scott appointed a Comprehensive Health Planning Task Force on Maternal-Infant Care. The report of that group in 1974 recommended a regionalized system with graded levels of care. North Carolina Memorial Hospital became one of a small group of level III centers that would be responsible for providing specialized clinical services, including the transportation of sick newborns as well as outreach education, research, and organization and evaluation of care. As a result of these developments, as well as the general trend toward more specialized services for children, the premature and infant special care nursery of NCMH admitted increasing numbers of infants who had been referred from community hospitals in North Carolina.

Growth of the clinical services in neonatology paralleled that in the division of maternal-fetal medicine in the Department of Obstetrics and Gynecology. Between 1972 and 1991, the number of deliveries in NCMH increased from about nine hundred to more than two thousand per year. This increase was accounted for largely by referrals of high-risk pregnancies to the maternal-fetal medicine specialists. Whereas the low-birthweight rate for the state averaged around 8 percent, it reached 20 percent in NCMH. With the interests of both obstetricians and neonatologists centered on the fetus and newborn, the mutual distrust that had characterized relationships between obstetricians and pediatricians in earlier years was replaced by a spirit of cooperation.

In 1976, Dr. Kraybill received a three-year grant from the Kate B. Reynolds Health Care Trust that enabled the establishment of an infant transport program to bring critically ill newborns from the hospital of birth to the North Carolina Memorial Hospital. The program first relied on pediatric residents, nurses, and respiratory therapists, who transported babies in local rescue squad ambulances or army helicopters from Fort Bragg. Later, Dr. Lawson developed and trained a nurse and respiratory therapist team that carried out this mission successfully without a physician in attendance. Still later, under the leadership of Carl Bose, this program was expanded to become the pediatric transport service. Because of his experience in air medical transport in Utah, Carl assisted the North Carolina Memorial Hospital in its acquisition of a hospital-based helicopter in 1986. A hospitalwide transport program, Carolina Air Care, was developed by Bose in collaboration with Drs. Hansen, Griggs, Proctor, and others. Bose served as associate director or director of this program thereafter. The pediatric team became one of the first in the country to transport critically ill pediatric (nonneonatal) patients without physician attendance.

In June 1972, prior to Kraybill's arrival in Chapel Hill, the special infant care clinic for follow-up of premature and other high-risk infants had been started by Dr. Robert Gould, who became chief resident in 1974–1975. Dr. Gould thought the acronym (SICC) was phonetically appropriate for the patients that were seen there. Kraybill assumed responsibility for this clinic soon after his arrival in September 1972. Dr. Stuart Teplin, a pediatric developmentalist, became codirector of the clinic several years later. This multidisciplinary clinic became the site for several research projects, as well as providing specialty treatment for "graduates" of the NICU.

The increasing understanding of the pathophysiology of prematurity, and the technological advances that accompanied it, resulted in a lowering of the threshold at which survival was possible. By 1980, the survival rate of infants with birthweights 500–1000 grams was about 50 percent. But a price had been paid; with survival of ever smaller babies came some new and disquieting diseases, such as bronchopulmonary dysplasia and necrotizing enterocolitis. Retrolental fibroplasia, formerly thought a disease of the past, appeared once again in tiny babies despite careful control of oxygen levels.

The development of the North Carolina regional perinatal program, the development of the maternal-fetal medicine division, the increased survival rates of tiny premature infants, and the infant transport program all contributed to the growth of the clinical service and the educational programs related to it.

Responding to pressures created by the scarcity of NICU beds in North Carolina in the early and mid-1980s, Dr. Lawson initiated the first computer-based system to identify available neonatal intensive care beds in the state; this was the forerunner of the current statewide neonatal telecommunications and database systems linking all the neonatal intensive care units.

In the late 1980s, it was recognized that the medical care of sick newborns in North Carolina could not be done by physicians alone, particularly in the face of reduced time spent by house staff in the neonatal intensive care units. Several of the units in the state began to recruit neonatal nurse-practitioners (NNPs), specially trained nurses who could perform advanced practice under the supervision of neonatologists. A task force chaired by Dr. Alan Stiles was established by the North Carolina Pediatric Society to study the need for NNPs in the state. This multidisciplinary group found that there was a need. Inadequate numbers of trainees were being certified by the only program in the state, a certificate program at Pitt Memorial Hospital in Greenville. With this in mind, the task force recommended establishment of other programs in North Carolina and disseminated information about hiring and training of NNPs outside the state.

The neonatal nurse-practitioner program at UNC was established in July 1991 with the completion of training of Peggy McCracken, a neonatal intensive care nurse with interest in advanced practice. The division of neonatal-perinatal medicine sponsored Ms. McCracken's training at the neonatal nurse-practitioner certificate program at Georgetown University from August to December 1989. Beginning in January 1990, she began her clinical training at UNC under the direction of Dr. Stiles and the other neonatology attending staff. This was an intense hands-on training period with emphasis on diagnostic skills, procedural skills, and patient management. In July of that year, she joined the faculty as a clinical assistant professor and became the first NNP at UNC Hospitals. Elizabeth Brown, another neonatal intensive care nurse, followed in the same training path in 1991. She joined the faculty in 1992. During the same year a third NNP, Maryellen Lane, who had trained in the Georgetown program and worked for several years at the Maine Medical Center in Portland, joined the group.

The NNP role at UNC has continued to evolve with both intensive care and intermediate care responsibilities for patient care, oversight of the neonatal advanced life support program for the hospital, and continued quality assessment for the division of neonatal-perinatal medicine. The program expanded in 1994 to hire a fourth NNP, David Francis, in expectation that further limitation of house staff time in the NICU will occur in the face of a continuing high NICU census. In part because of the program at UNC-CH, the School of Nursing is developing a master's degree program in nursing that will include training as an NNP. With evolution of the extended practice nursing role, such training will be important for supplying NNPs for North Carolina in the future.

Educational Programs

As in most other residency programs in pediatrics during the 1970s, the rapidly growing clinical demands of the NICU resulted in neonatology's taking an ever larger percent of resident time. This trend was tempered at UNC-CH by the presence of first-year residents from a number of other programs. Family medicine, anesthesiology, obstetrics, and the medicine-pediatrics programs all requested NICU experience for their first-year residents. These residents worked side-by-side with pediatrics residents in the nursery. This provided useful preparation for future practice, and the arrangement softened the impact of the later rulings by the Residency Review Committee limiting pediatric residents' neonatology experience. Unfortunately, for a variety of reasons, by the early 1990s only straight pediatrics and medicine-pediatrics residents rotated through the nurseries on a regular basis.

Given the limited time allocated to the third-year clerkship in pediatrics (six weeks, expanded to eight weeks in 1992) and the increasing complexity of the treatment of premature infants, medical students were not assigned to the NICU during their third year. Didactic teaching of neonatology was limited to two seminars for each student group. An elective acting internship in the fourth year launched the careers of a number of neonatologists.

In 1977, while Kraybill was still the only faculty member in the division, a fellowship program had been initiated. At first the fellowship was almost entirely clinical, but with the recruitment of research faculty, both laboratory and clinical research were incorporated into the program. When the Residency Review Committee in 1984 failed to accredit one third of existing programs because of inadequate research, the program at UNC-CH was accredited on first review. Dr. Stiles became director of the program in 1992. By 1994, seventeen fellows had completed the fellowship program and three were in training. Nine of the former fellows were in full-time academic positions.

A "minifellowship" in maternal-fetal-neonatal medicine was started in 1976 by Kraybill and Dr. Edward Bishop, then head of the division of maternal-fetal medicine. This innovative program provided an update of perinatal medicine for obstetricians, pediatricians, and family practitioners who came to Chapel Hill two days a week for four consecutive weeks. In many cases, an obstetrician and a pediatrician from the same community attended the course together. After the retirement of Dr. Bishop, Dr. Watson Bowes assumed obstetrical responsibility for this program in 1983. Its success was demonstrated by a number of physicians who returned to repeat the course every three or four years.

The expertise of Dr. Bose and others at UNC-CH in medical transport of sick newborns and children was shared with others beginning in 1986 through a symposium, which has been held annually since then. This symposium is now recognized nationally, attracting participants from across the United States, as well as a few foreign countries. Its success is due in large part to the codirectorship of Karen Metzguer, a nurse clinician-educator and a member of the division faculty. Because of Metzguer's contribution to this and other educational activities, she was appointed clinical assistant professor in 1991.

In 1984 Bose and Metzguer initiated a comprehensive outreach education program for perinatal health providers in central and southeastern North Carolina. This program, sponsored by the North Carolina Department of Environment, Health and Natural Resources, has become a model for other programs in the state.

Laboratory Research

D'Ercole's research, begun during his fellowship in pediatric endocrinology in 1974, delved into the role of the somatomedins, as they were called then, now designated insulin-like growth factors (IGF), in fetal and neonatal growth and development. Research into the regulation of fetal growth up until that time had focused almost exclusively on hormones and/or nutrients, or had relied on associations with a variety of environmental or disease factors. D'Ercole, together with Dr. Louis E. Underwood, set about to determine whether growth factors, such as the somatomedins, were stimulants of fetal growth. Their work began with the identification and characterization of specific somatomedin cell surface receptors in the human placenta. Not only did this finding raise the possibility that the somatomedins had actions in the placenta, but it also provided a source of a protein that specifically recognized somatomedin and, therefore, could be used to develop a practical and rapid assay for somatomedins. With such a placental receptor assay, sufficient somatomedin soon was purified (by Dr. Judson Van Wyk) to raise an antibody to somatomedin-C (IGF-I) and soon thereafter to develop a radioimmunoassay.

With these tools in hand, the research progressed quickly with the findings that somatomedins circulated in fetal blood from at least late in the first trimester of human gestation. They also showed that the somatomedins were predominantly bound to a variety of binding proteins. Using what now appear to be primitive techniques, D'Ercole and Underwood provided the first evidence that most if not all fetal tissues (from many species, including man) had somatomedin receptors. The later finding made it seem likely that the actions of the somatomedins were widespread. D'Ercole found that the somatomedins also were synthesized in most tissues (previously, they were thought to arise exclusively from the liver). This finding, taken together with the finding that specific receptors were widely expressed, suggested that the somatomedins acted near their sites of synthesis, i.e., in a paracrine or autocrine fashion, rather than like hormones that travel through the circulation to distant sites of action (endocrine mode of action). The latter hypothesis was novel at the time and led many scientists to reevaluate their thinking about the physiology of growth.

In these earlier years of D'Ercole's research career, the 1970s, D'Ercole and Underwood also were the first to discover that the Leprechaun Syndrome resulted from insulin resistance (a defective insulin receptor is often etiologic in this syndrome; however, the baby they studied was shown to have a still-undefined post-receptor mechanism of insulin resistance). D'Ercole also was among the first to prove biochemically that a defect in the thyroid hormone-receptor results in a thyroid hormone-resistant state.

In the 1980s, the research in the D'Ercole laboratory continued to test the hypothesis that IGF-I is synthesized in multiple tissues, where it acts in a paracrine fashion. These studies progressively utilized more sophisticated techniques and asked questions such as: What factors regulate IGF-I synthesis in specific tissues? Are cells from multiple tissues capable of responding to IGF-I? If so, how do they respond? D'Ercole's research was greatly aided by a number of uncommonly talented and enthusiastic trainees.

Dr. Alan D. Stiles, the chief resident in pediatrics in the 1981–1982 academic year, became interested in the research questions posed in the D'Ercole lab, and when not performing his other duties, developed a method to extract IGF-I from tissues. Armed with a valid method to assay tissue concentrations of IGF-I, D'Ercole, Stiles, and Underwood showed that growth hormone (GH) regulated IGF-I in many tissues, not only in liver as the dogma of the time stated. This work was published in the *Proceedings of the National Academy of Sciences* and was instrumental in convincing other scientists that IGF-I acted as a local agent rather than as a hormone that traveled to its sites of action through the circulation. The following year, Stiles went to Boston

Children's Hospital for fellowship training in the joint program in neonatology. During his fellowship he continued to collaborate with D'Ercole. One of his projects was to test the hypothesis that the local growth-promoting actions of IGF-I are important in regenerative growth. He chose the kidney as a model system because he knew that following a unilateral nephrectomy the remaining kidney grew to twice its normal size, and no known agent had been found to account for this growth. To test his hypothesis, Stiles performed unilateral nephrectomies in rats and showed that IGF-I kidney concentrations rose dramatically during the period of regenerative growth. This rise was not accompanied by an elevation of serum IGF-I and occurred even in rats that were made GH-deficient by hypophysectomy. This novel finding met with significant resistance and was rejected by several journals without substantive criticism. Today IGF-I is accepted as a major factor in renal growth and regeneration, and the precise molecular mechanisms of IGF-I's actions on renal growth and function are an intense area of research in many laboratories. In fact, the first clinical trials of IGF-I as a therapeutic agent for acute renal failure are underway.

Dr. Paul Kaplowitz, a former resident at UNC-CH, became the first pediatric endocrine fellow to work in the D'Ercole laboratory. Now a professor of pediatrics at Medical College of Virginia, Kaplowitz made extensive use of his PhD training in cell biology to investigate the actions of IGF-I. In a series of papers, he demonstrated unequivocally the capacity of IGF-I to stimulate the proliferation of embryonic and fetal mouse cells and of cell lines derived from human fetus. Dr. John Grizzard, a neonatology fellow, also worked in the D'Ercole lab. He characterized biochemically the receptors for IGF-I in the human placenta and fetus, and thus established the possibility of IGF-I actions during human in utero development.

Other work in the D'Ercole lab focused on biochemically characterizing proteins capable of binding IGF, IGF binding proteins (IGFBPs), which were found to be ubiquitous in the fetus, and on studies of the physiology of IGF-I in states of altered human fetal growth. While research was progressing well and productively, D'Ercole recognized that the newly emerging tools of molecular biology would have to become an integral component of his research if he were to remain productive.

The arrival of Dr. P. Kay Lund in the Department of Physiology greatly speeded this process. Lund, a PhD physiologist from Manchester, England, had recently completed a postdoctoral fellowship in molecular biology and gastroenterology at Massachusetts General Hospital. Dr. Van Wyk had convinced Lund that she ought to clone the cDNA for IGF-I, and thus she began a long and successful career investigating the molecular biology and physiology of the IGFs. Lund stimulated interest in molecular biology and was instrumental in transferring molecular technology to the D'Ercole lab. Billie Moats-Staats, a technician with D'Ercole who had previously earned a master's degree in cell biology at Kansas State University, decided to pursue her PhD with Lund. During her PhD training she cloned the cDNA and gene for ubiquitin and gathered valuable knowledge and experience that would serve her well when she later returned to pursue her research independently in the Department of Pediatrics in both the divisions of neonatology and endocrinology.

Studies in the D'Ercole lab, done in collaboration with the Lund lab, now focused on the mRNA for the IGFs (IGF-I and -II), their regulation and sites of synthesis. At about this time, Dr. Victor Han, a neonatologist, arrived from the University of Western Ontario and was the next exceptionally talented fellow to work in the D'Ercole lab. Han's primary interest was in the mechanisms of neural development, and therefore he initially spent time in the lab of Dr. Jean Lauder, professor of anatomy and cell biology, to learn techniques of neuronal culture. Having mastered these techniques quickly, he returned full time to the labs of D'Ercole and Lund to learn molecular biology. He also decided to develop a new method that was emerging, called in situ hybridization histochemistry (ISHH), a technique that uses RNA or DNA probes to identify the cellular sites of specific mRNAs. With ISHH in hand, Han was able to demonstrate the specific sites of IGF synthesis in the human fetus. This study, published in *Science*, was one of the first to use this technique and firmly established the IGFs as important agents in human development. Prior to accepting a faculty position at the University of Western Ontario, Han completed numerous studies relating to the role of growth factors in embryonic and fetal growth and set the tone for his continuing prolific research career.

During this time D'Ercole began a collaboration with Drs. Richard Palmiter (University of Washington, Seattle) and Ralph Brinster (University of Pennsylvania). Palmiter and Brinster had been the first to successfully create transgenic (Tg) mice and to employ them to answer biologic questions. Having developed a number of lines of GH-overexpressing Tg mice, they were now trying with limited success to generate IGF-I Tg mice in order to dissect the direct actions of each GH and IGF-I. The power of transgenic technology intrigued D'Ercole and he decided to use a sabbatical year in the Palmiter lab. The collaborative work on the IGF-I Tg mice progressed nicely, but the project that D'Ercole undertook in the Palmiter laboratory was a failure. Nonetheless, D'Ercole learned a great deal of molecular biology which he brought back to Chapel Hill.

On his return to Chapel Hill, he began mentoring his first PhD candidate, Zonghan Dai. Dai, who had a master's degree from the Institute of Developmental Biology in Beijing, had been recruited by Van Wyk on a recent trip to China. Dai quickly learned English and began molecular biology research on the mechanisms of IGF-I's actions. He completed his PhD in near record time and published several studies dealing with the mechanisms of IGF-I's autocrine actions before going to Duke University for postdoctoral training. Concurrently, D'Ercole did a study with Tg mice, again in collaboration with Palmiter and Brinster, demonstrating that IGF-I can replicate the somatic growth-promoting actions of GH. He showed that GH-deficient mice that

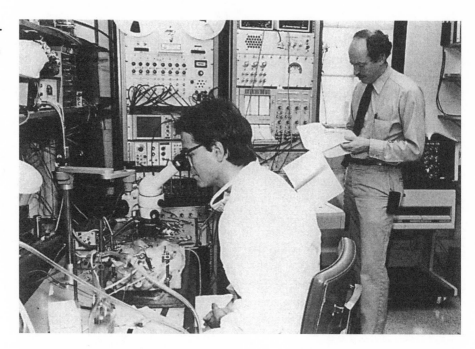

ectopically expressed a transgene for IGF-I grew normally, and he was able to confirm the hypothesis that Van Wyk and others had conceived in 1972. D'Ercole also began an independent transgenic mouse research program. The latter path proved arduous and extraordinarily time consuming, but with the aid of the new transgenic facility in the program in molecular biology and biotechnology the new research was under way. In the ensuing few years, he found that IGF-I-overexpressing Tg mice have large brains with markedly enlarged neurons and a dramatic increase in myelin, and that ectopic expression of IGFBP-1, an inhibitor of IGF-I action in the brain, causes brain growth retardation. As the Boat years ended, D'Ercole's interests had turned to the neuroscience aspects of IGF-I physiology.

Dr. Lawson's research was relevant to a number of important problems in pediatrics and neonatology. Upon arrival at UNC, he concentrated in the area of development of pulmonary surfactant and other aspects of pulmonary physiology. Dr. Carl Bose, then a fellow, collaborated on a project that demonstrated that induced diabetes in pregnant rabbits resulted in reduced synthesis of fetal lung surfactant. In collaboration with investigators in the pulmonary division of the Department of Medicine, Lawson was involved in several projects studying flux of water and electrolytes across the respiratory epithelium of the human fetus and newborn. These projects culminated in a new concept that transient tachypnea of the newborn is due to delay in the normal ionic shifts of sodium and chloride across the respiratory epithelium at birth and in the immediate neonatal period. Another project with clinical application established that lung water and effective pulmonary blood flow could be measured using a miniaturized adaptation of the "bag in a bottle" rebreathing technique. This resulted in clinical studies showing the potentially deleterious effect on pulmonary blood flow of positive end-expiratory pressure in mechanically ventilated infants.

During the early 1980s, Lawson resumed investigations, begun during his fellowship, of respiratory control in newborns. He developed a newborn animal model that allowed extensive studies of respiratory reflexes and their effect on central control of respiration. This work has been continually supported by the National Institutes of Health, including a Research Career Development Award from 1982 to 1987. Lawson's research received additional support and an award for best research grant in 1982 from the United Cerebral Palsy Foundation.

Throughout the period that included his being chief of the division, Lawson maintained his research laboratory, which was continuously funded by grants from the NIH. Maria Czyzyk-Kreska, PhD, MD, was recruited from the UNC-CH Department of Physiology as a research assistant professor in 1991. Drs. Lawson and Czyzyk-Kreska completed cellular studies of the development of neuronal networks in respiratory control. In conjunction with David Milhorn, PhD, in the Department of Physiology, they began to concentrate on molecular mechanisms affecting development of the oxygen chemosensory mechanisms in developing mammals. This resulted in a grant to study how oxygen regulates development of the central neuronal pathways, which in turn regulate respiratory responses to hypoxia. Another grant supported the study of mechanisms by which oxygen regulates gene expression of tyrosine hydroxylase. In 1994, Dr. Lawson was appointed a regular member of the human embryology and development-1 study section of the NIH.

Building on the interest in the control of cell proliferation and growth factors, Dr. Stiles established a laboratory to examine cellular mechanisms of cell growth when he returned from Harvard to join the UNC-CH faculty in 1986. He had drawn on his longstanding collaboration with Drs. D'Ercole, Underwood, and Van Wyk and his orientation to lung development during his fellowship training at the joint program in neonatology with Dr. Barry Smith. At the time of his return, his interests included the mechanisms leading to abnormal lung growth, but studies had focused at the organ and cell culture level. It was apparent that to investigate the mechanisms involved in controlling lung cell proliferation, the studies would have to include molecular biology tools. Collaborating with D'Ercole and Moats-Staats, he first described the production and action of insulinlike growth factor I from fetal lung fibroblasts. This established an autocrine action of this growth factor, a mode of activity previously thought to apply only to tumor cells. The final proof of this was shown by using antisense oligodeoxynucleotides (a tool that inhibits translation of specific RNA and so inhibits protein synthesis) to inhibit production of IGF-I in fetal lung fibroblasts. Dr. George Retsch-Bogart, a fellow in pediatric pulmonary, joined Dr. Stiles as his first fellow shortly after his arrival and successfully demonstrated that adult airway epithelial cells express receptors for IGF-I and are dependent on IGF-I to proliferate. Dr. Wayne Price, a fellow in neonatal-perinatal medicine who later joined Drs. D'Ercole and Stiles, has investigated the role of the IGF binding proteins during the process of lung development. He has continued his research as a research assistant professor working with this research group. A major step in developing this area of research at UNC occurred when a project examining the role of the IGF system in lung development was included in the pediatric SCOR grant in 1990, formalizing collaborations between the pediatric pulmonary and pediatric infectious disease divisions.

Though interest in the IGF system and lung development remains a primary focus, a second area of interest has evolved with the cloning of a previously undescribed growth-related gene from lung cells, called BB1. The BB1 gene is thought to encode a small protein active in late G1 of the cell cycle which is critical for DNA synthesis initiation. This discovery has led to a broadening of interest to include oncogenes, transcription regulation, and translational controls. A third area of interest involves repair following lung injury. This has included studies with IGF-I and damaged airway epithelium, collaborating with Dr. Margaret Leigh in the pediatric pulmonary division, and the role of proteoglycans in injury and repair with Dr. Kathleen Veness-Meehan in the division of neonatal-perinatal medicine.

Dr. Veness-Meehan's interests in distal lung development and the pathophysiology of injury in the developing lung were complementary to many of Dr. Stiles's interests and served as the basis for a strong collaborative relationship between the laboratories. The focus of Veness-Meehan's research was hyperoxic lung injury, a field relevant to clinical neonatology and the bronchopulmonary dysplasia seen so commonly in premature infants who require mechanical ventilation and supplemental oxygen in order to survive. Her studies of oxygen-induced injury in the newborn lung utilized molecular biology as well as biochemical studies of extracellular matrix components such as collagens and proteoglycans and the influence of substances such as vitamin A. Much of Veness-Meehan's early work was supported by the American Lung Association of North Carolina, and in 1992 Dr. Veness-Meehan was awarded the Venable Research Award for her work in retinol deficiency and hyperoxic lung injury.

Investigations into lung injury eventually led back to lung development, particularly the processes of alveolarization and septal formation. As her focus centered more and more on the role of the matrix proteoglycans in these processes, Veness-Meehan recognized her need for a scientific mentor. In 1993 Dr. Stiles introduced her to Dr. Bruce Caterson, a researcher in the Department of Orthopedic Surgery and one of the leading experts on proteoglycan synthesis and metabolism. In 1994, with Dr. Caterson as her sponsor, Veness-Meehan was awarded a five-year NIH Clinical Investigator Development Award for her studies of matrix-associated proteoglycans in lung development and lung injury.

Dr. Veness-Meehan's research interests were not limited to the laboratory. Her concern for the stresses imposed on parents by having a critically ill newborn led her to Dr. Karl Bauman in the School of Public Health and a doctoral candidate, Ms. Suzy Teall. They initiated a study of stress, social support, and affectionate behaviors of adolescent mothers and their infants in the NICU. Veness-Meehan's interest in bioethics was the basis for her work with Dr. Mia Doron, a former fellow in neonatal-perinatal medicine at UNC-CH, and their study of ethical decision making in the care of marginally viable premature infants.

Clinical Research

The late 1970s and 1980s saw increasing clinical research by the neonatology group and others in the Department. In 1979, Drs. Kraybill and Harned became principal investigators in a multicenter study of patent ductus arteriosus in premature infants, organized by Dr. Alexander Nadas, pediatric cardiologist at the Boston Children's Hospital and coordinated by the Harvard School of Public Health. This study demonstrated the efficacy and safety of a new lyophilized intravenous preparation of indomethacin in closing the ductus arteriosus in premature infants with respiratory distress syndrome.

Kraybill initiated clinical research studies of chronic lung disease in prematures. A statewide population-based study in North Carolina revealed wide differences in rates of bronchopulmonary dysplasia (BPD) among the ten newborn intensive care units that could not be explained by differences in birthweight distribution of the patients. Further epidemiologic studies of this phenomenon showed that the differences were attributable, in part, to differing treatment practices. Babies receiving mechanical ventilation who were relatively overventilated were at higher risk for BPD. This finding confirmed a widely held but previously unproven theory.

Other studies by Kraybill, in collaboration with Dr. Teplin and other investigators in the Center for the Study of Development and Learning, compared long-term developmental outcomes of extremely low birthweight infants with those of matched controls who had been born at term. These studies showed the influence of psychosocial as well as biological factors as determinants of neurodevelopment in extremely premature infants. A longitudinal study demonstrated that at age seven years, very low birthweight (VLBW) infants who had had chronic lung disease (CLD) in infancy had poorer language and memory function and performed less well in reading and mathematics than VLBW infants who had not had CLD. These studies, and his 1985 sabbatical leave at the Hastings Center (Institute of Society, Ethics and the Life Sciences) in New York, provided background for Kraybill's being appointed to the chairmanship in 1992 of the Committee on the Protection of the Rights of Human Subjects.

Drs. Carl Bose and others in the division investigated lung function in infants with respiratory disease. Bose, Kraybill, and others became investigators in clinical trials that showed the efficacy and safety of a synthetic surfactant for treatment of hyaline membrane disease in premature infants. These and similar national and international trials were organized by Dr. Walker Long, senior clinical scientist at Burroughs Wellcome Corporation and former fellow in the division of neonatal-perinatal medicine at UNC-CH. Upon his return from sabbatical leave in 1993, Dr. Bose initiated studies of the effect of nitric oxide in infants with pulmonary hypertension.

Facilities

The concept of the modern newborn intensive care unit (NICU) had its roots in Chapel Hill. Dr. Edward Curnen observed, in the mid-1950s, that premature infants and sick full-term infants shared similar needs for medical expertise, nursing care, and specialized equipment. Until then it had been standard practice to care for these two groups of patients in different locations, with separate staffs. Premature infants were outside the mainstream of pediatric patient care, isolated in premature nurseries that were off-limits to students, residents, and most staff pediatricians, as well as parents. Sick full-term infants were treated on the general pediatric wards. In December 1956, with the opening of the premature and infant special care nursery of North Carolina Memorial Hospital, Dr. Curnen had brought these two groups together in a prototypical newborn intensive care unit. In his characteristic modesty, Dr. Curnen never claimed credit for this important contribution to neonatology, yet his concept was at the heart of highly touted nursery designs that were published soon thereafter by more flamboyant pediatricians.

A rapidly planned and implemented renovation of the premature and infant special care nursery occurred in 1970. Dr. Knelson and Dr. Harned sketched the basic layout and location of utilities in one weekend. The construction was done by an NCMH crew. This was to have been only the first of three phases that would further expand the unit toward the east.

But after an auspicious, trend-setting beginning, the nursery facilities of North Carolina Memorial Hospital did not set any further records. After accepting the position in neonatology in June 1972, but before moving to Chapel Hill, Kraybill made an "emergency" trip to Chapel Hill at Denny's request, to provide "final input" to plans that would completely relocate all the nurseries to 4 East. Head nurse Miss Martha Russell was openly skeptical, if not cynical, about the completion of the project, saying, "It will be 1980 before we move into the new nurseries." Her dire prediction was not wrong. Phases two and three of the Knelson-Harned plan did not occur, and the first phase of the unit that they designed was to serve until 1981, when the NICU opened on 4 East. But the final phase of the relocation, the placement of the intermediate care nursery in adjacent space on 4 East, did not occur until 1992. For more than two decades, well-intentioned plans for expansions and renovations were repeatedly delayed, even derailed, by budgetary problems, institutional bureaucracy, and perhaps a lack of solid commitment to the needs of newborns in the face of the rapidly growing needs of other, more highly visible departments in the hospital.

With the construction of a new labor and delivery suite on the fourth floor of the new patient support tower, the nurseries were finally relocated to contiguous space on 4 East in 1981. But in the years between drawing of the plans and occupancy, the space had become inadequate and the design had become obsolete. The space first thought to be available had been encroached upon by the labor and delivery suite; the remaining space was configured badly because of immovable obstacles in the renovated space, some of which were not anticipated. As a result, when the unit opened, immediate renovations of the NICU space were necessary and the space intended for intermediate care was not usable. Only the (full-term) newborn nursery and the intensive care nursery were eventually occupied. The intermediate care nursery, which had been moved to the seventh floor as a temporary measure in 1979, remained there until 1992. The space on 4 East that had been intended for the intermediate care nursery was first relegated to storage, then renovated in 1987 to accommodate more NICU beds. The maneuver that made possible the realization of the Knelson-Harned vision of 1970 was the move of the (full-term) newborn nursery to 4 bed tower in 1990. This finally permitted the opening, in 1992, of an adequate intermediate care nursery on 4 East, adjacent to the NICU. This was accomplished through a plan, developed under Dr. Lawson's leadership, that utilized an unnecessary corridor, some adjacent offices, and the space that had been vacated by the move of the newborn nursery.

From 1987 through 1992, renovations and expansion resulted in a net increase in the combined neonatal intensive care unit and the intermediate care nursery from twenty-six to thirty-six beds. By 1994 the number of admissions to the combined units reached eight hundred per year. The rising number of admissions and the increasing survival of tinier babies in the early 1990s made ever more urgent the construction of completely new facilities that were planned as part of the long-awaited North Carolina Children's Hospital.

Eleven years (1970–1981) had gone by between the building of the Knelson-Harned phase 1 and the NICU relocation to 4 East. Another eleven years (1981–1992) elapsed before the ICN was finally also placed on 4 East, next to the NICU. Will it be another eleven years (1992–2003) before the new facilities open in the North Carolina Children's Hospital?

Reflections on a Quarter Century of Neonatalogy

During the first quarter century of the new specialty that came to be called "neonatology," remarkable progress occurred. The threshold of viability of premature infants moved ever downward in birthweight and gestational age; survival rates of prematures with hyaline membrane disease improved from about 10 percent to better than 90 percent. Much that occurred during those years resulted from the (sometimes) happy marriage of science and technology. A large body of essential knowledge was gained from the biomedical research that began to flourish in the decades following World War II and continues to the present. The application of this knowledge to the treatment of newborns was made possible by equally impressive technological advances. But another element in the successful care of high-risk newborns and their families is less apparent. It is the acknowledgment of the human values that enter into the difficult decisions about treatments that have been made possible by the scientific and technological advances. These three components—science, technology, and human values—must operate in appropriate balance if society is to realize the full benefits of this new specialty. But repeatedly since the 1940s, one or another of these three elements has been out of step with the other two. Many of the iatrogenic tragedies of neonatology, most notably retrolental fibroplasia, resulted from technology being applied before adequate scientific investigation had taken place. More recently, science and technology together have outstripped our ability to recognize and apply the human values that must ultimately determine when to use, and when to withhold, the available technology.

The future of neonatology is hard to predict; few would have foreseen the remarkable events of the past. One is tempted to pronounce that the threshold of survival for premature infants has surely reached a plateau at about twenty-four weeks' gestation and 500 grams. But then, only a quarter century ago similar pronouncements had been made to the effect that the limit was thirty weeks and 1,000 grams. It is possible that unforeseen breakthroughs will result in survival of even smaller and less mature infants, but a further lowering of the threshold of survival should not be considered a high priority. One hopes, instead, that the last decade of the twentieth century will bring the realization of more important goals—the reduction of the prematurity rate and the lessening of the long-term morbidity of the extremely low birthweight survivors.

ERNEST N. KRAYBILL

ACKNOWLEDGMENTS

The author is grateful to Floyd Denny, Herbert Harned, John Knelson, and Martha Russell, who provided historical details about neonatology in NCMH prior to 1972, and to Carl Bose, Joseph D'Ercole, Edward Lawson, Alan Stiles, Wayne Price, and Kathleen Veness-Meehan for their descriptions of individual research, teaching, and clinical activities that became parts of this chapter.

FACULTY

Bose, Carl L. BA, Duke, 1970; MD, Emory, 1974; Inst, Ped, 1979–80; Asst Prof, Ped, 1983; Assoc Prof, Ped, 1986; Prof, Ped, 1995; Chief, Div Neonat, 1993.

D'Ercole, A. Joseph. AB, Notre Dame, 1965; MD, Georgetown, 1969; Asst Prof, Ped, 1977; Assoc Prof, Ped, 1981; Prof, Ped, 1986.

Knelson, John H. BA, Manchester College, 1955; MD, Northwestern, 1960; Asst Prof, Ped, 1969; Adj Assoc Prof, Ped, 1972–78; Chief, Div Neonat, 1969–71.

Kraybill, Ernest N. BS, Eastern Mennonite College, 1958; MD, Univ Penn, 1962; Asst Prof, Ped, 1972; Assoc Prof, Ped, 1976; Prof, Ped, 1983; Chief, Div Neonat, 1972–87.

Lawson, Edward E. AB, Harvard, 1968; MD, Northwestern, 1972; Asst Prof, Ped, 1978; Assoc Prof, Ped, 1982; Prof, Ped, 1987; Chief, Div Neonat, 1987–93; Interim Chair, Ped, 1993–95.

Price, Wayne A. BS, Furman Univ, 1981; MD, Med Univ SC, 1985; Res Asst Prof, Ped, 1991–92; Clin Asst Prof, Ped, 1993.

Stiles, Alan D. BA, Univ NC at Chapel Hill, 1974; MD, Univ NC at Chapel Hill, 1977; Asst Prof, Ped, 1986; Assoc Prof, Ped, 1992.

Veness-Meehan, Kathleen. BS, State Univ College NY, 1979; MD, Univ Rochester, 1983; Asst Prof, Ped, 1990.

FELLOWS

Year	Name	Current Position
1977–79	Charles D. Yoder, MD	Priv Pract, Neonatol (Asheville, NC)
1977–80	Carl L. Bose, MD	Prof, Ped Neonatol; Chief, Div Neonatol, UNC-CH
1978–80	John L. Dolcourt, MD	Assoc Prof, Ped Neonatol, Univ Utah
1979–81	Walker A. Long, MD	Res Assoc Prof, Ped Cardiol, UNC-CH
1980–83	Cheryl A. Kennedy Caroll, MD	Teach Staff, Neonatol (Columbus, GA)
1981–84	Jeannine Gingras, MD	Res Assoc Prof, Ped Neonatol, UNC-CH (Carolinas Med Ctr, Charlotte)
1982–83	John Grizzard, MD	Priv Pract, Radiol (Petersburg, VA)
1983–85	Clarence W. Gowen, MD	Assoc Prof, Ped Neonatol, Eastern VA School of Med
1984–87	Deborah A. Donlon, MD	Clin Asst Prof, Ped Neonatol, Univ South Florida
1985–87	Joseph L. Brady, Jr., MD	Priv Pract, Neonatol (Charlotte, NC)
1986–88	Jamil H. Khan, MD	Asst Prof, Ped Neonatol, Eastern VA School of Med
1987–89	Brian R. Wood, MD	Asst Prof, Ped Neonatol, Eastern VA School of Med
1988–90	Terri M. Snidow, MD	Priv Pract, Neonatol (Richmond, VA)

1988–91	Wayne A. Price, MD	Asst Prof, Ped Neonatol, UNC-CH
1989–92	Ellyn Pearson, MD	Public Health (Silver Spring, MD)
1990–93	Mark Wright, MD	Neonatol, US Naval Hospital (Portsmouth, VA)
1991–94	Rita Makhlouf, MD	Priv Pract, Neonatol (Houston, TX)
1991–94	Mia W. Doron, MD	Vis Asst Prof, Ped Neonatol, UNC-CH
1992–95	Arthur Shepard, MD	Priv Pract, Neonatol (Albany, GA)
1992–95	Martin McCaffrey, MD	Neonatol, US Naval Hospital (San Diego, CA)
1993–	Edward Lee, MD	In training, UNC-CH

CHAPTER TWENTY-THREE

Nephrology

PEDIATRIC nephrology was among the last of the pediatric subspecialties to develop and was certainly among the last to arrive at UNC. This reflected in part the shortage of trained pediatric nephrologists and the willingness of the adult nephrology service to serve as consultants. Nevertheless, an ambulatory renal clinic was established in 1957 under the leadership of Dr. George K. Summer. Dr. Summer assumed this position not from any burning desire to take care of renal patients, but because his own interests in protein metabolism had led him to do a fellowship in Dr. Louis Welt's renal physiology laboratory. Dr. Summer's clinic took care of children with nephrotic syndrome and with glomerulonephritis, and shared its time and space with the cystic fibrosis clinic run by Dr. Annie Scott. This sharing was not by accident, as Dr. Scott encouraged Dr. Summer to set up the protocol and technique for doing the sweat test for diagnosis of cystic fibrosis.

When Dr. Summer took a sabbatical leave from July 1962 through June 1963, he asked the rising chief resident, Dr. Gus Conley, to oversee the clinic in his absence. Dr. Conley then became the first of several senior residents to oversee the clinic, as Dr. Summer did not return to clinical medicine at the end of his sabbatical. It is important to note that at this time there were still no routine microchemistries available at NCMH and that scalp-vein needles had been present only over the last three or four years. To get a serum creatinine on a patient remained somewhat of an ordeal. Pediatric renal transplantation and dialysis were not even being considered at UNC during this time. Each of the pediatric attendings was expected to be sufficiently competent to care for any renal patient on the general service; Dr. Summer does not recall ever being asked to consult on a hospitalized patient with renal disease.

In July 1966, Dr. Conley returned from the Air Force to join Dr. Robert

Gus Conley

Senior and Dr. Charles Sheaffer in the expanding Chapel Hill Pediatrics Clinic. At this time it was Dr. Denny's policy that all outside physicians with admitting privileges must have some role in teaching of house staff and students. Although Dr. Denny favored Dr. Conley's joining the endocrine outpatient service, he was convinced that the renal clinic needed a permanent figure. The bargain was sealed with words from Dr. Denny not to be forgotten: "I'm going to pay you a salary for this activity. Not much, to be sure, but one that binds you to us on that day, and not in the office even when it's busy."

During the ensuing five years, the clinic was expanded to take care of children with urinary tract infections as well as the occasional child with systemic lupus erythematosus and/or hypertension. The expansion into the evaluation of urinary tract infections was an interesting one in that the radiology service was not convinced that a voiding cystourethrogram (VCUG) was a necessary part of the evaluation. Dr. Conley then persuaded the radiologists to loan him a fluoroscopic room and a radiologic technician so that he could do his own VCUGs. This situation continued for several years until it became obvious to the radiology department that the test was an asset in the evaluation of children with urinary tract infections and that it was also a potential income producer for the radiology department. Though the radiology department was convinced of the value of this procedure, it is interesting that it took another decade or so to convince the Pediatric Department.

As the clinic expanded its role in the follow-up of hospital patients with renal disease, it also began to serve as a consultant service to referring physicians for these same illnesses. It was apparent that the major lack in the nephrology service at this time was an inability to provide inpatient consultations. The adult nephrology service had been consulted for years, but in general they were very uncomfortable with small children, particularly so with small children with obstructive uropathy. Dr. Christopher Fordham was performing most of the renal biopsies at NCMH during this time. Dr. Conley had been his intern when Dr. Fordham had done the first renal biopsy at NCMH in 1961. When the pediatric house staff felt that a renal biopsy would be important in the management of a particular patient, that patient would have to be presented to Dr. Fordham. Since doing biopsies on pediatric patients was not his favorite occupation, it was customary when a biopsy was thought necessary to send the intern in charge of the patient to sit in Dr. Fordham's office, suggesting the necessity of the biopsy. Although Dr. Fordham did not do all of the requested biopsies, the house staff had a reasonable success rate.

When Dr. Fordham left UNC for Georgia in 1969, Dr. Louis Welt began to do biopsies on the adult service but was not interested in doing them on school-age children. He did offer to teach Dr. Conley the technique, and thereafter pediatric renal biopsies were done with less difficulty. The technique in those days was to obtain an intravenous pyelogram in order to document two kidneys and approximately where they were. The patient would be taken to the pediatric treatment room on the seventh floor, and marks would be made on his back approximately where the kidneys were thought to be according to the intravenous pyelogram. The patient was given a cardiac cocktail, and the biopsy was done. Dr. William Huffines, a pathologist, would be present to document visually that there was renal cortex in the specimen. Following that, the patient would be returned to his room on the seventh floor. Compared to today's method of doing them with ultrasound guidance, it is a tribute to the human body that there were not more complications.

As the 1970s arrived, it became increasingly clear that the Pediatric Department was in need of a full-time pediatric nephrologist. Dialysis, renal transplantation, and the care of neonates with obstructive uropathy were not procedures that could be done without that level of skill. Dr. C. Richard Morris was such a person. He had received his pediatric training at Baylor University where he was highly regarded; he then took a renal fellowship under Dr. Norman Levinsky, a kidney physiologist at Boston University School of Medicine. Dr. Morris arrived at NCMH in July 1971 and under his leadership the load of patients with renal diseases increased almost exponentially. Dr. Morris became inundated by the requirements for teaching and patient care and never was able to follow through with research that he had initiated in Boston.

The outpatient clinic was expanded to a full day a week from its previous half day a week in order to cover children with obstructive uropathy in a combined clinic with the pediatric urology service, headed by Dr. James Mandell. This clinic allowed the joint follow-up of children with posterior urethral valves, renal dysplasia, hydronephrosis, and other forms of obstructive uropathy. In addition, the clinic expanded to include those children with tubulointerstitial renal disease and those who had renal lithiasis. This clinic worked so well that on several occasions the "three musketeers" (Morris, Conley, and Mandell) were asked to present their findings and approaches at various meetings around the state from Linville to Tarboro. In addition, Dr. Morris began consulting in Charlotte one afternoon a month in the renal clinic at Charlotte Memorial Hospital.

The inpatient pediatric nephrology service likewise increased immediately upon Dr. Morris's arrival, and subsequently peritoneal dialysis and hemodialysis became available to our inpatients. However, until the arrival of Dr. Fred Smith in 1989, children requiring these procedures when Dr. Morris was not physically present often were transferred to neighboring institutions for care.

Pediatric renal transplantations began at NCMH in 1976 with the successful transplantation in a large adolescent. Repeating somewhat the story of obtaining renal biopsies, there was a certain uneasiness in the Surgery Department about undertaking this procedure in pediatric patients. As the NCMH experience grew with pediatric patients, and especially with the beginning of the division of pediatric surgery, smaller and smaller patients were able to be transplanted. During the mid-1980s a kidney transplant was carried out in a child with congenital nephrotic syndrome who had been unable to maintain growth secondary to his protein losses. A bilateral nephrectomy was accomplished, and the patient was maintained on peritoneal dialysis so that he could regain his nutritional status and grow to sufficient size to accept a transplant. Our ability to continue that program has varied with the skill and desire of members of the surgical department, forcing a more recent patient with congenital nephrotic syndrome to be transplanted at the University of Minnesota. UNC is currently averaging five to six renal transplantations in children per year.

In addition to the active inpatient and expanded outpatient services, Dr. Morris has integrated the teaching of nephrology with that of the adult nephrology service. Presentations of patients as well as reviews of the current literature are accomplished during meetings that are open to both house staff and students. Dr. Morris has also established a pediatric resident and student rotation on pediatric nephrology in conjunction with the Pediatric Nephrology Department at Duke University. Our students and residents who elect this rotation spend approximately 60 percent of their time at UNC and the other 40 percent at Duke. The Duke students and house officers have equal access to this program, which seems to be growing in popularity. The regular nephrology elective now includes a day and a half of pediatric nephrology in the outpatient clinic in addition to their rotation on the adult nephrology service. The pediatric nephrology rotation and the pediatric part of the regular nephrology rotation have received high praise from the students and residents because of its organization and coverage of pertinent topics. Dr. Morris has received accolades from the students and residents for his efforts in teaching.

W. GUS CONLEY

FACULTY

Conley, William G. III. BS, Univ W Va, 1956; MD, Univ W Va, 1958, and Med Coll of Va, 1960; Clin Inst, Ped, 1966; Clin Asst Prof, Ped, 1969; Clin Assoc Prof, Ped, 1977; Clin Prof, Ped, 1987.

Mandell, James. AA, Univ Fla, 1965; MD, Univ Fla, 1970; Asst Prof, Surg and Ped, 1979; Assoc Prof, Surg and Ped, 1984–85.

Mesrobian, Hrair-George J. BS, Am Univ Beirut, 1973; MD, Am Univ Beirut, 1978; Dir, Ped Urol, 1985–94; Asst Prof, Surg and Ped, 1985–92; Assoc Prof, Surg and Ped, 1992–94.

Morris, C. Richard. BS, Baylor Univ, 1958; MD, Baylor Univ, 1962; Asst Prof, Ped, 1971; Assoc Prof, Ped, 1977.

Smith, Fred G. BS, UCLA, 1951; MD, UCLA, 1955; Clin Prof, Ped, 1987; Clin Prof, Ped, 1989.

FELLOWS

Year	Name	Current Position
1974–76	Robert L. Chevalier, MD	Genentech Prof and V Chair, Ped; Dir Res, Child Med Ctr, Univ Va.

CHAPTER TWENTY-FOUR

Neurology

THE neurology division of the Department of Pediatrics did not establish full identity until nearly two decades after the founding of the Department in 1952. It has always been shared with the Medical School's overall neurology program, initially the division of neurology in the Department of Medicine and, after 1975, the Department of Neurology. During more than a decade this sharing was relatively informal. Indeed, pediatric neurology was not recognized nationally as a subspecialty until 1957, when training criteria were set up. Our first fully qualified pediatric neurologist, Dr. James Etheridge, arrived in 1965, with a joint appointment in both the Department of Pediatrics and the division of neurology. Though his office and laboratory space were located within the division, the funding for his position came primarily from pediatrics. Yet the first listing of pediatric neurology as a division of the Department of Pediatrics occurred much later, apparently in 1972.

INITIAL EXPERTISE

Considerable knowledge of neurology in infants and children existed at UNC well before Dr. Etheridge's arrival. Some of this depended on Dr. Harrie Chamberlin, who joined the new Department of Pediatrics as a young instructor and that Department's second faculty member in January 1953. While trained as a pediatrician, he had had a year of internship in adult neurology and also had experience with the mentally retarded. Dr. Thomas Farmer, chairman of the division of neurology in the Department of Medicine, who arrived at UNC in 1952, had far more experience in the field. He and Dr. Norman Allen, who joined Farmer's division in 1955, became both consultants and mentors for Dr. Chamberlin. The latter, with their backing, saw or consulted on the majority of both neurological and developmental pediatric problems during the early years, in addition to sharing in the overall development of the Department of Pediatrics.

Dr. Chamberlin was Dr. Farmer's junior by seven years at Harvard College, followed by the wartime three-year program at the Harvard Medical School. The year in adult neurology comprised his initial postdoctoral training on Harvard's service at the Boston City Hospital under Derek Denny-Brown and Raymond Adams (Houston Merritt had gone on to New York). Aside from a four-bassinet nursery in which there was almost no patient turnover (one infant, with toxoplasmosis, was there for the entire year), there unfortunately was virtually no contact with children. Consults on the hospital's pediatric service were minimal. The latter was run by Dr. Joe English, a crony of Boston's Mayor Michael Curley, one of the last major city bosses. Not only did English not wish neurology consultations but, now in 1945–1946, he did not believe in penicillin, which had to be given by secret vocal order from his house staff! Though Chamberlin greatly admired Denny-Brown and Adams and the department did have one social worker, he increasingly came to feel that his mentors' research aims made them more interested in what the neuropathology would show than in their patients' overall welfare. This is not criticism, for their research was invaluable in the giant strides being made in the understanding of many neurological conditions, and the setting was that of an inner-city hospital nearly half a century ago.

During a subsequent two-year stint as an Army medical officer, working in both internal medicine and neurology, Chamberlin decided to shift his career to pediatrics. He was encouraged by a long talk with Dr. Adams, who correctly predicted that one day he would be combining both disciplines. Four and a half years of pediatric training followed, at Massachusetts General, at Yale (three years including the chief residency), and at Boston Children's. They included a valuable six months with Dr. Herman Yannet at the Southbury Training School for the mentally retarded and exposure to Byers, Paine, Lombroso, and Matson at Children's (Crothers, whom Chamberlin knew when a medical student, had retired).

One of the most important and happiest events that occurred for Chamberlin during his recruitment visit to Chapel Hill in the summer of 1952 was a luncheon with Farmer in the old dining hall (now the lobby) of the Carolina Inn. There he found that Farmer knew all his past teachers in neurology even better than he did and recognized the opportunity, under Farmer's guidance, to apply his somewhat limited neurological knowledge to children, to expand it and, indeed, to do just what Adams had predicted. If there had ever been any question about joining Dr. Edward Curnen, chairman of the new Department of Pediatrics at UNC, this experience clinched the decision.

Dr. Farmer's background in pediatric neurology was far more extensive. After graduating from Harvard in 1935 he obtained an MA in physiology and psychology at Duke before entering Harvard Medical School, obtaining his MD in 1941. Following an internship at the University of Pennsylvania Hospitals he began neurology training at Boston City Hospital under Denny-Brown, Merritt, and Adams. There he saw many child neurology patients in consultation, but all this had to be done at night on surreptitious requests of the pediatric residents. The senior pediatric physicians (none associated with Harvard) were opposed to help from Harvard's neurology service, the same situation that Dr. Chamberlin was to encounter three years later. Subsequently, Dr. Farmer received a Rockefeller fellowship to study under David Bodian at the poliomyelitis research center at Hopkins. There, because of his developing interest in child neurology, he spent considerable time with Dr. Frank Ford, whose textbook was virtually the bible in the field. After service in the Navy, Farmer returned to Hopkins to work with J. E. Moore in research on the efficacy of penicillin in neurosyphilis and then moved on to join the Department of Neurology faculty at the Southwestern School of Medicine in Dallas. Four years later he came to UNC to start the new division.

While in Dallas Dr. Farmer shared his interest in child neurology with Dr. Gilbert Forbes, then at the Texas Children's Hospital where there were many child neurology patients. In fact, he spent as much time with pediatric neurology problems as he did with adults. Initially he and Dr. Forbes planned to write a child neurology textbook together, but this plan was shelved when Dr. Forbes transferred to Rochester and Dr. Farmer to Chapel Hill. Eventually Dr. Forbes did contribute a chapter to all three editions of Dr. Farmer's textbook.

Dr. Norman Allen, another adult neurologist who had also trained at Harvard Medical School and on Dr. Denny-Brown's service at Boston City Hospital, arrived in Chapel Hill in 1955. He soon became a second important consultant for Dr. Chamberlin. He was especially interested in neurochemistry, having trained with Al Pope at Harvard. His research thus related to a number of neurological problems that manifest themselves in children.

EARLY DEVELOPMENTS

Despite the fact that Dr. Curnen and he comprised the only full-time pediatric faculty, Chamberlin was promptly able to establish weekly pediatric neurology conferences. These were the first regularly scheduled subspecialty conferences in the Department of Pediatrics except for those in pediatric radiology and were attended by students, house staff, and a few faculty from both pediatrics and neurology. Soon Chamberlin was sharing closely with the division of neurology and occasionally presenting patients at neuroradiology or neuropathology conferences. Farmer kindly recommended Chamberlin for associate membership in the American Academy of Neurology and membership in the Association for Research in Nervous and Mental Disease. Later Chamberlin attended national meetings of both, thus further expanding his horizon.

SPACE

Not until Dr. James Etheridge established his own office and laboratory space in the division of neurology in 1965 was any specific space allotted to pediatric neurology per se. Beginning in 1971 Etheridge's successors were given space in the research portion of the Biological Sciences Research Center (BSRC), in the division for disorders of development and learning as joint members of the faculty of that program, or (after 1976) in the Department of Neurology.

FUNDING

Sources of funding varied. Chamberlin, Farmer, and Allen were supported by their own departments, in which they held full-time appointments. Etheridge (1965–1969) was funded largely by the Department of Pediatrics. The Department of Medicine did contribute 24 percent at the start, but this $3,500 contribution remained the same as his salary increased. Later, most of the support for pediatric neurology faculty came from sources other than pediatrics. Dr. Lorcan O'Tuama (1971–1983) was initially 25 percent funded by medicine, 25 percent by pediatrics and 50 percent by the Biological Sciences Research Center, with medicine paying his medical faculty practice plan (MFPP) benefits. Following the initiation of a Department of Neurology in 1975, the 25 percent contributed by pediatrics was transferred to neurology. Dr. Charles Swisher (1972–1975) was funded entirely by the division for disorders of development and learning (DDDL) grants until 1974–1975 when, due to DDDL budget constraints, 47 percent of his salary was shifted to a combination of the Department of Pediatrics and Pediatric Area Health Education funds and 10 percent to the Department of Medicine. The salary for Dr. Jeffrey Allen (1975–1976) was split three ways equally between the DDDL, the Department of Medicine, and the Department of Pediatrics. There has been no input from the Department of Pediatrics into the salaries of pediatric neurologists since final funding arrangements for the Department of Neurology were completed in 1976.

CLINICAL GROWTH OF THE DIVISION

In the early years, all clinic patients with neurological problems, including seizure disorders, were funneled into one pediatric clinic day each week. The majority of developmental problems were also seen on that day for neurological assessment. Beginning in 1962, increasing numbers of the latter were seen in a specialized developmental evaluation clinic. Beginning a few years later, patients with convulsive disorders were evaluated on a separate clinic day. Consultations on similar problems were also made on the pediatric wards.

Demand grew rapidly. As early as 1957 Dr. Chamberlin had written, on request, an article for the now defunct *Tri-State Medical Journal* entitled "The Increasing Significance of Neurology in Pediatric Teaching and Research." In it he estimated that nearly a quarter of the children admitted to our pediatric service were "referred for evaluation and treatment of conditions involving the nervous system." He estimated that proportion to be slightly higher in the pediatric clinic. These figures may have been somewhat skewed by the fact that at that time he was the only member of the three North Carolina medical school faculties who concentrated specifically on neurological and developmental problems. But the eventual initiation of similar clinics at Duke and at Bowman Gray did not reduce the case load in Chapel Hill.

Psychological evaluation, eventually by pediatric psychologists, was an important adjunct to the full evaluation of a significant portion of the patients studied in the pediatric neurology clinic. Joint management with the division of physical therapy and frequent consultation by the division of orthopedics were routine for infants and children with cerebral palsy. As the DDDL evolved from the original, much smaller developmental evaluation clinic, it supplied consultation either on the spot in the pediatric clinics or occasionally by complete referral from a variety of disciplines: physical therapy, occupational therapy, speech and language, special education, behavioral psychology, developmental pediatrics, and others.

Certain specialized areas were also singled out for new programs, such as an interdisciplinary birth defects clinic initiated during the 1970s under the guidance of Dr. Robert Herrington, which focused particularly on neonates with meningomyelocele and its complications. A clinic for children with muscular dystrophy and other degenerative muscular disorders developed under the leadership of Dr. Colin Hall in the division (later department) of neurology.

RESEARCH IN THE DIVISION

Time pressures in the early years, derived from the rapidly increasing case load and the need to share in the overall development of the new Department of Pediatrics, left limited opportunity to focus on research projects in pediatric neurology. Research by members of the division of neurology often overlapped into this area, however. During the late 1950s and early 1960s, Farmer and Allen conducted an extensive study of familial cerebellar disorders, including a search for a neurochemical basis for some of them. Research by the neurology residents was mainly clinical, including studies of subarachnoid hemorrhage, progressive muscular atrophy, and amyotrophic lateral sclerosis. Chamberlin, who had had no research training, did share in some clinical research studies: the anticonvulsant effects of a derivative of Tridione, with Butler and Waddell in the Department of Pharmacology; the association of poliovirus with some cases of acute cerebellar ataxia, with Curnen; and study of a series of patients with hydranencephaly, with Norman Allen and Jim Halsey, a neurology resident (who later became chairman of the Department of Neurology at the University of Alabama).

Research by the pediatric neurologists who later joined the medical faculty can best be evaluated by a review of their bibliographies. One of Etheridge's interests concerned the interrelationship between severe hypoglycemia and brain damage. O'Tuama focused primarily on basic laboratory research, much of it dealing with the blood-brain barrier. Swisher studied the neuropathology of several neurological conditions, including Hallervorden-Spatz disease, and shared in a neurogenetic analysis of the frequent congenital anomalies in Lumbee Indians. Jeffrey Allen became interested in the subtle effects on the developing nervous system of drugs used in oncology and published several important articles on this following his departure for Sloan-Kettering in New York in 1976. Dr. Robert Greenwood, who arrived in 1977 with a strong background in research to head the pediatric neurology division, initially concentrated on various aspects of seizure disorders. Later he set up his own laboratory and now focuses on more basic neurochemical studies.

TEACHING IN THE DIVISION

Weekly pediatric neurology conferences for students, house staff, and faculty were among the earliest regularly scheduled subspecialty conferences in the Department of Pediatrics. Training was given to the pediatric clinic residents and, beginning in the fall of 1953, to assigned fourth-year medical students. Later, neurology residents were to provide additional support, including help with the pediatric neurology conferences. Either Dr. Farmer or Dr. Allen was usually available for consultation to Dr. Chamberlin when necessary. Dr. Chamberlin also provided neurological and developmental assessment consultation on the pediatric ward and, during his attending duties, he tended to emphasize these areas.

During the early years, teaching in the pediatric neurology clinic was augmented by help from two outside pediatric practitioners, Dr. Emily Tufts and Dr. J. W. Lynn, for both of whom Chamberlin provided backup. Time available for clinic teaching received a major boost when Dr. Ruth Dillard shared in the clinic, with a one-year hiatus, from 1958 until 1963. An able young instructor in the Department of Pediatrics, she was especially effective with developmental problems. Pediatric house staff were also often shown patients, the majority of them with disorders of development, whom Chamberlin evaluated in his private clinic, which frequently required a full day each week.

In January 1962 Chamberlin founded the interdisciplinary developmental evaluation clinic (DEC). In this new setting initially only one developmentally handicapped child and his family were evaluated in considerable depth each week. One of the pediatric residents, or occasionally a fourth-year student, alternated with a neurology resident to carry out the pediatric neurological evaluation of this child under Dr. Chamberlin's guidance and later to share in the extensive interdisciplinary conference concerning the child, his family, and management plans. The neurology resident also made pediatric neurology consultations on the ward, presenting the patients to Dr. Chamberlin.

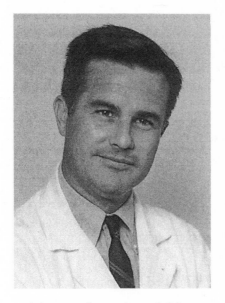

Jim
Etheridge

By 1965 Chamberlin's focus of effort was shifting to the expansion of the DEC into what was to become the DDDL, and Dr. James Etheridge took over primary responsibility for training in pediatric neurology. Indeed, Etheridge's arrival was a giant step toward the establishment of a full-fledged pediatric neurology unit, for he was our first faculty member who had been specifically trained as a pediatric neurologist. He had received his pediatric training in Charlottesville, followed by neurology training at the Mayo Clinic, and was fully certified in the field. Although he attended for one month a year in adult neurology, the remainder of his clinical activity was focused on children, and he held appointments in both the division of neurology and the Department of Pediatrics. A highly successful teaching and consultative child neurology service now developed.

Among outreach training activities perhaps the most important in the 1950s and early 1960s, well before Etheridge's arrival, was a regular program of interaction between the division of neurology in Chapel Hill and the Departments of Neurology in North Carolina's other two medical centers. This was also a forum for research presentations and hence a stimulus to further research. A portion of this activity focused on topics from pediatric neurology. Initially there were biweekly meetings with the Department of Neurology at Duke, over a period of about ten years while Dr. Charles Kunkle was chairman. Held alternately at Duke and Carolina, they occurred during dinnertime in the cafeteria special dining rooms, where a resident or attending gave either a clinical or research presentation. Eventually, in the late 1950s when Dr. James O'Toole arrived to head a Department of Neurology at Bowman Gray, he asked to join. The meeting site, now involving all three departments, was thus shifted to the Burlington Holiday Inn off I-85. At some of these sessions an outstanding visiting neurologist was invited: Raymond Adams, Denny-Brown, Houston Merritt (each several times), Philip Dodge, McDonald Critchley, and others. Denny-Brown was most impressed by one of the later sessions in Burlington, saying, "We can't even get that many neurologists together in Boston!" Chamberlin recalls working hard on two of his own presentations, one on kernicterus and another on what was known (in 1956) of the genesis of congenital defects of the nervous system acquired in utero. All these sessions were good to excellent and they only ended after Dr. Kunkle left Duke and each of the three departments had become increasingly complex and involved within its own medical center.

Among other early approaches to outreach were interactive FM radio programs. The division of neurology as well as the Department of Pediatrics occasionally shared in these, as did other Medical School departments. Each broadcast was linked in with the staff lounges of various hospitals with arrangements for subsequent call-in questions, several of which were usually promptly received. One of these programs, in February 1962, on convulsive disorders in children, which Chamberlin shared with Farmer, was especially memorable. After they had finished their presentations there was not a single call. Finally Victor Herring, a former pediatric resident practicing in Tarboro, took pity on them and called with a question but explained that everyone was glued to their television sets, as John Glenn had just been launched into orbit!

DEVELOPMENT OF THE SUBSPECIALTY OF PEDIATRIC NEUROLOGY AT UNC

The year 1957 had been a watershed for pediatric neurology, for it was then first officially recognized as a subspecialty. The American Board of Neurology and Psychiatry and the American Board of Pediatrics had established a joint committee that hammered out a training plan. Five years of training were required, two in pediatrics and two in adult neurology, both in programs approved by their respective boards, plus at least a year in pediatric neurology (later these requirements were revised). Each neurology program had to be specifically approved to train in pediatric neurology. Prior to this, there had been prominent specialists in child neurology but they had all basically been trained "on the job": Frank Ford, Bronson Crothers (who received the Howland Award from the American Pediatric Society), Randolph Byers, Philip Dodge, and others. But, at last, specific training requirements had been established.

Thus, in 1957, Chamberlin, the only member of the Department of Pediatrics with neurological training, faced a dilemma: whether or not to follow this training course and become a pediatric neurologist. On the surface, because he was well trained in pediatrics and had already had a year of adult neurology, it seemed logical to do so. But he was already an assistant professor, owned a house, had three children, and was not eager to uproot and return to adult neurology, presumably at a center where pediatric neurology was already developed. In addition, he was already particularly interested in mental retardation and related developmental problems and a somewhat different course seemed indicated to expand on this. After discussing the situation individually with Drs. Dodge, Byers, Adams, and Richmond Paine, he ultimately decided to continue on in Chapel Hill.

Eight years later, when Etheridge arrived to take over responsibility for pediatric neurology, Chamberlin was deeply involved in the field of mental retardation and the full range of developmental disorders. The DEC, which he founded in early 1962, had grown rapidly and, evolving into the DDDL, soon would fill two large floors of a new building. Eventually it would be comprised of some thirty-five faculty with appointments in twelve departments

Lorcan
O'Tuama

within seven different graduate schools. Thus Etheridge's arrival was particularly timely, for Chamberlin no longer had adequate time for in-depth participation in pediatric neurology activities.

Following Etheridge's departure in 1969, Dr. Marcel Kinsbourne, Dr. John Griffith, and others from Duke helped out in the pediatric neurology clinic during a truly difficult time. Finally, in 1971, Dr. Lorcan O'Tuama, trained at Boston Children's, took over in pediatric neurology.

Although Chamberlin was now less involved with pediatric neurology per se, it had been his hope to maintain a strong link with Farmer's division by recruiting a pediatric neurologist for the DDDL. In 1971, when it finally appeared that adequate funds could be available to accomplish this the following year, Philip Dodge, at Washington University in St. Louis, who understood the needs of Chamberlin's program, contacted him concerning one of his pediatric neurology fellows, Dr. Charles Swisher. This proved to be especially fortuitous, for Swisher, whose wife was a speech pathologist, was highly enthusiastic about the DDDL's interdisciplinary process. A position was found for her in the Department of Speech and Hearing Sciences and both were recruited, remaining until 1975. Though 100 percent on DDDL funds for the first two years, and 90 percent on DDDL and other pediatric funding during the third year, Swisher shared fully in division of neurology activities as well and made major contributions to both programs. Between 1972 and 1975, under his and O'Tuama's influence, four trainees began fellowships in pediatric neurology: Fred Stowe, Douglas Dove, David Sperry, and Philip Lesser. Each of them spent considerable time in the DDDL under Swisher's guidance. In addition, Swisher shared the responsibility for a full-time pediatric DDDL fellow and the training of various pediatric residents who rotated through the program.

Chamberlin recalls those three years as the most balanced and the most satisfying of the DDDL's history, at least with respect to neurology and pediatrics. But it was not to last indefinitely. In 1975 Swisher's wife was offered an impressive post at Northwestern and, having brought her to Chapel Hill, Swisher felt it his turn to give her priority. That summer he left to join the faculty at Michael Reese. Also in 1975 DDDL grants did not keep up with increasing costs and it became necessary to ask for help to support the pediatric neurology position from the Departments of Pediatrics and Medicine (which still included the division of neurology). The DDDL's contribution dropped to 33 percent, with 33 percent coming from each of the other sources.

With Farmer's help, Dr. Jeffrey Allen was recruited to fill Swisher's position as a junior faculty member, simultaneously completing his final year of pediatric neurology training. Very different from Swisher and less enthusiastic about the DDDL setting, he nonetheless proved to be an excellent teacher. Tragically, his only child was found in February to have a rhabdomyosarcoma. Thus, following surgery and some chemotherapy here, the Allens returned to New York for continued but unsuccessful therapy at Sloan-Kettering.

In 1975 the division of neurology was finally given departmental status, a step originally agreed to when Dr. Isaac Taylor was dean but not activated until this time by Dean Fordham. This initiated a search for a new chairman, culminating in the appointment of Dr. James Hayward from UCLA. To recruit him additional funds had to be accumulated, leading to the withdrawal from the DDDL in 1976 of 66 percent of the funds that had been used to support the pediatric neurology position. Knowing that it would be impossible again to fund the entire position from DDDL grants due to steadily increasing fiscal constraints, Chamberlin met with Fordham to explain the importance of keeping a link between the DDDL and pediatric neurology. A vigorous attempt to prevent the withdrawal was to no avail. Among the several effects on the DDDL of inability to keep up with escalating salaries and other costs, this was probably Chamberlin's biggest disappointment.

Although Chamberlin no longer played a role in the pediatric neurology unit of the new Department of Neurology, that unit has continued to grow and is under able leadership. In 1977, again through Philip Dodge, Farmer and Hayward were finally able to recruit Dr. Robert Greenwood, who has

Bob
Greenwood

Mike
Tennison

stayed to the present (O'Tuama left in 1983). He has proved an excellent choice, with a solid base in both clinical child neurology and research. With Dr. Hayward's arrival the Department of Neurology had moved into the Burnett-Womack building, allowing new laboratory space for several physicians and several newly recruited PhD staff.

Following O'Tuama's departure, Dr. Michael Tennison was recruited in 1983 as the second pediatric neurologist. A few years earlier he had been a resident on the service. He and Greenwood now make a very stable twosome that cares for patients on the pediatric service and runs the pediatric neurology clinic. About 1986 it was agreed with the Department of Pediatrics that they might have a primary service rather than merely a consultative one, designating certain children as pediatric neurology patients. Previously much time had been wasted on admission of complicated patients from the clinic, such as those with difficult convulsive disorder problems whom they knew well but whom a less experienced pediatric resident had never seen. Now the attending in pediatric neurology and the attending in pediatrics work together jointly. The system is working well and is far more streamlined and efficient. As of this writing a third pediatric neurologist, Dr. O'Neill D'Cruz, who trained at the University of Wisconsin, has joined the division (1991).

CONCLUSION

This report should not conclude without further mention of Dr. Farmer's textbook, *Pediatric Neurology*, which served to put Chapel Hill on the map as a center with expertise in that field. Farmer had long felt that something smaller than Frank Ford's giant tome was needed. The first edition, published by Harper & Row in 1964, included twelve other contributors, six from UNC: Allen, Downie, Morris, and Jenkins from the division of neurology, Chamberlin from Pediatrics (who wrote the chapter on mental retardation), and Dugger from Neurosurgery. The volume was well received and a Spanish edition was published. Expanded editions appeared in 1975 and again in 1983, the last with twenty-five contributors including, besides Chamberlin, two other members of the Department of Pediatrics, Stephen Kahler and Arthur Aylsworth. Chamberlin, who wrote the chapter on mental retardation for all three editions, found it an interesting though increasingly difficult challenge as the field became more and more complex. By its nature the format had to be somewhat different from that of other chapters, but it was useful to DDDL students and others to find the subject encapsulated into thirty-five double-columned pages. But by then a multivolume pediatric neurology textbook and several single-volume textbooks, including that by John Menkes, had appeared and it was decided not to continue with further editions.

HARRIE R. CHAMBERLIN

FACULTY

Chamberlin, Harrie R. AB, Harvard, 1942; MD, Harvard, 1945; Inst, Ped, 1953; Asst Prof, Ped, 1955; Assoc Prof, Ped, 1959; Prof, Ped, 1970; Prof Emeritus, Ped, 1984; Dir, Div Disorders of Devt and Learning, 1966–84.

Etheridge, James E., Jr. BA, Univ VA, 1951; MD, Univ VA, 1955; Asst Prof, Ped/Med (Neurol), 1965; Assoc Prof, Ped/Med (Neurol), 1969.

O'Tuama, Lorcan A. Belvedere College (Dublin, Ireland), 1957; MB, BCh, BAO, Univ College (Dublin), 1962; Asst Prof, Ped/Med (Neurol), 1971; Assoc Prof, Ped/Med (Neurol), 1975; Prof, Ped/Med (Neurol), 1981–83.

CHAPTER TWENTY-FIVE

Pulmonary Medicine and Allergy

HISTORICAL OVERVIEW

THE roots of the pediatric pulmonary division reside within the pediatric infectious disease and the adult pulmonary medicine divisions at the University of North Carolina, with dynamic influences from new faculty who came from the well-established pulmonary program at Case Western Reserve University in Cleveland. Even though a true pediatric pulmonary division was not defined until 1983, there had been a wealth of expertise in lung disorders at UNC. The pediatric infectious disease division had fostered special clinical interests in lung infections, particularly respiratory viral infections, tuberculosis, and blastomycosis, as well as chronic lung disorders such as bronchiectasis, cystic fibrosis, and sarcoidosis. These activities are reviewed more extensively in the chapter on the infectious disease division.

A separate pulmonary identity began to evolve in 1977, when Gerald Strope, as an infectious disease fellow, received pulmonary training within the adult pulmonary fellowship training program under the direction of Philip Bromberg. Following completion of his fellowship training, Dr. Strope remained on faculty, first in the infectious disease division (1979–1983) and then in the newly formed pediatric pulmonary division (1983–1987). He developed expertise in pulmonary function testing, infant apnea, obstructive sleep apnea, and mechanical ventilation, as well as management of the children with acute and chronic lung infections who were seen in a combined infectious disease and chest clinic. Dr. Strope's research interests centered around lung physiology. He supervised a program for assessing lung function longitudinally in children followed at the Frank Porter Graham Child Development Center which addressed questions about whether early respiratory viral infections influence lung growth and lung health. In parallel, he developed a system for measuring respiratory mechanics in hamsters infected with a parainfluenza virus using body plethysmography and demonstrated increased airway resistance and responsiveness to methacholine in infected animals. Dr. Strope maintained close association with both the pediatric infectious disease and adult pulmonary divisions, a framework that was important for training pediatric pulmonary fellows Marianna Henry (1980–1983) and Margaret ("Magee") Leigh (1982–1985), as well as establishing lines of collaboration that continue today.

Jerry Strope

The arrival of Tom Boat as chairman in 1982 broadened the pulmonary perspective at UNC. Dr. Boat brought extensive experience and expertise in cystic fibrosis gained from working with Dr. di Sant' Agnese at the National Institutes of Health and with the well-established cystic fibrosis center at Case Western Reserve University. In addition, he brought his research program focused on characterization of airway mucous glycoproteins and modulation of airway secretion. Pi-Wan Cheng, PhD, one of Dr. Boat's key coinvestigators, moved his carbohydrate biochemistry laboratory from Cleveland to Chapel Hill, thereby enabling Dr. Boat to maintain his research interaction while administering the Department. The following year, Dr. Boat was able to recruit Robert E. Wood, PhD, MD, another of his Cleveland coworkers, to come to UNC to build a pulmonary program with an emphasis on flexible fiberoptic bronchoscopy.

Dr. Wood's arrival in August 1983 marked the establishment of a pulmonary division. Other division faculty then were Drs. Jerry Strope, Tom Boat, Pi-Wan Cheng, and Marianna Henry, who had just completed her fellowship training under Jerry Strope's direction. The two pulmonary fellows at that time were Margaret Leigh (second-year fellow) and Ed Pattishall (first-year fellow). Dr. Wood's arrival also marked the birth of pediatric flexible fiberoptic bronchoscopy at UNC. Dr. Wood had taught himself "how to drive" pediatric flexible bronchoscope prototypes when he was at the NIH as a fellow and then at Cleveland. He demonstrated that this instrument could be used to obtain important information about airway disease and infection. His experience was the most extensive of any individual in the world. Indeed, Dr. Wood had trained most of the pediatric bronchoscopists. In his early days at UNC, Dr. Wood's participation in chest conference discussions focused on defining the usefulness of bronchoscopy as a diagnostic tool. Because of the intensity of his discussions, some of the house staff referred to Dr. Wood as a

Bob Wood

"used car salesman trying to sell bronchoscopy." However, it was only a matter of weeks before key members of the faculty "saw the light of bronchoscopy." At a memorable chest conference, Floyd Denny turned to Dr. Wood and said, "Bob, why don't you bronchoscope that child?" The volume of bronchoscopies steadily increased thereafter (as detailed in the section on bronchoscopy below).

Most of the subsequent additions to the faculty were individuals who received their fellowship training at UNC. In 1985, Margaret Leigh completed her fellowship training and was appointed assistant professor of pediatrics. Her research interests focused on airway epithelial biology with a particular emphasis on response to respiratory viral infection and reflected her multidisciplinary training as a fellow with mentorship from Tom Boat and Pi-Wan Cheng in the pulmonary division as well as Wally Clyde, Floyd Denny, Fred Henderson, Albert Collier, Johnny Carson, and Ed Hu in the infectious disease division. During her fellowship, she had identified the postnatal ferret as a model for studying maturation and differentiation of tracheal, pseudostratified, ciliated epithelium. In 1989, George Retsch-Bogart completed his fellowship training at UNC and was appointed research assistant professor in the pediatric pulmonary division. His research interests were directed at the role of growth factors, particularly the insulin-like growth factors (IGFs), in modulating airway epithelial cell proliferation and differentiation. Research mentors during his fellowship had been Joe D'Ercole in the endocrine division and Alan Stiles in the neonatology division. In 1991, Terry Noah completed his fellowship training and was appointed research assistant professor in the pediatric pulmonary division. His research had focused on release of cytokines from airway epithelial cells in response to insults such as ozone exposure or infection with respiratory viruses. Key mentors and collaborators were Bob Devlin and Suzanne Becker at the Environmental Protection Agency, Human Studies Section, at UNC and Fred Henderson from the infectious disease division. In 1994, Pierre Barker completed his pediatric pulmonary fellowship training and was appointed research assistant professor. His research focused on regulation of ion and water flow across airway epithelium during the perinatal transition from a "secretory" epithelium in the fetus to an "absorptive" epithelium in the newborn. During his fellowship, key mentors were Ric Boucher in the adult pulmonary medicine division and John Gatzy in the Department of Pharmacology. All four of these UNC-trained young faculty had outside research funding that provided over 70 percent of their salary support.

In the midst of these additions, Jerry Strope left UNC in 1987 to accept a faculty position at Eastern Virginia Medical School, where he assumed directorship of a newly formed facility to care for patients who were chronically ventilator-dependent. Also, for a brief period (1986–1988), Arno Zaritsky, a pediatric intensivist, joined the pulmonary division while he was establishing a separate critical care division. Prior to the arrival of Dr. Zaritsky, the pediatric pulmonary division provided a major portion of attending coverage in the pediatric intensive care unit and Dr. Wood was director of the pediatric intensive care unit between 1984 and 1986. After Dr. Zaritsky established the critical care program and recruited additional intensivists, the pulmonary division faculty decreased and ultimately ceased attending coverage in the pediatric intensive care unit.

In the early stages of the pulmonary division, asthma had not been a major focus. Dr. Craig LaForce, an allergist in private practice, had one half-day clinic per week at UNC to see asthma and allergy patients as well as to teach the pediatric house staff. Dr. LaForce was "housed" in the pediatric pulmonary division. Then, in 1992, Dr. David Peden, an allergist/immunologist from the National Institutes of Health, joined the pediatric pulmonary division as a full-time assistant professor. He expanded the focus on asthma within the division and in 1994, established a comprehensive asthma clinic attended by both an allergist (himself) and pulmonologists. Referring physicians send their complicated patients with reactive airway disease for evaluation by both pulmonary and allergy specialists. This combined approach expanded the fellowship training in asthma to include allergy skin testing and strategies to control allergies. Because of this added emphasis on asthma and allergies, the division changed its name to the division of pulmonary medicine and allergy in 1994. That year, Dr. Wood resigned and Dr. Leigh took over as chief of the division.

MAJOR CLINICAL INTERESTS

Cystic Fibrosis

In 1974 Dr. Jerry Fernald from the infectious disease division established a cystic fibrosis center at UNC. With development of the pulmonary division, the cystic fibrosis center roster steadily increased from 70 patients in 1982 to 403 patients in 1993. In the early 1990s, the UNC Cystic Fibrosis Center was the fastest growing center in the country, and in 1993, more cystic fibrosis patients were evaluated and treated at the UNC center than any other center in the country. The philosophy of the center focused on aggressive management of pulmonary infections. Dr. Wood established a research protocol to obtain lower-airway secretions by bronchoscopy from infants with cystic fibrosis and demonstrated that their bacterial colonization patterns were variable. Cultures of the bronchoalveolar lavage fluid yielded only oropharyngeal flora in some patients but demonstrated heavy growth of *Staphylococcus aureus* and/or *Pseudomonas aeruginosa* in others. Based on these findings, the UNC pulmonary group was the first to routinely use bronchoscopy to obtain lower-airway cultures to direct antibiotic therapy in patients who were unable to produce sputum. Most of the large CF centers have adopted this aggressive approach to identifying and treating lower respiratory infections in young cystic fibrosis patients who cannot expectorate sputum.

Another major advance in cystic fibrosis management at UNC was establishment of a lung transplantation program for patients with end-stage lung disease in 1989 when Tom Egan, a cardiothoracic surgeon with expertise in double-lung transplantation, was recruited to UNC. Shortly thereafter, cystic fibrosis centers around the country began to refer their cystic fibrosis patients with end-stage lung disease to UNC. While most of these patients were young adults, several pediatric patients were evaluated and subsequently underwent lung transplantation. Now the lung transplantation program at UNC is one of the most successful in the country.

Bronchoscopy

Bronchoscopy opened new approaches to evaluating airway and lung diseases. First, this diagnostic tool provided a mechanism for "seeing" airway anomalies such as laryngomalacia, vocal cord paralysis, subglottic stenosis, tracheomalacia, and bronchomalacia that produced wheezing and stridor. In addition, bronchoscopy-directed bronchoalveolar lavage provided access to lower-airway secretions for culture and cytopathic analyses, expanding our ability to evaluate the etiology of lower-airway diseases in infants and young children who are unable to expectorate sputum. In 1988, Kathleen ("K. C.") Blair, RN, was recruited to UNC as a bronchoscopy nurse. She had worked with Bob Wood in Cleveland and had extensive experience in assisting endoscopies and monitoring sedated infants and children. This addition greatly enhanced the efficiency and productivity of the pulmonary division, which has since been performing 350 to 400 bronchoscopies per year. Another factor influencing the bronchoscopy program was the addition of a pediatric otolaryngologist, Amelia Drake, in 1989 within the Surgery Department. She is a second-generation faculty member at UNC; her father, Newton Fischer, was also an otolaryngologist and professor in the Surgery Department, and her mother, Janet Fischer, was a professor in the adult infectious disease division. Amelia has had a close working relationship with the pulmonary division. She provides the surgical expertise to correct the airway lesions identified by bronchoscopy; the pulmonary division provides the expertise in bronchoscopy needed for subsequent evaluation of her patients postoperatively. A combined conference is held twice a month for Amelia Drake and the pulmonary division to review bronchoscopy videotapes and provide

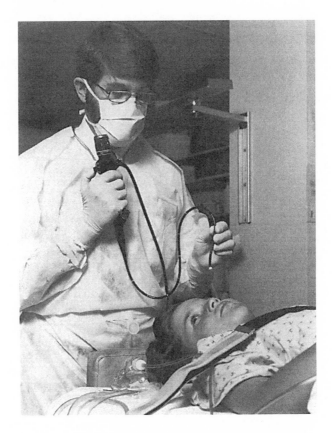

Bob Wood poised with his flexible broncho-scope

patient follow-up. This conference has become a key component of the fellowship training program.

After his arrival at UNC, Dr. Wood continued to conduct yearly bronchoscopy courses to train pediatric pulmonologists from around the country and around the world. Most of these courses have been held at UNC. In 1985 and 1986, the course was held in Davis, California, to provide more access to rhesus monkeys at the primate center there. However, with the acquisition of better airway models, Dr. Wood was able to decrease the need for animals in the practical laboratory sessions. This course has always been full, with a long waiting list reflecting its extraordinary reputation. Because of the increased interest by European pulmonologists, additional courses were conducted in Davos, Switzerland, in 1989, 1991, and 1993. These courses were coordinated by Dr. Martin Schoni in Davos and conducted by the faculty coordinated by Bob Wood. All of the UNC pulmonologists have been instructors in the bronchoscopy courses. These courses have greatly enhanced the reputation of the institution and have provided national and international exposure for our faculty. Clinical, research, and teaching activities centered around bronchoscopy at UNC were centralized in 1994 with the establishment of a bronchoscopy center at UNC directed by Bob Wood.

Marianna
Henry

RESEARCH ACTIVITIES

The research activities of the pulmonary division have focused on areas that complement the major clinical interests, specifically respiratory viral infections, reactive airway disease, airway epithelial cell biology, and cystic fibrosis. Dr. Strope's research on airway reactivity associated with viral infections provided a foundation for subsequent faculty research. Dr. Marianna Henry, in conjunction with Dr. Strope, coordinated lung function studies of the children at the Frank Porter Graham Child Development Center that demonstrated the normal pattern of lung growth in young black children and the influences of wheezing-associated respiratory viral infections on level and growth of lung function. Subsequently, Dr. Henry and Dr. Fred Henderson from the infectious disease division established a large epidemiologic study to define factors, including wheezing during early childhood (usually associated with viral infections), wheezing during later childhood (usually allergy-associated), and tobacco smoke exposure, that influence lung growth and airway reactivity in five hundred children eight to eleven years of age followed by a pediatric practice in Raleigh. Subsequently, Dr. Terry Noah demonstrated that viral respiratory infections stimulated cytokine expression by airway epithelial cells both in cell culture and in the nasal cells and secretions from children with naturally acquired respiratory viral infections. In other studies, Dr. Margaret Leigh defined the influence of influenza infection on mucus secretion in the ferret model and characterized the specificity of influenza virus attachment to ciliated cells. Dr. David Peden's research has centered around airway reactivity, particularly in response to environmental pollutants and in association with sinusitis.

Another central focus for research was airway epithelial biology. Drs. Pi-Wan Cheng and Tom Boat continued their studies characterizing composition and regulation of mucin secretion by airway epithelium. One of their primary objectives was to determine the basis for abnormal secretions in cystic fibrosis. They determined that neutrophil elastase and pseudomonas elastase, abundant constituents in cystic fibrosis airways, were potent secretagogues. Also, they determined that cystic fibrosis mucins were more heavily sulfated than non-cystic fibrosis mucins, a characteristic that may influence the viscoelastic properties of mucins. In addition, Dr. Cheng isolated and cloned several of the enzymes involved in post-translational glycosylation of mucins. During her fellowship, Dr. Margaret Leigh determined that the tracheal

epithelium of newborn ferrets is immature and sparsely ciliated at birth but
undergoes differentiation during the
first four postnatal weeks. In humans,
this differentiation occurs prenatally, at
thirteen to twenty weeks of gestation.
The ferret model of airway cell differentiation became a focus of multidisciplinary studies that combined efforts of
Tom Boat, Margaret Leigh, and Pi-Wan
Cheng from the pediatric pulmonary
division; Johnny Carson, Albert Collier,
and Ed Hu from the infectious disease
division; and Ric Boucher from the
adult pulmonary division. Subsequently,
Dr. Leigh established an airway injury
model and began studies with the above
collaborators to determine if the events
in repair after injury recapitulate those

Margaret
"Magee"
Leigh

seen during normal development. Other research directed at airway epithelial
biology included Dr. George Retsch-Bogart's studies of the influence of IGF-I
and -II on airway cell proliferation and expression of these growth factors
during airway development and Dr. Noah's studies of cytokine expression by
airway epithelial cells (described above).

Research focused on cystic fibrosis included Dr. Wood's bronchoscopic
studies in cystic fibrosis infants (described above). In addition, Dr. Wood has
used bronchoscopic techniques to quantitate deposition of aerosolized drugs,
e.g., amiloride, in the lower airways of cystic fibrosis patients. More recently,
Dr. Terry Noah has used bronchoscopy to obtain lower-airway cells and secretions to assess cytokine expression. Several of the pediatric pulmonary faculty
and fellows, including Terry Noah, Magee Leigh, Pi-Wan Cheng, Pierre
Barker, Dave Thomas, and Giovanni Piedimonte, participated in studies with
the adult pulmonary group and the gene therapy center to investigate
approaches to gene therapy for cystic fibrosis.

FELLOWSHIP TRAINING PROGRAM

The pediatric pulmonary division has maintained an active fellowship
training program with two to six fellows in training in any particular year. All
of these fellows have received support from outside funding sources, including an NIH Fellowship Training Grant that jointly supports the adult and
pediatric programs, the Cystic Fibrosis Foundation, the American Thoracic
Society, the Parker B. Francis Foundation, and the Robert Wood Johnson
Foundation. Twenty fellows have been enrolled in the program as of January
1995. Upon completion of fellowship training, all but one of the "graduat-

ing" fellows has pursued an academic career. One graduate, Ed Pattishall, initially was on faculty at the University of Pittsburgh, but then accepted a position at Burroughs Wellcome overseeing their artificial surfactant studies.

Margaret W. Leigh

FACULTY

Barker, Pierre M. MB, ChB, Univ Cape Town, 1979; MD, Univ Cape Town, 1991; Res Asst Prof, Ped, 1994.

Boat, Thomas F. BA, Central College (Iowa), 1962; MS, Univ Iowa, 1964; MD, Univ Iowa, 1966; Prof, Dept Chair, Ped, 1982–93.

Cheng, Pi-Wan. BS, National Taiwan Univ, 1965; PhD, Case Western Res, 1974; Assoc Prof, Ped and Biochem, 1982.

Henry, Marianna M. BA, Univ NC at Chapel Hill, 1973; MD, Univ NC at Chapel Hill, 1977; Inst, Ped, 1983; Asst Prof, Ped, 1984; Assoc Prof, Ped, 1991.

Leigh, Margaret W. AB, Sweet Briar College, 1973; MD, East Virginia, 1976; Asst Prof, Ped, 1985; Assoc Prof, Ped, 1992; Chief, Div Pul Med and Allergy, 1994.

Noah, Terry L. BA, Univ Mich, 1981; MD, Univ Mich, 1985; Res Asst Prof, Ped, 1991; Invest, UNC Ctr Envir Med Lung Biol, 1991.

Peden, David B. BA, W Virginia Univ, 1980; MD, W Virginia Univ, 1984; Asst Prof, Ped, 1992.

Retsch-Bogart, George Z. BS, Univ Cincinnati, 1974; MD, Univ Cincinnati; 1978; Clin Inst, Ped, 1988; Res Asst Prof, Ped, 1989; Asst Prof, Ped, 1993.

Strope, Gerald. BA, Houghton College, 1965; MD, Rochester, 1974; Asst Prof, Ped, 1979; Assoc Prof, Ped, 1986–87.

Wood, Robert E. BS, Stetson Univ, 1963; PhD, Vanderbilt, 1968; MD, Vanderbilt, 1970; Assoc Prof, Ped, 1983; Prof, Ped, 1988; Chief, Div Pul Med and Allergy, 1983–94.

FELLOWS

Year	Name	Current Position
1977–79	Gerald Strope, MD	Assoc Prof and Dir, Dept Pul/All & Immunol/Rheum, E Virginia Med Ctr
1980–83	Marianna Henry, MD	Assoc Prof, UNC-CH
1982–85	Margaret Leigh, MD	Assoc Prof and Chief, Div Pul Med, UNC-CH

1983–86	Edward Pattishall, MD	Clin Res, Burroughs Wellcome (RTP, NC)
1984–87	Karen Voter, MD	Assoc Prof, Univ Rochester
1985–88	Andre Muelenaer, MD	Asst Prof and Dir, Pul, Child Med Ctr (Roanoke, VA)
1985–89	William Waltner, MD	Priv Pract (Bellingham, WA)
1986–89	Franco Piazza, MD	Asst Prof, George Washington Univ
1986–89	George Retsch-Bogart, MD	Asst Prof, UNC-CH
1987–90	Carlos Perez, MD	Asst Prof, Univ Cincinnati
1988–91	Terry L. Noah, MD	Res Asst Prof, UNC-CH
1989–92	Gary Albers, MD	Asst Prof, St. Louis Univ Child Hosp
1990–93	Chris Harris, MD	Asst Prof, Univ Cincinnati
1991–	William Ashe, Jr., MD	In training, UNC-CH
1992–94	Pierre Barker, MD	Res Asst Prof, UNC-CH
1992–	Peter H. Michelson, MD	In training, UNC-CH
1992–	David E. Thomas, MD	In training, UNC-CH
1993–	Michael Schechter, MD	In training, UNC-CH
1993–	Giovanni Piedimonte, MD	In training, UNC-CH
1994–	Hugh R. Black, MD	In training, UNC-CH

CHAPTER TWENTY-SIX

Rehabilitation

MUCH of pediatric care, with the exception of health care maintenance and acute infectious diseases, requires the efforts of ancillary services. While the usual pediatric subspecialists have programs to deal with some of the associated problems of their patients, several other specialists may be required to care for children with a number of complex structural defects, including those requiring frequent surgery.

With the success of polio immunization, the National Foundation–March of Dimes shifted its orientation to birth defects. It began funding research on the causes of birth defects and for programs to care for the problems associated with these diseases. In 1965, a National Foundation grant for a treatment center was awarded to the UNC Department of Pediatrics. Dr. Loren MacKinney became the director, with partial salaries provided for him, an orthopedic surgeon, a physical therapist, a social worker, and a secretary. Dr. MacKinney left UNC in 1968 and Dr. Charles Sheaffer became interim director until 1969, when Dr. Robert Herrington assumed that role. He remained the director and pediatric coordinator until his retirement in 1991, at which time Dr. Adrian Sandler became director of the program.

In the early 1970s, when the purpose of the original grant had been accomplished—establishing a birth defects clinic—its support was withdrawn. At that time, Dr. Abram Kanof, a retired pediatrician with rehabilitation experience assisting in the clinic, suggested that the name of the program be changed to pediatric rehabilitation—a description that has persisted.

Spina bifida, with its multisystem involvement, is the disorder most frequently encountered at the clinic and vividly demonstrates the need to integrate the care and maximize the potential of children with especially complex problems. The problems associated with the care of these children, the individuals providing the care, and the changes in treatment that have occurred in the past twenty-five years provide a framework for telling the history of pediatric rehabilitation at the University of North Carolina.

Dr. Robert Herrington, as chief of the rehabilitation clinic, soon became the pediatrician involved in making the decisions about the interventions required for children brought to the hospital because of meningomyelocele. Since the basic problem of spina bifida–meningomyelocele is a neural tube defect and the major associated problem is hydrocephalus, neurosurgery was pivotal in its care and decisions about individual cases needed to be made jointly by pediatricians and neurosurgeons. In fact, until the early 1950s when shunting of hydrocephalus was developed, there was very little hope of survival. At UNC in the late 1960s, Dr. Robert Timmons greatly facilitated the care of spina bifida because of his interest in pediatric neurosurgery. However, in 1971 he left Chapel Hill to enter private practice in Greenville, North Carolina. Until the arrival of Dr. Ronald Woosley in 1978, neurosurgical involvement with the rehabilitation program was often "catch as catch can." However, with Dr. Woosley's interest in pediatrics and his regular attendance in the clinic, a level of neurosurgical follow-up was provided that had not previously been experienced. With Dr. Woosley's departure in 1982, Dr. Douglas Jones, first a chief resident and then an attending from 1983 to 1985, continued sensitive neurosurgical involvement. In 1985, Dr. Jones joined Dr. Timmons in private practice and Dr. Stephen Powers, who had been on the attending staff from 1983, assumed the role of the neurosurgeon most interested in meningomyelocele. Recently, the importance of pediatric neurosurgery has been emphasized with the arrival in 1991 of Dr. Stephen Gudeman as head of the division.

In addition to aiding in making decisions as to interventions and in counseling parents after the initial diagnosis, Dr. Herrington assumed a major role in coordinating the medical care of these patients in the clinic. Although the treatment of spina bifida–meningomyelocele most often begins as an inpatient encounter, a great portion of the subsequent involvement is in an outpatient setting. This required establishment of an outpatient program with a preclinic planning session to prioritize the important needs of the scheduled patients. At the same time, the charts of the patients who had been seen the previous week were reviewed to be sure decisions regarding treatment had been properly implemented. To ensure that the ten to twelve patients were seen by as many as six to seven disciplines during a four-hour clinic often taxed the interpersonal relationships of all those involved. In the late 1980s, Dr. Herrington, previously primarily responsible for orchestrating this complicated program, was assisted ably by Dr. Mary Sugioka.

Historically, the approach to meningomyelocele changed significantly between the 1970s and the 1980s. Contrary to the English approach of total intervention, in the 1970s many U.S. centers, including UNC's, were very conservative. When parents wished intervention, it often fell to the pediatrician to find another more aggressive treatment center. In the early 1980s, when the

Baby Doe laws became a factor in the practice of medicine, even the most severe cases of spina bifida were considered for surgical intervention. The pediatrician's role then became one of counseling, often with a degree of conservatism. Even if no surgery was done, supportive care was given.

Another area of counseling that fell to the pediatrician was in prenatal diagnosis. In the late 1970s and early 1980s, elevated alpha-fetoprotein amniotic and maternal serum levels were recognized as an indication of a fetal defect. This, coupled with the perfection of fetal ultrasound imaging, allowed for very accurate antenatal diagnosis of neural tube defects. When such were identified, Dr. Herrington and Ms. Carol Hadler, the pediatric social worker then with the program, presented the options to the parents. It is of interest that very few parents chose to complete the pregnancy when a defective fetus had been identified during the first trimester.

In meningomyelocele, the orthopedic management is frequently very challenging because of muscle imbalances produced by spinal lesions. In the late 1960s and early 1970s, the junior attending orthopedic surgeons, Drs. Jack Childers and William Bowers, who were associated with the program, often were very conservative in their approach to these complicated problems. In 1976, Dr. Walter Greene, a UNC Medical School graduate and orthopedic resident with interest in pediatrics, first worked in the rehabilitation clinic. His interest in children with orthopedic disabilities intensified as he became involved with the problems encountered in the care of children with meningomyelocele. Following a fellowship at the Newington Children's Hospital in Connecticut, an internationally recognized pediatric orthopedic center, he joined the UNC faculty in 1978. From that time, the orthopedic care provided by the pediatric rehabilitation program has been outstanding and the scholarly activities of Dr. Greene have made innovative contributions to pediatric care.

Because of the orthopedic problems of children with spina bifida, the physical therapist played a paramount role in their management. The success of the complicated surgical manipulations is often dependent on the therapist's involvements in orthotic selection and in training in the use of the new neuromuscular combinations after orthopedic surgery. This need for physical therapy in rehabilitation programs was recognized by the National Foundation when funding was provided in the original grant to our institution. The first physical therapist associated with the program was Ms. Judy Bestwick. Her work with the birth defects program was tragically interrupted by a fatal auto accident in May of 1975. Her dedicated, enthusiastic, and enlightened approach set the stage for a long line of physical therapists involved with meningomyelocele patients. Working with Judy Bestwick in the early 1970s, Ms. Carol Parr, a physical therapist associated with the division for disorders of development and learning, continued to provide leadership until she left in 1977. During her association with the program, there began an overlapping succession of outstanding physical therapists: Mr. James Little in the early 1970s until he left to be the director of physical therapy at the Lenox

Baker Hospital; Ms. Jan Montwheiler from 1976 to 1978; Ms. Julie Aul from 1978 until the late 1980s; and Ms. Diane Damiano from 1979 until late 1983. Ms. Julie Brugnolotti continued in Diane's footsteps until 1988, when Ms. Kathy Howes started her service, continuing to the present.

The orthopedic care of a child with spina bifida would not be complete without the involvement of an orthotic specialist who might construct appropriate braces. Since their inception, the UNC Hospitals have depended on the private enterprise of Mr. Joseph Ferguson's Capital Prosthetic and Orthosis Program. Following his death in 1983, his son, Mr. Dan Ferguson, with the help of Mr. Curtis Jones and others, has continued to provide expert bracing for children with meningomyelocele.

Urological problems, especially cord bladder disorders, require special attention, and when Dr. James Mandell became an attending in 1979, these were addressed expertly. It was also at that time that clean intermittent bladder catheterization, the revolutionary approach to the spina bifida problems of neurogenic bladder, became accepted management. In 1978, Ms. Carol Sackett, a urology nurse specialist, began a dedicated and continuing involvement with the pediatric rehabilitation program. Working with Dr. Mandell, she applied her skills in establishing bladder and bowel management programs. Once urological surgical problems of spina bifida were accomplished, the most important aspects of the prevention of chronic renal disease, i.e., bladder and bowel management, fell to Ms. Sackett. Her expertise can be attested to by the fact that only one out of several hundred meningomyelocele patients has died of renal complications. Ms. Sackett's influence on the well-being of children with spina bifida extended beyond her participation in the immediate pediatric rehabilitation program. Her efforts and success in making the intermittent bladder catheterization program accepted in school systems throughout the state cannot be overemphasized.

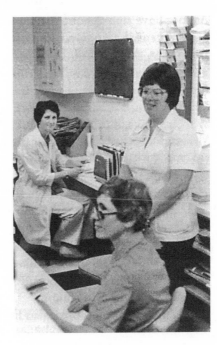

Important staff in the Pediatric Clinic (left to right): Trish Ross, Sharon Asbill, and Margaret Adams

Nurses have significantly contributed to the success of the pediatric rehabilitation program. Ms. Margaret Adams, the overall nursing supervisor of the pediatric outpatient department, was in charge of the nursing component of the rehabilitation program from 1969 until 1975, when she assigned this activity to Ms. Paula Mattocks. Since that time, Ms. Mattocks has essentially performed as a surrogate clinic director. In recent years, she has taken the responsibility for scheduling clinic visits, as well as coordinating the many ancillary tests a child might receive at a clinic visit. This was accomplished in addition to the normal clinic activities of observing accurate measurements, updating immunizations, and making public health nursing referrals, etc. Ms. Weiss Dykstra, a pediatric orthopedic nurse specialist, worked extensively with spina bifida patients. Tragically, she died in 1983; Ms. Sally O'Brian followed in her footsteps at the clinic, where she continues to be an important member of the rehab team. She, Paula Mattocks, and Carol Sackett still serve as important contacts for families of rehab patients.

There are many existing social programs that may assist patients with spina bifida and their families; however, the complexity of interactions in such programs can be overwhelming for even the most sophisticated families. The social worker is indispensable in helping families benefit from the programs that are available. The dedicated, enthusiastic efforts of the social workers associated with the rehab program are one of its outstanding facets. The succession of social workers began with Ms. Nancy Talbert, followed by Ms. Linda Howden starting in 1969; Ms. Jan Dunn from 1971 to 1974; Ms. Carleen Gilbert in 1978; Ms. Janice Ryan and Mr. Adams Wolford from 1979 to 1984; and Ms. Carol Hadler, who began an eight-year period of service in 1984. Ms. Hadler's efforts were particularly taxing, as she assumed much of the responsibility for helping families receive the benefits of Public Law 99-457. The major provisions of this law provide early intervention services for infants and toddlers and educational activities for children with handicaps beginning at age three. It was also during this period that antenatal diagnosis began to expand and Ms. Hadler provided help for women who had been identified as carrying a fetus with a neural tube abnormality.

Frequently, spina bifida children with their central nervous system abnormalities have significant learning disabilities. The evaluation of their educational potential is an important aspect of their management. Early in the children's lives, the physical therapists who are experts in performing the Denver Developmental Test could detect possible problems. But as the children approached school age, a more formal evaluation was necessary. For this reason, as well as because of the psychosocial and sexual problems encountered by the patients, a psychologist became important in the overall management. Although not specifically identified with the birth defects clinic, in the late 1960s and early 1970s Dr. Sandra Mills, as a pediatric psychologist, provided psychological expertise. In 1972, Dr. Brian Stabler began a postdoctoral fellowship which subsequently led to a permanent position in pediatric psychology. During these years, he was the program's "psychologist." From 1977 to 1993, Dr. Cynthia Wilhelm, first as a postdoctoral fellow under Dr. Stabler and subsequently as a psychologist in the vocational rehabilitation program, was the pediatric rehabilitation team's psychologist. In the mid-1980s, she directed the efforts of two outstanding pediatric psychology interns, Melissa Johnson and Julie Juenemann.

Occupational therapists also have been a part of the rehabilitation team. Assessment of physical capabilities and the selection of aids for independent living are important in the management of spina bifida. Ms. Lois Heying, Ms. Pat Moultin, Mr. Joe Saint Marie, Ms. Kay Cooper, and Ms. Suzanne Salsberg have provided expert service through the years.

All of the above specialists were involved as core members of this multifaceted team. In addition, other specialists were consulted for special procedures. For instance, the division of plastic surgery often has been called upon to help with the management of significant pressure sores so commonly associated with paraplegic patients. To give credit to all involved is impractical; however, Dr. Jefferson Davis has for the past five years enthusiastically cared for and provided follow-up care for many plastic surgical problems encountered. The Neurology Department has aided in treating seizure disorders.

A history of the pediatric rehabilitation program would not be complete without mentioning Ms. Vicky Stafford. As Dr. Herrington's secretary from 1975 to 1984, with her office in the pediatric outpatient department, she became the friend and often the first person of contact for the families of patients followed by the program.

ROBERT HERRINGTON

ADDENDUM TO DR. HERRINGTON'S HISTORY OF THE PEDIATRIC REHABILITATION PROGRAM

It was felt by the editors that this important program had not received the historical emphasis needed and especially that Dr. Herrington's role as the coordinator and often the chief decision maker needed to be detailed. Accordingly, an interesting taped interview was conducted by Dr. Harned with Dr. Robert Herrington to probe several additional aspects of the pediatric rehabilitation program.

Features of the program discussed in this interview included (1) funding of the program, (2) the types of patients cared for in this particular clinic, (3) the ethical considerations involved as the treatments of children with this condition have evolved, and (4) teaching and research.

Funding

Dr. Herrington indicated that from the time the support of the National Foundation was withdrawn until the present the rehabilitation program was self-sustaining. "Each of the various groups of allied ancillary services that were involved in the management of the patients assumed the responsibility for paying the individuals involved and this was done through a fee-for-service arrangement. I don't think that the fees collected from the patients anywhere made up for the salaries that the various people were receiving, but at any rate following the March of Dimes there was no program funding."

Types of Patients

Patients with spina bifida very quickly became the most frequently cared for in the rehab clinic. "The Rehab Program took care of patients who fell through the cracks—who didn't have a well-organized subspecialty group to take care of them." An exception was that of patients with cerebral palsy, who were handled in the rehab clinic early on but were subsequently shifted to a neurology clinic and a special orthopedic clinic. Other patients remained in the rehab clinic, including patients with isolated hydrocephalus and children with achondroplasia. Altogether, about 15 percent of the clinic's patients over the years were cases other than spina bifida.

Ethical Issues

"I had always been somewhat interested in ethical issues and certainly the problems encountered in the broad category of birth defects involved ethical issues."

When the Baby Doe laws went into effect and governmental agencies established guidelines for treating all possible conditions, decision as to treatment of these cases became more straightforward. The neurosurgeons would intervene in all cases where the parents desired this. Under these circumstances it was nearly impossible for a mother, in particular, to deny any treatment that would have any chance of success. Dr. Herrington found that now he was often leaning on the conservative side, since some treatments offered little hope of a reasonable outcome.

New ethical considerations arose with improved prenatal diagnosis. Serum alpha-fetoprotein levels needed to be obtained and could alert physicians to the presence of fetal neural tube defects. With ultrasound diagnosis possible during the first trimester, the possibility of abortion could be raised. If the diagnosis was made later in the pregnancy, this option was of course not available, but the family could be alerted to the implications of the fetal disorder and perhaps be prepared to deal with it better than if the diagnosis was made at birth.

Dr. Herrington described the work of Dr. Smithwells in England, who found that neural tube defects in animals could be prevented by folic acid treatment before and during pregnancy. Eventually this preventive measure was applied effectively to humans as a part of good prenatal care and certainly was vitally important for mothers who had had a previous baby with a neural tube defect. The pediatrician caring for these babies thus has to address many diverse ethical issues.

Teaching and Research

Despite the fact that pediatrics was the primary department involved in this program, pediatric residents were never required to rotate through the clinic. Orthopedic, urologic, and neurosurgical residents attended the clinic with their attendings and indeed, Drs. Mandell and Greene continued interest in these difficult patients from their residencies into their life work. Although no formal research designs were promoted, these specialists have published articles related to their work in the clinic. Several pediatric residents, including Drs. Marjorie Carr and Susan Hyman, took advantage of the teaching opportunities in this multifaceted program. Physical therapy students also attended the clinic. Third-year medical students attended the clinic for one session at times, but this exposure was considered to be rather light.

The interview ended with the thought that this program represents an excellent example of the interrelationships and expertise that can be brought to bear to provide care for very complex and at times devastating disorders.

HERBERT S. HARNED, JR.

CHAPTER TWENTY-SEVEN

Rheumatology and Immunology

Editor's Note: Efforts to establish an ambulatory clinic for children with rheumatologic diseases prior to 1981 were not successful. When I resigned as Department chairman in 1981, Dr. Fernald, the interim chairman, asked me to establish and direct such a clinic until a permanent division chief could be named. At that time we had two purposes for this move: We needed the service badly, and if we were successful it would help in recruiting a new chief. I was asked to do this because of my interest in rheumatic fever and because I had cared for most children with rheumatoid arthritis up to that time. Feeling inadequate to the task, I accepted with one stipulation—that we could attract Dr. Deborah Kredich from Duke to give us the needed expertise for us to be successful in this endeavor. Dr. Kredich agreed and was the prime mover in this clinic until Dr. Warren was recruited as chief in 1983. Dr. Nicholas Patrone, an internist in rheumatology fellowship, but interested in children's diseases, proved to be an extremely valuable contributor to our efforts. Others recruited as members of the pediatric rheumatology team included Dr. Cynthia Wilhelm, a psychologist from the Department of Medical Allied Health Professions; Mrs. Marion Kalbacker, pediatric clinical social worker; and Mrs. Mary Flynn, clinic nurse. Dr. Walter Greene, pediatric orthopedist, provided consultations as necessary. This group proved to be very compatible and developed an efficient and successful operation that formed the basis for the establishment of a formal division. Dr. Stein's story of the division continues below. (Floyd W. Denny, Jr.)

T HE rheumatology and immunology division was established as an independent departmental division in 1983, when Dr. Thomas Boat named Robert Warren, MD, PhD, as the first division chief. Dr. Warren completed his rheumatology-allergy-immunology combined fellowship at Duke University prior to arriving at UNC-CH. He established the multiple missions of the division. The first and foremost mission was to provide uncompromising service, accurate diagnoses, and superior patient care for patients with rheumatologic, autoimmune, and immunologic diseases. A consultative service, inpatient service, and two outpatient clinics were established. A hallmark of the outpatient clinics was the presence of a multidisci-

Bob Warren

plinary team including physicians, physical and occupational therapists, a social worker, a psychologist, and a nurse.

Established hand in hand with the patient care was a second mission: to provide education for postgraduate medical professionals (interns, residents, and rheumatology fellows). The monthly elective with Dr. Warren quickly became a popular selection among the residents, who were eager to learn more about rheumatologic diseases, immunodeficiency diseases, and the musculoskeletal examination.

The third founding mission was to establish a research program. The key emphasis was placed on basic laboratory research dedicated to exploring the pathogenesis of pediatric rheumatologic diseases. Dr. Warren's early investigations were focused on better understanding of rheumatoid factors in disease. He obtained initial funding through a development and feasibility grant awarded by the Multipurpose Arthritis Center.

The rheumatology and immunology division started with only a single full-time faculty member but strengthened its base by continuing collaborative programs with the rheumatology service at Duke University Medical Center. Dr. Warren invited Dr. Deborah Kredich to

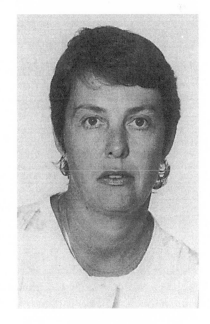

Debbie Kredich

Lenny Stein

continue her affiliation with the UNC rheumatology program. Dr. Kredich had established a rheumatology service at Duke University in 1971. She and Dr. Warren jointly participated subsequently in both UNC and Duke University clinics. These interactions fostered better communications and patient care between the two programs. In 1986 a collaborative grant was funded through the Arthritis Foundation to promote a higher level of programmatic interactions.

A new rheumatology teaching program was added in 1985. At the request of Carolinas Medical Center and under the sponsorship of the UNC AHEC program, the division initiated training of medical residents and medical students in Charlotte. Three clinics per year were established primarily to provide a teaching experience for pediatric trainees. In addition to trainee education, these clinics were especially important for patients who could not travel the distance to other established referral centers.

In 1986 Dr. Warren added to the division a second full-time faculty member, Dr. Leonard Stein. Dr. Stein trained in rheumatology and immunology at the University of Michigan and the Hospital for Sick Children in Toronto. The addition of Dr. Stein strengthened the clinical base; also, Dr. Stein brought with him interest and experience in studying B lymphocyte development. Dr. Stein added several new programs, which included a monthly journal club and X-ray conference. The division expanded in both patient service and research projects from 1986 to 1988. Dr. Warren continued his research on rheumatoid factors and received an NIH RO1 and a UNC Jefferson Pilot Award to further his work. Dr. Stein received a First Award to study B lymphocyte development and a RO1 award to develop and evaluate methods for early detection of HIV-1 infection in children.

The first of four postdoctoral fellows began training in 1988. Each of the fellows received training both at UNC-CH and at Duke University Medical Center. The depth and variety of the fellowship experience was enhanced by combining the strengths of both rheumatology programs. (A list of the fellows and their present positions is included at the end of this chapter.)

In 1988 Dr. Warren left UNC-CH to become head of pediatric rheumatology at Baylor College of Medicine and Dr. Stein became the new division chief. He began looking for a new full-time rheumatologist following Dr. Warren's departure and enlisted Dr. Ann Reed, who joined the division in 1990. Dr. Reed had trained in rheumatology at Northwestern. Her chief clinical and research interests were in juvenile dermatomyositis. Dr. Reed obtained a clinical investigator award to further her training and support her investigations of the role or interactions of HLA in patients with juvenile dermatomyositis.

Ann Reed

During the division's second decade the primary missions have continued with expansion of existing programs and the beginning of new initiatives. Provision of patient care continued as the primary mission. The arrival of Dr. David Peden in the pulmonary and allergy division added a broader foundation to the care and study of patients with immunodeficiency diseases. Dr. Peden's major clinical interests were in allergy, but he maintained a special interest in immunodeficiency and white blood cell abnormalities, an interest developed during his training at the National Institutes of Health. Dr. Peden participated in the rheumatology and immunology clinics as a special consultant.

The division continued its educational mission with expansion of the AHEC teaching program from three clinics per year to monthly clinics in 1995. These AHEC visits provided both lectures and hands-on teaching experiences for medical residents and students. In the area of postgraduate education two new programs were started. Dr. Stein began a collaborative venture with Dr. James Folds to develop a textbook for teaching first-year medical students about rheumatology and immunodeficiency. In the second project, Dr. Stein and Dr. Helen Cronenberger joined forces to develop interactive computer programs in rheumatology and immunology. Their pilot work was expanded following an award from the Arthritis Foundation. The mission to foster basic research also continued in the division's second decade. New research investigation was begun in collaboration with investigators in the School of Public Health. Members of the division became interested in understanding the potential impact of environmental agents on the immune system and interrelationships between environmental exposures and autoimmune diseases. The first divisional research project in this field of interest was undertaken to examine the impact of environmental pollution on the immune system in several communities in central North Carolina.

In early 1995 the pediatric rheumatology and immunology division moved from its longtime home in MacNider Building to the new Thurston Arthritis Center building. This exciting move brought the members of the arthritis center together from multiple sites on the UNC-CH campus. From this move the division expects a new era of collaborations to evolve, yielding even more successful patient care, teaching, and investigations in both biological sciences and clinical research.

LEONARD D. STEIN

FACULTY

Amoroso, Kathy. BA, Northwestern, 1980; MD, Duke, 1984; Clin Prof, Ped, 1990–94.

Kredich, Deborah W. AB, Univ Mich, 1958; MD, Univ Mich, 1962; Asst Clin Prof, Ped, 1982.

Reed, Ann M. BA, Univ of KY, 1978; MD, Med Coll of Ohio, 1984; Res Asst Prof, Ped, 1990.

Simpson, John. BS, Tufts, 1974; MD, Univ of SC, 1981; Vis Clin Prof, Ped Rheum/Immun, 1989–90.

Stein, Leonard D. BSc, Tulane, 1971; MD, Med Coll of GA, 1975; Asst Prof, Ped, 1986; Assoc Prof, Ped, 1989; Co-Dir, Div Ped Rheumatol, 1986–89; Dir, Div Ped Rheumatol, 1989.

Warren, Robert W. BA, Yale, 1972; MD, Washington Univ, 1978; PhD, Washington Univ, 1978; Asst Prof, Ped, Microbiol and Immunol, 1983–89; Dir, Div Ped Rheumatol, 1983–88; Co-Dir, Div Ped Rheumatol, 1986–89; Asst Dir, Clin Immunol Lab, 1987–89.

FELLOWS

Years	Name	Current Position
1987–91	Laura Schanberg, MD	Asst Prof, Ped Rheumat, Duke Univ
1988–91	Egla Rabinovich, MD	Asst Prof, Ped, Univ Chicago
1990–93	Robert A. Colbert, MD	Asst Prof, Ped, Univ Cincinnati
1990–93	Thomas G. Mason, MD	Consultant, Rheumat, Mayo Clinic
1993–96	Brandt Groh, MD	In training, UNC-CH

PART FIVE

Partners in
Pediatric Care

INTRODUCTION

As THE writing of the departmental history evolved, we became aware repeatedly of the complexities and diversities within the Department. Recognizing, as does Carl Sandburg, that the worst concept in our society is expressed in the word "exclusive," we challenged many of the major physician players to recount the histories of their particular divisions. These accounts were included in the previous section of the book. But even with this diversity of expression, many other voices need to be heard to provide a more complete chorus of the departmental activities over the years.

Physicians may tend to exaggerate their own importance in the overall provision of health care. From the patient's perspective, many others may seem equally important. This is especially true in the hospital setting of a large pediatric program such as that at our institution, where many care providers other than physicians play vital roles. Our Department has been blessed by having many extraordinary persons and organizations who have provided services to augment the basic functions of a physician-directed medical program. The contributions of the nursing staff have been immense and the leadership of the head nurses exceptional. Their contributions have been so pervasive that we have had considerable difficulty doing them justice in our descriptions of the work of the Department. The major daily involvement of other workers, including recreational therapists, social workers, school teachers, hospital volunteers, and administrators, also will be emphasized, including the many unique aspects of their endeavors. The activities of other health care partners, including physical therapists, occupational therapists, respiratory therapists, nutritionists, and the secretaries, have been included in some of the special summaries already presented and in those to follow.

Contributions of many nonphysicians have not been limited to persons within the hospital walls. Members of the Sigma Sigma Sigma sorority have contributed over $400,000 over many years to fund facilities and programs, often providing seed money that was multiplied many times to achieve departmental goals. Their ongoing support of the recreational therapy program at the hospital has been unparalleled in this country. The creation of our nearby, attractive Ronald McDonald House, a multimillion dollar facility providing a "home away from home" for families and children at nominal cost, has made up for many of the deficiencies in the physical settings of our wards.

Finally, the associations with the Department of Maternal and Child Health of the School of Public Health have been very important; these are addressed by Dr. Naomi Morris.

Herbert S. Harned, Jr.

CHAPTER TWENTY-EIGHT

Pediatric Nurses and Pediatric Nursing

Editors' Note: Writing the story of pediatric nurses and nursing at North Carolina Memorial Hospital was facilitated greatly by the presence still in the community of two key figures: Audrey Joyce Booth and Polly Johnson.

Audrey Booth was the first full-time maternal and child care nursing supervisor at NC Memorial Hospital. She arrived in Chapel Hill in 1954 and remained as pediatric nursing supervisor until 1965 when she left to head the renal dialysis unit at Durham VA Hospital. During Audrey's tenure at the University of North Carolina, she worked closely with the faculty of the School of Nursing, an association that is germane to this history and to Audrey's. After a short stint in Durham, she returned to the UNC School of Nursing where she held several positions: acting dean, director of statewide AHEC nursing activities, associate dean for operations, and director of development. She retired in 1985.

Polly Johnson began her association with NC Memorial Hospital as a staff nurse in the pediatric outpatient department in 1973. She became a nurse clinician in 1978. In 1983 she became the clinical nurse coordinator of the inpatient and neonatal nursing services, a position she held until 1986. She is still active in the North Carolina Board of Nursing as a practice consultant.

This history is written in two parts. The first is a summary of an interview by Floyd Denny on June 25, 1991, of Ms. Booth that covers the time from her arrival in 1954 to 1965. The second part was written by Polly Johnson and encompasses the time from 1965 until the early 1990s; it is divided into sections on inpatient and outpatient nursing. Both of these histories highlight important events and people and the association between nursing and pediatricians.

AUDREY BOOTH AND THE EARLY YEARS IN NURSING

AUDREY BOOTH was raised on a farm in southeastern Nebraska, traveling on horseback to a one-room school for eight years. The terrible drought and dust storms in the Midwest during the 1930s caused the Booth family to move to a small nearby town, Crete, the home of Doane College, a Church of Christ institution, so that the children could receive a college education. As she was finishing her time at Doane, she was steered by a wise counselor to the Nursing School of Western Reserve University (now Case Western Reserve University), where she received a master's degree in nursing in 1948. A stint as a camp nurse, experience with children with poliomyelitis at Omaha Children's Hospital, where she became director of nursing, and experience at Queen's Hospital, Honolulu, Hawaii, as assistant director and acting director of nursing, prepared her for coming to NC Memorial Hospital in 1954. In Hawaii, she worked with Mary Cheek, the director of nursing, who was to become the director of nursing at NC Memorial Hospital. Her satisfying experiences with Ms. Cheek's supervision and the possibility of getting a second master's degree in nursing at UNC were prominent driving factors for her coming to Chapel Hill.

Audrey arrived in Chapel Hill in May 1954, seventeen months after the opening of the pediatric beds on the seventh floor of the hospital. Rena Pittoti, the supervisor of the medical nursing services, had been responsible for the pediatric service until Booth's arrival. Audrey's memories of the early years as the nursing supervisor of the Maternal and Child Health Department were explored in some depth. The general impression gained from her recollections was the struggle to organize a competent pediatric nursing staff for developing Departments of Pediatrics and Surgery, warm association with her peers at NC Memorial Hospital and in the School of Nursing, good relationships with the pediatric faculty and hospital administrators, and epic episodes and hassles with a few surgeons and some pediatric house staff—but, in general, the work of a congenial group striving to attain the goal of good care of children at NC Memorial Hospital.

Some of Audrey's chief memories were of her close associations with other nurses and their constant struggle to develop a competent staff to care for children. She received help from Mary Cheek, director of nursing for the hospital, and assistant director Ethel Harrison, who was unusually adept at many things, especially those that were mechanical; she remembered these women especially warmly. Audrey recalled her very pleasant experiences with other nurses as well over the years. She mentioned specifically Sarah Usher, Laura Thompson, Bonnie Beard, Barbara Guiteras, and Martha Russell, all head nurses in the Department of Pediatrics. Audrey recalls very warm associations

with the faculty of the School of Nursing, where she had a clinical appointment. She mentions especially the nice
associations she had with Kit Nuckolls
and Beulah Gautefeld, who were pediatric faculty members. These close associations with the School of Nursing during these early years played a prominent
role in her return to the School of Nursing in a variety of capacities after
returning from the Durham VA.

Audrey
Booth

There were constant staffing problems; there never seemed to be enough
nurses and few had any pediatric nursing
training or experience. The establishment
of educational or inservice training for
the nursing staff helped solve the problem. This was started by Mary Cheek
with much help from Esther Sump, who
came from the School of Nursing to be
director of inservice education, and Helen Majette and Ethel Harrison from the
hospital staff. Through these efforts, a competent nursing staff was gradually developed.

Memory of less concerning issues related to dress codes for nurses during
the early years, lack of air conditioning, and racial segregation. She played
down any importance that dress codes may have had, feeling that what nurses
knew and did was so much more important than what they wore that this was
of little importance. There were vivid recollections of the tremendous heat
during the summer on the seventh floor, due to lack of air conditioning, as
well as the problems when air conditioning was being installed in the 1960s.
Audrey was surprised early at the general segregation of races in Chapel Hill,
as compared to Nebraska and Hawaii, but recalls that this was not a significant problem in pediatrics.

There were many recollections of faculty and house staff. The associations
with the pediatric faculty were almost universally good and warmly remembered. She has especially pleasant memories of working with Drs. Harned and
Chamberlin. Ed Curnen is remembered fondly and is described as "mild" and
"pleasant." She recalls problems in working with some of the surgical faculty,
especially Drs. Price Heusner and Richard Peters. There were "choice" words
for Heusner, but Peters was a close second; there were fewer problems with
other surgeons. Apparently many of the problems stemmed from bed assignments; accommodating pediatricians' and surgeons' needs for beds was a
constant problem. Several memories of interactions with house staff are vivid.
She remembers several hassles with Bill Davis, first chief resident, over bed
assignments. There were pleasant memories of bird hunting with Earle Spaugh

at the invitation of a patient's parents, and not so pleasant memories of a hair-raising ride with Woody Coley in the back of a truck transporting a polio patient in a respirator to Greensboro. They were accompanied by Margaret Moore, director of the Physical Therapy Department.

Audrey has nice memories of NC Memorial Hospital administrators, especially Dr. Robert Cadmus, the first hospital administrator. There was great admiration for him. He is described as an innovator and forward-thinking individual; she cites his ideas of an intensive care unit for patients in that category. She also remembers Gene Crawford and Joe Greer, assistants to Dr. Cadmus, as "personable young guys; I don't remember anything that wasn't okay."

Audrey also stressed her opinion of the importance of the Sigma Sigma Sigma sorority in the history of the Department of Pediatrics. She remembers helping Jud Van Wyk, who lived then in the Glen Lennox apartments, write the first proposal to start the playroom; it was done over a six-pack of beer. She recalls working with Elaine Hill in playroom matters and emphasized Elaine's great contributions to that project. The initiation of Elaine and Audrey into the Tri Sigma sorority is another highlight; white dresses and blindfolds are a part of her memory of the initiation process. We discussed at some length how the funds furnished by the sorority were parlayed into very sizable amounts to accomplish such things as building the seventh-floor isolation unit and outpatient playroom, helping with the burn unit, and more.

She describes with some painful feeling her leaving NC Memorial Hospital in 1965 to work in kidney dialysis at the Durham VA Hospital. The inability of the hospital to pay a reasonable salary to someone with her qualifications was one of the main reasons for leaving. She recalls with some satisfaction her role at a later time in improving this situation. The dialysis experience was a valuable lesson in chronic illnesses, but she was lured back to UNC with very responsible positions in AHEC and in the School of Nursing. Clearly her first love was with the institution that attracted her to North Carolina in the first place.

FLOYD W. DENNY, JR.

PEDIATRIC NURSING SERVICES

Pediatric Inpatient Nursing Services

1965–1969

Dorothy (Dottie) Merrow was hired in September 1965 as a second pediatric nursing supervisor until she resigned in August 1970 to take a faculty position at the UNC School of Nursing. By 1981, Dottie had left UNC to take a faculty position at East Carolina University's School of Nursing. Dottie had received her Master's of Science in Nursing degree from Duke University and taught four years at the Rex Hospital School of Nursing before coming to North Carolina Memorial Hospital in 1965. She had nursing administrative responsibilities for 7 East, 7 West, and the infant special care nursery (ISCN), a fifteen-bed unit on the fourth floor of the hospital. The head nurses on the seventh floor at the time of Dottie's employment were Bonnie Beard (7E) and Trish Ross (7W). Martha Russell, who had been the head nurse of the ISCN since its creation in 1956, left in 1963 to work at Vanderbilt Hospital and Charlotte Memorial Hospital before returning to the same head nurse position in 1966. Dottie describes her primary responsibilities during those years as managing the staffing of the units, clinical supervision, clinical teaching of the nursing staff, and being a general "fill-in-the-holes" person for the pediatric service. Ethel Harrison, who was the supervisor of the adult surgery service and the surgical intensive care unit, was very helpful to Dottie during her tenure in this position. They worked especially closely in providing the postoperative care for children undergoing open heart surgery. These children first went to the adult intensive care unit for immediate postop care and were later transferred back to 7 West for the remainder of their recovery period in the hospital.

The main attractions to the pediatric service that influenced Dottie's decision to take the supervisory position were the school program, the playroom for the children, and the open visiting hours for the parents. Cots were available for parents who wished to stay with their children, although Dottie had to thwart a move to remove the cots at one time during her tenure. Dottie recalls that the wife of Chapel Hill's first black mayor, Lillian Lee, was the hospital-based schoolteacher when she first came to the hospital in 1965.

As the pediatric service expanded during these years, nurses became involved in a number of activities beyond direct patient care. Regular interdisciplinary team meetings evolved, with a major emphasis on identifying and caring for the psychosocial needs, in addition to the medical needs, of the children. Team members included a pediatric social worker, psychiatrist, psychologist, schoolteacher, play therapist, and nurse along with the pediatric house staff. Parents were invited to participate in supportive group meetings (luncheons) coordinated by members of this psychosocial team. A rehabilitation team was developed to focus on the multiple needs of children with birth defects. It is important to note that not all hospitalized children were cared for on the pediatric units. Children with cystic fibrosis continued to be hospitalized in Gravely Hospital, the old tuberculosis hospital, until the midseventies. Charlie Foster was the head nurse of that Gravely unit, which did not have any direct organizational ties to the pediatric nursing service. As Dottie recalls, there were only infrequent and informal interactions between the pediatric inpatient and outpatient nursing staffs.

The nursing care delivery system was team nursing during this era. Team members included registered nurses, licensed practical nurses, and nurse's aides. Nurses cared for infants through adolescence on both 7 East and 7

West. With all private rooms, 7 West was the isolation unit. However, those children requiring the most "intensive" nursing care, regardless of diagnosis, were also cared for on this unit. During a rather severe nursing shortage in 1966–1967, pharmacy students began to administer medications on the pediatric units, a practice that continued throughout Dottie's tenure. She remembers that the pharmacy students did an excellent job. In addition, a second-level position was created for LPNs, and LPN IIs began to administer oral medications on the units. When a child required "intensive," one-to-one nursing care, such care was provided by a staff nurse without any additional staffing support for the rest of the service. As one might imagine, there were times when nurses were simply unable to meet all the nursing care demands of the children. Dottie also worked hard to get a pay differential for nursing staff on weekends but such salary practices were not adopted until the latter part of the 1970s. During this decade, the hospital also implemented the concept of ward managers who supervised the unit clerks and ordered supplies and equipment as well as managing the supply and capital expense budgets.

One of Dottie's most memorable experiences was the birth of Siamese twins in October 1965 and the ensuing nursing care they required in the infant special care nursery as they grew until ready for separation surgery (they were joined at the chest) and during their postoperative period. She remembers that both infants survived the surgery, although one died several months after hospital discharge. She also recalled the birth of the first set of triplets and a number of other "firsts" in the care of premature infants, and recounted finding, with some degree of horror, the introduction of phototherapy in the form of a number of fluorescent desklamps lined up over a baby's isolette. The house staff had "borrowed" the lamps from nearby offices for this new treatment regimen! No protection had been provided for the baby's eyes and, of course, no one had any idea about the amount of therapeutic (or otherwise) rays that the baby might be receiving. She also recalled the constant nursing care required by one boy with Guillain-Barré syndrome who was maintained on a ventilator for months that stretched into more than a year. At times, it was particularly difficult to provide this level of staffing. (It should be noted that the infant special care nursery, started in 1956, was the first of its kind in North Carolina, perhaps the first in the entire Southeast, as recalled by Martha Russell.)

All in all, this five-year period seems to have been the precursor to the age of pediatric specialization, when advances in treatment modalities saved the lives of smaller premature infants as well as the lives of other critically ill infants, toddlers, and school-age children. Thus, the nursing staff began its preparation for the age of intensive care and the specialty education required for nursing staff to move into this new age. The actual moves to a neonatal intensive care unit and a pediatric intensive care facility did not occur until the seventies.

DECADE OF THE SEVENTIES

This was a decade of many changes in inpatient pediatric nursing at North Carolina Memorial Hospital. Annette Ayer was hired in 1970 to succeed Ms. Merrow as the pediatric nursing supervisor. (This position was upgraded to clinical nurse coordinator within the state's personnel system during this decade.) She had received both her BSN and MSN degrees at Duke University, where she focused on nursing administration in the graduate program. She had accepted a staff nurse position in obstetrics at North Carolina Memorial Hospital six weeks before being appointed to the pediatric supervisory position. Much of Annette's administrative work focused on the need to increase staff positions to a more appropriate level for the increasingly complex care needs of the infants and children on the service. Annette remained in this position until 1981, when she resigned with plans to become more involved in community-based pediatric nursing. Unfortunately, Annette was diagnosed with breast cancer only a few months after her resignation from the coordinator role. She worked part time as a housewide supervisor at the hospital until shortly before her death in 1985.

With the opening of the bed tower (7A) in August of 1974, children were grouped according to ages and developmental needs for the first time: 7A was a twenty-six-bed unit for infants and toddlers, 7 East became the school-age unit, while 7 West remained the isolation unit throughout this decade. Bonnie Beard (Herje) remained as the head nurse of both 7 East and 7 West until the mid-seventies. Each of these units also had an assistant head nurse. Stephanie Yohe was the first head nurse of the baby-toddler unit, where she remained for the next fifteen years. Stephanie was instrumental in implementing primary nursing on this unit, the first pediatric unit to adopt this model of nursing care. Such a transition required the conversion of a number of nurse's aide and LPN positions to RN positions. This was slowly accomplished over the years of her tenure as head nurse.

By the early seventies, preparations were being made for the first pediatric intensive care unit. Terry Lucas, assistant head nurse on 7 West, coordinated the nursing efforts for the development of this unit. The original boys' ward on 7 East was converted to the first pediatric intensive care unit by the mid-seventies with June Schakne as the first head nurse of this all-RN unit. She remained in the head nurse position through the unit's move to the central core of the bed tower (7C). June resigned from her position in 1980 to pursue graduate nursing education at Emory University in Atlanta. Louise Taylor, daughter of Chancellor Ferebee Taylor, followed June as the head nurse of the PICU.

During the 1970s, nurses in the ISCN became involved in another "first" at the hospital. They began to stabilize critically ill neonates at outlying hospitals and care for them during transport to our hospital by ambulance, helicopter, or fixed-wing aircraft. At first these transports were carried out by both physicians and nurses. However, by the end of the decade only specially trained transport nurses and respiratory therapists were transporting these critically unstable infants from outlying hospitals. Susan Jones Vaughn and Karen Metzguer were two of the first neonatal nurses to become involved in this transport activity at NC Memorial Hospital. Once the transport team was well developed, Karen spent much of her time teaching nurses in these outlying hospitals (level I and II nurseries) how to prepare the critically unstable neonates for transport to our tertiary care center. This work was coordinated through the statewide AHEC system. Prior to the development of this transport program, those sick full-term babies and premature infants not born at NC Memorial Hospital were brought to the ISCN from outlying hospitals by public health nurses. With the advent of transport, the demand for nursery space as well as for qualified neonatal nurses grew rapidly. By the end of 1976, the ISCN had been split into the neonatal intensive care unit and the intermediate care nursery. Martha Russell served as the head nurse of the intermediate care nursery until her retirement in 1974. The first head nurse of the NICU was Susan Jones Vaughn, who served in that role until 1977. It is also important to note that the newborn nursery for healthy newborn babies became a part of the pediatric service by the end of this decade. Ann Mayberry was the head nurse at the time of this transition and has continued in that position to the present time.

With the increased subspecialization within pediatrics, the first clinical nurse specialist, Trish Greene, MSN, was hired to work with the pediatric hematology-oncology team. Another clinical nurse specialist, Carol Sackett, MSN, began working with children with complex urological problems in addition to her work with adults. Weiss Dykstra specialized in the care of children with orthopedic problems and also served on the first Pediatric Social Committee, an interdisciplinary team that focused on child abuse and neglect. By 1978, each unit had one nursing position devoted to education and precepting of staff in relation to the increasingly complex nursing care requirements of children in this tertiary care center. With advances in medicine and treatment modalities, nurses became involved in the care of children requiring central vascular catheters, cardiac and apnea monitors, hemodialysis, peritoneal dialysis, and chemotherapy. The shift to "high-tech" care required constant attention to the educational needs for both new and existing nursing personnel as the level of acuity increased for patients on all nursing units. This new age also required additional nursing staff positions at the RN level.

During the seventies, the hospital moved to a triad management style for each of the major services. In fact, there were two triads within the pediatric service, one for the nurseries and another for the general pediatric service. Each triad consisted of representatives from the Departments of Pediatrics, Nursing, and Hospital Administration. The pediatric clinical coordinator participated on both of these triads where decisions regarding long-range planning, annual budget development, and administrative policies related to servicewide issues were made. Each unit within the service also functioned within this triad model, with the head nurse, a pediatric faculty member, and the unit manager collectively making decisions regarding unit policy and practices that facilitated the delivery of both nursing and medical care on the unit. Head nurses had twenty-four-hour accountability for the nursing care provided on each unit. This meant that there were many sleepless nights and long hours spent ensuring proper "coverage" for their units.

THE EARLY EIGHTIES (1980–1981)

It was not until 1981 that supervisory coverage was provided twenty-four hours per day for the entire pediatric nursing service. The nursing supervisors on evening and night shifts were accountable for ensuring adequate staffing, including reallocation of personnel, within the entire service. Such on-site coverage relieved the constant pressure on the head nurses for singularly "running" their units. It also enhanced communication and collaboration among the seven nursing units: 7 East, 7 West, 7A baby-toddler, pediatric intensive care, neonatal intensive care, intermediate care nursery, and newborn nursery.

By 1981, there were over two hundred nursing staff employed on this 108-bed pediatric and neonatal service. Student nurses rotated through the general pediatric units and the newborn nursery. Collaborative research projects were being carried out by UNC nursing faculty and members of our nursing staff. Graduate nursing students obtained valuable experience in both clinical and administrative practica. All of these liaisons with the School of Nursing have benefited the pediatric nursing service in countless ways, including the implementation of new approaches to clinical nursing care and management techniques related to patient acuity, quality assurance, and personnel management.

SUMMARY

The evolution of nursing services from the mid-sixties to the early eighties reflected both the progress and increasing sophistication of pediatric and neonatal medicine, as well as the advances in nursing research and theory. It is not believed that any one "high-tech" development, research finding, or personnel maneuver had a greater impact than all the other influencing factors on the "growth and development" of this nursing service. Certainly, each nurse and each physician who cared for children on this service during this era had a major impact on the lives of these children and on the manner in which pediatric care was provided to and, most importantly, perceived by the families they served.

Pediatric Outpatient Nursing Services

1965–1969

Prior to 1969, the pediatric clinics operated six and a half days a week and offered a walk-in clinic on the second floor of the original clinic building. Nursing staff rotated through the entire outpatient clinic area rather than being permanently based in any one departmental area such as medicine, surgery, obstetrics, or pediatrics. During the hours of operation, the pediatric clinics were staffed by an aide, a licensed practical nurse, and one or two registered nurses. In 1967, Margaret Adams was hired as a staff nurse and in 1969 she became the first pediatric nursing supervisor. Margaret had received her BSN from UNC, practiced nursing in the Atlanta area, and then completed her master's of public health nursing degree at UNC before coming to the outpatient clinics. She remained in the supervisory position until a major reorganization of the pediatric clinics occurred in the early 1990s. Another long-term employee in the pediatric clinics was Trish Ross. After transferring from her assistant head nurse position on 7 West in the early seventies, she has coordinated the pediatric screening clinic until the present time.

In January 1969, the pediatric clinics moved to the new Spencer Love Building, and nursing staff became "home-based" for the first time. The subspecialty programs expanded to a full-day-a-week operation, in addition to the seven-days-a-week walk-in screening clinic. In order to cover all weekend and evening hours, nursing staff from the adult specialty clinics and the emergency room rotated through the pediatric screening clinic until the mid-seventies, when the complement of pediatric nursing personnel was sufficient to staff this area fourteen hours per day. Organizationally, the nursing staff was umbrellaed under the Department of Nursing for the entire hospital system until the early eighties, when the various departments within the School of Medicine became totally accountable for the fiscal operation and personnel management of their respective outpatient programs. Prior to this organizational change, the pediatric nursing supervisor was directly accountable to the clinical nurse coordinator of the outpatient department. June Watson served in this coordinator role until her retirement in 1979. Martha Stucker served in this role from 1979 until the total organizational shift to departmental management occurred in the early '80s and the position was abolished.

DECADE OF THE 1970S

During the 1970s, with the expansion of subspecialty clinics such as pulmonary, hematology-oncology, rehabilitation, and special infant care, nursing staff began to "specialize" as well. Trish Greene was hired as the first pediatric clinical nurse specialist in the mid-seventies. As a member of the pediatric hematology-oncology team, she provided care to pediatric oncology patients and their families on both an inpatient and outpatient basis until her resignation in 1980. Another nursing specialty was developed by Polly Johnson, the first nurse clinician, in the Pulmonary Clinic and UNC Cystic Fibrosis Center during the mid- to late seventies. Polly was initially involved in performing all the sweat tests throughout the hospital complex. She later trained laboratory personnel to perform this diagnostic test so she could concentrate her ener-

Polly Johnson and patient

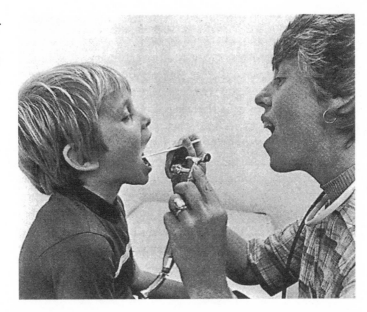

gies on family support and education as major components of both inpatient and outpatient care. In 1977, she and Brian Stabler, a pediatric psychologist, developed the first parent groups as well as groups for adolescents with chronic illnesses in the outpatient clinics. These groups were part of the services provided to clients in the CF Center program.

One of the major nursing achievements during the decade of the seventies was the development of an ongoing communication network with the public health nursing departments throughout North Carolina regarding the treatment plans and care needs of those children who came to the various pediatric subspecialty clinics. Credit for the development of this referral system and communication link with the public health departments goes to Margaret Adams. Because of her public health nursing background, she recognized the value in establishing and maintaining this vital link. Margaret also maintained an important clinical association with the division of continuing education in the School of Public Health and provided on-site short courses in clinic nursing practice for new public health nurses.

The seventies also saw the development of nurse-practitioner education and associated clinical preceptorships in the pediatric clinics. Faculty from both the School of Medicine and the School of Nursing precepted students in pediatric primary care. Having nurse-practitioner students in the clinic setting also increased the awareness of other health care providers regarding the advancing practice of nursing and the contributions that could be made by nurses in the field of primary health care. Both undergraduate and graduate students in the UNC School of Nursing received some of their pediatric clinical education in these clinics throughout this period of time.

THE EARLY EIGHTIES (1980–1981)

Nursing personnel continued to develop more specialized expertise and to participate as members of the multidisciplinary subspecialty teams in the pediatric clinic programs during this period. Polly Johnson helped develop the multidisciplinary team concept for a number of subspecialty programs, including diabetes and rheumatology clinics. She helped create the Young Adult CF Clinic, as well as start the first nursing clinic for the education of children with diabetes and their families. Although there never was a strong communication link between inpatient and outpatient pediatric nursing, communication did occur in some specialty areas. For example, Weiss Dykstra, an inpatient nurse, regularly participated in the rehabilitation clinic while Polly educated both the house staff and inpatient nurses in diabetes management and monitored the progress of many chronically ill children during their hospitalizations. Nurses also participated in collaborative research projects with physicians and other members of the health care team. Polly was a coinvestigator in a project regarding school achievement and absenteeism among children with chronic illnesses. Other investigators included Mary Glenn Fowler, MD, and Bobbie Lubker, PhD, a faculty member of the UNC School of Education. Because of her involvement in research as well as in the continuing education of nurses and pediatric house staff, Polly held adjunct appointments in both the School of Nursing and the School of Medicine at UNC.

Pediatric-Neonatal Nursing Services: 1982–1993

The decade of the eighties could easily be characterized as the era of high-tech nursing care with the introduction of more invasive treatment modalities, central vascular access devices, and the use of highly sophisticated equipment, including portable and computerized monitoring equipment. Coupled with the hiring of the first pediatric surgeon in 1983, followed by the hiring of the first pediatric intensivist in 1987, and shortly thereafter, the hiring of a second pediatric surgeon, the impact on both inpatient and outpatient nursing services was enormous. These years saw both an increase in specialty-focused care as well as a significant rise in the levels of acuteness of patients being cared for throughout the pediatric and neonatal nursing service. A patient classification and staff productivity system was introduced across all inpatient pediatric and neonatal units by 1985 to validate for hospital administration the need to reallocate nursing resources to a more RN-intensive staffing base. Not only were nurse's aide and LPN positions upgraded to RN-level positions, but the total number of RN FTEs was increased significantly to meet the higher acuity nursing needs of the children on this service. Along with increasing acuity levels of care came the increasing emphasis on quality management within the service.

The air transport service, originally limited to neonatal transport, was expanded to a hospital-wide flight transport program, which included the transport of critically ill and unstable children and adults as well as neonates.

Both the neonatal intensive care unit and the pediatric intensive care unit expanded their bed bases during this decade, the NICU from twelve to sixteen beds and the PICU from six to sixteen beds! Although the inpatient nursing service did not have any clinical nurse specialists, positions were created for "specialist" nurses for patients on subspecialty services such as oncology, orthopedics, dialysis, and pulmonary as well as for special services such as nutritional support.

In order to be more supportive of the families of children being treated at the hospital, the Ronald McDonald Corporation helped the medical community plan and realize the dream of building a home away from home for the pediatric service. The dream began in early 1983 and the Ronald McDonald House was officially opened in 1988. Tom Boat, as chairman of the Department of Pediatrics, and Polly Johnson, as the clinical coordinator of the inpatient nursing services, served on that first board of directors, helped raise money, and participated in the groundbreaking ceremony on Old Mason Farm Road. We must acknowledge the unending hours of work put in by Elaine Hill, the director of volunteer services at NCMH, who truly saw to it that our dream became a reality. Elaine was first a volunteer in the pediatric playroom on the seventh floor before taking over the entire volunteer services. She and her husband, John, played Mr. and Mrs. Santa Claus to the delight of the hospitalized children on Christmas Eves for more than twenty years until her retirement in 1990. Throughout her career in hospital volunteer services, Elaine worked closely with the nursing services to assure the appropriate care of patients and families.

Changes in the payer systems that began with the implementation of DRGs in the early eighties led to shorter hospital stays, a shift to same-day surgeries for most routine pediatric surgeries, and less time to prepare families for posthospital care. With the "push" to discharge these patients "sicker and quicker" and to provide more care on an ambulatory basis came the critical need for nursing to interface with those community-based agencies that would provide ongoing nursing care, family support, and teaching after hospital discharge. In order to respond to this need, the Nursing Department formalized a discharge planning program and hired a pediatric discharge planning nurse in 1989 to coordinate these activities for the entire pediatric-neonatal nursing service. Shelley Myles, a Canadian-educated nurse, became the first pediatric discharge planning nurse.

The organization of pediatric outpatient nursing services experienced a number of changes from the early eighties through 1993. Having first moved out from under the umbrella of the Department of Nursing to being accountable to the Department of Pediatrics of the School of Medicine, the nursing staff subsequently changed from being hospital employees to being employed under the University of North Carolina personnel system. Such a move was indicative of broad cost-containment measures being implemented across the hospital system. By the late eighties, a new ambulatory care center was being planned and decisions needed to be made by each department within the

Medical School as to which clinics moved and which ones stayed within the hospital. With the appointment of a new medical coordinator of the pediatric clinics in the early nineties, nursing services were again reorganized. At this time, the nursing supervisor position was replaced with a nurse-practitioner/clinic manager position. In 1992 Margaret Adams, who had held this supervisory position since 1969, moved into a full-time staff position in the hematology-oncology clinic program. Betty Compton, FNP, who had been hired in the primary care section of the Department of Pediatrics in the early eighties, became the nurse practitioner/clinic manager for what was now a larger and more geographically spread out clinic program. In February 1993, the pediatric primary care and continuity clinics moved to the new ambulatory care center, while most of the subspecialty clinics remained in the Spencer Love Building. The pediatric screening clinic also remained adjacent to the emergency department of the hospital, with Trish Ross continuing in her role as the primary nurse in this area.

The trend toward subspecialization and multidisciplinary approach to ambulatory pediatric services continued throughout this period, with the nurses specializing in each of the major pediatric subspecialty clinics. By the mid-eighties, the pediatric hematology-oncology clinic program had increased its client load and days of service and moved to the newly renovated quarters in the Gravely Building, where children and their families had a more supportive environment for day-long treatment therapies. In addition to her supervisory responsibilities, Margaret Adams served as the primary nurse in the hematology-oncology clinic. The pediatric pulmonary clinic experienced phenomenal growth in numbers of patients seen on an annual basis during this span of twelve years. Because of the advances in cystic fibrosis research and treatment modalities, much of which took place at UNC, patients and their families throughout the eastern United States were attracted to this treatment center. In 1983, Terry Lucas was hired to replace Polly Johnson as the cystic fibrosis and diabetes nurse clinician. Pam Stewart later filled that dual position until the patient volume in the cystic fibrosis center demanded the full-time services of a nurse clinician. The endocrine division was then forced to support a diabetic nurse clinician from their research trust funds.

On the inpatient pediatric and neonatal nursing services, the clinical nurse coordinator position changed hands several times between 1982 and 1993. After Annette Ayer's resignation in 1981, Martha Stucker, the clinical nurse coordinator of outpatient nursing services, took on the additional interim role of coordinating the pediatric and neonatal nursing services through January 1983. In February 1983, Polly Johnson was appointed as the clinical nurse coordinator for this nursing service after serving over eight years in the pediatric clinics programs. She had received her BSN degree from the Ohio State University and her MSN degree from Duke University. Polly served in the coordinator role until December 1986, when she resigned from the hospital system to become involved in the delivery of home care services. During her almost four-year tenure, probably the most frustrating management issue was the struggle to staff the six-bed pediatric intensive care unit. Since nursing in this critical care area required additional knowledge and skills, staff nurses from the general pediatric units could not be readily utilized to provide the level of care required. In order to maintain an adequate staffing pool for the PICU, the Nursing Department realigned the nursing staff of the PICU under the adult-focused critical care nursing services in 1986. This management arrangement continued until the expansion of the unit from six to sixteen beds, at which time the PICU returned to the pediatric nursing service. With the bed expansion, the staffing numbers were sufficient to accommodate the ebb and flow of nurses without needing to consider bed closings, a continual problem in the early eighties.

With the end of 1986, renovation and restructuring plans were in place for the entire seventh floor. By 1987, all the beds on the seventh floor were part of the pediatric service, with the adult neurology service having moved to another area in the hospital. These restructuring plans still maintained an age and developmental focus for each unit, but infants and toddlers would move to the older 7 East-West units, with the school-age and adolescent patients being housed in the newer bed tower area, where there was a bathroom in every room! The four-bed expansion of the neonatal intensive care unit was completed in early 1987. Susan Brunsen, clinical supervisor of the NICU during this time, carefully "dogged" that project to its completion.

In 1985, the triad management system that had been in place across all patient service areas of the hospital was discontinued. Nursing took over all administrative management, including fiscal, personnel, and equipment, for the inpatient services. Ward secretaries and the servicewide administrative positions were umbrellaed under nursing for each specialty service. The more traditional "head nurse" model was expanded to a broader unit-manager type of position, even though the title of this management position remained "clinical nurse supervisor." In this same year, long-range planning began for the organizational development of a North Carolina Children's Hospital. When North Carolina Memorial Hospital (NCMH) was restructured in the late '80s to become The University of North Carolina Hospitals, NC Children's Hospital was created as a component of this corporate hospital system. Planning also began for a freestanding women's and children's hospital to be built, hopefully by the end of the '90s, on the site of the old south wing of the hospital complex that for years housed the psychiatric inpatient and clinic services.

Following Polly's tenure, Julie Phipps was appointed to the clinical nurse coordinator position in 1987 and served for two years in that role. She came to this position from Pitt County Memorial Hospital in Greenville, North Carolina, where she had been the nurse manager of the neonatal intensive care nursery. Much of the earlier renovation planning started to become a reality during her tenure. Betty Tucker, who was hired in 1983 to replace the retiring Martha Russell as the clinical supervisor of the intermediate care nursery, also served as the interim clinical coordinator of the pediatric-neonatal nursing services after Julie's resignation. Betty deserves a lot of recognition for carrying on that dual role in the midst of such change and expansion of services.

In 1990, Terry Lucas was appointed as the clinical nurse coordinator of the combined maternal and child services. Terry had originally received a Diploma in Nursing from the Presbyterian Hospital School of Nursing in Charlotte, North Carolina. She later received her BSN degree at the University of Florida and her MSN degree from UNC-CH. Her appointment to coordinate the combined maternal and child services followed the retirement of Lib Warren, who served many years as the clinical nurse coordinator for the ob-gyn services. Terry remained in this coordinator position until late 1993.

By the end of the eighties, the inpatient pediatric nursing units were being converted from a developmental model where patients were grouped by ages to a subspecialty model where patients were grouped more by diagnosis and similarity of care needs across the pediatric age span. Such a reconfiguration was a major shift for the nurses to make. By the end of 1993, 7 E-W housed children on the subspecialty services of neurology, nephrology, gastrointestinal, and infectious diseases. In 1991, Shelley Myles moved from the discharge planner position to become the clinical supervisor of the 7 E-W units. Children on the hematology-oncology, pulmonary, and cardiology services were housed in 7 BT B/D. Jenny Spry, a UNC-CH graduate who started as a graduate nurse on the school-age unit, became the clinical supervisor of 7 BT B/D in 1990. By the late eighties, the pediatric surgery services had expanded to the point of having a twenty-bed unit on 6 West. Melody Watral, who had previously served as a staff nurse, a clinician, and a service-based supervisor, became the nurse manager of this new pediatric surgical unit.

After shifting both the postpartum and newborn nursery to the fourth-floor bed tower area and renovating the vacated area, the intermediate care nursery moved into a spacious twenty-bed unit adjacent to the NICU. Finally, by 1990, all the babies on the neonatal service were on the fourth floor—another dream realized after years of the ICN's existing in less than adequate space three floors removed from the core neonatal services! In 1991, another nursing "first" occurred with the hiring of neonatal nurse-practitioners in the NICU. By 1993, there were four NNPs involved in the neonatal program.

By the end of this 1982–1993 era, staffing had become more RN-intensive as well as subspecialized. The pediatric-neonatal service had grown from a 106-bed service to a 124-bed service for infants and children with complex health care problems and acutely unstable conditions requiring the resources of nurses, physicians, and other health professionals that were only available at the tertiary medical center level.

POLLY JOHNSON

CHAPTER TWENTY-NINE

Recreational Therapy Program: Robbie Page Memorial and Support of the Tri Sigma Sorority

Editor's Note: The vital contributions of Sigma Sigma Sigma (Tri Sigma), a national panhellenic sorority, enabled the Department to carry out many functions beyond its core medical programs. The full impact of this support has taken place throughout the major part of the lifespan of the Department. Dr. Curnen and Dr. Van Wyk were the prime movers in establishing this program at UNC. In the sections that follow, Dr. Van Wyk recalls the origins of these programs and then Dr. Harned reviews the major events that followed. He emphasizes the role of the leaders of the sorority in providing seed money for the creation of facilities and programs that have meant so much to the Department.

THE BEGINNINGS OF PLAY THERAPY AT NCMH

"A small amount of money has become available to fund rehabilitation programs in the clinical departments. These funds will be awarded competitively. If you wish to apply for these funds, please send me as soon as possible a summary of the specific programs that you wish to fund."
Memo from Dr. William Fleming to clinical department chiefs, 1956

WHEN this memo was written, NCMH had been open for only a few years, but long enough for certain deficiencies to have become apparent, particularly to new faculty recruited from well established programs. During the early years, recreation for children was entirely entrusted to

479

volunteers who read to the children and otherwise tried to keep them occupied. There was no play therapy program and the open porch at the east end of the seventh floor, which was supposed to be a recreation area for children, was unusable because the hospital incinerator continuously spewed ashes into this area. For this reason, the corridors of the seventh floor were full of ambulatory or wheelchair-bound children moving around without supervision; either that or they were sequestered in their individual rooms.

I was appalled by this state of affairs, having come from the Harriet Lane Home at Johns Hopkins where I had become accustomed to a well-developed play program under the direction of individuals trained in child development. Thus when Dr. Fleming's memo came across my desk, I suggested to Dr. Curnen that we apply for rehabilitation funds to start a play program. In making our proposal we insisted that rehabilitation was not limited to braces, eyeglasses, and physical therapy. When a child becomes ill, he/she tends to regress and, in our culture, we tend to forgive the child for such regression, allowing him/her to revert to more juvenile habits and behaviors, and generally making everyone miserable. For this reason, we articulated a program in which pediatric rehabilitation was defined as a process beginning from the moment a child became ill and that encompassed all those things that would limit this regressive tendency and optimize the child's normal development during his/her hospitalization. Although our proposed "rehabilitation program" would utilize play, which is the normal activity of a child, it would employ many other stratagems that would promote the earliest return of the patient to his/her own environment, and hopefully with developmental gains rather than losses. We proposed that such a program be staffed by professional play therapists who had been trained in child development.

Our application was approved; we, therefore, obtained funds to hire Ms. Kathryn McLaren, an MA in child development from Iowa State University, who was a leader in the play program at Johns Hopkins. (Ms. McLaren subsequently married Dr. William Pritchard, a neurosurgeon in Charlotte, and continues to live in North Carolina.) Ms. McLaren quickly teamed up with Margaret Moore, head of our physical therapy program, and worked with the house staff and volunteers in inaugurating this important function.

About this time, the president of the Tri Sigma sorority, Mrs. Robertson Page, had a son die at the age of five years of paralytic bulbar poliomyelitis. He had attended school only one day in his life and, according to his mother, had said that he always wanted to help other children. The chapters of the Tri Sigma sorority nationwide rallied around their national president and raised money that they wished to donate for poliomyelitis research. At this time, the National Foundation for Infantile Paralysis under Basil O'Connor had a monopoly on foundation support for poliomyelitis and did not welcome any challengers. Finally, Dr. Sydney Gellis, who was an advisor for the Poliomyelitis Foundation, was forced to turn the money down when it was offered by the Tri Sigmas to support research in Boston on the care of children with poliomyelitis. For this reason, the Tri Sigma Society decided to re-designate their money for pediatric rehabilitation rather than specifically for poliomyelitis, and the memorial committee focused on permanent projects involving brick and mortar.

Dr. Margaret Moore (EdD) was a key member of the original Robbie Page Memorial Fund Committee, and she encouraged Dr. Curnen to invite the leaders of the Robbie Page Memorial Fund to Chapel Hill to look over our play therapy program. Mrs. Lucille Morrison, the chair of the committee, and the other ladies were suitably impressed and charmed by Ed Curnen and Kathy McLaren and they saw real need. Their initial grant was used to install a sound system in each room so that suitable music could be played and books read to the children in all rooms simultaneously. Soon thereafter, Dr. Curnen challenged them to support the building of the playroom, as we now know it, over the old open deck on 7 East. This included a school area that was named later for Kristen Herrington, daughter of Dr. Robert Herrington, after she had been killed tragically in an auto accident on the 15-501 bypass.

During the early years, Dr. Curnen, and later Dr. Denny and I, tried to legitimize the discipline of play therapy and were always bedeviled by its name. We felt that the discipline of providing support for hospitalized children was a legitimate paramedical discipline that required a high level of specialized education and could not be demeaned by the term "play therapy." Unfortunately, the name continued to degrade our efforts. For a time, we tried to get Dr. Naomi Albanese, a dean at the University of North Carolina at Greensboro, to be involved and, in fact, that school supported several trainees on our seventh floor and was a strong supporter for a number of years. It was always our intention to have an academic program to educate young women and men as therapists in this important area and to do research relevant to the rehabilitation of sick children. Our concept has taken many turns, but, in effect, it has led to the establishment of what is now one of the leading such programs in the United States.

JUDSON J. VAN WYK

A LIVING MEMORIAL TO ROBBIE PAGE: THE RECREATIONAL THERAPY PROGRAMS ENDOWED BY THE TRI SIGMA SORORITY

From the perspective of the Tri Sigmas, the idea of a memorial to Robbie Page concentrated their energies in social service, which had been a powerful concern of the sorority. Since its founding in 1898 at the State Normal School in Farmville, Virginia (which evolved into Longwood College), and throughout many years of the national leadership of Mabel Lee Walton (covering the period from 1913 to 1947), this sorority had devoted major resources to social service. The YMCA, school libraries, projects alleviating tuberculosis, and war service in World Wars I and II gave way to emphasis on serving children, at first emphasizing library programs in local schools.

On September 1, 1951, a seminal event occurred in the history of the Tri Sigmas when Robbie Page died after contracting poliomyelitis only a few days previously. His mother, Mrs. Mary Hastings Holloway Page, who had been the national president for four years, lost her only son in this terrible tragedy. The sorority rose to the occasion and created a memorial to him that year, with the immediate goal of aiding in research on poliomyelitis, as described by Dr. Van Wyk. Starting with eighty cents from Robbie's own bank, this memorial has now dispensed over $400,000 to our programs alone, as well as other funds to several projects elsewhere.

The decision to divert the energies of the sorority from fighting polio to the rehabilitation of children was extraordinarily beneficial for the sorority as well as for the pediatric service at the North Carolina Memorial Hospital. Mrs. "Hastings" Page had attended Longwood College, where her mother and two aunts also had been members of the sorority. One of these aunts, Ms. Mabel Lee Walton, had become the main pillar of the sorority and had served as its president for thirty-four years, after which she had been succeeded by Mrs. Page. Chapel Hill was not far from the sorority's origins in Virginia. Dr. Margaret Moore, the chief of physical therapy at UNC, was one of the first members of the Robbie Page Memorial Fund Committee of Tri Sigma sorority and was aware of the needs and exciting plans of the Pediatrics Department at UNC. She became primarily responsible for guiding Mrs. Page and other delegates to our site. She has written a short history of the Robbie Page Memorial, which is available along with her other comments in our archives.

Dr. Curnen became a trusted friend of these wonderful people and a harmonious and lasting relationship was established. Dr. Denny also was able similarly to continue this friendship. Dr. Catherine Taylor, another important liaison with the sorority during Dr. Denny's tenure as chief of pediatrics and thereafter, has remarked on the excitement engendered as the sorority women met with him to discuss new imaginative projects. The Children's Room, with its portrait of Robbie, dedicated by his grandmother, Emily Walton Holloway, and his great-aunt, Mary Beall Walton, is nearly as meaningful to the sorority sisters as it is to those of us in the Department of Pediatrics and to the people we serve.

But before the Children's Room was completed, other projects were underway.

SUPPORT FOR FACILITIES

An intercom system was described in an article in the *Daily Tar Heel* on December 19, 1956. At a cost of $1,700, donated by the Tri Sigmas, Ms. McLaren was able to entertain children in their separate rooms. Her telling stories, playing phonographs, and tuning in children's radio programs were considered innovative procedures at that time. Individual toys were brought to the rooms for play. Ms. McLaren also organized group play activities in a small room at the east end of a seventh-floor corridor, the precursor of the fine

Margaret Moore hands Ed Curnen the first check from the Tri Sigma Sorority towards construction of the new pediatric playroom, while Kathy McLaren looks on

playroom to be described later. She supervised play commencing at 10 A.M., interspersing this between rounds and procedures.

In addition to support for this early program from the Tri Sigmas, more minor contributions were received from the Chapel Hill Rotary Club, the Community Church, and the Junior Service League. The Women's Auxiliary of Memorial Hospital and the Gray Ladies organization provided volunteer workers.

Dr. Curnen commenced working on plans for a comprehensive play area on the seventh floor in 1957. Two-thirds of a seven-hundred-square-foot area on the terrace on the east wing was initially assigned to this play area with the remainder for a small conference room and an interview area. As plans evolved, the playroom area alone was enlarged to seven times that of its earlier size and the total area to 2,280 square feet. The play area was conceived as also being used for the communal partaking of meals by the children, for physical therapy, psychotherapy, occupational therapy, and other group activities. A one-way mirrored screen was available for observation of the children's activities.

The Tri Sigmas' donation of $25,000 for this construction was matched by the state's Medical Care Commission in this first of successful "seedings" by the sorority. The beautiful "glassed-in" room that resulted had a commanding view from its south and east walls, contained storage cabinetry on its north wall, and even had a stone trough for water play, a sandbox, and a built-in sink, in addition to a television recessed into a wall. The Women's Auxiliary Hospital Shop contributed also to the construction of this facility, as well as several private donors. The playroom and conference room, constructed by an outside contractor, were completed in November 1958 and were dedicated several months later.

The new
playroom
and
conference
room under
construction
(1958)

The Tri Sigmas were enthusiastic about the success of this project and directed their attention to "seeding" other facilities. Dr. Curnen, an expert in infectious disease, saw the need of an isolation unit and planned to place this on the terrace at the west end of the seventh floor. Another donation of the Tri Sigmas of $25,000 was matched with $25,000 from the University and $63,000 from the state Medical Care Commission to aid in the construction of this eight-room unit, equipped with private baths in each room and with a large nursing station. Dr. Jack Lynch and his family also donated generously to this project. This unit was not completed until February of 1963, after Dr. Curnen had left for New York.

In 1962, the Tri Sigmas pledged $25,000, later supplemented by funds to cover additional costs, for a second playroom in the pediatric outpatient area. As the new Love Clinic Building evolved, completion of this project was delayed until October of 1969. Two other projects caught the attention of the sorority: an intensive care facility on the seventh floor and an adolescent lounge in the bed tower; these were completed in March of 1973 and November of 1975, respectively. The ninth-floor bed tower lounge also was made available at scheduled times for adult patients and provided office facilities for the Department of Recreational Therapy.

Annie Scott lectures on infant nutrition to medical students in the new pediatric conference room

PROGRAMS IN RECREATIONAL THERAPY

As each of these facilities was developed, new programs evolved. Initially, the play program under Ms. McLaren's direction involved volunteers only, five or six in the playroom at all times. By 1960, junior volunteers, later designated "candy stripers," began to assist. Arts and crafts, audiovisual programs, 16 mm movies, communal singing, "rhythm band" playing, and performances by guitarists and others were planned. Mrs. Elaine Hill has emphasized the important roles of the hospital volunteers in running the playroom during these early years before professional staffing was more complete.

Dr. Jack Lynch, a major donor toward seventh-floor expansion

Close coordination with the nursing service was arranged by head nurse Audrey Booth, to the extent that progress reports on all patients were kept by recreation personnel and appropriate comments placed in the medical records.

Operated on a six-day week, including four evenings in 1969, the playroom offered family-style lunches and evening meals. Toddlers and preschoolers received most of the attention during mornings, while the school-age children were attending classes in the adjacent school. Schoolchildren had more free afternoons and could be the focus of more attention then.

Specific programs were organized to teach the children what to expect at certain procedures, such as cardiac catheterization, using doll play with the child as the doctor. During 1970, this type of activity was extended to utilize

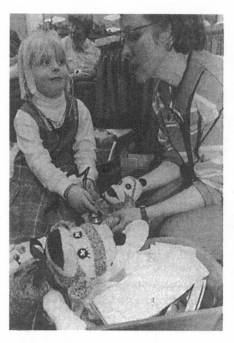

A "monkey doll," one of thousands produced by hospital volunteers, undergoes a cardiac check-up under the watchful eye of Laurie Reddick, pediatric recreation therapist [Credit: Chapel Hill News]

A future champion tests his mettle in the pediatric playroom

play techniques to reduce tension before more major surgical procedures. Later, play therapists actually attended some cardiac catheterization and renal procedures with the children. A videotape describing the cardiac catheterization procedure was prepared in 1978.

Age specialization became a feature of the recreation therapists' program in 1973 when toddler specialists, school-age experts, and adolescent-oriented therapists began concentrating on these age groups. Training for specializing in recreation therapy for burn patients was also developed as the play program began to include the Jaycee burn unit. The outpatient playroom also organized special programs, including preadmission tours of various facilities, permitting "playing out" of anticipated medical procedures such as ultrasound techniques, blood tests, and X-rays. Children staying in the twenty-four-hour observation area of the emergency room were also included within the reach of the outpatient playroom.

Imaginative new programs were added yearly; for example, in the mid-1970s "out-trips" into the community were made with some of those children who had been hospitalized for long periods. Educational programs on health care and safety were instituted, covering such topics as fires, poisons, bicycle safety, and dental care and using Walt Disney filmstrips and cassettes. The children did not escape being tested after these presentations to see what they had learned.

With Tri Sigma's assistance, a closed-circuit TV setup with thirty-seven sets and many appropriate videotapes was arranged for most of the children's rooms to reach the bedridden patients who could not be brought to the playroom.

Thus, although the playroom on the seventh floor remained the major facility, the play therapy program reached out to all children in the hospital.

Ms. Elizabeth Cozart in May of 1981 has described the therapeutic play activities at that time. She summarizes the sophisticated techniques used, including dramatic play with acting out of hospital encounters, storytelling with puppets, tape recording and "book" writing, and using visual aids such as allowing the child to run slide shows. Other activities were directed at employing directed expressive art, encouraging use of fine motor skills, and even using messy play. These methods indicate the extent to which recreational therapy has evolved during the existence of our program.

EDUCATIONAL PROGRAMS

Because there was no department of child development at UNC-CH, contacts were made early by Drs. Denny and Van Wyk with Dr. Naomi Albanese, the dean of the School of Home Economics, and with faculty members of the Department of Child Development at Women's College in Greensboro (now UNC-G). A pilot program was carried out, but no permanent liaison was achieved because of difficulties related to commuting. Plans turned toward affiliating with the Recreation Department at UNC-CH, and in 1967 a play therapy curriculum at the graduate level was initiated in that department. Dr. H. Douglas Sessoms, a professor of recreation administration, was instrumental in this endeavor. For the MA degree, two semesters of nine credit hours each and one summer session were required. Tri Sigmas supplied fellowship stipends of $200 per month plus tuition and the program started well with a carefully selected candidate for this "assistantship," Mr. William Lotito. He represented the first in a series of up to four assistants per year for the period to follow, with the Tri Sigmas paying for at least one each year and with the Bureau of Education for the Handicapped and the NC Memorial Hospital assuming additional funding. Student nurses and undergraduates from UNC-CH and from UNC-G, East Carolina, Clemson, University of Maryland, Indiana, Fairleigh Dickinson, University of Illinois, University of Georgia, and Longwood College were incorporated into the overall program even before 1980 and other schools have been represented since then.

A listing of the pediatric playroom staff and of the graduate assistants is included in *The History of Pediatric Recreation Therapy at North Carolina Memorial Hospital*, written by Ms. Barbara Salter, herself an assistant in 1980. This useful account also gives additional details of the "internship" itself and of the requirements for obtaining the support for this choice assistantship. Instructional materials prepared by the staff and graduate students are also listed, revealing the major contributions of such materials by Ms. Martha Early Rodenbeck, a recreation therapist from 1973 to 1976. This sixty-three-page history by Ms. Salter is recommended for the interested reader and is available in our archives.

CONTRIBUTORS FROM THE SORORITY

The Years Remembered of Sigma Sigma Sigma 1898 to 1962, published as a second edition in 1963 by the George Banta Company, Inc., of Menasha, Wisconsin, details the early history of the service provided by this outstanding sorority to its communities and the nation. Incidentally, the book was dedicated to the founders of the sorority and especially to Ms. Mabel Lee Walton, Robbie's great-aunt.

In a relationship as complex as that between the Tri Sigmas and the Department, many important players participated who have not been mentioned as yet. Among these many, Mrs. Lucille Amese Morrison, Mrs. Norma Caton Kitchen, Mrs. Margaret Freeman Dixon, Mrs. Mary Eileen Dobson, Mrs. Aubrey Christie Waddell, Ms. Emma Sloan, Mrs. Marie Dunham, and Mrs. Myrtle Holmes were mentioned specifically in the sorority's history of 1963. Other leaders later include Mrs. Evelyn Bone Bennett, Mrs. Sue Haynes Patton, Mrs. Helen Marie Snyder, Mrs. Gerry Johnson, Mrs. Martha Ward, Mrs. Margaret Munger, and Mrs. Ruth McCreary, who at the present time is the Tri Sigma who has been monitoring our programs most closely. Other important executives of the sorority whose names appear in our correspondence include Mrs. Needa Crawford, Mrs. Norma Larson, Ms. Nancy Beeker, Mrs. Debby Yates, Mrs. Carol Swango, and Mrs. Christine Longyear. Dr. Margaret Moore, in a recent letter, expressed how terribly proud she is of her "sorority and what it has accomplished." During her long tenure as an executive, she persuaded the sorority to keep the projects focused and directed attention to the needs at our institution.

Ms. Audrey Booth, who was the chief of pediatric nursing at important times, Mrs. Elaine Hill, who was the director of volunteers at the hospital, and Mrs. Harriett Brewer, who was the administrative manager of the Department of Pediatrics, were extremely important in arranging for the visits of the Tri Sigmas and in making the ladies feel at home in Chapel Hill. Mss. Booth, Hill, and Brewer were made honorary members of the sorority.

A complete listing of the many therapists who directed the children's recreation therapy programs at the hospital is included in the archives. These people were very familiar figures as they pursued their various roles in the Children's Room and elsewhere in the Department and must be credited for helping to make our service a relatively pleasant place for these desperately ill patients.

RECENT EVENTS

A recent supervisor of the playroom program, Mr. Darl Pothoven, sums up the important events of recent years.

In the 1980s, the support for graduate assistants continued, as did funding for some special projects. One such project was the replacement of all the televisions on the seventh floor. At the same time, a special closed-circuit television project, specifically for children, was developed and implemented in 1981. This project was given the name "Sigma Showcase," and featured children's programming of both an entertaining and educational nature. Sigma Showcase ensured that, for at least a few hours each day, pediatric patients would have access to wholesome television entertainment in their own rooms. Thanks to the ongoing Robbie Page Memorial Foundation Grant, the Sigma Showcase videotape library has expanded considerably over the years. Sigma Showcase continues today to be an important part of the daily television schedule.

Another major event of 1981 was the visit by the Robbie Page board to celebrate the twenty-fifth anniversary of the Robbie Page Memorial Playroom. This event was coordinated by Liz Shute Cozart, the recreational therapy supervisor. The service provided to hospitalized children over the past twenty-five years through the playroom was indeed something to celebrate. [Dr. Van Wyk's talk at this anniversary describing the early history is available in the archives.]

The year 1981 also saw the completion of Dr. Denny's term as chair of the Department of Pediatrics. He was succeeded by Dr. Thomas Boat. In honor of Dr. Denny's support of recreational therapy and his role in developing the relationship between Sigma Sigma Sigma and the hospital, one of the recreational therapy graduate assistantships was designated as the Floyd Denny assistantship.

In 1983, Liz Cozart moved away from Chapel Hill with her family and was succeeded as recreational therapy supervisor by Ms. Susan Gates. Shortly thereafter, Ms. Margaret Munger became chair of the Robbie Page Memorial Foundation board. The board approved a three-year grant to the Department of Recreational Therapy, which included as its major project the refurbishing of the Robbie Page Memorial Playroom. As this project was nearing completion in 1985, Mr. Darl Pothoven became the recreational therapy supervisor in pediatrics.

As hospitalized pediatric patients progressively became more ill, the importance of in-room services also increased. As portable videogame systems and VCRs became more common, Tri Sigma began providing resources of this type for use both in the playroom and in patient rooms. As recreational therapy began to expand the medical teaching element of its services, Tri Sigma purchased special medical teaching dolls to further assist in the preparation of children for surgeries and procedures. The playroom also continued to receive special attention as new equipment, including an aquarium, continued to be purchased to ensure that the children would have a top-notch play area.

In 1989, in recognition of the rapidly growing pediatric outpatient program, the Robbie Page board approved support for a third graduate assistant position, which was assigned to the outpatient recreational service area. At the same time, Ms. Carol Swango assumed the board's chair position. Funding continued for playroom equipment as well as for special equipment for patient rooms. For example, several multipatient rooms did not have wall-mounted televisions because of space and noise considerations. The Tri Sigma grant provided funds to purchase special televisions, mounted on movable arms, that could be positioned directly in front of the patient for viewing at low volume. These televisions could be moved out of the way to allow nurses to effectively perform their patient care duties.

Current projects underway or recently completed include another refurbishing of the playroom and the installation of videocassette players in the patient rooms. These projects are being coordinated by Ms. Dawn Widenhouse Lucas, a former Denny graduate assistant, who has been the recreational therapy supervisor since 1993. Dawn is actively involved in the planning process for the new North Carolina Children's Hospital.

The prospect of this state-of-the-art facility and of Tri Sigma's potential role in its development is exciting. There is every opportunity for the proud tradition of Tri Sigma's contribution toward serving the needs of hospitalized children through the Robbie Page Memorial Fund to continue well into the next century. Robbie would undoubtedly be delighted with the work that has been done in his name.

HERBERT S. HARNED, JR.

CHAPTER THIRTY

Social Work and Pediatrics,
1952–1993

DEPARTMENT OF SOCIAL WORK ADMINISTRATION

WITHIN six weeks of the opening of the North Carolina Memorial Hospital in September 1952, rudimentary social services were available through the efforts of Ann Bunce. Physicians (particularly "Yankees") who in their previous hospital settings had been accustomed to calling on social workers for making family assessments, identifying needs, and connecting families with community resources were at a loss both in understanding patients immersed in this Southern rural culture and in comprehending the lack of availability and accessibility of social services in North Carolina. In Chapel Hill in 1952, for example, there were no social agencies except for the Public Health Department; even the Department of Public Welfare required a long-distance call, which usually resulted in a busy signal on their single-line phone system to their Orange County offices in Hillsborough. Mrs. Bunce had had significant experience in public welfare in Syracuse, New York, and then with the Red Cross, first as Syracuse's home services field secretary, then overseas in hospitals during World War II. In Hawaii she met her husband, Paul, a urologist; after the war, while he completed his training at Johns Hopkins, she worked in the Harriet Lane Children's Hospital Admissions Department.

Because of her previous social service experience, Mrs. Bunce often was asked to consult informally with physician staff members in Chapel Hill. Subsequently the hospital director, Dr. Robert Cadmus, asked Mrs. Bunce to substitute the task of setting up a social services department for her previous volunteer activity of rolling bandages. With the assistance of one clerk and one telephone, Mrs. Bunce handled physicians' social service referrals, set up a community resources file, and established a $500 social services discretionary fund. After leaving the NCMH Department of Social Services in February 1953, Mrs. Bunce thereafter devoted her life to her home, her family, and volunteer services.

In January 1953 the hospital's first professional social worker, Rebecca Randolph, was employed. She was highly recommended by the faculty of the University of North Carolina School of Social Work, not only because her experience in child welfare was impressive, but especially because she had a master's degree in social work from the University of Pennsylvania. (In 1930–1950, UNC and UP were the only schools in the country to use as their psychological base the theories of Otto Rank rather than Sigmund Freud.) In the five years while she was director, 1953–1958, Ms. Randolph was able to build up the Social Services Department to four workers in addition to herself. Two student interns were assigned to the department from the UNC School of Social Work. Rather than having one worker who specialized and took all the referrals in pediatrics (or surgery or medicine, etc.), the patient referrals were rotated among the social workers. One would expect that Ms. Randolph, with her child welfare background and experience, would have been particularly helpful to the Pediatrics Department. She did mention by phone that working with the pediatric situations provided her happiest experiences because the Department of Pediatrics staff was so open and sharing. However, the hospital's physician staff generally did not find Ms. Randolph and her staff to be helpful in the ways they had learned to expect from past experiences with medical social workers, and she was asked to leave. She returned to child welfare in the Washington, DC area and now reports that she has had a successful and rewarding career. Although we have been in touch with her by phone on several occasions, unfortunately she has declined to be interviewed and to tell "her side of the story." The chief criticism of her work at UNC seems to have been that she was not used to working in a hospital setting and that she did not communicate well with the physicians. From her child welfare perspective, she was so involved in protecting the patient's confidentiality that she refused to write notes in the medical charts or often to discuss with others the patient's psychosocial and family information essential to the treatment of patients.

In the interim between Ms. Randolph's departure and the hiring of a new director, Carter Williams, MSW, was asked to serve as the department's administrator. Like Mrs. Bunce, Mrs. Williams was experienced in medical social work, as she had been employed at Duke's Department of Social Services as well as at Massachusetts General Hospital, Baltimore's Mt. Sinai Hospital, and Boston Lying-In Hospital. She was also the wife of a faculty physician, T. Franklin Williams, an internist. When she left this position, she too devoted her time to home, family, and community activities. Relevant to pediatrics, early in the 1960s she helped create the Chapel Hill Cooperative Preschool at the Community Church, which was thought to be the South's first racially integrated nursery school.

When she began her directorship, in order to mediate the conflicts between physicians and social workers, Mrs. Williams suggested that a study be done to determine needs and to better define the appropriate functions of social work in the North Carolina Memorial Hospital setting. A Sub-Committee on Social Services was set up under the leadership of Dr. Charles Burnett, chairman of the Department of Medicine. Ann Peters, MD, MSW, represented pediatrics on that important committee, which included seven physicians, a nurse, and a School of Social Work faculty member, Alan Keith-Lucas. At Mrs. Williams's recommendation, Ms. Josephine Barbour, the social work director of Massachusetts General Hospital (the first hospital in the country to establish a Department of Social Work, in 1905), was appointed as consultant. The report of that committee, including the very thorough recommendations of Ms. Barbour, appears in the appendix of Euzelia Smart's historical monograph, located in the library of the School of Social Work. Notably, Ms. Barbour recommended that the Social Services Department be centralized, i.e., that the divisions of the general hospital with its five social workers and that of psychiatry with its six workers be integrated; that the centralized department be administered by a director experienced in hospital social work; that there be clear and frequent flow of communication from social workers to physicians; and that the Sub-Committee on Social Services be established as a permanent School of Medicine Social Services Advisory Committee in order to continue to be available as a sounding board to the new director.

During the years 1959 to 1972 that Euzelia C. Smart was administrator of the Department of Social Work, she was able to implement the recommendations listed above. (The name was changed from Social Services to Social Work when the Department of Public Welfare changed its name to Social Services and confusion among NCMH patients was rampant.) Ms. Smart was well qualified in social welfare, medical social work, administration, and North Carolina culture. She was born in the North Carolina mountains, educated at Meredith College in Raleigh, and worked with the mountain women under the Works Progress and Emergency Relief Administrations during the depression. She had been commissioner of Public Welfare in High Point, North Carolina and during World War II was supervisor and hospital field director with the Red Cross in the Southeast Asian theater—serving in the Philippines, Japan, Korea, Australia, and New Guinea. After the war, she completed her MSW at Columbia, administered the social work program at the North Carolina Cerebral Palsy Hospital in Durham, and next was appointed to be director of social work at the University of Indiana Hospitals in Indianapolis. She was an active member of the American Hospital Association Society for Hospital Social Work directors and thus was up-to-date on current trends in hospital social work.

During the years of Ms. Smart's directorship at NCMH, she was able to integrate the psychiatric and medical social workers into a central department; she increased the staff size from four to seventeen; she sparked medical team members' sharing of responsibilities through the motif of social service rounds; she insisted that the social worker "follow the patient," both inpatient and outpatient (in contrast to other hospitals where social workers are assigned to outpatients only or inpatients only); and she organized the social workers into teams that reflected the clinical departmental structure of the UNC School of Medicine, i.e., pediatrics, medicine, ob-gyn, surgery, psychiatry, etc., thereby enhancing communication between social workers and other members of the medical team. Ms. Smart attributed her success to her ability to work closely with School of Medicine clinical faculty in identifying needs, and sharing information and treatment plans through individual conferences, chart notes, and social service rounds.

Within fifteen years after her retirement in 1972, Ms. Smart moved and settled into Carolina Meadows, a local life care community. Then in 1990, when she was eighty-two years old, she and her fiancé from the 1920s reconnected and were married. Now she is back at her home base in the North Carolina mountains where her husband, Wade Brown, lawyer and former mayor of Boone, is still consulted regarding legal problems by students at Applachian State University.

Before she retired, Ms. Smart identified her successor, W. Wallace Hill, with whom she had worked on a national committee of the American Hospital Association Society for Hospital Social Work directors. His MSW was from Rutgers; his experience included working with emotionally disturbed juveniles in a residential home and school social work. He discovered medical social work when he "filled in" in local community hospitals during the summers when schools were on vacation. Before coming to Chapel Hill, Mr. Hill had been director of social services at the Mary Fletcher (University of Vermont) Hospital in Burlington, Vermont. Mr. Hill first explored the NCMH department by coming to Chapel Hill as assistant director in 1971, a year before Ms. Smart retired. At that time he was involved in conducting various statistical and time studies in the department, which led to the projection of an overall departmental five-year plan. Mr. Hill's administrative style was to give his skilled senior staff freedom, support, and encouragement in building their individual clinical programs together with medical faculty. A major administrative talent lay in his quantitative contributions; the department became an early model for using computer-based statistics, which reflected the department's quality assurance program and responded to the cost-accounting era of hospital administration in the 1980s.

In 1972, early in Mr. Hill's directorship, an important event took place. The growth in staff, the proliferation of bureaucratic complexities (e.g., Medicare/Medicaid regulations), and their increasing specializations led to the administrative separation of the hospital and the School of Medicine. A separate hospital board of directors was appointed; the hospital thereafter reported directly to the state and was no longer subordinate to the Medical School. The relationships that Ms. Smart had developed with the clinical faculty of the School of Medicine continued as related to the care of patients;

however, since the overwhelming majority of the salaries of the social workers were increasingly from the hospital rather than the School of Medicine, the administrative and planning relationship with the school became less close.

Mr. Hill worked ceaselessly to develop the discretionary funds used mostly for lodging, meals, and transportation which were so essential to the young families who needed to be by the bedsides of their sick children but who were without adequate financial resources. Mrs. Bunce began with a $500 gift, Ms. Smart tapped other resources, but it was during Mr. Hill's administration that the following projects were developed: hospital volunteers' support of the meal ticket program; the creation of the Hospital Motel, then the Ronald McDonald House; Title XX transportation funding to help patients and their families travel to and from the hospital; church and Salvation Army financial support of the Food Cupboard on the pediatric floor; the Pediatric Holiday Card Project, which by 1993 had raised $50,000 for NCMH children's recreational and educational activities; and expansion of the department's Social Services Welfare Fund in general.

Mr. Hill became assistant director in 1990 and in 1993 retired in order to be more available to his family and to devote full-time efforts to developing statistical social work software. Scarlet Cardwell was appointed director in 1990. Her MSW is from the University of Tennessee and she had been the social work administrator at the Presbyterian Hospital in Charlotte, North Carolina.

PEDIATRICS CHIEF CLINICAL SOCIAL WORKERS

As mentioned above, it was Social Work Director Euzelia Smart who structured her proliferating staff into speciality areas and then teams. Alletta Hudgens, MSW, came to UNC in 1960 within six months of Ms. Smart's arrival and was assigned solely to pediatric cases. She was succeeded by another professional pediatric social worker, Esther Williams.

Dr. Harrie Chamberlin recalls that in 1961 he was involved in hiring the first social worker at the supervisory level for his developmental evaluation clinic: Jane Parker, MSW, who had been director of Public Welfare in Orange County, then worked not only purely in pediatrics but specifically with pediatric developmental evaluation clinic patients and their families. In 1964 Elaine Goolsby succeeded Mrs. Parker and was also involved in the evolution of the developmental evaluation clinic as it developed into the division for disorders of development and learning; eventually DDDL had a team of four professional social workers. When Mrs. Goolsby was appointed DDDL assistant director for clients, her associate Mr. Blan Minton became DDDL social work section head.

In 1964 Ms. Smart chose Ruth Paddison to be supervisor of the pediatrics team. Eventually each of the half-dozen social work teams was headed by a "chief clinical social worker," who served as a middle manager in an advisory

Virginia
Hebbert

capacity to the director. Ms. Paddison's experience had been in child welfare, especially adoption work, but not medical social work. After two years she returned to child welfare.

In 1967, when Ms. Smart heard that an old friend was returning to the Chapel Hill–Durham area, she persuaded Virginia Hebbert to take on the administration of the pediatric social work team. Ms. Hebbert was knowledgeable about medical social work, as she had taught such a course at the College of William and Mary and in the Philippines; she was experienced as a social work clinician in medical settings, particularly with children, as she had worked at Medical College of Virginia and at the Richmond Department of Public Welfare, as well as with placement of children in New York City and at the Children's Center in New Haven, Connecticut. She was experienced as a social work administrator, as she had set up the social work program at the St. James Hospital in Nanking, China, before militant communists took over the hospital, and had organized and headed the social work department at St. Luke's Hospital in Manila, Philippines.

When Ms. Hebbert began in the NCMH Department of Social Work, there were only two workers assigned to the pediatrics caseload, Edith Elliott (Wiggans) and Nancy Tolbert. When she left ten years later, the social work pediatric team had built up to ten workers.

Ms. Smart expected her supervisors to be "working" chiefs, i.e., to provide patient care in addition to being middle managers, advisors, and supervisors. Ms. Hebbert herself followed children treated in specialty clinics such as cardiology, endocrinology, neonatal disease, etc., until referrals from medical or nursing staff indicated the need for full-time service from a social worker. At that time, with input from the clinical staff, a full-time worker was employed to cover the clinic and its patients if they were hospitalized.

Ms. Hebbert's outstanding clinical contribution was—along with Drs. Cathy Taylor and Frank Loda—sparking, helping with the development of, and serving on the maltreatment syndrome team. From her early experience in placement of children in New York and Connecticut, Ms. Hebbert was sensitive to family cover-up of child abuse. At NCMH, she worked ceaselessly both to help maltreated children and to teach physicians and other professionals how to be suspicious of, diagnose, and treat child abuse. The NCMH maltreatment team appears to be the first of its kind in this country.

Ms. Hebbert says, "I was delighted and personally rewarded to work with

UNC physicians and nurses who became increasingly conscious of how the social situation affected a child's illness and the treatment needed. The pediatrics staff at UNC in that respect was far ahead of staff in any other hospital where I had worked previously."

When Ms. Hebbert retired in 1977, Wilma Peebles was appointed to assume the child clinical social worker position in pediatrics. Ms. Peebles was born and raised in Raleigh, had a BSW from North Carolina State, an MSW from Case Western Reserve, and had been teaching in an undergraduate social work program in Kentucky. Unfortunately, like Rebecca Randolph and Ruth Paddison, Ms. Peebles learned that she could not be maximally effective in a hospital setting. After just a year, she returned to the faculty of North Carolina State University and is now the dean of the Boston University School of Social Work. An experienced senior clinical social worker, Mary Rogan, was interim chief until the appointment of Juanita Todd in 1979.

Ms. Todd, like the other successful administrators depicted in this historical account, had had a wealth of experience, especially in medical social work: Red Cross in the District of Columbia and in Germany; family service in Dayton, Ohio; and the National Cancer Institute in Washington. Her immediate previous experience had been as chief clinical social worker on ob/gyn at the University Hospital in Indianapolis. (Although she had not been a member of that staff at the time Euzelia Smart was director, she was familiar with Ms. Smart's administrative patterns there: a central department that included both psychiatry and the general hospital, social work teams that reflected the medical school's divisions, speciality assignments, and thorough and close communication with physicians and the health team.) Ms. Todd now administers a team of seven full-time and five part-time professional social workers. Another senior worker, Marie Lauria, assists her chief in supervision of individual workers as needed and leads a monthly casework consultation group for social work pediatrics team members.

Under Ms. Todd's direction, the speciality areas developed initially by Ms. Hebbert have continued to grow. Ms. Lauria, chosen by Ms. Hebbert in 1974 to be the social work clinician with the pediatric oncology team, is still giving the highly skilled social care needed by these medically fragile, often terminally ill children and their families, but also is contributing to research and teaching through her work with the national Society for Oncology Social Workers and in the profession of social work in general. Examples of other challenging assignments in pediatric speciality areas that have initiated innovative program planning include the premature nursery, renal disease, neurology, endocrinology, pulmonary, genetics, cystic fibrosis, and rehabilitation.

COMPOSITION OF SOCIAL WORK STAFF

Although the NCMH Department of Social Work staff from the start has been composed primarily of females, it has consistently been racially integrated and always professionally qualified. Even on Ms. Randolph's small staff, all members had their master's degree in social work; Ms. Smart and Mr. Hill hired only a few social work assistants at the bachelor's level; and by the 1980s entering staff members were required not only to possess a master's degree in social work, but two years of experience as well. In 1990 the average experience for two-thirds of the staff was over eight years, and all had over three years' experience. No social work assistants ever were hired to cover pediatrics.

The hospital Social Services Department has been "avant-garde" as compared with most other NCMH departments in its racial composition. Ms. Randolph hired an African American social worker who later obtained her doctorate and directed the social work program at North Carolina Agricultural and Technical State University. When the North Carolina Memorial Hospital was integrated in the 1960s, African American social workers were involved in the planning strategies. However, it is sad to reflect that before the hospital was integrated, these professional persons were expected to use separate water fountains, rest rooms, and cafeterias! Both African American and Asiatic Indian social workers have served on the pediatrics team. Interestingly, as Elaine Goolsby, a native North Carolinian, has pointed out, social work staff members who have been born and raised in North Carolina—particularly, as she and many of the early NCMH patients, on a tobacco farm—have been in the minority.

SUMMARY

As described above, social work services in pediatrics evolved in a series of steps from identifying resources to help children and their families with concrete problems, to responding to referrals among a few social workers on a rotation basis, to assignment of social workers experienced in child welfare specifically to pediatrics, and most recently to the development of a significant social work response team with specific speciality assignments. Paralleling this, the pediatric social work service has contributed to development of community resources and to program planning for the hospital.

REFERENCES

Euzelia Smart. *Social Work—Program Planning and Development in Hospitals: An Historical Perspective*. Monograph. April 1976.

Audiotaped interviews with Ann Bunce, Elaine Goolsby, Virginia Hebbert, W. Wallace Hill, Euzelia Smart (Brown), and Carter Williams.

Telephone conversations with Rebecca Randolph.

Letter dated 11/1/88 from Dr. Robert Cadmus, first NCMH director.

Information obtained from various staff members, but especially Patsy Johnson, administrative assistant, Department of Social Work; Marie Lauria, pediatric oncology clinical social worker; and Juanita Todd, chief clinical social worker, pediatrics.

Discussions with pediatricians Harrie Chamberlin and Herbert Harned.

Memory/interpretation of Jean Harned, MSW, clinical social worker, ob/gyn, 1963–1972; educational director, 1972–1988. Mrs. Harned coordinated the hospital's field work program for twelve to fifteen social work students annually and acted as assistant social work director.

JEAN G. HARNED

CHAPTER THIRTY-ONE

The Hospital School

SCHOOL PROGRAMS IN THE EARLY
YEARS OF THE DEPARTMENT

P RECISE information regarding the exact time and circumstances of the foundation of the Hospital School cannot be given because few records of its earliest times have been located. Records do indicate that Mrs. Mary Milam started a volunteer tutorial service for hospitalized children in 1961. Mrs. Milam had moved to Chapel Hill when her husband, Dr. Franklin Milam, joined the staff of the State Health Department after a career with the Rockefeller Foundation. Mrs. Milam's teaching experience was from tutoring her three sons because the family spent many years in developing countries. During the first year Mrs. Milam worked alone. For the next two years, the program continued as a nonaccredited one while the number of volunteer teachers increased to four in 1962 and fifteen in 1963. Newspaper articles in 1964 mention two volunteers who were important to the progress of the school during these early times, Mrs. Frances Brinkhous and Mrs. Margaret Herrington. Also mentioned was that the school program was supported by "community clubs and Chapel Hill book agents" as well as the volunteer teachers.

An important event occurred in 1963 with the establishment of a small schoolroom adjacent to the Robbie Page Memorial Playroom. Kristen Herrington, daughter of Mrs. Herrington and Dr. Robert Herrington, a member of the pediatric residency staff, died in a tragic automobile accident and the schoolroom was established in her memory. The room was described in a news article of the time: "Soft beige-colored walls, thick wall-to-wall carpeting, a globe of the world on the teacher's desk and shelves of books (ranging from *The Green Fairy Book* to *Adventures in American Literature*) provide a cozy and comfortable setting for two hour classes each weekday."

The establishment of an accredited school program occurred in 1964 and was due to efforts of Drs. Erle Peacock and Donald Warren from the cleft palate center. When their oral-facial program, sponsored by the Crippled Children's Program, expanded from a summer session to a year-round program, they attempted to obtain a full-time teacher from the Special Education Program for the State of North Carolina. The Chapel Hill school system had not been able to provide funding, but Dr. Felix Barker of the state Special Education Program agreed to have one position funded for 1964–1965. Records are not clear on who filled this position, but it is believed it was Mrs. Lillian Lee.

In any event, Mrs. Lillian Lee and Mrs. Nathalie L. Harrison were the only two teachers for several years and played important roles during the early years. According to Dr. Warren, writing in 1966: "The State decided that not enough patients were enrolled in the Cleft Palate Center's residency sessions to support a full-time teacher for nine months, so the program joined with Memorial Hospital to set up one school program. The hospital, I believe, was provided funding through the Chapel Hill school system (which obtained its funding directly from the State for this) to employ two teachers, one being responsible for the Cleft Palate program when it held its session, and the other for the Hospital."

NATHALIE HARRISON'S INFLUENCE AND DIRECTION

Mrs. Nathalie Harrison proved to be the mainstay of the school program and perhaps was responsible more than anyone else for its long-term success. A former teacher in Georgia and Alabama schools, she received an EdM degree at UNC-CH in 1965. She came immediately to the hospital school and remained there except for the years 1969 to 1970, when she was employed as an elementary specialist for the EPDA Program, and 1977 to 1988, when she was director for Exceptional Children and Pupil Personnel Services for Chapel Hill–Carrboro city schools. She became the first principal of the hospital school in 1970 when it became large enough for official status as a school and remained in this position until 1977. She returned to the hospital school in 1988 and continued as principal until shortly before her untimely death in 1991.

Mrs. Harrison describes the school's operation in a 1967 article for *The Triangle*, the journal of the Tri Sigma sorority, one of the sponsors of the school. Mrs. Harrison captures the essence of the school program so completely in this article that it is quoted in its entirety:

"Give me some more take-aways to do. I like them."

These may not seem like words of praise to a teacher in a regular classroom, but to the teacher of the hospitalized child, they are indicative that the "treatment-teaching" program will be successful.

In working with the hospitalized child, we have found that the short-term educational program must fulfill both a psychological and an academic need. The hospital teaching program is beneficial in two important ways: first, and most important, studies have suggested that the child interested in the pursuits of life will recover more quickly, leave the hospital, and return to his normal environment. Second, the continuation of the education process prevents the "lost time" and the dread of returning to a class which has progressed beyond the student. Parenthetically, when parents are informed that their sick child is being assigned by the physician to "school," their outlook is brightened, which in turn is communicated to the child, reinforcing his will to become well.

In many instances, because of illness, the child may be both emotionally disturbed and academically retarded. One must be ever aware of the fact that the newly hospitalized child is removed from his familiar surroundings; that impending surgery or treatments will arouse anxiety; that distance or family obligations may prevent his parents from being with him; and that pain or discomfort compound all of these problems. In spite of all these factors, the child must continue to grow and develop; total child care demands that, along with consideration of physical well-being, steps must be taken to make the period of hospitalization a positive experience for the patient, and to provide a pattern of living as close to normal as possible. Essential to this is an educational program.

Dimock (Dimock HG: "The Child in the Hospital," Philadelphia, F. A. Davis Co., 1960) reports that the most important contribution of the hospital school is the filling of a psychological need, for it provides a normal, everyday activity for the child. The schoolroom affords familiar ground on which he may express himself. Kristen Herrington Memorial Classroom, at North Carolina Memorial Hospital, in Chapel Hill, offers all the familiar books, desks, globes, flash cards, and chalkboards found in the regular classroom. "We have one of these in my school back home," said by a newcomer indicates an important tie between the familiar setting at home and the unfamiliar one of the hospital.

Hospital school services are extended to all school-age children on the Pediatric Floor; South Wing, the psychiatric section; Gravely, the Tuberculosis Sanatorium; the Clinical Research Unit; the Hand House, a hand rehabilitation center; the Intensive Care Unit, for special care and burn cases; the Cleft Palate and Speech Rehabilitation Center, a resident eight-week program for children; and to any other areas of the Hospital where there are children of school age. One of the main problems, at the present, is trying to fill the demands of the many areas needing the services of the school. Thirty students a day may be a normal load for a classroom teacher; however, two teachers are over-loaded trying to teach this number when they are of varying ages and grade levels in school. Because of this diversity, one must be prepared to teach any subject on any level and often on short notice. Aside from teaching duties, the teachers attend meetings with the clinical staffs in an effort to contribute to total child care.

Unlike some hospitals, our program (after the physician's permission is given) is offered to all school-age patients on a voluntary basis. One finds that even the most reluctant pupils usually succumb to the peer pressure of "You aren't going to have school today? You'll be sorry when you get home if you don't." Some of the more reluctant children often stand in the door of the classroom for several days then ease quietly into a seat—another loyal supporter for the school program has been gained. Occasionally we find some children who continue their reticence to participate in school for the entire time of confinement; it is interesting to note that often this child's recuperative period is lengthy.

Effort is made to coordinate the hospital classes with the patient's home program. When the physician "prescribes school," a letter is sent to the child's regular teacher requesting the names of the texts and materials to be covered; the pupil's standing (e.g., scores on recent achievement tests, special strengths and weaknesses); the general levels of academic abilities and performance; his attitude toward school; his relations with peers; and his level of socio-emotional development. Using this information, we make appropriate lesson plans.

Two hours a day are planned for each child; often one does not have this full amount of time due to necessary interruptions, such as trips to X-ray, lab work, and treatment. When possible, the children are grouped according to age and ability, and attend school in the classroom. Patients who are restricted to their beds, because of traction, recent surgery, or other reasons, receive bedside instruction. The child depends on himself and the teacher for motivation and stimulation, so we try to offer as much variety as possible in teaching methods; essential to this effort are the audio-visual aids.

The Hospital School endeavors to put the child ahead of his home class to compensate for the time he will lose recuperating at home. Upon discharge, a letter is sent to the home teacher reporting the work completed, and, when hospital treatment or circumstances dictate, we offer recommendations. For example, an eight-year-old girl had been placed in a trainable class in her home school due to her poor speech and weak background. As far as her school was concerned, she was "untestable." After surgery, speech therapy, and special help in her school work, she became more intelligible; upon her return home, her school accepted our recommendations to place her in the first grade.

In some cases we feel that the child would profit more from remedial work, such as reading and arithmetic, rather than the pursuit of his normal prescribed program. The skills that he possesses can be strengthened, and new ones gradually added. We find that there is no stigma attached to dropping back a level in any subject at our hospital school, for the child need not be concerned about peer pressures or peer acceptance. For example, a twelve-year-old boy reported that he was in the fifth grade (this was confirmed by correspondence with his teacher), but when class work began we found that he was unable to read. Since a rather lengthy hospitalization period was to ensue, the rudiments of reading were begun and he was given numerous high interest, low vocabulary books and much encouragement. Upon discharge, he had gained enough confidence and background that he was able to enjoy reading for the first time. Through his newly acquired skills he attacked words, and, when he was unable to identify the word, he no longer was ashamed to ask for help.

A teen-age girl who had planned to drop out of school, get married, do anything except go back to school, though reluctant at first, became interested in assignments and worked well in class. On a return check-up visit, she told us that she now plans to finish high school.

Aside from information gathered on return visits, follow-up evaluations are made; letters are sent (one month after the discharge of the patient) to the home teacher of the long-term hospitalized cases requesting information as to the student's progress. The responses from the teachers have been favorable. Academically, due to the individualized instruction, our dischargees are often improved, and self-confidence and peer relationships are fostered. This is confirmed by the favorable reports from their resident teachers.

For the teacher, the rewards of hospital teaching are many. We experience a sense of accomplishment and satisfaction working with almost four hundred different children yearly. Many of these children we have had for lengthy periods, and some return from year to year. We feel that this program is a contribution to the welfare of the "whole child" in helping to occupy his free time in a constructive manner. In some instances, it offers an opportunity for those who have been unable to attend school at all because of their health. Also, we have had excellent acceptance and cooperation from the medical staff, nurses, play therapists, and others working with the children.

Our major problem area lies within ourselves. It is difficult to empathize and yet not be too sympathetic, to push just the proper amount for the good of the child and yet not demand too much. Through various experiences we learn that the hospital teaching program is our teacher, and we are the pupils. Learning must take place daily for teachers and children alike.

The status of the school in the later 1960s is shown in the following excerpt from an annual report of the hospital volunteers by Mrs. Margaret Herrington, chair of the Pediatric Teaching Committee:

> Pediatric teaching began the school year with an orientation held in the schoolroom on October 1. Mrs. Harrison and Mrs. Lee gave brief talks about the work of the school, after which coffee and cookies were served. Approximately twelve people attended. At the beginning of the year, there were ten volunteers working two hours each per week. This number decreased to five people working once a week, with one person working every other week. In addition to the volunteers, two practicum teachers have been working in the school program. They are University students who are candidates for master degrees in special education.

LILLIAN LEE AND OTHER IMPORTANT TEACHERS

In 1969 Lillian Lee, who contributed her skilled teaching over many years, and Mary Lou Pollock were the only teachers, although a third was added shortly for special education of children with cleft palates. Mary Lou attributes much of the success of the school program at that early time to the contributions of the hospital volunteers under Mrs. Elaine Hill and to Nathalie Harrison, who returned to the school as the first principal. The two division for disorders of development and learning classrooms, with their own teachers, also were part of the hospital school at this time. Ms. Pollock became school principal in 1977. When she left in 1983, the school personnel consisted of a principal, seven teachers, a secretary, and two educational aides. After Mary Lou left there was a succession of principals:

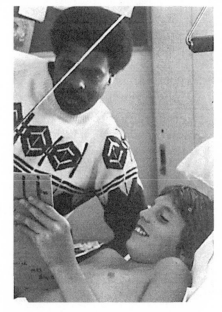

An orthopedic student-patient receives guidance from Major Geer

1983–1985	Sheila Breitweiser
1985–1987	Robin McCoy
1988–1991	Nathalie Harrison
1991–1992	Robert Sturey
1992–	Delores Paylor

This history would not be complete without mention of Mr. Major Geer, who joined the staff in 1970 and is still teaching in the school at the time of this writing. He was the first male teacher in the school and proved to be an ideal role model for the male patients admitted to the hospital.

MAJOR GEER'S SUMMARY OF PRESENT ACTIVITIES

Although records of the history of the school are sparse, Major Geer did furnish a description of some of the school activities about 1988. At that time Nathalie Harrison was principal and there were seven teachers and two aides. This document provides a summary of the philosophy, the programs, and the multiple locations where the school has extended its mission. It indicates that the concepts described by Mrs. Harrison in 1967 have been enforced and even broadened over the years.

STATEMENT OF PHILOSOPHY

The Hospital School provides educational services to chronically ill and hospitalized children at North Carolina Memorial Hospital. It is the intent of the school program to bridge the educational gap during a child's illness until she/he returns to the home school.

THE PROGRAM

School is a normal part of each child's daily life. When a child experiences limitations in his or her physical, mental, and/or emotional health, is unable to attend school for brief and/or extended periods of time, or requires hospitalization, normal educational progress is disrupted. Educational services at the hospital can help a child maintain academic progress during this period of treatment and convalescence. In addition, educational services can have a normalizing and therapeutic effect which stimulates and moves a child toward a more speedy recovery.

The responsibilities of the hospital teacher extend beyond regular teaching activities. These include but are not limited to the following:

Coordination with the home school in order to provide the most appropriate instructional services possible, both while hospitalized and upon the return home.

Scheduling which stresses flexibility due to a number of factors such as the physical condition of the child, limitations imposed by age and ability level, and existing scheduled medical treatment.

Instruction involving formal and informal assessments; adjusting to the expectations of the home, school, and capacity of the child; individual and small group instruction; and evaluation of the student's progress.

Reporting which includes maintaining a North Carolina Public School register for average daily membership, exceptional children reports as indicated, and corresponding with the home school.

Probably the most important responsibility of the hospital school teacher is that of child advocate with hospital staff, parents, and the home school to insure that the needs of the child are appropriately met.

The Hospital School provides educational services to the following areas:

Pediatrics	Outpatient Pediatric
Burn Unit	OB/GYN
Adolescent Psychiatry Unit	Orthopedics
Child Inpatient Psychiatry Unit	Rehabilitation Unit
Dialysis Unit	Ronald McDonald House
Hospital Cross Categorical Class	

At the time of this writing in 1993 the school continues to flourish and remains a vital part of the program for children at the North Carolina Children's Hospital.

FLOYD W. DENNY, JR.
HERBERT S. HARNED, JR.

CHAPTER THIRTY-TWO

Elaine Hill and Hospital
Volunteers: Their Role
in Pediatrics

THE hospital volunteers, and Mrs. Elaine Hill in particular, have played a very active role in supporting the programs of the Department of Pediatrics at the North Carolina Memorial Hospital. It is most fortunate that Mrs. Hill, the director of volunteer services at the hospital from 1967 until the early 1990s, was available for an interview. She knows more about volunteer activities at this hospital than any other person.

Mrs. Hill has had a very strong influence on a variety of programs vital to the operation of the Department of Pediatrics, including the playroom program, the "monkey doll" program, the school program, the volunteer "candy stripers," the lap parent program, college volunteers, sleeping-in programs for parents, the motel, health careers fairs, and the Ronald McDonald House. Insights into these programs can be gained from tracing Elaine's activities since her arrival in Chapel Hill in June of 1952, several months before the hospital opened officially.

Elaine was married to John Hill, a physician who was an important member of Dr. Butler's Department of Pharmacology. Coming from a sophisticated background in New York City, she was culturally shocked at first by the dullness of the little town of Chapel Hill in 1952. She soon became an active volunteer at the hospital to supplement her activities as a mother and as a member of the "family" of young faculty members. Her relationships with the Curnens and Burnetts were especially close.

Mrs. Hill was involved with many other projects of the hospital, including the health careers fairs, where teams from the pediatric recreation program and from pediatric nursing demonstrated their work, along with many other units and disciplines in the health care spectrum. Aware that the school guidance counselors were quite ignorant of the various health-related disciplines, the planners of the fairs directed their attention toward these people, as well as toward the pupils. These fairs became major projects involving visits to the hospital by as many as four thousand high school students at one time. They have been discontinued, perhaps because of their complexity and the demands on the time of the various exhibitors. Mrs. Hill believed that the exhibitors also benefited from participating in the fairs by reaffirming their own roles. Feedback from the school counselors indicated that the fairs proved to be one of the best field trips of the year for their students, but there is no way of knowing the impact of these fairs on the career choices of the individuals involved. At present, a very good program of seminars about health disciplines is being orchestrated by the volunteers, but this is probably no substitute for the elaborate fairs of the past.

Mrs. Hill has been president of the National Association of Directors of Hospital Volunteers, now composed of about fifteen hundred members, and she was responsible for organizing the North Carolina State Association of Directors. Ideas from these organizations have been supplemented by those procured at the volunteers' section meetings of the American Hospital Association.

THE PLAYROOM PROGRAM

The playroom initially had simply been a play space, but soon Mrs. Hill was involved with the planning of a new play area. She indicated that Dr. Curnen was aware of the interest of the Tri Sigma sorority in poliomyelitis research. Interestingly, she pointed out that the advent of the Salk polio vaccine resulted in the shift of the sorority's interest to programs other than research, and its membership responded totally to the concept of a play program for children proposed by Dr. Curnen at their national convention. (Other insights into the origins of the play program are described in the history of the Curnen years and in the chapter on the Robbie Page Memorial.) Mrs. Hill knew Mrs. Page, the president of the sorority, and helped to arrange some of the social functions for the Tri Sigs as they set up the Robbie Page Memorial. She was made an honorary "ex-collegiate" member of the sorority and blindfolded in a candle-lit ceremony; this was an unfamiliar role for her since she had not been a part of sorority life at her undergraduate colleges. Mrs. Hill acknowledges Ms. Audrey Booth's active role in organizing the early planning for the play program, which went far beyond the stages of "bricks and mortar." Elaine also was impressed by the manner in which the sorority has continued its interest and support during succeeding years. The play program and other programs relating to the Department of Pediatrics (the remodeling of the isolation ward, the Curnen conference room and teaching area, the outpatient playroom, and the intensive care area) provide models for how a college sorority can continue to perform good works long after graduation. A branch of the sorority was established at UNC for a time, but apparently it has not succeeded.

MONKEY DOLLS

The Tri Sigs came up with the idea of making dolls for the children, first creating "pinkie puppets." These permitted the child to place a hand in a cloth "body" and to move the plastic head. Within a few years, this idea had evolved into that of making the monkey dolls; these dolls proved to be so loved by the children and so meaningful to the volunteers, that some of them have since taken over this activity and have gone on to produce the dolls by the thousands.

Other aspects of the play program inaugurated during Mrs. Hill's tenure as its director included attendance at morning nursing reports to ascertain the conditions of the patients, instigation of a policy preventing physicians from examining or treating the children while they were in this sanctuary, and using the monkey dolls for playing imagined procedures, such as that of cardiac catheterization. Although these ideas may not have been entirely original at the North Carolina Memorial Hospital, and indeed Elaine admits that the monkey doll idea was generated at a national meeting, they proved to be very effective and meaningful. Elaine recalls a phone call from a parent whose child had been hospitalized years previously, requesting a substitute doll since the original had been "loved to death."

CANDY STRIPERS

For nine months following Dr. Denny's arrival, Elaine was the only staff person in the playroom and out of necessity she had to recruit many volunteers. In order to feed the children, offer music, movies, and crafts, provide story hours and family lunches and other activities, there was a need to recruit college students and teenagers. The latter were called "candy stripers" because of their red-and-white-striped uniforms. Started informally with a handful of girls, the program grew rapidly so that over ninety teenagers of both sexes volunteered during the first year. The program was started in the summer, but achieved such popularity that the candy stripers themselves voted for it to become a year-round activity.

SCHOOL PROGRAM

Mrs. Hill was less active for an interval of several years but did recall the conversion in 1963 of the observation area near the playroom into a schoolroom, when Margaret and Robert Herrington dedicated this space to the memory of their daughter, Kristen. Mrs. Hill's involvement with the Pediatrics Department again became vital when she assumed her role as director of volunteer services for the hospital in 1967. Soon, other programs were established.

LAP MOTHERS

A special type of volunteer was needed for the "lap mother's" role, later defined as "lap parents" since men also performed this difficult task. Volunteers were screened carefully and the nursing staff was alerted to the possible problem of excessive attachment of the "parent" to these very ill infants. On some occasions, these "parents" have also participated during stressful times before operations or other procedures. The volunteers were delegated heavy duties: Each lap parent was assigned to a single child and was required to come to the hospital at least five times a week.

COLLEGE VOLUNTEERS

The decision about whether a particular volunteer would be appropriate for pediatrics was always a joint decision by the volunteer and the director's staff (usually Mrs. Hill herself). For the college volunteers, it was rumored that volunteering was necessary to obtain admittance to medical, nursing, or physical therapy programs. The College Volunteers Group became enlarged to include as many as three hundred students at a given time and appointment of a full-time staff member was necessary to work with this group. This coterie of young people needed to take their roles as volunteers very seriously; if they did not, they would be dropped from the program and given a black mark. Mrs. Hill described registration day for the college student volunteers as similar to the lineup for basketball tickets. Students would get there ahead of time and camp on the floor in line. Pediatrics and the emergency room were the most popular choices for services.

OVERNIGHT FACILITIES

Among the hospital's problems, lack of facilities for overnight stays needed special attention. This was addressed in several ways by the staff aided by the volunteers. Chairs doubling as sleeping couches were selected so that parents could stay in the rooms. The Church of Christ near the hospital contacted the volunteer office and offered two apartments without charge. This shortage was relieved somewhat after 1967 when the nursing dormitory became available for use as a motel. The volunteers helped in the maintenance of this facility. Despite these accommodations, which were available also to patients and families from other services, these sleeping-in arrangements remained inadequate until the Ronald McDonald House became available.

RONALD MCDONALD HOUSE

In her interview, Mrs. Hill discussed the origins and implementation of the Ronald McDonald facility. The idea of applying for one of these units first came up at a meeting in 1983 of Mrs. Hill, Dr. Boat, William Petasnik (an important hospital administrator), and Juanita Todd (chief social worker on the pediatric service). After discussion with certain patients to determine the desirability of such a structure, this group approached the McDonald Corporation, which approved the project; $230,000 was made available for construction planning. Mrs. Hill became chief of the Real Estate Committee which searched for a suitable site. This was a difficult task since most of the University land in the vicinity was already being considered for other projects, other plots of undeveloped land were unavailable, and available housing that might have been converted to use as a motel-type of facility was inadequate. Finally, with the help of Chancellor Christopher Fordham and other administrators (including Garland Hershey and Gordon Rutherford), a 2.1-acre site was located near the Finley Golf Course. Funding was solicited from several foundations, the Glaxo Company, and other donors. Mrs. Hill then became chair of the Building Committee and helped to negotiate an incredibly low price ($1,300,000) for this spacious and well-kept building. Bricks and plumbing were donated; furnishings and many other items were discounted. Mr. Petasnik joked that Elaine had started this project with brown hair, but that this had since turned white from the intensity of her efforts. With this crowning achievement, the pediatric service now has a splendid, twenty-bed motel that is being run at capacity and has offered lodging for thirty-five hundred families during its first five years of existence. The mortgage has since been paid off, an endowment is accumulating, and, most importantly, an excellent facility is adding to the care generally provided by the pediatric service.

In retirement, Elaine Hill is still visiting the Ronald McDonald House daily and is aware of the details of its operation. She put in a nine-and-a-half-hour day on April 24, 1993, when the house celebrated its fifth year of operation.

Mrs. Hill admitted at the end of the interview that she has made a good life for herself since coming to Chapel Hill and has worked with fine people. She has been an important person in the development of the Pediatrics Department and has contributed to its mission of caring. We can all appreciate how her gracious personality and leadership qualities have contributed toward promoting of the causes of the Department.

HERBERT S. HARNED, JR.

CHAPTER THIRTY-THREE

The Chapel Hill Ronald McDonald House

THE outstanding Ronald McDonald House, also called the Carolina Pediatric Family Center at Chapel Hill, is situated at 101 Old Mason Farm Road adjacent to the Finley Golf Course. Since this home is for overnight stays for parents of children and for children who are patients themselves, the Department of Pediatrics has been involved in the operation of this house since its inception. We have asked Dr. Alan Stiles, who along with Dr. Stuart Gold has been a recent board member of the house, to summarize its mission and operation. We also have asked Mrs. Elaine Hill to reveal the early history of the house and to identify people who, along with herself, were prime movers in establishing this facility at Chapel Hill.

Dr. Stiles writes:

The Chapel Hill Ronald McDonald House opened in April 1988 and was the 113th in the United States and abroad. The establishment of the house was a joint effort of the community, the Department of Pediatrics, the UNC Hospitals, and the Ronald McDonald Children's Charities. Workers of varied backgrounds and skills—including pediatricians, pediatric nurses, social workers, and others sharing a common interest in the welfare of sick children being cared for at UNC Hospitals—planned all aspects of the house. The final product is a 14,273-square-foot facility with twenty bedrooms, kitchen and lounge facilities, and play areas located on Mason Farm Road about one mile from the hospital. The mission of the house is to serve as a short-term stay facility for pediatric patients at UNC Hospitals and their families. Support for operation of the Chapel Hill Ronald McDonald House comes from donations and fund-raising events. Only a fraction of the

The Ronald
McDonald
House

$240,000 budget (1994) for operations is recovered from room charges ($8.oo/night). No family is turned away from the house because of inability to pay.

Though many of the Ronald McDonald Houses have focused on patients with particular diseases, the Chapel Hill house in conjunction with the pediatric services at UNC Hospitals has set the priorities to reflect the large number of patients receiving intensive care and patients traveling great distances for outpatient diagnostic or therapeutic procedures. Taking this approach, the house has seen a steady increase in occupancy rate, now averaging greater than 90 percent. The average length of stay has remained about five days, reflecting the large number of families served by the facility. Another reflection of this utilization is the number of families now unable to stay at the house. For the first three years, virtually no families were turned away and stays were unlimited; now, more than three hundred families per year are unable to stay at the house despite a limitation of stay instituted in 1993.

With the establishment of an endowment fund in 1992, the house has entered a phase of fiscal stability and is now able to consider expansion to deal with greater utilization. The development of new programs including transportation and expansion of critical care units, as well as the shift to more outpatient diagnostic procedures, will likely lead to a greater need for house facilities. The house has become an indispensable resource for families and caregivers at UNC Hospitals and has allowed some normalization of life for families under the extreme stress of dealing with sick children.

In an interview on January 25, 1995, Mrs. Elaine Hill described the original conception of the facility. As director of volunteer services at the North Carolina Memorial Hospital, she was aware of the overwhelming difficulties of accommodating parents overnight at the hospital. Many of the patients' rooms at the hospital had not been designed for this and, as we all remember, parents were often found sleeping on chairs and couches and were forced to use common bathrooms which were grossly inadequate.

A house had been established at Duke primarily for oncology patients, and because this unit existed already in this vicinity, there was some question whether the McDonald organization would approve a unit associated with NC Memorial. Mrs. Hill probed this point by calling the McDonald's headquarters in Chicago and found that this was not a reason for turning down a request from us provided our patient mix was different from that at Duke. McDonald's indicated that we needed to have support from parents in particular for this venture. Support was soon obtained from influential parents, including Mrs. Gennie Polk and Mr. Roland Connelly. Dr. Robert Wells from the pediatric oncology division wrote a proposal for consideration by the regional McDonald's office in Raleigh.

Several boards for the prospective house were formed and Mrs. Hill, a longtime resident of Chapel Hill, was appointed chair of the Building Search Committee. This group visited other McDonald Houses in the region and then proceeded to visit almost every old house in Chapel Hill, including the Coker estate and Warner Wells's large house in the heart of the city. These houses in the historic district were unsatisfactory because of the red tape involved in redesigning them for the purposes envisaged. Old furnaces, inadequate parking, and distance from the hospital provided obstacles too great to overcome; the University then received the committee's fervent appeals. The present site was considered and the adjacent property owners in nearby Highland Woods were consulted. The neighbors there, many of whom were faculty members, were very sympathetic; Dr. Chris Fordham, the chancellor of the University, and his wife, Barbara, were in favor of the project, and others agreed that the land could be acquired for $1.00/year.

Mrs. Hill was later made chair of the actual Building Committee, a real challenge for her since she had "never even built a birdhouse" previously. Questionnaires were sent to other Ronald McDonald facilities and major decisions were made as to contractors (Venture Construction Company of Greensboro was selected) and interior decorators. Multiple small decisions needed to be carried out relating to placement of plumbing facilities, air conditioners, etc. Mrs. Hill reports that Bill Petasnik, the associate hospital director, was especially helpful in bringing the facility to reality. Mr. Petasnik along with Dr. Boat and Mrs. Nita Todd of the Social Work Department had sat in on early discussions of the house. Later, Eric Munson from the hospital and Jerry Fernald and Herb Cooper from pediatrics were involved in many decisions.

The living
room

The fund-raising went well and has been sustained ever since by the truly amazing participation of the Chapel Hill community. Initial grants from McDonald's Corporation for $200,000, from the Kroc Foundation for $25,000, and from the Kate B. Reynolds Foundation for $100,000 were supplemented by $100,000 from an anonymous donor who challenged one-to-one matching. Women's clubs, the Sertoma Club, and many other local organizations came to support the project, most of these from our own community, even though the main beneficiaries of the house would be those living away from Chapel Hill.

Furnishings for the house were obtained by the persuasiveness of the people who really believed in it. Mrs. Hill described a visit to a furniture store in Siler City which resulted in a pledge by Mr. Harold Hart and a business associate of forty bedframes, twenty nightstands, and twenty mirrors. (Mr. Hart's daughter had been a hospital volunteer when she was a UNC student.) Dr. Herb Cooper had an entree with people associated with the Hickory Merchandise Mart who supplied most of the downstairs furniture. In the offices and living room, only one couch and several lamps have been purchased— everything else has been donated and blends surprisingly well! The Herbert and Jean Harned library was furnished and endowed by the many friends and associates of Herb and Jean at the time of their retirement; the TV room by This End Up, the furniture company.

Over the years, pediatric leadership has been provided especially by Tom Boat, Jerry Fernald, Herb Cooper, Stuart Gold, and Mrs. Marie Lauria, social worker from the oncology division. Leadership by parents has been provided especially by Gennie Polk, Liz Ross, Roland Connelly, and Jane Gray. Barbara Hardin, the wife of Paul Hardin, the recent chancellor, has been very active as a volunteer and has opened her home to organize the important undergraduate volunteer group. Mike Haley, an owner of many franchises, and

Herb and Jean Harned, with a patient, share the dedication to them of the Ronald McDonald House library (1987)

Woody Durham, the UNC sports broadcaster, have organized the golf tournament which raises major funds for the house each year. House volunteers who have given thousands of hours of service include Geri Laport, Jackie Martinez, and Maurice Whittinghill. Major corporations, especially Glaxo and Burroughs Wellcome, have been "fairy godmothers" over the years. To see a more complete list of benefactors requires review of the house's newsletter, *The Tarhealer*, and the annual reports available in January of each year.

Special committees have been established to oversee the ongoing operations of the house, including committees for admissions, guest services, and house management.

Mrs. Hill did not gloss over the problems in this overall successful venture. There were many glitches during the building of the house that sometimes required immediate attention. An example was the finding during the final inspection hours before the gala opening in 1988 that a water heater was actually a boiler, preventing approval of the building scheduled to host the guests. Somehow, a true water heater was installed on time. Another problem was that the amount of the yearly contribution from McDonald's was not firm, since it depended on the prosperity of the company, making the budgetary process somewhat difficult.

Another problem has been the failure to establish a strong African American presence on the boards and committees of the house. This would be desirable because a substantial portion of the users of the house are African

Americans. Many efforts have been made to establish leadership by this group but have been only partially successful, except with the student volunteers.

Generally, the staffing of the house has been successful and an able group of people has been hired, but usually for short periods in this town of transients. Recent highly skilled persons include Mrs. Deborah Gerhardt, Mrs. Ellen (Crow) Armstrong (the present public relations director), and Mr. Bill Baxter (the present executive director).

We have paid attention in this account to the special people who have brought about this outstanding institution. Its links to the local and state business community can serve the Department and hospital well as plans are being laid for the ambitious North Carolina Children's Hospital.

HERBERT S. HARNED, JR.

CHAPTER THIRTY-FOUR

Harriett Dickey (née Brewer) and Department of Pediatrics Administration

Editors' Note: Harriett Dickey is the administrative manager of the Department of Pediatrics as this is being written in December 1993, a position she has held for twenty-five years. As the only administrative manager the Department has ever had, she has played a prominent role in the development of the Department. It was the opinion of the editors that her role was so important that she should have special recognition in this history. The following comments are derived from an interview of Harriett on September 2, 1993, by Dr. Floyd Denny, and from Dr. Denny's experiences with her during the last thirteen years of his chairmanship.

Harriett is a native of Hillsborough and except for one year at Lenoir Rhyne College in Hickory has never lived elsewhere. After attending UNC-CH she worked at Duke for one year before coming to work as a secretary for Dr. Harrie Chamberlin in August 1967 in what was then the developmental evaluation clinic or DEC. In September 1968 Lynn Kweeder, Dr. Denny's secretary and Department manager of several years, resigned and was replaced by Harriett. This was the start of a warm and very productive relationship that grew with the Department through Dr. Denny's and Dr. Thomas Boat's chairmanships and continues now under the leadership of Dr. Roberta Williams.

Harriett remembers that her year with Dr. Chamberlin was a good one. In her words, "He always liked to share the information that he had with you, so that was fun and exciting. He also was a great coach or a great boss as far as his wanting things done correctly. And for that being my first secretarial job it was good training." Harriett credits Lynn Kweeder for getting

Harriett
Dickey (*née*
Brewer)

her interested in the new job and remembers her as a "very warm and intelligent person."

The relative lack of complexity of the Department in the late 1960s compared to the early 1990s was discussed at some length. Harriett recalls that her job was always complex, but things got much more complicated as the years passed. She gave as an example: "The first thing I remember about working in the Department was the summers. We did not have medical students then. We had two attendings on the floor and during the month of August there were probably two attendings in the whole Department. Everybody else was off on their month's vacation. To compare that kind of laid-back atmosphere to what goes on today is quite a contrast; but we surely didn't think it was laid-back when we were living through it."

Shortly after Harriett became Denny's secretary the workload increased so that she assumed broad administrative duties in the Department, and subsequently her position was classified as administrative manager. This required that Denny have a separate secretary. There was a rather large number of secretaries in that position over the years. Several are remembered with extra warm feelings by Harriett and Denny. Sherri Davis was the first of these (her activities in the Department are included elsewhere in this history). Others mentioned by Harriett were Jane Martin, Peggy Davidson (subsequently Bernstein, when she married one of our chief residents) on two occasions, Karen Moore, and Jackie Olson. As the office got busier others were brought in to help with various duties; Jean Culberson is remembered fondly in that position.

A large part of the interview centered around Harriett's role in the Department and the relationship between her and Denny. Denny had an intense dislike for budgets and money and did not care much for schedules and many other administrative matters. Luckily Harriett liked these very much and quickly assumed responsibility for matters concerning them. At the same time Denny spent his time in overall direction of the Department, in teaching, research, and recruiting house staff and faculty. It proved to be an unusually good arrangement because there was always excellent communication between the two. She is remembered for her vast knowledge of Department and University administration, which she shared with faculty in a gracious manner.

When Denny resigned in 1981 Harriett seriously considered leaving the

Department. After some searching, however, she decided to stay and remembers this as a good decision. She enjoyed working with Jerry Fernald as the acting chair for the year before Tom Boat came, and remembers her years with Dr. Boat with pleasure. Academic medicine and the teaching hospital are changing so rapidly now, and not always for the better, in her opinion. In spite of this she has no regrets for having spent the last twenty-six years in the Department. She enjoyed working with Ned Lawson, the interim chair, and is now finding her place in the administration of Dr. Roberta Williams. When asked how much longer she is going to stay with the Department she replied, "Well, I don't know. I have a fourteen-year-old who will soon be in college, so. . . ."

FLOYD W. DENNY, JR.

ADDENDUM

This article about Harriett Brewer would not be complete without a statement from me regarding her value to me and to the Department over the years. I could not have functioned as I did without her. I shared everything with her because I valued her counsel and because I wanted one other person in the Department to be familiar with all departmental activities. Clearly, she has been one of the very important individuals in the successful growth of the Department. (FWD, Jr.)

CHAPTER THIRTY-FIVE

Maternal and Child Health

Editors' Note: The Department of Maternal and Child Health of the School of Public Health has played an important role in the activities of the Department of Pediatrics. In the section on the Curnen administration emphasis was placed on the vital role of Dr. Sidney Chipman in the Department's early years. We asked Dr. Naomi Morris to prepare the following summary of her view of the relationship between the two departments in later years. Dr. Morris was in the MCH Department during the tenures of three chairs—Drs. Chipman, Siegel, and Miller—in addition to her own. She participated in imaginative programs in collaboration with Pediatric Department members, as she describes. Finally, Dr. Harned has commented: "She might even have contributed to the growth of Floyd Denny, as well as the rest of the Department, in appreciating the importance of public health and community medicine." Her story follows.

I ARRIVED in Chapel Hill in late summer of 1961. We had come so that my husband, Charles E. Morris, could join the neurology faculty under Tom Farmer. On an earlier visit I had met Dr. Ann Peters, acting chair of the Department of Maternal and Child Health (MCH) at the School of Public Health while Dr. Sidney Chipman was away on a sabbatical.

It was during an earlier visit in 1961 that I first visited Dr. Denny in his office, telling him of my training at L.A. County Hospital and the Massachusetts General under Alan Butler, Nathan Talbott, and Fred Blodgett; my interest and subsequent experiences in ambulatory pediatrics; as well as my year in the Massachusetts State Health Department and MPH degree in Maternal and Child Health from the Harvard School of Public Health. He was very cordial, closing our discussion with the invitation, "If I can do anything to help you, please let me know." I was disappointed that he did not seem impressed with what my public health background in particular could offer the Department of Pediatrics, and as I left I said, "Thank you, and if I can do anything to help *you*, please let *me* know." I had really hoped to have some relationship with the Department of Pediatrics from the beginning, even though at the time I knew I was short of the inpatient training needed for board eligibility in pediatrics and that could be perceived as a significant limitation.

Naomi Morris

Joining Ann Peters in January 1962, I started immediately on research concerning day care used by employees of UNC, which was expanded to an Orange County survey. The experience was eye-opening. Upon Dr. Chipman's return he insisted that I present a paper at the next APHA meeting. He took over my training as a fledgling academic, and no one ever had a better mentor. He was exceedingly kind and helpful to me through all our years together in Chapel Hill, and we continue to correspond at least once a year.

When I arrived, Ann Peters, who had had some training in pediatrics in addition to her training in ob-gyn, was helping in the newborn nursery. When Dr. Chipman returned, he resumed his activities in the pediatric outpatient department, and he encouraged me to accompany him and participate as well. As time went on and my sons became involved in a longer school day, I gradually increased the time that I spent in professional activities and undertook regular duties in the pediatric outpatient clinic and in the (normal) newborn nursery. I especially enjoyed examining the newborns and training students and residents in this activity and in interacting with new mothers.

One year, when there was a sudden, unanticipated problem with state funding at the School of Public Health, Dr. Denny picked up one-third of my salary. I was complimented beyond words and really felt appreciated for the first time with this move. My interactions with the Department of Pediatrics became even more important to me, and I truly felt that I was able to contribute my perspective and to learn things important to public health. I particularly enjoyed Bob Greenberg and appreciated very much his Office of Equal Opportunity–sponsored clinic with its 51 percent community board. When he returned from his sabbatical in East Germany, he talked about how all children there were tracked from birth, receiving all their immunizations on time. This lockstep bothered him philosophically, and his quandary left a big impression on me that I have raised ever since with public health students. Computer tracking, of course, is just coming into its own in the United States at this time, but the issue of right to privacy is still being debated.

One study that I did in Chapel Hill had to do with patient satisfaction in several outpatient clinics at NC Memorial Hospital, including pediatrics. I believe that my findings became important when ambulatory activities were expanded and new patients were slow to come in.

I was involved in other studies that had less practical application but had theoretical implications, for which I sought the help of Lou Underwood, Jud Van Wyk, and Frank French. With Dick Udry (Carolina Population Center and MCH Department), I was studying biosocial aspects of sexual behavior, first of women, then of couples, then of adolescents. Lou, Jud, and Frank were all great collaborators and still continue to be involved, especially Frank and his lab. I will never forget one time when Jud asked me to present one of my studies to the pediatric faculty describing the role of pheromones in sexual arousal. I have always loved to hear Jud laugh. When the tube of liquid containing the "pheromones" was about to be passed around for people to smell, I accidentally dropped it. The material spilled and the room was filled with a basically obnoxious odor. I can still hear Jud laughing.

There were only three or four faculty in the Department of MCH when I first arrived. There were several nurses, including Louise Cantrell and Barbara Stocking, the latter remaining for many years and still living in Chapel Hill. Geraldine Gourley, the Department's first social worker, left in the mid-1950s but returned after I came. She now lives in a Chapel Hill retirement village.

In 1961 there were at most six students, and I remember another year when there were only three. All students were full time and tended to be doctors or nurses. With time the number in the class grew, and some pediatricians had additional part-time clinical responsibilities. As our program expanded, we enrolled people with other types of backgrounds, since public health experience was accepted in lieu of clinical training and increasing emphasis was placed on careers as advocates and administrators.

In the mid-1960s J. Richard Udry, a sociologist, was recruited from California to head up maternal and child health research projects. It was my responsibility and pleasure to work with him. Some of the work we were doing connected us to the pediatric endocrine division, as mentioned earlier. Other work connected us to the obstetrics faculty. My collaboration with Dick continues to this day.

Late in the sixties, recruitment began for another pediatrician to join MCH, with the idea that when Chip retired, the new person might take his place. The first pediatrician interviewed was Dr. Arden Miller, former dean of the University of Kansas School of Medicine; Dr. Miller was also interviewed for the vice chancellor for health affairs slot. MCH was disappointed when the latter position was offered Dr. Miller and he accepted it. Arden accepted a joint appointment in MCH and served as vice chancellor for five years.

Earl Siegel

The next pediatrician interviewed for MCH was Dr. Earl Siegel from California, who did accept the position. Dr. Siegel soon succeeded Dr. Chipman as chair of MCH. Dr. Siegel was interested in public health research and teaching, but not in clinical pediatrics. He said he had had his fill of that.

During Earl's tenure, I went on sabbatical to the island of Guam in the Marianas, where I did clinical pediatrics and served as advisor to the chief public health officer. Shortly after I came, I saw a case of tetanus in a five-year-old boy from the Philippines. Serving as a primary care pediatrician in a clinic sponsored by the Title V program for children with disabilities, I became aware of how easy it was for such children (and their parents) to receive little in the way of regular care, such as immunizations, anticipatory guidance, feeding advice, etc. The specialized clinics provided only specialized care, and so far as their parents knew, that was all they needed. I don't think that Guam was the only place where this has been the case. It was a great experience and added numerous anecdotes for my use in teaching, of which I did more upon returning to UNC.

I returned from my year away in 1971, and continued research, teaching, and service. I remember that while reviewing candidates for pediatric residency positions, Floyd said something to me about not wanting to accept too many women, because he did not want to be known as having a "sissy service." I am amused when I look at the gender of the UNC residents now, and even the Department chair!

But something else happened in the seventies; Floyd studied epidemiology at the School of Public Health. It did something to him, or maybe to me. Suddenly he was one of "us," someone with the broader, public health perspective. That, plus the development of community pediatrics as a division, brought MCH and the Department even closer together. Frank Loda and I definitely spoke the same language. We had a conversation in which we concluded that MCH and community pediatrics were philosophically identical with regard to child care and its context, and we worked together to capitalize on our understandings.

In 1973 I was promoted to full professor in MCH. Earl served as chair for seven years but in early 1975 became restless and resigned from a role that he found more and more burdensome. By this time, Dr. Miller had had five years as the vice chancellor and had stepped back into the MCH Department. Since the budget would not allow recruitment from the outside, it was apparent that Arden or I would have to be the next chair. In late summer 1975 I received a telephone call from Bernie Greenberg. He said, "Sweetie, I want you to be the next chair." I doubt anyone has ever been asked in those same words to become a department chair. At least, you would think it was a serious request. I loved Bernie Greenberg and appreciated the affection in his tone, but I still think about how the appointment was offered, with a chuckle and a question about what feminists would make of it.

While I was chair of MCH, the relationship with pediatrics became stronger than ever. I personally had research, service, and teaching bonds. Because of the similar Title V source of its funding and my growing involvement with the Children's Bureau (now Bureau of MCH in HRSA), I appreciated the University Affiliated Facility (UAF), directed by Harrie Chamberlin, more than ever. The preschool education program at the Frank Porter Graham School that had been started by Ann Peters and Hal Robinson was also under the pediatrics umbrella and of considerable interest to me. Knowledge of these activities has been of value to me as my own career has unfolded.

During academic year 1976, my husband was offered the chair of neurology at Chicago Medical School, to start in the fall of 1976. Although I remained through June of 1977 to allow my son David to finish at Chapel Hill High School, my chairmanship had to end after only two years. It was Chuck's turn to become a chair, I reasoned as we moved to the Chicago area.

Upon my leaving, Arden Miller became chair of MCH at UNC, and after him, the first nonphysician, Milton Kotelchuck. I know that the faculty has

Arden Miller

continued to grow, the number of students has become much larger, and the Department of MCH has been very productive and well known. I have been able to establish a similar Title V–funded MCH training program here at the University of Illinois School of Public Health, and in some of our projects we have collaborated with current faculty at UNC. I am a Fellow (Specialty Fellow) in the American Academy of Pediatrics, and have represented the American Public Health Association on the Academy Council on Pediatric Research for six years (with Tom Boat for a while). A new era is dawning because of the pressure for health care reform, and I can see that my MCH unit here will soon participate in a new ambulatory pediatric OB primary care center activity, perhaps in the role of facilitator/evaluator.

It is my understanding that the relationship between MCH and pediatrics at UNC has not been close since I left. Clearly personal factors have played a large role. I have wondered what made it so meaningful for me. Perhaps it was because I never practiced pediatrics in the complete sense, and so never became satiated. I have been fortunate to always have been able to do what I most enjoyed, and to have found wonderful, helpful, meaningful colleagues with whom to work. The Department of Pediatrics at Chapel Hill from 1961 to 1977 will always occupy a shining, warm spot in my memory.

NAOMI M. MORRIS

PART SIX

Pediatric Area Health Education Center Program

Editors' Note: A comprehensive review of the complex relationships between the Department of Pediatrics and the North Carolina Area Health Education Center Program is beyond the scope of this history. Instead, we have chosen to highlight elements of these relationships that we consider to be most important. We shall pay tribute to the vitally important role that Dr. Donal Dunphy played in these programs. We shall then stress the history of the important connections of the Department with the Area Health Education Centers at Charlotte, Greensboro, and Raleigh.

CHAPTER THIRTY-SIX

Donal Dunphy: The Right Man at the Right Time

D R. DONAL DUNPHY joined the UNC Department of Pediatrics in 1973, after a successful career as chairman of the department at the University of Iowa.[1] He was chosen by Dr. Floyd Denny to fill a unique position that would represent the Department of Pediatrics in the developing Area Health Education Centers (AHEC) program in North Carolina. During Don's tenure in that position, 1973 to 1989, the North Carolina AHEC program grew from three regional centers to a statewide system embracing all the health sciences and involving the state's four medical schools in nine regional centers serving all one hundred counties.

Don was born in Northampton, Massachusetts, and grew up in a family that placed a high value on education. An older brother became chairman of the Department of Surgery at the University of California, San Francisco; another brother became a lawyer and served as judge of a district court in Massachusetts. Don graduated from Holy Cross College and Yale University School of Medicine. His medical education was interrupted in his junior year by his treatment for tuberculosis. During that time Dr. Edward Curnen became his friend and mentor; although both Curnen and Dunphy would have major roles later in the UNC Department of Pediatrics, their careers never crossed in Chapel Hill. Don recalled that he was strongly influenced also by Dr. Grover Powers, the chairman of pediatrics at Yale who later

---

1. *Acknowledgments*: Some of the information in this chapter is taken from the transcript of an interview of Dr. Dunphy by Dr. Floyd Denny on September 27, 1991, about one year prior to Dr. Dunphy's death. Information was provided also by Mrs. Sandra Dunphy, Mr. John Payne, and Dr. Herbert Harned.

Colin and
Sandi
Dunphy at
the unveiling
of Don
Dunphy's
portrait

became an important advisor to the UNC Department of Pediatrics during its formative years. As a result of Dr. Powers' influence, Don remained at Yale for his residency in pediatrics, then stayed an additional two years as instructor in the department. Later, while in private pediatrics practice with Dr. Richard Olmsted in Connecticut, Don pursued part-time fellowship training in cardiology at Yale for two years. In 1953 he was drafted into the U.S. Army and served two years in Germany. After that experience Don was ready to return to academic medicine.

Two UNC chairmen of pediatrics tried to hire Dunphy as a faculty member. The first was Dr. Curnen, whose efforts in 1955 were unsuccessful. In Dunphy's words: "Ed didn't really have a position but he created one. It was half with the School of Public Health and the state, and half in the Department." (Later chairmen would copy that tactic of putting together all available funding sources to hire needed faculty members.) Don felt he needed to get back into a more traditional academic setting and took a faculty position at the University of Buffalo under the chairmanship of Dr. Mitchell Rubin.

Eighteen years later, Dr. Denny's efforts finally brought Dr. Dunphy to UNC, but it wasn't easy. In the meantime Don had been chairman of the department at the University of Iowa but had resigned after twelve years. He said later, "After about ten years a chairman loses his clout with the dean." After resigning the chairmanship Dr. Dunphy planned to "get out of the new chairman's hair and also out of mischief, as it were . . ." by taking a fellowship in pulmonary medicine and allergy at Jewish Hospital in Denver, then returning to the department at Iowa to provide those needed skills. But Dr.

Denny had another idea. Denny had caught the vision of a pediatrics department that would extend beyond the campus at Chapel Hill to encompass the entire state. This idea of "a medical school without walls" had been at the core of the 1970 Carnegie Foundation Report that UNC President William Friday had helped develop. Dean Reece Berryhill had begun to implement this concept already in the late 1960s. The result was the creation in 1972 of the North Carolina AHEC program. This program, initially funded by a federal grant, placed UNC faculty members in regional centers where they interacted with community-based practitioners as they taught medical students and residents.

In the early 1970s Dr. Denny devoted large amounts of his time and energy to developing the pediatric parts of this program. But by 1973 he realized that the increasing demands of a growing department would not permit him to continue doing so. He decided that he would hire a new faculty member to take over that responsibility and saw Dr. Dunphy as a prime candidate. He and Dunphy had known each other for years through the Association of Pediatrics Department Chairmen. Under Dunphy's leadership at Iowa the department had developed an outreach program that encompassed the entire state. Denny saw this as a model that was needed in North Carolina.

Dr. Dunphy responded politely, but without enthusiasm, to Dr. Denny's first invitation to consider a job at UNC. He decided to visit Chapel Hill, only because it was convenient to do so, on a return trip from giving American Board of Pediatrics oral examinations in South Carolina. But as he spent time with Dr. Denny and Mr. Glenn Wilson, the first director of the North Carolina AHEC program, it became increasingly evident to him that the AHEC position would provide an exciting opportunity. He said later, "The idea of moving the medical school off campus and having a substantial part of resident training and student training in the countryside, so to speak, was unique."

Dr. Dunphy was appointed professor of pediatrics at the UNC School of Medicine in 1973. His assignment in the Department was to assume responsibility for the pediatric programs that had been developed in the Charlotte, Wilmington, and Area L (Edgecombe, Halifax, Nash, Northampton, and Wilson Counties) AHECs and to oversee other off-campus pediatric activities. Later Glenn Wilson asked Don to take on an AHEC role that was broader than pediatrics and Don agreed to do so. In that capacity he advised Wilson, and later Wilson's successor, Dr. Eugene Mayer, on issues that cut across all the health science disciplines that are included in AHEC.

Dunphy's background and personality were well suited to the AHEC job. He was the perfect diplomat. A colleague remarked: "With a chew of tobacco in his mouth Don Dunphy could have mingled easily with the farmers of Eastern North Carolina." He was equally at ease in the highest councils of the University and of academic pediatrics at the national level.

Under Dr. Dunphy's leadership pediatrics became a major component of the North Carolina AHEC program. He built a base of off-campus training sites from which many pediatric activities grew. Six of the nine regional centers were affiliated with UNC-CH. Currently, three of these, Wake AHEC in Raleigh, Charlotte AHEC, and Greensboro AHEC, with a total of twenty-four full-time pediatrics faculty members, provide pediatrics clerkship experience for about one-half of UNC medical students. Fourth-year students serve acting internships in pediatrics in the teaching hospitals of those AHECs. For the recently created ambulatory care selective students may choose pediatric sites within the regions of the six UNC-affiliated AHECs, as well as in those affiliated with the other three medical schools. UNC Hospitals pediatrics residents receive about one-fourth of their clinical experience in Wake Medical Center (Wake AHEC) and the Moses H. Cone Hospital (Greensboro AHEC), while the Charlotte AHEC has a freestanding, UNC-affiliated residency training program in pediatrics. Seven divisions of the UNC Department of Pediatrics provide consultation clinics throughout the AHEC system. Virtually all members of the Department participate as faculty in continuing medical education in the regional AHECs across the state.

In his role as AHEC liaison for pediatrics, Don defused several potentially explosive situations that were the inevitable result of the unprecedented educational innovations that AHEC brought. In one center, older practitioners seemed threatened by the presence of a UNC faculty member who did things differently; in another, those responsible for existing teaching programs were reluctant to accept help from the University. Don earned the respect and confidence of both "town" and "gown." Upon his retirement the Greensboro AHEC named an annual pediatrics lecture in his honor.

Don's abilities were recognized as well by people outside the Pediatrics Department. He served the dean on important medical school committees including searches for department chairmen. His many administrative positions included those of associate chief of staff of North Carolina Memorial Hospital, codirector of the medicine-pediatrics residency training program, and director of the newborn nursery. For two years he served as acting chairman of the Department of Family Medicine. At the national level, Don was a member of the American Board of Pediatrics as well as the Residency Review Committee.

Don had an endless supply of jokes that he loved to tell. He was intolerant of pomposity and usually deflated it with a hilarious comment. He broke the monotony of long meetings by shooting spitballs and flying paper airplanes. This unassuming man with the ready smile and quick sense of humor was the right man at the right time for the UNC Department of Pediatrics and the North Carolina AHEC program. He played a critical role in the transformation of an educational experiment into the foremost AHEC program in the United States.

Don had a large group of friends; none, except his family, were closer than the circle of former pediatrics chairmen living in Chapel Hill, who in later years met monthly for lunch.[2] Don's indomitable spirit and the love of family and friends sustained him during the long illness that preceded his death on September 12, 1992.

ERNEST N. KRAYBILL

---

2. This was the infamous OLFA Club. The interested reader is referred to page 574 in this history for a description of this organization.

CHAPTER THIRTY-SEVEN

The Charlotte Connection

T HERE are two separate but closely related parts to the development of "the Charlotte Connection." One concerns Drs. J. C. Parke and Griggs C. Dickson and the other is the Area Health Education Centers program at Charlotte Memorial Hospital (now Carolinas Medical Center). While Dr. Parke, a 1954 graduate of the UNC School of Medicine, and Dr. Dickson, a 1955 graduate and pediatric resident in 1956–1957 and 1959–1960, were on the staff of the Department of Pediatrics at U.S. Naval Hospital, Portsmouth, Virginia, they decided they wanted to practice pediatrics together and chose Hartsville, South Carolina, as the appropriate site. This is germane to this history in that Dr. Reece Berryhill was influential in choosing that site because of the UNC–Cokers of Hartsville connection and Hartsville was Denny's hometown. Thus, the groundwork was laid for future associations between these pediatricians and UNC pediatrics.

The story continues with Parke and Dickson leaving Hartsville and starting a practice in Charlotte, North Carolina, in 1963. In 1964 they began to make monthly visits to Chapel Hill to assist in student teaching in the ambulatory clinic, Parke in the birth defects and hematology clinics and Dickson in general pediatric and cardiology clinics. In 1968 Parke was named the first chairman of the Department of Pediatrics at Charlotte Memorial Hospital and continued until 1974 to make monthly visits to Chapel Hill to meet with third-year students on the inpatient service and to visit in the genetics and hematology clinics. Dickson's visits ceased in 1968, to enable him to spend more time in his practice.

Charlotte Memorial Hospital was established at its present location on Blythe Boulevard in Charlotte, North Carolina, in 1940. The name was subsequently changed to Charlotte Memorial Hospital and Medical Center and

J. C. Parke

more recently to Carolinas Medical Center. The hospital is the largest of the fifteen facilities within the Charlotte-Mecklenburg Hospital Authority. A freestanding, rotating intern training program was established in 1942–1943 and at the present time there are 181 residents in thirteen approved residency programs including dentistry. This includes 20 pediatric residents.

The faculty in the early years of the rotating intern program were "volunteers" from the attending staff of the clinical departments. An elected chief of each of the clinical departments provided the administrative support for both the clinical and teaching functions. These individuals were very committed and well remembered by previous house staff and hospital administration. In fact, participation in the teaching programs was a big factor for both generalists and subspecialists to choose Charlotte-Mecklenburg for their practice of medicine and surgery.

In 1962, the board of trustees and the physicians of the teaching clinical departments expanded the educational programs at Charlotte Memorial Hospital. The decision was made to employ a full-time director of medical education, and Bryant L. Galusha, MD, a pediatrician in private practice in Charlotte, was chosen. He was the first full-time faculty member and began his duties in August 1962. He received his MD from Western Reserve University and his pediatric residency at the University Hospital in Cleveland.

In 1963 Dr. Galusha and others met with Dr. Reece Berryhill, dean of the School of Medicine at UNC, to explore an affiliation between programs in Charlotte Memorial Hospital to support the expansion of educational programs in Charlotte. Dr. Galusha remembers that Dr. Berryhill stated, "Prove to me that you are serious and worthy of the support and we will support you" (a classic Berryhill reaction).

The 1971 affiliation between UNC and Charlotte Memorial Hospital was cemented in 1972 through the development of the Area Health Education Centers program, the Charlotte AHEC being among the first established. This agreement allowed the development of UNC student rotations to Charlotte and established a mechanism for the physicians in Charlotte to have clinical appointments on the faculty of the clinical departments at UNC. Dr. Galusha became the director of the Charlotte AHEC in 1974, a position he held until 1984, when he resigned to become the executive vice president of the Federation of State Medical Boards. He then became field representative for the Accreditation Council of Graduate Medical Education, a position he held from January 1991 to June 1994. He is now retired and resides in Charlotte.

Dr. Galusha was very successful in the expansion of the intern-residency teaching program through successful recruitment of house staff and the expansion of "volunteer" faculty to teach the house staff. Community physicians have always been most cooperative in their participation in the teaching program. In July 1968 a full-time director of the pediatric residency program, James C. Parke, Jr., MD, was employed. He served in that capacity until 1991 when he was named director of pediatric research. Prior to 1968 Dr. Galusha had done much of the teaching of pediatrics to students and residents.

The second full-time faculty member to join the Department of Pediatrics was Robert P. Schwartz, MD, in July 1974. He had been a pediatric intern and resident at Charlotte Memorial Hospital and completed a fellowship in pediatric endocrinology at Duke University Medical Center. Bob was an excellent teacher and provided meticulous patient care and consultations. He became president of the North Carolina Pediatric Society and is well known throughout the state. He resigned his position at Carolinas Medical Center in June 1992 to accept the position of professor of pediatrics and director of the pediatric residency program at the Bowman Gray School of Medicine.

The first neonatologist, Mary Anne Rathbun, MD, was employed as director of newborn services in July 1977 and by 1994 there were eight neonatologists on the full-time faculty. Prior to 1977 Dr. Parke served as the newborn specialist, including care of the preterm infants; he successfully took the sub-board examination of neonatal/perinatal medicine of the American Board of Pediatrics and was certified in November 1979.

Frank S. Grass, PhD, was employed as director of the cytogenetics laboratory in July 1978 and was assistant director of the clinical genetics center. Dr. Parke had established the cytogenetics laboratory and a clinical genetics service in 1971, and Dr. Grass was instrumental in developing a prenatal diagnosis program. The cytogenetics laboratory has been designated as the Parke Cytogenetics Laboratory by Carolinas Medical Center. In July 1991, J. Edward Spence, MD, joined the full-time faculty and was named director of the clinical genetics program.

The first full-time faculty person in pediatric critical care was Marty B. Scott, MD, in July 1988. He resigned the position and moved to Fort Lauderdale, Florida, for private critical care practice in June 1991. For the next two years, full-time pediatric faculty maintained resident education and patient care services in critical care until July 1993, when three intensivists joined the full-time pediatric faculty: Edwin S. Young, Jr., MD (director of pediatric critical care), Otwell D. Timmons, MD, and Mark Uhl, MD.

The thirty-one full-time faculty employed in the Department of Pediatrics since August 1962 are listed below. Nineteen of these were employed between 1962 and 1991 and twelve have been employed since 1991. Seven of the thirty-one faculty have resigned their faculty positions at Carolinas Medical Center. There are currently twenty-three full-time faculty in the Department.

In July 1991, when Dr. Parke resigned the position of chairman of the department to become director of pediatric research, Valya E. Visser, MD, who had joined the full-time faculty in July 1983, assumed the position of interim chair. Michael E. Norman, MD, accepted the position as full-time chair of the department in May 1994 and is director of the pediatric residency training program. Dr. Visser is associate chair.

Dr. Norman, a pediatric nephrologist, held several positions in the Department of Pediatrics at the University of Pennsylvania School of Medicine from 1971 to 1983. Since that time, he has been professor of pediatrics and associate chairman of the Department of Pediatrics at Jefferson Medical College and chairman of the Department of Pediatrics at the Medical Center of Delaware in Wilmington. He has been received with enthusiasm and great expectation by the Department of Pediatrics at Carolinas Medical Center.

The roles of the "volunteer" and full-time faculties have remained much the same over the years. At the present time, the "volunteer" faculty play a major role in the education of residents on both the inpatient and outpatient services. Both primary care and subspecialty pediatrics and pediatric surgical specialists actively participate in the teaching program and in patient care services. Currently the chairman of the Department of Pediatrics is a full-time employee of Carolinas Medical Center and the Charlotte-Mecklenburg Hospital Authority and the elected representative from the practicing pediatricians is titled the chief of the Department of Pediatrics. There are 112 active staff members in the Department of Pediatrics and 23 of these are full-time faculty.

I cannot overemphasize the cooperation that exists between full-time and "volunteer" faculties in the education programs at Carolinas Medical Center. The AHEC program brought medical students from the University of North Carolina School of Medicine for both third- and fourth-year rotations, and the number of students at Carolinas Medical Center continues to increase annually. The students bring challenges and stimulation to our faculties. In this time of health care reform, I think that opportunities exist to broaden and enhance primary care education for students as well as for house staff. The "volunteer" faculty has provided and can expand educational opportunities for house staff and students.

FULL-TIME FACULTY, CAROLINAS MEDICAL CENTER DEPARTMENT OF PEDIATRICS

Bryant L. Galusha, MD
    Director, Medical Education   8/62–5/84
    Director, Charlotte AHEC   1972–1984

James C. Parke, Jr., MD
    Chairman   7/68–6/91
    Director, Pediatric Residency Program   7/68–6/90
    Pediatric Endocrinology   7/91–

Robert P. Schwartz, MD
    Assistant Chairman   7/74–6/92

Director, Pediatric Residency Program 7/90–6/92
Pediatric Endocrinology

Mary Anne Rathbun, MD
Director, Newborn Services 7/77–
Neonatology

Frank S. Grass, PhD
Director, Parke Cytogenetics Laboratory 1978–
Assistant Director, Clinical Genetics Center

Docia E. Hickey, MD
Assistant Director, Newborn Services 7/80–
Neonatology

Richard D. Kenney, MD
Director of Ambulatory Pediatrics–Adolescent Medicine 8/82–12/91

Valya E. Visser, MD
Associate Chair 7/83–
Neonatology

Lucinda Dykes, MD
Neonatology 7/87–6/88

Laurie Dunn, MD
Neonatology 10/87–9/88

David G. Fisher, MD
Neonatology 7/88–

Marty Scott, MD
Director, Pediatric Critical Care 7/88–6/91

David G. Rupar, MD
Chief, Infectious Disease 8/88–

Thomas J. Kueser, MD
Neonatology 7/89–

James A. Taylor, MD
General Pediatrics 7/89–6/91

Patricia R. Neal, MD
Neonatology 7/89–

Thomas Kuhn, MD
Director, Child Developmental and Behavioral Pediatrics 9/90–11/92

J. Edward Spence, MD
Director, Clinical Genetics Program 7/91–

Suzette Surratt Caudle, MD
Director, Term Newborn Nurseries 8/91–

Marsha J. Rhodes, MD
General Pediatrics 6/92–

Director, Pediatric Clinics

Paul Charles Engstrom, MD
  Neonatology   7/92–

Andrew M. Davey, MD
  Neonatology   7/92–

Mary K. Rogers, MD
  General Pediatrics   8/92–
  Medical Director, Child Abuse Program   1/94–

Edwin S. Young, MD
  Director, Pediatric Critical Care   7/93–

Otwell D. Timmons, MD
  Pediatric Critical Care   7/93–

Mark W. Uhl, MD
  Pediatric Critical Care   7/93–

Roberta S. Gray, MD
  Nephrology   2/94–

Richard T. Parmley, MD
  Director, Pediatric Hematology/OncologyServices   3/94–

Charlotte Ann Brown, PhD
  Director, Clinical Molecular Genetics   4/94–

Michael Edward Norman, MD
  Chairman, Department of Pediatrics   5/94–
  Director, Pediatric Residency Program

Philippe F. Backeljauw, MD
  Pediatric Endocrinology   7/94–

STUDENT AND RESIDENT EDUCATION

In January 1973, a third-year medical student from UNC, Patrick Mullen, elected to spend his clerkship at Charlotte Memorial Hospital. In the same month a fourth-year UNC medical student, Donny Goodman, spent an acting internship there. Those two students began the UNC student rotations in the Department of Pediatrics at what has become Carolinas Medical Center. A total of nine third-year and four fourth-year medical students elected to take their six-week clerkship in pediatrics each rotation. By 1980, twenty-four third-year students and thirteen fourth-year students took rotation at Carolinas Medical Center. More recently, twenty-four to twenty-eight third-year students have elected clerkships and thirteen fourth-year students have taken an acting internship or elective rotations at Carolinas Medical Center.

Additional support for the pediatric residency program at Carolinas Medical Center was arranged with the Department of Pediatrics at UNC School of Medicine to allow pediatric residents to take subspecialty electives at UNC. This was especially helpful in the years when subspecialty faculty were not available at Carolinas Medical Center. The rotations are shown below.

Rotations by Pediatrics Residents at UNC-CH

Dates	Number of Residents and Subspecialty Electives Taken
1979–80	2 residents, Pediatric Nephrology
1980–81	1 resident, Pediatric Nephrology
1981–82	1 resident, Sports Medicine
1983–84	1 resident, Pediatric Nephrology
	1 resident, Pediatric Hematology-Oncology
	1 resident, Pediatric Pulmonary
	1 resident, Sports Medicine
1986–87	2 residents, Pediatric Nephrology
1987–88	2 residents, Pediatric Pulmonary
	3 residents, Pediatric Hematology-Oncology
1992–93	1 resident, Pediatric Emergency Medicine

Growth of the Pediatric Residency Program

1964–65	The pediatric residency program is established with a single resident (Henry Stockwell, MD)
1968–69	3 pediatric residents, 2 interns
1977	The program is expanded to 5 residents at each level (PL-1, PL-2, PL-3)
1987	The program is expanded to 6 residents at each level
1991	The program is expanded to 7 residents at each level
July 1968–July 1989	109 residents complete the pediatric residency program at Carolinas Medical Center

AHEC Consultation Clinics by UNC-CH Pediatric Faculty

Date	Name	Monthly Specialty Clinics
1/76–6/78	J. Hugh Bryan, MD	Pediatric Hematology-Oncology
5/77–1994	Richard C. Morris, MD	Pediatric Nephrology
10/85–	Robert E. Wood, MD	Pediatric Pulmonary
	Marianna M. Henry, MD	
1985–1990	Robert W. Warren, MD	Pediatric Rheumatology-Immunology
1990–	Leonard Stein, MD	
8/93–6/94	Judson J. Van Wyk, MD	Pediatric Endocrinology
	Louis E. Underwood, MD	

Pediatric faculty from the University of North Carolina School of Medicine have supported the pediatric residency program at Carolinas Medical Center as visiting lecturers and subspecialty clinic attendings.

In addition, since 1978 Dr. J. Falletta of Duke University Medical Center has been a visiting lecturer and attending in pediatric hematology-oncology.

RESEARCH

The pediatric research program has been especially productive under Dr. Parke's guidance; as noted earlier, he was made the director of pediatric research in 1991. An indication of this productivity has been the publication of peer-reviewed research papers, book chapters, and abstracts. Basic studies in genetics and vaccine development, two of Dr. Parke's interests, are noteworthy. Other investigations include studies of AIDS in children, the therapy of newborns with meconium aspiration, and several studies of sickle cell disease. Dr. Parke and his group were very important contributors to the development of the *Haemophilus influenzae* vaccine, which has been so successful in reducing the occurrence of severe infections due to this common bacterium.

JAMES C. PARKE, JR.

CHAPTER THIRTY-EIGHT

The Greensboro Connection

FORMAL medical education in Greensboro began in 1946, when Edward P. Benbow was appointed to the newly approved pediatric internship at Sternberger Hospital.* Dr. Benbow was supervised and taught by a group of local pediatricians, including Drs. Marion Keith, Jean McAllister, and Samuel Ravenel. This internship program continued until the Moses H. Cone Memorial Hospital (MCMH) opened in 1953. In 1954, MCMH began offering a rotating internship, with up to ten positions. Later a two-year general practice residency was added. These programs were phased out in the 1960s, however, because of difficulty in recruitment.

The staff and administration of MCMH concluded that affiliation with a medical school offered the best prospect for a successful program in medical education and approached UNC about the possibility of such an affiliation. Dean Reece Berryhill and the UNC School of Medicine were in the process of forming the division of education and research in community medical care (established in 1965). As a result, negotiations were slow and questionably productive. As stated by Dr. William Herring, MCMH threatened to "go to Duke"; that four-letter word "generated shock waves on the UNC campus, and affiliation was approved in December 1965."

---

* Information compiled in part from:

Herring, W. B. The history of medical education in Greensboro. In *The History of Medicine in Greensboro, North Carolina, During the 19th and 20th Centuries*, R. L. Phillips, ed. The Printworks, Greensboro, 1991, pp. 70–99.

Sharpless, M. K. History of pediatrics in Greensboro. Phillips, *Op cit.*, pp. 130–184.

Martha
Sharpless

Dr. Floyd Denny, chairman of the Department of Pediatrics at UNC, was one of the preparers of the agreement finally approved by the dean and by the trustees of MCMH in December 1966. This document acknowledged a state-wide obligation of the School of Medicine and approved the establishment of teaching services in pediatrics and internal medicine at MCMH. Dr. William Herring, then at UNC, was appointed director of the medical teaching service, and Dr. Martha Sharpless, then practicing pediatrics in the Ravenel Clinic in Greensboro, was appointed director of the pediatric teaching service. After residency training in pediatrics at Chapel Hill, Dr. Sharpless had been Dr. Curnen's first chief resident at Columbia University. These two, Drs. Herring and Sharpless, remained the sole full-time, salaried faculty of the MCMH teaching programs for the next six years.

The first new residency program was an internship in mixed medicine-pediatrics, later evolving into a three-year program in family practice. Full three-year programs in internal medicine and pediatrics were begun in 1972; Dr. Jane Foy was the first resident to complete her pediatric training at MCMH, in 1974. (Dr. Foy, after an interlude at Johns Hopkins School of Medicine, returned to Greensboro and became medical director of the Child Health Clinics of the Guilford County Health Department, an integral part of the current teaching program in pediatrics.) During the early years, the training programs were supported by regional and community program grants, a training grant for family practice from the National Institutes of Health, contributions from the hospital, and faculty practice income.

UNC, under the leadership of Mr. Glenn Wilson, applied under the aegis of the Health Manpower Act of 1971 for funds for the establishment of Area Health Education Centers (AHEC) and was awarded $8.5 million. MCMH agreed to join the AHEC program in 1974 and received $3.5 million for construction of new educational facilities. A "definitive" educational building, the west wing of the current MCMH facility, was completed in 1980. Although the Greensboro AHEC has other regional programs, the three medical residency programs have been the major effort since their establishment.

Senior medical students from UNC, Bowman Gray, and other medical schools began serving as acting interns in 1967, first in family practice and subsequently in medicine and pediatrics when those programs began. Pediatric residents from MCMH, in turn, did subspecialty rotations at nearby medical schools, especially UNC. In Greensboro, Dr. Sharpless remained the major teacher for students and residents alike, with help in attending from the local private pediatricians. In addition, pediatric faculty members from Chapel Hill traveled to Greensboro each Wednesday morning, on a rotating basis, to conduct pediatric grand rounds and to round on the inpatient service with Dr. Sharpless, the students, and the residents.

The pediatric faculty at MCMH was enlarged by the addition of Dr. Robert Dillard in neonatology in 1973 and Dr. DuBose Ravenel in general pediatrics in 1976. Dr. Ravenel was director of the pediatric teaching service briefly but was replaced by Dr. David Silber in 1982. Dr. Silber came to Greensboro from Southern Illinois University with a special interest in medical student teaching. Dr. Stewart Schall, pediatric cardiologist, was recruited the same year from Chapel Hill. Dr. Silber further expanded the faculty in 1988 with the addition of Drs. Ola Akintemi and Kaye Gable. Dr. Akintemi was a graduate of the MCMH pediatric program and had trained in academic pediatrics at Case Western Reserve University in Cleveland; Dr. Gable, a Bowman Gray trainee, came to Greensboro from private pediatric practice in Forsyth County. In the meantime, in 1985 Dr. Donald Smith, a private pediatrician in Greensboro, was appointed vice president for medical education at MCMH and director of the Greensboro AHEC.

The freestanding pediatric residency was maintained at MCMH until 1989. In the mid- to late 1980s it became apparent that such programs would have increasing difficulty in filling with qualified residents, so negotiations were begun with Dr. Thomas Boat, chairman of pediatrics at UNC since 1982, to merge the training programs. The plans for merger were finalized in 1988–1989, with qualified residents in the MCMH program transferring in July 1989 to UNC to complete their training.

In return, residents from the UNC program began rotating to MCMH, as had already been the case with the Wake Memorial Medical Center in Raleigh. Dr. Silber decided to step down as director of the pediatric teaching service at MCMH, and Dr. Myron Johnson was recruited as his replacement.

Since July 1989, four PGY-2 and/or -3 residents from Chapel Hill (from the pediatrics and medicine-pediatrics programs) plus two or three PGY-1 residents (including UNC family practice residents as well) have rotated each month to MCMH. The pediatric teaching service at MCMH continues to train family practice residents from MCMH, with rotations during the PGY-1 year on inpatient pediatrics, ambulatory

Myron
Johnson

pediatrics, and neonatology and with electives during the PGY-2 year as desired by the resident. Inpatient training for all residents is on the pediatric ward at MCMH; training in ambulatory pediatrics is primarily at the Child Health Clinics of the Guilford County Health Department, directed by Dr. Jane Foy and staffed by several part-time pediatric faculty members.

In 1992, MCMH began having third-year UNC medical students for their full pediatric clerkship. (Previously, some students had spent one week at the child health clinics.) Dr. Silber remained on a half-time basis as the director of the clerkship for third-year medical students until 1995. MCMH continues to have one fourth-year student each month as an acting intern in pediatrics as well.

RESEARCH

In addition to teaching and patient care at MCMH, pediatric staff have remained active in research. Dr. Sharpless, who had a year of fellowship in pediatric infectious diseases at the Columbia Presbyterian Medical Center, pursued her interest in clinical research after the founding of the pediatric program at Moses Cone. She published papers on aspergillosis and atypical mycobacterial infections, as well as on her new interest, child abuse and neglect. Moses Cone was also for a few years a satellite clinic for the UNC studies on pediatric leukemia; the local participants included Laurence Ransom, MD, board certified in neonatology and pediatric hematology, and John Lusk, MD, an internal medicine hematologist. Dr. Johnson has remained active since his arrival in Greensboro in studies regarding the acute phase response and the role of apolipoproteins in atherogenesis and in screening for the risk of development of coronary artery disease.

The neonatology division at Moses Cone, which is now separate from pediatrics, served as one of the clinical trials centers for the evaluation of surfactant in the treatment of respiratory distress syndrome of prematures. In addition, Peter Gal, PharmD, and Stewart Schall, MD, from the MCMH Department of Pediatrics, have been actively involved in published studies with the neonatology division regarding the use of indomethacin for closure of patent ductus arteriosus.

HOSPITAL FACILITIES AND PROGRAMS

Moses H. Cone Memorial Hospital

Residency Programs at MCMH, 1993–94:
    Family Practice: 20 residents
    Internal Medicine: 15 residents
    Pediatrics (affiliated with UNC): no separate residents
    Pharmacy: 4 residents

Total Bed Capacity: 548

Pediatric Ward: 29 beds (6 "step down," 23 acute care)

Pediatric Outpatient Clinic: approximately 275 visits/year

Emergency Department: Staffed by full-time emergency physicians
Children under one year of age are seen by the pediatric residents; those over one year are seen by emergency department physicians, with pediatric consultation as necessary

Women's Hospital of Greensboro

"Normal" Newborn Nursery: approximately 3,900 deliveries per year, of which ~1,400 are patients of the pediatric teaching service (only MCMH family practice residents rotate on the newborn service)

Neonatal Intensive Care Unit: 36 bassinets, 4 full-time neonatologists; average daily census approximately 25; no resident coverage

PEDIATRIC TEACHING SERVICES: 1993–1994

Moses Cone Memorial Hospital and Women's Hospital, Full Time

A. Myron Johnson, MD, director, pediatric teaching service; professor of pediatrics, UNC

Olakunle Akintemi, MD, assistant professor of pediatrics, UNC

E. Kaye Gable, MD, assistant clinical professor of pediatrics, UNC

Chon Lee, MD, clinical instructor of pediatrics, UNC

Stewart Schall, MD, pediatric cardiology; associate professor of pediatrics, UNC

Kathryn Wyatt, PhD, pediatric psychologist

MCMH and Women's Hospital, Part Time

Theresa Bratton, MD, pediatric allergist

Susan Farrell, MD, medical director, developmental associates; associate clinical professor of pediatrics, UNC

William Hickling, MD, pediatric neurologist; assistant clinical professor of pediatrics, UNC

Prabhakar Pendse, MD, pediatric surgery; clinical associate professor of pediatrics, UNC

J. Laurence Ransom, MD, neonatal medicine; clinical associate professor of pediatrics, UNC

McCrae Smith, MD, neonatal medicine

Elizabeth Wanek, MD, pediatric surgery

Child Health Clinics, Guilford County Health Department

Jane Foy, MD, medical director; associate clinical professor of pediatrics, UNC
Faith Crosby, MD
Deborah Leiner, MD
Edwin Farrell, MD

A. MYRON JOHNSON

CHAPTER THIRTY-NINE

The Raleigh Connection

THE association of the Department of Pediatrics with Raleigh pediatrics started with the articles of affiliation between the Wake Medical Center and the School of Medicine, the University of North Carolina, dated September 28, 1971. In March 1972 there was an official proposal for affiliation between the Department of Pediatrics at UNC and the "Wake County Hospital System." This document included a rather detailed account of the establishment of adequate inpatient and outpatient pediatric services which would be a cooperative venture between the Department and the Raleigh pediatricians working through Wake Hospital. Greater detail of the association was covered in a letter from Dr. Floyd Denny to Dr. Bernard Herman, chief of the pediatric staff at Wake Hospital, dated June 6, 1972. At that time Dr. J. W. Lynn, recently retired from the State Health Department and an employee of Wake Hospital, was caring for all children admitted to the Wake nurseries, inpatient service, and outpatient clinic in facilities that were all very small and inadequate for good care. Only about one-third to one-half of Raleigh pediatricians were on the Wake staff and few private patients were admitted to the hospital there. The stage was set for the development of pediatrics at Wake Medical Center.

Dr. William Hubbard recalls some of his personal involvement in these events as he entered the private practice of pediatrics in Raleigh. He was finishing his chief residency at UNC in June 1972 and searching for an appropriate practice site. Arrangements were made for him to help establish the Wake service while his practice was getting started and while the Department of Pediatrics at UNC was identifying the first full-time pediatrician to head the Wake service. The greatest need appeared to be in the newborn nurseries, so Hubbard agreed to take care of all of the babies in the newborn and special care nurseries, for an annual "salary" of $5,000. Hubbard was joined by Dr. Wallace Brown in 1973 and Dr. Jerry Bernstein in 1974; they established Raleigh Pediatric Associates, PA, which has played a prominent role in the development of the Wake Hospital service. He describes the situation since his arrival in 1972:

> Since that time Raleigh Pediatrics Associates has continued its special relationship with the teaching program. We attend on the ward for three out of twelve months of the year. The other pediatricians in Raleigh take a week or two at a time. We continue to give noon lectures to the house staff and students and each rotation of students comes through our office on two occasions. At the first group visit, we sit and talk about a career in primary care and give them an opportunity to learn about the nonmedical side of being a primary care physician. Each student comes back a second time and sees patients with one of us. We view this as an opportunity to serve as a model and to give them the flavor of outpatient pediatrics in a private practice.

Dr. David Ingram, the present chief of pediatrics at Wake Medical Center, recruited to the Wake faculty in January 1974, picks up the story at this point in a note to Dr. Denny:

> The program started in July, 1973 when Dr. Archie Johnson, a neonatologist, was named Chief of the Pediatric Service. He set up a Neonatal Intensive Care Unit of 8 beds; J. W. Lynn continued to run the clinic (then one room with almost 5 visits a week!). In 1973 the ward had 18 beds and about 20 babies in the newborn nursery. There were 2 interns, 1 resident, and 4 students who rotated every 3rd night—it was very scary for them. Dr. Terry Salter and Dr. Tom Irons remember that as interns it was terrifying to be alone in the NICU and on the ward.
>
> Dr. Ingram arrived in January, 1974 and took over the noon lectures and the wards and also covered the NICU in Johnson's absence. The private doctors helped to attend on the NICU and wards. The house staff increased to 6 which helped considerably and the clinic expanded to 2 rooms! Dr. Steve Gehlbach worked from August 1974 to October 1976 half time and helped in several areas. Dr. Jim Thullen came in August 1975. He took over the

David
Ingram

NICU and expanded it—working every night for 2 years until Dr. Ross Vaughan joined him in August, 1977. They worked every other night, on call, for 9 years until Dr. Tom Young arrived as the third neonatologist. Dr. Laurie Dunn, the fourth neonatologist, came in 1989. By 1994 they were responsible for a 28 bed, level III NICU and a 40 bed well baby unit at Wake, as well as an 8 bed unit at Rex Hospital.

Archie Johnson was frequently away and resigned as the Director in 1976. David Ingram was Acting Director until 1977 when Mike Durfee was hired as Director. He became involved in adolescent care, and Ingram replaced him as Director in 1980.

Durfee developed an off-site teen clinic (Wake Teen Medical Services) and this became the site for adolescent training for 1 resident per month. The general clinic has expanded to day and night clinics with 10 rooms and 12,000 visits per year. The ward in 1994 had 22 beds including a 3 bed PICU. There were 15 residents, 1 acting intern, and 4 3rd-year medical students at a time. There are specialty clinics in neurology, cardiology, child abuse special infant care, and a clinic for complicated chronic cases.

After Dr. Gehlbach left in 1976, Dr. Susanne White came and took over the clinics until 1988. She was a "real saint" and especially cared for teenage mothers and their children as well as covering child abuse work with Ingram. She was replaced by Dr. Mythali Rajan in 1988, who took over the day clinic. Dr. V. Denise Everett arrived in 1987 and took over most of the child abuse work; she sees 400+ cases of sexual abuse per year and works full time at this.

Raleigh Pediatrics and the private community have been very supportive. In 1994 there were 99 pediatricians on staff, all admitting to the teaching service. Forty-five of them rotate as the ward attendings in 2 week blocks. They really enjoy being attendings. Raleigh Pediatrics (Drs. Hubbard, Brown, Bernstein, Foster, Hedgepeth, Kartheiser & Blair) has a "full time faculty equivalent" (FTE) which is paid by Wake AHEC.

The budget has gone from $70,000/year to $2 million/year. In 1994 the AHEC moved into a new $14 million AHEC clinic office building with a 24 room pediatric clinic. A 16-bed pediatric ER is

Susanne White

under development and a pediatric intensivist has been recruited for our PICU (covered by private pediatricians for 5 years so far).

The Pediatrics Teaching Service has an excellent relationship with the Wake Health Department under the medical direction of Dr. Peter Morris (a former UNC resident) who also runs the PICU, teaches in the night clinic and also got the Wake Hospital Teaching Award in 1993. Few Health Department doctors can do all those things!

We've been able to do a number of research projects leading to publication (probably in the range of 35 in refereed journals and many more in unrefereed journals). These have involved antigen detection, venereal diseases, physical findings in sexually abused children, neonatal sepsis, the use of surfactant, and PCBs in breast milk. We have had a research lab for the pediatric faculty for the last 20 years.

DAVID L. INGRAM

Editors' Note: Dr. Ingram added the following personal note at the end of his history:

I've had lots of fun over 20 years at Wake Medical Center, seen lots of children, especially those with infections, enjoyed Thursday conferences on ID, attending at UNC, and working with our inhouse faculty, the private community, pediatricians, residents, and students. We've worked hard to utilize the private community in our teaching of students and residents. They've done a good job and have enjoyed it. It's been fun to see the program grow.

THE HISTORY OF NEONATOLOGY—WAKE AHEC

With the help of funds from hospital volunteers and a negative-pressure respirator donated by the March of Dimes, Dr. Archie T. Johnson started the first intensive care nursery at Wake in July 1973. The first facility (two rooms) barely had enough space for fourteen isolettes and was staffed by one nurse for every three infants. Three UNC pediatric residents per month assisted Dr. Johnson in providing intensive care services around the clock. The faculty appointment and the direct affiliation with the Department of Pediatrics at UNC has been the foundation upon which the neonatal unit has subsequently grown and developed at Wake.

Before departing into family practice and administrative work, Dr. Johnson recruited Dr. Jim Thullen as director of neonatology in 1975. Through his leadership, four full-time neonatal faculty were recruited and retained. Dr. Ross Vaughan arrived in 1977, Dr. Tom Young in 1986, and Dr. Laurie Dunn in 1989. The unit at Wake developed as one of the original ten tertiary neonatal referral centers in the North Carolina Regional Perinatal Program. It has provided services to Wake County (8,000 deliveries) and Johnston County (750 deliveries) and has taken overflow referrals from UNC, Duke, and other

centers. Over the past twenty years, the
nursery has undergone three renovations, to sixteen beds, then nineteen beds,
then finally to twenty-eight beds. The
last major renovation, completed in
1989, was carefully designed around
the environment that patients, families,
and staff encounter, featuring smaller
rooms with restricted noise and controlled lighting. It is a "developmentally
supportive, friendly" unit emulated by
many in the Southeast and the country.
In September 1990, with the new unit
completed and a fourth neonatologist
on board, Dr. Thullen accepted a six-
month sabbatical at the Children's Hospital in Göteborg, Sweden, and recommended Dr. Ross Vaughan as the next
director. Five physician extenders (nurse-

Jim Thullen

practitioners, physician assistants) were recruited along the way to nurseries
and follow-up clinics at Wake. Growth in Raleigh and the Research Triangle
has resulted in competition from surrounding hospitals for neonatal services.
Dr. Vaughan, therefore, entered into an agreement with Rex Hospital in 1991
and Raleigh Community Hospital in 1992 to direct full-time neonatal coverage for these hospitals.

The goals of neonatology at Wake AHEC have been centered around the
provision of neonatal care and follow-up services, continuous medical education, and clinical research. All faculty promotions were based on scholarly
activities and innovative programs outlined by the late Dr. Donal Dunphy. In
the early years, we published our experience with respiratory distress syndrome (RDS) in a district referral center. This was followed by our work with
Dr. David Ingram in trying to differentiate early onset group B strep pneumonia from RDS by antigen detection in blood, urine, and tracheal aspirates.
In 1977, we received a sizable five-year grant to collaborate with the NIEHS
on a prospective study of environmental pollutants and their effect on infant
growth and development. Placental tissue and breast milk were analyzed in
911 mother-infant pairs in North Carolina, followed by standardized developmental assessments in the nursery (and first five years of life). This grant
supported the personnel we needed to develop expertise in the area of lactation education and support services. It also provided the normal growth and
development standards with which to compare our survivors of the NICU.

Mary Tully, our research coordinator for the NIEHS grant and now a certified lactation specialist, was also interested in and available to our intensive
care nursery. She has been instrumental in the proper collection, storage, and
utilization of human milk. She has published, with Dr. Thullen, a paper on

Ross
Vaughan

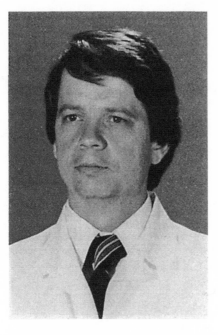

successful relactation of an infant with essential hypernatremia secondary to inadequate lactation. Ms. Tully and Dr. Thullen have developed the first human milk bank in North Carolina, recruiting donors and pooling and processing milk for its utilization in premature infants.

The concept of a developmental team originated because we chose to involve ourselves from the beginning with the long-term familial and societal consequences of neonatal intensive care. What started out as a small weekly clinic has expanded to a multidisciplinary team with three clinics a week. Four full-time child developmental specialists—Melissa Johnson, PhD; Jim Helm, PhD; Marie Reilly, PhD; and Joan Dietrich-Comrie, MS, CCC-SLP—now provide expertise in infant development for our patients, families, and staff within the nursery and for the public and private sector in the neonatal follow-up clinics. In 1989 we were certified as one of five training sites in the country for the Neonatal Individualized Developmental Care and Assessment Programs (NIDCAP). The Wake NIDCAP training, directed by Dr. Jim Helm, is part of a program developed and certified by Heidelse Als, PhD, and her colleagues at Harvard.

"High tech" came to our nursery in 1985 with Barry Mangum, PharmD, joining forces with Dr. Young in 1986 to develop a drug manual to unify drug administration policies. In 1987 they developed *Neodex* and distributed this manual to neonatal services in North Carolina. Their success convinced Ross Laboratories to publish and distribute this manual nationally as *NEOFAX*. The first edition was presented at the SPR meeting in 1987 and has been edited annually. To date, fifty thousand copies of the sixth edition have been distributed as of 1993 in the United States and about twelve foreign countries. Dr. Mangum and Dr. Young have also been invaluable in their contributions in infusion technology and our computerized neonatal database.

The focus of our efforts in neonatology at Wake AHEC goes well beyond the walls of the intensive care nursery with our commitment to teaching. In 1977, we began training family practice residents from UNC and Duke. This has grown to where now all faculty are involved in teaching that includes precepting medical students during their pediatric clerkship and supervising internships and externships in psychology, special education, physical therapy, and speech and language pathology. Opportunities for multidisciplinary input are afforded through daily rounds and lectures. In addition, there are ongoing teaching relationships with other professionals in clinic practice; for example, Dr. Thullen has conducted monthly seminars with early interventionists in the community for over fifteen years.

We are indebted to the administration at UNC, Wake AHEC, and Wake Medical Center for providing the site and supporting personnel conducive to facilitate teaching and medical education in Wake County. We are likewise thankful to the Wake County Department of Health and our obstetrical and pediatric colleagues for their ongoing support of our activities. Last, we are thankful for the many babies and families that we have touched over the years and who have taught us the most about neonatology.

JAMES D. THULLEN

WAKE TEEN MEDICAL SERVICES

Editors' Note: The Wake Teen Medical Services are an integral part of the Wake Area Health Education Center program and the brainchild of Dr. Michael Durfee. Dr. Durfee was chief resident pediatrician at UNC in 1965–1966. After private practice of pediatrics in Virginia he returned to Chapel Hill in 1975 as a Robert Wood Johnson Clinical Scholar, then was head of the Wake AHEC program from 1977 to 1980. Because of his deep interest in adolescents, and because of the paucity of services for this important group of patients, he established Wake Teen in 1977 as an arm of the Wake Pediatric Department and part of the Wake AHEC. The following is his story of his unit.

Wake Teen Medical Services (WTMS) was organized to provide affordable, accessible physical and mental health services for adolescents and their families in Wake County. A community needs assessment survey indicated the need for a multidisciplinary program to fill a gap in the health care delivery system for the county's sixty thousand teenagers. Disorders of the "new Morbidity" (Robert J. Haggerty, 1975) were the original focus of the clinic and continue to constitute its mission in the 1990s. Out-of-the-mainstream teenagers were initially chosen as the subpopulation most in need of the diverse services offered by the center. Since becoming a community-based facility, however, WTMS has broadened its socioeconomic base to include teens and young adults from all walks of life, while con-

Mike Durfee

tinuing its commitment to reaching youth who are dropping through the cracks of the traditional service delivery system.

Serving as a site for health care professionals in training, this outpatient facility is a part of the statewide Area Health Education Center system. Linkages with the major systems within the community, i.e., juvenile court, mental health clinics, schools, residential homes, etc., have been responsible for the success of the program in meeting its threefold goal of providing service, educating the community about the needs and concerns of teenagers, and teaching health care professionals about the specialized care of this group of children.

Because of the general practice nature of the clinic and the realities of a low-budget endeavor, no formal studies of outcome variables related to specific intervention strategies have been made. Indicators of success of the program include the fact that the number of patient visits has increased 250 percent in the past six years. Acceptance by the professional community has been confirmed by two surveys of referral sources, and community acceptance has been confirmed by the United Way accreditation process that resulted in a 47 percent increase in funding in 1987 and a 25 percent increase in 1989.

Wake Teen is unique in that its comprehensive approach to adolescent health care focuses on the needs of the whole person rather than on a particular problem. This project started by utilizing the results of the needs assessment to plan a program tailored to the teenagers of this community, and understood from the outset the clients' need for accessibility, confidentiality, and meeting after school hours. Consequently, a staff—consisting of family therapists; a nutritionist specializing in sports nutrition; nurse-practitioners specializing in family planning, health education, and sexually transmitted diseases; and a pediatrician specializing in the behavioral and emotional problems of adolescents—has been developed to provide a wide range of services to the community.

The clinic's emphasis on the family-covered approach to treating adolescents has resulted in the community's viewing Wake Teen as a positive, essential community resource and has allowed it to avoid being targeted for protest by special interest groups so often critical of teen clinics.

Funding by private foundations, universities, United Way, community groups, and patient-generated fees has made the clinic relatively immune to the vicissitudes of governmental politics. However, this "freedom" has created other dilemmas for the agency. The ever-present need for community fund-raising efforts, required to establish a stable and consistent funding base necessary to ensure continuous, effective operations, has been an enormous drain on administrative time and energy.

Our experience with this program would lead us to conclude that a project such as Wake Teen could be reproduced elsewhere. Six years of experience in the community has taught us the wisdom of the public health concept of viewing the community as the patient when dealing with teenagers as the "identified patient." We found that enlisting the support of community systems and funding sources requires three things: (1) knowledge that adolescents have a new set of health needs and concerns that can be locally determined, (2) a group of professionals dedicated to multidisciplinary health care linked with other systems in the community, and (3) a population sensitive to the needs of youth.

MICHAEL F. DURFEE

PAST AND CURRENT FACULTY, WAKE MEDICAL CENTER

Archie Johnson, MD
    Adjunct Associate Professor   1973–78
    Director, Pediatric Teaching Service

David L. Ingram, MD
    Professor   1974–
    Director, Pediatric Teaching Service

Stephen H. Gelbach, MD
    Assistant Professor   1974–76

James D. Thullen, DO
    Clinical Professor   1975–

Michael F. Durfee, MD
    Professor   1977–94
    Medical Director, Wake Teen Medical Services

Ross L. Vaughan, MD
    Clinical Associate Professor   1977–
    Director, Neonatal Service

Susanne T. White, MD
    Assistant Professor   1979–88
    Director, Day Clinic

Thomas E. Young, MD
    Clinical Associate Professor   1986–

Laurie L. Dunn, MD
    Clinical Assistant Professor   1987–

Mythali Rajan, MD
    Clinical Assistant Professor   1988–

V. Denise Everett, MD
    Clinical Assistant Professor   1988–

PAST AND CURRENT FACULTY, RALEIGH PEDIATRICS

William C. Hubbard, MD
    Clinical Professor   1972–

Wallace D. Brown, MD
    Clinical Professor   1973–

Jerry C. Bernstein, MD
    Clinical Professor   1974–

Sharon M. Foster, MD
    Clinical Associate Professor 1983–

J. Randy Hedgepeth, MD
    Clinical Assistant Professor 1986–

Karen A. Kartheiser, MD
    Clinical Assistant Professor 1989–

Elizabeth I. Blair, MD
    Adjunct Clinical Assistant   1991–
    Professor

PART SEVEN

Expanding Horizons: Our National Role

INTRODUCTION

A s the reputation of the Department grew and its activities diversified, new affiliations of national importance developed. The American Board of Pediatrics moved to Chapel Hill under the leadership of Dr. Robert Brownlee. The distinguished *Journal of Pediatrics* editorship was established at UNC within the division of community pediatrics, where Dr. Joseph Garfunkel daily peruses a large number of submitted articles. The OLFA Club of retired chairs of pediatrics was organized, its name defying literal translation. This organization meets monthly in this area to solve all the problems of pediatric education and the world in general. It has consisted of as many as nine active or retired chairmen from many regions of the country. This concentration of pediatric brain power that has moved to this area has contributed to the trend nationally in selecting the Research Triangle area for an intellectual base. Recently, during a visit here, the president of Yale, Dr. Richard Levin, complained with a slight touch of bitterness that all the professional intellectual societies—including Sigma Xi, the National Center for the Humanities, and others—seemed to be moving to this region.

The roles of faculty members in national organizations are listed in the histories of the various subspecialties and general histories of the eras of the three chiefs. Suffice it to say that the two pediatric academic societies, the Society for Pediatric Research and the American Pediatric Society, have been well represented by members of the Department. Dr. Denny has been president of both societies and Dr. Boat president of the SPR.

CHAPTER FORTY

The American Board of Pediatrics

THE history of the relationship between the UNC Department of Pediatrics and the American Board of Pediatrics probably can be traced to the early 1940s when Drs. Robert Brownlee and Floyd Denny were medical students at Vanderbilt University, Brownlee one year ahead of Denny.* They were members of the same medical fraternity, both came from South Carolina, both were destined to be pediatricians, and both were disciples of Dr. Amos Christie, then chairman of the Department of Pediatrics at Vanderbilt. As this history will recount, it was this association and friendship that eventually resulted in the Board moving to Chapel Hill. The most important part of this history involves Brownlee and his relationship to the Board. The following history will start with Brownlee—where he came from and how he became involved in moving the Board to Chapel Hill. This will be followed by a brief history of the Board in Chapel Hill and a summary of the performance of UNC residents on Board examinations.

Brownlee was born in Due West, South Carolina, where his father was an administrator at Erskine College, where Brownlee was educated. From there he went to medical school at Vanderbilt and became interested in pediatrics because of the influence of Amos Christie. This was during World War II, so after a pediatric internship he entered the Army for two years, in payment for his medical education at the Army's expense. After the Army he returned to Vanderbilt to finish his pediatric residency before moving to

---

*This history was prepared from information obtained from a taped interview of Dr. Robert Brownlee by Dr. Floyd Denny on July 26, 1991, and from records of the staff meetings of the Department of Pediatrics.

Anderson, South Carolina, to practice pediatrics with a classmate, Harold "Stonewall" Jackson. This lasted only a couple of years when he and Jackson moved to Greenville, South Carolina, and joined two other Vanderbilt graduates, Bill Deloache and Willie Mills, in a new pediatric practice named for our old chief—the Christie Pediatric Group. Brownlee's association with this practice lasted until 1970, when he became director of the pediatric education program for the Greenville Hospital System, a position he held through 1975, when he joined the American Board of Pediatrics as its associate executive secretary. Before 1976 he had been associated with the Board in a number of roles: examiner, secretary, and then president.

Robert Brownlee

In January 1976, when Brownlee joined the Board, its offices were in Philadelphia and Chicago. The Chicago office was being closed down by Dr. Howell Wright, the previous executive secretary, as he became emeritus in 1977. Brownlee then became executive secretary with offices in the Children's Hospital of Philadelphia. Shortly after his arrival in Philadelphia he began to contemplate a permanent home for the Board, and because of his earlier background considered a site in the Southeast. It was at that time that he contacted Denny regarding a possible move to Chapel Hill.

The first discussions of the possible move took place in 1977 during an airplane ride from Atlanta to Jacksonville, Florida, and the subsequent bus ride to Sawgrass Club, the site of the annual meeting of the American Society of Pediatrics Department Chairmen. After several visits to Chapel Hill by Brownlee and his wife, Judy, an agreement was made for the Board to move to Chapel Hill on July 1, 1978.

The first offices of the Board were in the NCNB building on Franklin Street. Up to that time, although the Board had its own examination committee, the National Board of Medical Examiners in Philadelphia handled all of the staff work. The Board began to expand its duties quickly and in Brownlee's words "grew from an administrative agency to a professional agency." It quickly assumed all aspects of the examination process. The NCNB space became too small with the increasing activities, and in 1983 the Board moved into its own building in Silver Cedar Court which, with an addition in 1991, gave the Board twenty-six thousand square feet of space!

On moving to Chapel Hill Dr. Brownlee became a professor in the Department and assumed attending duties in the outpatient department. In addition, in agreement with departmental needs and wishes, he began to develop a process for house staff evaluation. Working with a departmental committee, he developed a system for evaluation that is still in use today. This system was used by the Board to promote the evaluation of house staff in residency training programs all over the country. While the exact forms might not be used by other departments they serve as a guide and have proved very useful.

A number of other Board activities deserve mention. Recertification examinations for pediatricians were developed and subspecialty boards were formed in cardiology, hematology-oncology, neonatology, endocrinology, gastroenterology, and most recently in infectious diseases. All of these have required more staff to help Brownlee, in addition to the usual volunteers from practice and academia. Bill Deloache, an original partner in practice in Greenville, made regular trips to Chapel Hill to help Brownlee with extra duties. Harold Meyer, a pediatrician from Philadelphia, joined the Board as a full-time employee for seven years. Dr. Fred Smith, the chairman at Iowa, spent a year of sabbatical working with the Board and the Office of Educational Development in the School of Medicine. He later joined the staff full time in 1989. Dr. Thomas "Tim" Oliver also joined the staff full time after relinquishing the chair at Pittsburgh in 1987. Dr. William Cleveland, another Vanderbilt product, spent long periods in Chapel Hill helping in the exam process. Meyer, Oliver, and Smith also assumed teaching duties in the Department and have been very valuable additions to the faculty. Dr. Brownlee retired as president of the Board in 1992 and was replaced by Dr. James A. Stockman, formerly chairman of the Department of Pediatrics at Northwestern University.

Several departmental members have been involved actively in Board activities. Don Dunphy, Joe Garfunkel, and Tom Boat probably have been the faculty who devoted the most time to overall Board work. Several Department members have been involved heavily in the development of subspecialty boards: Underwood in endocrinology, Ulshen in gastroenterology, Lawson in neonatology, and McMillan in hematology-oncology. Although Denny played a pivotal role in bringing the Board to Chapel Hill, Brownlee has expressed disappointment in Denny's reluctance to be involved in Board activities. Denny's explanation for this was his disillusion in the examination process stemming from his years on the pediatric board committee of the National Board of Medical Examiners, including chairing the committee. Denny realized the importance of the Board but decided not to participate in a process in which he was uncomfortable.

In assessing the success of the Board in Chapel Hill and the value of the Board to the Department, Brownlee and Denny give a resounding positive response with the strong belief that many more fruitful years of association lie in the future.

Although the following section is not strictly history of the American Board of Pediatrics and the UNC Department of Pediatrics, the editors decided that it was appropriate to include here the information that is available regarding the UNC house staff performance on board examinations.

UNC RESIDENTS' PERFORMANCE ON THE
AMERICAN BOARD OF PEDIATRICS

Efforts to obtain from the American Board of Pediatrics the meaningful results of the performance of the graduates of the UNC pediatric house staff program were not fruitful because the criteria of grading the exams changed over the years, thus making any meaningful assessments impossible. A search in the minutes of the departmental meetings did, however, give some information in this regard. The data outlined below give some comparison between the scores of our residents and those of other programs. They do not allow any assessment of the relative scores of our graduates over the years.

The first information available was in 1968–1970, when twenty UNC residents performed as shown in Table 1.

TABLE 1.

Subject Area Covered	Average UNC Score	No. of U.S. Teaching Services' with Score >560
Newborn	559	3
Metabolism	563	3
Growth and Development	565	2
Infectious Diseases	583	5
General	589	4
TOTAL	584	4

Only one program scored 580 or more. Thus, for the period 1968–1970 the UNC graduates were #1 in the United States!

From 1971 to 1975 the number of UNC residents taking the boards was not recorded, but results were as listed in Table 2. Thus, for the period 1971–1975 the UNC graduates scored in the top 10 percent of all U.S. programs.

TABLE 2.

Subject Area Covered	Average UNC Score	Median Score, All Programs	UNC Rank among 240 Programs	Chance Range, 2SD
Newborn	500	469	60	26–94
Metabolism	503	461	55.5	31–80
Growth and Development	510	426	31	11–55
Infectious Diseases	554	455	2	1–11
General	540	462	7.5	2–22
TOTAL	525	447	18.5	7–43

In 1976, nine UNC residents took the boards with the results listed in Table 3. The range of scores for all U.S. programs was 194 to 570. Thus, the UNC residents were the highest or equal to the highest in the United States.

TABLE 3.

Subject Area Covered	UNC Average Scores
Infection and Immunity	558
Growth and Development and Psychiatry	513
Metabolism and Genetics	526
Ill Health	549
Data Gathering	567
Data Assessment	560
Problem Management	538
TOTAL	570

No data can be found for the performance of the UNC residents from 1977 to 1978. Departmental minutes from March 4, 1980, contain the following comments on the results from 1979: "While the pediatric residents' program mean was slightly above the mean for all programs, there was a lot of scatter among individual scores, from low to high. While there was concern that performance was down there seemed to be no clear cut explanation for the present trend."

The last data available are shown in the table on the following page. Note that this table refers to the written examination only. The mean scores of our residents and the proportion passing the written exam attest to the high caliber of the UNC residency program in the 1980s.

The summary includes residents who completed two or more years of general pediatric training in the UNC program. Residents are listed by the year of PL-2 training.

FLOYD W. DENNY, JR.

TABLE 4. Residents from UNC Program Compared with All Programs

PL-2 Year	Number	Mean Score*	Median Score	Score Range	Number Passed First Written Exam (%)		% Passed First Written Exam (All Programs)
1981	11	569	550	470–710	11	(100)	77
1982	9	509	500	380–630	9	(100)	79
1983	13	538	540	360–690	12	(92)	78
1984	10	537	540	440–650	10	(100)	78
1985	12	509	515	400–600	10	(83)	73
1986	13	527	530	350–650	12	(92)	76
1987	10	534	605	240–650	9	(90)	76
1988	13	555	580	440–670	13	(100)	79
1989	12	549	565	410–710	12	(100)	78
1990	11	558	620	400–650	10	(91)	82
1981–90	114	539	550	240–710	108	(95)	77

*The mean score for first-takers who are recent graduates of U.S. or Canadian medical schools is 500.

CHAPTER FORTY-ONE

Joseph Garfunkel and *the* Journal of Pediatrics

Dr. Joseph Garfunkel's association with the Department began when he explored several possibilities for relocating the base for the *Journal of Pediatrics* from Springfield, Illinois, to a place where expertise in pediatrics was more widely available. During this search, he sent a letter to Dr. Denny in 1983 inquiring if there might be interest in his moving to Chapel Hill and bringing the *Journal* with him. Dr. Denny, who had been a member of the editorial board of the *Journal* and realized its importance, responded positively. The transfer of this prestigious journal was soon under way, as Drs. Boat and Denny worked out the details of Dr. Garfunkel's appointment as professor at the University of North Carolina. Dr. Garfunkel's appointment and office were established in the division of community pediatrics.

Since joining the Department, Dr. Garfunkel has contributed greatly to its programs. In addition to basing the *Journal of Pediatrics* in Chapel Hill, he has become a popular attending physician in the outpatient department and newborn nurseries. From his broad base of knowledge, he has actively participated in the teaching sessions of the Department, including grand rounds, Journal Club, "eating meetings," and residents' rounds. He is recognized as one of the senior counselors in the Department. For his multiple contributions in teaching residents, he was awarded the Residents' Teaching Award in May of 1993.

In association with his duties as an editor he has created scientific writing seminars for aspiring academicians, locally as well as nationally. He has worked closely with Drs. Harvey Hamrick, Edward Lawson, and Martin Ulshen, who are associate editors of the *Journal of Pediatrics*. These associations and the development of close personal relationships in the Department have offered scientific stimulation and camaraderie. The presence in Chapel

Hill of the *Journal* and of Dr. Garfunkel himself has added to the prestige of the University of North Carolina as a center of excellence in pediatrics. Since the American Board of Pediatrics is located now in Chapel Hill, a claim can be made that this town is now the "Capital of Pediatrics," vying with the so-called "City of Medicine" down the road.

Joe
Garfunkel

In an interview recorded for our archives, Dr. Garfunkel provides background information about his own involvement with the *Journal* and about his philosophy relating to its operation.

First, some personal background information. He was taught in the Bahamas in a school system modeled on that of England, where much attention was paid to literature and the form of language. He attended Penn State University as an undergraduate and spent time while in the U.S. Navy at the University of South Carolina. He found this to be a pleasant enough experience so that he later looked with favor on settling in the South in Chapel Hill, as did his wife, Jerry. Dr. Garfunkel's medical school and pediatric training was at Temple University and St. Christopher's Hospital for Children in Philadelphia, where he came into very close contact with one of the great pediatricians of this era, Dr. Waldo E. "Bill" Nelson. Early in his career, he was convinced by Dr. Nelson to leave private practice to assume the duties of chief of the outpatient department of St. Christopher's Hospital during the development of that institution as a major teaching center.

Dr. Nelson later persuaded him to assume the role of assistant editor of the *Journal of Pediatrics*. This journal, which at one time had been the official journal of the American Academy of Pediatrics, had fallen on bad times when the academy decided to establish its new journal, *Pediatrics*. For some time Dr. Nelson had to solicit articles at pediatric meetings to keep the older journal afloat. Dr. Garfunkel, rightfully, expresses his admiration for Dr. Nelson, who not only reinvigorated the *Journal*, but also coedited and later edited the major pediatric textbook, known initially as the *Mitchell-Nelson* and later as the *Nelson Textbook of Pediatrics*. In addition, Dr. Nelson developed a fine Department of Pediatrics at Temple and was largely responsible for locating the Temple pediatrics program solely at St. Christopher's and for building this hospital into a strong institution.

Dr. Garfunkel indicated that Dr. Nelson was a vigorous taskmaster who instilled in his associates strong work habits and attention to duties. These included being called out on weekends to Dr. Nelson's home to edit sections

of the textbook or articles. Any such orders from "The Boss" were obeyed
because they were valuable learning experiences. Among other "commands"
from Dr. Nelson was the one persuading Dr. Garfunkel to become the associate editor of the *Journal*. Fortunately, this resulted in a continuity of high standards that has persisted over more than two decades.

After a short time at the Harrisburg Pennsylvania Polyclinic Hospital, Dr.
Garfunkel moved on to become chairman of pediatrics at the new medical
school at Southern Illinois University. Here he maintained a heavy workload
as he simultaneously developed that department while maintaining his role as
associate editor of the *Journal*. In 1977, he was appointed editor in chief, a
position he continues to occupy. The load of papers that required review
increased from the twelve hundred submissions yearly during Dr. Nelson's
stewardship to eighteen hundred in the early 1980s. This enormous responsibility was taking its toll in overwork to the extent that Dr. Garfunkel felt
he should resign his chairmanship. Since he had accomplished his mission of
establishing the department at SIU, he now could concentrate his primary
efforts on maintaining the standards of the *Journal*.

Although the number of submitted articles has stayed relatively constant
over the years, fewer papers from the United States have been submitted
recently. More and better foreign articles, especially from Western Europe,
Japan, South Africa, and Israel, have been reviewed in recent years. The overall 25 percent acceptance rate, very low for medical journals, has been maintained. By preserving the standards set by Dr. Nelson, Dr. Garfunkel has continued the process of careful editing and critical reviewing, but has added
many new features that ensure the continued preeminence of the *Journal of
Pediatrics*.

Dr. Garfunkel's imprint on the *Journal* bridged his periods of editorship at
SIU and at the University of North Carolina. His major change in organization during his editorship has been altering the editorial board frequently
enough to instill "young turks" in key roles. He prides himself on the number of these young people who have gone on to become departmental chairs.
He also points out very forcefully in his interview that he has found an
"inverse relationship between the quality of reviews of the individual articles
and the rank of the reviewers." This is not to say that more "seasoned"
reviewers cannot be important in making major decisions, but the younger
reviewers generally do a better job of attending to detail, submitting timely
and thorough reviews, and presenting unbiased opinions.

The review process was described in interesting detail. The papers arrive
several times daily on his desk at the Medical School. Dr. Garfunkel reads
them within twenty-four hours and usually submits them to two reviewers
from a master list. The return from a reviewer occurs usually in about a
month; a delay beyond two months is unacceptable. When the reviews are in
conflict, Dr. Garfunkel makes the decision—"The buck stops here!"

Sometimes extensive rewriting is needed and suggestions are made to
improve the language for the *Journal of Pediatrics*. This process is not con-

sidered necessary by some editors of journals, including some of those in the field of pediatrics. Missing from many of the papers submitted now are the careful department screening processes of the types that Dr. Nelson insisted upon before the articles ever left his pediatric department. Dr. Garfunkel believes this screening now should be the responsibility primarily of the division chiefs. Departments have grown to the extent that chiefs of service simply cannot perform this function adequately, but division chiefs sometimes now are not monitoring the articles optimally either.

In organizing the many courses that have instructed potential authors, including fellows and faculty members at UNC, on the art of writing medical articles, Dr. Garfunkel again has aimed at the young people coming up through the ranks.

In addition to his modifications of the organization of the *Journal*'s editorship, Dr. Garfunkel has introduced many changes in the makeup of the *Journal* itself. He has introduced sections on behavioral pediatrics and on adolescent medicine and is planning to introduce a review of important articles appearing in other journals.

Since coming to Chapel Hill, Dr. Garfunkel has been pleased by the community, with its music, theater, and spectator sports, especially basketball. He acknowledges readily the considerations shown him by Dr. Boat and Dr. Denny. But perhaps even more important, he enjoys the relationships with the young house staff and his patient responsibilities, which keep him refreshed.

Dr. Garfunkel, responding to questions about the future of the *Journal*, indicated that there were new challenges to medical journals, in particular from the electronic media. He revealed that indeed there already are purely electronic medical journals in existence. He still believes there will always be a place for "libraries and the printed word." A second challenge is from increased subspecialization, which may not produce as many articles of wide appeal, even though these may represent the most important advances. For example, articles on molecular biology may not easily be interpreted for the generalist. The proposed training of more primary care physicians may result in the demand for more articles where epidemiological considerations and outcome research are particularly important. These types of articles may appeal more to the generalist. However, the content of the *Journal* in large part must depend on which articles are actually submitted and competitive articles of the type that may provoke general interest will need to be received.

Dr. Garfunkel is very humble in comparing himself to Dr. Waldo Nelson, but it is quite apparent that the *Journal of Pediatrics* has been in the hands of an outstanding editor for the last fifteen years. Dr. Garfunkel has infused the new knowledge pouring into his office into our Department's activities and into the wider realm of pediatrics throughout this country in an exemplary manner.

HERBERT S. HARNED, JR.

The OLFA Club

THE OLFA Club is the latest and least prestigious of the organizations to emanate from the Department of Pediatrics. OLFA is an acronym for old (OL) farts (FA). The requisites for membership are two: having been a chair of a department of pediatrics, and being an old fart. Some outsiders have expressed concern regarding the appropriateness of the word "fart" in the club's name. Webster's Unabridged Dictionary defines this word as one that is "sometimes used of a person as a generalized term of abuse." It is hard to imagine a more apt description of a former pediatric department chairman. This short history will provide a description of the club's origins, a listing of its members, and a brief description of its activities.

The club began gradually in the mid-1980s when Donal Dunphy, Joseph Garfunkel, and Floyd Denny, who had offices located near each other in the Medical School, began to have occasional lunches together. At the time this seemed a natural thing to do—we all were approaching retirement age, all had been pediatric department chairmen at one time, and we enjoyed each other's company. After this had gone on for some time a decision was made (very lightly) that we should organize ourselves into some type of official group. This led to our having regular but informal monthly lunches. The details concerning the naming of the club are now vague, but in due course we decided to call ourselves OLFAs; the "Club" was added later. We very quickly decided on the two requisites for membership mentioned above. The qualification of former chairmanship was clearly determined but there was, and remains, considerable confusion regarding the definition of "old fart"; more about this later. We decided that there would be no rules, no dues, no agenda, and we would enjoy lunches together once a month.

Dunphy, Garfunkel, and Denny were charter members, and clearly satis-

fied both criteria for membership. Dr. Thomas "Tim" Oliver, former chairman at Pittsburgh, joined the American Board of Pediatrics in 1987, and Dr. Fred Smith, former chairman at Iowa, in 1989. Both clearly satisfied membership criteria and were welcomed into the fold. Dr. Samuel L. Katz resigned as chair at Duke in 1990 and was admitted as a full member. Our group numbered six for several years, until Don Dunphy's death in 1992. At this writing, the only other full member is Dr. Jerome S. "Jerry" Harris, who was the chairman at Duke before Katz. Two other members remain on probation: Dr. James A. Stockman, former chair at Northwestern, who joined the American Board of Pediatrics as its president in 1992, and Dr. Michael Simmons, former chair at Utah, who became dean of the UNC School of Medicine in 1994. Both fulfill the former chair requirement for membership, but both are presently in their fifties and it is not clear that they qualify as old farts. The debate continues at this writing, but both enjoy all benefits of membership in the club. Dr. Robert "Bob" Lawson, former chairman at three medical schools, was offered membership, and was clearly eligible, but decided to retire in Winston-Salem and was unable to accept. We have three honorary members, all highly qualified but living in other parts of the country. The most qualified of these is Dr. Waldo E. "Bill" Nelson of Philadelphia; the others are Dr. E. A. "Ted" Mortimer, retired but still active at Case Western Reserve University, and Dr. Robert E. "Bob" Merrill, who is retired and living in Texas.

Generally, the activities of the club do not extend beyond the monthly discussion luncheons at which many of the problems of the world, the country, the university, and even child care are solved. There is, however, one exception to this limited activity schedule. In 1991, Dr. Wallace D. Brown, a former UNC resident and a pediatrician in Raleigh, approached us on behalf of the Practice Consultants for Pediatrics and asked us to plan and execute a program on a particular aspect of the history of pediatrics. The Practice Consultants, a Triangle group usually involved in studying and exploring the evolving changes and problems in pediatrics, wanted a lighter touch at one of their dinner meetings and felt that the OLFAs could be the group to provide it. We accepted the challenge and the first year, with the help of Dr. Brown and the National Foundation, described what poliomyelitis was like before the availability of vaccine; this included the demonstration of an "iron lung" found in a hospital storeroom. The program was a tremendous success and we have been asked back for yearly repeats. Topics since that time have included: in 1992, tetanus and diphtheria; in 1993, rheumatic fever; and in 1994, a potpourri including pellagra, premature and full-term newborn feeding and nutrition, contagious disease hospitals, and end-stage renal disease.

The OLFA Club has received national attention for its uniqueness. Certainly, there are few areas in the country where nine former pediatric departmental chairmen would live in close enough proximity to form such a club. This demonstrates the strength of pediatrics in the Chapel Hill area.

FLOYD W. DENNY, JR.

PART EIGHT

The House Staff

INTRODUCTION

THE house staff has always commanded the central position in the heart and mind of the Department. The three chairs did not deviate from this prioritization, ensuring that attention given to house staff was always of the highest order. This included efforts to recruit, to educate, and to care for them personally. These efforts clearly resulted in a house staff that was of superior caliber and as admired and respected as any in the country. This is documented by scores on American Board of Pediatrics examinations (see chapter 40). While house staff endeavors have been very serious for the most part, they have also involved many pleasurable activities, as some of the accounts to follow will reveal.

Social functions have also been important. To its trainees, the Department has been known for its congenialty and for promoting fun in learning. To establish a friendly atmosphere, the chiefs and their wives have organized an incoming party for residents and their "special others," as well as a gala party during the Christmas season. The residents, their wives, husbands, and children and various other associates of the Department have also participated in an important spring outing. At this event, a classic baseball game has been played with the house staff vying against the faculty and various "ringers." Errorless play has occasionally occurred. Yearly awards at this picnic for jobs well done and compassionate care have been featured and the Curnen Book Award has had special significance. The organization of this massive event (which occurred rain or shine) by the administrative staff—including Harriett Brewer, Sherri Davis, and Sharon Asbill especially—has been excellent.

In recent years, a whitewater canoe trip down the treacherous Haw River was added to test the mettle of some of the incoming residents. Surviving this, the recruits could be pretty well assured that they would be able to handle any challenges presented during the next three years.

We begin this section by recounting the central role played by Sherri Davis in a chapter entitled "The Keeper of the House Staff." Three chapters follow on official activities that were developed to enrich the house staff program. An unusual and extremely productive association with the pediatric residency program of Portsmouth Naval Hospital is described in some detail. This is followed by chapters describing the Thomas F. Boat Evening of Scholarship, the Floyd W. Denny Pediatric Society, and a short description of the medicine-pediatric residency training program. We end the story of the house staff with a list of house staff members by year from 1953 to 1995.

An annual
Spring
Picnic at
Storybook
Farm

Upper right:
Doug
Willson
announces
house staff
awards

Middle:
Carl Bose
relaxes with
colleagues
and their
families

On the Haw

The reminiscences of residents from all three "eras" of the Department, in which they were invited to "tell it like it was," were originally scheduled to be included in this section of the book. As all of the parts of the history were being assembled, it was decided to include the appropriate reminiscences in the sections on each of the eras. The editors found these to be the most interesting part of the history and recommend them to the reader.

CHAPTER FORTY-THREE

Sherri Davis: The Keeper
of the House Staff

Editors' Note: Mrs. Sherrilyn C. Davis, known by one and all as Sherri, played a vital role in the success of the Department, especially in relationship to the house staff. In seeking an appropriate title for this chapter the word "keeper" came to mind but was not appealing at first. On consulting Webster's International and Unabridged Dictionary and finding "keeper" described as "one who keeps something" (as by watching over, guarding, maintaining, supporting, restraining), it was decided that "keeper" described perfectly Sherri's role with the house staff. We asked Sherri to describe for us her experiences with and relationships to the house staff over the years. The following is her contribution.

JULY 1, 1965

NEW interns on my first day in pediatrics. I guess that sort of set the tone for the years to follow.

During that time the departmental office was comprised of Dr. Denny, Lynne Kweeder, the "departmental secretary," and myself. My primary responsibilities included transcribing Dr. Denny's considerable dictation, coordinating the residency applications/applicants, and general support to the house staff.

Dr. Denny's dictation presented quite a challenge, since I came to this job with no experience in medical terminology. Dr. Denny is a great dictator, but I did spend quite a lot of time getting acquainted with Dorland's Medical Dictionary. And even that didn't prepare me for his occasional medical slang! I finally learned not to spend hours searching for a word and just to ask him what he was saying.

Residency recruitment was quite different then. Candidates would usually call or write us about a week in advance of their intended visit. We tried to schedule only one or two candidates on any day; however, there would occasionally be a "drop-in" candidate. This tended to make me a little crazy, and the candidates would usually spend some time waiting in the Medical School library (which was across the hall from our offices) while I tried to find people to interview them. Women candidates were indeed rare, and my recollection is that they faced tougher scrutiny than did the men. A candidate sporting a beard or mustache was pretty much rejected on sight.

Sherri Davis

The candidate interviews were pretty much as they are now—interviews with a couple of faculty members and lunch with a resident. However, we very frequently were called upon to find a place for the candidate to sleep. Fortunately, there were more call rooms than were needed at that time, and those rooms doubled as guest rooms.

General house staff support was easy. The group was fairly small, and they met in Dr. Denny's office every morning for rounds, so we got to know everyone quickly. (Just as an aside, Denny rounds were very important; the residents were waiting at Dr. Denny's office when he came in each morning.) Senior residents were required to make a presentation for eating meeting, rather like they do now. Helping with the preparation for these presentations was part of my job. Because of this I became fairly adept at working with mimeograph masters, learning how to cut and splice as necessary. (Remember, there were no photocopy machines!) It sometimes turned into a real ordeal if last minute revisions were needed, but since the group was so small, we managed to get it done without too much stress.

Things were a little easier then because not so much was expected in the way of paperwork. Everyone knew we were limited by how many carbon copies our spanking new electric typewriters could make, so only a few people would get a copy of any letter or document. There was no such thing as a pressure-sensitive copy form. This helped to keep our files smaller. All course or conference handouts were prepared in the office; there was no Copy Center. Reprints were much more important. Otherwise you could go to the library and make notes from an article if you didn't have the journal. The first copy machine our department bought was a "wet process." We had to hang the copies up to dry for a few minutes before we could use them.

WINTER 1968-69

The departmental office underwent some restructuring, as Dr. Denny needed a personal secretary. I already knew I would be leaving in the summer of '69. However, there was a job opening in the peds infectious disease division, and I moved to that.

Things were very "chummy" in the ID office. Dr. Clyde had built a small secretarial desk which fit quite nicely into the hallway. The hot plate for heating up lunch was on a shelf on the other side of the hallway.

My job duties in the ID office included the usual dictation for the attendings and fellows and typing manuscripts. However, it also included keeping the accounts and staying on top of the many supply orders necessary in operating a lab. This was a totally new experience. I have no idea what the opinion was of the job I did there, but I do not recall ever feeling that I really had a grip on things in that job.

SEPTEMBER 1972

I returned to the Department of Pediatrics after a three-year absence. The Department was eager to establish a job as "physician liaison," and this is what I set out to accomplish. The job also included being secretary to the chief resident. For the first time I found myself sitting in a room on the seventh floor. I think this made a lot of difference in general house staff support.

The addition of a "physician liaison" was merely an attempt to formalize the communications of the residents with the referring physicians. Each time a patient was admitted or discharged I would send a letter to the referring doctor outlining the diagnosis, who the primary physician in the hospital was, and what the follow-up plans were. This forced me to talk with the ward teams daily to keep track of the admissions and discharges.

At this time I also began the coordination of the third-year clerkship, which was then in the process of being completely revamped by Dr. Morris and the Third-Year Teaching Committee. About the same time the Medical School was accepting third- and fourth-year medical students who transferred from East Carolina to do their clinical work in Chapel Hill. This went on for a few years until the new medical school of Greenville was up to full speed. Somewhere along in these years we began the residency program at Wake.

AUGUST 1979-JUNE 1980

The Department was very gracious in allowing me to take a year's leave of absence to accompany my husband to the University of Washington for a sabbatical.

JULY 1980

The physician liaison position was abolished, and I returned to work part time as the student coordinator (third and fourth year) and secretary for the chief resident. By this time the chief resident's job had become much more administrative and the program at Wake was in full swing. The workload for the chief resident was expanding quickly, and I was permitted much more participation in the coordination of the program. Being "in the thick of things" on the seventh floor made it easy for me to be more involved with the residents on a daily basis, and the chief residents and I began to encourage more social occasions as a kind of support service to the house staff. Each year the "atmosphere" of the off-duty activities changed a bit with the personality and style of the chief resident. There were the "poker game" year, the "women's brunch" years, and the "bowling years," along with all the softball and volleyball teams and tennis tournaments.

My very heavy involvement in house staff orientation began in the summer of 1984 when the chief resident delivered her baby by C-section about four or five days before the orientation was to begin. That went off pretty well as far as I could tell, so I just sort of assumed that responsibility for the following summers as well. By that time we were no longer having to stage our own ACLS course, so it was primarily a matter of setting up a schedule and directing traffic for a few days. But it did give me a chance to work with the residents from their first day here, and that really made it easier in the long run.

SUMMER 1988

The residency recruitment was moved from the departmental office to the Pediatric Education Office and another secretary was hired to help. This gave me a chance to work with the residents from the very beginning. Although recruitment is very stressful on all of us in the Education Office, it is exciting to be involved in the selection of new interns.

We have found that our interactions with the candidates before the match and with our new interns after the match have a direct effect on the "tone" of the program. I do feel that the training years should produce some positive memories for our trainees, and that this office should work to eliminate unnecessary stresses. We try very hard to keep things as open as possible and to project an atmosphere of collegiality and mutual support. I credit this atmosphere with the fact that I am able to continue my relationship with our residents long after they leave Chapel Hill, talking with them frequently by phone, enjoying their letters and pictures of their babies. I guess the bottom line is that this job has given me the opportunity to develop friendships with many, many people all over this country and has thus enriched my life more than I ever would have dreamed on July 1, 1965.

SHERRI DAVIS

THOUGHTS ON SHERRI

Editors' Note: Sherri continues in her important role in the Education Office as this is being written in 1994. After Sherri contributed the above we asked one of the recent chief pediatric residents in 1991– 1992, Dr. Maria Britto, to respond with her reactions to the above and her relationships with Sherri. Her account follows.

May 1987

Enjoying the final months of freedom prior to the start of internship. Happy to have matched at UNC. Suddenly a deluge of mail from Chapel Hill —everything from housing suggestions to forms for confirming my citizenship. My father calls, someone named Sherri has called to be sure I know that orientation starts in June, not on July 1.

June 1987

A hectic time filled with meeting new people and being terrified of things to come. Knowing within the first day that Sherri is the one who always has the scoop and who has anticipated a crisis (and solved it) before you even knew it was coming. Wondering if all might be lost on that fateful day on the Haw when all the interns made it down the river, but Dr. Leigh, Sherri, and husband Ed were nowhere to be seen. Really being scared when Dr. Leigh paddled down alone—in Sherri's canoe, which was bent at a 90-degree angle. Finally, Sherri and Ed arrived—safe but swearing off all further intern canoe trips. (At least the canoe could be bent back to something nearly straight.)

July 1989–June 1991 (It's All a Blur)

Signs posted on the call room door to keep us out of trouble and to help us be good citizens: recycling center locations, voter registration deadlines, schedule deadlines, and dire warnings if the mailboxes were not cleaned out soon. In the summer, wonderful zucchinis and tomatoes in the call room. In the winter, random acts of kindness (banana bread or cookies), and all year round, something good to eat in the little jar on her desk (enough sugar to get you through afternoon checkout rounds). More important, a door that was always open—for finding out critical information (who's attending when I'm on ID consult service) and for just listening at the end of a terrible night on call.

July 1991

Chief residency: confirmation of my suspicion that Sherri really does keep the whole residency running. Discreet reminders: "Usually about this time the chiefs. . . ." Along with righthand woman Karen Kelly, providing total organization of the recruiting effort—including being at the loading dock at just the right time to pick up those intern candidates' lunch sandwiches. Placing the infamous "Do Not Disturb" sign on the chiefs' door whenever anything particularly onerous was going on, and assuring us that such things happen every year. Orchestrating the spring picnic: grocery lists for the chiefs, including the number of cases of beer (regular and lite). Gathering up the forwarding addresses and assuring us all that we'd always have a place to stay in Chapel Hill.

MARIA T. BRITTO

CHAPTER FORTY-FOUR

Pediatric Residency Rotation: Naval Regional Medical Center, Portsmouth, Virginia

IN THE late 1950s, an important program was established which directed pediatric residents from the U.S. Naval Regional Medical Center in Portsmouth, Virginia, to rotate through the pediatric subspecialty services at the North Carolina Memorial Hospital. By arranging this, the program at Portsmouth supplemented its own excellent service and enhanced its status as a pediatric training center. But, especially during the early years, the pediatric service at the North Carolina Memorial Hospital benefited from the participation of these very good trainees who added to our small house staff. During their three-month rotations on our subspecialty services, they performed the same duties and underwent the same instruction as did the members of our own house staff. The models for some of these rotations served as templates for the hundreds of rotations by residents to follow.

This joint program was organized in an informal manner that would now be impossible. We have been unable to find evidence of a written agreement establishing this program or detailing financial arrangements during the tenures of Dr. Edwin Leach or Dr. Frederick B. Becker as chiefs of the pediatric service at Portsmouth during the 1950s. As far as can be ascertained, there was no cost to the University of North Carolina at any time.

Dr. Becker had been brought to Portsmouth in 1955 to plan a two-year residency program which culminated in 1957 or 1958, when it was approved by the Bureau of Medicine and Surgery and the accrediting bodies of the American Medical Association. Dr. Becker became chief of the pediatric residency program in 1958. At this time, Dr. J. C. Parke, then a pediatric resident at Portsmouth and now a member of the AHEC faculty at Charlotte, worked with Dr. Becker in setting up three-month residency rotations at the University of North Carolina, which began in 1958. Dr. Parke recalls that Dr.

Edward D. Greaves, now with the Kaiser Medical Group in northern California, was the first resident to rotate. Dr. Parke also recalls that the next resident to rotate, in 1960, was Dr. Richard E. Sand, who now practices pediatric allergy-immunology in St. Paul, Minnesota.

Precise information about the operation of this program during its early phases is sketchy since no reports were demanded. Some historical details have been gleaned from reports of the UNC pediatric departmental meetings and from correspondence from Dr. James L. Hughes, who was chief of pediatrics at Portsmouth from 1967 to 1975, following the tenure of Dr. Melvin Museles.

A note in the departmental meeting minutes of June 20, 1961, indicates that the rotation was in operation, with Navy residents coming for experience in cardiology and endocrinology. In 1963, Dr. Melvin Museles became head of the pediatric program at Portsmouth. A note in the minutes indicates he visited Chapel Hill in the latter part of 1963. In July of 1965, the minutes revealed that the rotation was "running smoothly," and a similar note appeared in the minutes of March 1967.

The information supplied by Dr. Hughes in correspondence with Dr. Denny in April 1993 emphasizes the great success of his total program in the training of residents, but also indicates the significant contributions of the University of North Carolina:

Enclosed is a copy of the letter I received from F. Howell Wright, MD in November 1973. I inserted the bracketed names for 1971, 1972 and 1973. My former secretary wrote me in the fall of 1975 to indicate that our guys headed the list in 1974, too, but she didn't include the names of the test takers so I can't verify this.

Dear Capt. Hughes:

Your assumption is correct that the candidates from your service who took the written examination of the American Board of Pediatrics in the years 1971, 72 and 73 gave the best performance of all of the 204 programs in the United States and Canada which were ranked. Only programs with five or more candidates were analyzed for the ranking. The last column of the printout indicates the statistical probability that the rank assigned in each of the categories and the total test might have varied by chance. Thus, if you read the last columns, they indicate that there is no statistical probability that the performance would be less than the numbers indicated.

Comparison of Your Program with Other Programs on
ABP Written Examination 73–73
Number of Programs Ranked = 204

Program U S N   *Program No. 49-1*

1971	1972	1973
Dr. Phil Lesser	Dr. Garrett Burris	Dr. Ed Cortes
Dr. Tom Lohner	Dr. Jerry Reed	Dr. Hap Duffey
Dr. Norm Pryor	Dr. Bill Robertson	
Dr. Bob Vanderberry		

Subscore	Your Mean	Median All Programs	Your Rank	Chance Range in Rank
Newborn	594	466	1.0	1.0–2.0
Metabolic Dis	627	460	1.0	1.0–1.0
Growth & Dev	590	426	1.5	1.0–4.0
Infectious Dis	588	455	1.0	1.0–3.0
General	604	459	1.0	1.0–1.0
Total Test	623	445	1.0	1.0–1.0

My congratulations to you on the excellent showing maintained by your service.

Sincerely yours,
[signed]
F. HOWELL WRIGHT, MD
Executive Secretary
Central Office

FHW:mc

The Naval residents who performed so well on these examinations are remembered well by those of us who participated in their training. Other residents who rotated through the North Carolina Memorial Hospital are listed at the end of this section with the realization that this information is incomplete and does not list some of the residents who participated in the program before 1965 or after 1975.

In 1974, at the request of the Navy, a formal document of understanding was drawn up, substituting for the informal conversations and exchanges of letters that had been considered adequate in the past. This document, reproduced completely here, formally detailed the programs that had actually been in effect for approximately fifteen years.

Memorandum of Understanding
Between
The University of North Carolina at Chapel Hill
and
Naval Regional Medical Center, Portsmouth, Virginia

General

1. The University of North Carolina at Chapel Hill has established an approved professional program of special training in preparation for Pediatrics and such program requires bonafide residents enrolled therein to obtain clinical learning experience as set forth in the curriculum of the said University of North Carolina at Chapel Hill.

2. The Naval Regional Medical Center, Portsmouth, Virginia, which is under the jurisdiction of the U.S. Navy, has an approved residency program in Pediatrics. The Chairman of Pediatrics is responsible to make full use of the available clinical facilities and to make such innovations and changes as required to improve this program. Affiliation with university medical centers is one means of accomplishing this end.

3. It is to the benefit of the Naval Regional Medical Center, Portsmouth, that its Pediatric Residents be permitted to rotate through the Pediatric Department of the University of North Carolina at Chapel Hill, thereby increasing their clinical learning experience. Such rotation will contribute to the education of the residents in pediatrics and improve the Pediatric Program.

4. INSOFAR as the Commanding Officer deems it consonant with his command's mission, the Naval Regional Medical Center, Portsmouth, Virginia will:

   a. Provide the Chairman of the Department of Pediatrics, The University of North Carolina at Chapel Hill, with the names and numbers of the residents to be assigned and the dates they will be assigned.

   b. Prohibit the residents from accepting any fees or remuneration for services performed other than those salaries and fees paid the residents by the United States Government as Medical Corps Officers.

   c. Prohibit the publication by the residents of any material relative to their clinical experience at The University of North Carolina at Chapel Hill that has not been approved for release for publication by the Naval Regional Medical Center, Portsmouth, Virginia, and The University of North Carolina at Chapel Hill.

5. The Chairman of the Department of Pediatrics at The University of North Carolina at Chapel Hill, will:

   a. Make available his clinical and related facilities to those designated residents of the Naval Regional Medical Center, Portsmouth, Virginia for the purpose of obtaining clinical experience and training. Such experience and training will be given under the supervision of the teaching staff of the Department of Pediatrics School of Medicine.

b. Enforce such rules and regulations governing the residents and their conduct as may be promulgated by the Commanding Officer of the Naval Regional Medical Center, Portsmouth, Virginia.

c. Be responsible for such health examinations and protective measures as The University of North Carolina at Chapel Hill School of Medicine find necessary for the resident.

d. Be responsible for such protective measures for the residents under the licensure regulations of the State of North Carolina as required, as the residents will not be licensed physicians in the State of North Carolina. These protective measures are to include medical liability coverage that is sufficiently adequate, appropriate, and firm to protect the residents.

6. It is further understood and agreed that the Commanding Officer of the Naval Regional Medical Center, Portsmouth, Virginia, will, upon notice from the Chairman of the Department of Pediatrics, The University of North Carolina School of Medicine at Chapel Hill, that further participation by a resident(s) is not desirable, forthwith withdraw such resident(s) from participation in the program.

Training

7. The term of training shall be from 1 July 1976 to 1 July 1978 and be for periods of *10* weeks each for residents at the PL-3 level, primarily in the areas of infectious diseases, hematology/oncology, neurology, child development, endocrinology and cardiology. Termination of training will be effected by either The University of North Carolina at Chapel Hill, Department of Pediatrics, or the Naval Regional Medical Center, Portsmouth, Virginia, upon written notice to the other when deposited in the United States Mail, and directed to the party to whom notice is being given, at the address as set forth below.

Floyd W. Denny, MD   School of Medicine
Professor and Chairman   University of North Carolina at Chapel Hill
Department of Pediatrics   Chapel Hill, North Carolina 27514

Christopher C. Fordham, MD   University of North Carolina at Chapel Hill
Dean, School of Medicine   Chapel Hill, North Carolina 27514

Claiborne S. Jones   University of North Carolina at Chapel Hill
Vice Chancellor for Business Chapel Hill, North Carolina 27514
   and Finance

W. J. Jacoby, Jr.   Commanding Officer
Rear Admiral, Medical   Naval Regional Medical Center
Corps, USN   Portsmouth, Virginia 23708

After this statement was signed during Dr. Hughes's tenure, similar documents were required during subsequent years. Other chiefs of pediatrics at Portsmouth have included Dr. Jack Thomas and Dr. William M. Bason. The liaison continued until March 1984, when Dr. Boat received the following letter terminating this program:

> For the past fifteen years the Pediatric Residency Program at the Naval Hospital, Portsmouth, VA has sent each of its residents to North Carolina Memorial Hospital at Chapel Hill, N.C. for two months in order to supplement their educational experiences in pediatric subspecialties that were not available at this facility. The relationship has been an academically rewarding experience for our residents.
>
> During the past ten years there has been a significant expansion in the pediatric subspecialty capabilities at this hospital, and almost all of the primary needs of the residency program can now be provided for at the Naval Hospital. Therefore, it is no longer cost effective to continue sending pediatric residents from the Naval Hospital, Portsmouth, VA to the North Carolina Memorial Hospital. Current plans are to discontinue the rotation at Chapel Hill after the completion of this academic year on 30 June 1984.
>
> Enclosed are two original Memorandums of Understanding for the period of February 1984 to July 1984. If the agreement is acceptable, please obtain Doctor Bondurant's signature and return one original to this facility. The other is for your files.
>
> The termination of the formal relationship between the Pediatric Residency Programs of the Naval Hospital, Portsmouth, VA and the University of North Carolina is regrettable since our residents have significantly benefitted from their experiences at Chapel Hill. I thank you and the University of North Carolina for the many years of support.
>
> John N. Rizzi
> Captain, Medical Corps, U.S. Navy
> Commanding Officer

Thus ended another piece in the history of the developing Department at the University of North Carolina. It was the impression then, and now, that this program added appreciably to our activities, mirroring the sentiments expressed by Captain Rizzi above.

It is impossible to measure from the information available how important these subspecialty rotations were for the participating trainees. We cannot assess their effects on the future accomplishments of these doctors. We can say that the residents sent to the Department from Portsmouth for the most part were eager, cooperative, and capable people who compared very favorably with our own full-time residents. Our records do show that three residents later spent fellowships in the Department: Douglas Gregory in the division for disorders of development and learning and Drs. Charles Bullaboy and Anthony Woodall in cardiology.

Partial listing of the Portsmouth Naval residents who participated in NCMH rotations:

1965	Robert Edwards (Succasunna, NJ)
	Frank Mancuso (Portsmouth, VA)
1966	Joseph Asiaf (Brockton, MA)
	William Hinz (Iron Mountain, MI)
	Harry Mangold (Fairfax, VA)
1967	Larry Hall (Roseburg, OR)
	J. Ruel McMillian (Rome, GA)
	Regis Storch (Easten, MD)
1968	Foster Eich (Florence, AL)
	James Heaster (?)
	Bruce McDonald (Bridgeport, CT)
1969	Phillip Lesser (Charlotte, NC)
	Thomas Lohner (Bonita, CA)
	Norman Pryor (Orlando, FL)
1970	Edgar L. Cortes (Corpus Christi, TX)
	Depew "Hap" Duffey (Baltimore, MD)
	Robert Vanderberry (Raleigh, NC)
1971	Garrett Burris (LA?)
	Jerry Reed (TX?)
	William Robertson (Louisville, KY)
1972	Charles Brett (Greensboro, NC)
	Richard Gendron (Johnson City, TN)
	E. Clifford Russell (Richmond, VA)
1973	Raoul Morin (Johnson City, TN)
	Larry Shivertaker (Orange Park, FL)
	Eric Wulfsberg (Baltimore, MD)
1974	Walter Ashe (Greenville, TN)
	Robert Creutz (CT)
	Robert Stein (Kansas City, MO)
1975	Walter L. Gilbert (Norfolk, VA)
	Douglas Gregory (Portsmouth, VA)

FLOYD W. DENNY, JR.

CHAPTER FORTY-FIVE

The Thomas F. Boat Evening of Scholarship

Since 1985 the intellectual highlight of the Department of Pediatrics has been its annual Evening of Scholarship. This was conceived by Dr. Boat as a festive evening in which pediatric residents and fellows could present the results of their scientific studies to their peers and faculty members. Although initially proposed as an Evening of Research, several members of the faculty suggested that Evening of Scholarship be substituted, since the term "research" often conjured up a limited image of wet bench research. Such a perception might have a negative effect on the main goal of the exercise, which was to encourage each of our pediatric house staff to engage in some sort of scholarly activity beyond their usual ward and clinic assignments. Such activities might range from a case report and review of the literature about some disease to a sophisticated laboratory or epidemiologic study. Since its inception the Evening of Scholarship has developed into a showcase event in the Department's spring calendar.

The inaugural event, held April 16, 1985, in the Carolina Inn, consisted of five preprandial platform presentations beginning at 5:30 P.M., followed by a two-hour social hour and dinner, and then five more presentations. The postprandial presenters had the daunting challenge of keeping the audience awake. Poster sessions were added in 1988, and after some experimentation, the format was modified to begin an hour earlier and to include all of the platform presentations before dinner. A popular feature was a melding of the poster session and social hour in a relaxed setting that fostered meaningful interchanges among faculty, house staff, and fellows. Since 1991, six to eight platform presentations have been given before the social hour, and eight to thirteen posters have been presented during the social hour. The venue has also been changed from the Carolina Inn to the Morehead Building and then to the Kenan Center.

In 1993 the Evening of Scholarship was renamed "The Thomas F. Boat Evening of Scholarship" in recognition of Dr. Boat's seminal role in establishing the series and his unflagging advocacy of research and scholarship during his tenure as chair of the Department.

A few days before the 1989 Evening of Scholarship, Dr. Boat asked Dr. Van Wyk to make a few remarks after dinner. With so little advance warning, the speech was a short one, but one that established the tradition of a formal after-dinner talk by one of our faculty members. These talks are followed by presentation of certificates to all residents and fellows who have presented papers. The after-dinner speakers to date and their topics are listed below:

1990	Dr. Cambell McMillan	"The Human Need to Explore and Define the Unknown"
1991	Dr. H. Neil Kirkman	"The Value of Incongruities"
1992	Dr. Floyd Denny	"To Be a Scholar"
1993	Dr. Thomas Boat	"The Importance of Basic Research for Clinical Program Development"
1994	Dr. Joseph Garfunkel	"From Bench to Bedside and Return"
1995	Dr. Judson J. Van Wyk	"Pediatrics in the Year 2010: Five Years After Completion of the Human Genome Project"

The Evening of Scholarship in many ways has been similar to an artistic production. The stars have been those who presented papers, but the show could not have gone on had it not been for the hardworking steering committee and support staff. The first organizing committee was chaired by Dr. Edward Lawson. Subsequent chairs have been Drs. Robert Warren, William Henry, Leonard Stein, and John Carson. Karen Kelly and Sherri Davis have provided essential support services.

After a decade of scholarly evenings it is possible to discern trends and analyze some of the results of this innovative program. More than anything else, review of the titles and abstracts reveals the diversity and high quality of scholarly endeavors within the Department of Pediatrics. Each of our clinical divisions has been well represented. Cutting-edge research has run the gamut from molecular and cellular biology to sophisticated epidemiologic studies, and from clinical case reports to detailed studies of risk factors for specific diseases.

The kind of hoped-for scholarly efforts of house staff were well represented on the first program. Robert Covert reported on an infant who had suffered an intracranial hemorrhage in utero that later was proved to be secondary to an intrauterine viral infection. David Grossman and Hugh Craft reported on a project carried out under the supervision of Dr. Desmond Runyan to establish (for prognostic purposes) a method of scoring the severity of illness in patients admitted to our intensive care unit.

Our postdoctoral fellows quickly recognized the Evening of Scholarship as an invaluable opportunity to fine-tune their presentations for national spring meetings. Thus, papers submitted by MD and PhD postdoctoral fellows in the subspecialty training programs have outnumbered those submitted by our house officers.

The Evening of Scholarship has proven to be an enormous success by any standard, although the number of original submissions by active house officers has diminished, particularly in recent years. Of the 60 presentations from 1985 to 1990 (56 platform and 4 posters), 21 (35 percent) were presented by members of the house staff, whereas, of the 104 presentations from 1991 to 1995 (47 platform and 57 posters), only 18 (17 percent) were presented by house staff. In 1995 only 1 of the 18 submissions came from active house officers, although many of the presentations came from postdoctoral fellows who had been pediatric residents at UNC. Could it be that exposure to the Evenings of Scholarship while they were residents played a part in their subsequent career choices?

The topics presented to date and their respective presenters are listed on the following pages.

LEONARD D. STEIN

EVENING OF SCHOLARSHIP PRESENTATIONS, 1985–1995

1985

Covert, R. F., MD   *In utero* intracranial hemorrhage associated with congenital viral infection.

Denfield, S., MD   Myopathic cardiac diseases and persistent pulmonary hypertension: Etiologies and diagnosis.

Etzel, R. A., MD   Serum cotinine measures passive smoking in young children.

Gowen, C. W., MD   Nasal electric potential difference and response to amiloride superfusion in neonates.

Grossman, D. C., MD   Severity-of-illness scoring for pediatric intensive care unit patients.

Lachiewicz, A. M., MD   Hereditary renal disease and preauricular pits: A report of a kindred.

Leigh, M. W., MD   Glycoconjugates and their release vary with age in ferret trachea.

Myones, B. L., MD   The structural characteristics of complement receptor type 2 (CR2).

Pattishall, E. N., MD   Childhood sarcoidosis.

Spinola, S. M., MD   Molecular epidemiology of non-typable *Haemophilus influenzae* colonization in children: A longitudinal study.

1986

Brawley, R. W., MD   Multiple nosocomial infections in intensive care units.

Casella, S. J., MD   Insulin-like growth factor II binding to the type 1 somatomedin receptor.

Charest, N. J., MD   Isolation and characterization of complementary DNA (cDNA) for rat acidic epididymal glycoprotein (AEG): An androgen-regulated sperm-binding protein.

Homer, C. J., MD   The effect of maternal work during pregnancy on birth-weight.

Homer, C. J., MD   Socioeconomic indicators and perinatal outcome: North Carolina.

Lachiewicz, A. M., MD   Declining IQ scores of young fragile X males.

Muelenaer, P. A., MD   The immune response of infants to primary respiratory syncytial virus infection.

Myones, B. L., MD   Depletion of erythrocyte (E) complement receptor 1 (CR1) and increase of C3dg/E in patients with juvenile rheumatoid arthritis (JRA).

Spinola, S. M., MD   Antigenuria following *Hemophilus influenzae* type b poly-saccharide vaccination.

Toledo, C. H., MD   Identification and characterization of mRNAs for soma-tomedin/insulin-like growth factors (Sm/IGFs) in chicken embryo.

Voter, K. Z., MD   The relationship of lower respiratory illness in the first six years of life to lung function and airway reactivity in adolescent males.

Weston, B. W., MD   Effect of socioeconomic factors on survival in multiple myeloma.

1987

Buck, S. H., MD   Neonatal asymmetric septal hypertrophy associated with maternal terbutaline use.

Davenport, M. L., MD   Somatomedin-C/Insulin-like growth factor I (Sm-C/IGF-I) and IGF-II mRNAs during lung development in the rat.

Davis, K. P., MD   Carbon monoxide exposure in infants: A possible relationship to risk of sudden infant death syndrome.

Downs, S. M., MD, MS   Computer summaries of medical records.

Inamine, J. M., MD   Evidence that *Mycoplasma pneumoniae* reads the UGA Opal (Stop) Codon as tryptophan.

Kaplan, A. H., MD   *Corynebacterium aquaticum* infection in a patient with chronic granulomatous disease.

Kelly, D. P., MD   An extreme case of familial obesity.

Klein, S. C., MD   Characterization of trypsin-released high molecular weight glycoconjugates from ferret tracheal explants.

Muelenaer, P. A., MD   Urinary hydroxyproline excretion in young adult males exposed experimentally to nitrogen dioxide.

Muelenaer, A. A., MD   Ventilatory response to hypoxemia and hypercarbia of two strains of mice with different central nervous system serotonin levels.

Repaske, D. R., MD, PhD   Genetic locus of autosomal dominant neurohypophyseal diabetes insipidus is in or near the arginine vasopressin gene.

Voter, K. Z., MD   Postnatal development of mucocilliary transport in ferrets.

1988

Benaron, L. D., MD   Immunomodulatory effects of calcium channel blockers.

Bishop, W. P., MD   Proteolytic cleavage of a 15-20 kD N-terminal fragment from hepatic epidermal growth factor (EGF) receptor does not inhibit EGF binding.

Buck, S. H., MD   Management of occult central hyperthermia in cardiogenic shock.

Davenport, M. L., MD   Plasma concentrations of insulin-like growth factor II (IGF-II) are not changed by short-term fasting and refeeding.

Downs, S. H., MD   The circumcision decision.

Hall, S. H., PhD   Cyclic AMP-mediated hormone stimulation of *c-fos* mRNA levels in rat Sertoli cells.

Inamine, J. M., PhD   Nucleotide sequence analysis of the P1 operon of *Mycoplasma pneumoniae*.

Kaplan, A. H., MD   Short courses of antibiotics for febrile neutropenic patients.

Kelly, D. P., MD   Identifying attention deficits which impair cognition and spare activity.

Khan, J. H., MD   Somatomedin C/insulin-like growth factor during fetal lung development.

Lubahn, D. B., PhD   Cloning of the human androgen receptor cDNA and gene.

Piazza, F. M., MD   Wheezing-associated lower respiratory illness in early childhood and later lung function in non-asthmatic black children.

Retsch-Bogart, G. Z., MD   Effects of IGF-I on tracheal epithelial cell proliferation.

Weingold, D. H., MD   In vitro activity of a psoralen conjugated to insulin.

Wood, B. R., MD   Power spectral density of phrenic neurograms in newborn piglets.

1989

Bishop, W., MD   Characterization of tyrosine phosphorylation in isolated rat small intestinal epithelial cells.

Blair, E., MD   Growth factors and gonadotropin dependent ovarian granulosa cell differentiation: Roles of PDGF and TGF-B.

Crotser, C., MD   Nonorganic failure to thrive: A subgroup classification.

Downs, S. M., MD   Decision analytic approach to the management of the febrile infant.

Ferkol,T., MD   The babies' breath study: Predicting lower respiratory illness severity in infants.

Oetting, M., MD   Shocking revelations.

Piazza, F., MD   Attachment of influenza A virus to ferret tracheal epithelium at different maturational stages.

Rackoff,W., MD   Neuroblastoma at NCMH: 1965–1985.

Smith, B., MD   Serum lipid and lipoprotein profiles in elite age-group endurance runners.

Walker, J., MD   High dose growth hormone (GH) treatment of short children increases insulin secretion but does not impair glucose homeostasis.

Wood, B., MD   Characterization of the frequency dependence (transfer functions) of flow and pressure in small endotracheal tubes.

1990

Bates, A. S., MD   A critical appraisal of the quality of journal articles that evaluate diagnostic tests.

Crowe, J. E., Jr., MD   Immunodominance of T-cell epitopes: Implications for RSV vaccine design.

Downs, S. M., MD   Decision analysis and occult bacteremia: Chapter two.

Hillery, C., MD   The effect of fibrinogen binding on the phosphorylation of glycoprotein IIb/IIIa in resting and activated platelets.

Hollinger, B. R., MD   B-Receptor-mediated increase in cerebral blood flow during hypoglycemia.

Klein, J. D., MD   Adolescent risk behavior and media use.

Kupfer, S. R., MD   Identification of a glucocorticoid responsive element in Epstein-Barr virus.

Lannon, C. M., MD   Compliance with pediatric cholesterol screening.

Margolis, P. A., MD   Lower respiratory illness in infants and low socioeconomic status.

Marschke, K. B., MD   Androgen receptor binding to GRE/PRE-like sequences in androgen responsive genes.

Noah, T., MD   The use of an epithelial cell line as a model system to study the effects of pollutants on human airway epithelium in vitro.

Price, W. A., MD   Expression of insulin-like growth factors I and II messenger ribonucleic acid in fetal rats treated with dexamethasone.

Quigley, C., MD   Molecular defects in the androgen insensitivity syndrome.

Repaske, D. R., MD   Cloning a carboxy-terminal domain of the rat cGMP-stimulated phosphodiesterase by polymerase chain reaction.

Smith, B. W., MD   Effects of discontinuing competitive running on HDL-cholesterol in elite age-group distance runners.

Thissen, J. P., MD   Restriction of dietary protein produces resistance to insulin-like growth factor-I (IGF-I).

1991

Akinbi, H. T., MD   The role of insulin-like growth factor-I in DNA synthesis of the fetal lung fibroblast.

Cuenca, R. E., MD   IL-1ß and TNF-α differentially induce GRO gene in HT29 colon carcinoma cell line.

De Bellis, A., MD   Point mutations in the androgen receptor gene associated with androgen insensitivity syndrome.

Downs, S. M., MD   A cost-effectiveness analysis of intraosseous infusion as a prehospital skill.

Estabrooks, L. E., PhD   Characterization of chromosome 4p deletions and rearrangements.

Frederickson, D. D., MD   Focus group results—barriers to breastfeeding among rural North Carolina participants.

Freed, G. M., MD   Pediatrician compliance with new Hib vaccine recommendations in North Carolina.

Froelich, M. E., MD   Evaluation of headache characteristics and behavioral factors in children with headache.

Hillery, C. A., MD   Stoichiometry of glycoprotein IIIA phosphorylation in whole platelets and in vitro.

Mason, T. G., MD   Acute rheumatic fever in West Virginia: Not just a disease of children.

Noah, T. L., MD   Histamine-induced release of mediators from a human bronchial epithelial cell line.

Rabinovich, E., MD   Rheumatologic evaluation of patients with cystic fibrosis.

Schanberg, L., MD   Characterization of the human CD7 gene and potential regulatory elements.

Scharenberg, A. M., MD   PKC redistribution within CA3 stratum oriens occurring during acquisition of NM conditioning in the rabbit.

Shepard, A. J. III, MD   Administration of interferon gamma to osteopetrotic mice stimulates bone resorption.

Smith, B. W., MD, PhD   Anaerobic threshold of trained swimmers.

Thissen, J. P., MD   Clearance of serum insulin-like growth factor I (IGF-I) in protein-restricted rats.

1992

Barker, P. M., MD   Solution transport by explants of proximal and distal fetal rat lung in late gestation.

Barnes, D. M., MD   Antibiotic sensitivity patterns of *Streptococcus pneumoniae* isolated from children in day care.

Brown, G. R., MD   Pediatric firearm fatalities in North Carolina: 1986–90.

Colbert, R. A., MD   Rheumatic manifestations of HIV in children.

Dai, Z.   Insulin-like growth factor-I's (IGF-I) autocrine actions require secretion and interaction with its receptor on the cell surface.

Frederickson, D. D., MD   Breastfeeding promotion using incentives in WIC.

Frederickson, D. D., MD   Severe hypoglycemia is associated with diabetic ketoacidosis in type I diabetes.

Harris, C. E., MD   Gene transfer to primary airway epithelial cells employing molecular conjugate vectors.

Hummel, B. L., Jr., MD   A case of ligenous conjunctivitis with similar lesions in bowel and lung.

Larson, M. C., MD, MPH   Infant mortality in eastern North Carolina: Look at the problem in two counties.

Lindsay, R. L., MD   Convergent recall and active working memory deficits in mathematics disabled students.

Makhlouf, R A., MD   The role of IGFs and IGFBPs in altered fetal lung growth: Pulmonary hypoplasia model.

Pearson, E. B., MD   A trial of vitamin A supplementation in very low birth-weight infants at risk for bronchopulmonary dysplasia.

Pucilowska, J. B., MD   The effect of dietary protein supplementation on IGFs and IGFBPs in children with shigellosis.

Van Horn, S. E., MD   Alcohol use practices in students utilizing student health services.

1993

Backeljauw, P. F., MD   Effects of prolonged IGF-I treatment in children with growth hormone insensitivity syndrome (GHIS).

Barker, P. M., MD   Effects of gas composition and culture supplements on liquid secretion by distal lung of the fetal rat.

Bejjani, B. A., MD   Congenital absence of the vas deferens: A primarily genital form of cystic fibrosis.

Boney, C. M., MD   Human IGFBP-1 transgenic mice exhibit brain growth retardation.

Caldwell, C. R., MD   Tracheobronchitis: An under-recognized disease entity in critical care.

Charlton, P., MD   Immunocytochemical localization of BP-4 in the rat brain.

Colbert, R. A., MD, PhD   The role of the B pocket in allele-specific peptide presentation by HLA-B27.

Doron, M. W., MD   Increased incidence of sepsis at birth in neutropenic low birthweight infants of pre-eclamptic mothers.

Frederickson, D. D., MD   Relationship of sudden infant death syndrome to breastfeeding duration and intensity.

Hopper, J. A., MD   Fever in pediatric patients.

Lemozy, S. T., MD   Intraperitoneal insulin infusion by implantable pump, subcutaneous insulin infusion by external pump, and insulin multiinjections: Comparative evaluation in thirty insulin dependent diabetic patients.

Lucier, T. S., PhD   An ordered genomic library of *Mycoplasma genitalium*.

Makhlouf, R. A., MD   The role of the IGF system in oligohydramnios-mediated lung growth retardation.

Miller, L., PhD   PCR detection of *Mycoplasma pulmonis* in experimentally infected mice.

Pearson, E. B., MD   Patterns of decision making and death in neonatal intensive care.

Reid, L., MD   Mapping a tumor suppressor gene in 11p15.5.

Reinstein, L. J., MD   Evidence for adenosine A2 receptors on Kupffer cells: Relation to liver graft survival after transplantation.

Reitnauer, P. J., MD, PhD   A comparative study of prenatal diagnosis and perinatal autopsy.

Thomas, D. E., MD   Characterization of the static and dynamic functions of the respiratory system in the transgenic CF (knockout) mouse.

Winesett, D. E., MD   Effect of enteral nutrients on proglucagon expression in small bowel.

1994

Ashe, W. S., Jr., MD   The role of insulin-like growth factors in the repair of airway epithelium following acute injury.

Backeljauw, P. F., MD   Therapeutic trial of IGF-I in a patient with Donohue syndrome.

Barker, P. M., MD   Pathways for Cl-secretion in the CF "knockout" mouse fetal lung.

Bejjani, B. A., MD   Genetic disorders that masquerade as multiple sclerosis.

Boney, C. M., MD   Insulin-like growth factor-I (IGF-I) and IGF binding protein (IGFBP) expression during adipogenesis.

Charlton, P. A., MD   Molecular genetic approach to function of the neuroendocrine peptides galanin and GMAP.

Freed, L. H., MD   Determinants of patient satisfaction and intention to return for follow-up visits.

Heim, R. A., PhD   Characterization of a mutation in the neurofibromatosis (NFI) gene is confounded by a NFI related gene.

Hollinger, B. R., MD   Mediators of the relationship between religiosity and adolescent alcohol use.

Kufuor, N. K., MD, MPH   High-yield production of recombinant adeno-associated virus vector by the use of molecular conjugate.

Lucier, T. S., PhD   An ordered genomic library and genetic map of the *Mycoplasma genitalium* chromosome.

Michaelson, P. H., MD   The effect of ozone on growth factor production following in vitro exposure of human airway epithelial cells.

Realini, A. D., MD   Interruption in the medical interaction.

Reitnauer, P. J., MD, PhD   Spina bifida, developmental delay and neuroblastoma associated with an extra dicentric marker chromosome 15.

Szczepaniak, D. A., MD   Expression of (1,3) fucosyltransferase genes in human tissues.

Tepperberg, J. H., PhD   An inherited cryptic translocation between chromosomes 13 and 15, detected by FISH, in a child with Angelman syndrome.

Thomas, D. E., MD, PhD   Analysis of safety consideration of adenoviral vectors and immunologic and inflammatory responses in gene therapy.

Winesett, D. E., MD   Expression of IGF-I and Type 1 receptor mRNA in small bowel during fasting or total parenteral nutrition in rats.

1995

Ashe, W. S., Jr., MD   Expression of IGF system proteins during repair of airway epithelium following acute injury.

Avellar, M. C. W., PhD   Complex androgen response element in intron 1 of the 20 kDa protein gene contains binding sites for androgen dependent rat ventral prostate nuclear proteins.

Britto, M. T., MD   Patterns of health care utilization among North Carolina adolescents with sickle cell disease or cystic fibrosis.

Gregory, C. W., PhD   Localization of androgen-regulated DNA/protein interactions in the intron 1 androgen response elements (AREs) of the 20 kDa protein and C3 subunit genes.

Heidenreich, A. C., MD   Inducible nitric oxide synthase expression increases in response to neural/endocrine factors.

Heim, R. A., PhD   New mutations in the neurofibromatosis 1(NFI) gene detected by screening for truncated proteins.

Kaiser-Rogers, K. A., PhD   A derivative chromosome composed of 18P and 21Q associated with different phenotypes in a mother and son.

Kufuor, N. K., MD   Chromosome integration of DNA plasmids mediated by adeno-associated virus (AAV) inverted terminal repeats.

Lindquist, S. W., MD   *Bordetella holmesii* sepsis in an asplenic adolescent.

Lucier, T. S., PhD   The genetic basis for resistance to macrolide and lincosamide antibiotics in an in vitro deprived strain of *Mycoplasma pneumoniae*.

McCaffrey, M. W., MD   Effect of L-arginine infusion on infants with persistent pulmonary hypertension of the newborn.

Michelson, P., MD   Characterization of the nasal inflammatory response of extrinsic asthmatics following ozone exposure.

Raburn, D. J., PhD   Stage specific expression of a follicle stimulating hormone-induced antiproliferative factor, B-cell translocation gene 1 (BTG1) in testis.

Rittmeyer, C., MD, MPH   Prevention of necrotizing enterocolitis in preterm infants with enteral immunoglobulin: Meta-analysis and cost-effectiveness analysis.

Shapiro, H. L., MD   The child behavior checklist is an insensitive predictor of student health center visits for functional problems at a school for visually impaired children.

Shepard, A. J., MD   Mitotic activity in the dentate gyrus following hypoxic-ischemic insults in mice carrying a transgene for human insulin-like growth factor binding protein 1.

Såvendahl, L. S. G., MD, PhD   Low proconvertin (Factor VII) and impaired blood clotting due to growth hormone deficiency in rat.

Szczepaniak, D. A., MD   Post-transcriptional regulation of the plasma (1,3) fucosyltransferase gene (FUT6): Alternative splicing, polyadenylation, and isoform expression.

Thompson, J. W., MD   The effectiveness and costs of HIV testing strategies in pregnant women.

Tsuruta, J. K., PhD   Ligands for the IGF-II/cation-independent mannose 6-phosphate receptor modulate gene expression in spermatogonia, pachytene spermatocytes and round spermatids.

Yi, Ping, PhD   Developmental regulation of insulin-like growth factor-1 (IGF-1) gene expression in the brain of transgenic mice expressing an IGF-1-luciferase fusion gene.

CHAPTER FORTY-SIX

The Floyd W. Denny
Pediatric Society

OVER the first two decades of the Department of Pediatrics, no formal alumni gatherings as such occurred. Attendance at state pediatric society meetings involved nearly all faculty and many of the house staff on a regular basis so that perhaps the need was not as apparent. In the early 1970s, the idea for a pediatric alumni organization began to develop. In late 1974, Dr. Denny asked Jud Van Wyk and Jerry Fernald to begin planning for a pediatric alumni reunion for the fall of 1975. Plans included a brief scientific program on Friday afternoon with participants all being drawn from our own alumni and faculty ranks. Since Dr. Curnen had retired in 1974, it was proposed that the seventh-floor conference room be dedicated to him in recognition of his leadership as the first chairman but also in recognition of his role in soliciting the support from the Sigma Sigma Sigma sorority with which the conference room and playroom on the seventh-floor pediatric unit were built.

1975

The first Pediatric Alumni Club meeting was held October 3–4, 1975, in 103 Berryhill Hall. Speakers included Nelson Ordway (first pediatric cardiologist), Robert Winters (former resident and fellow), John Raye (former resident and chief resident), and Ray Antley (former resident). Over one hundred attendees signed in at registration and enjoyed the presentations from these former members of the Department, which ranged over a wide subject area.

Following the afternoon scientific session, a large group gathered in the seventh-floor conference room where Harrie Chamberlin led the program dedicating the Edward C. Curnen, Jr., MD Pediatric Library and Conference Room. Special guests attending were Dr. and Mrs. Curnen, Dr. Berryhill, and

Floyd Denny welcoming John Raye, chair of the Department of Pediatrics at the University of Connecticut and former chief resident, at a Denny Society meeting

Dr. Christopher Fordham (who was dean at that time), as well as employees and faculty members who were here in the 1950s. Representatives of the hospital, Tri Sigma sorority, and the original leadership in the Departments of Nursing, Physical Therapy, and many others were present. In addition to the ceremony, everyone was pleased with the completely remodeled seventh- floor conference room and photographs of Dr. Curnen and colleagues during his tenure, a photograph in memory of Annie Scott, MD, and even snapshots of a young Floyd Denny at the bedside with two interns in the class of 1960–61 (Emmy Lou Cholak and Brian Luke).

Jerry Bernstein and Gus Conley put on a social hour and banquet at The Ranch House attended by all participants and their spouses. By request there was no formal after-dinner program. An interesting note is that some of the registrants were concerned with the high price of the banquet, to wit, $16 per person!

The following morning many former residents joined Dr. Denny in a clinical grand rounds presentation on the ward. Others visited around Chapel Hill before returning to their homes.

During this original meeting, officers were nominated for the new Pediatric Alumni Club, with Jerry Bernstein president, George Hemingway vice president, and Jerry Fernald secretary-treasurer. It was decided that meetings would subsequently be held every third year since annual meetings were deemed too frequent and in conflict with many other meetings and CME activities attended by our faculty and alumni.

1978

The second triannual Pediatric Alumni Society meeting was held October 27 and 28, 1978, again in 103 Berryhill Hall. The program was focused on David W. Smith, MD, visiting professor from the University of Washington in Seattle. Dr. Smith's area of expertise was factors influencing fetal development, and his two Friday afternoon lectures were entitled "Prenatal Hazards to Fetal Development, including Alcohol and Hydantoins" and "Hypothermia and Biomechanics in Morphogenesis Especially in Relation to Deformation." The scientific program led by Dr. Denny also included Dr. Van Wyk on "Regulation of Cell Growth" and Dr. Neil Kirkman on "Your Role in Genetic Diagnosis of the Dying Child."

A pig pickin' and informal evening were held at the Canterfield Club, an old restored and expanded log cabin near Dr. Denny's home on Highway 54 west.

On Saturday morning, "Rounds with Dr. Denny" focused on recent progress in research and teaching in the Department as presented by young faculty members, including Joe D'Ercole, Mike Durfee, Fred Henderson, Edward Lawson, David Stempel, and Martin Ulshen. Records show that sixty-five participants joined in the weekend scientific and teaching sessions with approximately twice that number participating in the evening social activities. Feedback indicated that everyone was very pleased with the format of the triannual meetings and the informality of the social interactions.

1981

As the next triannum began to near, Dr. Denny surprised us by announcing that he would step down as departmental chairman in May 1981. This provided the Pediatric Alumni Club officers the chance to initiate plans to honor Dr. Denny at the upcoming meeting. The officers met, drew up by-laws, and proposed that the organization be named the Floyd W. Denny Pediatric Society. A planning committee consisting of Jerry Bernstein, Jud Van Wyk, Lou Underwood, Harvey Hamrick, Wally Clyde, George Hemingway, and Jerry Fernald outlined a fund-raising campaign and program to honor Dr. Denny's years as chairman of the Department. The date was moved from the usual fall date to May 1981 to coincide with Dr. Denny's resignation. A fund-raising drive was mounted to establish support for a continuing annual professorship and all alumni and friends of the Department were invited to contribute.

The meeting began on Thursday, May 21, in a hospitality suite for early arrivals at the Holiday Inn. Friday morning was dedicated to registration, socialization, and tours of NC Memorial Hospital and the Medical School. A noon luncheon for wives was arranged by Anne Fernald with Barbara Denny at the Chez Condoret at University Square in downtown Chapel Hill. At 1:30 P.M. the scientific session opened with remarks from Jerry Bernstein and Dean

Stuart Bondurant. Wally Clyde moderated the first session, which began with a presentation entitled "Scientific Writing: The Agony and the Ecstasy" by Dr. Robert E. Merrill, a long-time friend of Floyd's. Wally Clyde then discussed "Mycoplasmas and the Practitioner" in recognition of his long association with Floyd in the laboratory. Next on the schedule were former residents in practice. Harvey Hamrick moderated this session and introduced Ellis Fisher, Pat Jasper, and Bob Wilson, who commented on their recollections of serving as house staff under Dr. Denny and his influence on their subsequent practices. After a break, Dr. Lewis Wannamaker, a long-time friend and colleague of Dr. Denny's in his fellowship and early faculty days, introduced the 1981 Floyd W. Denny Lecturer, Dr. Charles Rammelkamp. "Rammel" discussed the "History of Research on Group A Streptoccocus and Rheumatic Fever," including Dr. Denny's involvement in this subject area since his fellowship days.

Following the scientific session, nearly 250 people gathered at the Carolina Inn for a banquet in honor of Dr. Denny. This time we did break our rules and have an after-dinner program, but it was brief and certainly not scientific. Those who remember Bob Merrill's talk will undoubtedly agree! At the end Dr. Bernstein presented a portrait of Dr. Denny, which now hangs in the library next to the departmental suite in the Burnett-Womack Building.

The meeting was completed with a Saturday morning business meeting and second scientific session presented by faculty and staff who had worked closely with Dr. Denny. Dr. Albert Collier discussed "Research at the Frank Porter Graham Child Development Center," Frank Loda "Developments in Community and Regional and International Pediatrics," and Susan Gates "The Role of Recreation Therapy in the Care of Pediatric Patients."

During the business meeting it was announced that fund-raising efforts had succeeded in raising nearly $20,000, which would remain invested with the Medical Foundation, the interest to support a yearly Floyd W. Denny Visiting Professorship and the main speaker for subsequent triannual meetings. The new name of the society was approved unanimously with emphasis on the fact that it was to include not only alumni but all friends of the Department.

1984

The next triannual meeting was focused on "Infectious Disease in the Day Care Setting." The topic was timely, given the rapid increase in numbers of working mothers and children in day care. Also, the pediatric infectious disease group had focused for nearly twenty years on the epidemiology of respiratory infection in the community and it was felt that the topic should be of interest to many practicing pediatricians. Dr. Robert Yolken from Johns Hopkins University was the visiting Denny Society Professor for the meeting and brought to us his expertise in infectious causes of gastroenteritis, most notably rotavirus. The Friday program was done in the usual way with a ladies' noon luncheon with Barbara Denny and Barbara Boat at the Hotel Europa. Dr. Boat, the new chairman of the Department, welcomed attendees, and Dr.

Albert Collier moderated the scientific session, which included presentations by Dr. Frank Loda, "Overview"; Dr. Yolken, "Gastroenteritis"; and Dr. Stan Lemon, chief of adult infectious diseases, "Viral Hepatitis in Day Care Centers." Dr. Denny then discussed "Studies on Respiratory Infections at the Frank Porter Graham Day Care Center," Dr. Fred Henderson the "Etiology of Otitis Media," and Dr. David Ingram "Invasive *Haemophilus influenzae* Infections in the Day Care Setting." It was quite a program (we thought), but unfortunately attendance hit a new low. We were able to muster a sizable audience from our faculty and house staff but the single topic did not seem to draw many to what, in the past, had been a well-attended meeting.

The evening banquet was held at the Hotel Europa and was followed by a talk on "Cultural Politics of Day Care" presented by Nancy Scheper-Hughes, PhD, associate professor in the Department of Anthropology at UNC. This excellent presentation was very up-to-date and politically correct in terms of the role of women in today's society. The entertainment that followed was presented by the General Assembly (Barbershop) Chorus lined up by Jerry Fernald, who was a member of the group and sang with them that evening. Imagine his surprise and chagrin, and the delight of the audience, when the chorus opened with "There Is Nothing Like a Dame"! Perhaps the most important part of the evening program was the recognition of Jerry Bernstein, who had served as president of the Pediatric Alumni Society since its inception in 1975. Dr. Ellis Fisher, president-elect, thanked him for his work and dedication to the society and presented him with a plaque in honor of his nine years of service.

As a result of this less-than-successful fourth triannual meeting of the Denny Society, the officers took careful note of factors that seemed to influence good attendance at previous gatherings. Fifty former residents were surveyed for their preferences for future meetings. What we learned suggested that several topics were needed to develop a program of broad interest. Although well-known outside speakers were popular, most preferred to hear from former faculty and house staff. We also found that newsletters and announcements had a way of ending up in the "dead letter office"; henceforth all mailings were sent first class, return postage guaranteed. We also finally realized that meetings for wives were inappropriate with the growing number of women entering pediatrics. With all these pros and cons in mind, we proceeded to plan for the next triannual meeting.

1987

"Current Topics in Pediatric Medicine" was the theme of the fifth triannual meeting held October 16–17, 1987. The meeting began with a highly successful luncheon for former chief residents with Drs. Curnen, Denny, and Boat. All but one or two of the nearly fifty former chiefs gathered around the giant table in the Dean's Conference Room to renew acquaintances and talk about old times.

Ed Curnen shares a joke with former residents at the 1987 Denny Society meeting

The scientific session began with "Current Topics in Pediatric Cardiology." Bill Henry introduced Dr. Roberta Williams, chief of the pediatric cardiology division at Los Angeles Children's Hospital, who spoke on "Recognition and Management of Cardiovascular Disease in the Fetus." Dr. Alex Nadas had been invited to attend but was unable due to a medical problem. His topic, interestingly enough, was to be "Pediatric Cardiology in 1987 as Perceived by Rip Van Winkle." The second half of the Friday afternoon program was on "Current Topics in Pediatric Infectious Diseases," moderated by Dr. Denny himself. Dr. Mary Glenn Fowler spoke on "AIDS in the School-Age Child" and Dr. Campbell McMillan on "AIDS in Childhood Hemophilia." These were very appropriate topics since testing for HIV had begun in the spring of 1985 and AIDS was becoming an increasing, although still quite rare, problem in pediatrics. The final topic, "Recent Trends in Rheumatic Fever," presented by Dr. Denny, emphasized the apparent resurgence of rheumatic fever in certain areas of the United States.

The evening socializing consisted of a pig pickin' and country music at the Five Oaks Clubhouse off the Old Chapel Hill Road. Music was presented by the Piney Mountain Boys, a group in which our own Art Aylsworth was a regular performer. On Saturday morning, following a brief business meeting, another innovation in programming was tested: four workshops, done in rotations so that participants could attend two of their choice. Drs. Arno Zaritsky, PICU chief, and Bill Henry presented "Principles of Pediatric Resuscitation"; Dr. Lou Underwood presented a workshop on "Management of Diabetes in Pediatric Practice"; "Update on Attention Deficit Disorders in Childhood" was given by Drs. Mel Levine and William Coleman; and "Special Stains and Exams Using the Office Microscope" was presented by Dr. Harvey Hamrick. At noon on Saturday a first-class reception for Dr. and Mrs. Herb Harned was held at the Europa Hotel. Arranged by Jud Van Wyk, this gathering began with champagne on a sunny outside terrace and a string quartet playing. A luncheon and dedication of the Herbert and Jean Harned Library in the newly completed Ronald McDonald House followed. The eloquence of Bill Henry and the self-styled poetry of Herb Harned were highlights of the gathering.

1990

Following the outline of the previous successful meeting, the sixth triannual gathering was held October 12–13 at the Omni Europa Hotel. An open luncheon for all former residents and spouses was held, with the Boats and Dennys as hosts. In recognition of the career of Dr. Campbell McMillan, the afternoon scientific program was comprised of presentations related to his interests and accomplishments. Dr. Howard Pearson, a long-time friend of Dr. Mac and chair of pediatrics at Yale, spoke on "The Clinician, the Scientist: A Medical Dilemma." Dr. Gary Jones, a new member of the hematology-oncology division, spoke on "Long-Term Effects of Therapy on Survivors of Childhood Cancer." Jack Benjamin, a former resident and fellow in hem-onc, presented "Me, Thee and the FEP, Reflections of a Private Practitioner." Finally, the highlight of the afternoon was "Reflections on the Natural History of Progress," presented in his uniquely philosophical style by Dr. Mac. This was so impressive that it is presented in this book in its entirety in the history of the division of hematology and oncology.

The evening social hour and pig pickin' was held at the new Skipper Bowles room next to the Dean Smith Center with entertainment provided by the ever-popular "General Assembly" Barbershop Chorus. The following morning a repeat of the four workshops included "Minor Surgical Skills and Procedures in the Pediatric Office" by Dr. Jeff Davis (plastic surgery); "Continuing Care in the Pediatrics Office of the Infant with BPD" by Drs. Alan Stiles and Ernest Kraybill; "Radiology for the Practicing Pediatrician" by Dr. David Merten, chief of pediatric radiology; and "Newer Procedures in Management Strategies of the Pediatric Gastroenterologist" by Drs. Martin Ulshen and Steve Lichtman. A wonderful reception for Dr. and Mrs. McMillan arranged by Herb Cooper was held Saturday noon at the Morehead Banquet Hall and attracted a large number of friends from the University community, the state, and beyond. It should be noted that this was not Dr. McMillan's retirement but a genuine outpouring of appreciation and affection for one of the most popular faculty members the Department has ever had. A portrait of Dr. Mac was presented at the end of the festivities and presently hangs in the Curnen Conference Room on the seventh floor of the Children's Hospital. Dr. McMillan's retirement occurred in January 1993, the bicentennial year of the University, when many alumni contributed to a resident education fund in his honor.

1993

Since 1993 was the year Floyd Denny would reach his seventieth year and, therefore, mandatory retirement from the University faculty, plans were begun for a special program. The Executive Committee, consisting of David Williams, Wally Brown, Meade Christian, and Jerry Fernald, mindful of the work already begun on this history of the Department, decided that the theme should be "40 Years of Pediatrics at UNC." After a great deal of planning, involving many but particularly the leadership of Jud Van Wyk, Herb Harned, Harrie Chamberlin, Meade Christian, Wally Brown, and Muff Carr, an extraordinary program was developed. The Friday afternoon meeting was held at the new Friday Center with introductions by President David Williams and the interim chair of the Department, Ned Lawson. Harrie Chamberlin presented "The Curnen Years," beautifully illustrated with photographs from the 1950s.

"The Denny Decades" included a videotape interview with Dr. Denny by Jud Van Wyk, followed by presentations from Herb Harned, Cam McMillan, Neil Kirkman, and John Raye. Finally, "The Boat Era" was reviewed by Tom Boat, Bob Wood, and Jake Lohr. One of the highlights of the gathering was dozens of photographs taken over the forty-year period and displayed by Herb and Jean Harned around the lecture hall and at appropriate locations throughout the weekend.

The Saturday morning program began with members of the present house staff in a skit reminiscent of Saturday morning Denny rounds from the '60s and '70s. The caricatures were extremely appropriate and entertaining and kept the crowd, including Drs. Denny and Boat, laughing in their seats. Special recognition should go to Muff Carr, who wrote the script for the skit.

Following the skit, a Pearls Session was presented by Alan Stiles and other former house staff, faculty, and present faculty. The morning wound up with a College Bowl under the direction of Meade Christian. Participants were residents from the oldest house staff (Griggs Dickson and Paul Glezen) and members of the present house staff. Joe Garfunkel served as the quizmaster and Tom Boat and Floyd Denny as judges. No one will remember which team won but it was a fun occasion and allowed for medical and humorous allusions to events from the four decades of UNC pediatric history.

As expected, attendance at this meeting surpassed all others in the history of the society, with approximately 250 guests attending the social hour and banquet for Floyd and Barbara Denny at the new George Watts Hill Alumni Center. Upon arrival at the banquet hall, everyone was stunned by the enormously elaborate floral arrangements on every table and a flower-bedecked gazebo/bar in the middle of the room. We were hastily assured that we were not financially responsible for these decorations, which had cost in the neighborhood of $25,000! A wedding reception for a scion of the Pepsi-Cola fam-

Upper: Denny Resident Rounds: Skit at the 1993 Denny Society meetings (Paul Monahan doing the "Denny dip")

Middle: The ARF's (Kim Buenting, Jim Alexander, Nancy Chaney Wight, Dick O'Brien, and Griggs Dickson) score a point in the quiz competition

Lower left: The Quiz Moderator (Joe Garfunkel)

Lower right: Floyd Denny and Tom Boat relax as they judge the quiz competition.

All photos by Dan Crawford

The Denny family: Tim, Barbara, Floyd, Zoe, and Mark (1993) [Credit: Dan Crawford]

ily had taken place the previous evening, and the decorations were left for our enjoyment! Following the meal, comments on Dr. Denny's career were made by David Williams, president and emcee; Jerry Fernald, associate chairman and long-time member of the infectious diseases division; Dave Tayloe Sr., long-time friend of the Department and representative of the North Carolina Pediatric Society; and Dean Stuart Bondurant. In recognition of Floyd's long service to the Department, the Denny Society Members presented him with a check to help finance construction of a special chair to go with an antique desk of his father's which he had recently restored. Ann Hamrick, representing the faculty wives, presented Barbara Denny with a beautiful vase by one of the area's distinguished potters in recognition of her long-time support of the Department and, in particular, of Floyd Denny himself. The evening ended with an announcement from president-elect Harvey Hamrick of plans for a fund-raising effort with a goal of $100,000, the interest from which would be sufficient for a first-class visiting professorship focused on resident education for the Department of Pediatrics.

In summary, it is fair to say that the UNC pediatric alumni gatherings over the span of twenty years were successful and served to bring many of the graduates together at appropriate intervals. In addition, the original fund-raising provided for an annual resident award ($250), attendance of pediatric house staff at annual NC Pediatric Society meetings ($1,000), support of the Evening of Scholarship ($1,000), and purchase of an IBM PS/2 computer for the society secretary to expand and update the mailing list for the departmental newsletter, *Pediatric Perspectives*. For a period of several years, support of an alumni gathering at the American Academy of Pediatrics was attempted. However, attendance was never really satisfactory and this project was abandoned. Alumni gatherings at the spring research meeting received support up through the end of the Boat era. These were discontinued at that time because the meetings of the Denny Society served the same purposes and were more successful.

GERALD W. FERNALD

CHAPTER FORTY-SEVEN

Medicine-Pediatrics Residency Training at the University of North Carolina

T HE internal medicine–pediatrics residency program consists of four years of combined training in internal medicine and pediatrics; graduates are board-eligible in both clinical disciplines. The two departments at UNC were pioneers in developing this unique program, which was adopted by many U.S. teaching hospitals twenty years later. The objective of the UNC program is to train clinicians to provide comprehensive and competent primary or specialty care to patients of all ages.

This type of training grew out of the flexible internship training common at many academic centers in the 1960s; at UNC during this time our program was frequently referred to as the medicine-pediatrics residency. In 1967, dual certification through a four-year training program was approved by the American Board of Internal Medicine and the American Board of Pediatrics. It was probably a resident at UNC who first petitioned the boards to allow this dual training.

Interest in the program grew slowly. The program at UNC was "formalized" in 1980 when four residents were accepted through the National Residency Matching Program ("the match"). Combined programs were first listed in the Graduate Medical Education Directory ("the green book") in 1983. The first national meeting regarding medicine-pediatrics issues took place in 1986. Because of the significant variability in curricula among programs, guidelines were developed in 1988 by the American Board of Internal Medicine and the American Board of Pediatrics which emphasized education rather than service, as well as integration and continuity in training. The Medicine-Pediatrics Program Directors Association was formed in 1991.

Despite modest beginnings, medicine-pediatrics training is becoming well-established as a discipline. In 1980, there were four med-peds programs with nine post-graduate year-1 (PGY-1) positions offered in the match; in 1995, there were ninety-three programs listed in the match with 405 PGY-1 positions offered.

The combined internal medicine–pediatrics program at UNC has enjoyed strong support from the Departments of Medicine and Pediatrics; early leadership was provided by Drs. Floyd Denny and Louis Welt. Dr. Andrew Greganti, the first program director, provided excellent leadership at both an institutional and national level; he was followed by Dr. Romulo Colindres. Current program director Dr. Carole Lannon was one of the first medicine-pediatrics graduates to lead a residency program; she was president of the Medicine–Pediatrics Program Directors Association in 1994–95 and is helping begin a graduate network, the Medicine-Pediatrics Physicians Association.

As of July 1995, there were fifty-five graduates of the medicine-pediatrics residency program at the University of North Carolina. Almost two-thirds have followed a primary care career path. Most of these graduates are in practice; some have earned public health degrees and are involved in community-based research. Several graduates are affiliated with primary care training programs. About one-third of the graduates have obtained subspecialty training. Several of these subspecialists treat both adult and pediatric patients in their clinic practices (nephrology, gastroenterology, endocrinology, rheumatology, hematology, and pulmonology). In recent years, there has been increased interest in primary care. For example, of the twenty-four residents who finished training at UNC between 1988 and 1995, twenty-one are involved in primary care. Sixteen of those are in primary care practice, and five are in academic primary care positions.

CAROLE M. LANNON

CHAPTER FORTY-EIGHT

Pediatric Department House Staffs

INTRODUCTION

THIS chapter lists the house staff trained in the Department of Pediatrics from 1952–1953 to 1995–1996. The listing of those individuals being trained as pediatricians was straightforward and gave us no problems. The listing of those being trained in pediatrics and internal medicine proved more difficult because schedules changed over the years. In the earlier years, the house staff who received any part of their training in pediatrics in a given year are listed below. Those spending the entire year in the Department of Medicine are not listed for that year. As noted below, the structure of the entire medicine-pediatric program changed in 1988 with all residents spending time each year in both medicine and pediatrics. This is reflected in the way these residents are listed.

For parts of the time covered by this history, especially in the earlier years, house staff from several other clinical services spent varying amounts of time as residents on the pediatric service. These included trainees from the Departments of Anesthesiology, Family Medicine, and Obstetrics. They are not listed here because these residents did not have a primary appointment in the Department of Pediatrics.

HOUSE STAFF LISTS

1952–1953

Second-Year Assistant Resident:
  William H. Davis

First-Year Assistant Resident:
  Earle F. Spaugh

Interns (1/1/1953–6/30/1953):
  George W. Brice   Frank C. Niblock

Rotating Interns:

Charles Adams	Wayne Boyles	John Chapin
Elwood Coley	Nicholas Love	Charles Vernon
Walter Feinberg	Daniel Martin	John Watters
Larry Gladstone	James Morris	James White
James Grimes	John Porter	George Wolff
Gordon Heath	Charles Starling	
William Joyner	Lewis Thorp	

1953–1954

Chief Resident:
  William H. Davis

Second-Year Assistant Residents:
  Earle F. Spaugh   George K. Summer

First-Year Assistant Residents:
  Elwood Coley   Marilyn Michaels

Interns:
  Benjamin Johnson   James S. White

Rotating Interns:

O. B. Bonner	Angus E. Holmes	Edward Thorne
Richard Borden	Harry H. McLean	Edward Viser
Carl Butenas	Alfred Senft	George L. Wilkinson
Alton Coppridge	James Earl Somers	
John Herion	Arthur G. Sherman	

Medical Interns Rotating through Pediatrics:
  William B. Blythe   Morris H. Lampert

1954–1955

Senior Assistant Residents:
  Elwood Coley   Earle Spaugh

First-Year Assistant Residents:
  Joseph D. Corpening   James S. White   Robert W. Winters
  Charles C. Stamey

Interns:
  Richard Borden   Annabelle T. Craddock   Hugh C. Hemmings

Rotating Interns:

Willis Jackson Brant	Tally Lassiter	Joe Robinson
Robert D. Breer	Katherine R. Melton	Thomas F. Stallings

Robert A. de Napoli	James R. Morton	William H. Weinel
Franklin M. Draper, Jr.	Jacqueline Noonan	
Joe C. Ebbinghouse	Charles C. Owens	

1955–1956

Second-Year Assistant Residents:

Charles Stamey	James White	Robert Winters

First-Year Assistant Residents:

Sacha H. Field	Sara L. Hoyt	James F. Morris
Hugh Hemmings		

Interns:

James Grimes	William C. Powell

Mixed Interns:

Griggs Dickson	Oliver Roddey	Henry M. Ware
Forrest K. Huntington	Clarence W. Taylor	Robert W. Wellenborn

1956–1957

Chief Resident:
Sacha Field

Second-Year Assistant Residents:

Hugh Hemmings	Sara Hoyt	James F. Morris

First-Year Assistant Residents:

Griggs Dickson	James E. Grimes	William C. Powell

Interns:

Robert F. Castle	Thomas H. Gardner	Victor G. Herring III
Wilma L. Castle		

Mixed Interns:

Wade H. Brannon	Malcolm McLean	Robert L. Murray
William E. Easterling	Lee G. Miller	Clarence Taylor
Forrest K. Huntington	Alfon B. Mosca	Pat Thompson

1957–1958

Second-Year Assistant Residents:

Richard B. Patterson	Robert J. Senior	Barbara Wilmer

First-Year Assistant Residents:

Robert F. Castle	Thomas H. Gardner	Harry Meyer
Wilma L. Castle		

Interns:

Boyd W. Cook	Faith Kung	Magdalena Maas

Mixed Interns:

Alan Brown	Robert T. Herrington	Bryce Templeton
Thomas Dulin	Martha Leas	
Edward Fleming	John Olson	

1958–1959

Chief Resident:
Robert J. Senior

Second-Year Assistant Residents:

Robert F. Castle	Wilma L. Castle	Harry Meyer

First-Year Assistant Residents:

Boyd W. Cook	Faith Kung (Currie)	James H. McCallum, Jr.
Robert T. Herrington		

Intern:
Magdalena Maas

Mixed Interns:

John S. Gaskin	Marie Lipsett	David Satin
Charles C. Hunter	John N. Lukens	John Semmelmeyer
Harry D. Jameson	Ralph S. Park	Reginald Tucker
William Kessler	Richard Porus	
Hervy Kornegay	Ann Ruhman	

1959–1960

Chief Resident:
Griggs Dickson

Second-Year Assistant Resident:
Faith Kung (Currie)

First-Year Assistant Residents:

Anne Preston Askew	Roland E. Schmidt	Charles Waters, Jr.
Marie F. Lipsett		

Interns:

Eugene E. Gould	Maria Reyes	Martha Sharpless

Mixed Interns:

J. Kelly Dixon	Robert Mann	Hugh Riddlehuber
Arthur Feldman	Adrian Pollock	Frank Shaw
Carl Harris	Mark Reiss	Roger Spencer

1960–1961

Chief Resident:
Frank French

Second-Year Assistant Residents:

Anne Preston Askew	Roland Schmidt	Charles Waters
W. Paul Glezen		

First-Year Assistant Residents:

Carlos Serrano	Martha Sharpless	Frank Shaw

Interns:

Joel Berne
Gerald Fernald

Emmy Lou Heiman
(Cholak)

Joseph Swanton

Mixed Interns:

Marvin Corn
James K. Dixon II
Arthur I. Feldman

Carl M. Harris
Charles M. Louden
Abraham M. Mizrahi

Mark D. Reiss
Bryce Templeton

1961–1962

Chief Residents:

Frank French

Paul Glezen

Second-Year Assistant Residents:

Joanna Dalldorf
Stephen Friedland

Robert Herrington

Frank Shaw

First-Year Assistant Residents:

William G. Conley
H. Bee Gatling

Carlos Serrano

Joseph Whatley

Interns:

H. David Bruton
William M. Clarke

Brian Luke

Fred Meyerhoefer

Mixed Interns:

Michael Bokat
Michael L. Connell
Donald Freeman

Alan Greenberg
John R. Marchese
Hubert Matthews

Peter Simkin
John Stephenson
Linn Turner

1962–1963

Chief Resident:

William G. Conley

Second-Year Assistant Residents:

John Fletcher

Bee Gatling

Margaret Wyatt

First-Year Assistant Residents:

William M. Clarke

Fred Meyerhoefer

John Stephenson

Interns:

James Conlee Pickens
Mary Louise Smith

Daniel Torphy

Leland W. Wight, Jr.

Mixed Interns:

Robert L. Abney
George L. Branch
Lawrence M. Cutchin

Jasper R. Daube
John T. Harrington
Willie G. Peacock

Carl S. Phipps
Edwin C. Shuttleworth
Forrest F. Weight, Jr.

1963–1964

Chief Resident:
William M. Clarke

Second-Year Assistant Residents:

Bee Gatling	John Stephenson	Louis Underwood
Fred Meyerhoefer		

First-Year Assistant Residents:

Robert L. Abney	Lawrence M. Cutchin	Leland Wight
George L. Branch	James C. Pickens	Margaret Wyatt

Interns:

Conrad Andringa	Charles M. Hicks	Robert Wilson
Michael Durfee	David Williams	

Mixed Interns:

William H. Cook, Jr.	George Hemingway	Charles Rathke
Branch Fields, Jr.	Richard Honsinger	Robert A. Shaw
Robert Gayler	Everett Moody	Lloyd Tarlin

1964–1965

Chief Resident:
James C. Pickens

Second-Year Assistant Residents:

George Branch	Benjamin Robbins	Leland Wight
Charles M. Hicks		

First-Year Assistant Residents:

William H. Cook, Jr.	Charles Rathke	Robert Wilson
Michael Durfee	David Williams	

Interns:

Charles Hunsinger	Jane Morley Kotchen	John Moore

Mixed Interns:

John Beard	John Vincent Mumma	Bryan Simons
Joseph Allen Cook	John R. Raye	Theodore Tapper
John R. Fisher	David Rosin	

1965–1966

Chief Resident:
Michael Durfee

Second-Year Assistant Residents:

Bob Edwards (Navy)	Frank A. Loda	David Williams
Ricci Larese (Navy)	Jerry Smith	Robert Wilson

First-Year Assistant Residents:

Ray Antley	Charles Hunsinger	John R. Raye
John Beard	John A. Moore	Robert A. Shaw

Interns:

James O. Burke, Jr.	Balaam Thal Elliott, Jr.	R. Beverly Raney, Jr.
Richard M. Doughten	Richard T. O'Brien	

Mixed Interns:

Roscius N. Doan	Joseph E. Kelleher, Jr.	Jesse R. Peel
Peter E. Dorsett	Eugene W. Lariviere	Daniel P. Stites
Ralph M. Gibson	Vasiliki Moskos	William T. Whitney

1966–1967

Chief Resident:
Robert L. Abney

Second-Year Assistant Residents:

Charles Hunsinger	John A. Moore	John R. Raye
Patrick Jasper		

First-Year Assistant Residents:

James O. Burke	Robert Kindley	R. Beverly Raney, Jr.
Balaam Thal Elliott, Jr.	Richard T. O'Brien	

Interns:

John T. Benjamin	Thomas E. Digby	William P. Kanto
Morton L. Cohen	William C. Hubbard	

Mixed Interns:

Richard A. Finch	William L. Gurnack	William C. Rawls
Wesley C. Fowler	Howard T. Hinshaw	Henry (Harry) Smith
Edward L. Goldblatt	Stephen J. Lerman	William Beverly Tucker

1967–1968

Chief Resident:
John R. Raye

Second-Year Assistant Residents:

James O. Burke	Robert Kindley	William Sayers
Balaam Thal Elliott	R. Beverly Raney, Jr.	

First-Year Assistant Residents:

John T. Benjamin	Thomas E. Digby	Henry (Harry) Smith
Morton L. Cohen	Patrick Jasper	

Interns:

Meade Christian	William Kagey	Mary Sugioka
Harvey J. Hamrick	John Kiesel	

Mixed Interns:

Thomas Bisett	Lester Haddad	Larry Rankin
John Douglas	William T. Hawkins	Mary Restifo
Glenn David Gardner	George D. Hopper	Jonathan Wise

1968–1969

Chief Resident:
  William Sayers

Second-Year Assistant Residents:

John T. Benjamin	Thomas E. Digby	Henry (Harry) Smith
John Beard	William Hubbard	

First-Year Assistant Residents:

Thomas Bisett	Harvey J. Hamrick	Philip Littleton
Meade Christian	George Hemingway	

Interns:

George Bensch	Kenneth Graupner	Thomas Saari
Peter Dawson	Abram Patterson	

Mixed Interns:

John Batjer	Charles Post	Roberta Williams
Wallace Brown	George Toma	Kay Woodruff
Thomas Mettee	Elizabeth Vaughan	Peter Zawadsky

1969–1970

Chief Resident:
  George Hemingway

Second-Year Assistant Residents:

Thomas Bisett	Harvey J. Hamrick	Robert Shaw
Meade Christian	Richard O'Brien	

First-Year Assistant Residents:

George Bensch	Najwa Khuri	Thomas Saari
Wallace Brown	Abram Patterson	

Interns:

George Robin Beck	Allen E. Cato	Lore Knetsch
John Hugh Bryan	Elias G. Chalhub	Robert H. Pantell

Mixed Interns:

C. Ellis Fisher	Michael A. Newman	Morris Schoeneman
Lee Hyde	Joseph Russell	Martin H. Ulshen

1970–1971

Chief Resident:
  Harvey J. Hamrick

Second-Year Assistant Residents:

Willis A. Archer	Peter Dawson	Abram Patterson
George W. Bensch		

First-Year Assistant Residents:

George Robin Beck	C. Ellis Fisher	W. Beverly Tucker
John Hugh Bryan	Robert H. Pantell	

Interns:

Earl W. Bryant	Bernard Guyer	Ross Vaughan
Irwin P. Cohen	Kathleen Salter (Keagy)	Susan B. Wolschina

Mixed Interns:

Mary Jo Freitag	Robert W. McDermott	M. Eugene Sherman
James P. Hampsey	John Phillip Moyer	Rick Suberman

1971–1972

Chief Resident:
William Hubbard

Second-Year Assistant Residents:

George Robin Beck	C. Ellis Fisher	Robert H. Pantell
George G. Bonham	Benton B. Levie	

First-Year Assistant Residents:

Jerry C. Bernstein	Mary Jo Freitag	Kathleen Salter (Keagy)
Irwin P. Cohen	Bernard Guyer	Susan B. Wolschina

Interns:

Eugene L. Borkan	Robert E. Gould	Charles H. Richman
Robert H. Cohan	Edgar W. Little	
Rene C. Duffourc	George E. Miller	

Mixed Interns:

Robert L. Blake	Jeffrey D. Jones	William W. Webb, Jr.
Vernon B. Hunt	Sara H. Sinal	Blane Yelton

1972–1973

Chief Resident:
C. Ellis Fisher

Second-Year Assistant Residents:

Jerry C. Bernstein	James Smithwick	Susan B. Wolschina
Fred Henderson	William Straughn	

First-Year Assistant Residents:

Edwin A. Farrell	Robert E. Gould	George E. Miller
Susan E. Farrell	Edgar Little	
Michael A. Gilchrist	Thomas Mettee	

Interns:

Peggy Falace	Robert W. Little	Mary Ann Williams
Emlen H. Jones	Thomas Murphy	
Gregory Hayden	Robert Chevalier	

Rotating Four Interns:

Henry Atkins	George Broze	Stanley M. Lemon
Daniel Barco	Franklin Cashwell	Donald Middleton

1973–1974

Chief Resident:
  Jerry C. Bernstein

Second-Year Assistant Residents:

Edwin A. Farrell	Michael A. Gilchrist	Emlen H. Jones
Susan E. Farrell	Robert E. Gould	Edgar Little

First-Year Assistant Residents:

George J. Broze	Gregory F. Hayden	Thomas F. Murphy
Earl W. Bryant	Thomas G. Irons	Mary Ann Williams
Robert L. Chevalier	Robert Little	(Morris)

Interns:

Michael L. Bramley	Carol M. Hagberg	Paul L. Sutton
David A. Clark	Ronald B. May	Halbert Woodward, Jr.
Anne Francis	Samuel H. Pepkowitz	

Rotating Four Interns:

Susan G. Birkemeier	S. Wayne Smith	Joseph E. Williamson
Dale Newton		

1974–1975

Chief Resident:
  Robert E. Gould

Second-Year Assistant Residents:

Earl W. Bryant	Gregory F. Hayden	Robert Little
Robert L. Chevalier	Thomas G. Irons	Thomas F. Murphy

First-Year Assistant Residents:

Michael L. Bramley	Carol M. Hagberg	Samuel H. Pepkowitz
David A. Clark	Emlen H. Jones	Paul L. Sutton
Peggy Falace	Ronald B. May	Halbert Woodward, Jr.
Anne Francis	Donald Middleton	

Interns:

Richard C. Andringa	John Myracle	William Wilson
Jon M. Fusselman	Anne Scholl	Charles Yoder
Jennifer Margolis	Michael Sharp	Eleanor Weissberg

Rotating Four Interns:

Charles W. Lapp	Christopher H. Snyder	Gerald L. Strope
Charles A. Mangano		

1975–1976

Chief Residents:

Carol M. Hagberg	Samuel H. Pepkowitz

Second-Year Assistant Residents:

Michael L. Bramley	Anne Francis	Donald Middleton
David A. Clark	James McQueen	Halbert Woodward, Jr.

First-Year Assistant Residents:

Richard C. Andringa	John Myracle	Michael C. Sharp
Jon M. Fusselman	Dale Newton	Christopher Snyder
Jennifer Margolis	Anne Scholl	Gerald Strope
Eleanor Weissberg	William Wilson	Charles Yoder

Interns:

Jeffrey Bomze	Craig LaForce	Teresa Salter
John Dolcourt	Dennis Mayock	Hugh Wells
Robert Hoyer	Evan Pattishall	Susanne White
Douglas Klaucke	William Rhead	

Rotating Four Interns:

Bernard Branson	Howard McMahan	Wanda Radford
Thomas Higgins		

1976–1977

Chief Resident:

Halbert Woodward, Jr.

Second-Year Assistant Residents:

Richard Andringa	John Myracle	Christopher Snyder
Randy Forehand	Dale Newton	Gerald Strope
Jon M. Fusselman	Anne Scholl	David Tayloe
Jennifer Margolis	Michael C. Sharp	Eleanor Weissberg

First-Year Assistant Residents:

Jeffrey Bomze	Craig LaForce	William Rhead
Bernard Branson	Charles Lapp	Teresa Salter
Jack Dolcourt	Dennis Mayock	Hugh Wells
Robert Hoyer	Evan Pattishall	

Interns:

Marjorie Carr	Paul Kaplowitz	Karen McCoy
Nancy Chaney	Karen Lowenstein	William Turk
Jerry Hood	Rubin Maness	Margaret Zwerling

Rotating Four Interns:

Holcombe Grier	Michael McCauley	John Roberts
Walker Long		

1977–1978

Chief Resident:

Randy Forehand

PL-3 Residents:

Jeffrey Bomze	Robert Hoyer	Evan Pattishall
Bernard Branson	Craig LaForce	Teresa Salter
Douglas Clark	Charles Lapp	
Jack Dolcourt	Dennis Mayock	

PL-2 Residents:

Marjorie Carr	Walker Long	Mary Sugioka
Nancy Chaney	Rubin Maness	Susanne White
Jerry Hood	Karen McCoy	Charles Willson
Paul Kaplowitz	William Turk	Margaret Zwerling

PL-1 Residents:

Arlen Collins	Melinda Paul	John Shahan
John Davis	Judith Ratner	Douglas Willson
Sharon Lail	Mitchell Reese	

Rotating Interns:

Henrik Anderson	Ray Mitchell	James Tiedeman
Lenore Buckley	John Ticehurst	William Waltner

1978–1979

Chief Residents:

Nancy Chaney	Karen McCoy

PL-3 Residents:

Juan Cardenas	Paul Kaplowitz	Susanne White
Marjorie Carr	Rubin Maness	Charles Willson
Jerry Hood	William Turk	Margaret Zwerling

PL-2 Residents:

Arlen Collins	Thomas Miller	Mitchell Reese
John Davis	Randy Pasternak	John Roberts
Holcombe Grier	Melinda Paul	Douglas Willson
Sharon Lail	Judith Ratner	

PL-1 Residents:

Teresa Bilz	Diane Edwards	Peter Morris
Katherine Chino	Seth Hetherington	James Spaeth
Tina Ciesiel	Jeannine Leatherman	Alan Stiles

Rotating Residents:

Ann Collier	Suzanne Landis	Stanley Spinola
Elizabeth Gamble	John Pecorak	James Strickland
Wanda Kotvan	Alice Pentland	

1979–1980

Chief Resident:

Charles Willson

PL-3 Residents:

Arlen Collins	Sharon Lail	John Roberts
Jack Davis	Thomas Miller	Douglas Willson
Holcombe Grier	Melinda Paul	
Marianna Henry	Mitchell Reese	

PL-2 Residents:

Teresa Bilz	Seth Hetherington	John Pecorak
Lenore Buckley	Wanda Kotvan	James Spaeth
Katherine Chino	Jeannine Leatherman	Stanley Spinola
Tina Ciesiel	Ray Mitchell	Alan Stiles
Diane Edwards	Peter Morris	William Waltner

PL-1 Residents:

Nita Coleman	Harry Guess	Patricia Robinson
Hugh Craft	Susan Hyman	Richard Waller
Joan Fine	Dana Ketchum	

Flexible A (1-year program):

John Bourgeois	Bruce Duncan

Flexible B (4-year program):

Sharon Foster	Shannon Kenney	Richard Sigmon
John Grizzard		

1980–1981

Chief Resident:
Douglas Willson

PL-3 Residents:

Teresa Bilz	Seth Hetherington	Ann Smith
Lenore Buckley	Jeannine Leatherman	Alan Stiles
Katherine Chino	Ray Mitchell	William Waltner
Tina Ciesiel	Peter Morris	
Diane Edwards	John Pecorak	

PL-2 Residents:

Nita Coleman	Harry Guess	Rick Sigmon
Hugh Craft	Susan Hyman	Stanley Spinola
Joan Fine	Wanda Kotvan	Richard Waller
John Grizzard	Patricia Robinson	

PL-1 Residents:

Ann Bailey	Ruth Ann Etzel	Peter Saviteer
Elizabeth Coulson	Barbara Hodge	Robert Valley
Cindy Devore	Edward Pattishall	

Flexible A (1-year program):

Susan Lipton	Liliana Visscher	Chris Yeakel

Flexible B (4-year program):

Michael O'Shea	Rupa Redding-Lallinger	Paul Sorum
Camille Porto		

1981–1982

Chief Resident:
Alan Stiles

PL-3 Residents:

Hugh Craft	Harry Guess	Patricia Robinson
Diane Edwards	Susan Hyman	Michael Schur
Joan Fine	Thomas Jones	Stanley Spinola
John Grizzard	Wanda Kotvan	Richard Waller

PL-2 Residents:

Ann Bailey	Barbara Hodge	Peter Saviteer
Betsy Coulson	Shannon Kenney	Rick Sigmon
Cindy Devore	Michael O'Shea	Paul Sorum
Ruth Etzel	Edward Pattishall	Robert Valley
Sharon Foster	Rupa Redding-Lallinger	

PL-1 Residents:

David Burchfield	Holley Manbeck	Jeffrey Schlactus
Elman Frantz	Larry Nickens	Edward Spence
Linda Goodwin	John Santamaria	Karen Zuidema (Voter)

Flexible Residents:

Febe Brazeal	David Goff	Nancy Robinson
Matt Gillman		

1982–1983

Chief Resident:

Hugh Craft

PL-3 Residents:

Ann Bailey	Barbara Hodge	Peter Saviteer
Cindy Devore	Shannon Kenney	Rick Sigmon
Ruth Etzel	Steve McCombs	Robert Valley
Sharon Foster	Edward Pattishall	

PL-2 Residents:

David Burchfield	Linda Goodwin	John Santamaria
Febe Brazeal	Claudia Nelson	Jeff Schlactus
Elman Frantz	Larry Nickens	Edward Spence
Matt Gillman	Michael O'Shea	Karen Voter
David Goff	Rupa Redding-Lallinger	

PL-1 Residents:

Robert Covert	David Grossman	Kathryn Morton
Marsha Davenport	Henry Harvey	Regina Rabinovich
Perry Anne Futral	Thomas Monk	Susan Sajeski (Pitts)

Flexible Residents:

Joseph Barnes	Diane Edge Judge	Carole M. Lannon
Carolyn Chantry		

1983–1984

Chief Resident:
Robert Valley

PL-3 Residents:

David Burchfield	Larry Nickens	Jeffrey Schlactus
Elman Frantz	Michael O'Shea	Edward Spence
Linda Goodwin	Rupa Redding-Lallinger	Karen Voter
Claudia Nelson	John Santamaria	

PL-2 Residents:

Joseph Barnes	Perry Futral	Carole M. Lannon
Febe Brazeal	Matt Gillman	Thomas Monk
Robert Covert	David Goff	Franco Piazza
Marsha Davenport	David Grossman	Susan Pitts
Diane Edge Judge	Henry Harvey	Regina Rabinovich

PL-1 Residents:

Douglas Cannon	Randy Hedgepeth	Gene Soares
Gary Eddey	Julie Kavanagh	Nancy Tang
Patricia Friedman	Joan Perry	Susan Warren (Denfield)

Medicine-Pediatrics (first year):

Douglas Clark	Steven Klein	Jackson Smith
Carol Ford		

1984–1985

Chief Resident:
Rupa Redding-Lallinger

PL-3 Residents:

David Annibale	Matt Gillman	Franco Piazza
Febe Brazeal	David Goff	Susan Pitts
Robert Covert	David Grossman	Regina Rabinovich
Marsha Davenport	Henry Harvey	
Perry Futral	Thomas Monk	

PL-2 Residents:

Joseph Barnes	Randy Hedgepeth	Jackson Smith
Douglas Cannon	Julie Kavanagh	Gene Soares
Douglas Clark	Steven Klein	Nancy Tang
Carol Ford	Carole M. Lannon	Susan Warren (Denfield)
Patricia Friedman	Joan Perry	

PL-1 Residents:

James Alexander	Kathleen Foster-Wendel	Virginia Nichols
Jay Anderson	Sally Harris	Charles Toledo
Elizabeth Andrew	Gregory Kirkpatrick	
Scott Buck	Terry Murphy	

Medicine-Pediatrics (first year):

Robert Dunmire	Tony Patriarco	Mary Roy
Cheryl Hillery		

1985–1986

Chief Resident:
Regina Rabinovich

PL-3 Residents:

David Annibale	Susan Warren Denfield	Carole M. Lannon
Joseph Barnes	Patricia Friedman	Joan Perry
Douglas Cannon	Randy Hedgepeth	Gene Soares
Douglas Clark	Julie Kavanagh	Nancy Tang

PL-2 Residents:

James Alexander	Sally Harris	Virginia Nichols
Elizabeth Andrew	Cheryl Hillery	Tony Patriarco
Scott Buck	Michele Humlan	Mary Roy
Robert Dunmire	Gregory Kirkpatrick	Jackson Smith
Carol Ford	Steven Klein	Charles Toledo
Kathleen Foster-Wendel	Terry Murphy	

PL-1 Residents:

Elizabeth Allen	Franklin Israel	Karen Sennewald
Robert Brown	Donald Kees	Brent Weston
Thomas Ferkol	Kathleen MacCarthy	
James Hubbard	Shanti Reddy	

Medicine-Pediatrics (first year):

Joanne Dykas	Robert McClure	Donna Vegeais
Andrew Kaplan		

1986–1987

Chief Resident:
Susan Warren Denfield

PL-3 Residents:

James Alexander	Sally Harris	Terry Murphy
Elizabeth Andrew	Michele Humlan	Virginia Nichols
Scott Buck	Gregory Kirkpatrick	Jackson Smith
Carol Ford	Steven Klein	Charles Toledo

PL-2 Residents:

Elizabeth Allen	James Hubbard	Shanti Reddy
Robert Brown	Frank Israel	Karen Sennewald
Robert Dunmire	Andrew Kaplan	Donna Vegeais
Joanne Dykas	Donald Kees	Brent Weston
Thomas Ferkol	Robert McClure	
Cheryl Hillery	Tony Patriarco	

PL-1 Residents:

Ann Bates	Timothy Johanson	Martin Nygaard
Kim Bullock	Karen Kartheiser	Wayne Rackoff
Catherine Davis	Kristen Moffitt	
Stephen Downs	Robin Newton	

Medicine-Pediatrics (first year):

Dean Meisel	David Repaske	Edward Ward
Jennifer Preiss		

1987–1988

Chief Resident:
Scott Buck

PL-3 Residents:

Elizabeth Allen	James Hubbard	Tony Patriarco
Robert Dunmire	Frank Israel	Shanti Reddy
Thomas Ferkol	Donald Kees	Karen Sennewald
Cheryl Hillery	Terry Noah	Brent Weston

PL-2 Residents:

Ann Bates	Karen Kartheiser	Wayne Rackoff
Catherine Davis	Robert McClure	David Repaske
Stephen Downs	Dean Meisel	Donna Vegeais
Joanne Dykas	Kristen Moffitt	Nancy Walton
Timothy Johanson	Martin Nygaard	Edward Ward
Andrew Kaplan	Jennifer Preiss	

PL-1 Residents:

Jane Benton	Marvin Hall	R. Edgar Timberlake
Sandra Botstein-Glick	Deanna Mitchell	David Weingold
James Crowe	Laura K. Noonan	
Janet Flaton	Debra Shah	

Medicine-Pediatrics (first year):

Lisa Benaron	Kimberly Kylstra	Douglas Nelson
Maria Britto		

1988–1989

Chief Resident:
Thomas Ferkol

PL-3 Residents:

Ann Bates	R Everette Frericks	Martin Nygaard
Mary Elizabeth Carter	Timothy Johanson	Wayne Rackoff
Catherine Davis	Karen Kartheiser	David Repaske
Stephen Downs	Kristen Moffitt	Nancy Walton

PL-2 Residents:

Sandra Botstein-Glick	Marvin Hall	Debra Shah
James Crowe	Deanna Mitchell	R. Edgar Timberlake
Janet Flaton	Laura K. Noonan	

PL-1 Residents:

David Barnes	Christina G. Flannelly	Marguerite Oetting
Mary Q. Barnes	Christopher Foley	Henry Shapiro
Elizabeth Blair	Mary (Molly) Froelich	Bryan Smith
Susan Cohen	Bonnie Hamilton	

Medicine-Pediatrics*

Fourth Year:	*Third Year:*	*Second Year:*
Joanne Dykas	Dean Meisel	Lisa Benaron
Donna Vegeais	Jennifer Preiss	Maria Britto
	Edward Ward	Kimberly Kylstra
		Douglas Nelson

First Year:

Elizabeth Dixon	Bryan Hollinger	Sheryl Scott
George Dodds		

1989-90

Chief Residents:

Ann S. Bates	Timothy Johanson

PL-3 Residents:

Sandra Botstein-Glick	Deanna Mitchell	Vicki B. Teague
James Crowe	Laura K. Noonan	Ed Timberlake
Janet Flaton	Julio Reinstein	Sharon Van Horn
Marvin Hall	Debra Shah	

PL-2 Residents:

Henry Akinbi	Christopher Foley	Marguerite Oetting
Mary Q. Barnes	Mary (Molly) Froelich	Henry Shapiro
Elizabeth Blair	Dawn M. Grinenko	Bryan Smith
Susan Cohen	Bonnie Hamilton	Hani Zreik
Christina Flannelly	Rita A. Makhlouf	

PL-1 Residents:

Noah Archer	Rebecca S. Cochran	Barry L. Hummel
Laura Bellstrom	Robert E. Couch	Patrick A. Jarvie
Kathryn Bishop	Diane M. Duffy	Renee Tuttle

---

* In 1988 the administrative structure of the Medicine-Pediatrics program was changed from being managed by each department where the resident was located to being managed as a separate free-standing unit. This is reflected in the change in listing beginning with 1988–89.

Virginia Brack   Sefanit Fassil
Kilian H. Brech   Theresa L. Hamel

Medicine-Pediatrics

Fourth Year:	*Third Year:*	*Second Year:*
Dean Meisel	Lisa Benaron	Elizabeth Dixon
Jennifer Preiss	Maria Britto	George Dodds
Edward Ward	Kimberly Kylstra	Bryan Hollinger
	Douglas Nelson	Sheryl Scott

First Year:		
Mark Dickinson	Kristine L. McVea	Darby Sider
John A. Hopper		

1990–1991

Chief Residents:

Marvin Hall   Laura K. Noonan

PL-3 Residents:

Henry Akinbi	Christopher Foley	Marguerite Oetting
Mary Q. Barnes	Mary (Molly) Froelich	Henry Shapiro
Elizabeth Blair	Dawn M. Grinenko	Bryan Smith
Susan Cohen	Bonnie Hamilton	Hani Zreik
Christina Flannelly	Rita A. Makhlouf	

PL-2 Residents:

Noah Archer	Robert E. Couch	Barry L. Hummel
Laura Bellstrom	Ruth Crosby	Patrick A. Jarvie
Kathryn Bishop	Diane M. Duffy	Art Shepard
Virginia Brack	Sefanit Fassil	Renee Tuttle

PL-1 Residents:

Amina Ahmed	Paul E. Monahan	Shelley Schoonover
Michelle I. Amaya	Scott D. Reeves	Clay A. Stanley
Laurie O. Beitz	Pamela J. Reitnauer	Jennifer F. Tender
Amy S. Henderson	Christopher Rittmeyer	
Chon Lee	Andrew Scharenberg	

Medicine-Pediatrics

Fourth Year:	*Third Year:*	*Second Year:*
Lisa Benaron	Elizabeth Dixon	Mark Dickinson
Maria Britto	George Dodds	John A. Hopper
Kimberly Kylstra	Bryan Hollinger	Kristine L. McVea
Douglas Nelson	Sheryl Scott	Darby Sider

First Year:		
Annamaria T. Kausz	Steven P. Stout	Justin J. Wu
Paqui D. Motyl		

1991–1992

Chief Residents:
Maria Britto   Doug Nelson

PL-3 Residents:

Noah Archer	Robert E. Couch	Barry L. Hummel
Laura Bellstrom	Ruth Crosby	Patrick A. Jarvie
Kathryn Bishop	Diane M. Duffy	Renee Tuttle Schust
Virginia Brack	Sefanit Fassil	Art Shepard

PL-2 Residents:

Amina Ahmed	Amy S. Henderson	Christopher Rittmeyer
Michelle I. Amaya	Chon Lee	Andrew Scharenberg
Laurie O. Beitz	Paul E. Monahan	Shelley Schoonover
Ildy Edenhoffer	Scott D. Reeves	Clay A. Stanley
Theresa L. Hamel	Pamela J. Reitnauer	Jennifer F. Tender

PL-1 Residents:

Paul O. Adholla	Susan B. Daly	Michele C. Larson
Kay Lynn Anderson	Carol M. Delahunty	Colleen M. Moran
Anshu J. Batra	Barbara B. Dentz	Nicole P. Shepard
Kimberly B. Buenting	L. Shannon Dudley	Josephine Young
Kimberly J. Clausen	Timothy P. Garrington	
Christopher Croasdale	David B. Goldenberg	

Medicine-Pediatrics

Fourth Year:	*Third Year:*	*Second Year:*
Elizabeth Dixon	Mark Dickinson	Annamaria T. Kausz
George Dodds	John A. Hopper	Paqui D. Motyl
Bryan Hollinger	Kristine L. McVea	Steven P. Stout
Sheryl Scott	Darby Sider	

First Year:

Elizabeth B. Buck	P. Christopher Tobin	Robin A. Yurk
Julian C. Ferris		

1992–1993

Chief Residents:
Laura Bellstrom   Virginia Brack

PL-3 Residents:

Amina Ahmed	Chon Lee	Andrew Scharenberg
Michelle I. Amaya	Paul E. Monahan	Shelley Schoonover
Laurie O. Beitz	Scott D. Reeves	Clay A. Stanley
Ildy Edenhoffer	Pamela J. Reitnauer	Jennifer F. Tender
Theresa L. Hamel	Christopher Rittmeyer	

PL-2 Residents:

Paul O. Adholla	Carol M. Delahunty	Kim McDermott

Kay Lynn Anderson
Anshu J. Batra
Kimberly B. Buenting
Susan B. Daly

Barbara B. Dentz
L. Shannon Dudley
Timothy P. Garrington
Michele C. Larson

Colleen M. Moran
Nicole P. Shepard
Josephine Young

PL-1 Residents:

Mark A. Anderson
Bassem A. Bejjani
Linda H. Butler
Aldon R. Collier
J. Genaro Diaz
Melissa G. Eaton

Margaret F. Farmer
Laura E. Heyneman
Jennifer R. Hoare
Niveen Y. Iskander
Ron L. Kaplan
Rachel C. Laramee

Scott W. Lindquist
Virginia J. Schreiner
Jacqueline E. Wanebo
Teresa L. Wooten

Medicine-Pediatrics

Fourth Year:
Mark Dickinson
John A. Hopper
Kristine L. McVea
Darby Sider

Third Year:
Annamaria T. Kausz
Paqui D. Motyl

Second Year:
Elizabeth B. Buck
Julian C. Ferris
P. Christopher Tobin
Robin A. Yurk

First Year:
Karen H. Albritton
Iris D. Bazing

Daniel A. Coles

Laura J. Csaplar

1993–1994

Chief Residents:
John A. Hopper

Pamela J. Reitnauer

PL-3 Residents:

Paul O. Adholla
Kay Lynn Anderson
Anshu J. Batra
Kimberly B. Buenting
Carol M. Delahunty

Barbara B. Dentz
L. Shannon Dudley
Timothy P. Garrington
Michele C. Larson
Kim McDermott

Colleen M. Moran
Nicole P. Shepard
Albertina Smith-Banks
Josephine C. Young

PL-2 Residents:

Mark A. Anderson
Bassem A. Bejjani
Linda H. Butler
Aldon R. Collier
J. Genaro Diaz

Melissa G. Eaton
Jennifer R. Hoare
Niveen Y. Iskander
Ron L. Kaplan
Rachel C. Laramee

Scott W. Lindquist
Virginia J. Schreiner
Jacqueline E. Wanebo
Teresa L. Wooten

PL-1 Residents:

Martha Feher
Jay M. Gillenwater
William O. Haddock
Barbara L. Hipp
Sheila M. Knerr
Robert Krzeski

Robert K. McClure
Margaret R. Morris
Edward M. Pickens
Anthony D. Realini
Courtney L. Robertson
Blair V. Robinson

Brenda B. Surles
Melinda C. Taylor
W. Randal Westerkam
Genon M. Wicina

Medicine-Pediatrics

Fourth Year:	*Third Year:*	*Second Year:*
Annamaria T. Kausz	Elizabeth B. Buck	Karen H. Albritton
Paqui D. Motyl	Julian C. Ferris	Iris D. Bazing
	P. Christopher Tobin	Daniel A. Coles
	Robin A. Yurk	Laura J. Csaplar

First Year:		
Lorraine H. Freed	Timothy J. Joos	David N. Thies
Patrick L. Godwin	James E. Kurz	
Kenny D. Hefner	Lisa F. Patterson	

1994–1995

Chief Residents:

Kimberly B. Buenting   Josephine C. Young

PL-3 Residents:

Mark A. Anderson	Niveen Y. Iskander	Jacqueline E. Wanebo
Bassem A. Bejjani	Ron L. Kaplan	Lynn M. Wegner
Linda H. Butler	Rachel C. Laramee	Teresa L. Wooten
Aldon R. Collier	Scott W. Lindquist	
Melissa G. Eaton	Virginia J. Schreiner	

PL-2 Residents:

Martha Feher	Mary Anne Mayo	Blair V. Robinson
Lorraine Freed	Robert K. McClure	Brenda B. Surles
Jay M. Gillenwater	Margaret R. Morris	Melinda C. Taylor
Barbara L. Hipp	Edward M. Pickens	Genon M. Wicina
Sheila M. Knerr	Courtney L. Robertson	

PL-1 Residents:

Rebecca L. Benton	Meghan B. Guerin	Cynthia A. Schadder
Amy Bingham (Fowler)	Michael W. Hauser	Adrea Gist Theodore
James W. Britt	Jeffrey C. Johnson	Dan F. Via
Brian H. Cassidy	Alexia Keller-Gusman	Jill C. Wright
Jennifer E. Charlton	Lucy S. Miller	
Peter T. Chu	John W. Rusher	

Medicine-Pediatrics

Fourth Year:	*Third Year:*	*Second Year:*
Elizabeth B. Buck	Karen H. Albritton	Patrick L. Godwin
Julian C. Ferris	Iris D. Bazing	Kenny D. Hefner
P. Christopher Tobin	Daniel A. Coles	Timothy J. Joos
Robin A. Yurk	Laura J. Csaplar	James E. Kurz
		Lisa F. Patterson
		David N. Thies

First Year:

Barbara A. Bergdolt	Susan R. Mims	Jon E. Simon
David L. Hill	Bruce M. Robinson	James A. Visser

1995–1996

Chief Residents:

Ron L. Kaplan	Virginia J. Schreiner

PL-3 Residents:

Muge Calikoglu	Sheila M. Knerr	Blair V. Robinson
Martha Feher	Mary Anne Mayo	Brenda B. Surles
Lorraine Freed	Margaret R. Morris	Melinda C. Taylor
Jay M. Gillenwater	Edward M. Pickens	Genon M. Wicina
Barbara L. Hipp	Courtney L. Robertson	

PL-2 Residents:

Rebecca L. Benton	Meghan B. Guerin	John W. Rusher
James W. Britt	Michael W. Hauser	Cynthia A. Schadder
Brian H. Cassidy	Jeffrey C. Johnson	Adrea G. Theodore
Peter T. Chu	Lucy S. Miller	Dan F. Via
Amy Bingham Fowler	Lisa Marie Ferrari	Jill C. Wright

PL-1 Residents:

Benjamin S. Alexander	Sabine U. Endrigkeit	Claudia C. Prose
Ann S. Baldwin	L. Bradford Hurst	Robert S. Spies
Jane G. Buss	Wendy G. Lane	Dorota A. Szczepaniak
Jennifer L. Campbell	Ann B. Lenox	Irene S. Tsang
J. Rebecca Daumen	Kristi L. Milowic	Mark S. Wainwright
Andrea M. Dunk	Jeanne S. Park	

Medicine-Pediatrics:

Fourth Year:	*Third Year:*	*Second Year:*
Karen H. Albritton	Patrick L. Godwin	Barbara A. Bergdolt
Iris D. Bazing	Kenny D. Hefner	David L. Hill
Daniel A. Coles	Timothy J. Joos	Susan R. Mims
Laura J. Csaplar	James E. Kurz	Bruce M. Robinson
	Lisa F. Patterson	Jon E. Simon
	David N. Thies	James A. Visser

First Year:

Paul R. Chelminski	Suzanne Lazorick	Mark D. Piehl
Darla L. Hatch	Kay M. Lowney	Barbara A. Porter

Biographies of the Early Greats of the Department

CHAPTER FORTY-NINE

Sidney S. Chipman

Dr. Sidney (Chip) Chipman was a major contributor to the early development of the Department of Pediatrics. Indeed, without his help and that of Dr. Arthur London, Drs. Curnen and Chamberlin would have had difficulty fulfilling the extensive responsibilities of pediatric teaching and service prior to Dr. Nelson Ordway's arrival in 1954.

Much of the following information is derived from a taped interview of Dr. Chipman at his retirement home in Pennswood Village, Newtown, Pennsylvania on May 17, 1988 by Dr. Harrie Chamberlin.

Dr. Chipman grew up in a small town in New Brunswick, Canada, and graduated from Acadia College in Nova Scotia. After medical school at McGill University he received residency training under Rustin McIntosh at Babies' Hospital in New York City. He then practiced general pediatrics in Connecticut for ten years (1932–42). Chip described the great satisfaction he had in practice and how he "by all odds did very well." But he also noted that "it put a lot of difficulties in the way of your family life" and he felt that he saw far too little of his two boys. It was perhaps for this reason that, after three years in the army (1942–1945), he resumed practice for only about six months and then, completely switching direction, went to the Yale University School of Public Health. He obtained his MPH degree there in 1947. While at Yale he had some contact with Grover Powers, for whom he developed great respect. Prior to coming to UNC Chip was on the faculty at the Louisiana State University School of Medicine for three years, where he worked with Nelson Ordway.

Dr. Chipman was the founder and first chairman of the Department of Maternal and Child Health in the UNC School of Public Health. Eventually that department would be judged by many to be the premier Department of

Sidney
Chipman

Maternal and Child Health in the United States. Dr. Chipman had arrived in Chapel Hill in 1950 and was fairly well established when Dr. Curnen arrived two years later. With the heavy responsibility of developing his own department, Chipman was under no obligation to aid in the launching of the Department of Pediatrics. Nevertheless, he contributed, quietly but effectively, to the new department that was developing under Dr. Curnen's leadership in the School of Medicine. Chipman was attending on the newborn service for long periods, attended senior staff conferences regularly, and gave occasional lectures and seminars. For several years he carried full ward-attending duties for six weeks each summer. Even after the Curnen years he continued to play a significant role in the Department.

Quiet, gentle, and modest, Dr. Chipman (in the words of his close friend, Dr. Nelson Ordway) "had the manners of a real patrician; he was not in the least stuffy but had a certain formality." Yet he could be as warm and amusing as any of his colleagues when one came to know him. His modesty is revealed in some of his reflections on his career and his years at Carolina. Chipman expressed regret that "in my years in medical school and in pediatric residency training I did not have enough exposure to research or research methodology. It wasn't until I got to the School of Public Health at Yale and the atmosphere at North Carolina that I really realized my short-comings and regretted that I hadn't done more. Research was hardly mentioned during my residencies." He also wondered whether he "did an adequate job in explaining to the Department of Pediatrics what a department of maternal and child health was all about. Our relationship was very cordial but not entirely satisfactory." He indicated that "the concept of community pediatrics was relatively unheard of in the 50s and 60s" and that "this perhaps explains why the relationship was not as close as it might have been. But I have no criticism of Ed Curnen or of Floyd Denny during that period."

Dr. Chipman chaired the Department of Maternal and Child Health until his retirement in 1970. After a period as acting chair of the Department of Maternal and Child Health at the University of Michigan, he and his wife Christine retired to Bradford, Vermont. They moved to Pennswood Village, a retirement home in Newtown, Pennsylvania in 1980. Chip considered Chapel Hill a wonderful place to live. "We had tremendous years in Vermont but I do sometimes wonder whether I should ever have left Chapel Hill." His further explanation of this revealed the unpretentiousness that characterized the man. "But I made the decision that I didn't want to retire in a community in which I'd had a certain amount of respect and made a certain number of achievements."

Following Christine's death Chipman married Harriet Shaw, a close mutual friend of his and Christine's. For many years he returned with Harriet to Nova Scotia every summer.

HARRIE R. CHAMBERLIN

CHAPTER FIFTY

Arthur H. London, Jr.

"PHYSICIAN, teacher, friend"—the words beneath a portrait hanging in the library in the pediatric clinic at UNC Hospitals that was dedicated to him tell us all we really need to know about Arthur London. He played a significant role in the history of pediatrics at UNC and in North Carolina, particularly the Piedmont area; and his influence through his teaching may be felt nationally.

Arthur was born in Pittsboro, North Carolina, in 1902. He was the second of five sons in a prominent family. His father was in the textile manufacturing business and also president of the local bank. With the family's status in the town it was natural that Arthur participate in the community activities. As his brother, Lawrence, tells, "Debating was a big thing in a small town and Arthur was a leader on the high school debating team." This training may have led to his subsequent ability to make a point with authority! He played high school baseball and was active in the first Boy Scout troop in Pittsboro. He began a long and dedicated service to the church by teaching in Sunday school. However, the association that may be most important in the development of his career and contributions was with Dr. William B. Chapin.

Dr. Chapin was a family physician in Pittsboro and Arthur as early as the age of ten would make house calls with him—first in a horse-drawn buggy and later in a Model T Ford. This experience gave him a generous exposure to the practice of medicine. Dr. Chapin wanted Arthur to become a physician, learn specifically about the treatment of children, and come back to help him. This was accomplished.

Two significant qualities of Arthur's life became apparent in his high school years. One was scholarship, as evidenced by his graduating at the top of his class. The second was generosity, as shown by his giving to a financially less fortunate person a tuition-free grant to UNC that he himself had been awarded.

After his college years at UNC, Arthur completed in 1925 the school's two-year medical program. It was during this time that a close and longstanding friendship was established with Dr. Reece Berryhill, who was subsequently to become dean of the Medical School at UNC.

Arthur London

In 1927 Dr. London completed medical school at the University of Pennsylvania. He stayed in Philadelphia for his internship at the Methodist Episcopal Hospital. He then did a year of residency at Cincinnati Children's Hospital, subsequently returning to be chief resident and instructor of pediatrics at the University of Pennsylvania. He returned to Durham, North Carolina, in 1930 to begin his practice of pediatrics.

Arthur's service commitments vary from humble to distinguished. On returning to Durham in 1930 he began fulfilling the request of his mentor, Dr. Chapin, by setting up a free pediatric consulting clinic in Pittsboro. He attended this clinic weekly. In an effort to promote good nutrition, he established a feeding clinic at Durham's Lakeside School. In 1939 he became a member of the Durham County Board of Health, serving for thirty-five years, five years of which he was the chairman. He served as chief of pediatrics at both Watts and Lincoln Hospitals in Durham. He served as president of the North Carolina Pediatric Society and as district chairman of the American Academy of Pediatrics. As a result of these latter two positions, he became involved in a study that was of national importance.

In 1944 the American Academy of Pediatrics felt it was necessary to formulate a plan for the health care of children in the postwar period.[1] They recommended that a survey be made of existing services and facilities in the United States. A committee composed of representatives from the American Academy of Pediatrics, the American Pediatric Society, and the Medical Advisory Committee of the Children's Bureau was selected. They recommended that North Carolina be the pilot state for devising the procedures used in collecting information. It was at this time that Arthur was president of the North Carolina Pediatric Society and district chairman of the Academy of Pediatrics;

---

1. Report of Committee on a Consideration of Child Health in the Postwar Period. *Journal of Pediatrics*, 1944, 25:625.

thus he was made a member of the Committee for the Study of Child Health Services of the American Academy of Pediatrics.

The North Carolina study was reported in the April 1948 *North Carolina Medical Journal*[2] and the national study was presented in a book published by the Commonwealth Fund, entitled *Child Health Services and Pediatric Education*, in 1949.[3] The use of the information and its application to pediatrics in North Carolina was subsequently reported in 1950 by Drs. London and Davison in the *JAMA*.[4]

Indirectly Dr. London may have played a role in the creation of what we now know as the UNC School of Medicine. Until 1951 the school was a two-year program. Early in the 1940s comments by Dr. Reece Berryhill in the minutes of the medical faculty[5] suggest that plans be formulated for expansion to a four-year program. A study by national consultants was commissioned and in 1946 it formally endorsed the proposition.[6] Thus began an intense period of lobbying by Dr. Berryhill and others. Mrs. Norma Berryhill has revealed that during this time Arthur's close friendship and support were most important in Dr. Berryhill's efforts to obtain legislative approval.[7]

Dr. London's demeanor was important in achieving the respect that he commanded as an administrator, as a practitioner of pediatrics, and as a teacher. His carriage, penetrating eyes, and authoritative voice created respect, sometimes tinged with fear. He was, however, a humble rather than arrogant person. He did not tolerate insincerity or frivolous matters, but if a person was honest and open he or she would be warmly received. Mrs. Mae Newton, former pediatric nurse at Watts Hospital, said, "He was the kindest soul you ever met and if you had a problem he would go all out to help you."[8] These were some of the characteristics that endeared him to the faculty at the newly established Department of Pediatrics at UNC in the 1950s.

Teaching was a significant and important part of Arthur's professional life. Dr. William L. London, a nephew and associate in the practice of pediatrics, said that Arthur loved teaching more than any other activity. Certainly students loved his teaching.[9]

For a number of years he taught pediatrics at Watts Hospital School of

---

2. Child Health Services in North Carolina, Supplement to the *North Carolina Medical Journal*, Vol. 9, April 1948.

3. *Child Health Services and Pediatric Education*. American Academy of Pediatrics. The Commonwealth Fund, New York, 1949.

4. London, Arthur H. Jr., and Davison, W. C.: Pediatric Care Under the North Carolina Plan. *JAMA* 1950, 143:1232–1235.

5. Medical Faculty Meeting. UNC School of Medicine, October 6, 1943.

6. North Carolina Medical Care Commission National Committee for Medical School Survey, Committee Reports. School of Medicine. July 1, 1946.

7. Personal conversation, Mrs. Reece Berryhill.

8. Personal communication, Mrs. Mae Newton.

9. Personal communication, Dr. William L. London.

Nursing in Durham. He was a clinical professor of pediatrics at both Duke and UNC, where medical students and house officers were privileged to have him in attendance on the wards and in the clinics. For those at UNC he may be most vividly remembered for his weekly slide presentations of pediatric problems. Arthur, throughout his career, took pictures of every conceivable medical problem that could be graphically depicted. With these slides and his years of experience he gave classic lectures.

Dr. London was awarded the University of North Carolina School of Medicine Distinguished Service Award in 1957. In 1971, five years before his death, the library in the outpatient clinic at UNC Hospitals was dedicated to him. This was most appropriate because that is where he gave his memorable talks.

For those who knew Arthur London it can truly be said he was a physician, teacher, and friend.

ROBERT T. HERRINGTON

ADDENDUM

by Floyd W. Denny, Jr.

One of my first memories of the Department of Pediatrics at UNC when I was making the decision to come to Chapel Hill is of Arthur London. I was very impressed with this rather austere-appearing and plain-talking man who was described to me as one of the most important practicing pediatricians in North Carolina and the most important one to our fledgling Department. This proved to be true in every possible and imaginable way. In a short time, we developed a warm and comfortable friendship. We did not always agree on departmental and academic matters but our disagreements were never acrimonious. I soon learned that I could always rely on his support in matters that really counted. His very wise counsel regarding the associations between the Department and practicing pediatricians was always helpful. I got the very definite feeling that he had put his "stamp of approval" on the Department and me; this clearly was important to us when we depended so much on the practicing pediatricians for patients and much of the teaching in the ambulatory clinic. He was a master clinician; Jud Van Wyk and I especially remember getting consultations from him on our tough patients. As mentioned by Bob Herrington above, Arthur was most noted for his teaching, especially his weekly sessions in the clinic, with students and house staff, who remember his stories of patients he had seen, all illustrated with his extensive slide collection.

Probably most important to the Department, however, was that Dr. London served as a role model for scores of students and house staff. He clearly loved his work, and had a large referral practice in addition to serving as a primary care pediatrician for hundreds of children. He exuded the aura of the successful and happy pediatrician and he shared this readily with many budding pediatricians during their formative years.

Two episodes involving Arthur stand out in my memory because they indicated so clearly to me his basic character. The first was after he had been diagnosed as having carcinoma of the head of the pancreas. This was shortly after Barb and I moved to our "farm" in the country and the occasion was the year-end picnic at Storybook Farm, an affair he rarely missed. Arthur was too ill to drive so I picked him up in Durham to bring him to Storybook. We stopped at my place, which was on the way, for Arthur to see my new home. Much to my horror our vicious Airedale terrier, Sam, had not been cooped up and charged at Arthur as he got out of the car. I was certain that this was the end of Arthur, and consequently of me. As Sam drew near Arthur was unperturbed, but simply stared at her, who about ten feet away drew to a halt. Barb and I differ on the rest of the episode. I remember that Sam turned away; Barb remembers Sam coming up to Arthur to be petted. This seemed to me a very apt portrayal of Arthur's indomitable will and character, the kind of effect he had on me and could have on others—including my dog Sam.

The other memory is of Arthur during my visits with him in his last few days. He had declined any anticancer therapy and was dying rapidly. I was tremendously impressed with his serenity and his dignified manner as death approached. I remember hoping that I, under such circumstances, could be half so brave.

Arthur was more than a friend and teacher, he was an advisor, confidant, supporter, and probably above all a great role model—overall one of the very important people to our Department as it was developing.

CHAPTER FIFTY-ONE

Nelson K. Ordway

THE arrival of Nelson Ordway in Chapel Hill in the summer of 1954, to become the third full-time member of UNC's two-year-old Department of Pediatrics, was a rare happy side effect of a dark period in our country's recent history. The McCarthy era was at its height and Nelson, then chairman of the Department of Pediatrics at LSU, was under heavy fire for strongly supporting one of his faculty, accused of being a communist for belonging to an antisegregationist organization. Nelson held his ground and, because he had tenure, could not be fired. Just before a unit of the Eastland Committee was about to investigate the university, however, he was told that his department would receive no further funding as long as he remained chairman. At this he resigned.

Nelson is not sure how Ed Curnen first learned of his plight, but evidence suggests that it was through Grover Powers at Yale, for Nelson had been on Yale's junior faculty from 1941 until his move to New Orleans in 1947. Curnen had overlapped Ordway at Yale during 1946–1947, but they had been in different departments.

There were three primary circumstances that drew Nelson to Chapel Hill: he and Lou Welt (in UNC's Department of Medicine) had been medical school classmates at Yale and fellow AOA members, and Lou encouraged him to come; Sidney Chipman, a close friend of Nelson's at LSU, had just moved to Chapel Hill to be the first chairman of the Department of Maternal and Child Health; and at UNC there was no pediatric cardiologist, a field in which Nelson had developed considerable expertise.

This brief account of Nelson's contributions and background focuses primarily on his years in our Department of Pediatrics. An expanded mini-biography is present in the historical archives of the Department. Much is

Nelson
Ordway

drawn from a long recorded interview with him, conducted by Harrie Chamberlin in 1988.

THE EARLIER YEARS

Nelson Ordway was born in October 1912 and spent much of his boyhood in Maine, graduating from the Bangor High School in 1929, well before his seventeenth birthday. Before matriculating at Yale he spent a year in Switzerland at the École Internationale de Genève. His junior year at Yale was also spent abroad, in Germany at the University of Freiburg. Following graduation with membership in Phi Beta Kappa he entered the Yale School of Medicine, receiving his MD cum laude in 1938. Postdoctoral training consisted of a year as a pediatric intern at Yale and two years as a rotating intern at the University of Pennsylvania Hospital. During the war years (1941–1945) he returned to Yale as a research assistant in pathology, studying the pathological effects of various poison gases, and then (1945–1947) became an instructor in pediatrics. In 1947 he was appointed an assistant professor of pediatrics at LSU, rapidly moving up to become department chairman five years later. But after two more years he moved to Chapel Hill.

UNC

At UNC Nelson found, as he phrases it, a "gemütlich" environment (warm, friendly, comfortable). His previous departments, Yale and LSU, had also been small. Everyone was supportive and he eventually knew almost the entire Medical School faculty. He constantly received strong backing from Ed Curnen, even when he had to spend considerable time sharing in the authorship of a medical compendium. He found that Ed brought in staff primarily for their attributes as "persons," supporting them in whatever they wished to do.

Though broad gauged in his knowledge and approach to pediatrics, Nelson's special focus was on pediatric cardiology. He introduced the techniques of cardiac catheterization into the Department of Pediatrics at Yale under the guidance of Jim Warren, in Yale's Department of Medicine, and brought them first to LSU and then to UNC. Because no image intensifiers yet existed, the procedure had to be carried out in darkness. At first patients had to be sent to Duke for cardiac surgery, but Richard Peters presently filled this need.

Ernest Craige and Daniel Young soon extended cardiac catheterization to adults, using the same clinical laboratory, but Nelson feels that he continued to do more catheterizations than they.

But there were other foci of interest and teaching. Nelson often lectured on parenteral fluid therapy and also developed an easy to prepare formula for an oral rehydration mix which was dubbed "Na-K-glucose," appropriate since his first two initials are "N.K." Partly because of a retarded son, he shared an interest with Harrie Chamberlin in mental retardation. He recalls the November 1956 Ross Conference on Etiologic Factors in Mental Retardation as a special event, developed by the Department and probably the first international conference ever held, at least in the Americas, on this subject. Believing that every well baby examination should include a developmental appraisal, he fashioned a simple streamlined approach largely based on Gesell techniques. As a small booklet, it was widely used locally until the appearance of Frankenberg's standardized Denver Developmental Screening Test.

Nelson had often participated in the excellent LSU outreach program, initiated by Myron Wegman, to various state medical society meetings. He thus enjoyed similar trips about North Carolina with Emory Hunt and the interactions with primary physicians. But he could never become entirely used to the before-dinner invocations. They had been unusual in predominantly Catholic Louisiana. He recalls one in particular with considerable amusement that ended with the special flourish "and, Oh Lord, deliver us from the evils of socialized medicine."

Nelson's decision to leave for New Haven after only three and a half years in Chapel Hill was due not so much to dissatisfaction with UNC as to a strong personal attraction to Yale. With the exception of an undergraduate year abroad and two postdoctoral years at the University of Pennsylvania, he had been at Yale from 1930 until 1947. Going back to New Haven was like "coming home."

TEACHING, RESEARCH, AND
PROFESSIONAL AFFILIATIONS

Nelson has always considered himself to be a general pediatrician despite greater emphasis on several specific areas: pediatric cardiology, especially congenital heart disease, fluid and electrolyte abnormalities, the neonate, and infant and early child assessment. He holds American Board Certification in pediatric cardiology.

As a teacher Nelson conveyed an infectious enthusiasm that was particularly stimulating in a one-to-one or small group setting. Formal lectures, though they captured the interest of the audience, were usually a bit less effective. Some of Nelson's most inspiring teaching, possibly that most often remembered by many of his students, came from informal contacts. At UNC in the mid-'50s with only sixty medical students to a class, this form of contact was frequent. His teaching philosophy owed much to Grover Powers and

Grover's weaving of humanity into medicine. Nelson's eclectic approach and wide experience in varied settings made him an especially interesting mentor.

Although over fifty publications, most of them in refereed journals, and eleven abstracts are listed in Nelson's bibliography, he disavows any claim to in-depth research. Others might disagree. He was a coauthor of several publications during the war years on pathology resulting from exposure to various poisonous gases. His papers dealing with congenital heart disease range from case reports to far more basic studies. He greatly admired Bob Winters and published studies with him on recovery from salicylate intoxication, but modestly claims that the thinking behind them was mostly Bob's. He feels that his most important research contributions were probably made during a visiting professorship in Cali, Colombia (1964–1965), studies of sodium and potassium ion shifts back into cells during rehydration following severe infantile diarrhea.

Nelson was impressively ingenious. In his tiny laboratory, converted from a washroom at the entrance to the clinic building auditorium, he adapted a method for measuring arterial oxygen content. He developed an audible drip method for assessing fluid flow rates in the dark cardiac catheterization laboratory. Among several similar original creations, he produced a simple mathematical model for estimating the initial reduction of the indirect bilirubin level by single and repeated exchange transfusions. The organization of his developmental appraisal booklet also reflects considerable ingenuity.

Nelson is a member of the Society for Pediatric Research, the American Pediatric Society, the Ambulatory Pediatric Association, and the American Public Health Association. As a member of the American Academy of Pediatrics, he chaired its Committee on International Child Health for five years (1970–1975). He also holds membership in the Société Française de Pédiatrie, the Sociedad Latinoamericana de Investigación Pediátrica, and pediatric societies in Venezuela and Colombia. He has been a consultant on diarrheal disease for both WHO and the Pan American Health Organization.

OBSERVATIONS

It is impossible to encompass all the facets of Nelson's life and character in this brief report. Indeed, that would be impossible under any circumstance. But a series of observations may help to impart a feel for some of these facets.

Due to his year of study in Switzerland before entering Yale and his college junior year at the University of Freiburg, Nelson has long been fluent in both French and German. He learned to speak Spanish relatively adequately during his sabbatical year in Cali. His facility with languages has enabled him to present a paper in Vienna in German, to teach and lecture in Lyon in French, and to teach and lecture in Spanish in various parts of Latin America. But he feels that the great contribution from his overseas experiences has not been the learning of languages, but the development of knowledge and understanding of other peoples. He emphasizes that one learns to accept them and their way of life even if one cannot totally identify with them.

Nelson's decision to accept a fellow in pediatric cardiology from Lyon while he was at UNC led to several amusing events and stories. Dr. Robert Verney's only request before he arrived with his wife was that his living quarters should have a bidet. His English was so poor that initially he and Nelson conversed in French. As mentioned earlier, cardiac catheterizations had to be done in complete darkness. Nelson's most hilarious story about Bob describes the latter when he was slowly feeding a catheter into a patient but it never appeared on the fluoroscopic screen. Nelson was feeling a bit uncomfortable when Bob suddenly asked, "What is that wet thing going down my leg?" It appears that he was catheterizing his scrub pants!

Nelson also has an exquisite feel for the English language and for grammar. Within weeks of his joining the Department, he was listening to this writer give a brief presentation on secretory otitis media at a luncheon meeting for residents and faculty. About halfway through a note was passed down to him from Nelson which read as follows: "I'm sorry, Dr. Chamberlin, but you are going to have to say *secrétory*. You have no choice. You may, however, say *excrétory*, if you wish to sacrifice orthoepistic elegance for Emersonian consistency."

Nelson's pet annoyance was the use of the term "parental fluid therapy" by an occasional student. To illustrate what the student was referring to, he had on his office wall a large drawing, so labeled and executed by Ernie Craige, of a distinctly maternal monkey feeding her young.

Yet, incongruously, despite his being a stickler for the proper use of English, Nelson's handwriting is unintelligible to virtually everyone, about the worst that any of us had ever seen. If his written grammar was not perfect, there was almost no way that we could know it.

As the reader must now already know, Nelson has a rich sense of humor. The first annual departmental picnic, entitled "Pediatrics Spring Refresher," was his idea. It was held on a lot owned by the Chamberlins across the bypass (now entirely grown up in woods). Nelson even prepared and mimeographed the flyer that announced it, along with a map. On the top was a can marked "SMA," but obviously overflowing with beer. Following the "Who" ("H.O.'s, Nurses, Technicians and Secretaries plus assorted wives, husbands and children"), the response to "Why" was given as "Vernal Euphoria of Senior Staff."

The annual student-faculty shows in the early days were always delightful and clever affairs. As Nelson said, in contrast to Yale's, "You can even bring your children." He had a part in one of them, but his most vivid memory is that of Tom Farmer as the cymbalist in a band; with a percussion hammer he would strike his knee, whereupon his foot would slam into the cymbal!

In the mid-'50s, the campus bell tower was sounding each quarter hour with a faulty sequence of the familiar Cambridge or Westminster quarters. Nelson, whose window faced the tower, was alternately amused and annoyed by this. After he informed the chairman of the Department of Music of the problem it was finally corrected. During the subsequent four decades the carillon sequence has remained correct and Nelson now jokes that his action represents his one lasting contribution to the University of North Carolina!

Nelson's personal life has met with more tragedy than most of us have faced. His second son, Peter, has always been severely retarded, along with having considerable autistic behavior. Although he remained with the family for years and received abundant love and support, the extent of his disability eventually made this impossible. For decades he has lived in residential schools for the retarded. Many years have passed since he last recognized members of his family. The following inscription always hung on the wall in Nelson's office. It reads in part:

> As one star differs from another in glory,
> So do the children of men differ in power and strength.
> Each child of God, even if not richly endowed,
> Has his place in the great scheme of life. . . .

In 1975 Ernestine, Nelson's wife and mother of their four children, died after a prolonged fight with cancer. She was sixty-four. Her loss left a painful void. But two years later he married Jane Menapace, a gracious lady with grown children of her own. Outgoing, strongly supportive, and sharing in many of Nelson's interests including his love of travel, she seems the perfect match. A visit with them in their lovely new home, surrounded by the intriguing fauna and flora of a mountainside in the Arizona desert, is a true pleasure.

CONCLUSION

Near the conclusion of our interview Nelson was asked what phases in his professional life had given him the most pleasure. He named four: his interaction with Sidney Chipman and Myron Wegman at LSU; his relationship with Milton Senn at Yale; his experiences in Latin America; and his years with the Indian Health Service. As mentioned earlier, it is not easy to capture the complexity of his many interests. He is a kind of late Renaissance man in his constant eagerness to learn more of the many aspects of the world around him. Highly compassionate, consistently humane, and deeply honest, he is a champion of the underdog and of the deprived and for the rights of all of us. It is appropriate to close with a quotation from his address to the graduating medical school class at LSU in May 1953, at the peak of the McCarthy era:

> Free inquiry, thorough knowledge, clear thinking, fearless expression
> of what we believe true, intolerance only of those forces which would
> suppress truth: these are the obligations upon us as citizens of a free
> America and a free world. And interpreted in the light of the Mosaic
> admonition to "love thy neighbor as thyself," these are also our rights,
> to which we add the sanctity of our personal thoughts and opinions.

HARRIE R. CHAMBERLIN

CHAPTER FIFTY-TWO

Annie V. Scott

I T WAS sheer good fortune that brought Dr. Annie V. Scott to our Department, where she spent the final phase of her professional career as a clinical professor, from 1954 until 1964.* Stern, indomitable, and taciturn, yet deeply admired and beloved, Dr. Scott had already contributed far more than most manage in a lifetime, as a teacher and model for medical students and as a physician and friend to thousands of infants, children, and their parents in China, well before she came to Chapel Hill. Over a span of thirty-one years, from 1920 until 1951, broken only by an occasional short leave and by World War II, she had made China her home. When the communist regime made it impossible for her to stay longer, she returned to Columbia's Presbyterian Medical Center, where she had taught during the war. It was when she turned sixty-five that Dr. Rustin McIntosh called Dr. Curnen on her behalf. Though she was to join a department not yet two years old, for her it was a return to her roots.

Annie Scott was born and brought up on a farm in rural Guilford County where she attended the Pleasant Garden High School. She was already twenty-one when she decided to attend the North Carolina Normal and Industrial College, much later to become the University of North Carolina at Greensboro. It was there that she set her goal to become a physician, graduating in 1914. Taking advantage of a fellowship at the Women's Medical College in Philadelphia, she received her MD there in 1918. Two years of post-

---

* An expanded form of this report, particularly of Dr. Scott's years in China, is present in the archives section of the department history.

Annie Scott

doctoral training followed in New York, at the Lying-in Hospital and at Bellevue.

In 1920, under the auspices of the Presbyterian Board of Foreign Missions, Dr. Scott sailed for China. It was the first of five separate trips that she would make to a totally different world, a world with thousands of years of history yet incessant instability, of beauty yet brutality, of floods and famines, with a different spectrum of diseases, new peoples and new languages, a world that was to be hers during the most active years of her life.

Although pediatrician-in-chief at the North China Medical College for Women in Peking, she initially focused on the study of Mandarin. Not only was this essential for communication in northern China, but it enabled her in 1932 to write a book in Mandarin, *The Care and Feeding of Infants and Children,* carried through three editions. In 1924 her medical school was merged with the Cheeloo Medical College and Hospital of Shantung University in Tsinan (now Jinan), 250 miles to the south. Dr. Scott was one of five faculty chosen to make the move.

By 1929 the new school had a faculty of twenty-four, British, American, and Chinese. There were two pediatric faculty, with Dr. Scott the chair as associate professor, later to be promoted to professor.

But the path to this stage clearly was not an easy one. Though she never mentioned it, from the age of eleven, probably due to Legg-Perthes disease, Dr. Scott had to adapt to a severe limp. Roads to local villages were often poor to nonexistent. An early photograph shows her standing in a dry riverbed with a group of coolies alongside her litter, which is slung between two mules.

The space problem in the clinic would have made the early situation in Chapel Hill seem luxurious. That pediatrics had had a late start and was slow to gain space sounds a familiar theme. In the late '20s she wrote:

> It is satisfying to see our clinic growing. We look back to the day when we began in the wash-basin corner of Skin Clinic and, because we were too noisy, were moved into the hall. After another year we acquired one room and then, after two more years, a total of four rooms, one of which was for weighing and one for the isolation of contagious diseases.

The first "Baby Clinic" was established at Cheeloo by Dr. Scott in 1926. A portion of a description of the daily routine is intriguing:*

> Dr. Scott and her two student helpers are at home to all the sick babies in Tsinan, together with their retinue of parents, sisters, brothers, aunts and amahs. Imagine, if you can, a small room with such a family delegation in tow of Baby Wang! The work begins as the doctor examines as best she may whatever spots the anxious mother will let her observe of the child's much swaddled anatomy. Windows and doors must remain closed, for mothers simply refuse to undress their children in a room reeking with fresh air. . . .

Diseases rarely seen in the United States were common. Kala-azar (leishmaniasis) was endemic and was the subject of two articles that she wrote in 1932 for the *Archives of Diseases in Childhood* and of another in the *Chinese Medical Journal*. But tuberculosis and malnutrition absorbed much of her time and interest: 52 percent of the schoolchildren tested in Tsinan showed positive tuberculins. A plan to study changes with age in this percentage was developed, but had to be deferred due to inadequate staff and funding. Two decades later she would finally carry out this plan, but in Alamance County, North Carolina, with the assistance of others in our young Department of Pediatrics.

During much of the time that Dr. Scott spent in China, the country was in turmoil. The Japanese were moving southward from Manchuria, communist and Kuomintang armies were already clashing, and local warlords vied with each other in many areas. Yet the hospital and medical school continued to function, although they were often overloaded with wounded soldiers. In May 1928, a major battle between Chiang Kaishek's Kuomintang forces and the Japanese took place in the immediate vicinity of Tsinan. Several aerial bombs were dropped and casualties were heavy. Foreigners had been advised to leave, but the hospital staff stuck it out.

None of this could deter Annie Scott. Even on her brief furloughs she felt constantly drawn back to China. In a letter written while on brief observer status in the Harriet Lane at Hopkins, she states, "I just long to be back in China where work is pressing. I feel so superfluous here." The letter is dated "December 7, 1925." Fortunately there would be exactly sixteen more years before her status in China would suddenly change. At news of the bombing of Pearl Harbor, she was forced to leave and was evacuated on the *Gripsholm* back to the United States.

During the war years in New York, as an instructor in pediatrics at Columbia's College of Physicians and Surgeons, Dr. Scott came into contact

---

* A quote by Mrs. A. P. Jacot from a description of the Cheeloo Baby Clinic in "Cheeloo Sketches, Shantung Christian University," published in 1928 by the American Presbyterian Church Educational Department, Box 330, Nashville, TN.

with the research of her friend, Dr. Dorothy Anderson, on the newly identified entity, cystic fibrosis. It was an exposure that would determine the focus of a major portion of her own work a decade later in Chapel Hill.

By 1946, soon after the war ended, she was back in Tsinan, rebuilding her department. When the communists took over she was allowed to stay on. Indeed, she remained in China as long as almost any American. But after the Chinese entered the Korean War, failure to leave risked indefinite internment. In early 1951, she set off on a somewhat hazardous but successful journey to Hong Kong.

Dr. Scott now returned to Dr. McIntosh's service, this time as a visiting professor. Again, among her other activities, she was able to work with Dr. Anderson. But in 1954, after only three years, she had reached Columbia's mandatory retirement age. Because of Dr. McIntosh's call to Dr. Curnen in Chapel Hill, a new group of pediatricians, their house staff, and their students were now to have the opportunity to know her.

Yet she was a complete stranger to all of us on her arrival. She initially seemed so distant that some of us wondered whether we could ever know well this new clinical professor. On rounds and in conferences she seemed a dour Scot and said almost nothing. But as one came to know her better one gradually realized, as Dr. Curnen states, that she had "a fine dry sense of humor and a tremendous range of pediatric knowledge. On rounds she never offered opinions but, if there had been controversy, on the following day I would usually find a pile of journals on my desk with markers in them," references that shed additional light on the discussions. She turned out to be a good teacher, especially in small groups; "very effective at the bedside," Dr. Curnen continues, "though not so able as a lecturer."

Childhood tuberculosis and cystic fibrosis continued to be Dr. Scott's major interests. Great emphasis was placed on proper nutrition. Teaming up with Dr. George Summer to perfect the use of the diagnostic sweat test, she shared with him in developing the first real clinic for cystic fibrosis in North Carolina. It lost its status only after her departure in 1964, Dr. Summer's transfer to the Department of Biochemistry, and Dr. Alexander Spock's arrival at Duke. Dr. Gerald Fernald, who took over in 1968, feels that such a firm foundation had been established that one can trace the outstanding clinical and research activity now ongoing in cystic fibrosis in both the Departments of Medicine and Pediatrics back to Dr. Scott's early contributions.

Almost from the start, Dr. Curnen emphasizes, "she set an extraordinary example for the house staff on the virtue of making extreme efforts to help patients even when the condition seemed beyond help. She was relentless in pursuing her care of difficult patients." She often visited these patients three or four times a day and made it clear to ward personnel that she expected meticulous care. The house staff, often under pressure from the care of other patients whose future they considered to be brighter, frequently found this difficult. Dr. Summer states that occasionally they would quickly disappear in the other direction when they saw her coming off the elevator with her characteristic limp and determined appearance, pushing the little wheeled cart on which she carried her records and any heavy equipment. Some were said almost to be "terrorized"! Yet, beneath her stern exterior there was a gentleness and compassion to which her patients quickly responded. It is Dr. Summer's feeling that her firm, strongly directed, no-nonsense manner in any professional situation was largely the result of having been a physician-in-chief in China for so many years, where hardships were many but where she refused to be deterred. "When focused on a specific task," Dr. Judson Van Wyk has stated, "she could never be turned aside."

Dr. Scott was the liaison pediatrician between the North Carolina Memorial Hospital and the Gravely Sanitarium, which was then under separate management. She played an integral part in the tuberculosis detection program, which included the research project on the rate of increase in the incidence of positive tuberculins with age, carried out in the Alamance County Schools. Dr. Sidney Chipman, chairman of the Department of Maternal and Child Health, who shared with her on this study, states that "she was a remarkable individual who contributed a great deal and was a wonderful person to work with." When asked whether he did not at times find her rather stern and forbidding, he replied, "Oh yes. The few times I disagreed with her she made it perfectly clear that she disagreed with me! But it was always a happy relationship."

In time the faculty came to know Dr. Scott's less severe, nonprofessional side. We learned that she loved gardening and had experimented with watercolor painting. Those of us who were fortunate to share dinner with her in her little apartment off McCauley Street were treated to marvelously cooked Chinese food and absorbing reminiscences of her experiences in China. Though it had taken time, we began to call her "Annie" and she was addressing us and our wives by our first names.

But Floyd Denny, who arrived in 1960 to replace Dr. Curnen, was at a disadvantage. To her Floyd, though thirty-five years her junior, was an authority figure and she could not bring herself to address him by anything but his last name. Floyd longed to have it otherwise. Now, years later, he delights in the story of almost imploring her on one occasion to call him Floyd. "Yes, Dr. Denny," was the response. After that she never once addressed him by name, either first or last!

Several awards were presented to Dr. Scott in these later years. But for her the most important recognition came in 1967 from her old college, now the University of North Carolina at Greensboro, at its seventy-fifth anniversary convocation. There she was awarded an honorary Doctor of Science degree with the citation, read by Chancellor Ferguson, commending her for "distinguished achievements in the field of medicine and for a lifetime of service to humanity." It was difficult to suppress our own feelings of admiration and pride for her as we watched her standing there, unsmiling but clearly deeply happy.

Three years before this someone had noted Annie Scott's birthdate, 1889, back in Chapel Hill. Somehow she had been a kind of Rock of Gibraltar, not a person who really ages, and no one had thought to check. But by then it was nearly three years since she should have retired! It was Floyd Denny's sad task to have to tell her so. She worked in a well baby clinic for the Guilford County Health Department for a time, living with her sister. Later she moved to High Point's Presbyterian Home. The writer recalls a fine spring morning in the late '50s when he, Dr. Scott, and others were driving through beautiful country-side along old NC 54 toward Graham. We were heading for one of the Alamance County schools to further the tuberculin test study. Obviously thinking of her childhood in rural central North Carolina, Dr. Scott seemed almost overcome with the loveliness about her as she told us what it meant to her.

Yet she had always dreamed of returning to China. When she died in 1975 there had been no possibility of fulfilling that dream. But it would have meant much to her to know that within the next decade at least six members of the Department of Pediatrics would visit the country that had been so much a part of her life. Those of us who had worked with her often thought of her while we were there.

She was beloved by us all and it was a great privilege to have known her.

HARRIE R. CHAMBERLIN

PART TEN

Looking to the Future

CHAPTER FIFTY-THREE

The Department of Pediatrics in 1996 and Beyond

THIS history of the Department of Pediatrics was intended in 1993 to end at the conclusion of the Boat years. The project turned out to be far more complicated than we had believed and did not permit completion as scheduled. The great growth in our Department from one with two full-time pediatricians, as described by Dr. Blythe in the foreword, to the present large and enormously productive staff of over seventy professionals engaged in teaching, research, and patient care has been the essence of this historical account. As we finally "go to press" in mid-1996 it seems appropriate that we take a look at the past three years and a glimpse at what the future holds in store.

Edward E. Lawson, interim chair, 1993–95

Dr. Edward "Ned" Lawson served as the interim chair from 1993 to 1995 and provided superb leadership in maintaining the momentum of the Department during this period. The role of interim chair is an especially difficult one, and the challenges facing Dr. Lawson were every bit as daunting as those faced by previous chairs. These challenges included participating in the conceptualization and fine planning of the new North Carolina Children's Hospital, dealing with indi-

Roberta G.
Williams,
chair, 1995–

vidual cases stemming from our increasingly litigious society, and facing the problems of new health care delivery systems, in addition to administering a very complex Department. Ned earned the great respect of his associates in the Department during this difficult time.

A widely representative search committee, under the chairmanship of Joseph W. Grisham, Kenan Professor and chair of pathology, recommended to Dean Michael Simmons that he appoint Dr. Roberta Williams, "one of our own," to succeed Dr. Boat as Department chair. Roberta is a 1968 graduate of our School of Medicine. She was a medicine-pediatric resident at UNC for one year, then received pediatric training at Babies' Hospital in New York and cardiology training at Boston Children's. Following faculty time at Harvard she became chief of pediatric cardiology at UCLA. She arrived in Chapel Hill in April 1995. It seems clear that she possesses in abundance those leadership qualities that will assure that our Department will continue to occupy its position of excellence and leadership in the United States. As we approach the twenty-first century the Department's bright future seems assured.

THE EDITORS

Index

INDEX